Medicine, patients and the law

Manchester University Press

CONTEMPORARY ISSUES IN BIOETHICS, LAW AND MEDICAL HUMANITIES

Contemporary Issues in Bioethics, Law and Medical Humanities, edited by Rebecca Bennett and Simona Giordano, of the University of Manchester, was established to publish internationally respected book-length works – primarily monographs and edited collections, but also specialist textbooks – in contemporary issues in bioethics, law and the medical humanities and as such welcomes proposals from this range of academic approaches to pertinent issues in this area. The series focuses on the strong foundations and reputation of the University of Manchester's world-leading scholars in bioethics and law, and its internationally respected Centre for Social Ethics and Policy. Works from across the humanities, brought to bear on contemporary, historical, and indeed future bioethical questions of the highest social and moral concern and interest, will find a perfect home within this series.

From reason to practice in bioethics: An anthology dedicated to the works of John Harris *Edited by John Coggon, Sarah Chan, Søren Holm and Thomasine Kushner*

The freedom of scientific research: Bridging the gap between science and society *Edited by Simona Giordano in collaboration with John Harris and Lucio Piccirillo*

Law and healing: A history of a stormy marriage
Margaret Brazier

Margaret Brazier, Emma Cave and Rob Heywood

Medicine, patients and the law

Seventh edition

MANCHESTER UNIVERSITY PRESS

Published by Manchester University Press
Oxford Road, Manchester M13 9PL
www.manchesteruniversitypress.co.uk

British Library Cataloguing-in-Publication Data
A catalogue record for this book is available from the British Library

ISBN 978 1 5261 5716 4 hardback
ISBN 978 1 5261 5717 1 paperback

This edition first published 2023

Typeset by Newgen Publishing UK
Printed in Great Britain by Bell & Bain Ltd, Glasgow

Contents

Part III
MATTERS OF LIFE AND DEATH

Table of cases

A

B

C

D

E

F

G

H

I

J

K

L

M

N

O

P

S

V

W

X

Y

Z

Decisions of the European Court of Justice are listed below numerically. These decisions are also included in the preceding alphabetical list.

Table of statutes

N

O

P

R

S

Table of statutory instruments

R

V

Table of European and international material

Regulations

Preface

One problem no author of a book on medical law will face is an insufficiency of subject matter. Parliament and the law courts have ensured that we have much to write about and should there be any risk of idleness our colleagues in medicine continue to develop new technologies requiring attention. The seventh edition of *Medicine, patients and the law* grapples with significant legal change on issues including public health, healthcare research, medical malpractice, the care of young children and organ transplantation. The United Kingdom's withdrawal from the European Union (colloquially styled Brexit) means that, more than ever, the law is in flux. The European Union (Withdrawal) Act 2018 repealed the European Communities Act 1972, but retained most EU laws as UK domestic law and gave the Government extensive powers to amend retained EU law by secondary legislation. The EU must be distinguished from the European Convention on Human Rights (ECHR) of which the UK remains a Member State for the present. There is pressure to repeal the Human Rights Act 1998, which makes Convention rights enforceable against public authorities in the UK, and indeed to withdraw from the ECHR itself. We can only apologise to our readers for the number of times they will encounter the phrase 'at the time of writing'. We have tried to identify sources to guide the reader through this tumultuous period of change.

I wrote the first edition of this book in 1987 after extensive discussions and debates with Professors Harry Street and Gerald Dworkin, who were initially to have co-written the book with me. Harry Street's untimely death, and Gerald Dworkin's many other commitments, prevented those original plans coming to fruition. Professor Emma Cave joined me as co-author for the fourth edition in 2007. Emma and I are delighted to welcome Professor Rob Heywood as the third member of our team. Planning this edition, I envisaged a three-way split of the first drafts of the chapters. In the event, poor health meant that Emma and Rob took on virtually all the hard graft of preparing the manuscript and I offered comments and advice. I trust I was not too irritating.

In 1987 there was much less medical law to write about. In 2022 every chapter of the book could easily grow into a book in its own right. We cannot cover every key issue in the depth that we might wish to. We hope that the work remains readable to a broad audience and offers a picture of the way that law and medicine relate to each other which will engage the interest of students, lawyers, health professionals and the general public. We are all affected by how law regulates medicine. As before, we do not attempt to cover mental health law as such. To do so would double the length of the book. We do, in Chapter 7, address complex and seemingly intractable questions about vulnerable patients, mental capacity and consent to treatment. We do not seek to cover the immense body of case-law from the Court of Protection, instead choosing illustrative examples.

This edition, like the previous sixth edition, is published by Manchester University Press. We are proud to be part of the Contemporary Issues in Bioethics, Law and Medical Humanities series at the Press and grateful to our editors, Lucy Burns and Thomas Dark, and our series editors, Rebecca Bennett and Simona Giordano, for their continued support. We want to thank all our colleagues at Manchester, UEA, Durham and elsewhere for their unstinting help and advice. Colleagues from the disciplines of law, bioethics and medicine have listened patiently as we tried out ideas on them and advised us as the work progressed. We owe a particular debt over many years to Neil Allen, Sarah Devaney, Kirsty Keywood, Sara Fovargue, Danielle Griffiths, Alexandra Mullock, Anna Nelson, Chloe Romanis, Craig Purshouse and Suzanne Ost. We thank our students (a number of whom are doctors and nurses) who challenge our views and force us to think again on many issues. We are especially grateful to Eliza Bechtold, who helped us with preliminary updates, Rachel Jenkins for proof reading and advice in the final stages and Jordan Buck for invaluable assistance with the table of cases and the index. Finally, this edition could not have been written without the support, patience and encouragement of our families, Rodney and Victoria Brazier, Simon, Hannah and Tom Cave, and Nicola and Isabella Heywood. I am grateful to the Leverhulme Trust for the award of a Leverhulme Trust Emeritus Fellowship (EM-2018-067/8) which assisted my research into medico-legal history.

Any criticism of medical practice in this book is the result of academic endeavour and not personal experience. We are grateful for the care our families have received from general practice and NHS hospitals. We care passionately about the NHS. Were all care of the standard that we have received, this book would be shorter.

No book on this subject is ever wholly up to date. This book is (we trust) up to date to March 2022.

Margaret Brazier

Introduction

The law's relationship with medicine has become a highly publicised affair. Rarely a day passes without media coverage of some new controversy surrounding medical practice, or medical ethics. In the COVID-19 pandemic, decisions about research, allocation of resources, vaccine priorities and mandate were everyone's business. Cases relating to the rights and responsibilities of doctors and patients feature regularly in the Law Reports. The medical profession finds itself in the limelight. One day doctors are hailed as saviours. The next they are condemned as authoritarian or uncaring. Advances in medical science, extending life at one end and bringing new hope to the childless at the other, have given rise to intricate problems of law and ethics. At every level of medical practice, law plays a role. Doctors cannot escape the reach of the law. For many practitioners, the rise in the number of malpractice claims is their main concern. Despite legislation designed to tackle a perceived 'compensation culture' doctors still fear an epidemic of US proportions. Notwithstanding the 'duty of candour', some doctors refuse to risk an apology or even to explain what went wrong lest their careers and reputations suffer should the patient choose to litigate. Patients still find the pursuit of any grievance frustrating. In 2022, people also seek a greater say in their own treatment, and in doing so have the backing of the Supreme Court in *Montgomery v Lanarkshire Health Board*.[1] Patients are no longer prepared to be patient. At the same time, how far patients who claim rights are also subject to responsibilities is increasingly debated.

It is not only the narrow question of our own health needs that concerns people today. Many of the recent scientific developments are controversial. Extending the 14-day limit for research on embryos, uterus transplants, gene editing, human cloning, all excite controversy. Older controversies about abortion, organ donation and assisted dying get no less difficult with time. The purpose of this book is to examine how medical practice is regulated, to analyse the rights and responsibilities of doctors and patients, to look at the provision of compensation for medical wrongdoing or error, and to explore the framework of legal rules governing those delicate questions of life and

1 [2015] UKSC 11.

death when medicine, morals and the law overlap. It is easy to perceive law's relationship with medicine as one of conflict, mirroring conflict between doctors and their patients. We suggest that this is a 'false' conflict. What the medical profession, patients and the public have a need for are:

(1) that the medical profession is properly regulated;
(2) that where possible, the rights and obligations of patients, doctors and other health professionals are clearly defined;
(3) that there is an adequate, fair and rational system of compensation for patients suffering injury;
(4) that there are effective means of investigating medical accidents and errors;
(5) that the law (together with professional guidelines) offers comprehensive guidance on those areas of medical practice of moral and ethical sensitivity.

Sources of law

In contrast to most European countries, the law of England is not neatly encapsulated in any Code. The task of the non-lawyer seeking to establish their rights and duties is far from easy. The law relating to medical practice is to be discovered from a variety of sources. Parliament has enacted several statutes governing medical practice. Since the first Medical Act in 1858, the regulation of medical practice and the disciplining of the defaulting doctor have been entrusted by Act of Parliament to the General Medical Council (GMC). The Medical Act 1983 is now the governing statute but it has been substantially amended. The organisation of the health service has been governed by countless statutes on the National Health Service (NHS), consolidated in the National Health Service Act 2006, and subject to major reform in 2012. The Health and Care Act 2022 brought about yet more fundamental change to the NHS. The Medicines Act 1968 (also heavily amended) is concerned with the safety of drugs. A number of other Acts of Parliament, such as the Abortion Act 1967, the Human Fertilisation and Embryology Act 1990 (as amended), the Human Tissue Act 2004, the Medicines and Medical Devices Act 2021 and the Mental Capacity Act 2005, are crucially relevant to questions about medicine, patients and the law. An Act of Parliament can create only a general framework of legal rules. Acts of Parliament, therefore, commonly empower government ministers to make subsidiary regulations known as statutory instruments. These regulations may determine crucial questions. For example, most of the duties of general practitioners within the NHS are dealt with by regulations and not by Act of Parliament.

When the UK was a member state of the European Union (EU), EU laws applied in the UK as in all member states and had a significant impact on health laws in the UK. In the chapters that follow we deal with several EU laws that affect medicine and patients, such as the 1985 Community Directive on liability for unsafe products, which resulted in the Consumer Protection Act 1987, and the General Data Protection Regulation, which governs the processing of personal information. Free movement allowed patients to travel to other countries for treatment and facilitated the mobility of health professionals.

The relationship between the UK and the EU changed fundamentally when the UK voted to leave the EU in a referendum in 2016. The following year the Prime Minister, Theresa May, notified the President of the European Council that the UK would invoke Article 50 of the Treaty of the EU. Tense negotiations followed and a Withdrawal Agreement was eventually negotiated. It is important to note that EU law must still be considered in relation to a number of questions relating to medicine and the law. The EU (Withdrawal) Act 2018 repealed the European Communities Act 1972 and provided that EU law already applying in the UK would be retained to facilitate continuity. A raft of amendments instituted largely technical change to make sure EU law could operate in the UK context. The UK withdrew from the EU on 31 January 2020 and a transition period ended on 31 December 2020. At that point the UK became a 'third country', losing the benefits of EU systems, but gaining opportunities for advantage through a bespoke approach. Notwithstanding EU Exit, the value of alignment with the EU makes EU law an important driver of change in the UK.

The European Union must not be confused with the European Convention on Human Rights. That Convention is a separate treaty to which the United Kingdom is a party. The Convention seeks to establish the rights of the individual and directly addresses questions such as rights to life, to privacy, and to found a family. The Human Rights Act 1998 renders rights granted by the Convention enforceable against public authorities in the United Kingdom. Domestic courts must take into account the jurisprudence of the European Court of Human Rights. As we shall see, the Act has transformed areas of medical law and, as a living instrument, that potential has not diminished with time. If the Conservative government repeals the Human Rights Act 1998, the Convention will remain relevant and any change to medical law resulting from repeal of the 1998 Act is likely to be gradual and incremental.

Conventions, statutes and statutory regulations alone by no means paint the whole picture of English medical law. Much of English law remains judge-made; the common law of England. Decisions, judgments handed down by the courts, form precedents for determining later disputes and define the rights and duties of doctors and patients in areas untouched by statute. The common law largely governs the patient's right to determine their own treatment, parents' rights to control medical treatment of their children and, as we shall see, several other vital matters.

We deal with English law. The common law is not confined to England. Decisions of courts in the USA, Canada and elsewhere are mentioned from time to time. Such judgments do not bind an English court. They can be useful as examples, or warnings, showing us how the same basic principles of law have developed elsewhere. Finally, it must be remembered that for the lawyer, Scotland counts as a foreign country. Scotland maintains its own independent legal system and, post-devolution, enjoys the power to legislate independently on most issues relating to medical care. Scotland has, for example, enacted its own Human Tissue (Scotland) Act 2006. On many of the questions dealt with in this book, English and Scottish law coincide. Occasionally, the law in England and Scotland diverges. We confine ourselves in general to stating the law as it applies in England and Wales, noting that the Welsh Assembly has gained increased powers to legislate independently of the Westminster Parliament. Wales was the first devolved country to provide for an opt-out system for cadaver organ donation. The problems of law and medicine addressed in this book are common to the United Kingdom as a whole and well beyond the shores of this country.

Part I

Part I of this book now begins by looking back at some of the history of law's engagement with medicine. We seek to show that contrary to claims that medical law is 'comparatively young', questions of medical law have troubled the courts and the legislature for several centuries. We also argue that assumptions that until the late twentieth century judges consistently deferred to medical opinion are misguided. Chapters 2 and 3 examine the overall framework of medicine today. How does the law seek to ensure that patients are treated by competent, qualified doctors practising ethical medicine? The government has proposed regulatory reform of the healthcare professions. Does the GMC meet patients' needs in 2022? What rights do we enjoy in the context of healthcare and how has the Human Rights Act affected medical law? Law can, at best, only set basic standards of behaviour. So in Chapter 4 we explore some of the ethical principles and dilemmas in modern medicine. Then in the final chapter of this first Part, we examine that critical component of any doctor–patient relationship, the necessity for trust and confidence. Can we be assured that our doctors will respect our privacy so that we can feel confident enough to be wholly frank with them? In what exceptional circumstances should that duty of confidence be breached to fulfil some more pressing responsibility to others?

Part II

In this Part, we examine what remedies the law affords a patient dissatisfied with the medical care they received. A patient may feel that they have not been fully consulted or properly counselled about the nature and risks of treatment. They may have agreed to treatment and ended up worse, not better. Consequently, the patient may seek compensation from the courts. Or they may simply want an investigation of what went wrong, and to ensure that their experience is not suffered by others. It is the rise in litigation that has caused so much anxiety among doctors.

The law relating to medical errors, often described as medical malpractice, operates on two basic principles. (1) The patient must agree to treatment. (2) Treatment must be carried out with reasonable skill and care on the part of all the members of the medical profession involved. Any doctor who operated on or injected, or even touched, an adult patient against her will might commit a battery, a trespass against the patient's person. A doctor who was shown to have exercised inadequate care of their patient, to have fallen below the required standard of competence, would be liable to compensate the patient for any harm caused in the tort of negligence. In short, to obtain compensation, the patient must show that the doctor was at fault. And if they sue for negligence, they must show that the doctor's 'fault' caused their injury.

We shall see that the law is a remedy only for more specific and serious grievances against a doctor. It is in any case an expensive and unwieldy weapon. Many patients have complaints, particularly about hospitals, which do not amount to actionable negligence. They complain about being kept waiting, inadequate visiting hours, or rudeness on the part of NHS staff. We shall look in this Part at extra-legal methods of pursuing complaints against a hospital or a doctor, and we consider if the whole system for compensating medical errors should be replaced by a no-fault compensation scheme. Nor do we limit our examination to faults alleged against medical practitioners. Many medical mishaps arise from the dangers inherent in certain drugs. We consider the liability of the drug companies and attempts by government to ensure that available medicines are safe. We end Part II by considering the controversial role of criminal law in relation to medical malpractice including institutional failings and systems errors.

We should say a word about legal 'language' today. The person who initiates a legal action, for example the patient suing a doctor for battery or negligence, used to be referred to as the plaintiff. When Lord Woolf recommended radical reforms of the civil justice system, some of which are discussed in Chapter 9, he also proposed that old-fashioned language should be changed into plain English. So today, the patient bringing a claim against a doctor is simply called the claimant. Where we discuss cases decided before 1999, we use the old term plaintiff. Defendants, thankfully, remain just that, defendants.

Part III

The first two Parts of this book focus on the relationship of doctors and patients, both the framework of that relationship and how the law deals with conflict when a patient is dissatisfied with the care that they have received. Part III looks at the dramatic questions in medical law where what is at stake is not only what an individual patient may be entitled to, but also what society should allow. The range of questions addressed is broad. Others are omitted simply on grounds of space. We consider if parents who find themselves with an unplanned child after receipt of negligent medical advice or treatment should receive compensation to meet the cost of raising that child. What duties are owed to an unborn child, and should pregnant women continue to enjoy legal immunity from liability to their future children? We venture into the troubled waters of the reproductive technologies, seeking to explain and analyse the law governing such matters as the time limit for embryo research, human cloning, hybrid embryos. We also attempt to address practical questions – how to define parental status, 'male pregnancy', what happens when surrogacy arrangements go wrong and the problems of overseas surrogacy. Medical research, new laws introducing deemed consent arrangements for deceased organ donations and the especial problems around the medical care of children are addressed. We end (appropriately) by examining laws relating to the end of life, and debates about assisted dying.

Law matters

Medical law has altered beyond recognition in the thirty-five years since the first edition of this book. No one who reads a newspaper, watches television or accesses social media can be unaware of the sorts of questions which we address. On an almost weekly basis, new initiatives or new laws are proposed. Sometimes it seems as though the dizzying pace of reform reflects little thought about the whole picture. More attention is paid to policy and ethical debate than law. There is insufficient rigorous analysis of what the limits of the law's remit should be. One set of lawyers, doctors and patients' groups addresses the adequacy (or inadequacy) of malpractice litigation. Ethicists, journalists and legal theorists join doctors and theologians in debating the grand moral dilemmas of medicine. Lay people tend not to get much of a chance to have their say until some controversy breaks, such as the scandals around abysmal standards of care at Shrewsbury and Telford Hospital NHS Trust.[2] For all these reasons, this book seeks to concentrate more on law than ethics as such, and to attempt to locate our discussions of the law in a practical context. We hope that we can dispel the myth that law is 'boring'. We hope that our discussion may cast some light on what the role of the law should be in the context of modern medicine.

2 DHSC, *Final Report of the Ockenden Review* (2022) HC 1219.

Part I

MEDICINE, LAW AND SOCIETY

Chapter 1

THE PRACTICE OF MEDICINE: YESTERDAY

1.1 Introduction

Medical law, both in the sense of regular engagement with medicine by the courts and Parliament, and in the academic study of how English law relates to medical practice, is often thought to be 'new'. A law student in 1968 interested in how law regulated medical practice would not find a course in medical law to whet their appetite for knowledge. Should they decide to do their own research, focusing on the past hundred years or so, they would find relatively little evidence of much activity. Two leading academics, Ian Kennedy and Andrew Grubb, writing in 2000, described medical law as 'a comparatively young subject', which only emerged in English law as an area of importance in legal practice or as an academic discipline over the last two decades of the twentieth century.[1]

Moreover, it was often assumed that when the courts or Parliament were asked to consider questions about medical practice, or moral dilemmas arising from advances in medical science, judges and legislators deferred to the doctors, accepting that 'doctor knows best'. Not until the 1980s, triggered by Kennedy's incisive attack on aspects of medical practice and judicial spinelessness in his Reith lectures, published in 1981 as *The Unmasking of Medicine*, was medical law born as a respectable area for academic study.[2] The subject grew apace. Medical law is a popular module on virtually every law degree. When the first edition of this textbook was published in 1987 there were two other comparable texts as opposed to at least twelve in 2022. Our seventh edition is nearly twice the length of the first.

If medical law was only born just over forty years ago, is there any useful purpose in examining yesterday? If there is a history of judges showing blind deference to medical practitioners, would we want to copy it? To understand what history offers, we look further back in time to uncover a longstanding relationship of law, medical practice and medical science. There is ample evidence that the law courts, Parliament and the Crown regularly engaged with medicine. Medical law in England has a history dating back to at least

1 A Grubb (ed), *Kennedy and Grubb: Medical Law* (3rd edn, 2000) Butterworths, 3.
2 I Kennedy, *The Unmasking of Medicine* (1981), Allen and Unwin.

the thirteenth century and providing little evidence of consistent deference to medical brethren until late in the nineteenth century.[3] We do not address medical law as an academic discipline here.[4]

Medico-legal history demonstrates that fundamental questions of law and ethics in relation to medicine endure over the centuries. The same questions are asked again and again. Persistent questions cluster around a number of themes, including regulation of medicine, the legal framework of the doctor–patient relationship, matters relating to human bodies, and conflict between popular opinion and science.[5] One central question is simple to ask and fiendish to answer. Is healthcare different from other businesses or occupations? Other important questions include: does the state have responsibilities to protect citizens from poor or dangerous medical practice? Who defines poor practice? Doctors have sought to assert that only they can define and distinguish between good and bad practice. Or, are patients to be regarded as consumers – free to make choices and to expect healthcare workers to implement those choices? The doctor or nurse is merely a technician, fixing the body, as the plumber fixes a defective water tank.

1.2 Medico-legal history

History has no easy answers to problems of the regulation of either practice or science. It may provide a model to inform those answers. For example, from the sixteenth until the twentieth century a contract model dominated provision of medical care, a model which can cast light on the pros and cons of advocacy of consumerist medical law today.

Medical law is not confined to consideration of professional regulation and the doctor–patient relationship; it also addresses how law responds to, and regulates, developments in biomedical science. We live in an era of amazing advances in medical technologies, embracing interventions undreamt of even a century ago. What history can there be? In many cases 'new' developments have 'old' roots. Artificial wombs are on the horizon, feeding into the eternal debate on the status of the fetus and what constitutes 'born alive'. In the absence of specific legislation, 'old' law remains relevant to 'new' medicine.[6]

1.3 Finding the history

Parts I and II of this book focus on the regulation of medical practice and the doctor–patient relationship. Part III *Matters of Life and Death* (and Chapter 4

3 M Brazier, *Law and Healing: A History of a Stormy Marriage* (2023) Manchester University Press.

4 See M Brazier and J Montgomery, 'Whence and Whither "Modern Medical Law?"' (2019) 70 *Northern Ireland Legal Quarterly* 5.

5 Ibid.

6 S Maclean, *Old Law, New Medicine: Medical; Ethics and Human Rights* (1999) Pandora.

of Part I) (*inter alia*) addresses responses to ethical dilemmas in relation to medicine, such as abortion, reproduction and end-of-life care. In current parlance those matters might be labelled as bioethical controversies. In relation to much of Parts I and II, the question is whether there is any history worth investigating, given that medicine and the legal system now appear so different. In Part III addressing ethical problems, history is 'hiding in plain sight'. You cannot examine these topics in medical law without encountering history, though you may not realise that you are doing so. In 2000, the Court of Appeal was asked to rule on the legality of separating conjoined twins in an operation which would inevitably kill the weaker twin. All three judges extended their exposition of the law back several centuries.[7] The question is not whether there is any history, but rather whether the history is outdated, based on superstitions rejected by people today, and, some have argued, riddled with religious dogma.[8] This chapter addresses regulation of practice and the doctor–patient relationship. Some history of the law relating to ethical dilemmas will be found in Chapter 4 and Part III.

Delving into medico-legal history is challenging. Not much has been written by modern English medical lawyers on their subject's history. Older cases are difficult to read. Early law reports are often partial, written in Norman French or Latin. Moreover, English common law was obsessed with procedure. Substantive issues relating to principles of law were buried under turgid disputes about whether the correct writ was served. Perseverance is worthwhile. B Abbott Goldberg commented 'in these dusty, fusty antiques are the first glimmers of modern law of the quality of medical care'.[9]

1.4 Ancestors, medicine and the law

Illness and injury have plagued humanity for as long as humans have walked the earth. What medical care was accessible to our ancestors? If there was little access to medical treatment there would be little call for law. Assumptions that until relatively recently only the rich had access to medical care have been proved wrong. Margaret Pelling has written 'early modern people were obsessed with health, with its fragility and with the means of preserving it'.[10] Moreover, there is evidence that laypeople, consumers of healthcare, sought rights over their own lives and bodies'.[11] Even if there is evidence that ordinary people had access to healthcare and resorted to law to assert their rights, given that medicine was very different, can anything be learned? David Wootton commented:

7 *Re A (Children) (Conjoined Twins: Surgical Separation)* [2000] Lloyd's Rep Med 425, CA.

8 G Williams, *The Sanctity of Life and the Criminal Law* (1957) Alfred A Knopf.

9 B Abbott Goldberg, 'Horseshoers, Doctors and Judges and the Law on Medical Competence' (1978) 9 *Pacific Law Journal* 107, 115.

10 M Pelling, *The Common Lot: Sickness, Medical Occupations and the Urban Poor in Early Modern England* (1998) Routledge, p 5.

11 Ibid, p 8.

> [I]f we define medicine as the ability to cure disease then there was very little medicine before 1865. The long tradition that descended from Hippocrates, symbolized by reliance on bloodletting, purges and emetics, was almost totally ineffectual, indeed positively deleterious.[12]

Treatments available before late in the nineteenth century were often brutal and, as Wootton says, 'ineffectual'. Consulting astrological charts, standard practice in Tudor England, would not be part of diagnosis today. Should an injury to a leg be so traumatic that amputation was the only option, the sixteenth-century surgeon would carry out surgery similar to today. But there would be no anaesthesia or antibiotics. Although some ancient remedies have still proven to be useful (leeches are again applied to clean wounds), the utility of 'treatments' is not the key factor in assessing historical relationships between law and medicine. Human bodies have changed little. Human nature is much the same. The patient in 1623 was not much different to his descendant in 2022.

1.5 'Doctors' looked different!

When we ask who were the doctors providing treatment, the picture becomes complicated. In the Middle Ages, the Universities of Oxford and Cambridge were empowered to issue licences to practise. A university licence required a lengthy academic education involving very little study of medicine.[13] The Church was a major provider of healthcare in the monastic hospitals. After the decline and ultimate dissolution of the monasteries, different groups of healers competed for custom in a 'medical marketplace'. England followed the continental tripartite division of medicine of physicians, surgeons and apothecaries, often described as orthodox practitioners. Physicians considered themselves to be the most learned of the orthodox and the apex of the medical hierarchy. They aspired to equal social status with the lawyer and the clergyman and claimed a monopoly in practising 'physic'. Physic may be loosely defined as embracing diagnosis, prognosis and recommendation of remedies. Physicians did not get their hands dirty or engage in trade. Attending his patient, the physician would diagnose disease by taking a history, sniffing the patient's urine and consulting his astrological charts. Then he would advise remedies. If he recommended bloodletting or surgery, the actual procedure would be carried out by a surgeon. Surgeons in medieval and Tudor England were perceived as more like craftsmen than gentlemen. Should the physician prescribe medicines, an apothecary would dispense the medicine. Apothecaries, however, had a broader role than just making up medicines ordered by physicians. Outside London, apothecaries were more like modern general practitioners.

[12] D Wootton, *Bad Medicine: Doctors Doing Harm Since Hippocrates* (2007) Oxford University Press, pp 64–66.

[13] M Pelling and C Webster, 'Medical Practitioners' in C Webster (ed), *Health Medicine and Mortality in the Sixteenth Century* (1979) Cambridge University Press, pp 189–194.

Other 'healers' crowded the marketplace. Herbalists offered alternative remedies to orthodox medicine; traditional healers (such as bone setters) learned their trade informally, often from family members. 'Quacks' peddled dubious remedies. In the sixteenth and seventeenth centuries, female midwives licensed by the Church cared for birthing women and their babies.[14]

1.6 Medical corporations

Orthodox 'doctors' belonged to their own medical corporation, each one regulating its members and representing their interests. From 1518, the College of Physicians claimed to be the pre-eminent authority on medical practice, although the surgeons created the first 'professional' association of doctors, setting up the Fellowship or Guild of Surgeons in 1368. Although representing the elite surgeons, often educated at one of the famous medical schools in Europe, the Fellowship remained small in numbers, and much routine surgery was performed by barbers, some of whom, barber-surgeons, specialised in medical procedures. In 1540, London surgeons were forcibly united with the barbers to form the Barber-Surgeons Company, further diminishing their social standing. In 1745 an Act of Parliament dissolved the unhappy union and, in 1800, the surgeons were granted a Royal Charter. The Company became the Royal College of Surgeons. Apothecaries were originally part of the Grocers' Company. In 1607, they obtained separate status within the Grocers' Company and in 1617 broke from the Grocers becoming the Society of Apothecaries. Unions with barbers and grocers reinforced the physicians' claim that surgeons and apothecaries were little different to blacksmiths and shopkeepers. The three corporations were in constant conflict. The law courts were the battlefield. There is an abundance of case-law in which the medical corporations challenged each other, and, from time to time, united to drive unlicensed healers out of business.

1.7 Regulation – wasted centuries?

Long before the Medical Act 1858 established the General Medical Council (GMC),[15] Parliament and the Crown also engaged in regulating medical practice. The volume of Royal Charters and statutes addressing regulation of medicine would fill a whole book. The fundamental questions about the purpose and form of regulation do not change. The two earliest Parliamentary interventions identified those questions, and proposed answers.

In 1421, a Bill presented to Parliament sought to license and regulate the practice of physic and surgery, to be enforced by the Sheriffs across the realm. The Bill deplored the practice of physic by 'many uncunning and unapproved' so that 'every man be he never so lewd' could take upon him practise 'to great harm and slaughter of many men'. Chaos following the death of Henry V

14 S Fox and M Brazier, 'Regulating English Midwives c1500–1900' (2020) 20 *Medical Law International* 308.

15 See 2.7–2.16 below.

meant that those proposals for a national regulator were never implemented.[16] The failure of the Bill was the first of a long list of missed opportunities to establish a unified system of regulation well before 1858. Unfortunately, one injunction from the Bill – '[N]o woman use the practise of physic' – throve for nearly five hundred years.

In 1511, Parliament enacted 'An Act concerning Physicians and Surgeons' requiring any man practising 'physic' or surgery to be licensed by their local bishop unless he was a graduate of Oxford or Cambridge.[17] Its Preamble declared that 'physic' and surgery require great learning and yet are 'daily within this realm exercised by a great multitude of ignorant persons' including 'common artificers, as smiths, weavers and *women*.' Such unlearned people:

> [P]artly use sorcery and witchcraft, and apply such medicines unto the disease as be very noxious, and nothing meet therefore to the high displeasure of God, great infamy to the faculty, and the *grievous hurt, damage and destruction of many of the king's liege people, most especially of them that cannot discern the uncunning from the cunning* [our emphasis].

Both the 1421 Bill and the 1511 Act proposed *external* licensing of practitioners and crucially declared that the purpose of licensing was the protection of the public (the king's liege people) rather than the protection of the interests of licensed practitioners. Not until 2002 was the Medical Act 1983 amended to declare that the main objective of the GMC is 'to protect, promote and maintain the safety of the public'.[18] While both Bill and Act decried the proliferation of unlicensed healers, they emphasised the danger that people could not judge if a practitioner had any qualifications to practise, and distinguish the 'uncunning from the cunning', laying the foundations of the policy driving the 1858 Act in establishing the Medical Register. Note, too, that tension still pervades the relationship between allopathic and alternative medicine.[19] And the rise of the latter has created a 'medical market' not that much different from 1511.[20]

1.8 Self-regulation

The 1511 Act introduced *external* licensing. Medical practitioners advocated self-regulation, arguing that they were best placed to assess fitness to practise

16 JH Raach, 'English Medical Licensing in the Early Seventeenth Century' (1944) 16 *Yale Journal of Biology and Medicine* 267.

17 3 Henry VIII c 5. The Act was not repealed until 1948 by the Statute Law Revision Act. In theory any physician or surgeon practising without an episcopal licence before 1948 practised unlawfully: JR Guy, 'The Episcopal Licensing of Physicians, Surgeons and Midwives' (1982) 56 *Bulletin of the History of Medicine* 528–542.

18 The Medical Act 1983 (Amendment) Order 2002, SI 3135/2002. See 2.8 below.

19 J Stone and J Matthews, *Complementary Medicine and the Law* (1996) Oxford University Press, pp 21–36.

20 B Lyons, 'Papist Potions and Electric Sex: A Historical Perspective on "Proper Medical Treatment"' in S Fovargue and A Mullock (eds), *The Legitimacy of Medical Treatment: What Role for the Medical Exception?* (2016) Routledge, pp 51–67.

and protect patients. The high point of self-regulation is seen in the powers granted to the London College of Physicians. Established in 1518 by physicians close to the King, the College Charter, confirmed by statute in 1522,[21] granted the College exclusive powers to license those permitted to practise 'physic' in London, or within a seven-mile area around London.[22] The London-centric focus resulted from the concentration of educated physicians in the capital and the lucrative London market for practitioners. Elsewhere local Guilds governed trades and crafts in most major cities.[23]

The College enjoyed the power to determine who was qualified to practise 'physic' and, via its Censors, exercised draconian powers to search for and punish unlicensed practice or *mala praxis* (malpractice). Its jurisdiction was not limited to its own members. The College exercised powers far in excess of the GMC at any time, including sentencing offenders to prison. Some judges, notably Sir Edward Coke, were highly critical of powers which allowed the College to be investigator, prosecutor and judge of violation of its rules,[24] criticisms levelled at the GMC four centuries later.[25] The College strove to compel other practitioners to submit to its authority. The surgeons and apothecaries used the courts to challenge the College with mixed success.[26] One strategy was to provoke a *cause celebre*. An individual acting as proxy for the surgeons or apothecaries defied the College and when found guilty of malpractice or unlicensed practice resorted to the common law courts, often triggering protracted litigation exemplified in *Bonham's Case*. Thomas Bonham was imprisoned for both malpractice and unlicensed practice. He succeeded in his suit against the College for false imprisonment.[27] In 1703, an apothecary, William Rose, defeated the College in the highest court in the realm, the House of Lords. The judgment allowed apothecaries to diagnose and give advice, not just make up medicines as directed by a physician, ie to practise physic, as long as the advice was given gratis and the apothecary charged only for his medicines.[28] While the College scored some victories in subsequent cases, the overall result was stalemate.[29] In practice, especially in the provinces, the tripartite division was breaking down. Dual qualified surgeon-apothecaries provided most families' care.

21 'The Privileges and Authority of Physicians in London' 3 Henry VIII c 5.

22 The College might have acquired a national role in examining candidates for an episcopal licence on behalf of the local bishop: see Brazier, *Law and Healing*, p 46.

23 RS Roberts, 'The Personnel and Practice of Medicine in Tudor and Stuart England: Part I: The Provinces' (1964) 6 *Medical History* 365–366.

24 *Dr Bonham's Case* (1609) 77 English Reports 646, 652.

25 Chief Medical Officer's Report: *Good Doctors Safer Patients* (2006) Department of Health.

26 Brazier, *Law and Healing*, pp 52–61.

27 HJ Cook, 'Against Common Right and Reason: The College of Physicians Versus Dr Thomas Bonham' (1985) 29 *American Journal of Legal History* 301.

28 *William Rose (Plaintiff in Error) v The College of Physicians (London)* (1703) 2 English Reports 857, discussed in HJ Cook, 'The Rose Case Reconsidered; Physicians, Apothecaries and the Law in Augustan England' (1990) 45 *Journal of the History of Medicine and Allied Sciences* 527.

29 Brazier, *Law and Healing*, pp 62–67.

Despite their internecine battles, orthodox practitioners still shared a visceral hatred of unlicensed healers, and again the courts were the fora in which the battle of *Orthodox v Others* was played out, designed to drive the latter out of the market. If a patient died after treatment by an unlicensed healer, campaigning doctors would assist the family at the inquest pressing for a verdict of manslaughter and the healer's prosecution for manslaughter. To boost conviction rates, the orthodox argued that if a patient treated by an unlicensed healer died within three days of treatment a presumption of guilt should arise and the accused would have to prove it was not his gross negligence which caused the death.[30] As we will see later, the judges rejected any such presumption.

1.9 Medical reform

By the end of the eighteenth century the failure of the existing system for regulation became apparent to all but the diehard corporations. A raft of different groups pressed for legislative reforms. With the apothecaries in the vanguard,[31] several pressure groups advocated different models for regulation.[32] We address only three.

In 1793, a group naming themselves the General Pharmaceutical Association of Great Britain (GPAGB) presented proposals to the medical corporations. All three of the ancient corporations opposed the proposals and, when a petition was presented to Parliament, ensured it made no progress. Nonetheless, the petition had interesting features which were to become key to reforms embodied in the Medical Act 1858, including the following: A 'competent court' should be established with '*full power to make such bye laws and regulations as may be thought most conducive to the welfare of the public and the profession*' [our emphasis]. Harking back to 1421, self-regulation was to be qualified by a requirement that regulators act for the welfare of the public not just the profession.

In 1806, the College of Physicians presented its own proposals, reviving and extending its claim to dominance. The College sought statutory powers to regulate all medical practice in England and Wales. No one would be permitted to practise medicine, surgery, midwifery or pharmacy without a licence from the College, which would set the entry standards and requirements for professional conduct for each branch of medicine. The College's attempt to restore and extend the old order met with little support. The Bill provided for an annual list of qualified practitioners, the forbear of the Medical Register, the lynchpin of regulation after 1858.

30 M Brazier, 'The Criminal Process and Medical Practitioners: Shield or Sword?' in M Henaghan and J Wall, *Law Ethics and Medicine: Essays in Honour of Peter Skegg* (2016) Thomson Reuters, pp 7–31.

31 The Apothecaries Act 1815 was an early flawed outcome of the pressure for reform; SWF Holloway, 'The Apothecaries Act, 1815: A Reinterpretation' (1966) 10 *Medical History* 107.

32 Brazier, *Law and Healing*, pp 68–74.

Criminalisation of quackery was high on the agenda of all the reformers. The London-based British Medical Association proposals summed up the fundamental objectives of many reformers; abolition of the tripartite system, unification of all branches of the profession to be regulated by a single national controlling body, elected by the whole profession. The protection of the interests of the professionals was the primary objective of many medical reformers to be ensured by the election of members of the regulatory body. Led by John Simon, who was to become England's first Chief Medical Officer (CMO), others contended that the primary function of regulation should be 'the service of the public'.[33] After sixteen failed attempts between 1830 and 1858, at long last the Medical Act was successfully enacted. It met with little enthusiasm, described by one leading reformer, Thomas Wakely, as 'half a loaf'.[34] The failure to criminalise the non-orthodox healers was especially galling to both the reformers and the medical corporations. Rejection of direct election was a blow to the general practitioners.

1.10 The Medical Act 1858

The Preamble read:

> Whereas it is expedient that Persons requiring Medical Aid should be able to distinguish qualified from unqualified Practitioners.

The Act began the slow process whereby a distinct profession emerged. Central to the 1858 Act was the creation of the medical register. Neither that Act nor its successors made it a criminal offence for an unqualified person to practise medicine. Should the authors of this book set up our own 'general practice', believing that we have learned enough medicine, we commit no crime even though we have no medical degree and are unlicensed to practise. Should we pretend to be registered, we could be prosecuted. The omission of provisions to criminalise unlicensed health workers bitterly disappointed many reformers. Two reasons may explain the omission. First the notion that the state should dictate who a patient should consult and what kind of treatment she might undergo was bitterly opposed. The Act itself went too far for some, who argued that reform would impose State medicine 'at the expense of English liberties' contending that 'the country has already got a State religion and a State education and it was now about to get State physic'.[35] Second, defining 'physic' in 1511 or 1858, or 'medicine' today is nigh on impossible. Is a father who gives his child a dose of paracetamol to lower his temperature practising medicine?

Defeat in 1858 for those who campaigned for the Council to be elected by the profession was reversed in the Medical Act 1886, which provided that five members of the Council should be directly elected. Many practitioners

[33] MJD Roberts, 'The Politics of Professionalization: MPs, Medical Men and the 1858 Medical Act' (2009) 53 *Medical History* 37, 40.

[34] Ibid, 37.

[35] T Duncombe MP cited in Roberts, 'Politic of Professionalisation', 44.

considered that the GMC's core function was to represent and safeguard doctors' interests. The very group of practitioners who had fought the old corporations' assertion of self-interest now claimed self-rule for the profession. They sought and won greater representation on the Council.[36] In 1983, a bloated Council comprised 104 members with elected representatives of the profession in the majority. 'Success' was short-lived. A damning report from the CMO charged that the GMC was 'dominated by professional interest, rather than that of the patient'.[37] Subsequent legislation radically changed the GMC, significantly reducing the influence of the profession. It is also worth noting that the 1858 Act allowed the appointment of lay members. No lay member was appointed until 1926. Lack of effective lay representation was to contribute to dissatisfaction with the GMC and the widely held view that the GMC failed to function as the nineteenth century CMO, John Simon, had proposed in 1858 in 'the service of the public'.[38]

1.11 Redress

Three millennia ago the Code of Hammurabi in ancient Mesopotamia declared:

> If a physician has performed a major operation on a lord with a bronze lancet and has saved the lord's life ... he shall receive ten shekels of silver ... if he causes the death of the lord his hand shall be chopped off.[39]

Redress for, and deterrence of, medical negligence has generated litigation for centuries. In medieval England, fear of litigation affected medical practitioners as much as it concerns doctors today:

> The medieval medical practitioner, *like his fellows of every age*, was vulnerable to accusations of negligence [our emphasis]. The least fortunate, or perhaps the most negligent, might find themselves liable to public prosecution, despite some recognition that treatment was hazardous. More commonly, the doctor might face a private lawsuit from a dissatisfied patient.[40]

We have seen that the College of Physicians could prosecute practitioners accused of *mala praxis* in London. Outside London, *mala praxis* was described by Chief Justice Holt as 'a great misdemeanour and offence at common law'.[41]

36 See R Smith, 'Profile of the GMC: 1978 and All That' (1989) 298 *British Medical Journal* (hereafter *BMJ*) 1297.

37 Chief Medical Officer's Report: *Good Doctors Safer Patients* (2006) Department of Health.

38 Roberts, 'The Politics of Professionalization', 40.

39 R Porter, *The Greatest Benefit to Mankind: A Medical History of Humanity from Antiquity to the Present* (1997) Fontana Press, p 45.

40 JB Post, 'Doctor versus Patient: Two Fourteenth Century Lawsuits' (1972) 16 *Medical History* 296.

41 *Dr Groenvelt's Case* (1695) 91 English Reports 1038, 1039. And see William Blackstone, *Commentaries on the Laws of England* Book III (2016) Oxford University Press, p 13 and see JW Willcock, *Laws relating to the Medical Profession with an Account of the Rise and Progress of the Various Orders* (1830) J & WT Clarke, p 89.

It would seem that the common law crime fell into desuetude during the nineteenth century.

1.12 Actions for negligence

As to private lawsuits, case-law from the fourteenth century and before addressed the same questions as we consider in Chapters 8 and 9. Today's law on liability for medical error is based on old cases. Duty[42] and standard of care,[43] informed consent,[44] experimental treatment,[45] and vicarious liability[46] all have their origins in cases decided before the twentieth century. Older cases may look different. While the principles defining medical negligence derive from cases centuries old, litigation often took a different form. In 2023 a claim for negligence will usually be initiated by the aggrieved patient. In 1623 the patient would normally have contracted with the doctor for his services. Patients unhappy with their treatment would simply not pay and the 'doctor' would initiate legal action suing for debt. The patient would defend failure to pay arguing that the 'doctor' was negligent.

1.13 Blind deference?

While there is evidence to show that medical law is far from new and has long been an important area of legal practice, is there evidence to support the assumption that, when the courts engaged with medicine, judges had always endorsed a tradition of deference to their medical brethren?[47] For about forty years after the 1957 case of *Bolam v Friern Hospital Management Committee*,[48] judges for the most part uncritically deferred to 'responsible medical opinion' to determine the obligations of doctors to patients, for example, in judging malpractice, establishing what patients should be told before consenting to treatment,[49] and defining the best interests of mentally incapacitated patients.[50] 'Responsible medical opinion' was a matter for the medical profession itself to define. Post 1981, the battle against *Bolam* dominated law in practice and academic debates. Yet, until late in the nineteenth century, judges generally declined to offer any sort of privilege to doctors, showing little inclination to accept medical opinion without question, or to favour licensed practitioners over unlicensed healers.

42 *Gladwell v Steggall* (1839) 132 English Reports 1283; *Pippin and Wife v Sheppard* (1822) 147 English Reports 400.
43 *Seare v Prentice* (1807) 103 English Reports 376.
44 *Slater v Baker and Stapleton* (1767) 95 English Reports 860.
45 Ibid.
46 *Hancke v Hooper* (1835) 173 English Reports 37.
47 H Teff, *Reasonable Care Legal Perspectives in the Doctor/Patient Relationship* (1994) Clarendon Press, pp 69–93.
48 [1957] 2 All ER 118.
49 *Sidaway Bethlem Royal Hospital* [1985] 1 All ER 643.
50 *F v West Berkshire Health Authority* [1989] 2 All ER 545

Judges saw no reason to give more credence to the opinion of a medical practitioner than to common practice in other occupations. Judicial language was at times scornful of the pretentions of the medical men. Directing the jury in the prosecution of an unlicensed healer for manslaughter, Park J said that in ascertaining whether the accused was criminally negligent, it mattered not:

> [W]hether the individual consulted be the president of the College of Physicians, the president of the College of Surgeons or the humblest bone-setter in the village.[51]

In civil claims for negligence, there is scant evidence that until late in the nineteenth century judges regarded a licensed doctor more favourably. A faint voice from the distant past to the contrary can be heard. In *The Oculist's Case* (1329)[52] a surgeon was sued after his treatment of a patient's eye resulted in the loss of the eye. Ibbetson notes the reluctance of Denum J to hold 'men of mystery' liable for professional incompetence.[53] Denum's sympathy for the medical practitioner was not shared by his successors. Simpson has suggested that the judiciary were not convinced that the licensed man was any more 'expert' or offered more effective treatments than an experienced but unlicensed healer.[54]

One caveat must be entered. The majority of cases reported are actions against surgeons and, to a lesser extent, apothecaries. There are few reported cases involving physicians. Goldberg notes that the eminent legal historian, William Holdsworth, 'simply lumps surgeons with smiths, horse doctors, innkeepers, vintners, butchers and carriers'.[55] Might physicians with their university degrees and social aspiration have attracted higher regard? The evidence from judgments relating to the powers of the College of Physicians is mixed, revealing sharp differences in judicial attitudes. In *Bonham's Case* in 1610, Coke CJ forcefully rejected the College's claim that only they could judge good or bad practice. He poured scorn on the College in colourful language:

> [N]o comparison was to be made between that private college and any of the universities of Cambridge and Oxford, no more than between a father and his children, or between the fountain and the small rivers which descend from it: the university is *alma mater* from whose breasts alone those of that private college have sucked all their science and knowledge.[56]

51 *R v John St John Long* (1831) 172 ER 172.

52 See J Baker (ed), *Baker and Milsom: Sources of English Legal History: Private Law to 1750* (2nd edn, 2010) Oxford University Press, p 381.

53 D Ibbetson, *A Historical Introduction to the Law of Obligations* (Oxford University Press) 1999, p 45.

54 AP Simpson, 'Quackery and Contract Law: The Case of the Carbolic Smoke Ball' (1985) 14 *Journal of Legal Studies* 366.

55 Abbott Goldberg, 'Horseshoers, Doctors and Judges and the Law on Medical Competence' 110.

56 *Dr Bonham's Case* (1609) 77 English Reports 646, 650.

The College was not to be the only expert judge of medical practice; any judge with a university education could find whether a medical case had been handled correctly or not.[57]

In 1695 in *Dr Groenvelt's Case*,[58] Coke's successor as Chief Justice, Holt CJ, was scornful of Coke saying the Court could make no judgment 'whether medicines were wholesome or not' for 'none but physicians can judge ... of it for that which is good physick for one person may not be for another'.[59] In Holt's words we espy 'glimmers' of *Bolam*.

In 1703, the landmark case of *Rose* undermined the physicians' claim to be the supreme arbiter of all medical practice.[60] The House of Lords rejected an attempt by the College to confine apothecaries to making up medicines as ordered by physicians, and to prevent them offering diagnoses or advice. No reasons were given. Perhaps one might surmise that their Lordships were unimpressed by the arguments of the College lauding the skill and beneficence of physicians and damning apothecaries as not '*bred* to have suitable skill'.

1.14 Rise of the expert

What of 'expert' witnesses called to testify what constituted common practice and reasonable skill? Yet again there is little evidence that until the nineteenth century the expert surgeon's opinion was accorded greater weight than that of the horse-doctor explaining good veterinary practice. The eminence of the defendant cut no ice with judges. In *Slater v Baker and Stapleton*,[61] the judges noted that proof of skill in general did not mean that there could not be particular cases when a practitioner acted rashly or unskilfully. In *Seare v Prentice*,[62] the trial judge was critical of a witness, Mr Kingston, suggesting that his 'vaunting' language must have diminished his credit with the jury. We should note that expert evidence in 1807 was not the same as today. Differences between evidence of fact and opinion were not clear-cut. The 'vaunting' Mr Kingston in *Seare* had himself performed corrective surgery on the plaintiff.

Clarification of the admissibility of expert evidence from witnesses who had no personal knowledge of the case opened the door to greater influence of expert evidence in medical malpractice claims.[63] Equally important was the development of genuine specialisms in medicine, particularly in obstetrics, and the growth of biomedical science. The impact of experts on the success of patient claims 1800–1900 is charted in research undertaken by Stein,

57 Cook, 'Against Common Right and Reason', 301, 317.
58 HJ Cook, *Trials of an Ordinary Doctor: Joannes Groenvelt in Seventeenth Century London* (1994) Johns Hopkins University Press.
59 *Dr Groenvelt versus Dr Burwell et al* (1698) 90 English Reports 883, 884.
60 *William Rose (Plaintiff in Error) v The College of Physicians (London)* (1703) 2 English Reports 857.
61 (1767) 95 English Reports 860.
62 (1807) 103 English Reports 376.
63 DM Dwyer, 'Expert Evidence in the English Civil Courts 1550–1800' (2007) 28 *Journal of Legal History* 93.

Guzelian and Guzelian.[64] Their survey of forty-nine reported cases (1800–1900) showed that in the eight cases where only the plaintiff-patient called an expert, the patient won. In the twelve cases where only the defendant called expert testimony the practitioner won. When both parties proffered expert evidence, the score was *Patients 8 : Doctors 21.*[65] From 1817 to 1828 all the cases in the survey were won by the patient. From 1828 to 1862 the result was a draw. After 1866 'practitioners effectively never lost again in the cases'.[66] The authors identify the Medical Act 1858 as a factor in the increased success rates for defendant-practitioners, arguing that the Act endorsed the competence of the registered doctor. In 1865, Alfred Swaine Taylor wrote that faced with competing evidence 'the default legal standard should be to absolve the medical practitioner under attack; he was after all a trained and presumably competent professional'.[67] Wilmot CJ's cautionary reminder in *Slater v Baker* that trained and competent professionals can still make mistakes seems to be forgotten.

1.15 The 'medical voice' and legislation

The increasing influence of medical expertise is also evident in legislation as illustrated in nineteenth century laws on abortion and dissection.

Until Lord Ellenborough's Act 1803, abortion was a common law misdemeanour but not a felony. Medical practitioners were largely invisible in either debates on fetal status or performing abortions, save where the mother's life was at risk. A succession of statutes from 1803 to 1861 made *unlawfully* procuring a miscarriage a felony and imposed draconian penalties on abortionists and women. The dominant voice in that legislative process was medicine. John Keown charted 'the increasingly restrictive development of the law against abortion between 1803 and 1861', concluding that Parliament was 'influenced to a significant degree by the emerging medical profession's condemnation of abortion and its proposals for reform'.[68] Note that the 1861 Act, via the presence of the word 'unlawfully', allowed for lawful abortions,[69] which proved to be abortions sanctioned by doctors. Contemporaneously, obstetrics emerged as a distinct specialty. The Obstetric Society was established in 1825, succeeded in 1858 by the London Obstetrical Society. The nascent male obstetricians with their 'shiny instruments and promise of "scientific expertise"'[70] sought a monopoly in the care of pregnant women and childbirth.

64 M Stein, C Guzelian and K Guzelian, 'Expert Testimony in Nineteenth Century Malapraxis Actions' (2015) 55 *American Journal of Legal History* 194.

65 Ibid, 203–204.

66 Ibid, 206.

67 A Swaine Taylor, *The Principles and Practice of Medical Jurisprudence Vol 1* (1st edn, 1865) Churchill, p 502.

68 J Keown, *Abortion, Doctors and the Law* (1988) Cambridge University Press.

69 See 16.2 below.

70 D Evenden, *The Midwives of Seventeenth-Century London* (2000) Cambridge University Press.

The Anatomy Act 1832 attracted huge controversy.[71] Medical education and medical progress required dead bodies to dissect. Demand vastly exceeded supply. Stealing fresh corpses from the grave, bodysnatching, became one means of meeting the need. There is little doubt that surgeons were complicit in practice and some were directly involved in grave robbing. Bodysnatching provoked fear and anger from the public yet failed to meet demand. Opposition to dissection itself was reinforced by horror at the prospect that your body, or the body of someone you loved, might well be dug up and sold to an anatomy school. The House of Commons set up a Select Committee to review the law and make proposals for law reform. From the start the Committee focused on the need to remove 'Impediments to the cultivation of the Science of ANATOMY'.[72] Feelings of aversion to dissection are noted and cursorily dismissed with a bland claim that such feelings were on the decline. The first Anatomy Bill, which in effect conscripted the bodies of the poor, failed in 1829. The Anatomy Act, which was little different in substance but more cleverly drafted, was enacted, provoking public disorder including the burning of the anatomy school in Sheffield.[73] Attitudes to medicine voiced in the Select Committee and parliamentary debate differed markedly to the scepticism of judges such as Coke. The difference may lie in the gradual evolution of a distinct medical science. 'Science' no longer embraced 'any body of knowledge that resulted from systematic and rigorous study'.[74] Theology and philosophy were deemed sciences. John Harrington, examining the interaction of medicine and the common law, explains how, in the mid to late 1800s, legislation gradually unifying the orthodox professions combined with the emergence of biomedical science based on laboratory investigation, rigorous testing and assessment of results granted medicine 'a position of unprecedented prestige and influence'.[75] 'Science' offered 'new certainties' to replace folklore and to challenge religion.

The history of dissection reveals other themes persisting across the ages, themes which re-surfaced in 2000[76] when it became widely known that organs and tissue were being routinely retained after post-mortem examinations without any or any adequate consent. The different values attached to bodies highlighted in the sometimes-literal battles fought over the Anatomy Act were seen to endure into the twenty-first century. The Bristol Inquiry Interim Report summed up the clash of values. 'For the parents of a deceased child, human material … is still thought about as an integral part of the child's body and thus are still the child. For the pathologists and clinicians, the material

71 R Richardson, *Death, Dissection and the Destitute* (2nd edn, 2000) University of Chicago Press.

72 Report from the Select Committee on Anatomy, 22 July 1828.

73 Brazier, *Law and Healing*, pp 239–240.

74 DL Faigman, *Legal Alchemy: The Use and Misuse of Science in the Law* (1999) WH Freeman, p 7.

75 JA Harrington, ' "Red in Tooth and Claw": The Idea of Progress in Medicine and the Common Law' (2002) *Social and Legal Studies* 211, 213.

76 See 21.2 below.

is regarded as a specimen or object. It is dehumanised.'[77] The organ retention 'scandal' also revealed continuing conflict between science and popular opinion exacerbated by condescending comments from some scientists and legislators, 'the educated elite'.

1.16 The Church, the Crown and Society

Developments in medicine do not take place in a vacuum. They need to be understood in the context of time and place. The influence of the Church, the relationship with the Crown, and the social status of medical practitioners are just three examples of the impact of context.

First, the Church. The influence of religious doctrine in laws touching on matters of life and death has been condemned,[78] imposing outdated Christian 'superstition' in a society in which fewer and fewer people practise its faith.[79] Even if religion plays a minor role in modern medical law, the close relationship of the Church, medicine and law shaped the evolution of medicine in several ways. Language used in talking about health workers recalls the era when monk-physicians provided much of the healthcare available. The word 'profession' echoes the vows made by priests and nuns. Doctors are expected to adhere to high standards of personal behaviour and can face disciplinary proceedings for misconduct unrelated to their technical fitness to practise. Proclamations from the Church issued eight centuries ago influenced the development of medicine. Canon 18 of the Lateran Council 1215 banned most clerics from undertaking surgery, opening up artificial divisions between physic and surgery which was to plague the regulation of medicine for centuries.

After the Reformation, the Church of England's role as a regulator of medical practice, licensing both surgeons and physicians in the provinces and regulating female midwives, demonstrates the close relationship of Church and State. The Church via it its parishes had the most effective system of administration in the realm.

The role of the Crown can be seen in the grant of royal charters and the relationship of monarchs with leading medical practitioners. The foundation of the London College of Physicians owed much to the regard in which Henry VIII held Thomas Linacre. The College Charter (1518) was entitled 'The Privileges and Authority of Physicians in London'. The grant of a monopoly in practising physic and the flood of legislation regulating all branches of practitioners testify to the singularity of medicine as different, of special concern to Crown and Parliament. And a consequence of the difference in 1518 was the emphasis on *privileges*. The physicians at least appeared to enjoy deference?

77 The Inquiry into the Management of Care of Children Receiving Complex Heart Surgery at the Bristol Royal Infirmary Interim Report, *Removal and Retention of Human Material* (2000).

78 G Williams, *Sanctity of Life and the Criminal Law* (1957) Alfred A Knopf.

79 E Wicks, 'Religion, Law and Medicine: Legislating on Birth and Death in a Christian State' (2009) 17 *Medical Law Review* (hereafter *Med Law Rev*) 410.

The College squandered its legacy, taking little notice of the intellectual developments on the continent, and as Porter comments 'subsided into [a] gentleman's club'.[80] In pursuit of the same gentlemanly status as the lawyer or the clergyman, the physicians sacrificed their opportunities to contribute to advances in medical science and to lead a coherent system of regulating all branches of medicine. They sought to avoid the stigma of manual labour and trade attached to the surgeons and apothecaries. The public attitude to medical practitioners early in the nineteenth century was summed up by Lady Chettam in George Eliot's novel *Middlemarch*, who preferred 'her medical man to be more on a footing with the servants'.[81]

From the late nineteenth to the twentieth century, immense changes in medicine, science and society transformed medical practice and the social standing of practitioners. For a short while, Lady Chettam's servants became the masters. Medical opinion was rarely questioned in the courts. In rare forays into legislation, into the regulation of evolving medical science and new technologies, Parliament deferred to the medical 'voice'. Medical opinion expanded its primacy to matters of ethics and social concern. To be a doctor was to join a highly respected profession. The medical men achieved much of what the ancient medical corporations had sought. One battle fought by the 'men' was, however, lost in 1876 when Parliament removed any legal obstacle to admitting women to the Medical Register.[82] And the age of deference was not to last long.[83]

80 Porter, *The Greatest Benefit to Mankind*, 288.

81 G Eliot, *Middlemarch* (1994) Penguin Classic, p 91.

82 Medical Act 1876.

83 M Brazier, 'The Age of Deference: A Historical Anomaly' in MDA Freeman (ed), *Law and Bioethics* (2008) Oxford University Press, pp 464–476.

Chapter 2

THE PRACTICE OF MEDICINE: TODAY

2.1 Medicine, patients and the law: the context

Public support for the National Health Service (NHS) was amply demonstrated in the weekly nationwide clap for the NHS at the height of the first wave of the COVID-19 pandemic in spring 2020. But approval for a service that is free at the point of delivery is marred by concerns about staffing, funding, waiting times, errors and scandals. In 2022, medicine and healthcare in England appear immersed in crisis after crisis. Events at Bristol,[1] Gosport,[2] Manchester,[3] Morecambe Bay,[4] Shropshire[5] and Stafford revealed a toxic culture of malpractice and a lack of compassion. Appalling suffering occurred at Stafford Hospital between 2005 and 2009. There was evidence of filthy conditions, food and water left out of reach of patients, and indifference to patient needs. Monitoring arrangements were insufficient, and a culture of fear prevented staff from reporting concerns. The Francis Inquiry – in which over 250 witnesses and over a million pages of documentary material were considered – investigated why the NHS system failed to detect these problems earlier.[6] Constant NHS reorganisation, regulatory gaps and ineffective communication contributed to the problem. Care of patients was not at the heart of the work of the Mid Staffordshire NHS Foundation Trust. Further policy change, reorganisation and the identification of scapegoats, it was concluded,

1 *Learning from Bristol, The Report of the Public Inquiry into Children's Heart Surgery at the Bristol Royal Infirmary 1984–1995* (2001) CM5207(1) (the Bristol Inquiry Report).

2 Right Rev'd James Jones KBE (Chair), *The Report of the Gosport Independent Panel* (2018) HC1084; and see Prof Richard Baker (Chair), *Gosport War Memorial Hospital: Deaths of Patients* (2013).

3 Shipman Inquiry, *Safeguarding Patients: Lessons From the Past – Proposals for the Future* 5th report (2004) Cm 6394 (The Shipman Inquiry).

4 Dr Bill Kirkup CBE (Chair), *The Report of the Morecambe Bay Investigation* (2015).

5 Donna Ockenden (Chair), *Emerging Findings and Recommendations from the Independent Review of Maternity Services at The Shrewsbury and Telford Hospital NHS Trust* (2020) HC1081; DHSC, *Final Report of the Ockenden Review* (2022) HC1219.

6 Robert Francis QC (Chair), *Report of the Mid Staffordshire NHS Foundation Trust Public Inquiry* (2013) HC947 (The Francis Inquiry).

would not bring about the necessary change. *Culture* change was needed, alongside clear standards, transparency, support for nursing, strong leadership and accurate information.[7]

The Francis Inquiry led to change across the tiers of regulation.[8] The Health and Social Care (Safety and Quality) Act 2015[9] now imposes an obligation on the Secretary of State to ensure that no avoidable harm is caused to service users. But the list of scandals that have dealt blow after blow to the reputation of the medical profession in the United Kingdom keeps growing. Some involve shocking treatment of vulnerable patients. In 2018 the Gosport Independent Panel found that over a 12-year period, up to 650 patients had died from lethal doses of painkillers given without clinical justification.[10] Appalling reports of degrading treatment of learning-disabled people in NHS establishments surfaced in 2006[11] and mistreatment of patients at Winterbourne View hospital in 2011 resulted in criminal prosecutions and imprisonment of staff.[12]

Many involve a failure to listen to patients. A particularly worrying picture emerges in relation to maternity care. In 2015 an independent inquiry into the deaths of mothers and babies at Furness General Hospital between 2004 and 2013 found significant failures of care. Staff colluded to conceal the truth and the regulators missed a series of opportunities to act.[13] A Health and Social Care Committee inquiry reporting in 2021[14] found that care is insufficiently personalised and that families are not properly supported when things go wrong. A Maternity Transformation Programme was launched and a Special Health Authority planned to conduct maternity investigations.[15] Most shockingly, the Ockenden Review of Maternity Care[16] looked into failings at Shrewsbury and Telford Hospital NHS Trust maternity unit, considering over 1,500 cases, mostly between 2000 and 2019. It concluded that the deaths of 201 babies and nine mothers could potentially have been avoided. Others

7 See further C Newdick, 'From Hippocrates to Commodities: Three Models of NHS Governance: NHS Governance, Regulation, Mid Staffordshire Inquiry, Health Care as a Commodity' (2014) 22(2) *Med Law Rev* 162.

8 See DHSC, *Culture Change in the NHS* (2015) CM 9009.

9 Amending the Health and Social Care Act 2008, ss 20(1) and 2(2).

10 Right Rev'd James Jones KBE (Chair), *The Report of the Gosport Independent Panel* (2018) HC 1084.

11 Healthcare Commission and the Commission for Social Care Inspection, *Joint Investigation into the Provision of Services for People with Learning Disabilities at Cornwall Partnership NHS Trust* (2006).

12 DHSC, *Transforming Care: A National Response to Winterbourne View Hospital: Final Report* (2012).

13 Dr Bill Kirkup CBE (Chair), *The Report of the Morecambe Bay Investigation* (2015).

14 Health and Social Care Committee, *The Safety of Maternity Services in England* (2021) HC19. And see Government Response (2021) CP513.

15 UK Parliament, Special Health Authority for Independent Maternity Investigations Statement made on 26 January 2022, UIN HCWS560.

16 DHSC, *Final Report of the Ockenden Review* (2022) HC 1219. And see DHSC, *Maternity and Neonatal Services in East Kent: Reading the Signals* (2022) HC 681. See 13.1 below.

were left with permanent and severe injuries. The report set out sixty actions for learning and improvement.

These so-called 'scandals' reflect poorly on individuals, but also on the NHS, which promises to ensure a safe service of the quality that patients and their families are entitled to expect.[17] A new Patient Safety Commissioner was introduced in 2022[18] on the advice of Baroness Julia Cumberlege's *First Do No Harm* report, which looked into how the healthcare system responds to reports of adverse events, focusing on three medicines and medical devices. The report concluded that 'The healthcare system is disjointed, siloed, unresponsive, and defensive. It does not adequately recognise that patients are its raison d'être'.[19]

2.2 Tiers of regulation

There are multiple tiers of regulation. First, personal regulation involves a doctor's individual commitment to a code of ethics, found in part in documents such as the Hippocratic Oath and the General Medical Council's (GMC's) *Good Medical Practice* guidance.[20] We consider the ethical responsibilities of doctors in Chapter 4. Second, professional regulation, which we consider below, is undertaken by statutory regulators such as the GMC and the Nursing and Midwifery Council (NMC); these are overseen by the Professional Standards Authority,[21] which monitors ten healthcare regulators, sets standards and enhances consistency. Finally, work-based regulation involves system and provider oversight, which we consider in the latter half of this chapter.

In recent years the medical profession has witnessed an unprecedented increase in all three types of regulation. Reforms of the GMC continue apace. Work-based regulations emphasise monitoring designed to ensure good practice rather than simply reacting to bad practice. The Health and Social Care Act 2012 removed tiers of management and streamlined arms-length bodies. The Act aimed to give *doctors* control – to 'liberat[e] the NHS from central control and political interference'.[22] It was hoped that transparency, competition and choice would promote a rise in standards and patient safety. The Francis Inquiry showed that this was not enough. The Health and Care Act 2022

17 See NHS Constitution (updated 2015), s 3(a).

18 Medicines and Medical Devices Act 2021, s 1.

19 Baroness Julia Cumberlege (Chair), *First Do No Harm: The Report of the Independent Medicines and Medical Devices Safety Review* (2020). And see 2.6 on the new Health Service Safety Investigations Body which will investigate to learn and improve rather than to attribute blame.

20 GMC, *Good Medical Practice* (2013) (updated 2019) is currently under review. In essence, the doctor must seek to show professionalism and be deserving of trust, a tradition dating back to the work of the nineteenth-century physician, Thomas Percival; see below at 4.2.

21 Section 222 of the Health and Social Care Act 2012 replaced the Council for Healthcare Regulatory Excellence (set up under ss 25–29 of the NHS Reform and Health Care Professions Act 2002), with the new PSA.

22 A Lansley, in *Transparency in Outcomes – A Framework for the NHS* (2010), p 3.

sought to better integrate services for patients and improve oversight of quality and safety. In 2022, the spotlight is very much on the healthcare regulators.

The various tiers of regulation do not always work in harmony. Work-based regulation is designed not only to enhance patient safety, but also to ensure the economic accountability of National Health Service (NHS) organisations. Job freezes and staff cuts have an impact on the level of care a hospital can provide. Economy and system pressures may compromise safety and reduce the ability of the individual health professional to offer the kind of care that they might wish to deliver.

2.3 The National Health Service

How well doctors can do their job is in part dictated by the environment in which they work. Though spending on the NHS has increased in real terms year on year, it has not matched increasing demands for care and the pressures of an aging population. The NHS operates in a system of finite – and increasingly limited – resources. The effects of austerity have been exacerbated by ever growing capacity of technology, an aging population and increased incidence of chronic disease. The NHS Long Term Plan 2019[23] set out a 10-year strategy to achieve priorities in light of a five-year financial settlement enshrined in the NHS Funding Act 2020, promising annual funds rising to £148.5 billion by 2024.

The Long Term Plan did not anticipate the COVID-19 pandemic, which put the NHS under considerable strain, as mortality and morbidity rose significantly and a staffing crisis saw health professionals retrained, brought out of training early or back from retirement. A cash injection attempted to ameliorate the extensive backlog flowing from the temporary cessation of routine services, moral distress and burnout suffered by some front-line staff, and the long-term sequalae of the virus referred to as Long COVID. In 2021 the National Audit Office (NAO) reported a significant backlog of elective and cancer care.[24] Despite £2.1 billion spent on contracts with the independent sector to help address the situation, by September 2021 only 68 per cent of patients needing treatment within sixty-two days of urgent referral received it on time. In addition, the NAO estimate that between 240,000 and 740,000 urgent referrals for suspected cancer were 'missed' due to the pandemic.

Funding issues are exacerbated by a steady stream of political reform, of which we provide only a brief account.[25] Aneurin Bevan's NHS Act 1946 established a comprehensive health service to improve the physical and mental health of the people of England and Wales with key services provided free at the point of delivery. In 1991, NHS Hospital Trusts were first created, and the

23 *The NHS Long Term Plan* (2019).

24 NAO, *NHS Backlogs and Waiting Times in England* (2021) HC 859.

25 The numerous NHS Acts were consolidated into the NHS Act 2006, the NHS (Wales) Act 2006 and the NHS (Consequential Provisions) Act 2006.

NHS divided into 'purchasers' and 'providers'. The Conservative government introduced the internal 'market' and general practitioner (GP) fundholding in 1995. GP fundholding was abolished by the incoming Labour government in 1997. Twenty-eight Strategic Health Authorities (SHAs) were created in 2001 to manage the performance of the NHS locally and 303 Primary Care Trusts (PCTs) provided health services. New emphasis was placed on decentralisation: a patient-led NHS. Focus on patient choice led to the reinstatement of competition between Trusts in 2004, and in 2006 the existing SHAs merged into 10 and the 303 PCTs merged into 152, reminiscent of the regional offices and Health Authorities abolished in 2001. PCTs were established in 2000 to plan and commission services for the locality. From April 2003, 75 per cent of the NHS budget devolved to PCTs.[26] PCTs could devolve their responsibilities to GP practices (or groups of GP practices), which were given indicative budgets and allowed to commission services.

A much bigger transfer of power followed the enactment of the Health and Social Care Act 2012, sometimes called 'The Lansley Act'.[27] The 2012 Act removed much of the strategic management of the NHS from governmental control. Around 170 organisations were disbanded, and 240 new ones created.[28] The Act split commissioning between local authorities, the NHS Commissioning Board (NHS England) and local consortia of GP practices called 'Clinical Commissioning Groups' (CCGs), which replaced Strategic Health Authorities and PCTs.[29]

Integration of health and social care has become increasingly important as the challenges of an aging population, including increased numbers of people with chronic conditions, are brought to bear. Its political prioritisation was signalled in the renaming of the Department of Health to the Department of Health and Social Care (DHSC) in 2018. The DHSC has overarching responsibility for healthcare services and for spending within budget. NHS England and CCGs received budgets for national and local commissioned services respectively. NHS England determined the services required and set a pricing structure, and NHS Improvement oversaw providers[30] and worked with NHS England to set 'the national tariff': a set of rules and prices used by providers and commissioners.[31] NHS England and NHS Improvement came together under a shared structure in 2019. CCGs commissioned planned and emergency hospital care, rehabilitation, most community healthcare and learning disability / autism services.

Critics feared that the integration would mean larger (potentially private) organisations providing care, with fewer providers operating over a longer

26 DH, *Sustaining Innovation through New PMS Arrangements* (2004), ref: 2545, p 7.
27 See (2014) 22(2) *Med Law Rev*, a special edition dedicated to the reforms.
28 National Audit Office, *The Performance of the Department of Health 2012–13* (March 2014), 1.4.
29 Health and Social Care Act 2012, ss 33–34.
30 Ibid, ss 61–71. Previously 'Monitor'.
31 Ibid, ss 115–127.

time span. In a judicial review, claimants argued that the Health Secretary did not have the power to introduce a new model, but Green J held that the integration of health and social care via a single provider was not contrary to the commissioner–provider split set out in the NHS Act 2006.[32] There were originally five claimants, including renowned physicist Professor Stephen Hawking who sadly died in March 2018.

Focus on choice and competition in the 2012 Act was viewed by many as an impediment. NHS England commissioned services from 'any qualified provider', including private companies. To qualify, the provider had to register with the Care Quality Commission (CQC) or meet equivalent requirements and be willing to comply with the NHS Standard Contract, for the price set in either the national tariff or by local commissioners. Section 75 required CCGs to put out to tender any contract over a financial threshold of £615k ('automatic competitive tendering'), which led to more private companies bidding for NHS work.

Wholesale reform of the controversial 2012 Act began modestly with proposals in the NHS Long Term Plan 2019 to merge many CCGs and introduce greater flexibility on the national tariff and procurement. More radical reform was set out in a white paper in 2021.[33] The Health and Care Act 2022 formalised new statutory 'integrated care systems' (ICSs)[34] to absorb CCGs and end the purchaser–provider split. The ICSs are made up of integrated care boards (previously CCGs) and integrated care partnerships (bringing the NHS and local authorities together). The aim is to forge strong collaborations between NHS providers, commissioners of local services (ICSs) and local authorities across geographical areas. The new ICSs are a regional tier reminiscent of the area health authorities abolished in the 1982 NHS restructure. Section 75 is repealed, ending the requirement to put services out to competitive tender.[35]

The reforms are unlikely to reduce private sector involvement, but we cautiously welcome a shift from competition to collaboration. How effective this will be will depend on how quickly trust can be (re)established. The NHS Plan was written before the COVID-19 pandemic which has sorely challenged the NHS. Will enhanced collaboration make up for the destabilisation that reorganisation brings?[36] As the population and economy changes, so the NHS

32 *R (Hutchinson and Others) v Secretary of State for Health and Social Care and the National Health Service Commissioning Board* [2018] EWHC 1698 (Admin).

33 DHSC, *Integration and Innovation: Working Together to Improve Health and Social Care for All* (2021) CP 381.

34 Health and Care Act 2022, ss 18–32.

35 Health and Care Act 2022, s 80 repeals Health and Social Care Act 2012, s 75 and revokes the National Health Service (Procurement, Patient Choice and Competition) (No 2) Regulations 2013 (SI 2013/500) made under s 75.

36 See H Alderwick *et al*, 'Will a New NHS Structure in England Help Recovery from the Pandemic?' (2021) 372 *BMJ* n248 arguing that previous major reorganisations 'delivered little measurable benefit' and that step change post-COVID would be preferable.

must adapt, but constant politically motivated change does not help health professionals do their jobs.

2.4 Angels or demons?

Good medical care requires more than sets of regulatory rules. Great demands are made of individual health professionals. Praised to the skies for their triumphs, few individuals attract greater public odium than the doctor or nurse who falls from their pedestal. The revulsion occasioned by Nazi atrocities in the concentration camps was nowhere as marked as in the case of Dr Mengele. That he used his skills as a doctor, taught to him that he might heal and comfort the sick, to advance torture and barbarism caused horror.

Public passion is rightly aroused by the likes of Mengele and Shipman, a Manchester GP and prolific serial killer. Passion is never far away from everyday relationships between doctor and patient. When doctors meet their patients' expectations, they are rewarded by admiration and affection. Woe betide them if they do not. One error, one moment of exasperation or insensitivity, may transform a beloved doctor into a hate figure. Consultants were once accorded godlike status. They inspired awe visiting the ward attended by a retinue of junior doctors and nurses. Their exalted status insulated them from personal contact with patients and protected them from the sort of complaints voiced freely to nursing staff. They paid a price. Gods are expected to work miracles. They are not expected to be subject to human error. When a consultant proved to be human, when medicine could not cure, the patient found it hard to comprehend failure and rightly or wrongly, often wrongly, regarded the doctor as personally incompetent.

Medical attitudes are changing. Family doctors are becoming a different breed. Many try hard to persuade patients to see their doctor as a partner in promoting good health. Doctors are urged to prescribe less freely and to talk more to their patients. The good GP is as interested in the prevention of ill health as its cure. A new generation of consultants is taking over in the hospitals. They are (in most cases) less grand and more prepared to listen to patients and nursing staff.

One 'bad apple', or even several, should not destroy the reputations of thousands of other medical practitioners who do their job diligently and compassionately. All professions have their miscreants. The medical profession should not be punished for Shipman's bizarre and apparently motiveless murders. The heart of the problem and the damage to the 'image' of medicine is that too little is sometimes seen to be done by the profession and its regulators to identify and remedy doctors' failings. It seems amazing that no colleague noted or acted on evidence of the number of apparently healthy patients on Shipman's list who died suddenly, in certain cases even in his surgery.

There are features of the profession of medicine which will render doctors more vulnerable to attack than other professionals. The doctor deals with the individual's most precious commodity, life and health. On a mundane level they may determine whether patient X is to be sanctioned to enjoy seven days off work for nervous exhaustion brought about by overwork, or classified as another malingerer.[37] At the other end of the scale, the doctor may hold in their hands the power of life and death. They are the person with the skill and experience. In their hands, as the patient sees it, rests the power to cure. As Ian Kennedy has said, the patient appears before the doctor 'naked both physically and emotionally'.[38] It is hard to overstate the power vested in doctors. The price of power is that those who exercise it must expect constant scrutiny from those subject to it and from the public at large. The age of deference is past. Doctors cannot be surprised when failure, incompetence or controversy attracts equal notoriety. Unfortunately, representatives of the profession sometimes react in an over-defensive manner, exacerbating the original criticism or complaint.

2.5 Whistleblowing

When healthcare goes badly wrong it will often be a health professional who brings the problems to public attention. The Public Interest Disclosure Act 1998 amended the Employment Rights Act 1996 to protect workers raising concerns from 'detriments' from their employers and prohibit so-called 'gagging clauses' insofar as they prevented workers[39] from making protected disclosures. Sections 17 to 20 of the Enterprise and Regulatory Reform Act 2013 made further changes to the 1996 Act, making employers vicariously liable for harassment or bullying of whistleblowers. The requirement to make disclosures in good faith was seen as too high a burden and was replaced with a stipulation that the worker believed the disclosure to be in the public interest.[40]

Protections of whistleblowers at Mid Staffordshire proved woefully inadequate.[41] An independent review chaired by Sir Robert Francis KC revealed that staff often felt unwilling to raise concerns due to fear of reprisals or poor expectations that it would lead to change.[42] The review recommended policy initiatives to change culture and support good practice, rather than wholesale reform of the 1996 Act. A new *Freedom to Speak Up* policy[43] was initiated in 2016 and new Regulations were set out to protect whistleblowers from discrimination when applying for new jobs within the NHS.[44]

37 I Kennedy, *The Unmasking of Medicine* (1981) Allen & Unwin, ch 1, p 9ff.

38 Ibid, p 8.

39 In *Day v Health Education England* [2017] EWCA Civ 329 a purposive interpretation of 'workers' was taken to protect trainee doctors. The case was remitted to the tribunal and dropped. See C Dyer, 'Junior Doctor Withdraws Claim that Whistleblowing Ruined his Career' (2018) 363 *BMJ* k4356.

40 See for example in *Ibrahim v HCA International* [2019] EWCA 2007 on subjective belief of best interests.

41 P Gooderham, 'Changing the Face of Whistleblowing' (2009) 338 *BMJ* b2090.

42 Sir Robert Francis QC, *Report on the "Freedom to Speak up?" Review into Creating an Open & Honest Reporting Culture in the NHS* (February 2015), 4.5.

43 NHSE&I, *Freedom to Speak Up: Raising Concerns (Whistleblowing) Policy for the NHS* (2016).

44 The Employment Rights Act 1996 (NHS Recruitment – Protected Disclosure) Regulations 2018, SI 2018/579.

Underlying cultural issues limit the effectiveness of legal protections. Annual NHS staff surveys suggest a gradual improvement in the number of staff confident that it is safe to raise a concern (72.5 per cent in 2020), but in 2020 19 per cent of staff had experienced bullying, harassment or abuse from colleagues.[45] Policies encouraging openness need to be matched with appropriate support.

2.6 A duty of candour

Increasing protections for whistleblowers are accompanied by emphasis on the duty of health professionals and providers to report errors and incidents. Professional guidance from the GMC requires doctors to be 'open and honest with patients if things go wrong'.[46] The 'duty of candour' is (since 2013) also a prominent feature of both the NHS Constitution and NHS Standard Contract and is reflected in licensing and registration requirements by which healthcare providers must abide.[47]

Regulation 20 of the Health and Social Care Act 2008 (Regulated Activities) Regulations 2014 makes provision for a *statutory* duty of candour applying to all providers.[48] It sets out financial implications for failing to be open with patients and families[49] and a criminal offence is committed when providers required by law to give information do so in a false or misleading manner. The first prosecution was brought in 2020. University Hospitals Plymouth Trust admitted not having communicated openly and honestly with a patient's family when an endoscopy procedure resulted in the patient's death.[50]

A potential restraint on openness flows from the criticism and legal action that can follow. The government consulted in 2016 and concluded that a 'safe space' would alleviate this problem.[51] The Healthcare Safety Investigation Branch (HSIB) was set up in 2017 to conduct independent investigations of patient safety concerns in England, operating on safe space principles.[52] Systemic weaknesses are identified and addressed without apportioning

45 NHS Staff Surveys, *NHS Staff Survey 2020 National Results Briefing* (2021).

46 GMC, *Good Medical Practice* (2013), para 55. And see GMC and NMC, *Openness and Honesty when Things go Wrong: The Professional Duty of Candour* (July 2015).

47 See 2.18.

48 SI 2014/2936 (as amended). Inserted by the Care Act 2014, s 81. And see Health (Tobacco, Nicotine etc. & Care) (Scotland) Act 2016 and The Duty of Candour (Scotland) Regulations 2018, which came into force in April 2018.

49 See, for example, CQC, 'Bradford Teaching Hospitals Fined for Failure to Comply with Duty of Candour' (2019) 17 January. The CQC issues a fixed penalty notice for failure to inform or to apologise in a timely manner.

50 CQC, 'Care Quality Commission Prosecutes University Hospitals Plymouth NHS Trust for Breaching Duty of Candour Regulation following Patient Death' (2020) 23 September.

51 DHSC, *Providing a 'Safe Space' in Healthcare Safety Investigations: Next Steps* (2017).

52 See 2.19 below.

blame or liability. Part 4 of the Health and Care Act 2022 put the renamed Healthcare Services Safety Investigations Body (HSSIB) on a statutory footing.

2.7 Entitlement to practise

One of the crucial functions of regulation is to ensure the competence of professionals offering services to the public. So who is entitled to practise medicine? Ten health and care regulators are overseen by the Professional Standards Authority for Health and Social Care. For reasons of space we will focus on the GMC. Other professional regulators include Social Work England, the General Chiropractic, Dental, Optical, Pharmaceutical and Osteopathic Councils, the Nursing and Midwifery Council, Pharmaceutical Society of Northern Ireland and the Health and Care Professions Council. The Government is committed to simplifying the legislative framework on professional regulation and may reduce the number of regulators.[53] Legislation is anticipated in 2023.

The GMC maintains a register of medical practitioners[54] and in 2009 the licence to practise was introduced[55] as part of reforms aiming to monitor doctors in order to assess their accordance with principles of Good Medical Practice.[56] Only registered practitioners can apply for a licence. Both registration and a licence are required to perform certain tasks such as writing prescriptions or signing death certificates and a criminal offence is committed when a person deliberately and falsely represents himself as being a registered and licensed practitioner or having a medical qualification.[57] However, unregistered and unlicensed practitioners can still use the title 'doctor'. No law expressly prohibits any unregistered, unlicensed or unqualified person from practising most types of medicine or even surgery. The rationale of the criminal law is that people should be free to opt for any form of advice or treatment, however bizarre, but must be protected from rogues claiming a bogus status and from commercial exploitation of untested 'alternative' medicine.

[53] Following a DHSC consultation on *Regulating Healthcare Professionals, Protecting the Public* (2021), the DHSC commissioned a review by KPMG. The Health and Care Act 2022, s 168 widens the scope of the Health Act 1999, s 60, creating new powers to remove a profession from regulation and abolish a regulator.

[54] The GMC will also regulate Physician Associates and Anaesthesia Associates (medically trained healthcare professionals who work alongside doctors and anaesthetists). See 2.14 below.

[55] The GMC (Licence to Practise) Regulations Order of Council 2009, SI 2009/2739, under powers derived from the Medicines Act 1983, Pt IIIA, s 29A(2).

[56] GMC, *Good Medical Practice* (2013) (currently under review). And see GMC, *Interim Standards for Physician Associates and Anaesthesia Associates* (2021).

[57] Medical Act 1983, s 49; and see *Younghusband v Luftig* [1949] 2 KB 354; *Wilson v Inyang* [1951] 2 KB 799; and see several BBC News stories: 'Banned Doctor Levon Mkhitarian Jailed after Treating 3,000 Patients' (2015) 17 July; 'Great Ormond Street Children's Hospital "Fake Doctor" Escapes Jail Sentence (2017) 27 March; 'Coventry Fake Doctor Jailed for Duping Elderly People' (2019) 2 May; 'Fake Doctor Medicated 164 Patients' (2019) 24 July.

2.8 A tradition of self-regulation

By virtue of the Medical Act 1983, the regulation of the medical profession was entrusted to the profession itself acting through the GMC, continuing a tradition of self-regulation, endorsed by Parliament, dating back to 1858. The GMC came under vigorous attack on the basis that its composition was biased in favour of the doctors. Its capacity to ensure that patients were treated by competent doctors truly fit to practise was doubted. Thus, although the Medical Act 1983 remains on the statute book, it has been radically amended.

Section 1A of the Medical Act 1983 sets out the central tenet of all attempts to reform the GMC:

> The over-arching objective of the General Council in exercising their functions is the protection of the public.

Section 1B sets out three secondary objectives:

(a) to protect, promote and maintain the health, safety and well-being of the public,
(b) to promote and maintain public confidence in the medical profession, and
(c) to promote and maintain proper professional standards and conduct for members of that profession.

Historically, while the GMC has policed admission to the medical register, little was done to ensure that a doctor continued to be competent, and up to date, in practice. They remained 'licensed' to practise, unless disciplinary proceedings, or health or performance procedures, were invoked against them. The Shipman scandal made clear that this was insufficient. After years of debate, Part IIIA of the 1983 Act introduced a scheme for revalidation of medical competence in 2012.[58] The GMC issues doctors a licence to practise on first registration. Doctors are required to renew that licence periodically, proving their continued competence through a scheme of continuing evaluation of practice.

If the absence of processes to monitor doctors' competence caused public concern, what were seen as feeble and apparently prejudiced disciplinary proceedings to deal with complaints against doctors aroused anger.[59] In 2002, the whole of the existing system for disciplining defaulting doctors, dealing with sick doctors, and addressing under-performing doctors was revised, but the critics were far from satisfied. Dame Janet Smith's inquiry[60] into the Shipman debacle led to a review of medical regulation by the Chief Medical Officer, Sir Liam Donaldson, who

[58] The GMC (Licence to Practise and Revalidation) Regulations Order of Council 2012, SI 2012/2685; GMC (Licence to Practise and Revalidation) (Amendment) Regulations Order of Council 2014, SI 2014/1273. GMC, *Guidance for Doctors: Requirements for Revalidation and Maintaining your Licence* (2018).

[59] See D Irvine, *A Doctors' Tale* (2003) Radcliffe Medical Press, in particular sections 3 and 4. Sir Donald Irvine was the President of the GMC from 1995 to 2002.

[60] The Shipman Inquiry.

concluded that the GMC was 'too secretive, too tolerant of sub-standard practice and too dominated by the professional interest, rather than that of the patient'.[61] Over the subsequent decade, reforms sought to boost public confidence. But the environment became increasingly hostile, and the GMC suffered a loss in the support and confidence of its registrants. Between 2005 and 2013, twenty-eight doctors who had died whilst under investigation by the GMC were confirmed or suspected suicide victims.[62] Matters reached a head in 2015. Paediatrician Dr Hadiza Bawa-Garba was convicted of manslaughter on grounds of gross negligence over the death of 6-year-old Jack Adcock and given a 24-month suspended sentence.[63] In 2017, the Medical Practitioners Tribunal Service (MPTS) suspended her for twelve months, having taken into account contributory systemic failures in the hospital. But the GMC appealed the decision, arguing that it was too lenient: it would not foster public confidence in the profession.[64] The GMC's appeal was successful at first instance, and Dr Bawa-Garba was struck from the medical register.[65] She subsequently appealed and won.[66] The medical profession was angry, in part at the criminal justice system, which we discuss in Chapter 10, but in particular at their regulator, the GMC. The GMC needed to do more to support doctors: to reduce the stress of investigations, speed them up and boost emotional support. In April 2019, Dr Bawa-Garba was able to return to practice under close supervision. As we shall see, reforms are proposed to breathe new life into professional regulation, and to enhance consistency across the health and care regulatory bodies. They have been a long time coming.[67]

2.9 Composition of the GMC

Who regulators are influences how confident the public will be in the process and objectivity of the regulatory framework. In 1983, the GMC comprised

[61] DH, *CMO's Report, Good Doctors, Safer Patients: Proposals to Strengthen the System to Assure and Improve the Performance of Doctors and to Protect the Safety of Patients* (2006), para 60.

[62] GMC, *Doctors Who Commit Suicide While Under GMC Fitness to Practise Investigation* (2014), chaired by Sarndrah Horsfall.

[63] Discussed fully at 10.4 below.

[64] For a critique on the nebulous term 'public confidence' see P Case and G Sharma, 'Promoting Public Confidence in the Medical Profession: Learning from the Case of Dr Bawa-Garba' (2020) *MLI* 20(1) 58.

[65] *GMC v Dr Bawa-Garba* [2018] EWHC 76 (Admin). Appeal denied in *Bawa-Garba v R* [2016] EWCA Crim 1841.

[66] *Bawa-Garba v GMC* [2018] EWCA Civ 1879.

[67] Law Commission report 345, Scottish Law Commission report 237 and Northern Ireland Law Commission report 18 (2014) Cm 8839 SG/2014/26 proposed to replace the various regulations with a single statute, providing a broad framework for the regulatory bodies and the Professional Standards Authority. A consultation (DHSC, *Promoting Professionalism Reforming Regulation* (2017)) looked at options. The Government response in 2019 promised further consultation. DHSC consultation, *Regulating Healthcare Professionals, Protecting the Public* closed in 2021 with draft legislation pending.

104 members. The lay element was less than 25 per cent. Doctors chosen by their peers dominated the Council. Such a large Council is on any analysis an unwieldy organisation to govern any profession, and in 2008 the numbers were whittled down to twelve lay members and twelve medical members,[68] and in 2012 numbers were halved again to six medical and six lay members.[69]

So what does the GMC do? The Medical Act lists four principal functions of the GMC:

(1) To provide advice for doctors on ethics and standards of professional conduct.
(2) To oversee medical education.
(3) To maintain a register of qualified doctors, to licence doctors and to 'revalidate' them.
(4) To investigate and (in some form) adjudicate allegations about the fitness to practise of doctors.

2.10 Advisory function

First, the Council is charged with providing advice for doctors on ethics and standards of professional conduct, standards of professional performance and medical ethics.[70] Reference to this advice is made throughout this book. The core guidance is contained in *Good Medical Practice*, which was first produced in 1995 and was comprehensively revised in 2006 and 2013 and is under revision again at the time of writing. *Good Medical Practice* (2013) is accompanied by a series of explanatory guides,[71] interactive case studies and learning materials.

2.11 Medical education

Second, the Council sets standards and outcomes for medical education, including postgraduate curricula, essentially performing a quality assurance role. The route to becoming a doctor begins with a medical degree. Requirements for undergraduate training are set out in *Outcomes for Doctors.*[72] A two-year Foundation programme follows.[73] A provisional licence to practise is awarded for F1 and a full licence at the start of F2, dependent upon demonstration of outcomes set by the GMC. At the end of the F2 year, doctors enter training in their chosen specialty or GP training. The GMC approves programmes for specialty training which, in England, are developed by the Joint Royal Colleges

68 GMC (Constitution) Order 2008, SI 2008/2554.
69 GMC (Constitution) (Amendment) Order 2012, SI 2012/1654.
70 See Medical Act 1983, s 35 as amended.
71 At the time of writing there are thirty-two explanatory guidelines promulgated by the GMC; see GMC, *Ethical Guidance for Doctors*, at www.gmc-uk.org/guidance/ethical_guidance.asp.
72 GMC, *Outcomes for Graduates (Tomorrow's Doctors)* (2018).
73 The Medical Act 1983, s 10A.

of Physicians' Training Board (JRCPTB) and overseen by Health Education England (HEE).[74] All doctors undergoing specialist training in the UK must be enrolled with JRCPTB. HEE sets out a quality framework, allocates education and training resources, and plans and develops the healthcare workforce. HEE has a series of regional units (HEE Local Offices, or 'Deaneries') to deliver the training, each overseen by a postgraduate Dean.[75] Those who gain a Certificate of Completion of Training (or equivalent) are entered onto the GP Register or the Specialist Register and are entitled to practise as substantive, honorary or fixed term consultants or as a GP.

What about doctors trained outside the UK? The GMC recognises certain postgraduate qualifications and has alternative routes to specialist registration. Checks by the GMC depend on where the doctor got their medical degree. Those trained outside the UK, the European Economic Area or Switzerland must, at the time of writing, pass a Professional and Linguistic Assessment Board (PLAB) test. A new common assessment for all doctors wishing to practise in the UK called the Medical Licensing Assessment is under development. From 2024, all UK and international medical students will take this assessment.

2.12 Maintaining a register

Third, the GMC is charged with the maintenance of the 'list of registered medical practitioners' and provides licences to practise. Doctors listed on the medical register have full, provisional,[76] specialist or GP registration.[77] All are accessible online. The GP register is a list of GPs eligible to work in the UK. It provides information for patients and aids pre-employment checks. The Specialist Register identifies medical practitioners by their specialties, accreditation and qualifications.

The GMC sets out criteria by which overseas qualifications may be accepted and from 2014 raised the required score on the International English Language Testing System. This followed an event where a German doctor, Daniel Ubani, on his first shift as an out-of-hours GP, prescribed a fatal dose of morphine to a pensioner in 2010.[78] At a fitness-to-practise hearing, Dr Ubani was struck from the register. The Medical Act 1983 was amended in 2014, to allow the Council to refuse a licence to practise when a medical practitioner has

74 Health Education England Regulations 2012, SI 2012/1290. HEE was reconstituted as a non-departmental public body by the Care Act 2014, s 96(1): Health Education England Regulations 2014, SI 2014/3215.

75 See Conference of Postgraduate Medical Deans, *The Gold Guide: A Reference Guide for Postgraduate Specialty Training in the UK* (8th edn, 2020).

76 See The GMC (Maximum Period of Provisional Registration) Regulations Order of Council 2015, SI 2015/92 setting a maximum period of provisional registration of 1,125 days.

77 Both set up under SI 2003/1250, Pt IV. Categories of doctors eligible for inclusion in the specialist register and GP registers are set out in the Postgraduate Medical Education and Training Order 2010, SI 2010/473, as amended.

78 And see *Gray v Germany*, App No 49278/09 (ECHR, 2014).

insufficient English language skills. The 2014 Order also introduced a new fitness-to-practise category of impairment due to language incompetence.[79]

Registration alone used to be sufficient to permit a doctor to practise medicine and hold themselves out as a medical practitioner. Amendments to the Medical Act[80] additionally require that doctors hold a licence to practise.[81] The licence is granted by the GMC at registration and is required of any doctor, private or NHS, part-time or full-time, if they wish to work in the NHS, write prescriptions or sign death certificates. Doctors need to show that their fitness to practise is not impaired at the point of registration and licensing with the GMC. Failure to declare relevant factors could lead to the doctor being struck from the register and losing their licence to practise. Doctors are also required to carry professional indemnity or insurance cover from the point of registration and failure to do so could amount to impaired fitness to practise.

Pressure on the NHS during the COVID-19 emergency resulted in the invocation of section 18A of the Medical Act. This provision allows temporary registration or licences to practise to be issued to suitable doctors willing to return to work post retirement, for the duration of an emergency.[82] Of the 15,000 doctors contacted, 11,865 volunteered to return to work,[83] along with 10,823 former nurses and midwives and overseas registrants[84] and social workers. Early provisional registration was also extended to 5,500 final year medical students. Many other health professionals urgently retrained to help at the front line. The humbling and overwhelming response of health professionals, carers and key workers brought the public out onto the streets to clap each Thursday at 8 pm for ten weeks and again for the NHS's 72nd birthday in July 2020.

2.13 Revalidation

Licensing was the first step towards 'revalidation', whereby doctors are appraised to ensure their general fitness to practise and compliance with *Good Medical Practice* guidance.[85] Revalidation forms a continuous assessment

79 Medical Act 1983 (Amendment) (Knowledge of English) Order 2014, SI 2014/1101; GMC (Licence to Practise and Revalidation) (Amendment) Regulations Order of Council 2014, SI 2014/1273.

80 The Medical Act 1983 (Amendment) Order 2002, SI 2002/3135, Pt V, inserts a new Pt IIIA 'Licence to Practise and Revalidation' into the Medical Act 1983.

81 The GMC (Licence to Practise) Regulations Order of Council 2009, SI 2009/2739 were revoked and replaced by the GMC (Licence to Practise and Revalidation) Regulations Order of Council 2012, SI 2012/2685, as amended. See 2.13 below.

82 And see Coronavirus Act 2020, ss 2–5 and Schedule 1.

83 GMC, 'COVID-19 – GMC Grants Temporary Registration to 11,800 Doctors' (2020) 27 March.

84 NMC, 'NMC Temporary Register Reaches Incredible Milestone as more than 10,000 Sign Up to Fight Covid-19' (2020) 17 April.

85 The GMC (Licence to Practise and Revalidation) Regulations Order of Council 2012, SI 2012/2685 as amended. Revalidation was rolled out for nurses and midwives in 2016.

based largely on local systems of annual appraisal. Doctors form a connection to a single organisation (their 'designated body') each of which appoints a senior doctor (a 'responsible officer') to oversee the governance systems and appraisals. At annual appraisals, doctors present a portfolio of supporting information. Every five years,[86] all doctors licensed to practise in the UK must show that they are up to date and fit to practise. This is judged according to an Appraisals Framework[87] based on the GMC's *Good Medical Practice* guidance. Responsible Officers can make one of three recommendations: approval, deferral or non-engagement with the process.

How has revalidation been received? A three-year review in 2017 concluded that revalidation has strengthened governance, 'has settled well and is progressing as expected'.[88] But research commissioned by the GMC suggested that only a 'significant minority' of doctors changed their practice as a result of revalidation.[89] Concerns were raised that the process was unnecessarily burdensome and that local support needed to be improved. New guidance was issued by the GMC to reinvigorate the process.[90]

2.14 Disciplining doctors – fitness to practise

The doctor's employer, like any other employer, may initiate disciplinary proceedings and as a result a doctor may face suspension or dismissal. The courts will not micro-manage NHS employers, but have shown willing to grant injunctive relief where there is evidence of irregularities.[91] The disciplinary procedures are complex and will not be dealt with in any detail here. However, note that being sacked from an NHS hospital will not of itself stop the errant or incompetent doctor practising medicine. They may simply move to the private sector. Only the GMC can act to ensure that an 'unsafe' doctor can no longer practise.

Complaints about doctors – whether they emanate from patients, other doctors or their organisations – can thus be put to the GMC, which may then investigate whether or not the doctor is fit to practise.[92] Only about 20 per cent of concerns received are investigated: The GMC is only concerned with issues that raise concerns about a doctor's ability to practise safely or threaten

[86] During the COVID-19 pandemic, some revalidations were moved back a year.

[87] GMC, *The Good Medical Practice Framework for Appraisal and Revalidation* (2011) updated (2013).

[88] *Taking Revalidation Forward: Improving the Process of Relicensing for Doctors – Sir Keith Pearson's Review of Medical Revalidation* (January 2017).

[89] J Archer *et al*, *Evaluating the Regulatory Impact of Medical Revalidation* (2018).

[90] See GMC, *Guidance for Doctors: Requirements for Revalidation and Maintaining Your Licence* (2018); GMC, *Guidance on Supporting Information for Appraisal and Revalidation* (2018).

[91] See, for example, *West London Mental Health NHS Trust v Chhabra* [2013] UKSC 80.

[92] Alternatively a complaint can be made through the NHS complaints process outlined in Chapter 11.

public confidence in the profession. There are two stages to the fitness-to-practise process – investigation and adjudication. Historically, the GMC was responsible for both stages; however, the dual role of prosecutor and adjudicator resulted in a loss of public confidence. Following public consultations, a new independent tribunal service was launched in 2012. The GMC investigates, whilst the Manchester-based MPTS, chaired by a judge, adjudicates. The two are operationally distinct. In 2015, the MPTS was put on a statutory footing, enhancing its independent status.[93]

Fitness-to-practise proceedings have been subject to several reforms. In 2004 three separate streams of health, performance and conduct were abandoned and complaints about doctors were analysed 'in the round'.[94] The 2004 Rules were amended in 2009, 2013, 2014, 2015 and 2017.[95] The focus has become whether the doctor's fitness to practise is 'impaired'; that is, whether by misconduct, health or other stated cause, the doctor can be considered unable to practise safely and effectively. In reaching a conclusion, regard must be had to the overarching objective of public protection, which incorporates the obligation to promote a safe NHS in which there is public confidence.[96]

Under section 35C(2) of the Medical Act 1983, as amended, impairment can result from all or any of the following:

- misconduct
- deficient professional performance
- a conviction or caution in the United Kingdom for a criminal offence, or a conviction elsewhere for an offence which, if committed in England and Wales, would constitute a criminal offence
- adverse physical or mental health
- not having the necessary knowledge of the English language
- a determination by another health regulatory body, in the United Kingdom or elsewhere, that their fitness to practise is impaired.[97]

At the investigation stage, the case examiners (one medical and one lay) can refer the doctor to an Interim Orders Panel where there is a clear need to protect patients or the public interest.[98] The panel has the power to impose an interim order restricting or suspending the doctor's right to practise pending

93 The GMC (Fitness to Practise and Over-arching Objective) and the Professional Standards Authority for Health and Social Care (References to Court) Order 2015, SI 2015/794.

94 GMC (Fitness to Practise) Rules 2004, SI 2004/2608.

95 SIs 2009/1913, 2013/815, 2014/1270, 2015/1964 and 2017/1049. See GMC, *Guidance to the GMC's Fitness to Practise Rules 2004 (as amended)*. The guide is not legally binding. Available at: www.gmc-uk.org/-/media/documents/DC4483_Guidance_to_the_FTP_Rules_28626691.pdf.

96 Medical Act 1983, ss 1A and 1B discussed at 2.8 above.

97 GMC, *Guidance to the GMC's Fitness to Practise Rules 2004*, para 4.

98 Medical Act 1983, s 35C(8).

the full investigation.[99] The GMC may conclude the case, agree undertakings with the doctor or issue a warning;[100] a measure introduced for cases which call for an official response, but which are not serious enough to justify restrictions on the doctor's registration, when either 'there has been a significant departure from *Good Medical Practice*' or 'a performance assessment has indicated a significant cause for concern'. Alternatively, the GMC can refer the case to the MPTS for a fitness-to-practise panel adjudication.

The powers of the MPTS are found at section 35D of the Medical Act 1983. There are three aspects to the hearing: the finding of facts; the decision on impairment; and the decision on sanction. During fact-finding, the Tribunal considers whether there is sufficient evidence of the facts alleged. In some cases, the facts will be disputed. The burden of proof rests with the GMC, which makes the allegations. The Health Act 1999 (as amended) replaces the criminal standard of proof (which was thought to be inappropriate and potentially too lenient on doctors) with a civil standard.[101] Doctors are now judged on the balance of probabilities rather than establishing proof 'beyond reasonable doubt'. The civil standard is a sliding standard that can be flexibly applied.[102] The more serious the matter, the greater the degree of probability required.

To make a decision on impairment, the Tribunal asks whether, on the basis of the facts, fitness to practise is impaired. If the answer is 'no', then, in common with the investigation stage, it can issue a warning[103] or take no further action. If the answer is 'yes', then the Tribunal proceeds to stage three and *in camera* makes a decision on sanction. There are four options:

(1) Undertakings
(2) Conditions (maximum three years)
(3) Suspension (maximum one year)[104]
(4) Erasure from the register.

Dr Bawa-Garba's case exposed the immense pressures on doctors under investigation by the GMC. In 2017, a government consultation considered how to address the culture of blame and to better support doctors.[105] In response, the government committed to bring about speedier, proportionate, more effective and less adversarial resolution.[106] A further consultation in 2021 explored

99 Medical Act 1983, s 41A.
100 Medical Act 1983, s 35C(6).
101 Health Act 1999, s 60A.
102 *R (N) v Mental Health Review Tribunal* [2006] QB 468, CA.
103 Medical Act 1983, s 35D(3).
104 Additional period of suspension cannot be applied to create an 'idle ground' between suspension and removal from the register: *Khan v General Pharmaceutical Council and Ors* [2016] UKSC 64; *Taylor v GMC* [1990] 2 AC 539. Further periods of suspension can, however, be applied on review: *Okpara v NMC* [2016] EWHC 1058.
105 DHSC, *Consultation: Promoting Professionalism, Reforming Regulation* (2017).
106 DHSC, *Promoting Professionalism, Reforming Regulation Government Response to the Consultation* (2019).

proposals to bring the various healthcare regulators into closer alignment.[107] Draft legislation will follow.

In future, the GMC will have greater discretion to decide which cases need to go forward to adjudication and which can be disposed of consensually. There will be fewer statutory rules and greater autonomy. Amending the 2004 Rules is cumbersome and slow: the government seeks to give the GMC greater flexibility over its operational procedures. In return, the government will demand greater accountability and transparency of the GMC. Statutory changes will ensure that doctors will no longer be asked to provide access to reflective practice material in fitness-to-practise investigations and statutory regulation by the GMC will extend to cover medical associate professions: Physician Associates, who support doctors in the management of patients and diagnosis, and Anaesthesia Associates, who are part of the consultant-led multidisciplinary anaesthesia team. It is clear also that limits will be placed on the GMC's right to appeal, which we explore in the next section. Other outcomes will be further debated, but it is proposed that conviction for certain offences such as murder, human trafficking and certain sexual offences will lead to automatic removal from the register. And there is likely to be better communication, throughout the process, with those who raise a concern.

2.15 Appeal of MPTS decisions

Since 2010, doctors can appeal against decisions to withdraw or refuse registration or a licence to practise under Schedule 3A of the Medical Act 1983.[108] Doctors have two routes to appeal. If they have received a warning, they can seek judicial review. If the MPTS panel has found that the doctor's fitness to practise is impaired, the doctor has twenty-eight days to appeal to the High Court under section 40(4) of the Medical Act 1983.

The court will decide if the decision of the fitness-to-practise panel was 'wrong'.[109] For example, the panel may have acted improperly, or the sanction might be disproportionate. In the latter case the court is entitled to prioritise the public interest – in particular public confidence and the standing of the profession.[110] The court has a range of powers. It can dismiss the appeal, quash, amend or substitute the direction, or remit the case back to the GMC fitness-to-practise panel.[111]

In 2010, Professor Walker-Smith and Dr Wakefield's names were erased from the register following a finding of serious professional misconduct. They were

107 DHSC, *Regulating Healthcare Professionals, Protecting the Public* (2021).
108 Under Medical Act 1983, Sch 3A (registration) and s 29F(1) (licence). The GMC (Registration Appeals Panels Procedure) Rules Order of Council 2010, SI 2010/476 sets out the procedure.
109 *GMC v Meadow* [2006] EWCA Civ 1390, [125]–[128].
110 See *Robert Allan Odes v* GMC [2010] EWHC 552 (Admin); *Cheatle v GMC* (2009) EWHC 645 (Admin).
111 Medical Act 1983, s 40(7).

both involved in a paediatric clinical trial, following which Dr Wakefield publicly made the link between the triple 'measles, mumps and rubella' (MMR) vaccination and autism, whilst Professor Walker-Smith made clear his support for the governmental policy on MMR. Dr Wakefield abandoned his appeal, but in 2012 Professor Walker-Smith's registration was restored after a successful appeal.[112] The panel had made errors and applied 'inadequate and superficial reasoning'. The GMC accepted the decision and made changes to its fitness-to-practise procedures as outlined above.

Doctors can appeal if they feel they have been dealt with harshly.[113] So, too, may the Professional Standards Authority for Health and Social Care (PSA)[114] appeal fitness-to-practise decisions made by the ten regulators, where it considers them unduly lenient, including when the person is acquitted.[115] This raises the potential for doctors to be challenged twice on the same conduct. In a 2015 referral to the High Court on the issue of leniency, Lang J stated: '[R]eference to having regard to double jeopardy when considering whether a sentence is unduly lenient is not … really apposite where the primary concern is for the protection of the public.'[116] Appeals are made to the High Court under section 29 of the National Health Service Reform and Health Care Professions Act 2002. Alternative Dispute Resolution reduces the number of cases that make it to court. Between 2004 and 2021, sixty-one appeals were heard in court.[117] A case study is provided by the PSA: a nurse was found to have repeatedly poked and struck with a broom handle a vulnerable patient with autism and to have then lied about her behaviour. The court upheld the PSA's appeal of a 12-month suspension and the nurse was struck from the register.[118]

Concurrently with the PSA's right to appeal, the GMC was given powers in 2015 to appeal decisions under section 40A of the Medical Act 1983, where it considered that the decision was not sufficient for the protection of the

112 *Walker-Smith v GMC* [2012] EWHC 503 (Admin).

113 See for example *Southall v GMC* [2009] EWHC 1155 (Admin). The Court of Appeal referred the case back to the GMC, which found him not guilty of serious misconduct in 2011. And see E Mahase, 'Manjula Arora: GMC Won't Challenge Appeal and Calls for Sanctions to be Dropped by Court' (2022) 377 *BMJ* o1538. And see 9.14 below.

114 The Council for Healthcare Regulatory Excellence changed its name to the PSA in 2012, pursuant to the Health and Social Care Act 2012, s 222.

115 *Ruscillo v Council for the Regulation of Health Care Professionals; the GMC and Another* [2004] EWCA Civ 1356. On the potential for 'double jeopardy' (being tried again for the same charge following acquittal) see *PSA v GMC & Uppal* [2015] EWHC 1304 (Admin), [9] per Lang J: '[R]eference to having regard to double jeopardy when considering whether a sentence is unduly lenient is not … really apposite where the primary concern is for the protection of the public.'

116 *Professional Standards Authority for Health & Social Care v GMC & Uppal* [2015] EWHC 1304 (Admin).

117 See PSA, *Cases Appealed*, at www.professionalstandards.org.uk/.

118 PSA, *Case Study: A Nurse who Repeatedly Mistreated a Vulnerable Patient in her Care*, at www.professionalstandards.org.uk.

public.[119] The PSA can join in such an appeal. It was this route to appeal that was taken in the case of Dr Bawa-Garba.[120] In 2019, the government accepted recommendations that these powers should be removed, with legislation expected in 2023.[121] None of the other health professional bodies has such a power and removal would go some way to restoring trust of the profession in the GMC. The PSA route to appeal will remain in order to protect the public interest. In the interim, between the Dr Bawa-Garba case and new legislation, the GMC brought additional appeals.[122] One involved transplant surgeon Simon Bramhall. He was convicted of assault in 2018 when he branded two livers with his initials during surgery. The Medical Practitioners Tribunal imposed a five-month suspension order in 2020 which the GMC (joined by the PSA) successfully appealed.[123] He was struck off the medical register in 2022.

2.16 Regulating the NHS

The first part of this chapter examined the regulation of individual doctors. We now turn to methods by which NHS organisations are regulated. In 2012 the Health Committee referred to the regulatory landscape as 'cluttered and opaque'. Attempts to streamline and simplify such a complex body as the NHS continue to challenge the reformers.

2.17 Criminal law sanctions

Individual doctors face sanctions when they fall short of good medical practice. But what of the employing organisation? In 2006, Southampton University Hospital NHS Trust became the first NHS Trust to be prosecuted under the Health and Safety at Work Act 1974 for failing to adequately manage two junior doctors. The Trust pleaded guilty to a charge of improper supervision and was fined £100,000 and ordered to pay £10,000 costs.[124] The Corporate Manslaughter and Corporate Homicide Act 2007, whilst not creating any new duties, has potential to improve accountability of companies and organisations, including healthcare businesses, for fatalities that result from system failures.[125]

119 The GMC (Fitness to Practise and Over-arching Objective) and the Professional Standards Authority for Health and Social Care (References to Court) Order 2015, SI 2015/794.

120 See also *Raychaudhuri v GMC* [2018] EWCA Civ 2027, where Bean LJ was critical of the GMC bringing an appeal under s 40A on the facts.

121 DHSC, *Williams Review into Gross Negligence Manslaughter in Healthcare* (2018), chaired by Prof Sir Norman Williams, rec 6; GMC, *Independent Review of Gross Negligence Manslaughter and Culpable Homicide* (2019), chaired by Leslie Hamilton, rec 21.

122 C Dyer, 'GMC Appeals Against Three Suspension Decisions It Says Were Too Lenient' (2019) 366 *BMJ* 15110.

123 *GMC v Bramhall* [2021] EWHC 2109 (Admin).

124 *R v Southampton University Hospital NHS Trust* [2006] EWCA Crim 2971.

125 Though the first prosecution against an NHS Trust was heard in 2016 and dismissed: *R v Cornish and Maidstone and Tunbridge Wells NHS Trust* [2015] EWHC 2967 (QB), discussed at 10.6 below.

And in the wake of events at Mid Staffordshire NHS Foundation Trust, the Criminal Justice and Courts Act 2015 created new offences of ill treatment or wilful neglect (discussed at 10.7 below). Individual care workers can be held liable under section 20 and the organisation as a whole can be considered to be guilty of the offence under section 21. Criminal law measures are discussed in detail in Chapter 10 below.

2.18 Working hours

Organisations must safeguard their patients, but also have a duty to protect their employees. Work-related stress amongst NHS staff is widespread,[126] and was intensified by high mortality rates, personal protective equipment deficiencies, and difficult working conditions in the COVID-19 crisis.[127]

Long working hours exacerbate the problem.[128] The European Working Time Directive,[129] implemented domestically in the Working Time Regulations 1998,[130] imposed a 48-hour week, subject to opt-out and rest breaks. Three important European Court of Justice rulings address the question of what constitutes 'working time'. In *SiMAP*[131] and *Jaeger*,[132] it was determined that on-call staff, resident at work out-of-hours, are considered to be 'working' whilst on duty, whether or not they are called to the bedside. However, whilst the rulings enforce safe standards of working, they also create considerable challenges around rotas, handovers and training.[133] A more sympathetic stance was taken in *Commission v Ireland*,[134] where the court considered that there was insufficient evidence to show that all time spent training junior doctors should be considered working time. The 1998 Regulation became retained EU law by virtue of the European Union

126 NHS Staff Surveys, *NHS Staff Survey 2020 National Results Briefing* (2021): '44% of all staff reported feeling unwell due to work related stress and pressure.' This is an increase of 4 per cent since 2019, while 26.5 per cent 'often think about leaving their organisation'.

127 See NHS England, *News: NHS Launches Mental Health Hotline for Staff Tackling COVID-19* (2020) 8 April.

128 'Junior Doctors Repeatedly Working Past Shift End, NHS Data Shows' *Guardian* (2019) 15 January: 'Almost 36,000 trainee doctors in England have worked beyond their contracted hours more than 63,000 times since 2015.' The *NHS Staff Survey 2020* (2021) showed that over half of staff worked additional unpaid hours on a weekly basis.

129 93/104/EC.

130 SI 1998/1833 (as amended).

131 Case C-303/98, *Sindicato de Medicos de Asistencia Publica (SiMAP) v Conselleria de Sanidad y Consumo de la Generalidad Valenciana* [2000] ECR I-7963.

132 Case C-151/02, *Landeshauptstadt Kiel v Norbert Jaeger* [2003] ECR I-8389.

133 See Prof Norman Williams (Chair), *Independent Working Time Regulations Taskforce to the DH, The Implementation of the Working Time Directive and its Impact on the NHS and Health Professionals* (2014).

134 Case C-87/14, *Commission v Ireland* [2015] ECLI:EU:C:2015:449. And see Court of Justice of the European Union, *Press Release No 80/15*, Luxembourg, 9 July 2015.

(Withdrawal) Act 2018[135] but the UK is no longer bound by EU employment law and change may follow.

2.19 Governance

NHS organisations are responsible for a rigorous system of clinical governance, the central aim being to ensure continuous quality improvement and consistency between organisations. A formal requirement for clinical audit in the NHS was first introduced in 1989.[136] Since that time there has been a bewildering array of reforms designed to enhance and monitor quality in the NHS.

Historically, the Commission for Health Improvement issued 'star ratings' to providers. This body was replaced with the Commission for Healthcare Audit and Inspection (the 'Healthcare Commission') in 2004,[137] which abandoned the star ratings in favour of an 'annual health check'. The Health and Social Care Act 2008 established the independent CQC, which, in April 2009, took over the regulation of both health and social care, in NHS, private and voluntary organisations.[138] From April 2010 all providers of adult healthcare were required to register with the CQC.[139] GPs and other primary medical services were required to register by 2013. Registration is dependent upon demonstration that the provider reaches outcome-based standards.[140] The registration status of Trusts is published on the CQC website. Monitoring is achieved through audit, annual quality accounts[141] and scheduled, responsive and themed visits.[142] Failure leads to sanctions.[143]

135 Note that the Working Time (Coronavirus) (Amendment) Regulations 2020, SI 2020/365 provided an exception to a ban on carrying forward untaken leave under reg 13 of SI 1998/1833 when many forewent leave due to the national effort to tackle COVID-19.

136 Secretaries of State for Social Services, Wales, Northern Ireland and Scotland, *Working for Patients* (1989) Cm 555.

137 Set up under the Health and Social Care (Community Health and Standards) Act 2003, s 41.

138 The Care Quality Commission (Additional Functions) Regulations 2009, SI 2009/410; The Care Quality Commission (Membership) Regulations 2008, SI 2008/2252, revoked and replaced by SI 2015/1479.

139 The Health and Social Care Act 2008 (Registration of Regulated Activities) Regulations 2009, SI 2009/660.

140 Health and Social Care Act 2008 (Regulated Activities) Regulations 2014, SI 2014/2936, Pt 3 (as amended); Care Quality Commission (Registration) Regulations 2009, SI 2009/3112, Pt 4 (as amended). And see CQC, *Guidance for Providers on Meeting the Regulations* (March 2015).

141 Health Act 2009, ss 8–10; The NHS (Quality Accounts) Regulations 2010, SI 2010/279 (as amended) and see the NHS (Clinical Commissioning Groups – Payments in Respect of Quality) Regulations 2013, SI 2013/474.

142 But see CQC, 'Routine Inspections Suspended in Response to Coronavirus Outbreak' (2020) 16 March.

143 The Health and Social Care 2008 Act as amended by the Care Act 2014 lists sanctions. See in particular ss 17 (cancellation), 18 (suspension), 29 (warning notices)

The CQC monitors, inspects and regulates health and care providers but it is not the only regulator of providers in the NHS. Several separate aspects of NHS governance were brought together under the banner of NHS Improvement from 2016. One was Monitor, which was originally set up under the Health and Social Care (Community Health and Standards) Act 2003 to authorise and monitor Foundation Trusts. Its role was expanded post-Health and Social Care Act 2012 to include responsibility (in conjunction with NHS England) for the system that reimburses providers of NHS-funded care, setting prices, promoting competition, and limiting anti-competitive practices.[144] Another was the NHS Trust Development Authority, a Special Health Authority, responsible for NHS Trusts' performance management (including governance and clinical quality). NHS Improvement merged with NHS England in 2019, and in 2022 NHS England took on the functions of the NHS Commissioning Board, Monitor and the NHS Trust Development Authority.[145]

Subject to exemptions, providers of NHS services require a licence.[146] If the conditions of a licence are flouted, fines can be imposed, or the licence revoked. New providers apply for an NHS Provider licence and CQC registration through a single process that monitors five areas: quality of care, access and outcomes; preventing ill health and reducing inequalities; people; finance and use of resources; and leadership and capability.[147]

The current model of regulation has limitations. The Francis Inquiry's concerns about effectiveness[148] and low public confidence in the CQC[149] led to a call for greater clarity of objectives, standards and results.[150] The CQC was at the centre of a scandal in 2013 when accused of failing to investigate a series of serious adverse incidents in maternity care at Furness General Hospital.[151] In the words of the Secretary of State, 'defensiveness and secrecy were put ahead of patient safety and care'.[152] Further reforms ensued. The CQC now focuses more centrally on assessing quality and providing the information necessary to

and 30–32 (urgent procedures and appeals). Sections 33–27 list offences. And see CQC, *Enforcement Policy* (February 2015).

144 In accordance with the Competition Act 1998 and the NHS (Procurement, Patient Choice and Competition) Regulations 2013 No 1, SI 2013/257 and No 2, SI 2013/500.

145 Health and Care Act 2022, ss 1, 33 and 36 respectively.

146 Exceptions are set out in The NHS (Licence Exemptions, etc) Regulations 2013, SI 2013/2677 (as amended).

147 See NHS, *NHS System Oversight Framework* 2020/21 (2021).

148 *Report of the Mid Staffordshire NHS Foundation Trust Public Inquiry*, chaired by Robert Francis QC, HC947 (February 2013).

149 Health Committee, *Accountability Hearing with the Care Quality Commission*, HC 592 (December 2012).

150 DH, *Hard Truths: The Journey to Putting Patients First* (January 2014) Cm 8777.

151 Secretary of State for Health, Jeremy Hunt, *Oral Statement on Morecambe Bay* (2013) 18 June, accessible at: www.gov.uk/government/speeches/oral-statement-on-morecambe-bay.

152 Ibid. And see Dr Bill Kirkup CBE, *The Report of the Morecambe Bay Investigation* (March 2015) pp 170–171 suggesting that whilst the CQC 'clearly failed to deal adequately with the Trust' there was not evidence of a deliberate cover-up.

allow NHS England and NHS Improvement to make the necessary changes. In a move reminiscent of the 2003 star ratings, the CQC now publishes ratings for all health and care providers. But at Whorlton Hall, County Durham, the media exposed abuse of patients with learning difficulties and complex needs notwithstanding a rating of 'good' from the CQC.[153] A Joint Committee on Human Rights report on the detention of young people with learning disabilities and / or autism said:

> We have lost confidence that the system is doing what it says it is doing and the regulator's method of checking is not working. It has been left to the media ... to expose abuse.[154]

As was evident in the Bawa-Garba case, poor treatment often has several causes. Poor doctors are created by poor systems. The HSIB was set up in 2017 to conduct independent investigations of patient safety concerns in NHS-funded care across England and make safety recommendations. It investigated around thirty safety concerns each year. For example, one investigation in 2019 focused on how to recognise when an infant is acutely ill after a 3-month-old infant was admitted to a hospital, discharged and then died of Meningococcus B four hours later on re-admission.[155] The aim was to review staff training and preparedness so future cases would not go unrecognised. HSIB espoused a model based on safety investigation techniques used in the aviation industry, focusing on identifying weaknesses rather than apportioning blame.[156] Originally funded by the DHSC and hosted by NHS England and NHS Improvement, under Part 4 of the Health and Care Act 2022 it was renamed the Health Services Safety Investigations Body (HSSIB) and made a fully independent public body, with powers to investigate and promote system learning in both the NHS and independent sector.

2.20 Bodies supporting the Department of Health and Social Care

The DHSC is a ministerial department with two Executive Agencies: the Medicines and Healthcare products Regulatory Agency (MHRA) and the Health Security Agency (UKHSA). The UKHSA replaced Public Health England (PHE)[157] part way through the COVID-19 crisis. There was criticism of PHE's role in developing mass testing facilities, though responsibility could also be attributed to underfunding and government decision-making. The MHRA

153 See David Noble QSO (Chair), *Report to the Board of the Care Quality Commission ('CQC') on how CQC Dealt with Concerns Raised by Barry Stanley-Wilkinson in Relation to the Regulation of Whorlton Hall Hospital and to Make Recommendations* (2020).

154 Joint Committee on Human Rights, *The Detention of Young People with Learning Disabilities and/or Autism* (2019) HC121, HL Paper 10.

155 HSIB, 'Recognition of the Acutely Ill Infant' (2019): www.hsib.org.uk/investigations-cases/recognition-acutely-ill-infant/.

156 See 2.6 above.

157 PHE was established in 2012 to protect and improve the nation's well-being.

was set up in 2003 to license and regulate medicines and devices. We examine its role in licensing products in Chapter 12 and in monitoring and regulation of clinical research in Chapter 18. The MHRA is advised by specialist boards and a range of expert advisory groups.

As we have seen, work-based regulation involves a system of clinical governance and performance management. The DHSC is supported by four arms-length regulators: the CQC referred to above; the Health Research Authority (discussed in Chapter 18), which balances the interests of the public and patients in medical research and the protection of research participants; the Human Tissue Authority, which regulates human tissue and organs (see Chapters 20 and 21); and the Human Fertilisation and Embryology Authority (HFEA), which is discussed in Chapters 14 and 15.

Several executive non-departmental public bodies provide central support and work to improve the sector: Health Education England is discussed at 2.11 above; the National Institute for Health and Care Excellence provides information, guidelines and standards on conditions, treatments and technologies (see Chapter 3); NHS Resolution manages clinical negligence claims (Chapter 9); and NHS Digital (Chapter 5) collates and produces information and, together with NHSX (which led on digital transformation), will be subsumed within NHS England in the impending NHS restructure.

2.21 Whither the NHS

The NHS does not stand still, nor should it. It is an organisation for the people and must evolve to take account of changing needs. But the scale and pace of reform have proved a great burden at a time of intense financial pressure. We have briefly examined systems of regulation at local, organisational, and national levels. Regulation serves a variety of purposes, which do not always coincide. Economic accountability may result in a health service that represents value for money. Resource allocation decisions and their local variations will inevitably result in injustice to some. Aggrieved patients may look to the law for redress, either if they are denied treatment, or if they are harmed by sub-standard treatment. There remains much to do to ensure confidence in both the 'new' systems for regulating medical professions, and the NHS itself.

Chapter 3

DOCTORS' RESPONSIBILITIES: PATIENTS' RIGHTS

3.1 Introduction

When we are ill, we want to be treated by competent doctors – that is why debates about regulation of the medical profession are so crucial. However, we may also wish to assert our own rights, especially in the context of decision-making. In the 2015 Supreme Court decision of *Montgomery v Lanarkshire Health Board*,[1] Lords Kerr and Reed highlighted the effects of human rights discourse on the doctor–patient relationship:

> [P]atients are now widely regarded as persons holding rights, rather than as the passive recipients of the care of the medical profession. They are also widely treated as consumers exercising choices: a viewpoint which has underpinned some of the developments in the provision of healthcare services.[2]

Patients are no longer content to be passive recipients even of 'good' care. They want a say in what 'good' care comprises. The pace of medical developments is such that, particularly in the context of reproductive medicine and genetics, new questions surface daily around the implications of certain kinds of treatment. These may concern entitlement to treatment, or how far choices about treatment belong to individual patients alone. Or they may focus on the role of the state. Or the interests of commerce may be involved. How does the law begin to address patient rights today? We begin by considering what relevance human rights have to medicine and turn in the latter half of the chapter to matters of resource allocation and access to medicine.

The United Nations General Assembly adopted the Universal Declaration of Human Rights in 1948. Article 25 protects an individual's 'right to a standard of living adequate for the health and well-being of himself and of his family' and incorporates a right to medical care and security in the event of sickness and disability. A series of nine human rights treaties (and their optional protocols) articulate the rights of certain groups. An individual whose rights are breached can complain to the monitoring body of each Convention, provided their state has ratified the Treaty and recognised the

1 [2015] UKSC 11. Discussed below at 6.12.
2 Ibid, [75].

competence of the Committee (usually by becoming a party to the optional protocols). In 1991, the UK ratified the Convention on the Rights of the Child 1989 (CRC) (discussed in Chapter 17). The Convention on the Rights of Persons with Disabilities 2006 (noted in Chapter 7) and optional protocol were ratified in 2009. Neither Convention has been incorporated into law in England,[3] but a Bill introduced in 2020 seeking to make Scotland the first country in the UK to directly incorporate the CRC into domestic law was passed in 2021,[4] and a duty incumbent on Ministers to have regard to the CRC was introduced in Wales.[5]

The forty-seven member states of the Council of Europe are bound by the provisions of the European Convention on Human Rights (ECHR), arbitrated by the European Court of Human Rights (ECtHR).[6] The ECtHR is an international court which sits in Strasbourg and hears applications from individuals and member states on potential breaches of the Convention. The Court is divided into various Chambers, which can make a judgment or, in very important or controversial cases, send the case to the Grand Chamber. Following a Chamber judgment, parties have three months to request referral to the Grand Chamber before the decision is considered final. The Grand Chamber can reconsider the case, but referrals are accepted only on an exceptional basis.

The Human Rights Act 1998 came into effect in 2000. It gives domestic effect to the ECHR. In practice, the English Courts referred to, and deferred to, the Convention for several years prior to 1998, in developing the common law. The Human Rights Act does not replace or eliminate existing common law principles. As Lord Reed made clear in 2013, the Convention is relatively broad and unspecific and cannot 'be treated as if it were Moses and the prophets'.[7]

Although the common law relating to healthcare developed piecemeal, with an apparent emphasis on wrongs rather than rights, in many instances the existing law may suffice to vindicate rights endorsed in the Convention.[8] Decisions

3 But ECHR rights should be read in domestic law as having regard to the UNCRC: *Dyer (Procurator Fiscal, Linlithgow) v Watson; JK v HM Advocate* [2004] 1 AC 379.

4 The United Nations Convention on the Rights of the Child (Incorporation) (Scotland) Bill 2020. The Supreme Court in *Reference by the Attorney General and the Advocate General for Scotland* [2021] UKSC 42 ruled that aspects of the Bill exceed the powers of the Scottish Parliament and so the Bill cannot become law in its current form and is delayed.

5 Rights of Children and Young Persons (Wales) Measure 2011, s 1.

6 On the relationship between the European Court of Justice and the European Convention on Human Rights note *Opinion 2/13 Re EU accession to the ECHR* [2014] ECR I 2454 (18 December 2014).

7 *R (Osborn) v Parole Board* [2013] UKSC 61 [56], discussed below at 3.3.

8 Consider, for example, *Esegbona v King's College London NHS Trust* [2019] EWHC 77 (QB), where damages were awarded for false imprisonment when a Trust failed to discharge a 68-year-old woman from hospital in breach of the Mental Capacity Act 2005.

of the English courts so far that address the Human Rights Act tend not to declare new rights, but to review whether the existing common law 'rights' are sufficient in the light of the Convention.[9]

Though some have expressed consternation about the way that the Convention changes English common law, controversial decisions often stem not from the Convention itself, but from the Strasbourg Court's changing interpretation of its Articles. The Convention is a 'living instrument' and this affords the Court significant discretion, which has proved contentious.[10] A growing faction seeks to distance English law from the Convention. Some argue for a wholesale decoupling, whilst others have suggested opting out of parts of the Convention.[11] Even if we remain party to the Convention, the Human Rights Act is under attack. The majority of the Commission on a Bill of Rights, reporting in 2012,[12] concluded that a UK Bill of Rights could replace the Human Rights Act, incorporating the UK's obligations under the ECHR whilst improving the sense of public ownership of the human rights regime. Plans to repeal the Human Rights Act[13] were shelved in 2022.

The form of human rights protection may be subject to change, but the legacy of the Convention and Human Rights Act in the context of medical law is likely to endure. It is to this we now turn.

3.2 The impact of the Human Rights Act 1998

Medical law, Ian Kennedy and Andrew Grubb declared, is essentially 'a sub-set of human rights law'.[14] The fundamental nature of the relationship between doctors and patients amply proves their point. At stake within the realm of medical law is our right to make our own decisions about how we live our lives and how we die. Our interests in privacy and in family life, in having or not having children, are central to our dealings with health professionals.

We should note that the ECHR addresses only a limited range of rights. There is no *positive* right to healthcare; there is no equivalent to Article 25 in the Universal Declaration of Human Rights. In a number of instances what the Convention confers are *negative* rights – ie prohibitions against certain kinds of infringement of basic freedoms, although the jurisprudence of the

9 See J McHale, 'Health Law in the UK as a Subset of Human Rights Law: Idealistic Aspiration or Coherent Reality?' (2019) 7(2) *Journal of Medical Law and Ethics* 179.

10 Lord Lester of Herne Hill QC, 'European Court of Human Rights and the Human Rights Act: British Concerns' (2012) 17(1) *Judicial Review* 1.

11 O Bowcott, 'UK Government Plans to Remove Key Human Rights Protections' *Guardian* (2020) 13 September.

12 Commission on a Bill of Rights, *A UK Bill of Rights? – The Choice Before Us* (2012).

13 Ministry of Justice, *Human Rights Act Reform: A Modern Bill of Rights* (2021).

14 I Kennedy and A Grubb, *Medical Law* (3rd edn, 2000) Oxford University Press, p 3. And see I Kennedy, *Treat me Right: Essays in Medical Law and Ethics* (1991) Clarendon Press, p 385.

Convention is moving to a greater recognition of *positive* rights. The Human Rights Act does not (whatever the media says) incorporate the Convention into English law. It renders the Convention enforceable against *public authorities*. The Act is relevant to disputes about enforced treatment or arguments that the Government are violating patients' privacy. Where what is at stake is a failure by the National Health Service (NHS) to provide certain sorts of care, or concerns about allowing, for example, insurers to demand medical details about you, the utility of the Act is diminished.

Even when a patient can bring their claim squarely within the ambit of a Convention right, they may find that the violation of their right is found to be justified. Many Convention rights are qualified. A good example is Article 8(1) – the right to respect for private and family life. In certain circumstances, Article 8(2) provides that infringement of the right may be justifiable; a violation of a patient's privacy could be held justified on grounds of public health, or for the protection of health or morals, as long as that infringement is proportionate. That means that interference with the individual's right must be shown to be 'necessary in a democratic society'. Moreover, Articles of the Convention may 'contradict' each other in certain circumstances, for example, Article 2 (life) and Article 8 (privacy). Finally, the jurisprudence of the ECtHR expressly endorses a doctrine oddly entitled the 'margin of appreciation'. That is, national jurisdictions are allowed a degree of freedom in defining their own criteria of public policy (morality).[15] English courts enjoy some degree of discretion to determine English views of ethical dilemmas in medicine.

Nor should you expect the ECtHR itself to be startlingly radical in relation to healthcare. Many European countries adopt a conservative approach to healthcare rights. For example, in relation to fertility treatment, Italy enacted legislation radically curtailing options for fertility treatment and effectively giving the force of law to Roman Catholic doctrine.[16] Be wary of arguments that English law violates the Convention where a consequence would be that other European countries are also in breach.[17] Remember that as the supreme arbiter of the Convention, the ECtHR is an international court with judges representing several jurisdictions.

3.3 How the Human Rights Act works

Understanding how the Human Rights Act works is important to assess how the Act may affect healthcare law. The Act does not directly incorporate the Human Rights Convention. In a claim against a private litigant, the claimant cannot sue for violation of Convention rights. The Act, first, requires that primary and subordinate legislation be interpreted where possible in a way which

[15] See *A, B and C v Ireland* [2010] ECHR 2032, see 14.8 below.

[16] Statute on Assisted Reproduction (Law 40/2004). Though see *Costa and Pavan v Italy*, App No 54270/2010 (ECHR, 28 August 2012).

[17] *SH v Austria*, App No 57813/00 (ECHR, 2011) (Grand Chamber) discussed in S McGuinness, 'Health, Human Rights and the Regulation of Reproductive Technologies in *SH and others v Austria*' (2013) 21(1) *Med Law Rev* 146.

is compatible with Convention rights[18] and renders it 'unlawful for a public authority to act in a way which is incompatible with a Convention right'.[19]

'Convention rights' are the fundamental rights and freedoms[20] set out in Articles 2 to 12 and 14 of the Convention, Articles 1 to 3 of the First Protocol (concerning rights to property, education and free elections) and Articles 1 and 2 of the sixth Protocol (abolishing the death penalty). Section 11 of the Act makes it crystal clear that Convention rights are in addition to, not in substitution for, rights and freedoms already endorsed at common law. It may seem odd that no express provision of the Act requires that judges develop the common law in a manner consistent with Convention rights. However, as noted above, English judges already, wherever possible, seek to ensure that the common law is consistent with such rights. More importantly, section 6 of the Act, which makes it unlawful for any public authority to act in a way incompatible with Convention rights, provides that courts are classified as public authorities. A judge hearing a patient's claim must, by virtue of section 6, consider compatibility with Convention rights and ensure consistency between common law and Convention rights.

However, the domestic rules on precedent are unaffected. If a decision of the Court of Appeal contradicts a decision of the ECtHR, the Court of Appeal in subsequent cases is bound by its previous decision. Only a higher court, the Supreme Court in this example, could hold that the Court of Appeal case was wrongly decided on the basis that it conflicts with a decision in the ECtHR.[21] For example, when Debbie Purdy argued that a lack of guidance on assisted suicide breached her rights under Article 8, the Court of Appeal[22] held that they were bound by the House of Lords decision in *Pretty*[23] where it had been found that Article 8(1) was not engaged under these circumstances. This is despite the fact that, subsequently, the ECtHR found that Dianne Pretty's Article 8(1) rights *were* engaged.[24] It was for the House of Lords (in their final decision before the Supreme Court was established) to 'untie the knot'. In a landmark ruling, the Law Lords allowed Debbie Purdy's appeal, so aligning domestic law and the Strasbourg jurisprudence.[25]

Not only do the rules of precedent delay the application of Strasbourg rulings in domestic cases, but section 2(1) of the Human Rights Act requires that domestic courts must '*take into account*' ECtHR jurisprudence, not follow it slavishly. The court can provide reasons why a Strasbourg decision should not

18 Human Rights Act 1998, s 3.
19 Ibid, ss 6–8.
20 Ibid, s 7.
21 *Kay v Lambeth London Borough Council, Price v Leeds City Council* [2006] UKHL 10. Applied in *Johnson v Havering London Borough Council and Secretary of State Affairs* [2007] EWCA Civ 26. For analysis see S Pattinson, 'The Human Rights Act and the Doctrine of Precedent' (2015) 35(1) *Legal Studies* 142.
22 *R (Purdy) v Director of Public Prosecutions* [2009] EWCA Civ 92.
23 *R (Pretty) v DPP* [2002] 1 AC 800, HL.
24 *Pretty v United Kingdom*, App No 2346/02 (ECHR, 2002) 35 EHRR 1.
25 *R (Purdy) v Director of Public Prosecutions* [2009] UKHL 44.

be followed where aspects of the domestic law were not fully appreciated.[26] The Supreme Court has also affirmed that it can look to the common law even if the jurisprudence of the European Court suggests a different interpretation of a Convention Article. *In R (Osborn) v Parole Board*,[27] the Supreme Court considered the relationship between domestic common law and Convention rights. Lord Reed made clear that Convention and common law are not distinct.[28] English law is and has long been permeated by human rights:

> The importance of the [Convention] is unquestionable. It does not however supersede the protection of human rights under the common law or statute, or create a discrete body of law based upon the judgments of the European court.[29]

Where a dispute falls within the domain of a Convention Article, the solution does not 'begin and end with the Strasbourg case law'.[30] *Osborn* is an important assertion of the primacy of the common law as a source of human rights law. The Supreme Court affirmed this approach in subsequent cases, emphasising the importance of developing the common law in areas falling within the scope of the Convention.[31]

Similarly, where a claim alleging violation of a Convention Right involves legislation, section 3 of the Act requires any court or tribunal to seek to interpret that rule in a way which is compatible with the relevant Convention Right. However, if such an interpretation is not possible, the courts are not granted powers to strike down legislation. The judicial role remains limited by doctrines of Parliamentary sovereignty. Section 4(2) provides that:

> If the court is satisfied that the provision is incompatible with a Convention right, it may make a declaration of that incompatibility.

The Government should then act to amend legislation to 'cure' the relevant incompatibility. Section 10 enables them to do so by secondary legislation making a 'remedial order'. Failure to act to remove the stated incompatibility would give rise to a claim against the United Kingdom before the ECtHR at Strasbourg. The dissatisfied patient could bring another claim suing the Government itself.

This can be illustrated by considering a controversial provision of the Human Fertilisation and Embryology Act 1990, which was the subject of a declaration of incompatibility. Section 28(6)(b) of the Act prior to its amendment by the Human Fertilisation and Embryology Act 2008 provided that if the sperm of any man was used after his death, he was not to be treated as the father of the child. Diane Blood[32] fought a long battle to be able to undergo insemination

26 *R v Horncastle* [2009] UKSC 14.
27 [2013] UKSC 61.
28 Ibid, [54]–[63]; [101]–[113].
29 Ibid, [57].
30 Ibid, [63].
31 *See A v BBC* [2014] 2 UKSC 25.
32 *R v Human Fertilisation and Embryology Authority, ex p Blood* [1999] Fam 151. See 14.15 below.

with her deceased husband's sperm. She ultimately gave birth to two sons after fertility treatment abroad. Section 28(6)(b) meant that the boys' birth certificates recorded the father as 'unknown'. Mrs Blood and her sons succeeded in their contention that the Act violated their rights to respect for private and family life endorsed by Article 8 and, in response, Parliament enacted the Human Fertilisation and Embryology (Deceased Fathers) Act 2003. The 2003 Act is now repealed but the 1990 Act has been amended to the same effect.[33]

For the healthcare professional, the most crucial element of the Act is the provision that 'Convention rights' are directly enforceable against public authorities, and that an individual who considers that her rights have been violated by a public authority can sue for damages. Where an individual considers that a public authority has acted in breach of Convention rights, a number of rather different outcomes must be considered. First, in many cases, the self-same rights conferred by the Convention are already recognised by the law of torts. For example, Article 5 provides for a right to liberty and security and protects the citizen against arbitrary detention. The ancient tort of false imprisonment protects that same fundamental interest. A patient alleging unlawful detention in hospital may not need to resort to claiming a breach of Article 5. They can sue in false imprisonment. In determining whether their detention was lawful, the court will be mindful of the provisions of Article 5 and the jurisprudence of the ECtHR.

The position is more complex when a Convention right is not so well established in domestic law. Privacy was not, though the common law has developed rapidly. The claimant might then choose to bring their claim directly under the Act alleging breach of Article 8, which requires respect for private and family life. If they elect for a Convention remedy alone, they can sue under the Act only if the defendant is a public authority. Were we to discover that the Department of Health and Social Care was bugging our offices, suing a government department would be straightforward. What if a tabloid newspaper splashed our medical history all over its front page? There is an argument that the newspaper, too, might be classified as a public authority, for section 6(3)(b) classifies as a public authority 'any person certain of whose functions are functions of a public nature'.[34]

Suppose, however, a private individual, a colleague, for example, invades our privacy by steaming open our private correspondence and finds letters from our doctors revealing an embarrassing medical complaint. What then? In practical terms, often some common law remedy may be found within which to frame a cause of action. The 'snooper' who peers through windows or opens our mail could be liable for harassment, or trespass to goods. If no common law remedy can be identified so that the defendant appears to be immune from liability, Article 6 of the Convention comes into play. Article 6 grants a right that, in determination of their civil rights and obligations, everyone is entitled to a fair trial. It grants a right of access to justice. If no remedy for violation of

33 See Human Fertilisation and Embryology Act 1990, s 28(5)A–I.

34 See 3.4 below.

Article 8 (right to privacy) appears to exist, the court must in effect develop a remedy,[35] or the court acts unlawfully in failing to implement Article 8. And the Government is in breach of the Convention in failing to provide a legal remedy, violating the citizen's right to access to justice.

Article 6 affects the development of the English law in two ways. Relatively rarely, Article 6 will come into play because the common law offers *no* remedy for violation of a Convention right. More commonly, the Article will be invoked in order to overcome some restriction on the claimant's common law right. A recent example of this flows from the exercise of the inherent jurisdiction of the High Court which has been found to exist in relation to vulnerable and incapacitated adults, even after the statutory regime in the Mental Capacity Act 2005 was introduced.[36] In *Mazhar v Birmingham Community Healthcare Foundation NHS Trust*,[37] 30-year-old Mr Mazhar had Duchenne Muscular Dystrophy and needed regular care. Difficulties with his home care provision resulted in him being removed from his home and the care of his mother to a hospital, without warning and in the presence of police officers. The Trust had made a successful emergency application under the inherent jurisdiction of the High Court on the basis of his vulnerability and undue influence from his mother. The Court of Appeal found that a lack of sufficient evidence to establish these factors and a failure to give Mr Mazhar the opportunity to be heard amounted to a breach of Article 6. Going forward, orders in respect of vulnerable adults under the inherent jurisdiction should not be made without notice to the individual save in exceptional circumstances.

3.4 Who can be sued?

As we have seen, the Act does not define public authority. Section 6(3) provides that public authority includes: (a) a court or tribunal, and (b) any person certain of whose functions are of a public nature. What does this mean for the NHS? National Health Service Trusts, including Clinical Commissioning Groups (CCGs) are public authorities. So are bodies such as NHS research ethics committees. 'Quangos' such as the Care Quality Commission are equally clearly public authorities, as are regulatory bodies such as the General Medical Council (GMC). Individual doctors, nurses and other health professionals working within the NHS are performing functions of a public nature and face potential claims under the Act (although normally such claims would be brought against their employer). General Practitioners and other non-employed NHS personnel might be more directly in the firing line. Professionals in private practice and private hospitals raise tricky questions.

35 *Campbell v Mirror Group Newspapers* [2004] UKHL 22. But see *Wainwright v Home Office* [2003] UKHL 53 where the Court deferred any responsibility for the creation of a tort of privacy to Parliament.

36 See 7.20 below.

37 [2020] EWCA Civ 1377. See also *R (TB) v CPS and South Staffordshire Healthcare NHS Trust* [2006] EWHC 1645 (Admin) and *Mehmet Günay et Güllü Günay v Turkey*, App No 52797/08 (ECHR, 2018): a claim in medical negligence that took seven years and four months to conclude breached Article 6.

Whilst a doctor is a public authority in relation to their NHS functions, the same does not apply to doctors in private practice. So if patient A contracts with Dr B to carry out surgery at Clinic C paying out of their own pocket, or via private health insurers, the relationship is entirely private. However, if patient A later sues Dr B or Clinic C, in determining the nature of the patient's redress, the court must seek to develop the common law consistently with the Convention on Human Rights. If this is not possible, patient A may have redress against the Government under Article 6 for violating their right to a fair trial to determine their civil rights and obligations.

Do private clinics treating NHS patients perform functions of a public nature? They will not be regarded as 'core' public authorities under section 6, but might they be viewed as 'hybrid bodies' under section 6(3)(b)? As we have seen, under section 6(3)(b) a public authority includes 'any person certain of whose functions are functions of a public nature'. However, section 6(5) provides that: 'In relation to a particular act, a person is not a public authority … if the nature of the act is private.' The test therefore relates to the particular act of which complaint is made.[38] In *Scott v LGBT Foundation Ltd*,[39] for example, Mr Scott claimed that his Article 8 rights were breached when the LGBT Foundation made an oral disclosure of confidential information to a third party. The LGBT Foundation received public funds, but the claimant did not access funded services and therefore the Foundation was not a hybrid public body for the purposes of the relevant act. The question is whether the act is a private act, or the discharge of a public function.[40]

Initially there was reluctance to give 'core' or 'hybrid' public authority status to private clinics, even when patients were funded by local authorities.[41] But an amendment to the Care Act 2014[42] extended the application of the Human Rights Act to cover *all* care arranged by or paid for (directly or indirectly, and in whole or in part) by an authority.[43] Is the application of the Act to largely private arrangements a step too far? We think not. The Francis Inquiry[44] serves as a stark reminder of the need to ensure that all people subjected to poor standards of care, regardless of how it is funded, are able to assert their human rights.

3.5 Who can sue?

Only a person who is a 'victim' of the alleged violation of the Convention can bring a claim under the 1998 Act. The concept of victim derives from the

38 See for example *London and Quadrant Housing Trust v R (Weaver) and Equality and Human Rights Commission* [2009] EWCA Civ 587.
39 [2020] EWHC 483 (QB). See 5.8 below.
40 See *Aston Cantlow Parish Church Council v Wallbank* [2003] UKHL 37, per Lord Nicholls [16].
41 *R (Heather) v Leonard Cheshire Foundation (Cheshire)* [2001] EWHC Admin 429; *YL v Birmingham City Council* [2007] UKHL 27.
42 Section 73(2).
43 Though not to privately arranged and funded residential and domiciliary care.
44 Discussed in Chapter 2 above.

Convention and jurisprudence of the ECtHR. A victim must be actually and directly affected by the act or omission which is the subject of the complaint. Though two or more victims based on the same facts can make a grouped application, there is no direct provision for interest groups to sue to vindicate Convention rights.

What does this mean in practice? Obviously, a claimant who is detained in hospital against their will can ground a claim on Article 5 (although a claim in false imprisonment may suffice).[45] A person who alleges that they have been experimented on without consent may have a claim under Article 3 (prohibiting inhuman or degrading treatment) or Article 8. However it may be difficult for individuals to fund claims about important principles. Interest groups will want to use the Convention to challenge and change existing law (for example, the ban on voluntary euthanasia). Will they be able to do so, given interest groups cannot sue as groups? It is not necessary to show that a claimant has actually already suffered from the consequences of an alleged violation. 'Victims' need only show a real risk of being directly affected by a breach. Abortion centre counsellors acting with women wishing to receive advice successfully challenged Irish laws prohibiting dissemination of any information about abortion.[46] Representative interest groups involving groups of victims are able to gain standing under the Act.

In the not-too-distant future, another issue may come to the fore. The Convention refers to 'human' rights but does not define human. Technological advances in artificial intelligence and enhancement may raise the potential for novel beings with the capacity for consciousness to claim human rights, and for intelligent animals or natural 'living' entities such as rivers to be found deserving of human rights.[47]

3.6 Convention rights

Reference will be made to relevant Convention rights throughout the chapters that follow. All that we do now is give a brief overview of those Convention rights that are likely to have the most significant impact in the rights and obligations of doctors and patients in England.[48] The COVID-19 pandemic is a stark reminder of the global nature of health rights, and the importance of public health, but whilst we make reference to the pandemic throughout the book the reader should look elsewhere for a detailed account of public health rights.[49]

45 But see 7.11–7.12 below.

46 *Open Door and Dublin Well Women v Ireland* (1992) 15 ECHR 244.

47 See DR Lawrence and M Brazier, 'Legally Human? "Novel Beings" and English Law' (2018) 26(2) *Med Law Rev* 309.

48 See T Murphy, *Health and Human Rights* (2013) Hart.

49 See for example, LO Gostin and BM Meier, *Human Rights in Global Health: Rights-Based Governance for a Globalizing World* (2018) Oxford University Press; SA Zweig *et al*, 'Ensuring Rights while Protecting Health' (2021) 23 *Health and Human Rights Journal* 173.

3.7 Article 2

Article 2 provides that 'Everyone's right to life shall be protected by law'. It imposes substantive obligations on the state to protect the right to life and prohibit deprivation of life, subject to certain exceptions, and a procedural obligation to protect the right 'by law'.

The state is under a positive obligation[50] to regulate so as to require provision of care that protects lives.[51] The European Court found a breach of Article 2 when a newborn baby died in an ambulance having been refused admission to public hospitals in Turkey due to lack of space.[52] There was a failure to provide emergency care and to properly investigate the incident that led to the child's death. The UK Supreme Court held in 2012 that a preventive operational obligation extends to safeguarding informal psychiatric patients from the risk of suicide,[53] but there has been reluctance to extend it further. The Court of Appeal found in *Maguire*[54] that the procedural operational obligation does not necessarily extend to vulnerable people in care homes where they reside there for residential purposes rather than for medical treatment. The case will be considered by the Supreme Court in due course. And in *Morahan*,[55] when a voluntary in-patient at a rehabilitation unit did not return at the agreed time and was found to have died of an overdose, it was found that the need for an enhanced investigation did not arise as there was no real and immediate risk of death which the state knew or ought to have known.

Does the positive obligation under Article 2 extend to situations in which a person objects to the treatment needed to save their life? In *Nottinghamshire Healthcare NHS Trust v RC*,[56] Mostyn J re-asserted the right of those with mental capacity to choose to harm or kill themselves. A Jehovah's Witness

50 See *Osman v United Kingdom* (1998) 29 EHRR 245.

51 Provided there is effective regulation, the Strasbourg Court has found that death resulting from negligence will not give rise to a claim: *Lopes de Sousa Fernandes v Portugal*, App No 56080/13 (ECHR, 2018) (Grand Chamber) 66 EHRR 28. And see *R (Parkinson) v HM Senior Coroner for Kent, Dartford & Gravesham NHS Trust & Sameer Hijazi* [2018] EWHC 1501 (Admin).

52 *Asiye Genç v Turkey*, App No 24109/07 (ECHR, 2015). See A Nisen, 'A Right to Access to Emergency Health Care: The European Court of Human Rights Pushes the Envelope' (2018) 26(4) *Med Law Rev* 693.

53 *Rabone v Pennine Care NHS FT* [2012] UKSC 2. See also *Savage v South Essex Partnership NHS Foundation Trust* [2008] UKHL 74 and discussion in J Varuhas, 'Liability under the Human Rights Act 1998: The Duty to Protect Life, Indirect Victims and Damages' (2012) 71(2) *Cambridge Law Journal* (hereafter *CLJ*) 263.

54 *R (Maguire) v HM Senior Coroner for Blackpool & Fylde* [2020] EWCA Civ 738. And see *R (Gardner and Harris) v Secretary of State for Health and Social Care and Ors* [2022] EWHC 967 (Admin), [287]–[291] finding no breach of Article 2 in relation to policies to discharge patients to care homes in the COVID-19 pandemic without isolating them. The policy was, however, found to be unlawful on the public law ground of irrationality.

55 *R (Morahan) v HM Assistant Coroner for West London* [2021] EWHC 1603 (Admin).

56 [2014] EWHC 1317 (COP).

with a history of self-harm was admitted to a psychiatric hospital having cut the brachial artery in his arm. He made repeated attempts to reopen the wound and signed an advance decision[57] withholding consent to blood products, even if his life was at risk. Mostyn J quoted John Stuart Mill's essay *On Liberty*:

> That the only purpose for which power can be rightfully exercised over any member of a civilised community, against his will, is to prevent harm to others. His own good, either physical or moral, is not a sufficient warrant ... Over himself, over his body and mind, the individual is sovereign.[58]

Mostyn J found that RC had capacity to refuse blood products.[59] There is a duty on public authorities to give effect to the right to life of persons under state control, but provided a patient has capacity, they retain the right to 'opt-out of the right to life granted to him by Article 2'.[60]

What limits may or must be placed on the right to life? When does such a right crystallise? Is it an absolute right entitling the patient to any possible treatment? How are competing rights of other patients to be addressed? Remember that such a right would necessarily impose an obligation to provide publicly funded care. The ECtHR has made it clear that where protection from disease requires use of state resources, individual countries are left considerable freedom to assess their own aims and priorities.[61]

Arguments have been unsuccessfully advanced that the Article 2 right to life also entails a right to die,[62] and that Member States must recognise the right to life of fetuses. Refusing to strike down national abortion laws, the European Commission has not applied Article 2 to fetuses in the first trimester of pregnancy.[63] In *Vo v France*[64] the ECtHR confirmed that the question of when a right of life accrued fell within the margin of appreciation allowed to contracting states.

3.8 Article 3

Article 3 provides that 'No one shall be subjected to torture or inhuman or degrading treatment or punishment'. It has been applied to offenders in prison who are denied medical treatment[65] but, except where a person is detained, there is reticence to recognise breach of Article 3 for failure to provide

57 Properly witnessed, as required under Mental Capacity Act 2005, ss 24–26.
58 *Nottinghamshire Healthcare NHS Trust v RC* [2014] EWHC 1317 (COP), [8] per Mostyn J.
59 Ibid, [42].
60 Ibid, [19] per Mostyn J. See 6.3 below.
61 *Osman v United Kingdom* (1998) 29 EHRR 245.
62 *R (Pretty) v DPP* [2001] UKHL 61, see 22.6 below.
63 See *Bruggeman and Scheuten v Federal Republic of Germany* [1977] EHRR 24; *Paton v UK* [1980] 3 EHRR 408 (discussed at 16.12 below). See 16.1 below for contrasting developments in the USA.
64 [2004] ECHR 326. See 16.1 below.
65 *McGlinchey and Others v United Kingdom*, App No 50390/99 (ECHR, 2003).

treatment.[66] It is conceivable, however, that horrific cases, such as the appalling standards of care and resulting morbidity and mortality at Mid Staffordshire NHS Foundation Trust,[67] severe mistreatment of residents of Winterbourne View hospital,[68] and failures to place children with severe mental health disorders in suitable care,[69] might breach Article 3.[70]

Are laws prohibiting voluntary euthanasia contrary to Article 3? An argument might run linking Articles 3 and 8. The case could be put, for example, that a patient dying of some terrible degenerative disease or suffering acute pain from terminal cancer was, by being denied the option of active euthanasia, subjected to inhuman and degrading treatment, contrary to Article 3. Moreover, if their doctor, or some other third party, was willing to help them die, preventing them from doing so might violate their privacy contrary to Article 8. We shall see that when Dianne Pretty,[71] a woman dying of motor neurone disease, sought to invoke Articles 3 and 8 to support her claim that her husband should be granted immunity from prosecution if he helped her to commit suicide, her claim failed. The House of Lords refused to interpret Article 3 to affirm a right to die with dignity. Her further appeal to the Strasbourg Court also failed.[72] Nor can Article 3 be relied upon to compel doctors to continue futile or inappropriate treatment. Leslie Burke, who suffered from a degenerative neurological condition, cerebellar ataxia, fought for the right to artificial nutrition and hydration in the event that he was unable to voice his wishes. He unsuccessfully sought to invoke Articles 2, 3, 8 and 14 to challenge guidance from the GMC which stated that where a patient's disease is severe and the prognosis poor, artificial nutrition and hydration will not always be appropriate, even if death is not imminent.[73] The Court of Appeal and the ECtHR turned his claim down.[74] Doctors cannot be forced to administer treatment which they believe to be clinically unnecessary, futile or inappropriate.

Article 3 will raise other questions about our existing common law. Might certain forms of non-consensual treatment fall foul of Article 3?[75] Consider

66 See *R v North West Lancashire Health Authority ex p A, D & G* [2000] 1 WLR 977, CA.
67 In *Z v United Kingdom* (2001) 34 EHRR 97, neglect and abuse of four children and failure of the state to protect them was deemed capable of violating Article 3.
68 See DH, *Transforming Care: A National Response to Winterbourne View Hospital: Final Report* (2012).
69 See *Re X (A Child) (No 3)* [2017] EWHC 2036 (Fam), Sir James Munby P, [36].
70 Equality and Human Rights Commission, *Close to home: An Inquiry into Older People and Human Rights in Home Care* (2011), p 28.
71 See *R (Pretty) v DPP* [2001] UKHL 61 (discussed at 22.6 below); and see *Rodriguez v British Columbia A-G* (1993) 82 BCLP (2d) 273.
72 *Pretty v UK* [2002] 2 FLR 45.
73 GMC, *Withholding and Withdrawing Life-Prolonging Treatments: Good Practice in Decision-Making* (2002), para 16. The guidance has since been updated. See at 22.18 below.
74 *R (Burke) v GMC* [2005] EWCA Civ 1003; *Burke v UK*, App No 19807/06 (ECHR, 2006).
75 See *Herczegfalvy v Austria* (1992) 18 BMLR 48. See *R (N) v M* [2003] 1 WLR 562, CA.

cases relating to naso-gastric feeding of patients with anorexia nervosa without their consent.[76] And how far does Article 3 impose obligations on health professionals to intervene in order to prevent harm caused by other individuals in the case of abuse or neglect?[77]

3.9 Article 5

The relevant parts of Article 5(1) provide:

> Everyone has the right to liberty and security of person. No-one shall be deprived of his liberty save in the following cases and in accordance with a procedure prescribed by law ...
>
> (e) the lawful detention of persons for the prevention of the spreading of infectious diseases, or persons of unsound mind, alcoholics or drug addicts or vagrants.

Article 5(1)(e) was relevant in the COVID-19 pandemic. Measures to prevent the spread of infectious disease were set out in Schedule 21 of the Coronavirus Act 2020.[78] Powers relating to potentially infectious persons allowed compulsory screening and assessment to protect the person, or others, or to maintain public health. They did not sanction compulsory medical treatment.[79] Provisions to make vaccination against COVID-19 a condition of work for care workers were introduced in 2021 and planned, but later abandoned, for all patient-facing healthcare workers in 2022.[80]

Outside the context of public health emergencies, the common law tort of false imprisonment already gives protection to the liberty and security of persons. A lacuna in mental health law came to light in *R v Bournewood Community and Mental Health Trust ex p L*.[81] L was a 49-year-old man who had autism and lacked capacity. He was an in-patient at Bournewood Hospital but was not detained under the provisions of the Mental Health Act 1983. Instead, he was detained in his best interests, under the common law doctrine of necessity.[82] The High Court held that L's detention was lawful and proper. But the case was successfully challenged in the ECtHR in *HL v United Kingdom*:[83] Detention

76 *Re E (Medical Treatment: Anorexia)* [2012] EWHC 1639 (COP), [126] per Jackson J.

77 Note that the Care Act 2014, s 42 imposes a duty on local authorities to make enquiries where an adult is at risk of abuse or in need of care. Contrast with the Social Services and Well-being (Wales) Act 2014 and the Adult Support and Protection (Scotland) Act 2007, which also impose such a duty on healthcare professionals.

78 The Act revoked the Health Protection (Coronavirus) Regulations 2020, SI 2020/129, made under the emergency procedure set out in the Public Health (Control of Disease) Act 1984, s 45R.

79 See also Public Health (Control of Disease) Act 1984, s 45E.

80 The Health and Social Care Act 2008 (Regulated Activities) (Amendment) (Coronavirus) Regulations 2021, No 1 and No 2 (SI 2021/891 and SI 2022/15) amended the Health and Social Care Act 2008 (Regulated Activities) Regulations 2014. Challenges to the policy were dismissed in *R (Peters & Anor) v Secretary of State for Health and Social Care and Anor* [2021] EWHC 3182 (Admin).

81 [1998] 3 All ER 299, HL.

82 *F v West Berkshire Health Authority* [1989] 2 All ER 545.

83 (2005) 40 EHRR 32.

under the common law was arbitrary and lacked sufficient safeguards. It was incompatible with Article 5. A change to the Mental Capacity Act 2005 was introduced in the Mental Health Act 2007, closing the 'Bournewood gap' and introducing (in 2009) Deprivation of Liberty Safeguards.[84] The Safeguards proved controversial. Not only were they costly and bureaucratic, but they were ineffective in protecting human rights.

In 2014, the Supreme Court in *P v Cheshire West and Chester Council*,[85] after an extensive analysis of the jurisprudence of the ECtHR, ruled that a deprivation of liberty occurs whenever a person who lacks capacity is subject to continuous control and lacks the option to leave. This is so even if the individual does not object and the restriction is 'normal' for their level of disability. Unsurprisingly the decision led to a huge rise in applications.[86] This pressure grew in 2019 when, in *Re D*, the Supreme Court held that parents could not give valid consent to the confinement of a 16- or 17-year-old child.[87] The Mental Capacity (Amendment) Act 2019 introduced a new scheme of 'Liberty Protection Safeguards' that, subject to implementation currently planned for late 2023, will apply from the age of 16.

3.10 Article 6

Article 6 provides that:

> In the determination of his civil rights or obligations or of any criminal charge against him, everyone is entitled to a fair and public hearing within a reasonable time by an independent and impartial tribunal established by law.

Article 6 incorporates a right to bring a civil case to court. As we shall see in Chapter 9, the scope of legal aid in clinical negligence cases was vastly reduced in the Legal Aid, Sentencing and Punishment of Offenders Act 2012 (LASPO). Does this have potential to breach Article 6? It is unlikely: Section 10 of LASPO operates as a 'human rights safety net' allowing funding in exceptional cases, though its limitations have led to sharp criticism.[88]

3.11 Article 8

Article 8 has had far-reaching effects. Article 8(1) provides: 'Everyone has the right to respect for his private and family life, his home and his correspondence.' Note the wording; the right is a right to *respect*. Does that connote an absolute claim to privacy? As with Article 2, the question arises of what kind of

84 Mental Capacity Act 2005, Sch A1 and 1A.
85 *P v Cheshire West and Chester Council and another; P and Q v Surrey County Council* [2014] UKSC 19.
86 See 7.12 below.
87 *Re D (A Child)* [2019] UKSC 42.
88 For example, Mostyn J describes the 'safety net' as a 'fig leaf' in *G and JG and JF and JFG* [2015] EWHC 564 (Fam), [14]; and see also [20].

obligations Article 8 creates. Does it impose positive obligations on the state to act to promote a right to privacy or simply a duty not to interfere with privacy?[89] It is clear that some sort of positive obligation is imposed by Article 8. Then we have to consider how to define parameters of private and family life. Prohibition of contraception, for example, obviously constitutes an interference with that right – interfering with intimate relationships. However, does regulation of third parties involved in assisted conception fall into the same category? In some cases, one person's right to private life may conflict with another's right to family life. Consider *ABC v St George's*,[90] where the High Court considered whether health professionals looking after a man who had tested positive for a genetic disease called Huntington's disease should have alerted his daughter, ABC, notwithstanding that the man would not consent to the disclosure. ABC was not successful in her claim for damages, but Yip J required that, in future, the interests of third parties in receiving information that they are at serious risk should be balanced with the patient's privacy rights.

Article 8 has contributed to a gradual shift away from medical paternalism and the upholding of patient choice. It was relevant to the development of the doctrine of informed consent in *Montgomery v Lanarkshire Health Board*[91] and instrumental in a notable victory for Debbie Purdy who sought clarification of the Director for Public Prosecutions' (DPP's) guidance on prosecution in cases of assisted suicide.[92] The DPP issued new guidelines in 2010.[93] Claims that the prohibition on assisted suicide breach Article 8 have not, so far, fared as well. In *R (Nicklinson) v Ministry of Justice*[94] the Court recognised that Article 8 was engaged, but were split on what action to take. Lady Hale and Lord Kerr found that the prohibition on assisted suicide was incompatible with Article 8, but the Court left the matter to Parliament to review.

We will see in Chapter 5 that the common law duty of confidentiality has changed in terminology, if not in substance, to the extent that, in 2004, Lord Nicholls recommended that the tort should be renamed, the 'misuse of private information'.[95] Could Article 8 be used to prevent certain information ever being sought from individuals? Article 8(2) graphically illustrates the qualified nature of certain Convention rights. It provides:

> There shall be no interference by a public authority with the exercise of this right except such as is in accordance with the law and is necessary in a democratic society in the interests of national security, public safety or the economic well-being

89 See *R v North West Lancashire Health Authority ex p A, D & G* [2000] 1 WLR 977, CA.

90 *ABC v St George's Healthcare NHS Trust and others* [2020] EWHC 455 (QB), following the Court of Appeal decision that the case should proceed to trial in [2017] EWCA Civ 336.

91 See *Montgomery v Lanarkshire* [2015] UKSC 11, [80] per Lord Kerr and Lord Reed. See 6.1 and 6.7 below.

92 *R (Purdy) v DPP* [2009] UKHL 45. See 22.7 below.

93 DPP, *Policy for Prosecutors in respect of Cases of Encouraging or Assisting Suicide* (2010).

94 [2014] UKSC 38, per Lord Neuberger [76], [99]–[110].

95 *Campbell v MGN* [2004] UKHL 22, [14].

> of the country, for the prevention of disorder or crime, for the protection of health or morals, or for the protection of the rights and freedoms of others.

Note the width of potential exceptions to Article 8(1). Breach of Article 8(1) must be necessary and proportionate. In a controversial 2021 ECtHR ruling, the Grand Chamber found that the Czech Republic's policy of compulsory routine vaccination of children against diseases such as tetanus, measles, mumps and rubella was necessary and proportionate.[96] Failure to comply can result in a modest fine and restrictions on preschool placements. The applicants claimed this policy breached their article 8 rights, but the Grand Chamber found the policy proportionate, compliant with children's best interests, and within the State's wide margin of appreciation. *Vavřička* did not concern COVID-19 vaccination, but both legally and politically, the case demonstrated the potential human rights compliance of a mandatory policy if herd immunity could not be achieved through voluntary measures.

Article 8 has protected reproductive rights, but the jurisprudence of the ECtHR illustrates both the complexity of Article 8 and judicial conservatism. In *Evans v United Kingdom*,[97] the Grand Chamber held that the UK had not exceeded its margin of appreciation under Article 8(1) in relation to the requirement under the Human Fertilisation and Embryology Act 1990 that Natalie Evans' partner's consent be required to implant their embryo in her uterus. Evans and her partner stored the embryos after her cancer treatment, but sadly their relationship ended and he refused consent to the implantation of the embryos.

A wide margin of appreciation also applies with respect to abortion, which in England, Wales and Scotland is governed by the Abortion Act 1967. In 2018, the Irish Health (Regulation of Termination of Pregnancy) Act followed an historic referendum to repeal the eighth amendment of the Irish constitution, which had enforced a near-total ban on abortion. Attention turned to Northern Ireland, where the Supreme Court held that prohibitions were incompatible with Article 8.[98] The Northern Ireland (Executive Formation etc) Act 2019 repealed sections 58 and 59 of the Offences Against the Person Act 1861, which makes abortion a criminal offence. A new framework was introduced by regulation in March 2020.[99]

3.12 Article 9

Article 9 protects religious freedom and conscience[100] providing:

> Everyone has the right to freedom of thought, conscience and religion; this right includes freedom to change his religion or belief and freedom, either alone or in

96 *Vavřička and Others v the Czech Republic*, App No 47621/13 (ECHR, 2021).
97 App No 6339/05 (ECHR, 2007) (Grand Chamber).
98 *Re an application by the NIHRC for Judicial Review (NI)* [2018] UKSC 27.
99 The Abortion (Northern Ireland) Regulations 2020, SI 2020/345.
100 For a full exploration of the role of conscience and the limits of conscientious refusal to participate in healthcare practices see 'Conscience and Proper Medical Treatment', a special edition of *Med Law Rev* (May 2015).

> community with others and in public or private, to manifest his religion or belief, in worship, teaching, practice and observance.
>
> Freedom to manifest one's religion or beliefs shall be subject only to such limitation as are prescribed by law and are necessary in a democratic society in the interests of public safety, for the protection of public order, health or morals, *or for the protection of the rights and freedoms of others.* [our emphasis]

This has a bearing on medical treatment decisions in a number of ways.[101] In *Re J*,[102] for example, the rights and freedoms of a non-practising Christian mother and the welfare of the child were balanced against a Muslim father's wish to manifest his religion by having his son circumcised. The Court of Appeal held that a failure to sanction the operation did not offend his rights under Article 9.

As we shall see, English courts have on a number of occasions overruled parental objections to treatment of their children contrary to their faith.[103] The classic example is where a court orders that a blood transfusion is given to a child of Jehovah's Witness parents. The parents might argue that requiring that their child undergo a transfusion violates the family's religious freedom and their right to respect for their family life (Article 8). Do the rights of the child, especially their right to life under Article 2, trump the parents' claims?

Article 9 is a qualified right. In *Chaplin*, the ECtHR upheld a UK judgment preventing a nurse from wearing a crucifix. The restriction was necessary to protect the health and safety of patients.[104] Article 9 protects doctors' rights to conscientious objection and freedom of thought and religion. As we shall see in 16.11 below, section 4 of the Abortion Act 1967 provides that no person is under a duty 'to participate in any treatment authorised by this Act to which he has a conscientious objection'.[105] In *Greater Glasgow and Clyde Health Board v Doogan*[106] two Roman Catholic midwives objected to having any involvement in the process of terminating pregnancy. Focusing

101 See J McHale, 'Health and Health Care Law, Faith(s) and Beliefs: New Perspectives and Dilemmas' 9(4) (2009) *Medical law International* 279 introducing a special edition of relevant papers.

102 *Re J (Child's Religious Upbringing and Circumcision)* [2000] 1 FLR 571 per Thorpe LJ, [12]. And see *Re S (Specific Issue Order: Religion: Circumcision)* [2004] EWHC 1282 (Fam). Female circumcision was prohibited in the UK under the Prohibition of Female Circumcision Act 1985 replaced by the Female Genital Mutilation Act 2003, as amended by the Serious Crime Act 2015, s 73 to allow the making of civil FGM Protection Orders.

103 See *Re S (A Minor) (Medical Treatment)* [1993] 1 FLR 376. See 17.10 below.

104 *Eweida, Chaplin, Ladele and McFarlane v United Kingdom* (2013) 57 EHRR 8.

105 See NHS England, *Standard General Medical Services Contract* (2017/18), para 9.7.2 '...where the Contractor has a conscientious objection to the termination of pregnancy, prompt referral to another provider of primary medical services, who does not have such conscientious objections'; and see discussion of *Greater Glasgow Health Board v Doogan and Anor* [2014] UKSC 68 at 16.11 below.

106 [2014] UKSC 68.

on the statutory construction of section 4 rather than the ambit of Article 9, the Supreme Court distinguished hands-on roles in terminations from administrative dealings. The latter are not covered by the right to conscientious objection.

3.13 Article 10

Nor must Article 10 be overlooked. Article 10 guarantees freedom of expression, a right embracing freedom of the press. All too often Articles 8 and 10 conflict and the courts must embark on a delicate balancing exercise.[107]

3.14 Article 12

Finally Article 12 might be thought to guarantee a right to reproduce as it states that:

> Men and women of marriageable age have the right to marry and found a family according to the national laws governing the exercise of that right.

Could Article 12 be used to challenge limitations on access to fertility treatment? In *Dickson v UK* the Grand Chamber of the ECtHR found that a refusal to allow access to artificial insemination facilities whilst in prison violated Article 8, but that no separate issue arose under Article 12, so it was not necessary to consider its application.[108]

3.15 Convention on Human Rights and Biomedicine

Patients' rights are not centre-stage in the ECHR. To raise a question about patients' rights, the relevant dispute must somehow be fitted into the pigeonhole of general rights. A further European convention, the European Convention on Human Rights and Biomedicine ('the Bioethics Convention'), directly addresses doctor–patient relationships. This Convention, agreed in 1997 by states party to the ECHR, has not been signed or ratified by the United Kingdom. We are not yet a party to that treaty.[109] Even if and when the United Kingdom does ratify this Convention, it will not have direct force. A patient will not be able to sue for violation of a right granted by the Bioethics Convention. Nor is there any right of individual petition to the ECtHR at Strasbourg. Nonetheless, articles of the ECHR may be interpreted with reference to the much fuller explanations and definitions of human rights offered in the Bioethics Convention.

107 Graphically illustrated *Campbell v Mirror Group Newspapers* [2004] UKHL 22.

108 *Dickson v United Kingdom* [2008] 46 EHRR 41. See M Eijkholt, 'The Right to Procreate is not Aborted' (2008) 16(2) *Med Law Rev* 284.

109 See J Montgomery, 'Bioethics after Brexit: An Opportunity to Rationalize Bioethics Governance in the United Kingdom' (2018) 18(2–3) *Medical Law International* 135, suggesting the UK becomes a signatory to the Convention 'to consolidate its connections with European values' and maintain influence in bioethics post-Brexit.

3.16 NHS Constitution

Section 1 of the Health Act 2009 made provision for the NHS Constitution.[110] Published in 2009,[111] and updated in 2012, 2013, 2015 and 2021, it applies to the NHS in England. The Constitution covers principles, values, pledges, patient rights and responsibilities, and staff rights and responsibilities. Patient rights focus on:

- quality of care and environment;
- respect, consent and confidentiality;
- informed choice;
- involvement in your healthcare and in the NHS;
- complaint and redress;
- access to health services; and
- nationally approved treatments, drugs and programmes.

These key areas will be explored throughout this book, but we will turn to the last two in the next sections.

3.17 Access to healthcare[112]

New medicines and devices are constantly becoming available but not all are accessible to patients. As we saw in Chapter 2, whilst some services are commissioned directly by NHS England, most of the commissioning of NHS services is currently undertaken by CCGs.[113] They are soon to be replaced by Integrated Care Systems that will plan, coordinate and commission health and care services in geographical partnerships.[114] There is a duty to commission the services necessary to meet the reasonable requirements of the population.[115] There is flexibility within the legislative framework as to how they go about this, but regard must be had to the need to promote the NHS Constitution[116] and to reduce inequalities between patients with respect to their ability to access health services.[117] Commissioning must operate within a prescribed budget:[118] Tough resource allocation decisions result.

110 See the NHS (Revision of NHS Constitution Guiding Principles) Regulations 2015, SI 2015/1462 modifying two of the guiding principles.

111 See also NHS, *The Handbook to the NHS Constitution* (2009), updated (2022).

112 See C Newdick, *Who Should We Treat? Rights, Rationing and Resources in the NHS* (2nd edn, 2005) Oxford University Press (hereafter Newdick). And note that special requests can be made for treatment of rare and complex conditions: see NHS England, *Individual Funding Requests for Specialised Services: A Guide for Patients* (2017).

113 National Health Service Act 2006, s 14C as amended by the Health and Social Care Act 2012.

114 ICSs are discussed at 2.3 above.

115 NHS Act 2006, s 3.

116 Ibid, s 14P.

117 Ibid, s 14T.

118 Ibid, s 223H.

Provided a decision is made fairly and rationally, the ECtHR is reluctant to interfere with the rationing decisions of member states. Article 3 might be invoked if the refusal of treatment constitutes 'inhuman or degrading treatment'[119] and Article 14 if the decision discriminates on the ground of disability or age. As we have seen, Article 2 will only assist if there is a failure to regulate so as to require provision of care. It has been held that Article 8 does not impose a positive obligation to provide treatment.[120] In *Condliff*,[121] a patient sought a gastric band operation to address his morbid obesity. The Trust's policy, however, was to perform the procedure only when the patient's body mass index was over 50. Mr Condliff therefore had to make an Individual Funding Request (IFR), which was denied. The Trust's decision was based on purely clinical factors. Social factors, including the adverse effect on his private and family life, were not considered relevant. Mr Condliff alleged that this policy breached his Article 8 rights. The Court of Appeal disagreed. Article 8 was not engaged and, even if it were, there were 'legitimate equality reasons' for the policy.[122] Mr Condliff subsequently made a second successful IFR based on relevant clinical factors.

In *UCL NHS FT v MB*[123] a patient with a complex mental health disorder refused to leave hospital. The hospital argued she was medically fit, and that it was particularly pressing that they free up beds in light of the COVID-19 outbreak. MB had been offered three months of twenty-four-hour care, but she argued this should be extended to a year. In law she was considered a trespasser and the hospital was granted an injunction to exclude her from the ward. MB unsuccessfully raised Articles 3, 8 and 14. The court found the risk of suicide was low and that there had not been discrimination.

If the ECHR fails to endorse a direct unequivocal right to healthcare, can we construct such a right from other sources? How are rationing decisions made in the NHS?

3.18 NICE

The Health and Social Care Act 2012 established an independent executive non-departmental public body called the National Institute for Health and Care Excellence (NICE).[124] This replaced the National Institute for Health and Clinical Excellence established in 1999,[125] and expanded its remit to incorporate social care.[126]

119 Note that in *Price v UK* (2001) 34 EHRR 1285 the prison authorities breached Article 3 in their deficient care of a prisoner who was a thalidomide victim.

120 *R v North West Lancashire Health Authority ex p A, D and G* [2000] 1 WLR 977, CA.

121 *R (on the application of Condliff) v North Staffordshire PCT* [2011] EWCE 910 (Civ).

122 Ibid, per Toulson LJ, [52].

123 *UCL Hospitals NHS FT v MB* [2020] EWHC 882 (QB).

124 Section 232.

125 See the National Institute for Clinical Excellence (Establishment and Constitution) Order 1999, SI 1999/220 (amended SI 2005/497).

126 Health and Social Care Act 2012, Pt 8.

NICE provides guidance, standards and advice to help the NHS deliver the best possible care within the resources available.[127] The functions of NICE are now set out in legislation which requires NICE to have regard to:

(a) the broad balance between the benefits and costs of the provision of health services or of social care in England,
(b) the degree of need of persons for health services or social care in England, and
(c) the desirability of promoting innovation in the provision of health services or of social care in England.[128]

The Institute is best known for its 'technology appraisals': assessments of the clinical- and cost-effectiveness of (mainly) new technologies, such as medicines, procedures and diagnostics. These assessments oblige the NHS to fund the recommended treatments and medicines, provided doctors deem them clinically appropriate.[129] This is reinforced in the NHS Constitution as a patient right.[130]

NICE currently makes technology appraisals on the basis of the cost per quality adjusted life year (QALY). The analysis combines how much a treatment will extend life and the quality of life improvement it will bring. It is then possible to work out how much a drug or intervention would benefit patients with a particular condition, compared with existing or no treatment. One QALY is equal to a year of perfect health. A calculation is made based on the estimated QALYs a person will have following a particular procedure or treatment and the likely cost per QALY.[131] QALYs have equal value, regardless of the nature of the problem they are designed to treat. Imagine, for example, a new drug costs £60,000 more than an existing drug but will give patients a year more good health. It would cost £60,000 per QALY gained.

Where the cost per QALY gained is over £30,000, a strong case must be made for funding.[132] Where the cost per QALY is between £20,000 and £30,000, the Institute sets out a list of factors that must be taken into account,[133] including consideration of certain non-health factors.[134] This goes some way toward

127 See NICE, *Health Technology Evaluations: The Manual: Process and Methods* [PMG36] (2022) setting out the methods, processes and timescales that NICE follows when carrying out health technology evaluations to provide recommendations on the use of new and existing medicines, products and treatments in the NHS.

128 Health and Social Care Act 2012, s 233. See also The National Institute for Health and Care Excellence (Constitution and Functions) and the Health and Social Care Information Centre (Functions) Regulations 2013, SI 2013/259, pursuant to the Health and Social Care Act 2012, s 237(1).

129 NHS Commissioning Board and Clinical Commissioning Groups (Responsibilities and Standing Rules) Regulations 2012, SI 2012/2996, reg 34.

130 NHS Constitution (updated 2015), section 3a: 'You have the right to drugs and treatments that have been recommended by NICE for use in the NHS, if your doctor says they are clinically appropriate for you.'

131 NICE website: *Glossary*, www.nice.org.uk/Glossary?letter=Q.

132 NICE, *NICE Health Technology Evaluations: The Manual* (2022), para 6.3.8.

133 Ibid, para 6.3.7.

134 Ibid.

addressing the problems which flow from the subjectivity of the quality of life assessment and the prioritisation of population health over the worst off:[135] The focus on quality of life can render those with co-morbidities or disabilities at a considerable disadvantage. Critics argue that the technology appraisals focus too heavily on cost-[136] (rather than clinical-) effectiveness.[137] Since 2013, a special route called the 'highly specialised technology appraisal' is available for so-called 'orphan drugs', which are designed to treat rare diseases that only affect small numbers of people.

The media react sharply when NICE fails to approve a new medicine.[138] A person aggrieved by a technology appraisal can bring an appeal on grounds that:

(a) in making the assessment that preceded the recommendation, NICE:
  (i) failed to act fairly, or
  (ii) exceeded its powers; or
(b) the recommendation is unreasonable in the light of the evidence submitted to NICE.[139]

Appeals have been lodged against a significant proportion of technology appraisals.[140] NICE's decisions are also subject to judicial review if illegality, irrationality or procedural impropriety can be established. For example, in *Eisai Ltd v National Institute for Health and Clinical Excellence*[141] the manufacturer of an Alzheimer's drug complained that the drug should be extended to mild sufferers of the disease. It was held that NICE acted unfairly in failing to make a full version of their economic model available during the appraisal process.[142] Contrast the 2020 case of *Cotter*.[143] NICE decided that a drug, sapropterin dihydrochloride, should require a technology appraisal before being

135 For analysis of competing goals see T Ottersen, 'Lifetime QALY Prioritarianism in Priority Setting' (2013) 39(3) *Journal of Medical Ethics* (hereafter *J Med Ethics*) 175.

136 According to H Dakin *et al*, *The Influence of Cost-Effectiveness and other Factors on NICE Decisions* (HERC Research Paper 05/14, 2014), '[c]ost-effectiveness alone correctly predicted 82% of decisions; few other variables were significant …'.

137 Health Committee – Eighth Report, *National Institute for Health and Clinical Excellence* (2013), paras 19–24.

138 See, for example, H Bodkin, 'Cannabis-based Medicines Blocked for Routine Use in NHS' *Telegraph* (2019) 8 August.

139 The National Institute for Health and Care Excellence (Constitution and Functions) and the Health and Social Care Information Centre (Functions) Regulations 2013, SI 2013/259, reg 9(3), pursuant to Health and Social Care Act 2012, s 238.

140 See NICE, *Past Appeals and Decisions*, www.nice.org.uk/about/what-we-do/our-programmes/nice-guidance/nice-technology-appraisal-guidance/technology-appraisal-and-highly-specialised-technologies-appeals/past-appeals-and-decisions.

141 [2008] EWCA Civ 438. See C Brasted and H Dedman, 'A Model Consultation' (2009) 159 (7373) *New Law Journal* (hereafter *NLJ*) 850; K Syrett, 'NICE and Judicial Review: Enforcing "Accountability for Reasonableness" Through the Courts?' (2008) 16(1) *Med Law Rev* 127.

142 But see *R (in the application of Bristol-Myers Squibb Pharmaceuticals Ltd) v NICE* [2009] EWHC 2722 (Admin).

143 *R (Cotter) v NICE* [2020] EWHC 435 (Admin).

utilised as a treatment for the rare inherited condition of Phenylketonuria (PKU), which inhibits the ability to metabolise protein. Cotter challenged the decision, arguing that a highly specialised technology appraisal would be more appropriate. It was thought that this might increase the chances of approval. The judicial review failed: NICE had correctly applied the criteria.

In addition to 'technology appraisals' and 'highly specialised technology appraisals', NICE also makes 'general recommendations'. Although general recommendations are not mandatory, there is a public law obligation to make rational decisions. In *Rose* it was held that a CCG which declined to offer treatment recommended by NICE should have justified their policy as a rational exception to the guidance.[144] The CCG could not refuse treatment simply because it disagreed with the evidence base set out by NICE. Elizabeth Rose was 25 and required treatment for Crohn's Disease, which might leave her infertile. NICE had issued guidance in 2004 recommending oocyte cryopreservation treatment, but the CCG declined to offer the procedure in light of evidence that the success rate was low. The High Court did not quash the refusal of treatment but did rule that the CCG's general policy of denying funding for oocyte cryopreservation was unlawful. General policies which conflict with NICE guidance require careful justification.

A recommendation can put additional stress on the strained resources of providers, as is clear from the following long-running legal battle. In a 2008 technology appraisal, NICE recommended a licensed product for the treatment of age-related macular degeneration, which causes gradual loss of vision. A group of CCGs prescribed an alternative drug, Avastin (by Roche), that was licensed for treatment of cancer but not for macular degeneration. The manufacturer of the licensed product argued that this policy undermined the right of patients to access NICE recommended treatments. In 2014 the Royal College of Ophthalmologists issued a statement that there was no clinical difference between Avastin and licensed drugs by Bayer and Novartis that were ten to twenty times more expensive. In 2018 guidance,[145] NICE concurred. Bayer and Novartis issued judicial review proceedings, but the High Court and then the Court of Appeal found that CCGs were free to choose Avastin 'off-label' for ophthalmic use on the basis of cost, provided there were no differences in efficacy or safety.[146]

3.19 Challenging NHS resource allocation decisions

So far, we have considered ways in which a patient denied treatment might claim a breach of their human rights or might challenge NICE guidance when it recommends that a treatment is not sufficiently clinically effective or cost-effective. Both avenues are limited. In this section we consider the

144 *R (Rose) v Thanet Clinical Commissioning Group* [2014] EWHC 1182 (Admin).

145 NICE, *Age-Related Macular Degeneration* NG82 (2018).

146 *Bayer and Novartis v NHS Darlington CCG and Anor* [2018] EWHC 2465 (Admin); [2020] EWCA Civ 449.

circumstances in which patients might challenge a particular decision not to fund their treatment.

In the domestic courts, early attempts to challenge decisions about access to healthcare met little success. In 1979, four patients who had spent long periods vainly awaiting hip-replacement surgery went to court alleging that the Minister had failed in his duty (then imposed by the National Health Service Act 1977) to promote a comprehensive health service and to provide hospital accommodation and facilities for orthopaedic surgery. The patients alleged: (1) that their period on the waiting list was longer than was medically advisable, and (2) that their wait resulted from a shortage of facilities, caused in part by a decision not to build a new hospital block on the grounds of cost. The patients asked for an order compelling the Minister to act, and for compensation for their pain and suffering. The Court of Appeal[147] held that (a) the financial constraints to which the Minister was subject had to be considered in assessing what amounts to reasonable requirements for hospital and medical services; and (b) the decision as to what was required was for the Minister, and the court could intervene only where a Minister acted utterly unreasonably so as to frustrate the policy of the Act. An individual patient could not claim damages from the Minister for pain and suffering. The patients lost the immediate legal battle. They gained valuable publicity. And the courts did not entirely abdicate control over the Minister. A public-spirited patient resigned to getting no damages themselves could (by way of an application for judicial review) still challenge a Minister whom they allege had totally subverted the health service (for example, a Minister using their position and powers exclusively to benefit private medicine at the expense of the NHS).[148]

The Court of Appeal rejected any legally enforceable right to healthcare actionable by a patient for his own benefit. Did any such right exist against local health providers? In 1987, the parents of two sick babies who needed cardiac surgery sought to enforce such a right on their sons' behalf. They applied to the Divisional Court for a court order that their sons be operated on. The health authority explained that lack of resources and lack of trained nurses meant that each baby kept missing out on his operation to other more urgent cases. The court refused to make an order that the operation be carried out immediately.[149] The parents had no right to demand immediate treatment for their sons. The health authority could do only what was reasonable within their limited resources, human and financial. It is difficult to see what else the court could have done in these cases. The court could not provide the

147 *R v Secretary of State for Social Services, ex p Hincks* (1980) 1 BMLR 93, CA. And see *R v N and E Devon Health Authority ex p Coughlan* [1999] Lloyd's Rep Med 306, CA.

148 Chances of success are not high, and the government of the day could always change the law, but they can be made to do it openly and not be permitted to pay lip service to a duty to a public health service which may have been abandoned.

149 *R v Central Birmingham Health Authority Ex p Walker* (1998) *Times*, 26 November; *R v Central Birmingham Health Authority ex p Collier* (1988) *Times*, 6 January, CA. See the highly critical analysis of Collier by Newdick, at pp 98–100.

resources needed to operate on all sick babies. In effect, the judges were being asked to decide that baby X needed surgery more urgently than baby Y, and judges are not qualified to make clinical judgements.

In *R v Cambridge District Health Authority ex p B*,[150] the Court of Appeal again demonstrated reluctance to become involved in questions of allocation of resources. B was a 10-year-old girl suffering from non-Hodgkin's lymphoma. In 1994, she received a bone marrow transplant from her sister. In 1995, she became ill again. The doctors treating her considered no further treatment should be given to prolong B's life. B's father obtained advice that there was a possible course of treatment. With further intensive chemotherapy, B stood a 10–20 per cent chance of remission sufficient to allow a second bone marrow transplant to succeed. The transplant itself stood a 10–20 per cent chance of success, offering B at best a 4 per cent chance of 'recovery'. The treatment package would cost about £75,000. The health authority refused to fund B's treatment. They argued (1) that such 'experimental' treatment was not in B's best interests and (2) that given the minimal prospects of successful treatment the cost could not be justified. Other demands on the limited budget took priority.

The trial judge, Laws J, was not convinced by the authority's case. He issued an order requiring the authority to reconsider the evidence in support of their decision not to treat B. They must do more than 'merely toll the bell of tight resources'.[151] The authority appealed. The Court of Appeal backed them unequivocally, rejecting Laws J's attempt to require greater transparency in decisions about allocating resources. The appeal court rested their decision largely on clinical grounds, on evidence from the doctors that the aggressive treatment proposed was not in B's interests, despite the contrary view of B's father and the child herself. Sir Thomas Bingham MR summed up judicial attitudes to problems in allocation of healthcare resources when he commented:

> Difficult and agonising judgements have to be made as to how a limited budget is best allocated to the maximum advantage of the maximum of patients. That is not a judgement which the court can make. In my judgement, it is not something that a health authority can be fairly criticised for not advancing before the court.[152]

So when will the courts intervene to question decisions about whom to treat, or what treatment patients may be entitled to? Successful challenges to decisions about provision of healthcare often depend on the patient identifying some obvious flaw in the decision-making process.[153] In *Fisher*,[154] a health authority refused to fund the costly drug beta interferon for any patient with multiple sclerosis. They operated a blanket ban on provision of the drug, failed to make any assessment of individual patients' needs and ignored a circular from the Department of Health advising that serious consideration be given to providing beta interferon to certain categories of patients with multiple

150 [1995] 2 All ER 129, CA.
151 (1995) 25 BMLR 16, at 17.
152 [1995] 2 All ER 129, at 137.
153 See Newdick, ch 5.
154 [1997] 8 Med LR 327.

sclerosis. The judge held that the authority failed to take a reasoned decision after consideration of all the relevant factors.

In *Booker*[155] it was held that an insurance payout following a road traffic accident, which enabled the claimant to purchase private care, did not absolve the NHS of its responsibility for providing a tetraplegic patient with nursing care. The decision was unlawful and irrational. The NHS Constitution provides that care is provided on the basis of clinical need. If the NHS wishes to recoup the costs of caring for a patient who is the victim of a tort, legislation is required. And in 2016, the National AIDS Trust successfully argued that NHS England should fund a preventive treatment used for those at high risk of contracting HIV.[156] NHS England failed in its argument that this 'public health function' was the responsibility of local authorities.

A notable 'victory' for patients denied access to treatment is found in *R v North West Lancashire Health Authority ex p A, D & G.*[157] The defendant health authority refused to pay for gender-reassignment surgery for the applicants. Such surgery was classified by the authority as a low priority along with cosmetic procedures such as face-lifts or hair transplants. Trans patients should be offered psychiatric and psychological services, but the authority would not 'commission drug treatment or surgery that is intended to give patients the physical characteristics of the opposite gender'. Statements in the policy document about exceptional cases based on overwhelming clinical need made it abundantly clear that in reality such a case would never be conceded. No one would be a sufficiently *exceptional* case to qualify. The Court of Appeal quashed the decision to refuse treatment to the applicant as 'irrational'. The authority had failed to evaluate the medical evidence relating to 'transsexuality', as it was then known. They dismissed forms of effective treatment without proper consideration:

> [T]he ostensible provision that [the authority] makes for exceptions in individual cases and its manner of considering them amount effectively to the operation of a 'blanket policy' against funding treatment because it does not believe in such treatment.[158]

Another patient victory, this time in relation to unlicensed drugs, occurred in *R (Rogers) v Swindon NHS Primary Care Trust.*[159] The Court of Appeal, overturning the High Court decision, held that Swindon Primary Care Trust's funding policy for the (as yet) unlicensed drug, Herceptin, was irrational and

155 *R (Booker) v NHS Oldham and Direct Line Insurance PLC* [2010] EWHC 2593 (Admin).

156 *R (National AIDS Trust) v NHS England* [2016] EWHC 2005 (Admin). See CF Hurley, 'Prevention is Better than Cure, but Who Foots the Bill? *R (National AIDS Trust) v NHS England*' (2019) 27(1) *Med Law Rev* 155.

157 [2000] 1 WLR 977, CA.

158 Ibid, per Auld LJ.

159 [2006] EWCA Civ 392. And see *Basma v Manchester University Hospitals NHS FT* [2021] EWCA Civ 278 (eligibility criteria for 10-year-old girl with Spinal Muscular Atrophy to access Nusinersen involved her being able to walk five steps. This was largely a factual rather than clinical judgement and so should take into account the family's evidence of her ability).

unlawful. Herceptin was licensed for late-stage HE-II, an aggressive form of breast cancer. Ann Marie Rogers (the applicant) was in the early stage of the disease. Some Trusts provided Herceptin in such cases, despite the fact that it was neither licensed nor approved by NICE. The Health Secretary, Patricia Hewitt, had previously announced that Herceptin, which costs £26,000 a course, should not be refused purely on grounds of cost. Trusts would still be able to refuse treatment where cost is a factor, but in this case, Swindon PCT had declared that cost was irrelevant to its decision. The court held that there was therefore no rational basis for refusing to treat Mrs Rogers. What then would provide a rational basis for refusal of unlicensed treatment? Resource availability, combined with clinical need and individual circumstances.

One option open to the court in cases where an irrational policy has led to treatment being refused is to remit the case back to the commissioning body. We give two examples. A 7-year-old child with PKU was denied an individual funding request for a drug called Kuvan. Due to severe autism and learning disabilities, this particular child would have difficulties sticking to the strict diet that would be needed, absent Kuvan, to prevent further impairment. The court found that the decision was irrational, and the matter was remitted to the panel to make a fresh determination.[160] A 50-year-old Welsh woman with stage 4 appendix cancer was denied an individual funding request to wash out her abdomen during surgery with heated anti-cancer medication. The High Court found that the funding panel had erred and remitted the decision back to them.[161] On this occasion, the panel subsequently approved the treatment, but a correctly applied procedure will not necessarily result in a patient being provided the treatment they seek.[162]

In other cases, the *application* of a lawful, rational policy is irrational. *R (Otley) v Barking and Dagenham NHS PCT*[163] concerns one such example. Victoria Otley had purchased cancer treatment privately. The drug proved effective, and she tolerated it well. She sought a further five cycles of the expensive drug, funded by her PCT. The policy was that the NHS body can refuse to fund treatment (taking into account financial restraints and the patient's circumstances) unless the circumstances are exceptional. The PCT decided that Victoria Otley's case should not be viewed as 'exceptional'. This policy was approved as fair and rational. However, it was applied irrationally. The court held that, because there were no other treatment options, her case was indeed exceptional.

A similar finding was made in *R (Ross) v West Sussex PCT*[164] where the refusal of a Trust to fund potentially life-saving cancer treatment was one which 'no reasonable Trust could have made'. What constitutes 'exceptional' circumstances must necessarily be considered on a case-by-case basis. The courts have

160 *R (SB) v NHS England* [2017] EWHC 2000 (Admin).
161 *R (Wallpott) v Welsh Health Specialised Services Committee* [2021] EWHC 3291 (Admin).
162 As in *R (Murphy) v Salford PCT* [2008] EWHC 1908 (Admin).
163 [2007] EWHC 1927 (Admin).
164 [2008] EWHC 2252 (Admin).

shown themselves prepared to scrutinise the process by which healthcare providers make decisions about what kinds of treatment they will provide and who will have access to such treatment.[165] However, if the healthcare provider can demonstrate that it has fully considered the case made to it, and addressed all the relevant considerations, but ultimately determined that other treatments and other claims must be given priority, courts remain unlikely to intervene.

NHS England is responsible for ensuring equality in access to and outcomes of healthcare, but decentralisation of budgets and commissioning freedom has potential to result in regional inconsistencies. Generic commissioning policies aim to ensure fair and consistent decision-making across the board, but there will inevitably be further recourse to the courts.

3.20 Timely treatment

Quality treatment is timely treatment. Section 3(a) of the NHS Constitution states that patients:

> ... have the right to access certain services commissioned by NHS bodies within maximum waiting times, or for the NHS to take all reasonable steps to offer a range of suitable alternative providers if this is not possible.

The NHS has obligations to provide treatment within a specified time frame (at the time of writing 92 per cent of non-urgent referrals should be seen in eighteen weeks and 85 per cent of urgent referrals for suspected cancer should be seen in two weeks). Waiting times data is collated by NHS England and this is used to monitor compliance with national standards.[166] The rules only apply to consultant-led treatment, so a patient needing a hearing test, for example, may have to wait longer. There are also exceptions where there are clinical reasons for delay (for example, obesity). The COVID-19 pandemic impacted considerably on waiting times. In July 2020, over 83,000 patients waited more than a year for treatment, notwithstanding efforts to restore services post first-wave lockdown.[167] The British Medical Association estimated that between April 2020 and October 2021 there were:

- 4.13 million fewer elective procedures; and
- 28.62 million fewer out-patient attendances.[168]

[165] But how should exceptionality be defined? See A Ford, 'The Concept of Exceptionality: A Legal Farce' (2012) 20(3) *Med Law Rev* 304.

[166] Set out in the NHS Commissioning Board and Clinical Commissioning Groups (Responsibilities and Standing Rules) Regulations 2012, SI 2012/2996, Part 9 (as amended). And see DHSC, *Referral to Treatment Consultant-led Waiting Times: Rules Suite* (2015).

[167] NHS England, *Consultant-led Referral to Treatment Waiting Times Data 2020–21*. England Level Timeseries (2020), www.england.nhs.uk/statistics/statistical-work-areas/rtt-waiting-times/rtt-data-2020–21/. See S Griffin, 'COVID-19: Waiting Times in England Reach Record Highs' (2020) 370 *BMJ* m3557.

[168] BMA, *Pressure Points in the NHS* (2021) 14 December, www.bma.org.uk/advice-and-support/nhs-delivery-and-workforce/pressures/pressure-points-in-the-nhs.

Where the eighteen-week target is not met, dissatisfied patients can access the NHS Complaints Procedure, discussed in Chapter 11. If the delay is severe (more than fifty-two weeks), NHS England might also impose contractual penalties. The onus is on the patient to contact the provider and ask for alternative arrangements to be made – some patients will choose to accept the delay, while others may attempt to avoid delay by requesting treatment in another country.

3.21 Treatment abroad

Prior to EU Exit, if you became ill on holiday in the EU, the European Health Insurance Card covered emergency treatment abroad. Now, most people making new applications will apply for a Global Health Insurance Card, which offers equivalent protection. But insurance is designed for emergencies rather than scheduled treatment. What if a patient requiring a knee replacement wants to go to Belgium or Germany rather than waiting in pain for months in the UK? Articles 56 and 57 of the Treaty on the Functioning of the European Union set out rights for European Union citizens to obtain medical treatment services in other member states. Regulation 3 of the Freedom of Establishment and Free Movement of Services (EU Exit) Regulations 2019 provides that, following EU Exit, rights under Articles 56 and 57 cease to be recognised in domestic law. Whilst this has impacted on cross-border treatment, the government has sought to retain certain arrangements for planned treatment in the EU. According to the 2021 version of the NHS Constitution:

> You have the right to authorisation for planned treatment in the EU under the UK EU Trade and Cooperation Agreement where you meet the relevant requirements.
>
> You also have the right to authorisation for planned treatment in the EU, Norway, Iceland, Lichtenstein or Switzerland if you are covered by the Withdrawal Agreement and you meet the relevant requirements.

The so-called 'S2' route that was set out in a European Regulation[169] is now expressed in the EU-UK Trade and Cooperation Agreement.[170] It covers direct arrangements between the UK and EU states for state-provided non-experimental care. The patient might not have to pay anything up front, but all healthcare must be authorised in advance. The conditions applied to residents of that country will apply to the patient, so if residents normally cover a proportion of the costs, then the patient will be held to the same terms. The patient can then apply for part or all of the contribution on return to the UK. Deficiencies in retained EU law post-EU Exit are addressed in regulations.[171]

[169] Regulation 883/2004 (EC) on the Coordination of Social Security Systems and Implementing Regulation 987/2009 (EC).

[170] Subject to certain differences: See T Hervey, 'Analysis 1 of the Brexit Deal: Healthcare Entitlements in the EU-UK Trade and Cooperation Agreement' *EU Law Analysis Blog* (2020), http://eulawanalysis.blogspot.com/. Deficiencies in retained EU law post-EU Exit are addressed in regulations.

[171] The Reciprocal and Cross-Border Healthcare (Amendment etc) (EU Exit) Regulations 2020, SI 2020/1348, amending a raft of 2019 regulations preparing for the possibility of a no deal Brexit.

Prior to EU Exit, a second route – the 'EU Directive on Cross-Border Healthcare'[172] – also extended to private care where the treatment was the same or equivalent to that which would be available under the NHS. The loss of this route restricts the options for those facing *undue* delay.[173] Pre-EU Exit, in *R (Watts) v Bedford PCT and the Department of Health*,[174] a 74-year-old woman was informed by Bedford Primary Care Trust (PCT) that she would have to wait a year for a bilateral hip replacement. She applied to have the operation in France, but the PCT refused, and reduced her wait to four months. Mrs Watts, who had to use a wheelchair and was in constant pain, went ahead with the operation in France, without the PCT's authorisation. The PCT refused to reimburse her because four months was the 'normal' waiting time for a hip replacement. Did the 'normal' four-month wait constitute 'undue delay'? The Court of Appeal referred the matter to the European Court of Justice (ECJ),[175] which held that when determining whether a proposed waiting time is acceptable, Member States must apply 'an objective medical assessment of the clinical needs of the person concerned in the light of all of the factors characterising his medical condition'.[176] If patients waited longer than doctors advised, regardless of NHS targets, the NHS must refund the costs where patients paid for treatment elsewhere in Europe.[177] Post-*Watts*, cross-border healthcare could be authorised at the discretion of the Secretary of State for Health, if treatment could not be given without 'undue delay', which was left undefined, and depended on the particular circumstances of the case.

Of course, another option available to the patient is to fund their own treatment abroad. As we shall see in Chapter 14, there is a thriving market in cross-border reproductive services such as IVF and surrogacy where people seek to take advantage of regimes which impose fewer restrictions or costs.

The step away from a 'European' right to healthcare coincides with vastly increased waiting lists flowing from the COVID-19 crisis.

172 Directive of the European Parliament and the Council on the Application of Patients' Rights in Cross-Border Healthcare (2011) 2011/24/EU. Regulations pre-empted the Directive and implemented the *Watts* judgment: The NHS (Reimbursement of the Cost of EEA Treatment) Regulations 2010, SI 2010/915 inserted a new s 6A and s 6B into the NHS Act 2006.

173 Case C-157/99, *BSM Geraets-Smits v Stichting Ziekenfonds VGZ and HTM* [2002] QB 409, [2001] ECR I-5473.

174 [2004] EWCA Civ 166, CA.

175 Case C-372/04, *R (Watts) v Bedford PCT and The Secretary of State for Health* [2006] QB 667. See JV McHale, 'Rights to Medical Treatment in EU Law' (Commentary) (2007) 15(1) *Med Law Rev* 99.

176 Ibid, [79].

177 Ibid, [113]–[114].

Chapter 4

MEDICINE, MORAL DILEMMAS AND THE LAW

4.1 Introduction

Medical ethics and bioethics make news, but are far from new. From the formulation of the Hippocratic Oath in Ancient Greece, doctors have debated among themselves the codes of conduct which should govern the art of healing. Today, philosophers, theologians, lawyers and journalists insist on joining the debate. Outside interest, or interference as doctors sometimes see it, is not new. Hippocrates was a philosopher. Major religions across the world pronounce on matters of medical ethics.[1]

The Hippocratic Oath makes interesting reading. Its first premise is that the doctor owes loyalty to his teachers and his brethren. Obligations to exercise skill for the benefit of patients' health come second. Abortion, direct euthanasia and abetting suicide are prohibited. Improper sexual relations with patients are banned. Confidentiality in all dealings with patients is imposed. In 2,500 years, these basic precepts of medical practice changed little. Dramatic changes in the kinds of moral and ethical problems confronting the doctor came only in the last fifty years or so. The art of the Greek philosopher physician became a science for many practitioners.

Science has given the doctor tools to work marvels undreamed of by earlier generations. *In vitro* fertilisation, pre-implantation genetic testing and gene therapy are no longer extraordinary. The technology to create artificial gametes is on the horizon.[2] Ectogestation may become a reality so that the fetus could be gestated in an artificial womb.[3] The list of technological 'miracles' is endless. They have placed in the hands of the doctors powers which humanity once ascribed to God alone. Technological advances can liberate but they

1 See, for example, DE Guinn, *Handbook of Bioethics and Religion* (2006) Oxford University Press.

2 A Klein, 'Early Mouse Fetuses Generated Without Sperm or Eggs for First Time' *New Scientist* (2019) 17 October.

3 See A Alghrani and M Brazier, 'What is It? Whose is It? Repositioning the Fetus in the Context of Research' (2011) 70 *CLJ* 51.

also have potential to control behaviour. Ectogestation might lead to greater choice, but if the female body is labelled as a source of danger, it could also enforce patriarchal ideals.[4]

Technological progress has been matched by social change. People are less willing to accept without question the decisions of those who exercise power, be they judges, politicians or doctors. Paternalism is out of fashion. Lawyers and philosophers, not to mention parents, wonder why the doctor is best qualified to judge whether a baby's quality of life is such as to make life-saving surgery desirable. The power of the doctor to end life, whether by switching off a ventilator, or by deciding not to give a patient a place on the active transplant list, disturbs us all. These moral dilemmas are just as acutely felt by doctors. Their difficulties are accentuated by the fact that the new technology cannot be made available to all those in need. There is just not enough money or resources in the National Health Service (NHS). Above all, the medical profession today faces a society more deeply divided on virtually every moral question than ever before. The public demands a say in medical decision-making on sensitive ethical issues. Yet from the hot potato of whether doctors should help couples to have a 'saviour sibling' to help their dying child, through the debates on abortion to treating children for gender dysphoria, the doctor who seeks guidance from public opinion will discover division, bitterness and confusion.

Questions of medical ethics arise throughout the whole field of medical practice. Most medical students receive education in ethics as an integral part of their studies.[5] Specialist bioethics training and academic courses offer further development. Several texts address medical ethics in detail.[6] Increasingly, those scholars who address the ethics of medicine speak of bioethics rather than *medical* ethics.[7] The change of terminology is not merely semantic. The most difficult dilemmas begin in the laboratory, not at the bedside. Consider xenotransplantation, whereby animals might be genetically engineered to produce organs compatible for transplant into humans with organ failure.[8] The essential question is whether science should continue to pursue the research

4 E Jackson, 'Degendering Reproduction?' (2008) 16(3) *Med Law Rev* 346; EC Romanis *et al*, 'Reviewing the Womb' (2020) 47(12) *J Med Ethics* 820.

5 GMC, *Outcomes for Graduates (Tomorrow's Doctors)* (2018) Outcomes 1: Professional values and behaviours, para 2.

6 Excellent texts on medical ethics include: TL Beauchamp and JF Childress, *Principles of Biomedical Ethics* (8th edn, 2019) Oxford University Press; BMA, *Medical Ethics Today: The BMA's Handbook of Ethics and Law* (3rd edn, 2012); JM Harris, *The Value of Life* (1985) Routledge. On the relationship of medical ethics and law see AM Phillips, AM De Campos and J Herring (eds), *Philosophical Foundations of Medical Law* (2019) Oxford University Press; J Miola, *Medical Ethics and Medical Law: A Symbiotic Relationship* (2007) Hart.

7 See R Chadwick and D Wilson, 'The Emergence and Development of Bioethics in the UK' (2018) 26(2) *Med Law Rev* 183.

8 S Fovargue, *Xenotransplantation and Risk Regulating a Developing Biotechnology* (2011) Cambridge University Press. In 2021 and 2022 there were significant advances in life-supporting genetically engineered pig-to-human kidney and heart transplantation: See 'Man Gets Genetically-Modified Pig Heart in World-First Transplant' *BBC News* (2022) 11 January.

that may transform such possibilities into reality. Scientists need education in ethics as much as doctors. Equally importantly, the term bioethics is seen as less doctor-centred than medical ethics. All health professionals confront ethical dilemmas. This book focuses on doctors. Much of what we say is relevant to other health professionals too, but each health profession faces its own particular variant of ethical debate.[9] The ethics of the doctor–patient relationship are touched on throughout this book. It is not and does not purport to be a book about medical ethics, or bioethics. Miola challenges the commonly held assumption that law and ethics form a cohesive unit.[10] They may clash or create a 'regulatory vacuum' where the law hands over the responsibility for decision-making to medical ethics, and professional guidance leaves matters to the conscience of the doctor. We focus primarily on the role of the law.

4.2 Ethics not etiquette

Were you to peruse the ethical guidance provided for doctors in the late nineteenth and early twentieth century, what you might find would have scant relationship to what most of us today think of as medical ethics. The doctor was envisaged as an English gentleman.[11] As long as they behaved in a gentlemanly and benevolent fashion, their own conscience and integrity would guide them towards ethical solutions in dilemmas surrounding how to treat a patient.[12] By 1963 formal guidance from professional bodies, notably the General Medical Council, offered somewhat more concrete advice.[13] Doctors were prohibited from sexual relationships with their patients or their patients' partners. They should not take advantage of their privileged access to patients' homes. They must avoid misuse of alcohol or drugs. They were not to tout for custom, nor must they disparage other doctors. Echoing the longstanding disdain for 'quacks', doctors were instructed to refrain from any collaboration with unqualified practitioners.[14] Advice centred on gentlemanly behaviour and without doubt some of the injunctions issued in earlier days had beneficial effects on patient care. However, what was styled ethics had at its core a code of etiquette. Doctors should conduct themselves in a particular way; they should show professional solidarity and practise benevolent paternalism.

9 See for example J Tingle and A Cribb (eds), *Nursing Law and Ethics* (4th edn, 2013) Wiley Blackwell; JF Sadler (ed), *The Oxford Handbook of Psychiatric Ethics* (2015) Oxford University Press; MD Dubber, F Pasquale and S Das (eds), *The Oxford Handbook of Ethics of AI* (2020) Oxford University Press.

10 J Miola, *Medical Ethics and Medical Law: A Symbiotic Relationship* (2007) Hart.

11 This model of 'ethics' was initiated by the Manchester physician, Thomas Percival, in his book on *Medical Ethics*, first published in 1808; see CD Leake (ed), *Percival's Medical Ethics* (1927) Williams & Wilkins.

12 See R Gillon, *Philosophical Medical Ethics* (1986) Wiley, ch 5.

13 See GMC archived ethical guidance from 1963 at www.gmc-uk.org/guidance/archive.asp.

14 See, for example, GMC 'Bluebook', *Professional Conduct: Fitness to Practise* (1985). And see 2.10 above on GMC's current advisory function.

The scale of grossly unethical abuse of medicine revealed in the wake of the Second World War destroyed any complacent culture of paternalist medicine. A series of codes of medical ethics were promulgated internationally. Moral philosophers began to subject medicine to a much more rigorous critical analysis. 'Critical' medical ethics emerged offering a framework within which ethical dilemmas could be the subject of debate and reflection. Beauchamp and Childress's seminal book *Principles of Biomedical Ethics*, now in its eighth edition, proved especially influential.[15]

Beauchamp and Childress formulated four basic principles, autonomy, beneficence, non-maleficence and justice, as a framework for ethical conduct. The four principles are a fashionable subject for attack.[16] They do not, and never sought to, provide easy answers to particular questions or offer a comprehensive ethical analysis. They do, as Gillon says, '… help us bring more order, consistency and understanding to our medico-moral judgements'[17]. The influence of the four principles, and their delicate relationship with legal principles, make it important that in any study of the law relating to healthcare a brief account is given of the four principles.[18]

4.3 Respect for autonomy – self-determination

Autonomy literally means self-rule, as opposed to heteronomy – rule by others. We should respect autonomous choices made by other people. Crude paternalism is the antithesis of respect for autonomy. Non-consensual treatment of a patient, even for their own good, violates their autonomy. Gradually, as we shall see in Chapters 6 and 7, English law, via principles governing consent to treatment, clothed the moral principle of autonomy in legal reality. The principle lies at the heart of the doctrine of informed consent. The landmark ruling of the Supreme Court in *Montgomery v Lanarkshire Health Board*,[19] made abundantly clear that patients are rights holders and the doctor's duty to disclose information 'takes its precise content from the needs, concerns and circumstances of the individual patient'.[20] *Montgomery* upholds the right of

15 TL Beauchamp and JF Childress, *Principles of Biomedical Ethics* (1st edn, 1979) (8th edn, 2019) Oxford University Press. See also HT Engelhard, *The Foundation of Bioethics* (2nd edn, 1996) Oxford University Press.

16 For example, K Clouser and B Gert, 'A Critique of Principlism' (1996) 15 *Journal of Medicine and Philosophy* 219. And see J Savulescu *et al*, 'Festschrift Edition of the Journal of Medical Ethics in Honour of Raanan Gillon' (2003) 29 *J Med Ethics* 265.

17 See Gillon, *Philosophical Medical Ethics*, p viii.

18 R Huxtable 'For and Against the Four Principles of Biomedical Ethics' (2013) 8(2–3) *Clinical Ethics* 39 notes that critics of the four principles have claimed them to be imperialist, inapplicable, inconsistent and inadequate. Huxtable argues that they nonetheless have a useful role, particularly for 'time-pressed clinicians' and students.

19 [2015] UKSC 11.

20 Ibid, [73] per Lords Kerr and Reed. See R Heywood and J Miola, 'The Changing Face of Pre-Operative Medical Disclosure: Placing the Patient at the Heart of the Matter' (2017) 133 *Law Quarterly Review* (hereafter *LQR*) 296.

patients to choose between or reject viable treatment options, but it also recognises the importance of shared decision-making.[21] Clinicians have a legitimate role in selecting reasonable treatment alternatives and can refuse to offer treatment that is not clinically indicated.[22]

Respect for autonomy does not demand unthinking deference to any choice made by another human being. To demand respect, a choice must be a maximally autonomous choice – an informed and free choice made by someone with the capacity to make such a choice. A very young child will 'choose' not to go to the dentist and 'choose' not to be injected with antibiotics. Their choice will be dictated by the nastiness of the procedure involved. They are not able to weigh the benefits of good dental care, or antibiotics to cure their streptococcal infection, against the immediate unpleasantness. An older person with severe mental disabilities may be similarly disabled from making any real choice. A paranoid schizophrenic may be constrained by their 'voices' to refuse treatment because they know that the doctor is Satan. The preferences expressed in such cases are not autonomous choices.

In setting boundaries of mental capacity, the law struggles with the concept of what constitutes an autonomous choice. The temptation to regard a choice you disagree with as non-autonomous is strong. The outcome of the choice should be irrelevant. A woman who rejects surgery for breast cancer where the prospects of complete recovery were good, but she could not tolerate any mutilation of her breast, makes a decision that we see as bizarre. The Jehovah's Witness rejecting blood transfusion does so on the basis of an interpretation of the Bible which not all of us share. Their choices remain autonomous choices, made by people able to reason, and on the basis of adequate information.

4.4 Beneficence – do good

An injunction to act beneficently requires doctors to frame their actions to benefit their patients. The needs of the patient should be the professional's preeminent concern. Patients should never be a means to an end. What does such a pious hope mean in practice? The ethics of clinical research have attracted much philosophical attention. The failure of doctors to act beneficently and the treatment of human participants as little more than research tools explains that emphasis on research ethics. Ethical professionals should put the individual's welfare first, even if to do so conflicts with their own interests, for example, their research objectives.

Another problem with beneficence might be that it could be seen as just another name for paternalism. The beneficent doctor does what they think is best for the patient. If natural childbirth is dangerous for the patient and the child she

21 Ibid, [82]–83] per Lords Kerr and Reed.

22 E Cave, 'Selecting Treatment Options and Choosing Between them: Delineating Patient and Professional Autonomy in Shared Decision-Making' (2020) 28 *Health Care Analysis* 4; E Cave and C Milo, 'Informing Patients: The Bolam Legacy' (2020) 20(2) *Medical Law International* 103.

carries, must the beneficent doctor perform a Caesarean section whether the patient likes it or not? The answer is no, because beneficence demands respect for autonomy. Professionals should offer their judgement on what is good for the patient, but doing good for the patient requires that ultimately, they accept *the patient's* decisions on what is good for them.

Translating the ethical imperative of beneficence into legal principle is tricky. The law imposes a duty of care owed by doctor to patients. That duty, however, generally involves not doing me any harm. English law does not impose any duty to be a Good Samaritan. Once a patient is admitted to hospital, staff must provide them with adequate and competent care. A doctor or nurse who witnesses a road accident but passes by on the other side commits no legal wrong. Yet if they fail to help when they could easily do so, they fail to act beneficently.[23]

Beneficence illustrates an important point about law and ethics. Ethics demands a higher standard of behaviour than the law requires. A competent surgeon who removes a patient's gallstones without mishap fulfils their legal duty of care. If they dismiss the patient's complaints of pain with scorn, make them feel like a child, and treat them as just another patient number, is the surgeon acting ethically?

4.5 Non-maleficence – do no harm

Raanan Gillon[24] says of non-maleficence: 'Among the shibboleths of traditional medical ethics is the injunction *Primum non nocere* – first (or above all) do no harm.' Gillon does not challenge the principle of non-maleficence as such. Its importance is self-evident, but what he rightly points out is that this principle cannot be absolute. Medicine often involves doing harm. Removing an inflamed appendix inevitably involves a degree of harm – risk, pain and scarring. The benefits obviously outweigh the harm in that case.

Practices which avoid all risk have ultimately done more harm than good. Sometimes acting beneficently at a population level will involve harm to some individuals, as in vaccination strategies involving a risk of adverse effects to a small number or when surges in demand in a pandemic crisis necessitate difficult resource decisions. Sometimes agonising dilemmas arise as was the case in relation to the conjoined twins, Jodie and Mary, separated by surgeons in Manchester in 2000.[25] Without surgery both girls would die. Separating Mary from her sister would and did result in her death. 'Do no harm' to Mary meant not doing good for Jodie.

[23] Though a doctor may face disciplinary proceedings as GMC guidance requires that in an emergency a doctor must provide to anyone at risk the assistance they could reasonably be asked to provide. GMC, *Good Medical Practice* (2013), para 26.

[24] See Gillon, *Philosophical Medical Ethics*, p 80.

[25] See *Re A (Children) (Conjoined Twins: Surgical Separation)* [2000] Lloyd's Rep Med 425. See 17.5 below.

4.6 Justice[26]

'[T]he idea that justice is a moral issue that doctors can properly ignore is clearly mistaken.'[27] Few would dissent from a proposition that doctors should treat patients justly. Justice in this context might be interpreted as meaning that patients are entitled to be treated fairly and equally by their doctors. King Charles should be treated no differently from a homeless person brought into Casualty after they are found unconscious in a doorway. Health professionals should not show preference for patients who enjoy a particular status or provide sub-standard care for patients of whom they disapprove.

Alas justice is much more complex. Within the NHS resources are limited. Not every treatment can be offered to every patient who may derive clinical benefit from such treatment. Imagine that King Charles and the homeless person both needed a liver transplant. The demand for donor livers far exceeds supply. How should a just decision be made about whether either of them should receive a transplant? King Charles turned 73 in November 2021. The homeless person is 35, but an alcoholic. His general health is extremely poor. Other contenders compete for livers, a number of them younger than King Charles and in better health than the homeless person.

We might agree that King Charles should not get a transplant just because he is King Charles.[28] We might agree that the homeless person should not be refused a transplant just because they are homeless. Is it relevant that if the homeless person continues to drink after surgery, the transplant is likely to fail? Even if they overcame their addiction their lifestyle may militate against success. Poor diet and no settled home will make it difficult for them to comply with the post-operative regime necessary to avoid rejection of the donor liver. There is a lively debate about how far lifestyle and/or 'fault' should affect access to NHS resources.[29]

The complexity of notions of distributive justice in healthcare, coupled with scarcity of resources, has resulted in health economists entering the debate. They have advanced the merits of an exercise based on 'quality adjusted life years' (QALYs) which measure health as years of life after treatment weighted by the patient's quality of life. QALYs embody an attempt to provide an objective framework to assess how society should determine priorities for treatment.

Both King Charles and the homeless person may do badly on a QALY test. Life post-transplant is unlikely to generate for anyone years of full health. Let us award King Charles four years of 0.50 health and the homeless person twenty

26 See generally, C Newdick, *Who Should We Treat? Law Patients and Resources in the NHS* (2nd edn, 2005) Oxford University Press.

27 See Gillon, *Philosophical Medical Ethics*, p 87.

28 He can of course simply opt for private care. Is it unjust that those who can pay can obtain whatever treatment they desire?

29 K Sharkey and L Gillam, 'Should Patients with Self-Inflicted Illness Receive Lower Priority in Access to Healthcare Resources? Mapping out the Debate' (2010) 36 *J Med Ethics* 661.

years at 0.25 health, the cost being the same for both 'patients'. King Charles scores 2; the homeless person scores 5; both will almost certainly lose out to younger, fitter patients. QALYs trigger another question. Should anyone get a liver transplant? Compare liver transplants with hip replacements. A woman of 50 having a hip replacement for arthritis may generate 15–20 QALYs at lower cost. Yet arthritis is not life-threatening. It is perhaps not surprising that the English courts have been reluctant to engage in questions of health resources.

As we saw at 3.18 above, the National Institute for Health and Care Excellence has had no such option. NICE relies on the QALY to bring a degree of objectivity into recommendations about health and care burdens and the potential of a new drug or intervention to improve outcomes and quality of life.

4.7 Autonomy and patients' responsibilities

Of Beauchamp and Childress's four principles, autonomy became *de facto* the dominant principle, especially in legal debate. So dominant did that one principle become that Daniel Callaghan declared: 'Nothing has exasperated me so much as the deference given in bioethics to the principle of autonomy.'[30] The emphasis on autonomy has meant, as Draper and Sorrell explain: 'Medical Ethics is one-sided. It dwells on the ethical obligations of doctors to the exclusion of those of patients.'[31] And in *R v Collins and Ashworth Health Authority ex p Brady*,[32] Kay J commented:

> [I]t would seem to me a matter of deep regret if the law has developed to a point in this area where the rights of the patient count for everything and other ethical values and institutional integrity count for nothing.

The notion of autonomy became distorted. Autonomy was wrongly understood as simply a right to what 'I want'. The doctor became little more than a technician delivering what the consumer-patient demands.[33] As Onora O'Neill[34] has eloquently pointed out, such an interpretation of autonomy is mistaken. Autonomy involves 'privacy, voluntariness, self-mastery, choosing freely, choosing one's moral position and accepting responsibility for one's choices'.[35]

30 D Callaghan, 'Can the Moral Commons Survive Autonomy?' (1996) *Hastings Centre Report* 41.

31 H Draper and T Sorrell, 'Patients' Responsibilities in Medical Ethics' (2002) 16 *Bioethics* 335.

32 [2000] Lloyd's Rep Med 355, at 367.

33 See M Brazier, 'Do No Harm: Patients Have Responsibilities Too?' (2006) 65 *CLJ* 397; and see G Laurie and JK Mason, 'Waxing and Waning: The Shifting Sands of Autonomy on the Medico-Legal Shore' in C Stanton *et al* (eds), *Pioneering Healthcare Law: Essays in Honour of Margaret Brazier* (2016) Routledge, ch 2.

34 See O O'Neill, *Autonomy and Trust in Bioethics* (2002) Cambridge University Press; O O'Neill, *A Question of Trust* (2002) Reith Lectures.

35 See R Faden and T Beauchamp (in collaboration with NMP King), *A History and Theory of Informed Consent* (1986) Cambridge University Press, p 7.

O'Neill adds to that list 'self-control' and 'self-determination'.[36] Expressing a non-reflective preference is not a manifestation of autonomy. Responsibility requires reflection on how our choices affect others. Making a case that patients owe ethical duties to others, including their doctors, is relatively easy. Clothing such ethical responsibilities with legal force is a harder task.[37] Reflecting, however, on patients' responsibilities forces us to consider the growing support for a view of communitarian ethics.[38] In judging the ethics of a particular course of action, the impact on the community, not just the individual, must be evaluated. The NHS Constitution balances patient rights with their responsibilities. The COVID-19 pandemic is paradigmatic of public health considerations trumping individual rights.

The dominance of autonomy in bioethics is tempered by an increasing shift from an individual to a relational model,[39] which recognises the 'social-embeddedness' of autonomy and the impact of a person's relationships and dependencies on the value of autonomy. For example, in 2020, the High Court recognised that a balancing exercise is needed between the interests of patients in having their information kept secret and the interests of third parties with whom there is a proximal relationship, who may have an interest in knowing the information to protect them from risk of harm.[40]

There has also been a recent resurgence of both soft[41] and hard[42] forms of paternalism. An example of the former is the government's adoption of Thaler and Sunstein's theory[43] to 'nudge' people toward beneficial health choices.[44]

36 See O O'Neill, *Autonomy and Trust in Bioethics*, p 22.

37 See Brazier, 'Do no Harm – Do Patients Have Responsibilities Too?'.

38 Note that GT Laurie, S Harmon and E Dove 'admit to their adherence to community ethics'. See GT Laurie, S Harmon and E Dove, *Mason and McCall Smith's Law and Medical Ethics* (11th edn, 2019) Oxford University Press, 1.20. And see D Callaghan, 'Principalism and Communitarianism' (2003) 29 *J Med Ethics* 287; A Etzioni, 'Authoritarian versus Responsive Communitarian Bioethics' (2011) 37 *J Med Ethics* 17.

39 See for example S McLean, *Autonomy, Consent and the Law* (2009) Taylor & Francis; J Herring, *Law and the Relational Self* (2019) Cambridge University Press.

40 *ABC v St George's Healthcare NHS Trust and others* [2020] EWHC 455 (QB), following the Court of Appeal decision that the case should proceed to trial in [2017] EWCA Civ 336.

41 N Levy, 'Forced to be Free? Increasing Patient Autonomy by Constraining it' (2014) 40 *J Med Ethics* 293.

42 S Conly, *Against Autonomy: Justifying Coercive Paternalism* (2012) Cambridge University Press; A Caplan, 'Why Autonomy Needs Help' (2014) 40 *J Med Ethics* 301.

43 RH Thaler and CR Sunstein, *Nudge: Improving Decisions About Health, Wealth and Happiness* (2009) Yale University Press.

44 I Johnston, 'How the Government's Successful "Behaviour Insights Team" has had a Profound Effect on Whitehall' *The Independent* (2014) 9 February.

4.8 Virtue ethics and the ethics of care

Virtue ethicists counter the dominance of autonomy in medical ethics by stressing the benefit of doing the right or virtuous thing in a given situation.[45] If your friend asks you for money with which he might travel to Switzerland to engage the services of the assisted-suicide clinic because he is suffering intolerably from a terminal condition, you may agree to help him because you respect his right to make his own choices, or alternatively, from a virtue ethics standpoint, you might help simply because benevolence, kindness and generosity requires it. Principalists revere autonomy, but it has less relevance to a virtue ethicist who might argue that decisions about death or abortion should be based on compassion.[46]

Feminists too find conventional theory lacking on the basis that it fails to take account of gender-specific disparities. Attention is directed to areas where women's interests have traditionally been neglected, such as birth control and pregnancy. But the resulting theories have significance far beyond reproductive issues. Harvard psychologist Carol Gilligan's 'Ethic of Care'[47] emphasises the importance to women of relationships. Instead of basing ethical theory on abstract principles, such as autonomy, the ethic of care addresses issues at a personal level. Health must be contextualised; physical and emotional needs must be taken into account.

4.9 To whom (or what) do we owe ethical obligations?[48]

Principles of medical ethics often conflict. Withdrawing treatment from a patient in a vegetative state may be seen to harm them. Yet continuing to keep them alive can equally be classified as harming them. Money spent on sustaining such a patient over several years deprives others of treatment in a cash-strapped NHS. Keeping X alive may be an injustice to Y. The trump card invoked to demand that the patient in a vegetative state be accorded priority centres around beliefs in sanctity of life. What we mean by sanctity of life, whether it is a trump card, is hotly debated.[49]

4.10 The sanctity of life: Judaeo-Christian tradition[50]

For the devout Roman Catholic sanctity of life is straightforward. Human life is a gift from God and is literally sacred. Any act which deliberately ends an

45 See generally, R Hursthouse, *On Virtue Ethics* (1999) Oxford University Press.
46 See, for example, L Van Zyl, *Death and Compassion: A Virtue-based Approach to Euthanasia* (2000) Ashgate; R Hursthouse, 'Virtue Ethics and Abortion' (1991) 20 *Philosophy and Public Affairs* 223.
47 C Gilligan, *In a Different Voice* (1982) Harvard University Press.
48 See Gillon, *Philosophical Medical Ethics*, chs 7 and 8.
49 M Brazier, *Law and Healing: A History of a Stormy Marriage* (Forthcoming) Manchester University Press, ch 6.
50 See J Finnis, *Natural Law and Natural Rights* (1980) Oxford University Press; O O'Donovan, *Begotten or Made* (1984) Oxford University Press.

innocent life is wrong. Life begins at conception and therefore abortion, and research on, or disposal of, an artificially created embryo, a test-tube embryo, is never permissible. Life ends when God ends it. No degree of suffering or disability justifies a premature release effected by us.

Yet even so there remain grey areas in the application of belief that life is sacred. Abortion is banned because the only intent of that operation is to kill the fetus. The Roman Catholic Church forbids abortion even when pregnancy threatens the woman's life. However, a pregnant woman with cancer of the womb may be allowed a hysterectomy albeit that the fetus will then die. This is called the doctrine of double effect. The operation for cancer incidentally destroys the fetus but that was not its primary purpose.

At the other end of life, the Church, while condemning euthanasia, does not demand that extraordinary means be taken to prolong life. Where is the line drawn? Should a severely disabled baby be subjected to painful surgery with a low success rate? Must antibiotics be administered to the terminal cancer patient stricken with pneumonia? The doctrine of double effect and the application of a distinction between ordinary and extraordinary means to preserve life have generated substantial literature and debate.[51] Nonetheless, the orthodox Roman Catholic remains fortunate in the security of their beliefs on the sanctity of life, beliefs shared by many fundamentalist Christians of the Protestant tradition.

Other practising Christians, who subscribe in essence to the doctrine of the sanctity of life, see further problems once they seek to apply their faith. Contraception is morally acceptable to the majority, and to many Roman Catholics now, although still officially prohibited by the Church. The exact point when life begins and becomes sacred becomes of the utmost importance to determine the morality of certain contraceptive methods. Abortion to save the pregnant woman's life is accepted by many Christians, as it always has been in the Jewish and Muslim faiths. Fetal life deserves protection but not at the expense of the pregnant woman's. This step taken, the extent to which the fetus's life may be sacrificed to the pregnant woman's has to be ascertained.

Is a threat to the pregnant woman's mental stability sufficient? What about the women who suffer rape? What is the status of the early embryo created in the test-tube? These and many other issues caused dissent within many Christian traditions. For example, a number of eminent Anglican theologians[52] argued that research on the early embryo is acceptable and raised no conflict within Christian doctrine. Other Anglicans remained adamantly opposed to any form of destructive research on embryos.[53] Nonetheless the adherent of any

[51] See, for example, the debate between J Finnis and J Harris in J Keown (ed), *Euthanasia Examined: Ethical, Clinical and Legal Perspectives* (1995) Cambridge University Press.

[52] See, for example, K Ward, 'An Irresolvable Debate' in A Dyson and J Harris (eds), *Experiments on Embryos* (1989) Routledge, ch 7.

[53] And note opposition to mitochondrial transfer procedures: BBC News, 'Churches Oppose Three-Person Baby Plan' (2015) 30 January.

religious faith enjoys a framework of belief. The sanctity of life has meaning for them because that life was given by God.

4.11 The sanctity of life in a secular society

Many still subscribe to some form of belief in a divinity or higher power. Churches are popular for weddings and funerals and thriving communities of Jews and Muslims remain committed to their traditions. Britain today is an overwhelmingly secular society where the majority of the population is uncommitted to any religious creed and those people practising any religious faith are a minority.[54] How many people retain a general belief in God as the Creator is open to question. For those who do not, what meaning has the sanctity of life? If life is not bestowed by God, on what grounds is it sacred?

Belief in the sanctity of life does survive the absence of religious belief. Taking life is as reprehensible to many agnostics and atheists as it is to the Christian or the Jew. Many non-believers have been more consistent in fighting for the sanctity of life than have certain warmongering Christian priests, or those 'Christians' who in the USA gather round the jails to celebrate the death penalty's return. What in a secular society is the basis of the sanctity of human life? To most people who are not philosophers the answer is simple. There is a deep and embedded instinct that taking human life is wrong. Life is a most precious possession.[55] All other possessions, all potential joys, depend upon its continued existence. An attack on one individual's right to life which goes unchecked threatens us all. Our autonomy is undermined. Our security becomes precarious.

The move away from a concept of life as God-given, however, has certain consequences. If at the basis of belief in the sanctity of life is a perception of the freedom of the individual, of the joy that life can bring, then the quality of life comes into account. Any right of the fetus to come into possession of their own life must be balanced against the pregnant woman's rights over her own life and body. When pain and disability cause an individual to cease to wish to live, then they should be free to end that life. It is theirs to do with as they wish. Individual choice becomes central to applying the concept of the sanctity of life. No one must interfere with an adult's choices on continued life. Whether any other adult can be compelled to assist a fellow to end their life raises more difficult questions. The concept of freedom of choice offers little guidance where an individual is incapable of choice. Nevertheless, this uncertain position commands a fair degree of generous support. People have an intrinsic right to life. Life is not 'inviolable'.

The secularised version of sanctity of life does not accept that only God can choose the moment of death.[56] Judges in the 1990s emphasised the importance

[54] On the secularisation of bioethics, see E Jackson, *Medical Law: Text, Cases and Materials* (5th edn, 2019) Oxford University Press, pp 12–27.

[55] See R Dworkin, *Life's Dominion: An Argument About Abortion and Euthanasia* (1993) Harper Collins.

[56] See E Jackson and J Keown, *Debating Euthanasia* (2012) Hart, p 37.

of sanctity of life in end-of-life decisions involving both adults[57] and children[58] and the term is still used by the judiciary today.[59] But the version of sanctity of life adopted by the courts supports a rebuttable presumption in favour of life. The courts have shown reluctant to engage in debate as to its meaning. In the case of *Newby*, Irwin LJ and May J in the divisional court found that, in the context of an assisted-dying claim, Parliament rather than the court is the appropriate forum for discussing sanctity of life:

> On issues such as the sanctity of life there is no consensus to be gleaned from evidence. The private views of judges on such moral and political questions are irrelevant, and spring from no identifiable legal principle.[60]

Given the conceptual ambiguity, one of us with Suzanne Ost has suggested that a more relevant term is 'reverence for life'. This would better encapsulate the value of human life and bridge gaps between different philosophical viewpoints.[61] Adoption of this term by the judiciary in favour of a focus on sanctity of life would aid the development of more coherent principles governing the circumstances in which the presumption in favour of life could be rebutted.[62]

4.12 The value of life: a different perspective[63]

A number of philosophers attack the very notion that 'taking human life is intrinsically wrong'. Life is seen as having no inherent value. Life has value only if it is worth living. Taking life is wrong because 'it is wrong to destroy a life which is worth living'.[64] Side by side with a move to concentrate attention on the quality of life alone comes a redefinition of human life deserving of protection. It is *persons*,[65] not all human animals, whose lives have value. Unless there is capacity for self-awareness, for the individual to recognise themselves as a functioning human person able to relate to other persons, they have no life

57 *Airedale NHS Trust v Bland* [1993] AC 789, at 808 per Sir Thomas Bingham MR.

58 *Re J (a minor) (Wardship: Medical Treatment)* [1991] Fam 33, at 43.

59 See for example *Aintree University Hospitals Foundation Trust v James* [2013] UKSC 67, [35] per Lady Hale; *Birmingham Women's and Children' NHS FT v JB and KAB* [2020] EWHC 2595 (Fam), [39] per Hayden J and *GOSH NHS FT v MX, FX and X (a child)* [2020] EWHC 1958 (Fam), [28] per Russell DBE J.

60 *R (Newby) v The Secretary of State for Justice* [2019] EWHC 3118 (Admin), [42].

61 M Brazier and S Ost, *Bioethics, Medicine and the Criminal Law Volume 3: Medicine and Bioethics in the Theatre of the Criminal Process* (2013) Cambridge University Press, p 89. And see discussion A Mullock and R Heywood, 'The Value of Human Life in Healthcare Law' in C Stanton *et al* (eds), *Pioneering Healthcare Law: Essays in Honour of Margaret Brazier* (2016) Routledge, ch 4.

62 R Heywood and A Mullock, 'The Value of Life in English Law: Revered but Not Sacred?' (2018) 36(4) *Legal Studies* 658.

63 See, in particular, two persuasive and lively works: J Glover, *Causing Death and Saving Lives* (1977) Penguin; JM Harris, *The Value of Life* (1985) Routledge & Kegan Paul. And see H Kuhse (ed), *Unsanctifying Human Life: Essays on Ethics* (2001) Wiley.

64 Glover, *Causing Death and Saving Lives*, ch 3.

65 Harris, *The Value of Life*, ch 1.

of the quality and kind which must be preserved. Certain consequences follow. A person who can reason must be allowed to judge for themselves whether continued life is worth it. A human who cannot reason for themself, who is not a person, may have that judgement made for them by others. Providing painless release for a person who considers their life not worth living, or an individual whose capacity for self-awareness has gone, so that they have ceased to be a person, becomes a moral action. The unborn are not persons. They have no rights against their mothers who are persons. Abortion is moral and it may even be considered immoral not to abort a seriously damaged fetus. Research on embryos to benefit existing persons, whether by improving treatment for infertility or seeking a cure for congenital disease, is not only morally permissible, but almost a moral imperative. Euthanasia of the hopelessly brain-damaged with no hope of recovery is acceptable and may, in strictly controlled circumstances, be non-voluntary.

4.13 Reverence for life and the medical profession

No doubt the disparity of views among the general population is reflected in the personal views of many doctors. Doctors, however, have to take decisions on matters that others merely debate. How far and in what fashion is reverence for life a central medical ethic? The Declaration of Geneva[66] included the following undertaking: 'I will maintain the utmost respect for human life from time of conception; even under threat, I will not use my medical knowledge contrary to the laws of humanity.'

When the Declaration was first formulated in 1947, 'the utmost respect for human life' no doubt imported to most doctors a prohibition on abortion, at any rate where the pregnant woman's life was not in danger, and a complete ban on any form of euthanasia. The Declaration was amended and updated in Sydney in 1968. By 1968, abortion on grounds other than immediate danger to the woman had been legalised in Britain and parts of the USA. Within a decade debate was to flourish within respected medical circles as to whether keeping alive all disabled babies was right, and whether prolonging the life of the sick and elderly had not been taken to extremes by modern medicine. The Declaration was amended again in 1984, 1994, 2005, 2006 and 2017. The most recent version contains an undertaking which simply reads: 'I will maintain the utmost respect for human life' as well as a new undertaking to 'respect the autonomy and dignity of my patient'.

What then does the obligation to respect human life entail? What it does not entail, and what has never existed in any code of medical ethics, is an injunction to preserve life at any price. The prevention of suffering is as much the doctor's task as the prolongation of life; the two cannot always be complementary. The doctor struggling to interpret and apply their obligation to respect life faces a number of quandaries.

[66] Adopted by the 2nd General Assembly of the World Medical Association, Geneva, Switzerland, September 1948.

4.14 The beginning and end of life

An admonition to respect human life would be easier to adhere to if there was agreement as to when life begins and ends. Few biologists see the fertilisation of the woman's egg as the beginning of a new life. They argue that egg and sperm are living organisms and point out that many fertilised eggs fail to implant. The fertilised egg may split into two, and in rare cases grow not into a baby but a hydatidiform mole. Fertilisation is just one step in a continuing process. At what stage then does life begin and attract respect?[67] We have noted the argument that the fetus has no status because it is not a person. A growing view appears to be that the fetus as potential life attracts increased status as it grows to full human likeness. This gradualist perception of the embryo resulted in the support for embryo research from most doctors' organisations in 1990 helping to ensure that Members of Parliament eventually voted to permit research for a period of up to fourteen days in the Human Fertilisation and Embryology Act 1990.[68]

The end of life too has no definite marker anymore. It can no longer be equated with the cessation of breathing and heartbeat.[69] A definition of death as the irreversible cessation of all activity in the brain stem[70] is generally accepted within the medical profession, although some doctors still occasionally express public doubts. For the lay public the decision to agree to switch off the life-support machine of a relative causes individual anguish, and anxiety occasionally surfaces that a desire for organs for transplantation might prompt too swift a pronouncement of death.[71]

If a patient is in a vegetative state having lost all cortical function, should we regard them as dead? Was Tony Bland alive in any real sense?[72] Is such a move euthanasia by the back door? The question of continuing to keep alive the unkindly named 'human vegetable' will not go away. It must be faced, not by a surreptitious moving back of the moment of death but by addressing ourselves to the question of whether the doctor may ever kill.[73]

4.15 Killing and letting die

Caring for a patient as they die in peace may be the last service their doctor can perform for them. Doctors and nurses tending the terminally ill in

67 S Pattinson, *Medical Law and Ethics* (6th edn, 2020) Sweet & Maxwell, 1–024 describes three positions on the moral status of the fetus: full, no or limited. The limited status view is that the fetus's fixed or gradualist moral status is less than the woman's, but not none.

68 Note that, at the time of writing, there are proposals to revisit the 1990 Act and the '14-day rule' in particular. See 15.1 below.

69 See Chapter 19 below.

70 *Re A* [1992] 3 Med LR 3033.

71 See Chapter 19.

72 See *Airedale NHS Trust v Bland* [1993] AC 789 HL. See 22.1 and 22.15.

73 See Chapter 22.

hospices are accorded the highest respect. The doctor's obligation to relieve suffering may on occasion cause them to refrain from prolonging life. Asked whether a doctor should invariably invoke every weapon of medical progress to prevent death, people of every shade of opinion would answer, no. For the Roman Catholic, the test would be whether 'extraordinary means' must be resorted to in order to prolong that life. Extensive surgery on a dying cancer patient offering them only weeks more life would be ruled out. Antibiotics to cure a sudden, unrelated infection pose a more difficult moral dilemma. For Muslims, Allah is the Creator of life and the One who will end life through natural death. There is a duty incumbent on individuals to strive for life, but this does not extend to an obligation to seek or continue futile treatment.[74] For most of us, religious or irreligious, this satirical rhyme sums up our attitude;

> Thou shalt not kill; but needst not strive
> Officiously to keep alive.

Scratch the surface of this popular attitude and problems emerge. What amounts to 'officiously' keeping alive? Is the doctor alone to judge when a life is worth living? Lawyers and philosophers often enjoy the argument such issues generate, doctors on the whole do not. They have to provide answers. Where a patient is sane, conscious and an adult, the dilemma has today a relatively easy answer, albeit no less painful. The patient decides whether treatment continues. The doctor, if they have been frank with the patient, has little choice but to leave it to the patient. They cannot lawfully give treatment without the patient's consent.[75] Suicide, if refusing treatment can be so classified, is no longer a crime. A more acute dilemma arises where the patient cannot make their own decision. Here the distinction between killing and letting die takes a central role.[76]

Not surprisingly, the distinction between killing and letting die has not been allowed to go unchallenged. It is subject to a three-pronged attack: (1) Technology makes the distinction between letting die and killing difficult if not impossible to put into practice. (2) It is argued that there is no valid moral distinction between killing and letting die. (3) Some writers have maintained that directly and painlessly killing a patient is a morally superior decision to leaving them to a slow undignified death.[77]

The problems posed for the doctor by the technology at their disposal cannot be side-stepped. An accident victim rushed into hospital is put on a life-support machine. All that can be done is done for them. They prove to be irreversibly brain-damaged but not brain-dead. Failing to put them on a machine would

[74] NI Abu-El-Noor and MK Abu-El-Noor, 'End of Life Decisions: An Islamic Perspective' (2014) 10(1) *Online Journal of Health Ethics*, DOI: 10.18785/ojhe.1001.04.

[75] See *B v NHS Hospital Trust* [2002] 2 All ER 449.

[76] In *Aintree v James* [2013] UKSC 67, [22] per Lady Hale, the Supreme Court held that treatment that is not in the incapacitated patient's best interests, because, for example, it is futile or overly burdensome, is unlawful.

[77] And see Lord Browne-Wilkinson in *Airedale NHS Trust v Bland* [1993] AC 789, at 885.

have meant allowing them to die. Is disconnecting the machine killing them[78] (though comatose patients disconnected from life-support machines have lived on for several years in some cases)?[79] Into which category, killing or letting die, does not feeding the patient fall? A newborn baby with severe disabilities may never demand food, may be unable to feed naturally from breast or bottle. Is omitting to tube-feed that baby killing or letting die? Into which category does failure to perform delicate and painful surgery to relieve hydrocephalus (water on the brain) fall? The difficulties of applying the distinction in practice can be enumerated endlessly.

So, why not abandon the distinction altogether? Several apparently persuasive arguments can be made in favour of such a change of direction.[80] The concept of the value of human life as dependent on self-awareness and the quality of life renders it moral to end a life once self-awareness has gone, or, as in the case of a newborn baby, where it has never developed. A patient still able to reason but living in pain, distress and disability retains the right to make their own judgement on their quality of life. If they are unable to reason the decision may be taken from them. Once quality of life, not life itself, is the determining factor, it follows that directly killing the patient may be a moral imperative. For if the patient's quality of life is such that life has no instrumental value, is it not kinder to end that life painlessly than let them drag on for more days, weeks or months in undignified 'sub-human' misery? If one accepts the basic premise that the value of human life is solely dependent on life being objectively 'worth living', then logically progress to acceptance that a doctor may sometimes kill their patient must follow.

Pure logic does not, however, govern most human reactions. *Involuntary*[81] euthanasia, ending a patient's life without any direction from them or a proxy acting on their behalf and without reference to their interests, is universally excoriated. *Non-voluntary* euthanasia, ending a life on the invitation of a proxy speaking for the patient and on the basis of a considered judgement of their best interests receives some support,[82] often invoking the justification of beneficence. *Voluntary* euthanasia, assisting a competent patient who desires to die, has a growing number of committed advocates. Nonetheless, any form of active euthanasia causes some disquiet and fears of a slippery slope that modest legalisation of voluntary euthanasia in limited circumstances may metamorphose into a ready acceptance of less than voluntary euthanasia.[83] The arguments against are dismissed with some scorn by the philosophers

78 *B v NHS Hospital Trust* [2002] 2 All ER 449.

79 See I Kennedy, 'The Karen Quinlan Case: Problems and Proposals' (1976) 2 *J Med Ethics* 3.

80 J Coggon, 'On Acts, Omissions and Responsibility' (2008) 34 *J Med Ethics* 576.

81 On the problems of terminology, see 22.1 below; and see *Mason and McCall Smith's Law and Medical Ethics*, 18.01–18.05.

82 See L Doyal, 'Dignity in Dying Should Include the Legalisation of Non-Voluntary Euthanasia' (2006) 2 *Clinical Ethics* 65.

83 See J Keown, *Euthanasia, Ethics and Public Policy: An Argument Against Legalisation* (2nd edn, 2018) Cambridge University Press, ch 1.

proposing a change of attitude. Suggestions that doctors are 'playing God' cut little ice unless you believe in God. Fear that powers to kill may be misused could be alleviated by proper controls. Instinctive revulsion is seen as an uninformed response.

The distinction between killing and letting die is unlikely to go away. First, the conception of life as in some sense 'revered' has a greater hold on the population as a whole than its detractors concede. Fewer people in the UK may now subscribe to belief in the God of the Bible, the Talmud or the Koran. Belief that humanity must set limits on what humanity may do is deeply ingrained. Second, the vision of the slippery slope to euthanasia (real or illusory)[84] for the unfortunate and the dissenter operates to deter acceptance of non-voluntary euthanasia. Today the hopelessly brain-damaged, tomorrow the mentally disabled, the day after opponents of the government, is the fear of many. Finally, and practically most importantly, even if the exercise of judging objectively quality of life is carried out in all good faith, how can it be achieved? Who will sit in judgement?

4.16 Reverence for life and the law

Legislating on moral and ethical issues created fewer problems for the Victorian parliamentarian.[85] Applying the common law posed no dilemma for the judge. He knew what was right and what was wrong. The Victorian was unperturbed by doubt, unconcerned by any feeling that his decision should mirror the moral attitudes of society as a whole. Divisions in moral attitudes, although they did exist, were not as deep as those pertaining today. Nor were the problems of medicine as complex. Death remained then an independent agent largely beyond the doctor's skill to combat.

Despite the plethora of ethical problems created daily by modern medicine and the changed moral climate, the law changes slowly. No statute expressly addresses the fate of the newborn infant with multiple disabilities who in an earlier age would have died whatever had been done for her.[86] So far, every attempt to legislate on euthanasia has stalled in its progress through Parliament.[87] The first test-tube baby, Louise Brown, was born in July 1978. Twelve years later Parliament finally enacted the Human Fertilisation and Embryology Act 1990 regulating IVF. Before that Act, the Abortion Act 1967 represented a legislative attempt specifically designed to tackle developments in medicine and altered moral outlooks. But the Abortion Act was piloted through Parliament not by the government of the day, but by David Steel MP by means of a Private Member's Bill. The troubled history of that Act,

84 See S Smith, 'Evidence for the Practical Slippery Slope in the Debate on Physician-Assisted Suicide and Euthanasia' (2005) 13 *Med Law Rev* 17.

85 See Chapter 1 above and Brazier, *Law and Healing*, ch 6.

86 See Nuffield Council on Bioethics, *Critical Care Decisions in Fetal and Neonatal Medicine* (2006).

87 At the time of writing, Baroness Meacher's Assisted Dying Bill 2021–22 is the first such Bill in seven years to reach the Committee Stage in the House of Lords.

a compromise which pleases few, perhaps explains why governments of all political colours shy away from entering the battlefields on the intrinsic and extrinsic value of human life. Attempts to amend the Human Fertilisation and Embryology Act 1990 relating to the time limit for abortion[88] unleashed an outburst of vitriolic abuse unknown in even the most hard-fought party political battle.

Political disinclination to engage in debate on the value of life means that to a large extent the regulation of the medical profession on issues of life and death has been left to the judges. In drawing up and applying codes of practice on the treatment of the critically ill newborn, the brain-damaged and the dying, the medical profession acts within the constraints of the criminal law of murder and manslaughter. The doctor's exposure to the law can be brutal. The law holds its hand from laying down the code of practice within which they work. Struggling to decide on whether treatment should continue, they act within guidelines agreed within their own profession but lacking statutory force. Ninety-nine times out of a hundred they can comfort themselves with the thought that no one will question their decision in these grey areas between living and dying. On the hundredth occasion they may face the spectre of prosecution for murder or attempted murder. The distinction between killing and letting die does not operate in the criminal law to debar a charge of murder. Allowing a patient to die, when it was the doctor's duty to treat them and the doctor knew that and intended that death would ensue, is as much murder as stabbing the patient to death.

The crucial issue once more is what is the content of the doctor's duty? When is it their obligation to prolong life? Left to decide that issue according to conscience and professional opinion most of the time, doctors not unnaturally are resentful that intervention when it comes may take the form of criminal prosecution for murder. Doctors do not see themselves as murderers. Even the most vehement and passionate member of '*pro-lifer*', believing that medical decisions as to the care of the newborn are frequently wrong, and err too often on the side of withholding treatment, would not place the doctor on the same moral plane as the person murdering in the course of robbery.

The reaction of the medical profession has often been that the law should keep out of medical ethics. Proposals to replace the existing and hazy common law with detailed legislative rules attract little enthusiasm.[89] Procedural rules about consultation, reference to codes of practice and the keeping of records of decision-making appear more acceptable. What doctors might welcome is such legislation that additionally promises immunity from prosecution to the doctor following the correct process. Such legislation would check the maverick. It would ensure that no one doctor whose standards deviate markedly from their fellows could pursue a course of treatment or non-treatment of

[88] But ultimately resulted in a 'liberalisation' of the law on late abortions: see s 37 of the 1990 Act (and see 16.4 below).

[89] J Havard, 'Legislation is Likely to Create More Difficulty than it Resolves' (1983) 9 *J Med Ethics* 18.

patients unacceptable to the majority. However, it would enshrine in the law a principle that such decisions are for the doctors alone. The rest of us would be excluded from any right to a say on these matters of life and death.

The ultimate decisions about life and death are not simply medical decisions.

This was the view expressed in an editorial in the *British Medical Journal* over twenty-five years ago.[90] We concur. The value of life is not a matter to be left for the doctors to decide and for the philosophers to argue over. The law's involvement to ensure that society's expectations are met is inevitable. The law is far from perfect in its operation. Reform in a society divided in its moral judgements is hard to formulate. Detailed legislation is probably undesirable even if such legislation could be agreed on. The variation in the circumstances confronting the doctor is too great. Rules cannot be invented that would meet every possible dilemma the doctor may face. The doctor's judgement cannot and should not be excluded. What can be done, if there is a will to do so, is to stimulate greater debate on the codes of practice under which the doctor works. Greater legal and lay involvement in their development should be encouraged. The gap between lawyer and doctor needs to be bridged. Doctors complain that lay people do not understand the full implications of the problems presented by the disabled and the dying and do not appreciate the complexity of modern medical technology. Greater openness and a greater willingness to involve those outside the medical profession in decision-making to bring about better understanding and better understanding of the problems of medicine will bring about better law-making.

However much any government might prefer to remain aloof from debates on medicine and morals, the developments in the uses of human tissue, genomics, embryology and assisted conception have forced the British, other European and Commonwealth governments to legislate:

(1) Legislation may be designed to protect patients from possible abuses, to prevent what is perceived as an undesirable practice creating risks of injury or exploitation.
(2) Legislation may be needed or need to be amended because gaps in the existing law place people in a legal limbo. As we shall see in Chapter 14, the provisions of the Human Fertilisation and Embryology Act 2008 relating to legal parenthood create chaos in the context of surrogacy. Questions of family law and status may be complex and sometimes controversial. Clear statutory answers are essential to safeguard the interests of the child.
(3) Developments in genetics and biotechnology may create, or exacerbate, several legal problems. Who owns genetic information, and how should access to that information be controlled? What property rights accrue from body products? If cells from a patient's body are used to develop a remedy to some disease, can they claim the ensuing profit made by a drug company? If a healthy gene taken from a patient's embryo is

90 [1981] *BMJ* 569.

used and inserted to replace a defective gene from the patient's sister's embryo, to whom does the gene belong? Can human genes be patented? All these questions require a legal answer and, if legislation does not provide the answer, expensive litigation will proliferate.

(4) Inadequate unclear laws generate distrust and anger. The fuzzy, toothless provisions of the now repealed Human Tissue Act 1961 contributed immensely to the outrage and agony occasioned by revelations of organ retention practices.[91]

(5) Finally, the most difficult of all aspects of legislation in this area is to decide what kinds of procedures are acceptable in our society. Are there medical advances whose implications are such that, though possible, they should be prohibited by law? The United Kingdom sanctions strictly controlled stem cell therapies, ie therapeutic cloning. Some European countries outlaw cloning altogether.

Legislating on what is permissible is fraught with difficulty. Emotions run high. In 1990 anti-abortion campaigners flooded Parliament with model fetuses. Pro-embryo research lobbies played to the cameras with touching and well-timed stories of the joy brought to previously infertile women by their 'test-tube' babies. The scientific possibilities are hard to grasp and science-fiction scenarios abound. Test-tube-baby technology creates fears of Aldous Huxley's *Brave New World*. Above all, each side in the moral debate is convinced they are right and the other is irretrievably wrong. What tends to be overlooked is this. In many ethical debates today, there is no answer that will be universally accepted as right. The question for legislators is not to find a right answer, to achieve a moral consensus, but to determine how in a liberal, democratic society legislation can be formulated in the absence of such consensus. To evade that task is to leave the scientists free rein to do as they see fit. To criticise them with hindsight is unfair and unproductive. Theologians, ethicists, lawyers and indeed all citizens must be prepared to grapple with these awkward moral dilemmas and, probably, be ready to compromise.

[91] *The Royal Liverpool Children's Inquiry Report* (2001) HC 12–II. See 21.2 below.

Chapter 5

A RELATIONSHIP OF TRUST AND CONFIDENCE

> Whatever, in connection with my professional practice, or not in connection with it, I see or hear in the life of men, which ought not to be spoken of abroad, I will not divulge, as reckoning that all such should be kept secret.
>
> The Hippocratic Oath

> I will respect the secrets which are confided in me, even after the patient has died.
>
> Declaration of Geneva (as amended 2017)

5.1 Introduction

Doctors, like priests and lawyers, must be able to keep secrets. For medical care to be effective, for patients to trust their doctor, patients must have confidence that they can talk frankly to them. In its latest guidance to doctors, the General Medical Council (GMC) puts it this way:

> Trust is an essential part of the doctor–patient relationship and confidentiality is central to this. Patients may avoid seeking medical help, or may under-report symptoms, if they think their personal information will be disclosed by doctors without consent, or without the chance to have some control over the timing or amount of information shared.[1]

An obligation of confidence to patients lies at the heart of all codes of ethics, but a comparison of the quotations above shows that the obligation is not necessarily absolute. The Ancient Greek physician undertook not to divulge that which 'ought not to be spoken of abroad'. He judged what fell into that category. The Declaration of Geneva is more stringent. Must *any* information given by a patient in confidence be kept secret for ever? A moment's reflection reveals the problems inherent in both absolute and relative obligations

[1] GMC, *Confidentiality: Good Practice in Handling Patient Information* (2017, updated 2018) (hereafter GMC, *Confidentiality*). And see commentary: C Stanton, 'Patient Information: To Share or Not to Share' (2018) 26(1) *Med Law Rev* 328.

of confidence. An absolute obligation leaves the doctor powerless to do anything but try to persuade their patient to allow them to take action if, for example, a patient tells them he is HIV positive but is still having unprotected sex with his wife who knows nothing of his condition, or when a depressed mother confesses her violent impulses towards her baby.[2] On the other hand, a relative obligation, which leaves doctors free to breach confidence when they judge that some higher duty to another person or to society applies, may deter patients from seeking necessary treatment. This may damage not only the patient but also those very people vulnerable when the doctor treats and does not 'tell'. The wife whose husband receives no advice about 'safe sex' and HIV, and the baby whose mother seeks no counsel may be more vulnerable if fears of breach of confidence prevent the husband and the mother getting any help at all because they are afraid to confide in a doctor.

In this chapter we look at the law on confidentiality as it affects doctors and adult patients and examine the role of the medical profession in enforcing the ethical obligation of confidence. The special problems affecting confidentiality and parents and children are considered in Chapter 17. Issues relating to confidentiality in medical research are considered in Chapter 18. The complexity of the law may surprise some. The number of occasions when the law allows or compels the doctor to breach confidence may shock many. We consider the 2016 General Data Protection Regulation (GDPR) and the Data Protection Act 2018, which set out a data protection regime designed to ensure that people can trust that their data will be used responsibly and fairly. The government launched a consultation in 2021,[3] proposing a replacement scheme to maximise on the potential of the digital sector. The chapter also explores what the patient is entitled to be told. From the patient's viewpoint the doctor's obligation of confidence exists to prevent the doctor passing on information about them to third parties. A relationship of trust requires that this should not happen. Trust also requires that the doctor be frank with the patient. Information about the patient should generally not be withheld from them. It is 'their' information not the doctor's and so we also ask how far patients are entitled to frankness from their doctors.

5.2 Breach of confidence: medical privacy

English law on breach of confidence developed haphazardly.[4] In some cases it is governed by statute. For example, section 33A of the Human Fertilisation

2 The Children Act 2004, s 11 places a duty on NHS Trusts (and others) to make arrangements to ensure that 'their functions are discharged having regard to the need to safeguard and promote the welfare of children'.

3 Department for Digital, Culture Media & Sport, *Data: A New Direction* (2021). As we go to press, the UK has proposed changes to the framework on privacy in the Data Protection and Digital Information Bill 2022 (Bill 143 2022/23), discussed at 5.19 below.

4 See Law Commission, *Breach of Confidence* (1981) Report No 110, Cmnd 8388, para 3.1.

and Embryology Act 1990 (as amended) makes fertility treatment a medical secret that cannot be passed on even to other doctors without consent, except in a medical emergency.[5] At common law, the core obligation requires doctors to respect patient confidences. Judges have shown themselves willing to act to prevent the disclosure of confidential information in a wide variety of circumstances. Often the obligation of confidence arises as an implied term of a contract, as is the case with the employee bound by his contract of employment to keep their employer's business to themselves. But the obligation of confidence can equally arise where no contract exists, or has ever existed, between the parties.

Confidentiality is not only a strong private interest, but there is also a public interest in keeping certain types of information private, and this is particularly true of medical information. In a very early case, action was taken to prevent publication of a diary kept by a physician to George III.[6] Much later, in 1974, a judge put the doctor's duty thus:

> [I]n common with other professional men, for instance a priest and there are of course others, the doctor is under a duty not to disclose, [voluntarily] without the consent of his patient, information which he, the doctor, has gained in his professional capacity, save ... in very exceptional circumstances.[7]

Today any attempt to understand the law governing medical confidentiality must take account of a bewildering array of sources. In addition to the case-law, it is necessary to take account of Articles 8 (right to privacy) and 10 (freedom of expression) of the European Convention on Human Rights (ECHR), and voluminous guidance from regulatory bodies and the National Health Service (NHS).

Article 8(1) of the ECHR states that: 'Everyone has the right to respect for his private and family life, his home and his correspondence'. The European Court of Human Rights has consistently upheld the right to privacy in relation to medical records. But it is not an unqualified right. The court has upheld seizure of medical records in criminal proceedings[8] and use of records in connection with social security benefits.[9] In *Z v Finland* the Court said:

> Respecting the confidentiality of health data is a vital principle in the legal systems of all the Contracting Parties to the Convention. It is crucial not only to respect the sense of privacy of a patient but also to preserve his or her confidence in the medical profession and in the health services in general.[10]

5 See criticism: C Repschlager, 'Does Fertility Treatment Still Need to be a Medical Secret?' *Bionews* (2019) 2 December.

6 *Wyatt v Wilson* (1820), unreported but referred to in *Prince Albert v Strange* (1849) 41 ER 1171, 1179.

7 *Hunter v Mann* [1974] 1 QB 767, at 772.

8 *Z v Finland* [1997] 25 EHRR 371.

9 *MS v Sweden* [1997] 45 BMLR 133.

10 [1997] 25 EHRR 371, [95].

5.2 *A relationship of trust and confidence*

In England, the Human Rights Act 1998 renders the Convention Articles enforceable against public authorities. In the United States of America, and many civil law jurisdictions, an all-inclusive cause of action for invasion of privacy is recognised. No right of privacy as such is even now recognised in English domestic law,[11] but the various aspects of English law which protect privacy, including the common law action for breach of confidence, have developed to take account of Article 8. The terminology has changed, leading Lord Nicholls to call for the renaming of the tort:

> The continuing use of the phrase 'duty of confidence' and the description of the information as 'confidential' is not altogether comfortable. Information about an individual's private life would not, in ordinary usage, be called 'confidential'. The more natural description today is that such information is private. The essence of the tort is better encapsulated now as misuse of private information.[12]

The common law principles developed incrementally by the judiciary long before the Human Rights Act remain important to an understanding of medical confidentiality, but now have to be applied with due regard for Convention rights. So, in *Campbell v Mirror Group Newspapers*,[13] to which we shall return, the House of Lords balanced human rights, Article 8 versus Article 10, rather than the traditional concepts of private and public interests, but Lord Hope commented that: 'It seems to me that the balancing exercise to which that guidance is directed is essentially the same exercise, although it is plainly now more carefully focussed and more penetrating.'[14]

Article 8 of the Human Rights Act strengthens the principles long contained in the common law action for breach of confidence, in which the basic general principles are these:

(1) The courts will intervene to restrain disclosure of information where the information is confidential in nature and not a matter of public knowledge, or trivial in nature.
(2) Where information is found to be private and confidential, any non-consensual disclosure requires justification in the public interest.[15]
(3) Once an obligation of confidence is created it binds not only the original recipient of the information but also any other person to whom disclosure is made by the recipient when that other person knows of the confidential status of the information.[16] As well as acting in advance to prevent the disclosure of confidential information, the courts may

11 *Wainwright v Home Office* [2003] 3 WLR 1137. And see *Douglas v Hello! Ltd* [2007] UKHL 21, [272].

12 *Campbell v Mirror Group Newspapers* [2004] UKHL 22, [14]. The term has since been adopted in a number of cases, such as *Hutcheson (formerly KGM) v News Group Newspapers Ltd* [2011] EWCA Civ 808, [22] and *Vidal-Hall v Google Inc* [2015] EWCA Civ 311.

13 [2004] UKHL 22, [157].

14 [2004] UKHL 22, [86].

15 *W v Egdell* [1990] 1 All ER 835, at 846, CA; *Campbell v Mirror Group Newspapers* [2004] UKHL 22.

16 *Campbell v Mirror Group Newspapers* [2004] UKHL 22.

where appropriate award compensation after information has been improperly disclosed.[17]

In *A-G v Guardian Newspapers (No 2)*,[18] Lord Goff broadened the scope of breach of confidence, stating that when information is entrusted to another person in *circumstances* imposing an obligation not to use or disclose that information without the consent of the giver of the information an initial confidential relationship is not required.[19] In *Campbell v MGN*[20] (which did not involve a doctor–patient relationship), the Law Lords ruled that the *circumstances* in which the information was obtained were irrelevant. The *nature* of the information was of paramount importance. The 'old' test of a confidential relationship covered the relationship of doctor and patient. Applying the new terminology, it remains the case that a 'reasonable expectation of privacy'[21] can be established when a patient divulges information about their health to their doctor and may extend to a broader class of health information.

5.3 Disclosure after death

Does death terminate any obligation of confidence to a deceased patient? You might ask why this should matter but consider just two examples. A senior cabinet Minister dies and within weeks her general practitioner (GP) publishes a best-selling book highlighting her multiple medical problems in graphic and prurient detail. A famous married actor dies, and his doctor tells the tabloid press all about his battle with HIV and bisexuality. Should the first doctor be allowed to profit from the abuse of his professional relationship? Do the widow and children of the actor have a claim to consideration? For many years the GMC has instructed doctors that 'Your duty of confidentiality continues after a patient has died'.[22] It was less clear whether the law imposed such an obligation surviving the patient until in *Lewis v Secretary of State for Health*[23] Foskett J took the view that the 'obligation of confidence is capable of surviving the death of the patient'.[24] Such he said were the expectations of the public and the profession. The legal obligation is not necessarily permanent, and the period of survival will depend on the sensitivity of the information in issue and the prospect of any harm done to surviving relatives.

17 *Cornelius v De Taranto* (2001) 68 BMLR 62.
18 [1990] 1 AC 109.
19 Ibid, 281.
20 *Campbell v Mirror Group Newspapers* [2004] UKHL 22.
21 Ibid, [21] per Lord Nicholls.
22 GMC, *Confidentiality*, para 134.
23 [2008] EWHC 2196. And see *Press Association v Newcastle upon Tyne Hospitals Foundation Trust* [2014] EWCOP 6. (LM had refused a blood transfusion on religious grounds and died. Peter Jackson J lifted a reporting restriction and reiterated that death does not automatically lead to loss of privacy protection.) And see 5.13 below.
24 *Lewis v Secretary of State* [2008] EWHC 2196, [24]; and see *Bluck v The Information Commissioner and Epsom and St Helier University NHS Trust* (2007) 98 BMLR 1.

5.4 Justifying disclosure

The challenging questions about medical confidentiality do not, however, lie in establishing a *general* duty of confidence, or expectation of privacy, but in determining what amounts to 'very exceptional circumstances' justifying breach of that duty.

First, disclosure will always be justified legally when the doctor is *compelled* by law to give confidential information to a third party. This may be by way of an order of the court to disclose records in the course of some civil proceedings. Doctors, unlike lawyers, enjoy no professional privilege entitling them to refuse to give evidence in court. Or it may be under some statutory provision, such as those Acts of Parliament requiring that specified diseases be notified to the health authorities.[25]

Second, the doctor may *voluntarily elect* to disclose information in certain circumstances. Where there is a public interest in disclosure of confidential and private information, the court will consider whether harm (to either physical or moral integrity) may be caused to someone as a result.[26] The public interest in disclosure must be balanced with the public and private interests in maintaining confidentiality. Thus, disclosure of private information requires justification.

In early judgments, the public interest 'defence' tended to concern disclosure of crime.[27] Gradually it has been accepted that that defence is not limited to crime, or even misconduct.[28] Two major cases remain central to an understanding of when public interests will justify a breach of medical confidentiality. In *X v Y*[29] a tabloid newspaper acquired, in breach of confidence from a health authority employee, information identifying two GPs who were continuing to practise after having been diagnosed as HIV positive. The authority sought an injunction prohibiting publication of their patients', the doctors', names. The newspaper argued that the general public, and the doctors' patients in particular, had an interest in knowing that the doctors were HIV positive. Rose J reviewed the evidence about transmission of HIV from doctor to patient where the doctor had received proper counselling about safe practice. He found that the risk to patients was negligible. Far greater risks arose from the possibility that if they could not rely on confidential treatment, people with AIDS, or who feared they might have AIDS, would not seek medical help. The judge, granting the injunction, said:

> In the long run, preservation of confidentiality is the only way of securing public health; otherwise doctors will be discredited as a source of education, for future individual patients will not come forward if doctors are going to squeal on them.

25 Public Health (Control of Diseases) Act 1984 (as amended); see 7.21 below.
26 *R v Department of Health ex p Source Informatics Ltd* [2000] 1 All ER 786; *Campbell v Mirror Group Newspapers* [2004] UKHL 22.
27 *Gartside v Outram* (1856) 26 LJ Ch 113, at 114.
28 *Lion Laboratories Ltd v Evans* [1984] 2 All ER 417, at 433.
29 [1988] 2 All ER 648.

> Consequently, confidentiality is vital to secure public as well as private health, for unless those infected come forward they cannot be counselled and self-treatment does not provide the best care ...[30]

By contrast in *W v Egdell*,[31] the Court of Appeal sanctioned a breach of confidence by a psychiatrist. W had been convicted of the manslaughter of five people and of wounding two others. He was ordered to be detained indefinitely in a secure hospital. He could be released only by order of the Home Secretary if he were found to be no longer a danger to public safety. As a step towards eventual release, he sought to be transferred to a regional secure unit. The transfer was not approved by the Home Secretary and W then applied to a mental health review tribunal for a conditional discharge. In support of his application his solicitors arranged for an independent psychiatric report from Dr Egdell. Dr Egdell's report was not favourable. He judged that W was still a dangerous man with a psychopathic personality, no real insight into his condition and a morbid interest in explosives. Unsurprisingly, W's solicitors withdrew their application for his discharge, but they did not pass on the report to the tribunal or the hospital where W was detained. Dr Egdell was concerned by the fact that his report was not passed on. He ultimately sent his report to the medical director of W's hospital and agreed that a copy of that report should be forwarded to the Home Secretary. W sued Dr Egdell for breach of confidence.

The Court of Appeal made it crystal clear that Dr Egdell did owe W a duty of confidence. Had he sold his story to the press or discussed the case in his memoirs, Dr Egdell would have been in breach of confidence. But the duty of confidentiality is not absolute. The public interest in medical confidentiality must be balanced against the public interest in public safety. If Dr Egdell's diagnosis was right, W remained a source of danger to others and he was entitled to communicate his findings to the director of the hospital now detaining W, and to the Home Secretary, who would have the final say on if and when W should be released into the community.

X v Y and *W v Egdell* did not mean that a doctor may *never* disclose that a patient is HIV positive, or that he may always disclose his concerns about a patient's mental health. In each case the powerful interest in maintaining confidentiality must be balanced against the danger ensuing if confidentiality is not breached. Only where there is a clear and significant risk of the patient causing harm to others which cannot be abated by any other means may confidence be breached.

As we have noted, more recently judicial assessment of public and private interests has involved the careful balancing of Convention rights. *Campbell v Mirror Group Newspapers Ltd.*[32] involved the disclosure of information concerning the health of a famous fashion model. Although the information

30 Ibid, at 653.
31 [1990] 1 All ER 835; applied in *R v Crozier* [1991] *Criminal Law Review* 138, CA.
32 [2004] UKHL 22.

was disclosed by the *Mirror* newspaper, rather than a medical practitioner, there are clear implications for medical privacy. The House of Lords balanced Campbell's right to privacy under Article 8, protected by the common law duty of confidentiality, with the freedom of the press, protected under Article 10. Both are qualified rights and neither has pre-eminence over the other. Campbell objected to the publication of furtively taken photographs and articles proving that she was attending Narcotics Anonymous. This, she maintained, was a breach of confidence for which she was entitled to compensation under the (then applicable) Data Protection Act 1998. By a majority, the House of Lords found in her favour, overturning the decision of the Court of Appeal. The special nature of medical information was recognised by Baroness Hale who stated:

> It has always been accepted that information about a person's health and treatment for ill health is both private and confidential. This stems not only from the confidentiality of the doctor–patient relationship but from the nature of the information itself.[33]

Article 8, like the common law, imposes only a relative obligation of confidence.[34] Article 8(2) provides:

> There shall be no interference by a public authority with the exercise of this right except such as is in accordance with the law and necessary in a democratic society in the interests of national security, public safety or the economic well-being of the country, for the prevention of disorder or crime, for the protection of health or morals, or for the protection of the rights and freedoms of others.

In *W, X, Y and Z*, the Court of Appeal balanced the reasonable expectation of privacy according to Article 8(1) and the public benefit (Article 8(2)):

> It is common ground that the test ... involves two questions. The first is whether the claimants have a reasonable expectation of privacy in relation to the Information. This question is judged objectively by reference to the reasonable person of ordinary sensibilities. If they do have a reasonable expectation of privacy, the second question is whether there has been a breach of their rights to privacy and confidentiality. This requires a balancing exercise of weighing the public benefit that would be attained by the transmission of the Information against the harm that would result from the interference with the rights.[35]

In this case, 'modest interference' with Article 8(1) for the purpose of debt collection was found to be 'in accordance with the law'.

33 Ibid, [145].

34 See also *Szuluk v United Kingdom* [2009] ECHR 36936/05 and *R (TB) v CPS and South Staffordshire Healthcare NHS Trust* [2006] EWHC 1645 (Admin).

35 *R (W, X, Y and Z) v Secretary of State for Health and Secretary of State for the Home Department, the British Medical Association* [2015] EWCA Civ 1034: MJ Taylor and J Wilson, 'Reasonable Expectations of Privacy and Disclosure of Health Data' (2019) 27(3) *Med Law Rev* 432.

5.5 The General Medical Council (GMC)[36]

A doctor facing a practical dilemma about whether she can lawfully disclose information in the public interest will want more specific guidance than that available from the judgments of the courts. Guidance is promulgated by several bodies, such as the British Medical Association[37] and the UK Caldicott Guardian Council, which is the national body for Caldicott Guardians: people responsible for protecting health and care information in NHS organisations and local authorities.[38]

Another primary source of such advice is the GMC's guidance, *Confidentiality: Good Practice in Handling Patient Information*, issued in 2017.[39] The GMC plays two roles in enforcing confidentiality. First the courts will give due regard to the profession's own view of the ethical obligations owed by its members in formulating consequential legal obligations.[40] That does not mean GMC guidelines are in any sense law or that the courts will slavishly follow the profession's view. But the guidance may be a good indicator of how the courts will resolve dilemmas as they come before them.

Second, aggrieved patients may prefer to complain to the GMC rather than take legal action in the courts. The medical professional in breach of confidentiality could face a finding of impaired fitness to practise and removal from the register. The civil action for breach of confidence is an excellent weapon for restraining threatened breaches of confidence. It may be less effective in offering redress to the victim of a breach of confidence, except in a commercial setting. If a trade secret is revealed by an employee and the employer loses profits, his loss can be measured by the courts and appropriate compensation ordered. The defendant may be obliged to hand over all his illegal profits. A breach of medical confidence rarely results in monetary loss but will give rise to indignity and distress for the patient. It used to be unclear if mental distress could give rise to damages for breach of confidence. In *Cornelius v De Taranto*[41] the judge at first instance awarded the claimant £3,000 in damages for mental distress caused by 'unauthorised disclosure of the confidential information' and subsequent cases have followed suit. However legal action may be expensive and the damages low.[42] The legal claim itself may attract unwelcome publicity

36 And see BMA, *Confidentiality and Disclosure of Health Information Toolkit* (2009) (updated 2018).

37 BMA, *Confidentiality and Health Records Toolkit* (updated 2020).

38 The UK Caldicott Guardian Council, *The Eight Caldicott Principles* (2020).

39 See also DHSC, *Confidentiality: Code of Practice* (2003) and NHS England, *Confidentiality Policy* (2016, as updated).

40 *Lewis v Secretary of State for Health* [2008] EWHC 2196 (QB), 19; *W v Egdell* [1990] 1 All ER 835, 843 and 850.

41 (2001) 68 BMLR 62. In 1981, the Law Commission had recommended the award of damages for distress. And see the Scottish decisions *AB v CD* (1851) 14 D 177; *AB v CD* (1904) 7 F 72; see GT Laurie, S Harmon and E Dove, *Mason and McCall Smith's Law and Medical Ethics* (11th edn, 2019) Oxford University Press, 6.69.

42 Though see *Mosley v News Group Newspapers* [2008] EWHC 1777.

and complaining to the GMC may remain a preferred option for many victims of breach of medical confidence.

The GMC makes it clear that patients have a right to expect that information about them will be held in confidence by their doctors.[43] We consider, first, information where the identity of the patient is disclosed, what the GMC describes as personal information. The doctor's duty is to maintain confidentiality strictly. The Guidance warns doctors to be vigilant in protecting confidential information. It rightly notes that 'many improper disclosures of information are unintentional'.[44] Technologies such as telemedicine, email and phone apps[45] facilitate new ways to communicate with patients and share information, but they also create new challenges around confidentiality. Notes should not be left lying around. Consultations with patients should not take place where they can be overheard by other patients or by staff not involved in the care of the patient. Doctors responsible for the management of records must make sure that all staff understand their responsibilities to secure patient confidentiality.

5.6 Disclosure with consent

Disclosure is self-evidently lawful if the patient expressly consents to disclosure. For consent to be informed, the doctor must ensure that the patient understands what is to be disclosed, the reasons for disclosure and the consequences thereof. The patient must be told to whom information will be given and how much information will be disclosed. But the model of informed consent that has developed with regard to treatment does not apply seamlessly with respect to health data. For example, some patients prefer to make decisions as part of a family group and the law's foundations in privacy and individual autonomy can rest uneasily alongside a relational autonomy approach.[46] Furthermore, Chico and Taylor[47] argue that the requirements of consent in relation to confidentiality do not necessarily need to mimic the requirements in relation to treatment. Complex and individualised informational requirements, they warn, may erode patient choice if alternative models to consent are developed to justify information sharing for treatment or research in the public interest.

In a number of instances consent may be implied rather than explicit.[48] Health care in the NHS is usually provided by a team of professionals and sharing

43 GMC, *Confidentiality*, introduction.

44 GMC, ibid, paras 118–119.

45 See 5.19 below. See M Sheppard, 'mHealth Apps: Disruptive Innovation, Regulation, and Trust—A Need for Balance' (2020) 28(3) *Med Law Rev* 549.

46 R Gilbar, 'Family Involvement, Independence, and Patient Autonomy in Practice' (2011) 19(2) *Med Law Rev* 192.

47 V Chico and R Taylor, 'Using and Disclosing Confidential Patient Information and The English Common Law: What are the Information Requirements of a Valid Consent?' (2018) 26(1) *Med Law Rev* 51.

48 MJ Taylor and J Wilson, 'Reasonable Expectations of Privacy and Disclosure of Health Data' (2019) 27(3) *Med Law Rev* 432 suggest that the 'reasonable expectation of privacy' could be interpreted to provide an alternative legal basis to implied consent.

information within that healthcare team will normally be lawful on the basis that patients usually understand that a number of different health professionals will play a role in their care.[49] The GMC makes clear that efforts must be made to ensure that patients are aware of this practice and that their wishes are respected should they decide to withhold consent.[50] Doctors must make sure that everyone within the team to whom information is disclosed understands that they are bound by a legal obligation of confidence. Moreover, the sharing of confidential information should be restricted to staff who are directly involved in personal care[51] but surveys have suggested that in practice a growing number of non-medical staff have access to confidential records.[52]

The jurisdiction of the GMC is limited to registered medical practitioners, but all NHS staff are subject to the law on confidence. Information confided by the patient to their doctor remains legally confidential when passed by the doctor to NHS administrators for storage. NHS England's *Confidentiality Policy*, issued in 2016, is clear that confidentiality binds everyone working within the NHS.[53] Disclosure within the service is justified only if required in the context of the patient's healthcare. Disclosure to third parties outside the service is permissible only with the patient's consent save in exceptional cases. The exceptions, for example where disclosure is required by law or in case of serious crime, correspond closely to the exceptions sanctioned by the GMC. Guidelines are enforced by the sanction of disciplinary action, or even dismissal, against staff members who break them.[54]

Concerns about privacy have led to risk aversion amongst health professionals. To encourage responsible data sharing, the NHS has endorsed the use of the NHS Number instead of the patient's name as the primary identifier in clinical correspondence. The Health and Social Care (Safety and Quality) Act 2015 inserts a new section 251A into the Health and Social Care Act 2012 requiring that a 'consistent identifier' – the NHS Number – be used to identify individuals.[55] There are several exceptions to the rule, which only applies where it is in the best interests of an individual who does not object. Section 251A does not permit anything that is inconsistent with either the common law duty of confidentiality or the Data Protection Act 2018.

49 GMC, *Confidentiality*, para 27.
50 Ibid, paras 26–29.
51 *I v Finland* (2008) 48 EHRR 740.
52 'NHS Breaching Citizens' Human Rights over Levels of Access' (2010) 10(5) *Privacy and Data Protection* 1.
53 NHS England, *Confidentiality Policy* (2016), 3.9: NHS staff are bound by the DHSC, *Confidentiality: NHS Code of Practice* (2003).
54 Note that all doctors in clinical practice should participate in clinical audit. Provided it is undertaken by the team providing the care, or their support staff, personal information may be disclosed if the patient is aware that personal information may be disclosed for audit purposes, has been informed and has not objected. GMC, *Confidentiality*, para 96.
55 The Health and Social Care Act 2012 (Consistent Identifier) Regulations 2015, SI 2015/1439 implements the reform.

5.7 Disclosure where the patient lacks capacity

What about the patient who lacks capacity to authorise disclosure of information, be they unconscious in an emergency department or suffering from some long-term impairment? A key question will be how much information doctors can share with family or carers. Under the Mental Capacity Act 2005 there is a presumption of capacity. A person will only be shown to lack capacity in relation to a specific decision where they are unable to make a decision for themselves[56] by virtue of the fact that they cannot understand, retain, weigh or use the information relevant to the decision.[57] A Lasting Power of Attorney (LPA) can be conferred on a third party under section 9 of the Act. An LPA can make decisions about the welfare or affairs of someone who lacks capacity. In connection, an LPA can in some circumstances request access to the person's health records under the Data Protection Act 2018, discussed below.

Under section 5 of the Mental Capacity Act, those providing care for someone who lacks capacity will not incur legal liability provided they have properly assessed the patient's capacity, and act in the patient's best interests. The Act provides a checklist for determining best interests.[58] So the question becomes: is the disclosure of information in the incapacitated patient's interests? And in many cases, it will be.[59]

Under section 4(7) of the Mental Capacity Act the doctor has a duty, where practicable, to consult appropriate persons about the patient's treatment. Discussing the condition of an unconscious patient in an emergency department and seeking advice on their treatment with colleagues and family members is proper and lawful.[60] However where a patient is conscious and objects to disclosure, doctors should be wary of releasing information to the family in the patient's 'medical interests'. Under section 4, best interests include, but are not limited to, medical interests. The patient's beliefs, values, and past and present wishes must also be taken into account. Only information that it is essential to share should be disclosed and in general there will be no need or justification to give details of past healthcare.[61] So if a patient is unconscious having suffered serious head and abdominal injuries, it may be lawful to discuss with her family her current condition and prognosis but not to disclose that examinations show that some years before she had terminated a pregnancy.

5.8 Disclosure to protect the patient

Doctors may sometimes wish to disclose information to protect their patient, and the GMC guidance is clear that if a patient who lacks capacity may be

[56] Mental Capacity Act 2005 s 2(1). On the 2005 Act generally, see below Chapter 7.
[57] Ibid, s 3.
[58] Ibid, s 4.
[59] GMC, *Confidentiality*, paras 41–49.
[60] See *R (S) v Plymouth City Council* [2002] EWCA Civ 388.
[61] GMC, *Confidentiality*, para 46.

at risk of neglect or abuse the doctor *must* inform[62] an appropriate person or authority promptly. What if a patient is vulnerable or very ill, but retains capacity?[63] Consider the dying patient. Not long ago, it was considered acceptable to ignore a patient's plea to keep knowledge of their illness from their family, or even to 'spare the patient pain' by telling their family, but not the patient, how close they are to death. The GMC today is clear that where the patient retains capacity, information may only be shared with the family with their consent.[64] There is no legal basis for compassionate paternalism. But what if death or serious injury may result to the patient, for example, the doctor becomes aware that their patient is the victim of escalating domestic abuse but the patient refuses to allow them to contact the police or social services? Can disclosure to protect the patient be made in such circumstances? Paragraphs 58 and 59 of the GMC guidance advise:

> If an adult patient who has capacity to make the decision refuses to consent to information being disclosed that you consider necessary for their protection, you should explore their reasons for this. It may be appropriate to encourage the patient to consent to the disclosure and to warn them of the risks of refusing to consent.
>
> *You should, however, usually abide by the patient's refusal to consent to disclosure, even if their decision leaves them (but no one else) at risk of death or serious harm* [our emphasis].

Note the word 'usually' may be seen as allowing for a truly exceptional case.[65] A competent patient is generally free to withhold consent to confidential information being disclosed, even if they will be harmed as a result. But the duty of confidentiality is not absolute. If the threat to the patient poses risk to others, their competent refusal to the disclosure of information could be overridden. A woman suffering abuse from her partner, who refuses to consent to information being disclosed to the police, might be overridden if she has children who are also at risk. What if the individual is warned that their confidential information could be passed on and it is subsequently disclosed without specific consent? In *Scott v LGBT Foundation Ltd*[66] Mr Scott challenged the legality of an oral disclosure by the LGBT Foundation of information to Mr Scott's GP. The Foundation considered Mr Scott to be at risk of suicide and was unable to provide him with the services he needed. He had been informed that information disclosed could be passed on if the Foundation considered him to be at risk. Striking out the claim, Saini J said:

> In my judgment, on the basis of these facts, it will not be possible for Mr Scott to make out at a trial a necessary element of this cause of action, namely that it

62 Ibid, para 55. This applies 'unless it is not of overall benefit to the patient to do so' in which case see para 56.

63 See E Cave, 'Disclosure of Confidential Information to Protect the Patient: The Role of Legal Capacity' (2015) (1–2) *Journal of Medical Law and Ethics* 7.

64 Ibid, para 37.

65 D Sokol, 'Is Doctor–Patient Confidentiality Dying a Slow Death?' (2018) 363 *BMJ* k4313 argues that there are times when referrals are made without proper justification, resulting in a loss of patient trust.

66 [2020] EWHC 483 (QB).

> was a breach of confidence for LGBT Foundation to convey (in a limited way and only to his GP) the information in the Disclosure. The general duty of confidence owed to Mr Scott was qualified by a permissive rider in the circumstances.[67]

In referral forms, the Foundation had stated 'We will try to get your consent first, but this may not always be possible', but the judge held that the forms 'are not to be read as contractual instruments' and that disclosures to keep the patient safe 'in extreme circumstances' could be justified in this case as a matter of common sense.[68]

The Social Services and Well-being (Wales) Act 2014[69] and the Adult Support and Protection (Scotland) Act 2007[70] expressly require doctors and other agencies to notify local authorities where an adult is at risk of abuse. Section 42 of the (English) Care Act 2014 imposes a duty on *local authorities* to make inquiries where it has a reasonable suspicion that an adult is experiencing or is at risk of abuse or neglect. It does not extend to doctors,[71] but NHS England encourages partnership and adherence to the principles of the Act.[72] The variability across devolved nations illustrates the inevitable tension between a desire to protect patients at risk and respect for autonomy.

5.9 Compulsory disclosure

When a disclosure of confidential information or production of medical records is required by law, the doctor has no choice but to comply, and compulsory disclosure is mandated in a variety of circumstances.

First, a doctor must give any information required by a court.[73] Privilege, in the sense of being free to refuse to give evidence relating to professional dealings with clients, is something usually enjoyed by lawyers alone and not shared by any other professional colleagues.[74] A doctor can be subpoenaed to

67 Ibid, [81].

68 Ibid, [82].

69 Section 128(1): 'If a relevant partner of a local authority has reasonable cause to suspect that a person is an adult at risk and appears to be within the authority's area, it must inform the local authority of that fact.'

70 Section 5(3): 'Where a public body or office-holder to which this section applies knows or believes – (a) that a person is an adult at risk, and (b) that action needs to be taken (under this Part or otherwise) in order to protect that person from harm, the public body or office-holder must report the facts and circumstances of the case to the council for the area in which it considers the person to be.'

71 After a 2018 consultation the Government decided not to introduce a mandatory reporting duty or a duty to act. See D Foster, 'Child Protection: Duties to Report Concerns' *House of Commons Library Research Briefing* (2020) 28 February.

72 NHS England, *Safeguarding Adults* at www.england.nhs.uk/wp-content/uploads/2017/02/adult-pocket-guide.pdf.

73 See, for example, *General Dental Council v Savery and others* [2011] EWHC 3011 (Admin) (medical records were lawfully obtained by the GDC without consent for the purposes of disciplinary functions. Sales J said (obiter) at [64] that it is good practice to inform patients.)

74 See JV McHale, *Medical Confidentiality and Legal Privilege* (1993) Routledge.

give evidence about their patient's health and may be forced to reveal intimate information. Doctors cannot withhold information from the court and they may be ordered to produce the patient's records. They do not have to volunteer their views or expertise but whatever questions they are asked they must answer. The protection for medical confidentiality in the courtroom lies in the judge's discretion. Judges will try to ensure that confidence is breached only to the extent necessary for the conduct of the trial. Doctors may be unhappy at having to break trust with their patient. They can be reassured that they are at no legal risk. Any breach of confidence made as a witness in court is absolutely privileged.

In exercising their powers to order disclosure of evidence or documents, courts strive to balance justice and confidentiality, giving due regard to Article 8 of the Convention. In *D v NSPCC*[75] the plaintiff sought to compel the NSPCC to disclose who had mistakenly accused her of child abuse. The court refused to make the order. The public interest in people feeling free to approach appropriate authorities to protect young children outweighed the plaintiff's private interest in unearthing her accuser. Thus, there will be some cases where the courts may refuse to help a party seeking to discover who gave damaging information about them to the police or some other authority. Particularly sensitive information may be allowed to be withheld from the court in the public interest.[76]

In the unusual case of *P v Griffith*,[77] Ms Griffith was sentenced to twelve months' imprisonment for contempt of court when she forged a court order in an attempt to obtain the medical records of a relation who lacked capacity. Ms Griffith sought the disclosure in connection with an application to the Court of Protection in relation to a dispute about her relative's best interests. The contempt was an interference with the administration of justice, but the court also acknowledged that it prejudiced the relative, given the confidential and private nature of medical records.

Next, the doctor may be compelled to hand over information to the police or other authorities before any trial commences. Several statutes demand that doctors answer questions if the police come and ask them. If a statute imposes a duty on 'any person' to answer police questions, any person includes doctors.[78] Their profession confers no exemption or privilege upon them.

75 [1977] 1 All ER 589.

76 See *AB v Glasgow and West of Scotland Blood Transfusion Service* 1993 SLT 36 (a Scottish court refused to order disclosure of the identity of a blood donor who had allegedly supplied infected blood); And *R (TB) v CPS and South Staffordshire Healthcare NHS Trust* [2006] EWHC 1645 (Admin) (successful judicial review of a crown court decision to obtain the reluctant consent of an unrepresented child witness in a sexual abuse case to disclose medical records, in breach of Article 8).

77 [2020] EWCOP 46.

78 *Hunter v Mann* [1974] 1 QB 767.

Provision is made for compulsory notification of certain highly infectious diseases and of sexually transmitted disease.[79] Section 45A of the Public Health (Control of Disease) Act 1984 makes expansive provision for compulsory notification of certain specific diseases such as cholera or typhoid and also provides that doctors should notify the appropriate authorities of any infection or contamination that 'presents or could present significant harm to human health'.[80] Abortions must be reported. Details of drug addicts are required under the Misuse of Drugs Act. Births and deaths have to be notified by doctors as well as registered by families.

Finally, a number of organisations concerned with health administration may require information in the course of performing their functions. These include the NHS Ombudsman, the Department of Health and Social Care and other NHS authorities.[81] Examining the individual items on the long list of circumstances when a doctor can be forced to hand over information concerning his patients, many can be justified on grounds of public interest. The trouble is that the list grows haphazardly.

Section 251 of the National Health Service Act 2006 (previously section 60 of the Health and Social Care Act 2001) grants the Secretary of State further powers to dilute patient confidentiality:

> (1) The Secretary of State may by regulations make such provision for and in connection with requiring or regulating the processing of prescribed patient information for medical purposes as he considers necessary or expedient—
> (a) in the interests of improving patient care, or
> (b) in the public interest.

The Health Service (Control of Patient Information) Regulations 2002[82] (COPI) implement this power. In a concession to opponents, a group now called the Confidentiality Advisory Group (CAG) was established with whom

[79] The NHS (Venereal Diseases) Regulations 1974, SI 1974/29 make provision for the tracing of sexual contacts, but also seek to ensure that the identity of patients and contacts remains confidential.

[80] And see the Health Protection (Notification) Regulations 2010, SI 2010/659, amended in 2020 (SI 2020/237) to add COVID-19 to the list of notifiable diseases. See 7.21 below.

[81] For example the Health and Care Act 2022, s 123 provides for regulations to determine that certain disclosures to the Healthcare Services Safety Investigations Body (set up to investigate incidents without apportioning blame and discussed at 2.6 above) do not breach the obligation of confidence. But powers must be used with proper regard for the patient's right to privacy under Article 8 of the Human Rights Convention; see *A Health Authority v X* [2001] EWCA Civ 2014.

[82] SI 2002/1438, as amended by the Care Act 2014, s 117. See discussion in M Taylor, 'Legal Bases for Disclosing Confidential Patient Information for Public Health' (2015) 23(3) *Med Law Rev* 348.

the Minister was required to consult on any regulations to be made under Section 60.[83] CAG approval is subject to review every twelve months.

The COVID-19 pandemic saw the rare invocation of regulation 3 of COPI in England and Wales, which deals with the processing of information for public health protection without an individual's explicit consent.[84] In compliance with regulation 3(4), the Secretary of State, informed by the independent advice of the CAG, served notices that certain NHS organisations would be required to process confidential patient information.[85] The purposes referred to in the notices were widely framed, encompassing research, planning, managing and understanding COVID-19, support for NHS Test and Trace, and 'identifying and understanding information about patients or potential patients with or at risk of COVID-19'. Regulation 4 provides that:

> Anything done by a person that is necessary for the purpose of processing confidential patient information in accordance with these Regulations shall be taken to be lawfully done despite any obligation of confidence owed by that person in respect of it.

In accordance with regulation 7, safeguards included regular review and undertakings that the NHS will control the data and limit use of identifiable data where possible. Data protection legislation continues to apply. The *BMJ* reported that some GPs posted privacy notices on their websites, typically stating:

> In order to look after your healthcare needs during this difficult time, we may urgently need to share your personal information, including medical records, with clinical and non-clinical staff who belong to organisations that are permitted to use your information and need to use it to help deal with the covid-19 pandemic.
>
> This could (amongst other measures) consist of either treating you or a member of your family and enable us and other healthcare organisations to monitor the disease, assess risk and manage the spread of the disease. Please be assured that we will only share information and health data that is necessary to meet yours and public healthcare needs.[86]

Others did not, and we fear that many patients were oblivious to the potentially wide-ranging access to their medical records during the pandemic.

[83] The CAG also advises the Health Research Authority on the use of confidential patient information.

[84] On regs 3 (public health protection) and 5 (public health improvement) see MJ Taylor, 'Legal Bases for Disclosing Confidential Patient Information for Public Health: Distinguishing Between Health Protection and Health Improvement' (2015) 23(3) *Med Law Rev* 348.

[85] See DHSC, *Coronavirus (COVID-19): Notice under Regulation 3(4) of the Health Service (Control of Patient Information) Regulations 2002 – General* (2020) 20 March. (One of several notices: the latest, at the time of writing, is set to expire in June 2022.)

[86] C Dyer, 'Covid-19: Rules on Sharing Confidential Patient Information are Relaxed in England' (2020) 369 *BMJ* m1378.

5.10 Disclosure in the public interest

As we have seen, the case-law makes it clear that the public interest can justify disclosure of confidential information without consent.[87] Article 8(2) sets out a list of exceptions to the right to respect for privacy, a list that, at first sight, looks broad enough to encompass a host of exceptions to the rule. So we need to examine carefully just when a competing public interest is sufficient to outweigh the public interest in medical confidentiality. The GMC explains the public interest in disclosure as designed 'to protect the individual or society from risks of serious harm, such as serious communicable diseases or serious crime or to enable medical research education or other secondary uses of information that will benefit society over time'.[88] We deal with the use of information for research and other secondary purposes in Chapter 18. Our focus here is on disclosure to protect individuals and society from harm. The doctor is faced with a balancing exercise weighing the harm done to the patient and the public trust by breaching confidence against the harm posed to others by the patient if he fails to act. A simple example will illustrate the point. A patient whose sight is failing and who has had several mini strokes insists on continuing to drive. She refuses to accept that she is medically unfit to drive, or to contact the Driver and Vehicle Licensing Agency (DVLA). She poses a risk of death or injury to other road users whenever she is out on the road. The GMC advises doctors that in such a case they not only may, but should, contact the DVLA.

5.11 Serious crime

An obvious example of a public interest justifying breach of confidence is the prevention of crime. But does this include any suspicion of a criminal offence that a doctor may learn of in the course of caring for his patients? When may, or must, doctors inform the police about criminal conduct on the part of a patient? If fifteen years after the event, a depressed patient, plagued by guilt, confesses to non-violent crimes committed in her youth, is her doctor obliged to inform on her? Contrary to popular myth, a doctor is under no general obligation to contact the police. Unless a statute specifically so provides, a doctor does not commit any offence by failing to tell the police of any evidence they may have come across professionally which suggests that a patient may have committed, or is contemplating, some crime.[89] A criminal offence is usually committed only when a doctor or anyone else accepts money to conceal evidence of crime.[90] Section 19 of the Terrorism Act 2000 imposes a duty on everyone, including doctors, to inform the police if they believe or suspect certain offences concerning funding terrorist activity have been committed. And section 26 of the Counter-Terrorism and Security Act 2015 introduced a

87 See in particular *X v Y* [1988] 2 All ER 648 and *W v Egdell* [1990] 1 All ER 835, CA.
88 GMC, *Confidentiality*, para 22.
89 Criminal Law Act 1967, s 5(5).
90 Ibid, s 5(1).

new 'prevent' duty incumbent on NHS Trusts and Foundation Trusts requiring mechanisms to refer cases appropriately where there is evidence of a risk of radicalisation. There are several Acts of Parliament that require doctors to disclose information if asked to do so by police,[91] but they are not compelled to volunteer that information.

If a doctor has reason to believe that the patient or a third party may commit a serious crime placing others at risk then, as with Dr Egdell, the doctor may lawfully contact the police or other appropriate authorities. So if a doctor makes a judgement that a new mother with acute post-natal depression is likely to harm her baby and he cannot persuade her to seek help, he acts lawfully in contacting social services and even in extreme cases the police and/or her family to protect the child. Many disclosures to prevent crime will, however, entail a breach of confidence with someone other than the 'criminal'. A rape victim refuses to go to the police but the evidence of the brutal attack on her indicates that other women may be at risk. In such cases, disclosure may be justifiable and the GMC advises doctors that if others are at risk from offenders using weapons or from domestic violence then the patient's refusal to involve the police may be overridden.[92]

What of cases where the public interest is not so much in the prevention of crime, but in the detection or prosecution of crime? The Serious Crimes Act 2015, sections 70–75 requires health and social care professionals to report cases of female genital mutilation in girls under eighteen. In many other cases, the choice remains the doctor's. In the context of confidential relationships outside the medical field, some case-law would suggest that the public interest justifies disclosure of *any* crime or misdeed committed or contemplated.[93] Within the doctor–patient relationship, freedom to disclose in the public interest should be more limited in scope. Doctors who suspect that another person is at risk of physical injury at their patient's hands must be free to act to protect that person. Preventing harm to others outweighs the private and public interests in confidentiality. The GMC advises that disclosure is defensible in relation to serious crime,[94] 'especially crimes against the person'. What the doctor should not do is hand over to the police information on each and every patient who transgresses the law. In *Re C*[95] a doctor and his colleague argued that their reputation had been damaged by 'misinformed press reporting'. They sought disclosure of a patient's medical records to set the record straight. Munby P refused their application, which would constitute an unjustifiable breach of the patient's confidentiality that could not be justified in the public interest. Parliament has legislated in numerous cases to compel breach of medical confidence. The courts should not be zealous to add to that list.

91 For example, the Road Traffic Act 1988, s 172 (information identifying the driver of a car involved in a road traffic collision).
92 GMC, *Confidentiality*, paras 65–66.
93 *Initial Services Ltd v Putterill* [1968] 1 QB 396, 405.
94 GMC, *Confidentiality*, paras 64–65.
95 *Re C (A Child) (Application by Dr X and Y)* [2015] EWFC 79.

The flaw in this argument is whether a doctor found to be in breach of confidence for disclosing a crime could be condemned by a court for taking steps to combat crime, performing a moral duty cast on every citizen. The doctor is distinguished from other citizens by the presence of a positive legal duty to his patient. Enforcing his duty to his patient benefits the public as well as the patient. Medical confidentiality is at the root of good healthcare. Should the courts, however, find that as upholders of the law they cannot condemn those who help bring lawbreakers to justice, the alternative solution is to fall back on the professional standard set by the GMC, and hold that breach of confidence is justified only in case of serious crime. The doctor may not break the law if he discloses details of petty crimes. He may be held accountable for professional misconduct. The legal and ethical standards do not need to be exactly the same.

5.12 Serious communicable diseases

Section 11 of the Public Health (Control of Disease) Act 1984 requires doctors to notify the proper authorities about certain infectious diseases but can doctors go further and warn those individuals who might be at risk from a patient with a serious communicable disease? May a GP alert a wife to the fact that her husband is HIV positive? The GMC advises that doctors *may* (not must) disclose such information to known sexual contacts.[96] Doctors are urged to do all they can to persuade the infected person to inform sexual partners. If persuasion fails, then the doctor should consider whether they should inform any sexual partner at risk of infection. Would the law support a doctor who did so? In defamation a defence protects any communication which the maker has a duty to impart and the recipient a legitimate interest in receiving. This defence does not apply in breach of confidence.[97] Here, the defence is that the public interest demands disclosure. Where a genuine risk of physical danger, injury or disease is posed to any third party, the public interest in individual security is sufficient to justify disclosure to that person so that they can protect themselves appropriately. Risk of harm must be established.[98] A simple belief that someone else, spouse or relative, is entitled to information is insufficient, even if they have an interest, and not merely a prurient interest, in the matters at stake.[99] The balance of public interest in favour of preserving confidentiality should be displaced only by a significant danger of physical harm.

And what of the risk a doctor may pose to patients? As we have seen in *X v Y*, the judge granted an injunction banning an account in the media of two

[96] GMC, *Confidentiality: Disclosing Information about Serious Communicable Diseases* (2017), para 13.

[97] Law Commission, *Breach* of *Confidence*, paras 6-94–6-96.

[98] It was not established in the Irish case of *Child and Family Agency v AA* [2018] IEHC 112: A Mulligan, 'Patient Confidentiality and Disclosure of HIV Status: Disentangling the Entitlement to Disclose from the Duty to Warn' (2021) 29(4) *Med Law Rev* 688.

[99] For example, that a parent might want to know if an adult daughter was HIV positive in order to offer her support but that interest, however caring it might be, will not suffice.

GPs diagnosed as HIV positive on the basis that the risk to patients in that case was negligible. There was no public interest in disclosure founded on the protection of others. That does not mean that it is never in the public interest to disclose information relating to individuals who have a serious communicable disease and pose a risk of transmission to others. It is not uncommon for surgeons to cut themselves in the course of surgery so that there is blood-to-blood contact between surgeon and patient. Certain forms of surgery, now styled exposure-prone procedures, carry a risk of cross-infection.[100] Such a risk is not limited to HIV. Hepatitis B[101] for instance is much more infectious than HIV but transmitted in the same manner. Other diseases with different modes of transmission may endanger patients, for example a health worker with untreated TB places all their patients at risk. The GMC gives very specific guidance[102] to doctors treating fellow health workers whose own ill health may endanger their patients either because they suffer from disease that they might pass on to patients or because their judgement or performance may be impaired, e.g., by the onset of a neurodegenerative disease. First, the affected worker has an obligation to seek and follow advice to protect their patients,[103] but if they fail to do so the doctor treating them *should* inform the health worker's employers or contracting body, or where appropriate the relevant regulator.[104] When there is a real risk of transmission of disease or a health professional's illness renders them unsafe to practise, the public interest in patient safety prevails, and the doctor acts lawfully in bringing the risk to the attention of those authorities charged to protect patient welfare.[105]

5.13 Freedom of the press

We have seen that exceptionally doctors may disclose information about patients with serious communicable diseases to protect others. The common law and Article 8(2) prioritise the protection of those others. What effect, however, does Article 10 of the ECHR have in such cases? Can the media rely on the right to freedom of expression in making public debates about burning issues that could compromise patient confidentiality? Openly identifying an individual healthcare worker who is HIV positive is highly unlikely to be lawful. A more difficult question arose in *H (A Healthcare Worker) v Associated Newspapers Ltd and N (A Health Authority)*.[106] H tested positive for HIV

100 For guidance on managing the risk of transmission from worker to patient see Public Health England, *HIV-Infected Healthcare Workers and Exposure Prone Procedures* (2014).

101 M Brazier and J Harris, 'Public Health and Private Lives' (1996) 4 *Med Law Rev* 171.

102 GMC, *Confidentiality: Disclosing Information about Serious Communicable Diseases* (2017), paras 5–6.

103 GMC, *Good Medical Practice* (2013), paras 28–29.

104 Ibid, para 25.

105 GMC, *Confidentiality: Disclosing Information about Serious Communicable Diseases* (2017), para 6.

106 [2002] Lloyd's Rep Med 210, CA.

while working as a health professional for a health authority, identified in court proceedings only as N. The health authority proposed to carry out a 'look back' exercise to notify patients treated by H and invite them to undergo HIV testing if they so chose. H sought an injunction to prevent N from notifying his patients and carrying out the 'look back' study. He provided details of at least some of his NHS patients with the utmost reluctance, and refused to supply any information about his private patients. H argued that, in his particular case, the risk to patients of HIV was so low that it did not justify breach of his or his patients' clinical confidentiality.

Before H's case against the health authority could be heard, the *Mail on Sunday* heard about the case. The newspaper planned to publish a story about H's condition and his dispute with the health authority. He sought a second injunction to prevent publication of any details identifying him personally or identifying either the health authority that employed him or his medical specialty. A temporary injunction was granted to him in the terms he sought. The newspaper retaliated with the headline 'Judge's Gag over Aids Threat to Patients'.

Gross J upheld the ban on publishing details of H's identity but would have allowed publication of the health authority's identity and H's specialty. H appealed. He argued that if the nature of his specialty and the name of his employing authority were in the public domain, he himself would be readily identifiable by a significant number of people, including some of his patients. The Court of Appeal acknowledged that H's case involved a difficult balancing exercise. They concluded that a ban on identifying the health authority should be imposed. Disclosing N's (the health authority's) identity would be likely to 'set in train a course of events' that could result in disclosure of H's identity and compromise his first action against the health authority to prevent the health authority conducting the 'look back' study. Patients might also be harmed by discovering the risk to themselves without immediate access to proper advice and counselling. The appeal court, however, was not convinced that a ban on identifying H's specialty was necessary. Such a restraint would inhibit legitimate debate on a matter of public interest. The Court of Appeal in *H* granted more weight to the interest in freedom of expression and public debate about the risks of HIV transmission and infected health workers than Rose J did in *X v Y*.

The influence of Article 10 of the ECHR (guaranteeing freedom of expression) is plainly seen in *Press Association v Newcastle upon Tyne Hospitals Foundation Trust*,[107] when the Court of Protection lifted reporting restrictions after the death of a Jehovah's Witness who had refused a blood transfusion. However, in *W v M (An Adult Patient)*[108] the mother, sister and partner of a woman in a minimally conscious state indicated they would be likely to drop

[107] [2014] EWCOP 6. See 5.3 above.
[108] [2011] EWHC 1197 (COP).

their case if the press intruded on their privacy. The Court of Protection had to consider whether it was lawful to withhold M's artificial nutrition, so the matter was clearly of public importance. Baker J held that the claims under Article 8 of M and her family took priority over Article 10 rights of freedom of expression and reporting restrictions were imposed.

5.14 Genetic information and confidentiality[109]

Especially difficult questions touching on medical privacy arise in relation to genetic and genomic testing and counselling, which can be arranged through the NHS, privately or 'direct-to-consumer' in order to discover health predispositions and sometimes traits and ancestry. This is a complex subject which we can give only cursory attention.[110] Genetics refers to the study of genes (heredity), and genomics to the study of the combined influence of a person's genes. NHS England has committed to sequencing 500,000 whole genomes by 2024 to better understand genetic disorders. The NHS Genomic Medicine Service was launched in 2018 to work toward equitable access to testing and to integrate genomic medicine into routine NHS care by 2025, and in 2020 the Genome UK strategy was launched 'to cement the UK's status as a global leader in genomics'.[111]

Because our genes are inherited, there are often familial implications to testing. Genomic testing of babies can help obtain a diagnosis but can also reveal incidental findings raising difficult questions about what and when to tell parents and the growing child.[112] In older patients, too, testing can reveal unexpected findings, can relate to future rather than current health implications and can give information that is predictive and uncertain. Professional guidance updated in 2019 sums up the dilemma:

> Providing the tested person with a right of veto over communicating such information may be unsound because it does not take sufficient account of the familial aspects of genetics. At the same time, respecting confidential information is an important aspect of clinical practice, and is vital in securing public trust and confidence in healthcare.[113]

109 See generally, M Taylor, *Genetic Data and the Law: A Critical Perspective on Privacy Protection* (2012) Cambridge University Press.

110 See further 18.18 below. And see E Jackson, *Medical Law: Text Cases and Materials* (5th edn, 2019) Oxford University Press, ch 9.

111 UK Government, *Genome UK: The Future of Healthcare* (2020) 26 September.

112 See Joint Committee on Genomics in Medicine, *Genetic Testing in Childhood* (2022); Nuffield Council on Bioethics, *Whole Genome Sequencing of Babies* (2018) London.

113 Royal College of Physicians, Royal College of Pathologists and British Society for Genetic Medicine, *Consent and Confidentiality in Genomic Medicine: Guidance on the Use of Genetic and Genomic Information in the Clinic* (3rd edn, 2019), p 8. And see Joint Committee on Genomics in Medicine, *Genetic Testing in Childhood* (2022).

Article 10(2) of the Oviedo Bioethics Convention states:

> Everyone is entitled to know any information collected about his or her health. However, the wishes of individuals not to be so informed shall be observed.[114]

Uncertainty surrounding the extent of the right not to know, its conceptual origins and relevance beyond genetics – to end-of-life care and healthcare research, for example – are the subject of much debate.[115]

One dilemma is this: If the patient tests positive for the BRCA 1 gene there is a 50 per cent chance that any sister of hers will also carry the gene and women with the gene are at 80–85 per cent risk of developing breast cancer. Regular screening and even an elective mastectomy can reduce the risk substantially. In this example it seems more likely that informing the sister at risk is justifiable to avoid serious harm as her health and life are at stake.[116] But what if the patient does not want this to happen?

GMC guidance suggests that in rare cases the doctor may overrule the patient's refusal to share information with relatives at risk of death of serious harm.[117] Could the doctor who decides the question of this conflict of duty in the patient's favour be at risk of a lawsuit if the risk of harm to someone else materialises?[118] In *ABC v St George's Healthcare NHS Trust and others*, a father, who was being treated under the Mental Health Act 1983, and his pregnant daughter attended joint family therapy sessions arranged by the second defendant, South West London NHS Trust. Out of respect of the father's wishes, his daughter was not informed of his diagnosis with the highly penetrant and incurable dominant genetic condition, Huntington's disease. When the daughter was inadvertently told about the diagnosis she was tested. Four months after the birth of her baby she was sadly found to carry the Huntington's gene. She brought a claim for wrongful birth. Had she known of the risk to her unborn child of inheriting the condition, she argued that she would have terminated the pregnancy.

The Court of Appeal[119] held that the daughter could potentially be owed a duty of care by the father's doctors if there was a sufficiently proximal relationship,

114 Convention for the Protection of Human Rights and Dignity of the Human Being with regard to the Application of Biology and Medicine: Convention on Human Rights and Biomedicine, Oviedo, 4 April 1997.

115 See R Chadwick, M Levitt and D Shickle (eds), *The Right to Know and the Right Not to Know: Genetic Privacy and Responsibility* (2014) Cambridge University Press.

116 See K O'Donovan and R Gilbar, 'The Loved Ones: Families Intimates and Patient Autonomy' (2003) *Legal Studies* 353.

117 GMC, *Confidentiality*, paras 73–76.

118 See the USA case *Tarasoff v Regents of University of California* (1976) 551 P 2d 334 (student medical centre at the University of California held liable for failing to warn a young woman of the risk posed to her by one of their patients).

119 [2017] EWCA Civ 336. See R Gilbar and C Foster, 'It's arrived! Relational Autonomy Comes to Court: *ABC v St George's Healthcare NHS Trust* [2017] EWCA 336, (2018) 26(1) *Med Law Rev* 125.

notwithstanding policy arguments to the contrary that a duty to 'third parties' could undermine trust and open the floodgates. The case was sent back to the High Court to determine the issue.[120] There, Mrs Justice Yip ruled that the second defendant, South West London NHS Trust, owed a duty of care because of their close relationship with the daughter which flowed from the therapy sessions. It was fair, just and reasonable for the Trust to balance the risks of disclosure and non-disclosure. But because this balance had been undertaken reasonably and responsibly, in this instance there was no breach.

ABC makes clear that the duty of confidentiality is not absolute and equally clear that the reasons for overruling confidentiality must be strong. There is no special law in the field of genetics: no recognition of an all-encompassing duty to prevent harm to third parties. But the case reiterates the importance of balancing the ethical duties to patients and others. Heather Widdows[121] has argued that individualistic ethical frameworks are flawed in the context of genetics – a view shared by an increasing number of ethicists. Lucassen and Parker have proposed a solution to the dilemmas posed by familial interests in genetic information.[122] According to their 'joint account' model, some types of genetic information are akin to a joint bank account and one family member cannot bar access to another. Their model has found much support.[123]

5.15 Genetic privacy[124]

Genetic information also helps us note the limits of confidentiality and that it falls short of a guarantee of privacy. An obligation of confidentiality binds the recipient of the confidence to keep private information secret. Imagine this scenario. X undergoes genetic tests to establish whether they have a gene rendering them susceptible to breast cancer. The test proves positive. A potential employer or insurer seeks to ascertain if they have undergone such a test and to find out the results. Doctors breach confidence if they release test results without the patient's consent. So the employer or insurer will simply demand that information from the patient themselves. The patient is free to refuse to divulge the test results. The consequence will be that they are turned down for the job, or refused insurance. Their 'right' to privacy means little. Genetic information is becoming more and more important in everyday life as understanding of the role genetics play in disease increases. Knowledge will enable individuals to lower their risk by adapting their lifestyle. It is already possible for a person to have the whole of their genome sequenced.

120 *ABC v St George's Healthcare NHS Trust and others* [2020] EWHC 455 (QB).
121 H Widdows, *Connected Self: The Ethics and Governance of the Genetic Individual* (2013) Cambridge University Press.
122 A Lucassen and M Parker, 'Genetic Information: A Joint Account? (2004) 329 *BMJ* 165.
123 C Foster, J Herring and M Boyd, 'Testing the Limits of the "Joint Account" Model of Genetic Information: A Legal Thought Experiment (2015) 41(5) *J Med Ethics* 379.
124 See 18.18 below.

Could Article 8 establish a right to keep personal information secret and make it unlawful to ask X questions about genetic test results? Alas, an employee or insurer may seek to invoke one of the justifications for violating privacy set out in Article 8(2). In X's case, where what is established by tests is a susceptibility to breast cancer, a 'defence' based on the protection of the health or freedom of others invoked by an employer is unlikely to succeed. Were she a potential airline pilot with a genetic susceptibility to heart failure the balance of argument might be different. Another argument that might be advanced in X's particular case might be on protection of 'economic well-being'. Can employers or insurers be forced to take on poor risks? Note though that Article 8(2) speaks of the economic well-being of the country, not of individual businesses.

Being able to control access to genetic information is important and if employers and insurers have unrestricted access to genetic information, the risk arises of the creation of a genetic underclass who struggle to find work and cannot for example gain the life insurance that any sensible person wants before taking on a mortgage. UK insurance companies have agreed to a voluntary moratorium on seeking access to genetic test results in relation to life insurance policies worth less than £500,000.[125] In relation to policies above the higher thresholds, the only government test approved (at the time of writing) is for Huntington's.

Can a judge require genetic testing to help settle a dispute? In the case of *Birtles*, two sisters battled over their father's estate.[126] One of the sisters applied to make the other sister take a DNA test to see if she was the biological daughter of the deceased. HHJ Matthews held that three questions were relevant: (i) whether the test would be sufficiently accurate (ii) whether the court had jurisdiction, and (iii) whether it ought to make the order in all the circumstances of the case. She held that 'the inherent jurisdiction of the court extends to directing that a party to proceedings give a saliva sample by way of mouth swab for the purposes of establishing paternity in a case where paternity is in issue'.

Birtles was referred to in a clinical negligence case, *Paling (A Child) v Sherwood Forest Hospitals NHS FT.*[127] The claimant alleged that the doctor had failed to treat an infant's hypoglycaemia, leading to serious brain injury. The doctor applied for whole genome sequencing of the child and parents to rule out a one in four or five chance of a genetic cause. Master Sullivan refused the application, drawing a distinction between the degree of invasion into a person's private life of a blood test or genetic test for a specific syndrome, and genome sequencing. Whole genome sequencing is a significant invasion into a person's private life and would require strong justification. It was not justified given the genetic cause was merely possible though could potentially be justified if a specific genetic cause was suspected or the cause was unknown but likely genetic.

125 HM Govt, *Code on Genetic Testing and Insurance* (2018) October.
126 *Nield-Moir v Freemen (Re Birtles Deceased)* [2018] EWHC 299 (Ch).
127 [2021] EWHC 3266.

Should we have laws to protect genetic privacy? Section 45 of the Human Tissue Act 2004 already outlaws the taking and analysis of DNA samples without consent. Would it make sense to legislate more generally to safeguard medical privacy? As we shall see, the GDPR contains express provisions concerning genetic data. Article 4(13) defines genetic data and Article 9 prohibits the processing of genetic data with limited exceptions.[128]

5.16 The data protection regime

Medical information is further protected by a regime of data protection. The EU GDPR was approved by the EU Parliament in 2016 and came into force in 2018. The GDPR and domestic Data Protection Act 2018 replace the EU Data Protection Directive 95/46/EC 1995 and domestic Data Protection Act 1998, which had become outdated due to the digital revolution. The GDPR was transposed into UK law following the European Union (Withdrawal) Act 2018. The Government has set out proposals to replace both the (now UK) GDPR and the 2018 Act with a new 'UK Framework of Citizen Data Rights'.[129] The (potentially contradictory) aims are to maximise the potential of the lucrative digital sector by enhancing flexibility and to 'ensure that privacy is protected' by giving people better control of their data. At the time of writing proposals are at an early stage and, in this section, we focus on the existing regime.

Article 5 GDPR sets out six overarching principles of:

(1) Lawfulness, fairness and transparency
(2) Purpose limitation
(3) Data minimisation
(4) Accuracy
(5) Storage limitation
(6) Integrity and confidentiality

As is clear from the sixth principle, the focus of data protection complements the law on confidentiality. Whilst in some cases claims regarding breach of confidentiality and data protection rules may overlap, a key distinction lies in the focus of the GDPR on the regulation of 'processing' of 'personal data' that are recorded electronically or manually.[130] Confidentiality, on the other hand, extends also to oral communications between doctors and patients.

Data protection is geared toward reinforcing the rights of individuals, strengthening the EU internal market and enforcement, modernising international transfers of personal data, and driving global data protection standards. It protects citizens' personal information regardless of where it is sent, processed

128 Article 9(1)–(4).

129 I Duncan Smith, T Villiers and G Freeman, *Taskforce on Innovation, Growth and Regulatory Reform* (2021) May, pp 67–82. This led (as we go to press) to the Data Protection and Digital Information Bill 2022.

130 GDPR Article 2(1). And see *Scott v LGBT Foundation Ltd* [2020] EWHC 483 (QB) (strike out claim confirming that the data protection regime does not apply with respect to oral disclosures).

or stored, including outside of the EU. The GDPR endows every data subject with the right to lodge a complaint with a supervisory authority for alleged infringement of the GDPR and to an effective judicial remedy. Additionally, Member States were obliged to implement rules on penalties applicable to infringements that are effective, 'proportionate and dissuasive', and to take all necessary measures to ensure effective implementation.[131]

The scope of the GDPR is wide: 'personal data' are defined in Article 4(1) as 'any information relating to an identified or identifiable natural person', and, according to Article 4(2), data are 'processed'[132] where they are (*inter alia*) recorded, collected, organised, structured, stored, altered, disclosed, disseminated, erased or destroyed. Articles 15–17 protect rights to access, rectification and erasure and Article 32 protects data security. Personal data breaches must be communicated both to the relevant authority (Article 33) and to the data subject (Article 34).

In accordance with the first principle, personal data must be processed under one of six legal bases set out in Article 6:

(1) Consent for one or more specific purposes
(2) Contract
(3) Legal obligation
(4) Vital interests such as when processing is needed to protect someone's life
(5) Task in the public interest
(6) Legitimate interests (but this cannot apply to public authorities processing data to perform an official task)

The preferable legal basis will depend on factors such as which organisation is processing the data and the purpose for their use. Where 'consent' is relied upon as the legal basis to process personal data, Article 9 sets out additional protections that apply to personal health data, requiring that consent should be both unambiguous and explicit; implied consent will not suffice.[133] As we discuss at 18.17 below, the Health Research Authority has advised that the 'task in the public interest' rather than 'consent' is generally a preferred legal basis for processing data in health research. This is because of potential power imbalances between researchers and the data subjects and because the Article 9 requirements can limit some types of research. It should be noted that even if consent is not the chosen legal basis for processing under the data protection regime, it remains relevant to the common law duty of confidentiality set out above.[134]

131 Ibid, Art 84.

132 See *Johnson v Medical Defence Union* (2007) 96 BMLR 99.

133 Defined as 'personal data related to the physical or mental health of a natural person, including the provision of health care services, which reveal information about his or her health status': GDPR Article 4(15).

134 Differences between the consent requirements under the data protection regime where consent is the legal basis for processing, and the consent requirements under the law of confidentiality, are explored in detail in ES Dove and MJ Taylor, 'Signalling Standards for Progress: Bridging the Divide Between a Valid Consent

Article 17 of the GDPR grants individuals, under certain circumstances, the right to erasure ('right to be forgotten') of personal data.[135] For example, the ruling has implications for doctors who were once subject to an online complaint, disciplinary proceeding or investigation by the GMC which is revealed in a search of their names.

5.17 The Information Commissioner's Office (ICO)

In the UK, data controllers are under a duty to notify the Information Commissioner's Office (ICO) as well as individuals concerning data breaches that risk affecting individuals' rights. The 2018 Act increased the maximum penalties for regulatory breaches from £500,000 to £17 million and creates new offences to address emerging threats.[136]

The Information Commissioner's Office is charged with upholding information rights. It is largely funded by fees paid by organisations processing personal data which must register with the ICO. It operates a complaints procedure and acts against those who have broken the law. For example, in 2019, a GP practice manager was fined for sending personal data to her personal email account, and a pharmacy was fined £275,000 for leaving medical records in unlocked containers.[137] And in 2021 a Scottish charity was fined £10,000 for inadvertently sending an email to 105 people which included email addresses and names of a number of people which could lead to assumptions as to their HIV status or risk.[138]

Proposals to reform the ICO set out in 2021 seek to impose a clearer strategic vision, improved accountability mechanisms and a new commitment to focus on the most serious threats to public trust and inappropriate barriers to data use.[139] The Data Protection and Digital Information Bill 2022 seeks to rename the ICO the 'Information Commission' and render it more susceptible to Government influence.

5.18 Anonymised data

Most of what has been said so far relates to information from which the identity of the patient can be ascertained. For many purposes, however, anonymised

to Use Patient Data Under Data Protection Law and the Common Law Duty of Confidentiality' (2021) 29(3) *Med Law Rev* 411.

135 And see landmark Case C-131/12, *Google Spain SL, Google Inc v Agencia Española de Protección de Datos, Mario Costeja González* (13 May 2014).

136 Data Protection Act 2018, Pt 6.

137 ICO, 'Former NHS Manager Fined for Sending Personal Data to her Email Account' (2019) 5 April; ICO, 'Action We've Taken: Doorstep Dispensaree Ltd' (2019) 20 December.

138 ICO, 'ICO Warning After Scottish Charity Reveals Personal Data in Email Error' (2021) 22 October.

139 Department for Digital, Culture Media & Sport, *Data: A New Direction* (2021), ch 5.

data about patients and their diseases is needed or wanted by diverse organisations. The government is putting increasing amounts of information in the public domain. The Information Commissioner's Office has responded to the 'big data revolution' with a code of practice on anonymisation.[140] Anonymised information may be necessary to carry out clinical audits, or to compile statistics about health needs, or for epidemiological purposes. Many of us might applaud such purposes. Commercial organisations such as drug companies may also seek access to such information to help them with marketing or product development. The GMC gives extensive advice on anonymising data and its disclosure.[141] It urges doctors to explain to their patients how such data are used and what benefits flow from exchange of information. Does the duty of confidentiality apply to anonymised information? In *R v Department of Health, ex parte Source Informatics Ltd*[142] the Court of Appeal held that where data was lawfully obtained, confidence would not be breached where the confider's identity was not disclosed. Patients have no property in information about them. Ethical safeguards now surround anonymised data. The law focuses on controlling information about us where we can be identified.[143] GPs, pharmacists and drug companies may still profit from information derived from us.[144]

5.19 A new direction?

As mentioned above, as we go to press the Data Protection and Digital Information Bill 2022/23 builds on a 2021 Government Taskforce[145] to enhance growth, secure new jobs, transform public services, enhance the power of research and improve data flow for the benefit of society. The strategy, which extends beyond health data, builds on experiences in the COVID-19 pandemic when international data sharing enhanced scientific research and united countries in a shared common goal to combat the virus. If the Bill is enacted, it will reform data protection laws within the existing GDPR framework, by

140 ICO, *Anonymisation: Managing Data Protection Risk, Code of Practice* (2012).

141 See GMC, *Confidentiality*.

142 [1999] 4 All ER 185; [2000] 1 All ER 786, CA. See 18.17 below.

143 But see criticism of Source Informatics in D Beyleveld and E Histed, 'Betrayal in the Court of Appeal' (2000) 4(3–4) *Medical Law International* 277: 'The Court of Appeal's reasoning does not clarify the duty of confidence, but virtually abolishes it in the face of competing commercial and research interests.' And see S Pattinson, *Medical Law and Ethics* (6th edn, 2020) Sweet and Maxwell, 6–023 who argues the decision is subject to challenge and that in light of *Campbell*, 'there is surely no room for a narrow interpretation of privacy that is incompatible with the well-established approach to that article'.

144 See further discussion of *Department of Health v Information Commissioner* [2011] EWHC 1430 (Admin), at 18.17 below. And for a recent example see S Barr, 'Coronavirus App Criticised for Advertising Face Masks by Samantha Cameron's Fashion Label' *The Independent* (2020) 18 October: the ad reported that sales would fund COVID-19 research, but it provoked anger from some recipients.

145 I Duncan Smith, T Villiers and G Freeman, *Taskforce on Innovation, Growth and Regulatory Reform* (2021) May, pp 67–82.

amending the Data Protection Act 2018. One of the most important proposals is to redefine personal data, but any attempts to narrow the definition will be monitored for compatibility by the European Commission. Data flow with the EU is dependent on the UK offering an adequate degree of data protection so that additional transfer mechanisms are not sparked. The focus on removing barriers and burdens and increasing data flows has potential to benefit health but it could also undermine the right to privacy set out above and, with it, public trust that is fundamental to health research.

5.20 Custodians of health and care data

A series of arms-length bodies have been created to collate, analyse, disseminate and protect health data. The NHS Information Centre for Health and Social Care was replaced by the Health and Social Care Information Centre, which in turn was replaced by NHS Digital in 2016. NHS Digital became England's central source of health and social care information for secondary use. NHSX was added in 2019 to focus on digital transformation. In 2021 it was announced that both NHS Digital and NHSX will be axed, and their roles subsumed within NHS England, where digital transformation will remain high on the agenda.

The data released are designed to benefit the community by providing measurements for research, planning, commissioning, performance and success.[146] NHS Digital can require providers to return certain data, including confidential data,[147] which it then processes and publishes in the form of statistics, health indicators, reports and audits.[148] Confidential information can only be released where there is a legal basis for doing so. In all other cases, the data are processed in the secure environment of NHS Digital and published in a form which reduces or eradicates the risk of the patient being identified. Data dissemination is overseen by the Independent Group Advising on the Release of Data (IGARD). IGARD makes general recommendations and scrutinises the appropriateness of requests for dissemination of confidential information[149] including personal data, pseudonymised data, and aggregated data which does not have small numbers supressed. NHS Digital has issued a Code of Practice on confidential information,[150] setting out five rules:

(1) Confidential information about service users or patients should be treated confidentially and respectfully
(2) Members of a care team should share confidential information when it is needed for the safe and effective care of an individual

[146] See HSCIC, *Information and Technology for Better Care: HSCIC Strategy 2015–2020* (March 2015).
[147] Health and Social Care Act 2012, s 256.
[148] Ibid, s 260.
[149] As defined in the Health and Social Care Act 2012, s 263(2).
[150] Required by virtue of the Health and Social Care Act 2012, s 263: NHS Digital, *Code of Practice in Confidential Information* (version 1.0, 2014) (updated 2018).

(3) Information that is shared for the benefit of the community should be anonymised
(4) An individual's right to object to the sharing of confidential information about them should be respected
(5) Organisations should put policies, procedures and systems in place to ensure the confidentiality rules are followed.[151]

Interestingly, Rule 4 goes beyond the requirements of the Health and Social Care Act 2012, which attracted criticism for its failure to require consultation with patients (where practicable) where disclosure is not designed to benefit them directly.[152] The rules make an admirable attempt to re-state the complex and sometimes ambiguous legal provisions discussed in this chapter in a simple and applicable format. Naturally there are caveats explored in the Code. For example, Rules 1 and 4 are subject to any legal requirements to provide information. And Rule 3 is dependent on the level of anonymisation deemed necessary given the value of the data, the likelihood of re-identification and the risks posed by the environment into which the data are released. The Code differentiates between anonymised and de-identified information. In the latter case, the individual may be identifiable if controls are not put in place. The Code also recognises that there may be 'exceptional circumstances' where confidential information must be used but requires that there must be a legal basis for doing so (informed consent, legal obligation or disclosure in the public interest).

5.21 Secure data sharing

The digital transformation of the NHS has been slowed by reliance on pre-internet systems and split responsibility across different agencies and organisation. One of the greatest challenges is to securely share data.[153] A failure to share data across the team of health practitioners assisting a patient risks error, delay and discontinuity. The Health and Social Care (Safety and Quality Act) 2015 inserted into the Health and Social Care Act 2012 a new duty[154] incumbent on the care team to share information to facilitate patient care where it is in the patient's best interests.

Outside the remit of patient care, the sharing of confidential data has proved more controversial.[155] Health data are a valuable resource. Patient health data might be utilised for research, health improvement or commercial gain. Since the 1980s, information on hospital admission has been collated and since

151 NHS Digital, *A Guide to Confidentiality in Health and Social Care* (version 1.1, 2013).
152 See J Grace and M J Taylor, 'Disclosure of Confidential Patient Information and the Duty to Consult: The Role of the Health and Social Care Information Centre' (2013) 21 *Med Law Rev* 415.
153 See 4.1 above.
154 Health and Social Care Act 2012, s 251B.
155 See JL Bell, 'Governing Commercial Access to Health Data for Public Benefit: Charity Law Solutions' (2020) 28(2) *Med Law Rev* 247 (suggesting that concerns might be ameliorated if public benefit is promised through the involvement of charity organisations).

2018 NHS Digital operate a national programme allowing patients to opt out of their confidential patient information being used for research and planning. Efforts have been made to expand the database to primary care. NHS England commissioned the now defunct care.data programme in 2013. It faced controversy from its inception and was delayed and then paused pending a review by the then National Data Guardian for Health and Care, Dame Fiona Caldicott,[156] whereupon it was terminated. Though patients were permitted to opt out, communication by leaflets left patients inadequately informed. Events in 2021 suggest a failure to learn from the care.data debacle. A second attempt to harness GP data in the General Practice Data for Planning and Research Programme was marred by failures to listen to and engage with the public and providers. It was paused when distrust led to high numbers of opt outs.[157]

Ongoing initiatives to enhance infrastructure and workforce literacy are combined with investment to improve data linkage with the aim of transforming access to data for research, planning and direct care. But they are dependent on public trust which is in short supply. In 2017, personal data of 1.6 million patients was shared with DeepMind, a unit of Google, breaching Data Protection laws.[158] Patients also fear poor data security, particularly after the global WannaCry ransomware attack in 2017.[159]

5.22 Patients' access to records

We turn now to the opposite side of the coin. Patients expect their doctors to keep their secrets. Can doctors have secrets from their patients? The law relating to confidentiality prevents doctors from improperly disclosing information from or about their patients. What if the patient seeks information about themselves? When can a patient demand to see their records?

An attempt to assert a common law right of access to all health records failed in 1995.[160] Health records are not 'owned' by patients. Until 1998 the statutory picture was confusing. Access was governed by the Access to Medical Reports Act 1988 and the Access to Health Records Act 1990. The Data Protection Act 1998 simplified matters and today access is governed by the Data Protection Act 2018 and the GDPR.[161] Under the 2018 Act, patients have a *prima facie* right to access all of their health records whether manual or computerised, as well as supplementary data.[162] This is commonly

156 National Data Guardian for Health and Care, *Review of Data Security, Consent and Opt-Outs* (2016). Dame Fiona died in 2021. She dedicated her career to the protection of confidential patient records and their use.

157 DHSC, *Data Saves Lives* (2022).

158 Information Commissioner's Office, 'Royal Free – Google DeepMind Trial Failed to Comply with Data Protection Law' *ICO: News* (2017) 3 July.

159 M Field, 'WannaCry Cyber Attack Cost the NHS £92m as 19,000 Appointments Cancelled' *Telegraph* (2018) 18 October.

160 *R v Mid-Glamorgan Family Health Services ex p Martin* [1995] 1WLR 110.

161 Note that the Data Protection Act 2018, rather than the Freedom of Information Act 2000, governs access to personal data.

162 Data Protection Act 2018, Pt 4, ch 3 and GDPR, Article 15.

referred to as a Subject Access Request. Furthermore, the information must be provided free of charge, though a reasonable fee might be charged if the request is repetitive or is excessive or 'manifestly unfounded' – a term that is not defined in the legislation. Access can be denied in certain circumstances listed in Schedules 2 and 3 of the 2018 Act. One such exception applies if access would be 'likely to cause serious harm to the physical or mental health of the data subject or another individual'.[163] The 'appropriate health professional'[164] is responsible for forming an opinion as to the applicability of the serious harm test. Part 6 of the 2018 Act allows the patient to apply to the court, so a judge can decide if access has been improperly refused. An NHS England initiative allows patients registered at practices with compatible systems and who register with the NHS App to access any new entries in their health records.[165]

Finally, the access provisions of the Data Protection Act 2018 apply only to living patients. Consequently, a small part of the Access to Health Records Act 1990[166] is preserved to enable executors of a deceased person's estate or members of his family to gain access to his records in an appropriate case.

Access is only possible if the record still exists. Most records are destroyed after a period of time. Different records are kept for different lengths of time.[167] The retention period for most adult health hospital records is eight years. The retention period begins when a record is no longer operational, such as when the patient has been discharged from care or has died. GP records are usually kept until ten years after a patient has died. In the course of the UK Infected Blood Inquiry into infection with Hepatitis and HIV of men, women and children given contaminated blood and blood products, many who sought their health records to help understand what had happened found that they had been destroyed, prompting claims of a cover-up.[168]

163 Ibid, Sch 3, Pt 2, para 2(2).

164 The term 'appropriate health professional' is defined as 'the health professional who is currently or was most recently responsible for the diagnosis, care or treatment of the data subject in connection with the matters to which the data relates…'. Ibid, Sch 3, Pt 2, para 2(1).

165 NHS Digital, *Access to Patient Records through the NHS App* at www.digital.nhs.uk.

166 Access to Health Records Act 1990, s 3(1)(f). See *Re AB* [2020] EWHC 691 (Fam) (personal representatives could apply for access to medical records of a deceased person to arrange storage and use of the deceased's sperm / embryos – the right was not limited to circumstances where a claim arose from the deceased's death).

167 The Public Records Act 1958 governs the safekeeping and disposal of health (and other public) records and the Health and Social Care Act 2008, reg 17 requires secure maintenance of accurate, complete and detailed records (regulated by the CQC). The Consumer Protection Act 1987 requires records to be held as proof of an activity against the possibility of a claim. See NHSX, *Records Management Code of Practice* (2020).

168 C Dyer, 'Medical Records Were Destroyed in Infected Blood Cover-Up, Inquiry Hears' (2018) 362 *BMJ* k4108.

One of the aims of the GDPR is to improve access to data, for patients, researchers and carers alike. By creating a new 'digital single market', the Regulation aims to establish trust and confidence in e-services, improve enforcement of data protection and facilitate economic growth. But progress is slow. The law is several steps behind the brave new big data world.

Part II

MEDICAL MALPRACTICE

Chapter 6

AGREEING TO TREATMENT

6.1 Introduction

There would be little support today, even from the most paternalistic doctor,[1] for the proposition that a sick adult should be compelled to accept whatever treatment his doctor thought best. No one suggests that adults who stay away from dentists out of childlike fear and to the detriment of their dental and general health should be rounded up and marched to the nearest dental surgery for forcible treatment. Few would deny the right of the adult Jehovah's Witness to refuse a blood transfusion,[2] even if in doing so they forfeit their life. Medical treatment normally requires the agreement of the patient. The right of the patient, who is sufficiently rational and mature to understand what is entailed in treatment, to decide for themselves whether to agree to that treatment is a basic human right. The right to autonomy, to self-rule rather than rule by others, is endorsed by ethicists as a right to patient autonomy. Two of their Lordships in *Chester v Afshar*[3] signalled that a patient's right to autonomy and dignity should today be accorded the highest priority by English law. Lord Steyn declared that in 'modern law, paternalism no longer rules'.[4] In 2015, the United Kingdom Supreme Court swept away the last vestiges of legal endorsement of medical paternalism in *Montgomery v Lanarkshire Health Board*.[5] Patients consenting to treatment must as a general rule be given appropriate information about the risks and benefits of that treatment that a reasonable person in the patient's position would want to know. No longer are patients only entitled to be told what doctors think it is appropriate to tell them. The much criticised decision of the House of Lords in *Sidaway v Royal Bethlem Hospital*[6] is now consigned to history. Lord Kerr and Lord Reed declared that:

1 And certainly not from the General Medical Council (GMC). See their guidance to doctors; GMC, *Decision Making and Consent* (2020).

2 See *Jehovah's Witnesses of Moscow v Russia* (2011) 53 EHRR 4.

3 [2004] UKHL 4, [17] and [24].

4 Ibid, [16].

5 [2015] UKSC 11 (hereafter *Montgomery*).

6 [1985] 1 All ER 643.

> [P]atients are now widely regarded as persons holding rights, rather than as the passive recipients of the care of the medical profession. They are also widely treated as consumers exercising choices.[7]

This chapter considers the relatively easy case of adults with mental capacity. Such an adult has a right to determine what is done to their body. In Chapters 7 and 17, we look at the law in relation to patients lacking capacity and to children, and we also address circumstances where legislation may endorse compulsory medical treatment. A person who intentionally touches another against that other's will commits a trespass to that person just as much as coming uninvited on to the person's land is a trespass to their land. The tort of battery is committed. Where a person consents to a contact no battery is committed. So a boxer entering the ring cannot complain of battery when they are hit on the chin by their opponent. Battery is any non-consensual contact. Conduct which constitutes the tort of battery may also amount to the crime of assault. We should also note that contacts resulting in serious bodily harm may still constitute a *criminal* assault, even when such contacts are wholly consensual. English law does not allow you to consent to, for example, sado-masochistic practices that cause actual injury to you.[8] Any such 'injury' must be justified by some good purpose. Medical treatment and surgery are acknowledged to be such purposes.[9] So, more controversially, are 'manly sports', thus justifying the boxers' mutual exchange of blows.[10] There remains a question of whether any kind of maverick or extreme 'surgery' might be beyond the privilege usually accorded to medicine and surgery.[11]

How do the rules relate to doctors? Any doctor examining a patient, or injecting or operating on a patient, makes contact with that patient's body. Normally the doctor commits no wrong because they do so with the patient's agreement. Should they fail to obtain a patient's agreement, or should a doctor force themselves on a patient, they commit the tort of battery, and the crime of assault.[12] Not only does the doctor infringe on their patient's autonomy, they also violate the patient's bodily integrity.[13] That crude scenario is unlikely, but

7 *Montgomery*, [75].

8 *R v Brown* [1993] UKHL 19.

9 See *Attorney General's Reference (No 6 of 1980)* [1981] 2 All ER 1057; Law Commission, *Consent in the Criminal Law* (1995) Consultation Paper No 139.

10 See *R v Coney* (1882) 8 QBD 534.

11 For example, extreme 'cosmetic' surgery involving amputation or gross facial disfigurement. See D Griffiths and A Mullock, 'The Medical Exception and Cosmetic Surgery: Culpable Doctors and Harmful Enhancement?' in S Fovargue and A Mullock (eds), *Transforming Wrong(s) into Right(s): The Power of 'Proper Medical Treatment'* (2015) Routledge. And see S Pattinson, *Law at the Frontiers of Biomedicine* (2023) Hart, chapter 5 on cybernetic biohacking.

12 See recently the findings of the inquiry into to the conduct of Ian Paterson, a breast surgeon who subjected patients to needless operations and was convicted of wounding with intent: *Report of the Independent Inquiry into the Issues raised by Paterson* (HC 31) (2020) (chair: Rev'd Graham James), discussed further at 10.7 below.

13 And so breaches Article 8 of the Human Rights Convention: see *Glass v United Kingdom* [2004] 1 FLR 1019, ECtHR; *Juhnke v Turkey* (2009) 49 EHRR 24, ECtHR.

not unknown. In *Border v Lewisham and Greenwich NHS Trust*[14] the claimant had a suspected broken arm and the doctor treating her in Casualty proposed to insert a cannula in her other arm. The claimant objected forcefully, worried that, as she had recently had lymph nodes removed, she might develop oedema. The doctor considered other options unviable and went ahead with the insertion of the cannula. The Court of Appeal held that in the absence of consent the insertion of the cannula inexorably led to a finding of breach of duty. What of the surgeon who correctly decides to treat cancer of the bone in the right leg by amputating that leg, but by error amputates the wrong leg, the left leg? Once the error is discovered the poor patient has to endure a further operation to remove the right leg. Or a patient's notes are mixed up and a woman who was scheduled for and consented to an appendectomy is given a hysterectomy. Both unfortunate victims can sue the surgeon in battery, because they did not consent to the operation performed. In a Canadian case, a woman who expressed her wish to be injected in her right arm was injected by the doctor in her left. She sued in battery and succeeded.[15]

In all the above examples, the surgeon or some other member of the hospital staff has been careless, so the patient could normally sue in negligence too. However, there are differences between the two torts. In battery, a patient need not establish any tangible injury, because the actionable injury is the uninvited invasion of his body. This is important. A doctor may, on medically unchallengeable grounds, decide that an operation is in the patient's best interests and proceed with the treatment. The patient's health may then improve. Yet if the operation was done without consent, a battery has still been committed. A doctor who discovered that his patient's womb was ruptured while performing minor gynaecological surgery was held liable to her for going ahead and sterilising her there and then, because she had not agreed to sterilisation.[16] A woman whose ovaries were removed without her express consent similarly recovered damages for battery.[17] The essence of the wrong of battery is the unpermitted contact. There is no requirement that the patient prove that if they had been asked to consent to the relevant treatment they would have refused, which in many respects makes it a more attractive proposition for a potential patient litigant than pursuing an action in negligence.

These cases can be contrasted with *Connolly v Croydon Health Service NHS Trust*.[18] Mrs Connolly claimed a battery had occurred when treatment was continued despite her withdrawal of consent. She consented to an angiography to investigate angina and was informed of the risk of complications. During the procedure it became apparent that there was a potentially life-threatening problem, and an angioplasty was performed. This caused significant pain and

14 [2015] EWCA Civ 8.

15 *Allan v New Mount Sinai Hospital* (1980) 109 DLR (3d) 536.

16 *Devi v West Midlands* AHA [1980] 7 CL 44. And see *Williamson v East London and City Health Authority* [1998] Lloyd's Rep Med 6 (woman consented to removal of breast implants but not to a mastectomy).

17 *Bartley v Studd* (1995) 2(8) *Medical Law Monitor* 1 (the surgeon was disciplined by the GMC).

18 [2015] EWHC 1339 (QB).

Mrs Connolly demanded that the procedure cease. Judge Collender QC held that she lacked capacity to withdraw consent at the relevant time and had not in fact done so. Had she maintained capacity she could in theory have made a valid withdrawal of consent to the procedure. As it was, her initial consent protected the doctors from an action in battery.

Two further points should be noted. Battery may be alleged by a patient who *says* they did not consent. First, on whom does the onus of proof lie? It has been held in England that the onus of proof lies on the patient in that they must establish that they did not agree.[19] Second, for what will the patient be compensated? In negligence, we shall see that a defendant is only liable for the kind of damage which they reasonably ought to foresee. In battery, the test is more favourable to patients. The defendant may be liable for all the damage which can factually be shown to flow from their wrongdoing. A doctor who injected a patient in the 'wrong' arm would be liable in battery *and* negligence for any unwanted stiffness in that arm, and for any adverse reaction which they ought to have contemplated in view of the patient's history. They would not be liable in negligence for a 'freak' reaction, but in battery they might be so liable. Nonetheless judges in England have sought to limit the scope of battery when it overlaps with negligence, mainly because they have sought to avoid subjecting a surgeon to liability in battery.[20]

A significant disadvantage with the tort of battery as a means of vindicating patients' rights was that for a claim to lie in battery traditionally there had to be direct *physical* contact between doctor and patient. A patient who agreed to take a drug orally, having been totally misled as to the nature of the drug, could not sue in battery. Had the doctor injected them with that self-same drug, a claim in battery would lie. Recently the courts have developed the criminal law to allow prosecution for causing grievous bodily harm where no direct physical contact took place,[21] leading to the possibility that if a doctor deceived a patient into taking a dangerous drug that made her seriously ill, the doctor could face criminal charges.[22]

6.2 Emergencies

What of the patient not in a fit state to give or communicate consent themselves? When the patient is unconscious,[23] treatment may have to be given

19 *Freeman v Home Office* [1984] 2 WLR 130.

20 See C Beuermann, 'Are the Torts of Trespass to the Person Obsolete? Part 2: Continued Evolution' (2018) 26 *Tort Law Review* 6.

21 *R v Ireland and Burstow* [1998] AC 147, HL; *R v Dica* [2004] 3 All ER 593, CA. Note the Domestic Abuse Act 2021, s 71 restates *R v Brown* and *R v Dica* for the purposes of establishing that consent to serious harm for sexual gratification is not a defence, and relevant exceptions.

22 See Law Commission, *Reform of Offences against the Person: A Scoping Consultation Paper* (2014) Consultation Paper 217, para 2.13.

23 Or otherwise unable to give or withdraw consent due to a lack of capacity. See discussion of *Connolly v Croydon Health Service NHS Trust* [2015] EWHC 1339 (QB) at 6.1 above.

immediately, before the patient can be revived and consulted. They may have been wheeled into Casualty after an accident. They may have agreed to operation X, in the course of which the surgeon discovers a rampaging tumour needing immediate excision. Where there is no available evidence of the patient's own wishes in such circumstances, section 5 of the Mental Capacity Act 2005 grants to doctors a general authority to act in the best interests of the patient and do whatever is immediately necessary to preserve the life and prevent any deterioration in their health.[24] The bystanders who rush to the aid of the unconscious accident victim and administer first aid, and the ambulance crew who bring them into Casualty, are equally protected from any claim in battery. This is the case even if the patient has attempted suicide.[25] Additionally, some patients with a mental health disorder are eligible for detention for assessment and treatment under the Mental Health Act 1983 without their agreement, even if they retain mental capacity.[26] Adults of sound mind, however, have a right to refuse life-sustaining treatment.[27]

Once the immediate threat to a patient's life has passed, other decisions may have to be taken before they regain consciousness. In practice, when a patient is unconscious or otherwise incapable of consenting to treatment themselves, the response of the hospital staff is to consult, when possible, with the patient's relatives or friends. What legal validity has a consent given by the relatives of an adult? The answer is none. Consulting relatives is courteous, but is legally significant solely in that as a matter of evidence it establishes that the doctor's consideration of the patient's best interests has been adequately informed as required by the Mental Capacity Act 2005, which stipulates that when forming an opinion on best interests, a decision-maker must take into account, amongst other things, the views of anyone engaged in caring for the person or interested in his welfare.[28]

One difficult problem arises when some (but inconclusive) evidence is forthcoming about the unconscious patient's own wishes. Consider, for example, a patient who is wheeled into hospital unconscious and needs an immediate blood transfusion. His wife says, truthfully, that he is a Jehovah's Witness and would refuse a transfusion. Can the doctor lawfully give a transfusion? The procedure is necessary, but the doctor knows the patient would be likely to refuse it. In *Malette v Shulman*,[29] a Canadian case, a young woman was brought unconscious into Casualty. She carried with her a card clearly stating that she was a Jehovah's Witness and that she would in no circumstances consent to a blood transfusion even if her life was in danger. The Canadian court held that the doctor who administered a transfusion committed a battery. There was in that case no question that the patient had taken pains to ensure that no doctor should be in doubt of her refusal of blood in any contingency.

[24] GMC, *Decision Making and Consent* (2020), para 63. See also 7.8 below.
[25] See J Herring, *The Right to Be Protected from Committing Suicide* (2022) Hart.
[26] See 7.19 below.
[27] *Re T (Adult: Refusal of Medical Treatment)* [1992] 4 All ER 649, CA.
[28] See Mental Capacity Act 2005, s 4(7).
[29] (1988) 63 OR (2d) 243 (Ontario High Court).

Attempts to argue that a refusal of treatment must be 'informed' by knowledge of the actual circumstances of treatment were rejected.[30] In the next section we will look at *Re T*,[31] where the English Court of Appeal overruled an apparent objection by T to a transfusion. The facts of the cases are markedly different as the evidence T truly and independently objected to transfusion was shaky, whereas Mrs Malette's convictions were beyond doubt. Sections 24 and 25 of the Mental Capacity Act 2005 now provide for a formal means of making an advance decision to refuse treatment. The Act requires that such an advance decision must be both in writing and witnessed.[32] However, in *Newcastle upon Tyne Hospitals Foundation Trust v LM*[33] the judge was satisfied that the informal, unwritten evidence that LM would never have agreed to a transfusion sufficed to require that her wishes be respected.

6.3 A right to say no?

Will the law ever set limits to a competent adult's right to refuse treatment? Are we free to reject life-saving treatment which others might consider it 'wicked folly'[34] to refuse? The theory is clear. In *Re T (Adult: Refusal of Medical Treatment)*,[35] Lord Donaldson declared that an adult patient 'has an absolute right to choose whether to consent to medical treatment, to refuse it or to choose one rather than another of the treatments being offered'.[36] Such an absolute right to autonomy 'exists notwithstanding that the reasons for making the choice are rational, or irrational, unknown or even non-existent'. In *Re T*, a young woman of 20 had suffered serious injuries in a road accident. She was thirty-four weeks pregnant and consented to a Caesarean section on the following day. Later that evening she was visited by her mother, a devout Jehovah's Witness. T was not herself a baptised Witness. After her mother's visit, T told doctors that she would not agree to any blood transfusion before or during surgery. She first enquired whether alternatives to whole blood were available, and was assured that such alternatives exist. She was given a form to sign evidencing her refusal of transfusion and absolving the hospital from liability for failing to administer blood should she haemorrhage. After delivery of a stillborn child, T lapsed into a coma and suffered life-threatening internal bleeding. The hospital argued that they could not lawfully give her a blood transfusion. Her boyfriend and father sought a court order authorising a life-saving transfusion. Notwithstanding his ringing endorsement of patient autonomy, Lord Donaldson and his brethren in the Court of Appeal granted that order.

30 Discussed in D Brahams, 'Unwanted Life-Sustaining Treatment' (1990) 19(335) *Lancet* 1209.
31 [1992] 4 All ER 649, CA.
32 Mental Capacity Act 2005, s 2(5) and (6).
33 [2014] EWCOP 454.
34 See, for example, the judgment of Lord Alverstone in *Leigh v Gladstone* (1909) 26 TLR 139 authorising forcible feeding of a suffragette prisoner.
35 [1992] 4 All ER 645, CA.
36 [1992] 4 All ER 649, at 652–653, CA.

The Court of Appeal held that on the facts of the case T's refusal of treatment was not an autonomous judgement. Her decision was 'flawed':

(1) The combination of the effect of her injuries and the medication she was taking impaired her mental capacity to decide whether or not to agree to blood transfusions.
(2) T lacked sufficient information to make a decision to refuse transfusion. While she was told there were alternatives to whole blood, she was not advised about their limited utility or warned that there were circumstances where, without transfusion, her life would be at risk. Lord Donaldson[37] criticised the doctors, whom he suggested were more anxious to disclaim any possible legal liability than to ensure that T was given comprehensible and comprehensive information.
(3) Pressure from T's mother may have constituted undue influence rendering her purported refusal of blood transfusion less than independent and voluntary.

These factors that were felt to cloud the nature of T's decision caused the Court of Appeal to conclude that T's rejection of blood could be disregarded. The right of the individual to decide whether to accept medical treatment was paramount but in 'cases of doubt, that doubt falls to be resolved in favour of preservation of life, for if the individual is to override the public interest, he must do so in clear terms'.

It may be tempting to regard *Re T* as judges saying one thing (upholding the rhetoric of autonomy) and doing another (rejecting an unusual belief which caused a young woman to risk sacrificing her life), which, as we will see, has happened not infrequently in a number of consent-related cases. Thus, *Re T* requires careful scrutiny. Do the facts in *Re T* support judicial doubts whether T ever made a truly voluntary and sufficiently informed choice to reject life-saving treatment?[38] In the next chapter we explore further whether some vulnerable patients who may not clearly fail the test for mental capacity may nonetheless, like T, be unable to make a real choice because of their circumstances or pressure from those close to them.[39]

Recent judgments indicate something of a change in judicial attitudes to adult Jehovah's Witnesses refusing blood, suggesting a greater willingness to accept the authenticity of the patient's wish to refuse blood even in marginally questionable cases. In *Newcastle upon Tyne Hospitals Foundation Trust v LM*[40]

37 [1992] 4 All ER 649, at 663, CA.

38 It may always be especially difficult to judge capacity retrospectively; see *NHS Trust v T* [2005] 1 All ER 387.

39 See *Local Authority v A* [2010] EWHC 1549 (Fam) and see 6.4 below.

40 [2014] EWHC 454 (COP). See also *Nottinghamshire Healthcare NHS Trust v RC* [2014] EWHC 1317 (COP): having embraced the Jehovah's Witness religion, RC executed an advance decision refusing blood products. Notwithstanding his history of serious mental illness, Mostyn J held he had capacity to execute the advance decision.

the hospital sought a declaration that it would be lawful not to administer a blood transfusion to LM. LM, a very sick woman aged 63, 'needed' a transfusion if she were to survive and even with the transfusion might still die. She had been a Jehovah's Witness for over forty years. In hospital, while still able to communicate, LM stressed that she would not want treatment with blood products even if that decision resulted in her death. At the time of the application to court, LM was sedated and in intensive care, and by that time lacked capacity to make or communicate any contemporaneous decision. LM had a long history of mental illness and had not executed a formal advance decision refusing blood. Nonetheless Jackson J held that LM, despite her mental illness, had enjoyed the capacity to decide whether to accept or refuse blood before she was admitted to intensive care and that her longstanding and consistent opposition to transfusions remained effective.[41] Jackson J apparently accorded greater weight to the beliefs of the patient than might seem to be the case in *Re T*. Two points might be noted. The treating clinician had made a decision that they did not consider it appropriate to force the transfusion on the patient, and the success of transfusion in preserving the life of the patient was far from certain.

In contexts far different from the very particular issue of blood products and Jehovah's Witnesses the principle of autonomy has been firmly endorsed by English courts. In *Airedale NHS Trust v Bland*, Lord Goff reiterated that the:

> ... principle of self-determination requires that respect must be given to the wishes of the patient, so that if an adult of sound mind refuses, however unreasonably, to consent to treatment or care by which his life would or might be prolonged, the doctors responsible for his care must give effect to his wishes, even though they do not consider it to be in his best interests to do so.[42]

In *B v An NHS Trust*,[43] Butler-Sloss P ruled that it was unlawful for doctors to refuse to switch off a ventilator keeping Ms B alive. Ms B suffered a haemorrhage in her spinal cord which left her paralysed from the neck down and wholly dependent on a ventilator to breathe. She asked her doctors to switch the ventilator off. She considered that death was preferable to survival in such a state. Her doctors disagreed. They thought that she could enjoy a reasonable quality of life living in a spinal rehabilitation unit. They expressed strong conscientious objections to 'killing' Ms B. When she first indicated her wish to have the ventilator switched off, psychiatrists questioned Ms B's mental capacity. However, she was ultimately adjudged competent to make her own decisions. The judge ruled that continuing to ventilate Ms B against her will constituted an assault on her and awarded her nominal damages of £100. She ordered that arrangements be made to transfer Ms B to a unit where doctors would be prepared to comply with her request. Butler-Sloss P unequivocally

[41] Alternatively, he held that if LM did lack capacity, blood transfusions were, given her faith, not in her best interests: see 6.14 below.

[42] [1993] 1 All ER 821, at 866; and see Lord Mustill at 889. See also *Secretary of State for the Home Department v Robb* [1995] 1 All ER 677.

[43] [2002] EWHC 429 (Fam); discussed at 7.4 below.

endorsed the value of patient autonomy. The crux of the matter will always turn on the capacity of the individual to make a valid choice – a subject explored further in the next chapter.

In *Re T*, Lord Donaldson's recognition of an unqualified right to refuse treatment as long as the adult patient was competent to make that decision was subject to a controversial *caveat*. He contended that an exception to that right might exist in 'a case in which the choice may lead to the death of a viable foetus'.[44] Pregnant women, and women in labour, might be excluded from the normal right to self-determination. A series of controversial cases followed *Re T* in which judges ordered women to submit to Caesarean sections.[45] Ultimately the Court of Appeal clarified the law, confirming that a pregnant woman 'of sound mind' retains exactly the same right to accept or refuse treatment as any other adult. As we discuss in detail at 13.23 below, women with serious mental health disorders are in a much more precarious position. Identifying when a person lacks capacity may be tricky, and judges may be naturally reluctant to stand by and watch a pregnant woman and her child both die.[46]

6.4 What is meant by consent?

Consent need not usually be written.[47] Consent may be implied from the circumstances. If a patient visits their general practitioner (GP) complaining of a sore throat and opens their mouth so that the doctor can examine their throat, they cannot complain that they never expressly said to the doctor: 'You may put a spatula on my tongue and look down my throat.' A patient visiting Casualty with a bleeding wound implicitly agrees to doctors or nurses cleaning and bandaging the wound. In an American case, an immigrant to the USA complained that he had not consented to vaccination. It was found that he had bared his arm and held it out to the doctor. His action precluded the need for any verbal consent.[48]

A patient for whom surgery or any form of invasive investigation is proposed will normally be asked to sign a consent form. Most Trusts now provide treatment-specific consent forms. In many cases supplementary procedures will require additional consent. However, the consent form might provide for additional procedures necessary to save life or serious injury, and they should cover anaesthetic procedures as well as surgery. Consent forms should ensure

44 [1992] 4 All ER 645, at 653, CA.
45 E.g. *Re S* [1992] 4 All ER 671.
46 See, for example, *Bolton Hospitals NHS Trust v O* [2003] 1 FLR 824 and *Re AA* [2012] EWHC 4378 (COP).
47 Sometimes legislation such as the Human Fertilisation and Embryology Act 1990 requires written consent; see *R v Human Fertilisation and Embryology Authority ex p Blood* [1997] 2 All ER 687, CA, discussed at 14.15 below. And see ss 2(5) and 3(5) of the Human Tissue Act 2004.
48 *O'Brien v Cunard SS Co* (Mass 1891) 28 NC 266.

that patients appreciate that they are entitled to ask questions and to demand explanations about what is to be done to them. As the Supreme Court in *Montgomery* has now made abundantly clear, patients are not passive recipients of what the doctor thinks best. However, a form is no more than some evidence of what the patient has agreed to. General Medical Council (GMC) guidance emphasises that consent should be seen as a process rather than a mere form filling exercise and that decisions should be recorded properly in the patient's medical records.[49] What is important is the substance of what the patient is entitled to be told and has been told, and what is then done to them. Clearly any action expressly prohibited by the patient, that is, additional procedures which on the form they state 'I do not wish to be carried out without further discussion', would constitute a battery if imposed on the patient. What would be the effect of a form within which a patient consented to any procedure that the surgeon saw fit to embark on? In the absence of the clearest evidence that the patient fully understood the 'blank cheque' which they handed to their doctor, such a form will be virtually irrelevant.[50] If the patient can show that, despite the form, they did not give any real consent to the procedure carried out, the surgeon will be liable in battery.

Some patients opt 'not to know' information, perhaps because they fear the psychological consequences. GMC guidance advises that if a patient states that they do not wish to discuss the details of a procedure with a health professional, then the latter should explain to the patient that they will need to be provided with some information in order to proceed. This should include details about whether the procedure is invasive, what level of pain or discomfort they might experience and what can be done to minimise this, anything they should do to prepare for the intervention and if it involves any risk of serious harm.[51]

6.5 Does it matter who operates?

As important to many patients as what the operation entails may be the question of *who* operates. If a patient agrees to surgery believing eminent consultant X will operate on them, is their consent invalidated if registrar Y operates? When a private patient contracts with consultant X that X will operate, the consultant is in breach of contract if they substitute someone else. Within the National Health Service (NHS), the patient would have to show that their consent was conditional on X operating and they would not have agreed to the surgery if anyone else proposed it. In *Jones v Royal Devon and Exeter NHS Foundation Trust*, the defendant Hospital Trust was held liable in negligence because a patient was not informed with sufficient notice about the substitution of a less experienced surgeon for the experienced surgeon originally proposed.[52] Disclosing this change at such a late stage denied the patient the opportunity to make an informed choice and thus undermined her right of

49 GMC, *Decision Making and Consent* (2020), para 54 and 55.
50 See *Chatterton v Gerson* [1981] 1 All ER 257.
51 GMC, *Decision Making and Consent* (2020), para 66.
52 [2015] 9 WLUK 420.

autonomy. Had she been provided with the information in a timely manner, it was more likely than not that she would have used that information to refuse the operation at that point and postpone it until the more experienced surgeon was available. The case was litigated in negligence, but there is also a possibility that an argument could also be made out in battery. The patient provided consent on the basis of being operated on by surgeon X, but where surgeon Y performed the procedure instead without the agreement of the patient, the terms of the original consent could be said to no longer apply and so there would be no valid agreement at all for the surgeon Y to proceed.

In practice, consent forms used within the NHS usually expressly provide that no assurance is given that any particular doctor will operate, but given the decision in *Jones*, it will be prudent for Trusts to make this possibility explicit to patients at an earlier stage of the process.

Where a patient is made aware of the potential for the eminent consultant to be swapped for a less experienced registrar, they would have no complaint if the registrar operates. If, however, the registrar lacked the experience to perform a particular operation, the patient will be able to sue the registrar and the consultant if harm ensues. They can sue the registrar for the lack of competence. They can sue the consultant (and the NHS Trust) for failure to provide proper supervision and for allowing an inadequately qualified member of the team to operate.

In 1984, it was reported that a vet was allowed by a surgeon friend to remove a patient's gall bladder. A patient operated on by a vet will have a claim in battery against the vet, however competent he may have proved to be. He agreed to a qualified doctor operating on him.[53] He no more agreed to surgery by a vet than to surgery by the authors of this book. An operation performed by a medical student will give rise to a claim in negligence if the student is not competent. A claim in battery may also lie if the patient was not expressly informed about the proposal to allow a student to operate. The patient consented to an operation and accepted, if they signed the standard form, that no particular practitioner undertook to operate. They consented to surgery performed by a practitioner, not an 'apprentice'. Teaching hospitals play a vital role, and the public interest requires that medical students train on real people. Nevertheless, any contact with a patient on the part of a medical student requires the patient's consent.

6.6 How much must the doctor tell the patient – informed consent?

For consent to mean anything the patient must be told what operation is to be performed and why it is to be done. Consent forms will usually certify that doctors have explained the proposed operation, investigation or treatment to the patient. What exactly must the doctor explain? All surgery under general

[53] See *R v Tabassum* [2000] Lloyd's Rep Med 404 CA, see 6.6 below.

anaesthetic entails some risk. Many forms of surgery and medical treatment carry further risk of harm, even if they are carried out with the greatest skill and competence. Patients have unsuccessfully sought to argue that if an operation entails an inherent risk, then they cannot be said to have given a real consent to that operation if they were not told of the risk. They contended that they had inadequate information on which to make a proper decision and they could not give an 'informed consent'; therefore a claim in battery should lie. Alternatively, they have contended with some greater success that if a claim in battery does not lie, they ought to be able to sue for negligence. The doctor's duty of care encompasses giving adequate information and advice. If they have given the patient inadequate information and the patient agreed to a risky procedure from which injury did ensue, the doctor, it is argued, is responsible for that damage.

Let us look first at the argument that if risks or side-effects inherent in an operation are not disclosed, then the patient has not really consented at all, and the surgeon is liable for battery.[54] In *Chatterton v Gerson*,[55] Miss Chatterton pursued such a claim. She suffered excruciating pain in a post-operative scar. Dr Gerson proposed an operation. The operation failed to relieve her symptoms. A second operation was carried out. Miss Chatterton was no better and subsequently lost all sensation in her right leg and foot with a consequent loss of mobility. She claimed that while Dr Gerson was in no way negligent in his conduct of the surgery, he failed to tell her enough for her to give her 'informed consent'. Her claim in battery failed. The judge said that a consent to surgery was valid providing that the patient was 'informed in broad terms of the nature of the procedure which is intended'. Any claim in relation to inadequacy of information about the risks or side-effects of treatment, or availability of alternative treatment, should be brought in negligence.

By contrast, a patient who agreed to an injection which she understood to be a routine post-natal vaccination, but which was in fact a long-acting contraceptive, Depo-Provera, succeeded in battery. Her doctor failed the test set in *Chatterton v Gerson*. He obtained her agreement to the injection leaving her totally unaware of, and misleading her, albeit in good faith, as to the nature of what was being done to her.[56] In another case, a bogus doctor, who persuaded several women to allow him to examine their breasts, claiming that he was conducting research into breast cancer, was convicted of indecent assault.[57] The women's 'consent' depended on their belief that he had medical qualifications and that the contact to which they agreed had a proper medical purpose. And a GP was found guilty of ninety offences of sexual assault by penetration and sexual assault by touching in relation to twenty-four patients.

[54] On the distinction between valid consent and informed consent, see E Cave, 'Valid Consent to Medical Treatment' (2021) 47 *J Med Ethics* e31.

[55] [1981] 1 All ER 457. The nature and purpose test for battery is cogently criticised by TK Feng, 'Failure of Medical Advice: Trespass or Negligence?' (1987) 7 *Legal Studies* 149.

[56] See *Potts v North West Regional Health Authority* (1983) *Guardian*, 23 July. See 13.2 below.

[57] *R v Tabassum* [2000] Lloyd's Rep Med 404, CA.

He argued he was practising 'defensive medicine' when he subjected healthy young women to cervical smears and intimate examinations.[58]

Other attempts to claim in battery, where the nature of what was to be done was honestly explained but the risks of the procedure were not fully explained, have failed just as Miss Chatterton's did.[59] In *Sidaway v Royal Bethlem Hospital* in the Court of Appeal, Lord Donaldson said: 'It is only if the consent is obtained by fraud or misrepresentation of the *nature* [our emphasis] of what is to be done that it can be said that an apparent consent is not a true consent.'[60] The House of Lords unanimously endorsed his views.[61] Lord Scarman, giving the most patient-oriented opinion on the information that patients should be given about treatment, nonetheless rejected battery as the legal mechanism to attain that end, and declared: '[I]t would be deplorable to base the law in medical cases of this kind on the torts of assault and battery.'[62]

The Canadian courts also view battery as an inappropriate remedy for inadequate counselling. The Canadian Chief Justice has said:[63]

> I do not understand how it can be said that the consent was vitiated by failure of disclosure of risks as to make the surgery or other treatment an unprivileged, unconsented to and intentional invasion of the patient's bodily integrity … unless there has been misrepresentation or fraud to secure consent to the treatment, a failure to disclose the attendant risks, however serious, should go to negligence rather than battery.

It is easy to understand why courts shy away from finding doctors liable in battery. The word itself is emotive. Doctors resent being accused of 'battering' their patients, being equated with 'the mugger who assaults his victim'[64]. However, distinguishing between battery and no battery on the *Chatterton v Gerson* test is not easy. Consider the example of a patient tested for HIV without his consent. He agrees to a blood test preparatory to surgery. He is never told that among the tests to be carried out on his blood is a test for HIV. Did he understand the nature and purpose of the test? He understood what would be done to him and that several tests would be carried out on his blood. Opinion about whether such a practice constitutes battery is divided.[65] Normally,

58 S Murphy, 'GP who Sexually Assaulted 24 Patients Jailed for Life' *Guardian* (2020) 7 February. And see *R v Shah* [2020] EWCA Crim 1676 for leave to appeal against sentence.

59 *Hills v Potter (note)* [1984] 1 WLR 641, at 653.

60 [1984] 1 All ER 1018, at 1026 and *Freeman v Home Office* [1984] 1 All ER 1036.

61 *Sidaway v Board of Governors of the Bethlem Royal and the Maudsley Hospital* [1985] 1 All ER 643.

62 [1985] 1 All ER 643, at 650.

63 *Reibl v Hughes* (1980) 114 DLR (3d) 1.

64 See Maclean (2004) 24 *Legal Studies*, at 399.

65 Discussed elegantly in J Keown, 'The Ashes of AIDS and the Phoenix of Informed Consent' (1989) 52 *MLR* 790. And see DR Chadwick *et al*, 'Implied Consent for HIV Testing in the UK: Time for a New Approach?' (2022) 9(1) *Lancet HIV* e63 claiming that the requirement for explicit consent is delaying diagnosis with associated morbidity and mortality and calling for the normalisation of HIV testing by implied consent.

express and detailed information about exactly what tests are proposed when blood is given is rarely sought or offered. Patients agree to tests so that doctors can find out what problems they may encounter and treat them safely. It is difficult to say that such patients, including the patient tested for HIV, do not understand in broad terms what is going on. Were some ruse employed to obtain consent the picture might be different. Imagine that a doctor suspects a patient is HIV positive and wants a test for that sole purpose. Fearing that the patient would refuse consent if asked outright, the doctor uses a pretext, for example, a suspicion of anaemia. Would you argue that the patient falls within the *Chatterton v Gerson* test, that his consent was obtained by fraud or misrepresentation? The difficulty is that what constitutes fraud is complex.

In the context of criminal law, the courts have tended to say that the fraud must deceive the victim about the very nature of what is being done to her.[66] The patient agreeing to the blood test, albeit believing the test is designed to check his red blood count, still understands what is being done. It may be civil and criminal law adopts different tests of fraud. In a case where a dentist was prosecuted for assault because, unbeknown to her patients, she continued to practise when suspended from the dental register, the Court of Appeal quashed her conviction for criminal assault.[67] The patients were not misled about what was being done to them, or as to the identity of the accused. Nonetheless, Otton LJ condemned the accused's conduct as reprehensible and suggested that a civil claim for damages might well succeed.

6.7 Negligence and a duty to inform

Where no question of misrepresentation arises, a claim based on failure to give the patient adequate information about proposed treatment lies in negligence. The doctor's duty of care to his patient includes a duty to give them careful advice and sufficient information upon which to reach a rational decision whether to accept or reject treatment. Lord Steyn emphasised in *Chester v Afshar* that 'a patient's right to an appropriate warning from a surgeon when faced with surgery ought normatively to be regarded as an important right which must be given effective protection whenever possible'.[68]

In the landmark decision in *Montgomery v Lanarkshire Health Board*[69] (hereafter *Montgomery*) the Supreme Court gave substance to that protection, overruling the earlier decision of the House of Lords in *Sidaway v Royal Bethlem Hospital*[70] (hereafter *Sidaway*) and establishing that patients are entitled to make their own choices about what risks to incur and thus doctors must provide the information that the patient needs to make that choice. Put briefly, the 'reasonable professional' test in *Sidaway* was replaced by a nuanced 'reasonable patient' test. We might note that the GMC beat the courts to this

66 *R v Clarence* (1888) 22 QBD 23.
67 *R v Richardson* (1998) 43 BMLR 21, CA.
68 [2004] UKHL 41, [17].
69 [2015] UKSC 11.
70 [1985] 1 All ER 643.

final rejection of *Sidaway* in its 2008 consent guidance. In its updated 2020 guidance, the GMC emphasises that the consent process requires doctors to initiate a dialogue with patients in order to ascertain a patient's values and what may be important information to them in the decision-making process. The emphasis is very much on partnership between doctors and patients and requires that doctors must 'give patients the information they want or need to make a decision'.[71]

6.8 Bye-bye *Bolam*

We noted at the start of this chapter that the decision of the Supreme Court in *Montgomery v Lanarkshire Health Board*[72] ended decades of judicial deference to medical paternalism. The Supreme Court forthrightly rejected any role for the *Bolam* test in information disclosure. As will be seen in Chapter 8, the *Bolam* test remains a crucial part of determining negligence in what might be styled 'ordinary' clinical negligence claims concerned with such matters as errors in treatment or diagnosis. The famous (or infamous) case of *Bolam v Friern Hospital Management Committee*[73] also raised questions of consent and information disclosure. Mr Bolam agreed to electroconvulsive therapy to help improve his depression. He suffered fractures in the course of the treatment. The risk was known to his doctor. He did not tell Mr Bolam. Mr Bolam alleged that the failure to warn him of the risk was negligent. The judge found that the amount of information given to Mr Bolam accorded with accepted medical practice in such cases and dismissed his claim. He added that even if Mr Bolam had proved that the doctor's advice was inadequate, he would only have succeeded if he could have further proved that, had he been that given that information, he would have refused consent to the treatment. The test of negligence according to McNair J was the test of responsible medical opinion.

Across the Atlantic, courts took a different approach and the doctrine of 'informed consent' was born. In *Canterbury v Spence*[74] a US court said that the 'prudent patient' test should prevail. Doctors must disclose to their patients any material risk inherent in a proposed line of treatment:

> A risk is material when a reasonable person, in what the physician knows or should know to be the patient's position, would be likely to attach significance to the risk or cluster of risks in deciding whether or not to forgo the proposed therapy.

The Canadian Supreme Court also rejected the 'professional medical standard' for determining how much the doctor must disclose. Emphasis was laid upon

71 GMC, *Decision Making and Consent* (2020), para 10.

72 [2015] UKSC 11.

73 [1957] 2 All ER 118. Earlier in 1954, Lord Denning held it to be entirely for the individual doctor to decide what to tell his patient, even if the doctor went so far as to resort to what his Lordship termed 'a therapeutic lie'; *Hatcher v Black* (1954) *Times*, 2 July; and see *O'Malley-Williams v Board of Governors of the National Hospital for Nervous Diseases* [1975] *BMJ* 635.

74 (1972) 464 f 2D 772, at 780.

'the patient's right to know what risks are involved in undergoing or forgoing surgery or other treatment'.[75] The Canadian court did allow that a particular patient might waive their right to know, might put themselves entirely in the hands of the doctors. And the court said that cases might arise where 'a particular patient may, because of emotional factors, be unable to cope with facts relevant to the recommended surgery or treatment and the doctor may, in such a case, be justified in withholding or generalising information as to which he would otherwise be required to be more specific'. The doctor could rely on a defence of therapeutic privilege. The High Court of Australia followed Canada in rejecting the *Bolam* test of professional opinion. In *Rogers v Whittaker*[76] failure to disclose a 1:14,000 chance of blindness in both eyes inherent in surgery was held negligent. The patient had made clear her concerns about risks of losing her sight altogether.[77]

Such a patient-oriented approach initially found little judicial support in England.[78] Miss Chatterton, who lost in battery,[79] also failed in negligence. The doctor, the judge said, did owe her a duty to counsel her as to any real risks inherent in the surgery proposed. He did not have to canvass every risk and in deciding what to tell the patient he could take into account 'the personality of the patient, the likelihood of misfortune and what in the way of warning is for the particular patient's welfare'. This standard Dr Gerson had met.

6.9 *Sidaway*

What amounts to a 'real risk of misfortune inherent in the procedure'? For thirty years the decision of the Law Lords in *Sidaway* entrenched in theory a test based *prima facie*[80] on professional opinion, applying the *Bolam* test. Following an accident at work, Mrs Sidaway had endured persistent pain in her right arm and shoulder. Later the pain spread to her left arm. In 1960 she became the patient of Mr Falconer, an eminent neurosurgeon at the Maudsley Hospital. An operation relieved the pain for a while. By 1973, Mrs Sidaway was again in pain. She was admitted to the Maudsley Hospital and

75 *Reibl v Hughes* (1980) 114 DLR (3d) 1.

76 [1993] 4 Med LR 79: discussed in D Chalmers and R Schwartz, 'A Fair Dinkum Duty of Disclosure' (1993) 1 *Med Law Rev* 189.

77 For an insightful comparative analysis of the different legal responses to information disclosure in the UK and the Antipodes see J Miola, 'On the Materiality of Risk: Paper Tigers and Panaceas' (2009) 17 *Med Law Rev* 76. And for a further comparative law review see *Montgomery*, [70]–[73].

78 Note that, far from being engrained in a long history of paternalistic tradition, the deference to doctors endorsed in *Bolam* only emerged in the late nineteenth century when the profession became more organised and coherent. See M Brazier and J Montgomery, 'Whence and Whither "Modern Medical Law"?' (2019) 70(1) *Northern Ireland Legal Quarterly* 5, 12.

79 See 6.6 above.

80 The speeches on the Law Lords in the majority indicate a measure of disagreement as to the exact role to be allocated to *Bolam*, a matter well addressed by the Supreme Court in *Montgomery*. See 6.12 below.

Mr Falconer diagnosed pressure on a nerve root as the cause of her pain. He decided to operate to relieve the pressure. Mrs Sidaway gave her consent to surgery. As a result of that operation Mrs Sidaway became severely disabled by partial paralysis.

Mrs Sidaway sued both Mr Falconer and the Maudsley Hospital. She did not suggest that the operation had been performed otherwise than skilfully and carefully. Her complaint was this. The operation to which she agreed involved two specific risks over and above the risk inherent in any surgery under general anaesthesia. These were (1) damage to a nerve root, assessed as about a 2 per cent risk and (2) damage to the spinal cord, assessed as less than a 1 per cent risk. Alas for Mrs Sidaway, that second risk materialised and she suffered partial paralysis. She maintained that Mr Falconer never warned her of the risk of injury to the spinal cord. Mr Falconer died before the action came to trial and in the absence of evidence as to exactly what the patient was told by her surgeon, the trial judge inferred that Mr Falconer would have followed his customary practice and would have warned Mrs Sidaway in general terms of the possibility of injury to a nerve root, but would have said nothing about any risk of damage to the spinal cord.

Ten years after the operation which left Mrs Sidaway paralysed, and seven years after Mr Falconer's death, the case reached the House of Lords.[81] The paucity of evidence about what actually happened when Mrs Sidaway and Mr Falconer discussed the proposed surgery rendered the case, as Lord Diplock put it, 'a naked question of legal principle'. What principle governed the doctor's obligation to advise patients and to warn of any risks inherent in surgery or treatment recommended by the doctor? The majority of their Lordships largely endorsed the traditional test enunciated in the case of Mr Bolam nearly thirty years before. The doctor's obligation to advise and warn his patient was part and parcel of his general duty of care owed to each individual patient. *Prima facie*, providing he conformed to a responsible body of medical opinion in deciding what to tell and what not to tell his patient, he discharged his duty properly. There being evidence that, while some neurosurgeons might warn some patients of the risk to the spinal cord, many chose not to, Mrs Sidaway's case was lost.

The Law Lords sought to emphasise that *Sidaway* should not be seen as endorsing the view that providing a doctor follows current medical practice in deciding what information to give their patients they will be immune from legal attack. The courts retain ultimate control of the scope of the doctor's obligation. First, for Lord Bridge and Lord Templeman, a crucial issue in Mrs Sidaway's case was that the risk of which she was not advised was a less than 1 per cent risk, and all the medical expert witnesses were agreed that it was a risk which many responsible neurosurgeons elected not to warn patients of. Had the risk been of greater statistical significance, their Lordships *might* have held in Mrs Sidaway's favour, even if expert medical witnesses supported non-disclosure. Lord Bridge gave as

81 *Sidaway v Board of Governors of the Bethlem Royal and the Maudsley Hospital* [1985] 1 All ER 643.

an example 'an operation involving a substantial risk of grave adverse consequences, for example [a] 10 per cent risk of a stroke from the operation'.[82] He went on to acknowledge that there might be cases where 'disclosure of a particular risk was so obviously necessary to an informed choice on the part of the patient that no reasonably prudent medical man would fail to make it'. Second, for Lord Diplock and Lord Templeman a vital question in the case was that Mrs Sidaway had not expressly inquired of Mr Falconer what risks the surgery entailed. For Lord Diplock the case concerned solely what information the doctor must volunteer. Lord Templeman said that Mr Falconer could not be faulted for failing to give Mrs Sidaway information for which she did not ask.

Nonetheless four out of five of the Law Lords in *Sidaway* rejected the transatlantic test that what the patient should be told should be judged by what the reasonable patient would want to know and demonstrated little enthusiasm for 'informed consent'.[83] Lord Scarman alone rejected current medical practice as the test of what a patient needed to be told. In a powerful dissent he asserted the patient's right to know. The patient's right of self-determination, his right to choose what happened to his body, was the factor which to Lord Scarman made the issue of advice given to the patient distinct from other aspects of medical care. The doctor should be liable 'where the risk is such that in the court's view a prudent person in the patient's situation would have regarded it as significant'.[84] But, albeit the patient's right of self-determination distinguishes advice given from other stages in medical care, advice before treatment cannot be totally separated from the doctor's general duty to offer proper professional and competent service. Doctors, in Lord Scarman's view, should be to a certain extent protected by 'therapeutic privilege', permitting a doctor to withhold information if it can be shown that 'a reasonable medical assessment of the patient would have indicated to the doctor that disclosure would have posed a serious threat of psychological detriment to the patient'.[85]

6.10 The road from *Sidaway*

While, in the immediate aftermath of *Sidaway*, the Court of Appeal[86] appeared to entrench an unmodified *Bolam* test and endorse the professional standard as the touchstone for information disclosure, the courts gradually began to chip

82 [1985] 1 All ER 643, 663.

83 In the Court of Appeal, Dunn LJ declared that, 'The concept of informed consent forms no part of English law'; *Sidaway v Board of Governors of the Royal Bethlem and Maudsley Hospital* [1984] 1 All ER 1018, 1030.

84 [1985] 1 All ER 643, 654.

85 [1985] 1 All ER 643, at 654. Lord Scarman recognised the right of a patient of sound understanding to be warned of material risks save in exceptional circumstances, yet he too found against Mrs Sidaway on the facts of the case. He held that she failed to establish on the evidence put forward by her counsel that the less than 1 per cent risk was such that a prudent patient would have considered it significant.

86 *Blyth v Bloomsbury Health Authority* [1993] 4 Med LR 151; *Gold v Haringey Health Authority* [1987] 2 All ER 884, CA. And see *Moyes v Lothian Health Board* [1990] 1 Med LR 471.

away at the professional standard and the role of *Bolam*, culminating in the Supreme Court decision in *Montgomery*. Eleven years before *Montgomery*, in *Chester v Afshar*[87] Lord Steyn said simply: 'Surgery performed without the informed consent of the patient is unlawful. The court is the final arbiter of what constitutes informed consent.'[88]

The trigger for change towards a more patient-oriented test came initially from the doctors themselves.[89] Professional practice changed markedly. Doctors now endorse more open disclosure of risks. Guidance from the GMC[90] now provides detailed instructions about the information that patients should be offered covering risks, benefits and burdens, uncertainties and other options. Advice should be tailored to the needs, wishes and priorities of patients, focusing on what matters to them about their health. Health professionals should take into account patients' wishes, fears and what activities are important to their quality of life. Consideration should also be given to the needs, values and priorities that influence patients' decision-making, their concerns and preferences about the options and their expectations about what treatment or care could achieve.

Judicial change came slowly. In *Smith v Tunbridge Wells Health Authority*[91] a claim was brought by a 28-year-old man who was not warned of the risk of impotence inherent in rectal surgery. His claim succeeded despite expert evidence that a body of surgeons did not warn patients of that risk. The judge, citing Lord Bridge in *Sidaway*, found that failure to warn such a patient of a risk of such importance to him was 'neither reasonable nor responsible'. Mere evidence of a medical practice did not counter allegations of negligence, reflecting the fact that judges should be concerned with what ought to have happened in a negligence case, not what does happen.[92] Practice must therefore be reasonable in the context of providing patients with an informed choice. In *Bolitho v City Hackney Health Authority*[93] the House of Lords stressed that, in relation to all claims of negligence against doctors, expert evidence

87 [2004] UKHL 41.

88 Ibid, [14].

89 'A fair criticism of the law may well be that, up until now, it has lagged behind developments and changing attitudes from within the medical profession.': R Heywood, 'RIP Sidaway, Patient-Orientated Disclosure – A Standard Worth Waiting For? *Montgomery v Lanarkshire Health Board*' (2015) 23(3) *Med Law Rev* 455, 466. Note, however, there are some potential problems with attempting to align completely professional and legal standards. See R Heywood and J Miola, 'The Changing Face of Pre-operative Medical Disclosure: Placing the Patient at the Heart of the Matter' (2017) 133 *LQR* 296.

90 GMC, *Decision Making and Consent* (2020), para 17 and 18.

91 [1994] 5 Med LR 334; and see *McAllister v Lewisham and North Southwark Health Authority* [1994] 5 Med LR 343; *Newell & Newall v Goldenberg* [1995] 6 Med LR 371; *Williamson v East London & City Health Authority* (1997) 41 BMLR 85; *Lybert v Warrington Health Authority* [1996] 7 Med LR 71, CA.

92 See JL Montrose, 'Is Negligence an Ethical or Sociological Concept?' (1958) 21 *MLR* 259.

93 [1998] AC 232.

advanced to support the defendant's case that he acted without negligence must be shown to be responsible. To rebut negligence a practice must have a 'logical and defensible' basis. In *Bolitho*, Lord Browne-Wilkinson seemed at one stage to suggest that in his clarification of the *Bolam* test he was not concerned with cases about informed consent.[94] That statement was not designed to exempt consent claims from judicial scrutiny, but simply to acknowledge that case-law stretching back to Lord Bridge in *Sidaway* already allowed scrutiny of information disclosure practice.[95]

More fundamental change came in *Pearce v United Bristol Healthcare NHS Trust.*[96] Mrs Pearce, who was expecting her sixth child, was two weeks past her due date of delivery. She discussed the possibility of induction with her obstetrician, who warned her of the risks of induction and Caesarean surgery but did not tell her that there was a 0.1–0.2 per cent risk of stillbirth associated with non-intervention. Mrs Pearce's child was stillborn, and she alleged that failure to warn her of the risk of stillbirth was negligent. The Court of Appeal held that she had not established negligence. The very slight risk of stillbirth arising from non-intervention, compared to the risks of intervention, was not a risk which the defendants were negligent in failing to disclose, especially in the light of Mrs Pearce's distressed condition at the time of the consultation. What is of interest in *Pearce* is that Lord Woolf's judgment in the doctors' favour departed radically from a simple test of whether the information offered to Mrs Pearce conformed to a reasonable body of expert opinion. Lord Woolf declared that 'if there is a *significant risk which would affect the judgement of a* reasonable patient, then in the normal course it is the responsibility of a doctor to inform the patient of that significant risk, if the information is needed so that the patient can determine for him or herself as to what course she should adopt' [our emphasis]. Lord Woolf seemed to suggest that the reasonable doctor must tell the patient what the reasonable patient would want to know,[97] and sought to replace the 'reasonable professional' test advanced by the majority in *Sidaway* with a 'prudent patient' test.

6.11 The impact of *Pearce*

Lord Woolf's formulation of a patient-focused test in *Pearce* appeared to be endorsed by the Court of Appeal[98] and tacitly approved by the House of Lords.[99] It seemed, notwithstanding *Sidaway*, to have become the 'standard formulation of the duty to disclose information to patients'.[100] In *Montgomery* before the Court of Session (*sub nom NM v Lanarkshire Health Board*), the

94 [1998] AC 232, 243.

95 See M Brazier and J Miola 'Bye-Bye Bolam: A Medical Litigation Revolution?' (2000) 8 *Med Law Rev* 85, 107–10.

96 [1998] 48 BMLR 118, CA. And see *AB v Leeds Teaching Hospital NHS Trust* [2004] EWHC 644 (QB); *Wyatt v Curtis* [2003] EWCA 1779 (Civ).

97 Brazier and Miola, 'Bye-Bye Bolam: A Medical Litigation Revolution?', at 110.

98 *Wyatt v Curtis* [2003] EWCA Civ 1779, [16].

99 *Chester v Afshar* [2004] UKHL 41, [15] per Lord Steyn.

100 See *Montgomery* [69].

Scottish Court of Appeal disagreed, and with something close to scorn the court dismissed submissions that *Pearce* replaced the reasonable doctor test with a reasonable patient test. *Sidaway*, the Scottish judges said, was binding on the English Court of Appeal, as it was on them. Lord Woolf's judgment in *Pearce* had been *ex tempore*. Had it been his intent to refine or qualify *Sidaway* the Scottish appeal court said that it was unlikely that he would have done so other than in a reserved judgment. The judgment in *Pearce* did nothing other 'than follow and endeavour to apply the majority view of the House of Lords' in *Sidaway*.[101] In response to submissions that the House of Lords in *Chester v Afshar* had endorsed the judgment in *Pearce* as modifying *Sidaway*, the Court of Session first dismissed any such remarks as obiter[102] and later rejected any argument that anything said in *Chester v Afshar* could be so interpreted. The case was appealed to the Supreme Court and the stage was set for the 'death of *Sidaway*'.

6.12 *Montgomery*: autonomy reigns?

Nadine Montgomery sued on behalf of her son born with cerebral palsy and other disabilities caused when he was starved of oxygen during his birth. Mrs Montgomery was small (just over five feet in height) and suffered from diabetes; both factors that might result in difficulties in labour including 9–10 per cent risk of shoulder dystocia described by an expert witness as 'a major obstetric emergency'[103] carrying risks to mother and child. In particular, there was a 0.2 per cent risk of a brachial plexus injury to the child leaving him with a paralysed arm and a very small (less than 0.1 per cent) risk of hypoxia in labour resulting in cerebral palsy. Sadly for Mrs Montgomery's son, both risks materialised. His mother argued that had she been given advice about the possible problems of vaginal delivery she would have opted for an elective Caesarean section. The Supreme Court unanimously upheld her appeal. The decision of the Court was delivered by Lord Kerr and Lord Reed with whom the other Justices agreed. Lady Hale added some additional observations focused in particular on the very specific context of childbirth and discussed later in Chapter 13.

The Court held that while assessment of the risks and benefits of treatment was properly regarded as part of medical expertise, the decision about whether those risks, benefits and alternative options should be discussed with the patient was not purely a matter of professional judgement. Such an approach ignored 'the patient's entitlement to decide on the risks to her health that she is willing to run (a decision which may be influenced by non-medical considerations)'.[104] *Bolam* has no role to play in determining what patients should be told.[105] The correct test is in essence that embodied in Lord Scarman's minority opinion in

101 *NM v Lanarkshire Health Board* [2013] CSIH 3 [26].
102 Ibid, [19]. *Chester v Afshar* being strictly speaking a case relating to causation only and not breach of duty.
103 Ibid, [8].
104 Ibid, [83].
105 Ibid, [84].

Sidaway, with the addition of a subjective branch to the disclosure test which focuses on the wants and needs of the particular patient before the health professional. Subject to an exception where non-disclosure is justified by the 'therapeutic exception' (discussed below at 6.15), the doctor has a duty to ensure that the patient:

> … is aware of any material risks involved in any recommended medical treatment, and of any reasonable alternative or variant treatments. The test of materiality is whether, in the circumstances of the particular case, a reasonable person in the patient's position would be likely to attach significance to the risk, or the doctor is or should be reasonably aware that the particular patient would be likely to attach significance to it.[106]

Applying that test to Mrs Montgomery's case the Court held that given the substantial risk of shoulder dystocia, itself a major obstetric problem requiring at best traumatic interventions that affect the mother, plus the very serious risks to the child compared to the very small risks of Caesarean delivery, the risk of shoulder dystocia was (as the defendant doctor knew) likely to affect a patient in Mrs Montgomery's position. Indeed, Mrs Montgomery had expressed her anxieties about vaginal delivery. In her own evidence the defendant very honestly said that she considered that, if the risk of shoulder dystocia was disclosed to patients such as Nadine Montgomery, they would simply then seek Caesarean delivery.

Note the importance placed by the judges on the entitlement of the patient to receive information on which to make their own choices. That choice may be to decline information, to 'delegate' their right to choose to their doctor.[107] That is in itself an autonomous choice.

Montgomery concerned information given to a patient in order that they could decide whether or not to undergo the proposed treatment. Must doctors also conform to the reasonable patient standard in disclosing post-operative risks? In *Spencer v Hillingdon Hospital NHS Trust*[108] the High Court held that the Hospital Trust breached their duty of care in failing to warn Mr Spencer of the risk and symptoms of post-operative deep vein thrombosis. The NICE guidelines were not entirely clear as to which groups of patients should be so warned. The 'ordinary sensible patient', however, would expect the warning and *Montgomery* makes this the focus of the duty to disclosure information.

6.13 Alternative treatments

Montgomery makes it clear that doctors must do more than simply discuss risks of treatment. To enable patients to exercise their right to make their own choices, the patient must be made aware of alternatives to treatment proposed by the doctor. The precise parameters of what health professionals must disclose to patients in terms of alternatives, however, remain unclear.

106 Ibid, [87].
107 Ibid, [85].
108 [2015] EWHC 1058 (QB).

Prior to *Montgomery*, in *Birch v University College London Hospital NHS Foundation Trust*,[109] Mrs Birch agreed to a cerebral catheter angiogram to test for a possible aneurysm in her brain. She suffered a stroke caused by the procedure and she had been fully warned of the risk of a stroke caused by the angiogram, but she had not been informed that there was an alternate and non-invasive procedure, magnetic resonance imaging (MRI). Her counsel argued that information about other options and their comparative risks was essential to discharge the doctors' duty to give Mrs Birch adequate advice on which to found her decision about whether or not to consent to the angiogram. The judge agreed. Albeit the issue of comparative risk was not addressed by Lord Woolf in *Pearce*, Cranston J held that:

> ... the duty to inform a patient of the significant risks will not be discharged unless she is made aware that fewer, or no, risks are associated with another procedure. In other words, unless the patient is informed of the comparative risks of different procedures she will not be in a position to give her fully informed consent to one procedure rather than another.[110]

The decision in *Birch* ought to be welcomed[111] and a similar expansive view of the need to provide patients with wider treatment information has been endorsed by the courts post-*Montgomery*. In *Webster v Burton Hospitals NHS Foundation Trust*, liability was imposed on the defendant Trust for the negligence of one of its consultant obstetricians.[112] It was held by the Court of Appeal that the claimant should have been provided with information of the unusual features (if not complications) of her pregnancy, as without it she was denied the opportunity to make an informed choice about proceeding with an induction or delaying the delivery. Had the relevant information been provided, the court found that she would have opted for the alternative of inducement and avoided the harm to her child.

Nevertheless, the courts post-*Montgomery* have still been seen to exercise a degree of caution when considering the scope of a health professional's duty to disclose alternatives, perhaps mindful of the fact that having to disclose the uncertainties associated with a multitude of different treatment options could subject health professionals to an unrealistic and perhaps impractical legal burden. In contrast to *Webster*, liability was denied in *Grimstone v Epsom and St Helier University Hospitals NHS Trust*.[113] In this case the claimant alleged that an orthopaedic surgeon was negligent in failing to disclose information about alternative hip-replacement options to her. After developing severe post-surgical complications, the patient contended that she thought she was agreeing to one type of implant, when in fact the consultant used another newer device. The claimant alleged that the defendant should

109 [2008] EWHC 2237.
110 [2008] EWHC 2237, [74].
111 See R Heywood, 'Medical Disclosure of Alternative Treatments' (2009) 68 *CLJ* 30.
112 [2017] EWCA Civ 62.
113 [2015] EWHC 3756. See LV Austin, '*Grimstone v Epsom and St Helier University Hospitals NHS Trust*: (It's Not) Hip to Be Square' (2018) 26(4) *Med Law Rev* 665.

have made her aware of the lack of data for the newer alternatives. Despite acknowledging the lack of information disclosure pertaining to the new device, McGowen J seemed to prioritise in her reasoning the fact that a reasonable body of doctors in the same position would not have given such information to a patient. On this basis, the claim failed.[114] The position taken by the judge is at odds with the rejection of the *Bolam* standard in *Montgomery.*[115] A complaint based on *Montgomery* would focus on whether the particular circumstances of the patient, known or ought reasonably to have been known to the consultant, ought to have triggered the need for enhanced disclosure of wider relevant information about the new hip-replacement device.

6.14 What about understanding?

Imparting information does not of itself assist the recipient to make an informed decision. If a patient is simply deluged with complex technical details and an array of statistics, they may be in no better position to make the choice right for them than if they had simply accepted the recommendation of their doctors. The GMC emphasises the importance of sharing information in a way that the patient can understand, seeking to check that the patient has understood and making available additional time and support where needed.[116] The courts have held that poor communication of risks by the medical team that led to the claimant being understandably confused did amount to breach of the duty to inform.[117] Is there a legal duty to seek to ensure that the patient does understand information properly communicated? In *Al Hamwi v Johnson*[118] the claimant misunderstood what she had been told of the risks of amniocentesis and radically overestimated the risk of miscarriage, believing it to be 75 per cent when in fact it was less than 2 per cent. On the basis of this misapprehension, she refused amniocentesis and went on to give birth to a disabled baby. The judge held that Mrs Al Hamwi had been presented with factually accurate information and the doctor had acted correctly in giving all the relevant information. The doctor should and did take steps to satisfy herself that the patient understood the information but this 'obligation does not extend to ensuring that the patient has understood'.[119]

In *Montgomery* the Supreme Court appears to indicate that the doctor has at least 'a duty to take reasonable care to ensure the patient is aware of any material risks'.[120] Notwithstanding this, precisely what reasonable steps a

114 [2015] EWHC 3756, [12] [iv].

115 See E Cave and C Milo, 'Informing Patients: The *Bolam* Legacy' (2020) 20(2) *Medical Law International* 103 for a discussion of other ways in which the *Bolam* test remains relevant in certain cases on information disclosure.

116 GMC, *Decision Making and Consent* (2020), para 22.

117 *Cooper v Royal United Hospital Bath NHS Trust* [2005] EWHC 3381.

118 [2005] EWHC 206; and see J Miola 'Autonomy rued OK?' (2006) 14 *Med Law Rev* 108. And note *Nathanson v Barnet and Chase Hospitals NHS Trust* [2008] EWHC 460.

119 [2005] EWHC 206, [69].

120 *Montgomery*, [87].

health professional must take to ensure that there is at least a certain level of understanding from the patient of what is being proposed is still unclear. The final report of the Cumberlege Review gives significant attention to the issue of understanding in the consent process.[121] The report suggests that more thought needs to be given to help patients conceptualise risk so that information is conveyed to patients in a way that is clear and meaningful.[122] One insightful recommendation highlights the potential benefits of patients talking to, or hearing from, others who have experienced the same intervention with or without complications.[123] The advantages of patient decision aids in the informed consent process are also illuminated, emphasising the need for them to be jointly developed with patients so that they accurately and fully reflect the patient experience and outcomes.[124]

Alongside these developments, there is some evidence that judges themselves are now beginning to at least think about, and offer advice on, how to assist patient understanding. In *Mordel v Royal Berkshire NHS Foundation Trust*, Jay J usefully set out some steps that could be taken in the future to improve the consent process in clinical settings.[125]

6.15 The therapeutic exception

For so long as the professional standard governed what information about treatment doctors must disclose, the question of 'therapeutic privilege' exceptionally allowing a doctor to withhold information when disclosure might risk damage to the patient's health was fairly muted in the UK. For if doctors only had to tell patients what fellow doctors thought they should know then in most cases the professional standard factored in such 'therapeutic privilege'. The Supreme Court in *Montgomery*, in departing from the professional standard, expressly acknowledges a role for what they call 'the therapeutic exception'. Doctors are entitled to withhold information reasonably considered detrimental to the patient's health[126] or in 'circumstances of necessity'.[127] The scope of any 'therapeutic exception' remains undefined.[128] Would a surgeon be able to justify withholding from a very elderly patient the frightening information about the risk of impotence in an operation the surgeon judged to be essential to maintain the patient's independent living? The Court warns that the therapeutic privilege must not be abused to allow doctors to prevent patients

121 Baroness Julia Cumberlege (Chair), *First Do No Harm – The Report of the Independent Medicines and Medical Devices Safety Review* (2020).

122 Ibid, 2.21.

123 Ibid.

124 Ibid, [2.22].

125 [2019] EWHC 2591 (QB); [2019] 10 WLUK 77.

126 Ibid, [88].

127 Ibid.

128 See E Cave, 'The Ill-informed: Consent to Medical Treatment and the Therapeutic Exception' (2017) 46 *Common Law World Review* 140; R Mulheron, 'Has *Montgomery* Administered the Last Rites to Therapeutic Privilege? A Diagnosis and a Prognosis' (2017) 20 *Current Legal Problems* 149.

making decisions that the doctor might see as contrary to the patient's best interests.[129] It is clear that any such defence must be based on cogent reasons relating to the welfare of that *particular* patient, and so not just based on the patient's age or the surgeon's view of the minimal risk. In *AB v Leeds Teaching Hospital NHS Trust*,[130] the defendants argued that giving families information about the retention of organs from their dead children would cause unnecessary distress, and might result in psychiatric harm. Gage J rejected a blanket plea of therapeutic privilege saying of the defence: 'In so far as it involved the exercise of a therapeutic privilege it was one that does not appear to have been exercised on a case by case basis.'

The GMC now advises that the 'therapeutic exception' is a limited exception and that health professionals should seek legal advice if they are considering withholding information from a patient on this basis.[131] Before *Montgomery*, Maclean warned of the ambiguity of therapeutic privilege and the lack of research into its use and effect.[132]

6.16 Causation

Proving that the doctor failed to give the patient a sufficient warning of some possible adverse risk or side-effect is not enough to ensure that a claim in negligence succeeds. The patient must also establish that, had they received such a warning, they would not have consented to the treatment in question.[133] They must show that the doctor's negligent failure caused the injury of which they complain. Despite grand statements about principles of informed consent, it was a narrow question of causation that directly concerned the Law Lords in *Chester v Afshar*.[134]

Miss Chester, a former journalist, had suffered from lower-back pain for many years. She was referred to Mr Afshar, a consultant neurosurgeon, who recommended surgery. Miss Chester, a private patient, consented to the operation. Unfortunately, the operation resulted in cauda equina syndrome. Miss Chester suffered significant nerve damage and became partially paralysed. Miss Chester's claim that Mr Afshar had not warned her of the 1–2 per cent risk of cauda equina syndrome was accepted by this trial judge. He held that the defendant was negligent in failing to give Miss Chester such a warning.[135]

129 [2019] EWHC 2591 (QB), [91].
130 [2004] EWHC 644.
131 GMC, *Decision Making and Consent* (2020), para 15.
132 A Maclean, *Autonomy, Informed Consent and Medical Law* (2009) at 205–208. And see 7.20 below re: vulnerable patients and the inherent jurisdiction.
133 In *Jones v North West Strategic Health Authority* [2010] EWHC 178, Mrs Jones's claim failed because as she was a Jehovah's Witness the judge ruled that she would have been unlikely to have consented to a Caesarean section with its increased risk of the need for a blood transfusion. And see *Nicholas v Imperial College Healthcare NHS Trust* [2012] EWHC 591.
134 [2004] UKHL 41.
135 The Court of Appeal refused leave to challenge the trial judge's findings of fact.

The question before the House of Lords was did Mr Afshar's negligence cause Miss Chester's paralysis? Miss Chester did not argue that, had she received such a warning, she would probably never have gone ahead with the operation. She did not say that a risk of paralysis was just too great, and she would put up with the pain. Nor did she try to claim that she would have sought out a different surgeon, or a different form of operation.[136] She said only that, had she been properly warned, she would not have gone ahead with surgery on that day. She would have taken time to reflect, to seek a second opinion and consult her friends. The House of Lords found in her favour by a majority of three to two.

The dissenting judges, Lord Bingham and Lord Hoffmann, applied the conventional principles of causation. Miss Chester had failed to show that, properly warned, she would have been likely to have refused to have surgery. She would most likely have had the operation albeit some time later. She would have been subject to just the same risk. Her 'injury would have been as liable to occur whenever the surgery was performed and whoever performed it'.[137] The majority considered that the patient's right to autonomy and dignity, the right to make an informed choice, justified 'a narrow and modest departure from traditional causation principles'.[138] Should Miss Chester lose her claim, in conformity with the normal rules on causation, Lord Hope argued that the duty on doctors to warn patients of risks of surgery would be rendered 'useless in the cases where it may be needed most'.[139] Lord Hope stressed that many patients might find a decision about whether to go ahead with risky treatment difficult. They could not with hindsight say definitively 'I would have said yes or no'. Many people might share Miss Chester's ambivalence. Patients who would find such a decision difficult should not be deprived of a remedy. Hence he agreed with the majority to modify the rules of causation, as he saw it 'modestly'. Lord Bingham saw any departure from those usual rules as 'substantial and unjustified'.[140]

At a practical level we may wonder in how many cases the modified rules of causation in *Chester v Afshar* will apply. Mrs Montgomery (as we have seen) lost her case on breach of duty in the Scottish Court of Session in *NM v Lanarkshire Health Board* but nonetheless the Court offered their views on the issue of causation had breach of duty been established. The Court accepted without question the finding of the judge at first instance that even had Nadine Montgomery been warned of the risk of shoulder dystocia, resulting in such an adverse outcome as in fact ensued, she would have followed the obstetrician's advice and agreed to attempt a vaginal delivery. Thus applying the traditional rules of causation Mrs Montgomery failed the 'but for' test. Her counsel also,

136 See *Chappel v Hart* [1999] 2 LRC 341.
137 [2004] UKHL 41, [8].
138 Ibid, [24] (Lord Steyn).
139 Ibid, [86] (Lord Hope).
140 Ibid, [9]; And see S Green, 'Coherence of Medical Negligence Cases: A Game of Doctors and Purses' (2006) 14 *Med Law Rev* 1; T Clark and D Nolan, 'A Critique of *Chester v Afshar*' (2014) *Oxford Journal of Legal Studies* (hereafter *OJLS*) 659.

however, sought to argue that *Chester v Afshar* should be interpreted to mean that if a grave risk of which the doctor should have warned the patient materialised, that sufficed to establish a causal link. The Scottish appeal court was unconvinced. In *Chester v Afshar* the proposed surgery was elective and so in the unusual circumstances of her case Miss Chester could argue that had she been warned she would have taken some time to deliberate and the outcome might have differed, 'The birth of a baby cannot simply be put off or postponed'.[141]

In the Supreme Court, the Scottish court's decision on causation was also overturned but by application of the traditional test of causation. The Justices first held that most exceptionally they might reject the usual assumption that the trial judge had fully considered all the evidence on causation. In the light of the defendant obstetrician's own evidence that Mrs Montgomery's likely reaction, and that of other women in her predicament, to information about the risks of shoulder dystocia would have been to ask for a Caesarean, the case on causation, on the simple 'but for' test, was amply made out. There was thus no need to address any possible application or extension of *Chester v Afshar*.[142] The full extent to which *Chester v Afshar* will modify traditional rules of causation remains to be seen, but in Australia there is evidence that the courts have retreated from the expansive approach to causation in negligent information disclosure cases that was adopted in *Chester*.[143] A legitimate question has therefore been raised as to whether judges may be tempted to use causation as a control device to mitigate against the patient-oriented standard of care.[144]

The Supreme Court decision in *Khan v Meadows*[145] demonstrates the use of another control device that can sometimes be deployed by the courts to limit recovery in clinical negligence actions. This is referred to as the scope of duty enquiry, which is a component of the remoteness of damage question. Ms Meadows was a carrier of haemophilia, a hereditary disease. Mistakes were made by her GP, Dr Khan, when she requested a test to determine her carrier status. In reliance, she believed she did not carry the gene and so did not request a test when she became pregnant. Her baby was born with haemophilia and also with autism. Dr Khan accepted liability with respect to the child's haemophilia but not the autism which Ms Meadows had not sought advice about. At first instance, Yip J applied the 'but for' test of causation and awarded £9m to cover losses associated with autism as well as haemophilia. Had the correct advice been given, this child with autism would not have been born. However, recovery with respect to the child's autism was overturned by the Court of Appeal and the Supreme Court dismissed the subsequent appeal. It is not sufficient to merely show 'but for' causation. Rather, the claimant

141 [2013] CSIH 3, [52].
142 *Montgomery*, [105].
143 See *Wallace v Kam* (2013) 250 CLR 37.
144 AM Farrell and M Brazier, 'Not So New Directions in the Law of Consent? Examining *Montgomery v Lanarkshire Health Board*' (2016) 42 *J Med Ethics* 85.
145 [2021] UKSC 21. See CP McGrath, 'A Khan of Worms: The Scope of Medical Advice' (2021) 80(3) *CLJ* 440.

must be able to show that the particular harm they suffered fell within the scope of the defendant's duty of care. As the harm associated with autism was not one of the risks that was intended to be addressed by Dr Khan's advice, he was not liable for costs associated with it. We wait with bated breath to assess the future direction of travel in regard to factual causation and remoteness of damage in UK law, but there are additional signs post-*Montgomery* of the courts adopting a restrictive approach.[146]

6.17 Rights, partnership and informed consent

Doctors' fears of litigation surrounding 'consent' are understandable. The sheer difficulty for both parties of recalling, reviewing, and interpreting conversations which took place years ago in a context a million miles from a courtroom should not be underestimated. The possibility that departing from the *Bolam* test will increase the unpredictability of the outcome of litigation[147] is acknowledged in *Montgomery*. The Justices however say expressly that:

> [A] degree of unpredictability can be tolerated as the consequence of protecting patients from exposure to risks of injury which they would otherwise have chosen to avoid. The more fundamental response to such points, however, is that respect for the dignity of patients requires no less.[148]

The Supreme Court welcomed informed consent with enthusiasm.[149] The Court rejected a number of the practical objections once seen as obstacles to a patient-centred approach to information disclosure, notably by Lord Diplock in *Sidaway*. It may be doubted if those objections were ever supported by adequate evidence[150] but the immense changes in society and medical practice led the Supreme Court to dismiss the view that patients do not want more information, and could not understand that information if they were offered it. In the age of the Internet and easy access to multiple sources of information 'it would be a mistake to view patients as uninformed, incapable of understanding information, or wholly dependent upon a flow of information from doctors'.[151] As to the argument that more information would lead

146 See *Diamond v Royal Devon and Exeter NHS Foundation Trust* [2019] EWCA Civ 585; *Correia v University Hospital of North Staffordshire NHS Trust* [2017] EWCA Civ 356.

147 Though not necessarily increase the incidence of litigation; *Montgomery* [93].

148 *Montgomery* [93].

149 But what exactly does informed consent entail? For an impressive analysis of the varied and variable meaning of 'informed consent', see A Maclean, 'The Doctrine of Informed Consent: Does it Exist and has it Crossed the Atlantic?' (2004) 24(3) *Legal Studies* 386.

150 *Montgomery*, [76].

151 *Montgomery*, [76]; and see R Heywood, 'Informed Consent in Hospital Practice: Health Professionals' Perspectives and Legal Reflections' (2010) 18 *Med Law Rev* 152; R Heywood, 'Medical Disclosure of Alternative Treatments' (2009) 68 *CLJ* 30.

to patients 'irrationally' refusing much-needed treatment, the Supreme Court offers a dual response. First the central principle in *Montgomery* embodies the tenet that patients have the right to take responsibility for risks affecting their own health and thus must be entrusted with their own choices.[152] Second in the focus on the particular patient, the concept of irrational choice largely evaporates. The circumstances of individuals differ so that what is rational to us may seem irrational to you or our doctors. Non-medical factors may outweigh a wholly scientific approach. Consider this scenario. A woman is told that radical mastectomy will very significantly maximise her prospects of recovery from breast cancer. She knows that if she loses a breast her partner will leave her and that psychologically she is unable to cope with the necessary mutilation. Who can say she is 'irrational' if she opts for the statistically less 'safe' option of lumpectomy? Or envisage an elderly man facing rectal surgery of the same sort as the operation involved in *Smith v Tunbridge Wells Health Authority*. The younger reader might consider that such a man would contemplate a small risk of impotence with greater equanimity than the 28-year-old Mr Smith. Who but the gentleman in question can judge that risk to his own remaining hopes in life?[153]

The judgment in *Montgomery* lauds informed consent. The Justices perceive positive benefits as much as an absence of negative factors agreeing with the GMC that partnership can 'have therapeutic benefits and is regarded as an integral aspect of professionalism in treatment'.[154] Despite some academic criticism, the judgment in *Montgomery* has been well received and the 'death of *Sidaway*' has attracted few mourners.[155] Yet perhaps *Montgomery* has still broader implications for medical law and not all are wholly welcome, and a number of important questions remain unanswered.[156] The judgment notes the change in provision of healthcare and the move away from old-fashioned doctor–patient relationships to a world of multiple health providers and the ever-encroaching role of managerialism. Responsibility for a range of decisions may become institutional rather than individual and the

152 *Montgomery*, [81].

153 For an interesting discussion on patient values and the importance of dialogue in the consent process, see J Herring *et al*, 'Elbow Room for Best Practice? Montgomery, Patients' Values, and Balanced Decision-Making in Person-Centred Clinical Care' (2017) 25 *Med Law Rev* 582.

154 *Montgomery*, [78].

155 For a positive view, see R Heywood, 'RIP *Sidaway*, Patient-Orientated Disclosure – A Standard Worth Waiting For? *Montgomery v Lanarkshire Health Board*' (2015) 23 *Med Law Rev* 455. For a searching critique of *Montgomery*, see J Montgomery and E Montgomery, '*Montgomery* on Informed Consent: An Inexpert Decision?' (2016) 42 *J Med Ethics* 89.

156 E Cave and C Milo, 'Informing Patients: The *Bolam* Legacy' (2020) 20(2) *Medical Law International* 103; S Devaney *et al*, 'The Far-Reaching Implications of *Montgomery* for Risk Disclosure in Practice' (2018) 24 *Journal of Patient Safety and Risk Management* 25; R Heywood and J Miola, 'The Changing Face of Pre-Operative Medical Disclosure: Placing the Patient at the Heart of the Matter' (2017) 133 *LQR* 296.

Court sees an evolving role for public law.[157] Patients may be 'widely treated as consumers'.[158] An image of the NHS as a 'health supermarket' is created where relationships become at best minimally important and the notion of partnership peripheral. The fiduciary nature of the doctor–patient relationship given legal shape in Canada,[159] where courts have sought to reclassify doctor–patient relationships by adapting equitable concept of the fiduciary relationship to embrace the doctor and their patient,[160] is not considered. Within such a relationship of trust the doctor's duty would equally be to make available to the patient that information which it seems likely that individual patients would need to make an informed choice on treatment. Such a change would not just endorse patients' rights but also enhance patient care[161] by fully recognising the alliance between patient and doctor, improving the quality of healthcare.[162]

It is somewhat ironic that just as the English courts endorse a patient-centred approach to consent, a number of philosophers begin to express doubts about the dominance of 'informed consent'.[163] Doubts are cast on how far legal rules truly represent the ethical value of autonomy.[164] It is argued that an unduly libertarian view of autonomy has prevented an adequate emphasis on responsibility and that obtaining informed consent has become a mechanistic process detrimental to good communication.[165] O'Neill argues that the goal of full or complete understanding is illusory. Therefore, the focus of informed consent should be on preventing coercion and allowing patients to control the amount and form of information they receive.[166] The Supreme Court does recognise

157 *Montgomery*, [75]. See E Jackson, 'Challenging the Comparison in *Montgomery* Between Patients and "Consumers Exercising Choices"' (2021) 29(4) *Med Law Rev* 595 pointing out information does not always lead to informed consumer choices and that this may be particularly so in the medical context.

158 *Montgomery*, [75].

159 *McInerney v MacDonald* (1992) 92 DLR (4th) 415; *Norberg v Wynrib* (1992) 92 DLR (4th) 449.

160 Alas, such a proposition was rejected by both the Court of Appeal and the Law Lords in *Sidaway* and by the Australian High Court in *Breen v Williams* (1996) 70 AJLC 772. See M Brazier, 'Patient Autonomy and Consent to Treatment' (1987) 7 *Legal Studies* 169, 189–91.

161 See A Grubb, 'The Doctor as Fiduciary' [1994] *Current Legal Problems* 112; P Bartlett, 'Doctors as Fiduciaries' (1997) 5 *Med Law Rev* 193; M Brazier and M Lobjoit, 'Fiduciary Relationship: An Ethical Approach and a Legal Concept' in R Bennett and C Erin (eds), *HIV and AIDS Testing, Screening and Confidentiality* (1999) Oxford University Press, p 170.

162 See H Teff, 'Consent to Medical Procedures, Paternalism, Self-Determination or Therapeutic Alliance' (1985) 101 *LQR* 432.

163 A Maclean, *Autonomy, Informed Consent and Medical Law* (2009) Cambridge University Press, ch 7.

164 See in particular, K Veitch, *The Jurisdiction of Medical Law* (2007) Ashgate.

165 See N Manson and O O'Neill, *Rethinking Informed Consent in Bioethics* (2007) Cambridge University Press.

166 O O'Neill, 'Some Limits of Informed Consent' (2003) 29 *J Med Ethics* 4.

the danger 'of bombarding the patient with technical information'[167] and stresses the importance of skilled communication.[168] The emphasis again must be on the informational needs of the patient in the clinic or the hospital bed. Those needs may not always fit neatly with a consumer-based 'supermarket' ethos and finally, as we will see in the next chapter, the health and social needs of capacitous but vulnerable patients challenge a wholly autonomy-based model of decision-making.

167 *Montgomery*, [90].

168 See, J Herring *et al*, 'Elbow Room for Best Practice? *Montgomery*, Patients' Values, and Balanced Decision-Making in Person-Centred Clinical Care' (2017) 25 *Med Law Rev* 582.

Chapter 7

CAPACITY, CONSENT AND COMPULSION

7.1 Introduction

In Chapter 6, the principles relating to consent to treatment by competent adults were examined. This chapter looks at two other dimensions of consent to medical treatment. When an adult is incapable of deciding for themselves whether or not to agree to treatment, how can treatment be lawfully authorised on their behalf? If an adult refuses to agree to treatment, can that refusal be overruled, either on the grounds that the patient 'irrationally' refused treatment which was in their interests, or because, untreated, their physical or mental condition threatens the safety of other people? As we shall see, the law is complex and raises fundamental questions of human rights, requiring examination of the European Convention on Human Rights and the United Nations Convention on the Rights of Persons with Disabilities.[1] Health professionals and health providers face challenging questions in ensuring that they both respect the rights of patients with mental disorders and also protect vulnerable patients from harm, including self-harm.[2]

The law relating to decision-making on behalf of people who lack mental capacity is now largely but not exclusively to be found in the Mental Capacity Act 2005. The Act is accompanied by a Code of Practice[3] addressing the health and other needs of people who lack capacity. A consultation on a new draft Code was launched in 2022.[4] If an elderly person develops dementia, decisions have to be made about where they should live, whether they need to move to a nursing home and what happens to their own house, just as much as what medical treatment they receive. Social care and medical care cannot be divorced from each other. Central to the Act was the creation of the Court

1 See P Bartlett, 'The United Nations Convention on the Rights of Persons with Disabilities and Mental Health Law' (2012) 75 *Modern Law Review* 752.

2 *Rabone v Pennine Care NHS Foundation Trust* [2012] UKSC 2. And see J Herring, *The Right to be Protected from Committing Suicide* (2022) Bloomsbury.

3 Office of the Public Guardian, *Mental Capacity Act: Code of Practice* (2007) (revised July 2013, updated October 2020).

4 See DHSC, *Consultation: Changes to the MCA Code of Practice and Implementation of the LPS* (2022) 17 March.

of Protection which determines a rising number of cases relating to disputed or controversial treatment of mentally incapacitated adults. The workload of the Court has become close to impossible.[5]

Doctors and nurses caring for a patient who lacks capacity to consent to treatment on their own behalf confront an awkward dilemma. What does the law allow and require them to do when an adult patient has such profound learning disabilities that they are unable to make decisions about their medical care? It is this kind of question that the Mental Capacity Act addresses. As we shall see, section 5 of the Mental Capacity Act allows actions to be taken to ensure a person lacking capacity received medical treatment in their best interests, subject to limits regarding the use of restraint or force.

In considering how English law should address the dilemmas posed by those who are unable to make their own decisions about healthcare, proper account must be taken of human rights law. However well intentioned, non-consensual treatment is in a sense still compulsory treatment. In order to treat a patient, especially if they are actively objecting to treatment, some element of restraint or detention may also be necessary.[6] Could such treatment violate Article 3 of the Human Rights Convention?[7] The European Court of Human Rights (ECtHR) set out some ground rules in *Herczegfalvy v Austria*.[8] The Court emphasised the vulnerability and powerlessness of patients lacking mental capacity. Treatment could lawfully be imposed on a patient where they are entirely incapable of deciding for themselves and where such treatment was a 'therapeutic necessity'. Where therapeutic necessity was conclusively established, the 'compulsory' treatment should not be regarded as inhuman or degrading.

Article 5 of the Convention protects the right to liberty. While Article 5(1)(e) allows for the detention of 'persons of unsound mind', English law was found wanting in the legal protection offered to patients lacking mental capacity who are hospitalised without either their own consent or any appropriate independent authorisation.[9] This meant that the Mental Capacity Act 2005 had to be amended by section 50 of the Mental Health Act 2007, which inserted provisions into the 2005 Act establishing the Deprivation of Liberty Safeguards (DoLS).[10] The recently enacted Mental Capacity (Amendment) Act 2019 has since introduced a new procedure for authorising a deprivation of liberty called the Liberty Protection Safeguards. It is intended that this will replace the DoLS system from late 2023. A revised single Code of Practice was released for consultation in 2022 to cover both the Mental Capacity Act 2005 and the new Liberty Protection Safeguards scheme under the 2019 Act.[11]

5 Select Committee on the Mental Capacity Act 2005, *Mental Capacity Act 2005: Post-Legislative Scrutiny* (February 2014), ch 6, paras 205–206. And see 7.12 below.

6 Extending in some instances to the use of restraint and 'reasonable force'; see *Norfolk and Norwich NHS Trust v W* [1996] 2 FLR 613.

7 See *ZH (A Protected Party) v Commissioner of Police for the Metropolis* [2013] EWCA Civ 69.

8 (1993) 15 EHRR 437 (ECtHR).

9 See *HL v United Kingdom* (2004) 40 EHRR 761, discussed at 7.11 below.

10 Discussed at 7.12 below.

11 Discussed in more detail below at 7.12.

The Mental Capacity Act needs to be distinguished from the Mental Health Acts of 1983 and 2007.[12] The Mental Health Acts regulate treatment for mental illness allowing (*inter alia*) for compulsory treatment and detention. Many people who may be mentally ill do not lack mental capacity. Few of those who lack mental capacity are eligible for compulsory treatment under the Mental Health Act. An independent review of mental health legislation in 2018 recommended reform to give patients more control over treatment and to more closely align the Mental Capacity and Mental Health Acts.[13]

The statutes alone are not enough to meet the legal questions arising from society's obligation to meet the needs of vulnerable adults. The inherent jurisdiction of the High Court endures, and a series of cases suggest that in exceptional cases when someone is classified as a 'vulnerable adult'[14] the courts can intervene to protect that person from neglect or abuse.

7.2 Not just about healthcare

The Mental Capacity Act addresses the whole range of decisions that need to be made once there is doubt that the individual can make their own choices about how they live their lives. The Act has generated an avalanche of case-law, coming close to overwhelming the Court of Protection set up to 'preside' over the Act.[15] Many of the cases arising from the Act are not directly about healthcare decisions. They address questions as diverse as marriage, where a person should reside, and if family members should remain in contact with them. Nonetheless such cases may have relevance to us in three senses. First, the case may clarify how we should apply the mental capacity test or understand the concept of best interests. Second, health is about much more than decisions about medical treatment. A safe and comfortable home may do more to advance the person's well-being than pills or potions. Finally, a number of cases address a mix of issues such as both where and with whom the person should live and, for example, what treatment they should receive for their epilepsy.[16] The diligent reader will need to explore the whole range of judicial decisions applying the 2005 Act and the courts' inherent jurisdiction. This chapter does not attempt comprehensive coverage and simply introduces the basic principles of English law in this area.

7.3 Not altogether new

In many respects the Mental Capacity Act codifies earlier case-law. There are few radical changes in legal principle. The test of mental capacity remains

[12] See P Bartlett and R Sandland, *Mental Health Law: Policy and Practice* (4th edn, 2013) Oxford University Press.

[13] DHSC, *Modernising the Mental Health Act – Final Report form the Independent Review* (2018). A Draft Mental Health Bill was published in June 2022.

[14] See *DL v A Local Authority & Ors* [2012] EWCA Civ 253 and see 7.20 below.

[15] *G v E and others* [2010] EWHC 621 (Fam), [4].

[16] *Re P (Adult Patient: Consent to Medical Treatment)* [2008] EWHC 1403 (Fam).

much the same. 'Best interests' continues to be the benchmark against which lawful treatment of a patient lacking capacity is normally to be judged. Earlier case-law remains relevant to illustrate how the Act will work. There are important changes in practice. A person can now, via a lasting power of attorney, appoint a proxy to make medical and personal decisions for them should they lose mental capacity. A court can exceptionally appoint a deputy (a kind of guardian) to act for a patient. The Court of Protection oversees the framework of the Act. Above all, what the Act should do is offer a uniform and comprehensive framework to help decision-making on behalf of people lacking mental capacity in all the aspects of their lives. Further guidance on the interpretation and application of the Act is found in the Code of Practice. The Code does not add any new legal requirements but provides guidance on the Act. At the time of writing, it is under review and a draft updated Code was consulted upon in 2022. Some – including court-appointed deputies, donees of a lasting power of attorney, and people working in a professional capacity, such as doctors and social workers – come under a legal duty to have regard to its provisions.[17] Failure to comply with the Code is taken into account in any relevant legal proceedings.

7.4 The threshold of capacity

The first question that needs to be addressed is how the law decides whether or not a person has the mental capacity to make their own decisions about medical treatment. Three different sorts of test could be used. A status test could assess intelligence and determine that all who fell below the requisite 'score' were incapable, and all above capable. A status test would designate a person as competent or incompetent for all legal purposes. An outcome test would judge the capacity of the decision-maker by the rationality or wisdom of the decision made. Neither test found favour with English law, which applies a functional test. The functional test, endorsed in case-law, is retained in the Mental Capacity Act. The relevant question becomes whether X enjoys the necessary understanding to embark on the particular enterprise in question – be it entering a contract, making a will, marriage, or consent to medical treatment.

The application of the functional test to consent to medical treatment is well illustrated in *Re C*.[18] C was detained in a special hospital. He had been diagnosed as suffering from chronic paranoid schizophrenia. In 1993, he developed severe problems with a grossly infected leg. Doctors judged his life might be at risk if they did not amputate the leg below the knee. Conservative treatment had no better than a 15 per cent prospect of success. C refused to consent to surgery. He sought an injunction preventing doctors amputating the leg

[17] See the Mental Capacity Act 2005, ss 42(4) and (5).

[18] [1994] 1 All ER 819; and see the similar case of *Heart of England NHS Foundation Trust v JB* [2014] EWHC 342 (COP). Compare the decisions that C and JB retained capacity with that of Kay J in *R v Collins and Ashworth Hospital Authority ex p Brady* [2000] Lloyd's Rep Med 355; and see *Surrey and Sussex Healthcare NHS Trust v MSAB* [2015] EWCOP 50.

without his express consent. There was no doubt C was mentally ill. He suffered from delusions, including a fixed belief that he himself had had a glittering career in medicine. Nonetheless, Thorpe J found that C was competent to make his own decision on the surgery in question and granted the injunction C sought. The test set out by Thorpe J for mental capacity in medical treatment involved three stages:

(1) Can the patient take in and retain treatment information?
(2) Does he believe it?
(3) Can he weigh that information and *make* a decision?

Despite his delusions, C remained capable of understanding what he was told about the proposed treatment and, in particular, he comprehended the risk of death consequent on refusing surgery.

The *Re C* test formed the basis of the test defining the threshold of capacity within the 2005 Act. Section 1 provides that a person must be presumed to have capacity unless proven otherwise.[19] No one is to be treated as unable to make a decision unless all practical steps have been attempted to help them to do so. A person is not to be treated as lacking capacity merely because they make an unwise decision.[20] Inability to make a decision must relate to an impairment of, or a disturbance in the functioning of, the mind or brain, which may be permanent or temporary.[21] Inability to make a decision depends on establishing that the person is unable:[22]

(a) to understand the information relevant to the decision,[23]
(b) to retain that information,
(c) to use or weigh that information as part of the process of making the decision,[24] or
(d) to communicate his decision (whether by talking, using sign language, or any other means).[25]

19 In *Re F* (case No 11649371) (2009, unreported) it was held that a reasonable belief that the patient *may* have capacity is sufficient to ground an application to the court to enable a full examination of the issue of capacity to be made without delay.

20 See s 1(4).

21 See s 2(1). In *A Local Authority v JB* [2021] UKSC 52 (a case on capacity to have sex), the Supreme Court confirmed that the correct approach is to establish whether P is unable to make a decision (applying s 3) before going on to consider whether there is a causative relationship between the inability to decide and an impairment of or disturbance in the functioning of P's mind or brain (applying s 2).

22 See s 3 and analysis in AR Keene *et al*, 'Taking Capacity Seriously? Ten Years of Mental Capacity Disputes Before England's Court of Protection' (2019) 62 *International Journal of Law and Psychiatry* 56.

23 See *Mental Health Trust v DD* [2014] EWCOP 13 (inability to understand (*inter alia*) significant risks of pregnancy to the woman's life).

24 And this includes a requirement to believe that information; *Local Authority X v MM* [2007] EWHC 2003 (Fam).

25 See *Re AK (Adult Patient) (Medical Treatment: Consent)* [2001] 1 FLR 129, CA. AK was in the terminal stages of motor neurone disease. He could communicate only by

The Act directs that what must be assessed is essentially the patient's capacity to understand[26] what is at stake and act on that information.[27] The rationality of the decision should not determine the capacity of the decision-maker. However, when doctors profoundly disagree with a patient's decision, they may be tempted to suggest that the patient lacks capacity. Butler-Sloss P warned against the dangers of succumbing to such temptation in *B v An NHS Trust*.[28] Ms B was a tetraplegic patient who sought to have the ventilator keeping her alive switched off. Her doctors challenged her capacity to make such a decision, citing alleged ambivalence in her views, her lack of understanding of other options proposed to her, and supposed depression. Butler-Sloss P found that Ms B retained full mental capacity despite her desperate plight. She warned that:

> It is most important that those considering the issue should not confuse the question of mental capacity with the nature of the decision made by the patient, however grave the consequences. The view of the patient may reflect a difference in values rather than an absence of competence.[29]

It would be foolish to suggest that outcome plays no role in determining mental capacity. Capacity is unlikely to be disputed unless others disagree with the outcome. Perhaps we should be more concerned about patients of borderline mental capacity who simply acquiesce in the wishes of their doctors or relatives? And the judges themselves do not wholly ignore outcomes. Butler-Sloss P herself said in a pre-2005 Act case, *Re MB (An Adult: Refusal of Medical Treatment)*:

> The graver the consequences of a decision, the commensurately greater the level of competence is required to take the decision.[30]

The importance of effective communication between patients and professionals cannot be underestimated. When a patient is known to be affected by some degree of learning disability or dementia, it may be too easy to assume a lack of capacity.[31]

barely blinking an eye to answer yes or no to questions. He indicated that he wished doctors to switch off the ventilator keeping him alive. The court granted a declaration that it was lawful to act on his instructions. AK retained mental capacity and extraordinary means made communication possible.

26 It is not necessary to show that the patient understands every detail of proposed treatment simply the salient features: *Mental Health Trust v DD* [2014] EWCOP 13, [15].

27 In *A Local Authority v JB* [2021] UKSC 52, [92] the Supreme Court held that 'the information relevant to the decision includes information about the "reasonably foreseeable consequences" of a decision, or of failing to make a decision, which consequences are not limited to the consequences for P.'

28 [2002] 2 All ER 449; see 22.4 below. In *Heart of England NHS FT v JB* [2014] EWHC 342 (COP), [7] Peter Jackson J warned that 'the tail of welfare' should not be allowed 'to wag the dog of capacity'. And see discussion of *S v Birmingham Women's and Children's NHS Trust* [2022] EWCOP 10 at 16.14 below.

29 [2002] 2 All ER 449, [100].

30 [1997] 8 Med LR 217, at 224, CA. And see *A Local Authority v JB* [2021] UKSC 52, [51] (Lord Stephens) recognising that the right to make unwise decisions depends on them being capacitous.

31 The Select Committee on the Mental Capacity Act 2005, *Mental Capacity Act 2005: Post-Legislative Scrutiny*, HL Paper 139 (March 2014) points to problems

In a number of recent cases, judges have struggled with the problem of how far an ability to appreciate the consequences of refusing treatment, to use or weigh the information given to them, may be seen as impairing capacity under the Act. *Connolly v Croydon Health Service NHS Trust*[32] is an unusual case in which the claimant withdrew consent part way through a procedure. During a routine angiogram, complications arose necessitating an emergency angioplasty. It was held that, at the crucial time, she lacked the capacity to withdraw her consent. In *A Local Authority v E*[33] E, who had been sexually abused as a child, had suffered for several years from severe anorexia nervosa and alcoholism. Her initial treatment in her teens appeared for a time to have succeeded and she studied medicine at university. But in 2006 she relapsed and was compulsorily detained under the Mental Health Act on at least ten occasions. At the age of 32, E, with the concurrence of her parents and the doctors treating her, decided that she wished to refuse all further treatment and receive palliative care only while she died of starvation. She signed an advance decision to that effect. Some months later as E's condition deteriorated the local authority applied to the court for guidance. The Court of Protection ruled that E lacked capacity at the time of the hearing as her obsessive fear of weight gain meant that she could not weigh the case for and against further treatment and the strong sedative medicine that she was receiving as part of her palliative care clouded her judgement. In relation to the earlier advance decision, evidence for her capacity at that point was equivocal and therefore it was not appropriate to apply that advance decision. Peter Jackson J recognised that E was in a Catch-22 situation: 'namely that by deciding not to eat, she proves that she lacks capacity to decide at all'. In *Northamptonshire Healthcare NHS FT v AB*[34] a 28-year-old woman with severe and enduring anorexia nervosa was also found to lack capacity to make decisions about food or weight gain, but in this case, it was found that it would not be in her interests to undergo non-consensual tube feeding. AB sought to appeal to address the Catch-22 situation. She would argue that the assessment of capacity should focus on her decision rather than her condition.[35] Tragically, she died before her application for permission to appeal could be listed.

E and AB's cases may be contrasted with two decisions[36] discussed in Chapter 6 where the wishes of two patients with long histories of mental illness to refuse blood in accordance with the tenets of Jehovah's Witness[37] beliefs were held to be capacitous. Perhaps the distinction is that for these patients, unlike E, any impediment to their ability to weigh and process information about

implementing the Mental Capacity Act and gaps between theory and practice. See also Government response: *Valuing Every Voice, Respecting Every Right: Making the Case for the Mental Capacity Act* (June 2014) Cm 8884.

32 [2015] EWHC 1339 (QB). See 6.1 above.

33 [2012] EWHC (COP) 1639.

34 [2020] EWCOP 40.

35 On which see E Cave and J Tan, 'Severe and Enduring Anorexia Nervosa in the England and Wales Court of Protection' (2017) 23(17) *International Journal of Mental Health and Capacity Law* 4.

36 *Newcastle upon Tyne Hospitals Foundation Trust v LM* [2014] EWHC 454; *Nottinghamshire Healthcare NHS Trust v RC* [2014] EWCOP 1317; see 6.3 above.

37 Even though RC was not a baptised Witness.

proposed treatments derived from a factor (faith) that was independent of their mental illness.

Note that section 2(2) of the Act indicates that lack of capacity may be due to temporary as much as permanent factors affecting the patient's mind or brain.[38] What of the patient whose understanding and reasoning powers fluctuate? At some times they comprehend what is asked of them and can act on information given to them. Days or even hours later their competence deserts them albeit to return at some later point. Fluctuating competence may be a result of psychotic disorder or, commonly, a consequence of dementia. Prior to the 2005 Act, the courts tended to find that patients with fluctuating capacity lacked capacity.[39] The Act continues to require an ability to understand and retain information, but section 3(3) states:

> The fact that a person is able to retain the information relevant to a decision for a short period only does not prevent him from being regarded as able to make the decision.

In theory, the functional test of capacity endorsed in the 2005 Act enables many patients with some degree of learning disability to retain capacity to authorise their own treatment, but one problem that has been identified with the capacity test is that it endorses a binary approach to the question.[40] That is, a patient either has capacity, or they do not. The distinction is often not that clear-cut though and the idea that a patient may have varying levels of capacity in regard to different decisions is not always acknowledged in the way that it should be.[41] However, recognising a broader spectrum of decision-making ability is not trouble-free.

Another issue is that a patient with learning difficulties might understand enough to authorise their own treatment but refuse to do so. The elderly patient with toothache may allow fear of the dentist to overrule their desire to be rid of the toothache. That outcome will be seen by others as undesirable. Those others will be tempted to say the patient is unable to make a decision. Care should be taken before rushing to enforce treatment in the patient's best interests. Several thousand indubitably competent people damage their dental health by staying away from the dentist. Just because a patient is labelled learning-disabled, or living with dementia, should we enforce their visit to the dentist? In laudable efforts to preserve what look to others as still valuable lives are the courts on occasion requiring that the patient proves their capacity rather than as the Act requires operating on a strong presumption of capacity?[42]

38 See discussion of *Re MB (An Adult: Refusal of Medical Treatment)* [1997] 8 Med LR 217, at 224, CA; see 13.21 below.

39 See *Re R (A Minor) (Wardship: Medical Treatment)* [1991] 4 All ER 177, at 187; *Re D (Medical Treatment: Mentally Disabled Person)* [1998] 2 FLR 22, at 24.

40 See E Jackson, 'From "Doctor Knows Best" to Dignity: Placing Adults Who Lack Capacity at the Centre of Decisions About Their Medical Treatment' (2018) 81 *MLR* 247. And see B Clough, The *Spaces of Mental Capacity Law: Moving Beyond Binaries* (2021) Routledge.

41 Jackson, ibid.

42 See Select Committee on the Mental Capacity Act 2005, *Mental Capacity Act 2005: Post-Legislative Scrutiny*, HL Paper 139 (March 2014), ch 3.

7.5 Treating adults who lack mental capacity

When an adult patient lacks capacity to consent to treatment on their own behalf, two closely related questions next have to be answered. On what basis is proposed treatment lawful, and, who authorises such treatment? Two principal tests are canvassed, 'best interests' and 'substituted judgement'. A 'best interests' test requires that decision-makers consider what the overall welfare of the patient demands. It is, in theory at least, an objective test. 'Substituted judgement' demands an attempt to discern what the patient would want were they able to decide for themselves. It is illustrated in a famous US case, *Re Quinlan*.[43] Karen Quinlan was a young woman who succumbed to sudden illness and lay in a coma supported on a ventilator. Her father applied to the court to be appointed her guardian and sought court approval to switch off the ventilator. The court authorised his decision on the basis of evidence that this was what Karen would have wished. The US court (1) endorsed a test of substituted judgement, and (2) granted Karen's father, her next of kin, powers to act on her behalf. In many civil law jurisdictions, as well as some states in the USA, the law allows next of kin to make decisions on behalf of adults who lack mental capacity,[44] just as English law empowers parents to consent to treatment on behalf of their young children. The Mental Capacity Act adopts a modified version of a best interests test and rejects any notion that next of kin should automatically enjoy proxy powers of consent.

Prior to the 2005 Act, the law left patients lacking mental capacity and their doctors in a legal limbo.[45] No one had legal authority to act as proxy and consent on behalf of the patient. Even if a patient was compulsorily detained under the Mental Health Act 1983, section 63 of that Act allowing doctors to dispense with the patient's consent applied only to treatment for mental disorder.[46] And, as we noted earlier, most patients who lack mental capacity are not detained under the Mental Health Act.[47] Nor could an adult lacking mental capacity be made a ward of court so that the court could authorise treatment.[48]

43 *Re Quinlan* 355 A 2d 664 (NJ, 1976).

44 A test controversially employed in extensive litigation in the USA surrounding the proposed withdrawal of artificial hydration and nutrition from Terri Schiavo. The application was supported by her husband and opposed by her parents. See *Respondent Michael Schiavo's Opposition to Application for Injunction* Case No: 04A-825, March 24, 2005 (Supreme Court, USA). See 22.14 below.

45 See *T v T* [1988] 1 All ER 613; and see the third edition of this work, pp 115–117.

46 So under the 1983 Act, doctors may require a detained patient to accept medication for schizophrenia but have no power to authorise surgery for a hernia. But it should be noted that judges tend to give mental disorder a wide meaning. In *R v Collins and Ashworth Health Authority ex p Brady* [2000] Lloyd's Rep Med 355, forcible feeding to prevent Ian Brady starving himself to death was held to constitute treatment for his mental disorder. And see 7.19 below.

47 Or are eligible to be so detained. Patients with severe learning disabilities who are treated in hospital are usually voluntary (or informal) patients.

48 See BM Hoggett, 'The Royal Prerogative in Relation to the Mentally Disordered: Resurrection, Resuscitation or Rejection' in MDA Freeman (ed), *Medicine, Ethics and the Law* (1988) Stevens.

One of the extraordinary features of the history of this area of law is that not until 1987 did this question trouble the courts.[49] In earlier times, perhaps no one gave much thought to the legality of treating patients lacking mental capacity? Doctors and families simply went ahead on the basis that 'doctor knows best'? The rise in medical litigation and increased concern for patients' rights began to worry doctors. Health professionals feared litigation both if they went ahead with treatment without consent, and if a patient suffered harm because they did nothing.

7.6 *F v West Berkshire Health Authority*[50]

The trigger for judicial action to clarify the legality of treatment of learning-disabled patients came about in the context of the sterilisation of adult women with learning disabilities. If the girl was under 18, she could be made a ward of court, and the court, if sterilisation was in her best interests, could authorise that radical surgery.[51] The first fully reported case relating to an adult, *T v T*[52] came to court in 1987 and the following year *F v West Berkshire Health Authority* reached the House of Lords. F was a 36-year-old woman, with severe learning disabilities. She was a voluntary patient in a psychiatric unit and had entered into a sexual relationship with a male fellow patient. The House of Lords granted a declaration stating that F might lawfully be sterilised. Lord Brandon declared:

> [A] doctor can lawfully operate on, or give other treatment to, adult patients who are incapable, for one reason or another, of consenting to his doing so, provided that the operation or other treatment concerned is in the best interests of the patient.[53]

Their Lordships made it clear that learning-disabled adults could lawfully receive medical care and treatment. The elderly confused lady with cataracts can have those cataracts removed. But *F* empowered doctors to decide on what treatment a patient received with no formal restrictions imposed on the exercise of that power. Operating on an old lady with cataracts is one thing, sterilising a learning-disabled woman is an intervention of a different order of magnitude.[54] Disquiet about the decision in *F v West Berkshire Health Authority* arose from a suspicion that the judgment benefited doctors rather more than patients. A declaration from a High Court judge protected doctors from subsequent litigation.[55] Particularly if there was some dispute between

[49] See *Re T* (14 May 1987, unreported); *Re V* (1987) *Times*, 4 June; *T v T* [1988] 1 All ER 613.
[50] See 13.4 below.
[51] See *Re B (A Minor) (Wardship: Sterilisation)* [1987] 2 All ER 206, HL.
[52] *T v T* [1988] 1 All ER 613.
[53] [1989] 2 All ER 545, at 551.
[54] Lord Griffiths dissented. He argued that a grave decision such as sterilisation with all its implications should not be left to doctors alone. He believed that it was open to the House of Lords to develop a common law rule that prior judicial approval was required before an operation as radical as sterilisation could be performed (pp 561–562).
[55] See J Bridgeman, 'Declared Innocent?' (1995) 3 *Med Law Rev* 117.

the patient's relatives, or relatives and carers, the doctor benefited from the court's intervention.

7.7 Defining best interests

The most fundamental problem with *F* was the way their Lordships defined best interests ruling that courts should apply the *Bolam* test. Treatment would be lawful if it conformed with a reasonable and competent body of professional opinion, albeit there might be another reasonable and competent body of professional opinion to the contrary.[56] In 1995 the Law Commission criticised the use of *Bolam* in this context. Their Report recommended that it 'should be made clear beyond any shadow of a doubt that acting in a person's best interests amounts to more than not treating a person in a negligent manner'.[57]

After a decade of rubber-stamping medical opinion, the courts adopted a much more proactive approach to best interests, well before the enactment of the 2005 Act. Refusing to authorise a vasectomy on a learning-disabled man, Thorpe LJ[58] emphasised that the decision about the patient's interests was one which the judge must make. It encompasses 'medical, emotional and other issues'.[59] *In Re S (Adult Patient: Sterilisation)*[60] concerned an application to carry out a hysterectomy on a 29-year-old woman with severe learning difficulties. Doctors and her mother were concerned about the risk of pregnancy and the woman also suffered from severe menstrual problems. She had a phobia about hospitals. Overturning the trial judge's decision that hysterectomy would be lawful, the Court of Appeal held that other less invasive alternatives should be tried first. Butler-Sloss P said: 'The *Bolam* test [is] irrelevant to the judicial decision, once the judge [is] satisfied that the range of options was within the range of acceptable opinion among competent and reasonable practitioners.'[61]

Thorpe LJ emphasised that what the medical expert witnesses offered was expert advice on the options for treatment. The court must exercise the choice the patient was unable to make. The patient's welfare in its broadest sense must be the paramount consideration.[62]

7.8 'Best interests' survives: the Mental Capacity Act

The Mental Capacity Act retained but reformed the best interests test to determine how a patient lacking capacity should be treated. Section 5 provides a

56 *Bolam v Friern Hospital Management Committee* [1957] 1 WLR 582 discussed fully in Chapter 8 and see MA Jones, 'Justifying Medical Treatment Without Consent' (1989) 5 *Professional Negligence* 178.

57 Law Commission, *Mental Incapacity* (1995) Report No 231, para 3.27.

58 See *Re A (Medical Treatment: Male Sterilisation)* [2000] 1 FCR 193, CA.

59 [2001] 1 FCR 193, at 200.

60 [2000] 3 WLR 1288.

61 Ibid, at 1299; and see *R (on the application of N) v Doctor M* [2003] 1 FLR 667.

62 See also *Simms v Simms* [2003] 1 All ER 669; *A v A Health Authority* [2002] 1 FCR 481.

statutory basis, the general authority, for any act done in relation to the care or treatment of a person lacking mental capacity. It provides that:

1. If a person ('D') does an act in connection with the care or treatment of another person ('P'), the act is one to which this section applies if –
   (a) before doing the act, D takes reasonable steps to establish whether P lacks capacity in relation to the matter in question, and
   (b) when doing the act, D reasonable believes –
      (i) that P lacks capacity in relation to the matter, and
      (ii) *that it will be in P's best interests for the act to be done* [our emphasis].
2. D does not incur any liability in relation to the act that he would not have incurred if P –
   (a) had capacity to consent in relation to the matter, and
   (b) had consented to D's doing the act.[63]

Section 5 has a broad application extending beyond medical treatment. Anyone who intervenes to assist a person lacking mental capacity is protected from liability in battery[64] if they act in that person's best interests. The passer-by who pulls a distressed elderly person with dementia out of the way of oncoming traffic falls within section 5. The paramedics who lift them into an ambulance, and all the doctors and nurses who tend them in hospital, act lawfully by virtue of section 5.

In *ZH v Commissioner of Police for the Metropolis*[65] a severely autistic and epileptic young man who could not speak was on a trip to the swimming baths with carers. He froze at the poolside and after some time the manager called the police. The claimant jumped into the pool and police then forcibly restrained him with handcuffs and leg restraints detaining him in a police van for forty minutes before releasing him to a carer. The Court of Appeal accepted that the officers acted in good faith believing that they were acting in the claimant's interests, but they failed to consult the carer present at the scene and their actions were 'hasty and ill informed' and thus not in the best interests of the claimant and outside the protection given by section 5.

The Mental Capacity Act seeks to give force where appropriate to the prior preferences of someone who later in life loses mental capacity. As we shall see:

(1) Some statutory force is given to advance decisions,[66] often called 'living wills', whereby a person gives directions about treatment which they should, and should not, receive if they become unable to decide such matters for themselves. Thus we could today set out our decisions about continuing treatment in circumstances where for us death would

[63] See further *Mental Capacity Act 2005: Code of Practice*, para 6.20.

[64] Note, however, that s 5 grants only immunity from battery. Should the patient's care be negligent, she retains her rights to redress.

[65] [2013] EWCA Civ 69.

[66] See Law Commission, *Mental Incapacity*, Part V.

become preferable to life. As we shall see, the Act only gives force to advance refusals of treatment and not to demands for future care.

(2) In section 9, the Act further empowers us to nominate our chosen proxy (attorney) by executing a lasting power of attorney to act for us should we lose capacity to act for ourselves. However, both advance refusals and lasting powers of attorney will work to reflect the wishes of the individual herself only in limited circumstances. First, the patient must at some point in their life have enjoyed the necessary mental capacity to execute such an instrument. Second, they must actually have done so, contemplated a future loss of capacity and acted to attempt to extend their autonomous choices beyond that sad event. The numbers of patients making advance decisions or creating lasting powers of attorney may well be small.[67]

(3) Most importantly, then, the Act follows the 1995 Law Commission's recommendation that any evaluation of best interests should take into account evidence of what the patient themselves might want. Section 4 of the Mental Capacity Act adopts (with some additions) the Law Commission's notion of a modified best interests test, a test incorporating elements of substituted judgement.

7.9 Modified best interests

Section 4 of the Mental Capacity Act sets out the test to be applied. The volume of cases addressing the best interests of incapacitated adults is immense and to do justice to even a quarter of the case-law would take a book of its own.[68] Many questions of best interests relate either to matters concerning contraception and pregnancy, or end of life. Such cases are more fully dealt with in Chapters 13 and 22. In this chapter we seek to introduce the broad principles relating to the best interests test. In determining best interests, decision-makers are first instructed that in making their decision they should not act merely on the basis of:

(a) the person's age or appearance, or
(b) a condition of his, or an aspect of his behaviour, which might lead others to make unjustified assumptions about what might be in his best interests.[69]

Simply because a patient is 94 does not justify assuming that they would be better off dead in some life-threatening emergency.

67 Sue Wilkinson and Celia Kitzinger set up Advance Decisions Assistance to support people exercising end-of-life choices. See https://adassistance.org.uk.

68 Two excellent resources are: (1) The 39 Essex Chambers Court of Protection team provides a range of guidance, reports, newsletters and case notes at https://39essex.com. (2) The Open Justice Court of Protection project enhances transparency of Court of Protection cases at https://openjusticecourtofprotection.org.

69 See s 4(1).

Next, when considering best interests, the decision-maker must consider if the patient is ever likely to recover the capacity to make their own decisions, and if so, when this may be.[70] Wherever possible, the patient must be allowed and assisted to participate in decisions as far as they are able.[71] So if X has suffered serious brain injuries in a road accident, only immediately necessary decisions should be taken by others while there remains the possibility that X will recover at least some of their reasoning powers. As X slowly recovers, where feasible, they should at least be consulted. In determining best interests, a decision-maker must consider as far as reasonably possible.

- the person's past and present wishes and feelings (and in particular any relevant written statement made by him when he had capacity).
- the beliefs and values that would be likely to influence his decision if he had capacity.
- the other factors he would be likely to consider if he were able to do so.[72]

In considering these matters, the Act further requires that a decision-maker seek the views of those people who may be best placed both to offer the views of the patient themselves and to judge their welfare.[73] So where possible the decision-maker must consult:

(a) anyone named by the person as someone to be consulted on the matter in question or a on matter of that kind,
(b) anyone engaged in caring for the person or interested in his welfare,
(c) any donee of a lasting power of attorney granted by the person, and
(d) any deputy appointed for the person by the court.[74]

This modified best interests test requires decision-makers to focus on the individual patient and make a judgement to promote their welfare, a judgement which takes proper account of any prior views that the individual may have expressed and involves the people most likely to know about their views. Substituted judgement becomes a part of best interests where such judgement can practically be discerned.[75] The dignity of every patient, including those who never enjoyed mental capacity, is given due regard. A patient may never have had the capacity to make judgements. Nonetheless they would

70 See s 4(3).
71 See s 4(4).
72 Section 4(6). See *Ashan v University Hospitals Leicester NHS Trust* [2006] EWHC 2624 (importance of religious faith).
73 The importance of such evidence is beautifully illustrated in *Sheffield Teaching Hospitals NHS Foundation Trust v TH* [2014] EWCOP 4.
74 Section 4(7).
75 See *Aintree University Hospitals Foundation Trust v James* [2013] UKSC 67, [24] per Lady Hale.

have displayed preferences and feelings, particular aversions,[76] or especial pleasures. Treatment which transgressed those aversions or removed those pleasures could only be in their interests if strong evidence supported its continuation, despite the distress occasioned to the individual. Note, though, that the requirement to take into account the patient's own views and feelings, what Mary Donnelly[77] has called the consultative model, is not without problems in practice. The patient may be unable to communicate save via their family or be heavily dependent on them to the extent that it becomes hard to discern which are the real views of the patient and which are the wishes of the family member.[78]

The statutory best interests test no longer conflates best interests with non-negligent care. In case after case the courts emphasise that doctors and courts assessing best interests must consider the question holistically looking at all the effects of a decision to adopt a particular treatment.[79] Such an approach allows weight to be given to social as much as medical factors.[80]

Problems arise when family members who care for, or are close to the patient, vehemently reject treatment that a court would conclude is in the patient's medical interests. The patient may need to be removed from their family to residential care if the family will not comply with recommended treatment and that will itself harm the patient. The courts are charged with the task of weighing competing harms.[81]

During the COVID-19 pandemic the Court of Protection was asked to consider several cases where people lacked capacity to consent to vaccination against COVID and their relatives considered the risks of a new vaccine to be problematic. In *Re E*[82] vaccination was considered to be in the best interests of a women lacking capacity who had consistently accepted vaccines throughout her lifetime, notwithstanding her son's concerns around the speed of the

76 'To take a simple example, it cannot be in the best interests to give the patient food which he does not like when other equally nutritious food is available.' Ibid, [24] per Lady Hale.

77 M Donnelly, 'Best Interests, Patient Participation and the Mental Capacity Act' (2009) 17 *Med Law Rev* 1.

78 See *Re P (Adult Patient: Consent to Medical Treatment)* [2008] EWHC 1403 (Fam), [19]; *A NHS Trust v DE* [2013] EWHC 2562 (Fam).

79 See *Aintree University Hospitals NHS Foundation Trust v James* [2013] UKSC 67, [26] per Lady Hale.

80 See, for example, discussion of *An NHS Trust v DE* [2013] EWHC 2562 (Fam) at 13.4 below.

81 See *Re P (Adult Patient: Consent to Medical Treatment)* [2008] EWHC 1403 (Fam); In *A Local Authority v WMA* [2013] EWHC 2580 (COP) it was held to be in WMA's best interests to move out of his mother's house and into a residential unit. WMA lacked capacity but wished to remain with his mother. His mother also opposed the move. But there was a history of neglect and WMA's lifestyle at his mother's house was isolated. HHJ Cardinal made the necessary authorisation of the associated Deprivation of Liberty.

82 [2021] EWCOP 7.

vaccine's development. But in *SS v London Borough of Richmond Upon Thames*[83] Hayden J held that it was not in P's best interests to have the vaccine against her wishes. It was clear to the court that 86-year-old P would have likely refused the vaccine if capacitous. The judge was told that anyone attempting vaccination 'had better be "kung fu experts" ' such was the force of her wish not to be vaccinated. The best interests determination is an individual one to be made on the basis of all relevant facts.

Provided it is performed in a kind and sensitive way, persuasion can be a useful tool in encouraging the patient to see the benefits of, and to eventually accept, a proposed course of action. In *Avon and Wiltshire Mental Health Partnership v WA*, Hayden J found that a young man lacked capacity to make decisions about nutrition and hydration, but that he should not be force-fed. Rather efforts should be made to persuade him to comply.[84] If persuasion ultimately failed, a clear refusal from a patient would still need to be respected in appropriate situations.[85]

The Law Commission revisited mental capacity in 2017. The main purpose was to address the unsatisfactory DoLS, which we discuss at 7.12 below, but the Commission also made certain recommendations of more general application, often with a view to enhancing compliance with the UN Convention on the Rights of Persons with Disabilities. One was a recommendation to enhance the emphasis on the patient's wishes and feelings through a modification of section 4(6) on best interests. The Commission recommended imposing an obligation on the decision-maker to give particular weight to any wishes or feelings of an incapacitated person when undertaking a best interests assessment.[86] A draft Bill was produced, but despite the suggestion being initially welcomed by the Government,[87] it was not included in the final version of the Mental Capacity (Amendment) Act 2019.

7.10 Serious medical treatment

Within the constraints of the modified best interests test, in the majority of cases relating to mentally incapacitated patients, doctors remain proxy decision-makers for their patients. The Law Commission's initial proposals in 1995 recommended that the general authority to make decisions in a patient's best interests should be subject to statutory restrictions.[88] Certain controversial radical and/or irreversible treatments would normally demand authorisation by the Court of Protection. The government rejected statutory restrictions on the general authority,[89] and the Act contains some more

83 [2021] EWCOP 31.
84 [2020] EWCOP 37, [102].
85 Ibid, [96] and [102].
86 Law Commission, *Mental Capacity and Deprivation of Liberty* (2017) Law Com No 372, recommendation 40.
87 DHSC, *Final Government Response to the Law Commission's Review of Deprivation of Liberty Safeguards and Mental Capacity* (2018) Statement UIN HCWS542, March.
88 See Law Commission, *Mental Incapacity*, Part VI.
89 *Making Decisions* (1999) Cm 3803, para 12.

limited safeguards.[90] Sections 30–34 of the Act set out special rules relating to the inclusion of people lacking mental capacity in medical research.[91] Section 37 obliges National Health Service (NHS) authorities to seek advice from an independent mental capacity advocate (IMCA):

(1) if it is proposed to provide serious medical treatment for a patient lacking mental capacity, and;
(2) if there is no one (other than professional carers or advisers) who can be consulted about the patient's best interests.[92]

Serious medical treatment is defined as:

> ... treatment which involves providing, withdrawing or withholding treatment in circumstances where –
>
> (a) in a case where a single treatment is being proposed, there is a fine balance between its benefits to the patient and the burdens and risks it is likely to entail for him,
> (b) in a case where there is choice of treatments, a decision as to which one to use is finely balanced, or
> (c) what is proposed would be likely to involve serious consequences for the patient.[93]

The 2017 Law Commission report proposed statutory reform. It recommended that the section 5 general authority should not be available for certain decisions, including the provision of serious medical treatment, unless written records were kept to note the steps taken to establish incapacity, to help the person make a decision, to determine their best interests and to incorporate any ascertained wishes and feelings.[94] However, like the proposal to amend the best interests test, this was not included in the final version of the Mental Capacity (Amendment) Act 2019.

As law and practice have evolved since the Mental Capacity Act came into force, the need for independent scrutiny of any intervention that is significant and/or life changing has been given force by the Mental Capacity Act Code of Practice and the jurisprudence of the Court of Protection. At the time of writing, the Code of Practice is under review. Interim guidance[95] strongly advises that any proposal to withdraw artificial nutrition or hydration that is

90 See also s 4(5) relating to the withdrawal of life-sustaining treatment (see 22.18 below).
91 See 18.11 below. See for discussion R Heywood *et al*, 'Lost Voices in Research: Exposing the Gaps in the Mental Capacity Act 2005' (2019) 19 *Medical Law International* 81.
92 And see the *Mental Capacity Act 2005 Code of Practice*, para 6.9.
93 The Mental Capacity Act 2005 (Independent Mental Capacity Advocate) (General) Regulations 2006, SI 2006/1832, reg 4.
94 Law Commission, *Mental Capacity and Deprivation of Liberty*, recommendation 41.
95 *Serious Medical Treatment, Guidance* [2020] EWCOP 2. And see draft MCA COP (2022), 6.32–6.39.

finely balanced, or where there is a difference of medical opinion or a lack of agreement, should be brought before the court.[96] Additionally, cases that do not concern life-sustaining treatment, but involve a serious interference with a person's human rights, should also be brought before the court, even if the parties agree. This will include proposals for a person lacking mental capacity to be an organ or tissue donor, or to carry out a non-therapeutic sterilisation, or proposals for experimental treatment or covert contraception. Finally, cases involving treatment that will require a deprivation of liberty that goes beyond the permissible restraints set out in sections 5 and 6 of the Mental Capacity Act may require an application to court, as we now consider.

7.11 Use of restraint and detention

Many patients who lack mental capacity will simply acquiesce in treatment. What of the patient who forcefully objects – the dentist moves towards them and the patient jumps out of the chair? Section 6 of the 2005 Act authorises the use of force and restraint, if such measures are necessary, and a proportional response to (1) the likelihood of the patient suffering harm if they are not treated and (2) the seriousness of that harm.[97] Sometimes, continuing treatment may require more than brief restraint. An elderly patient with dementia may need to be confined in their care home. A patient with anorexia nervosa who is to be fed forcibly will also need to be detained in hospital. Prior to the 2005 Act, judges were prepared to use common law powers to authorise detention in the patient's best interests.[98] Patients were deprived of their liberty without any of the safeguards that would apply to detention under the Mental Health Acts.

The inadequacy of the common law was highlighted in *R v Bournewood Community and Mental Health Trust ex p L*.[99] The House of Lords ruled that the common law powers derived from *F* could be invoked to authorise the *detention* of patients lacking mental capacity. L was 48 years old, autistic and severely learning-disabled. He could not speak and had very limited understanding. L was incapable of making any of his own decisions about his health or personal care. From 1994, after nearly thirty years in mental health units, L lived with paid carers. One day, in 1997, he became extremely agitated at his day centre. His carers could not be contacted. L was taken by ambulance to Bournewood hospital and ultimately admitted as a 'voluntary' informal patient. He was not formally detained under the Mental Health Act 1983. He remained in hospital for several months despite his carers' wish for him to return to their home. An action was brought on L's behalf, accusing the hospital of false imprisonment. The essence of the case was whether or not L had been unlawfully detained. The Court of Appeal ruled in L's favour. He had been detained against his will and no lawful grounds for his detention justified his treatment. The Law Lords by a bare majority held that L was *not*

96 As was made clear in *NHS Trust v Y* [2018] UKSC 46. See 22.20 below.
97 Mental Capacity Act 2005, s 6 (3) (a) and (b).
98 See *Re C (Detention: Medical Treatment)* [1997] 2 FLR 180.
99 [1998] 3 All ER 299, HL.

imprisoned in the hospital. He was kept in an unlocked ward and not actually restrained from leaving. The majority considered that evidence that had he attempted to leave he would have been restrained did not establish that he was detained against his will. All their Lordships agreed, however, that L was 'imprisoned' in the ambulance, but his detention was in any event lawful. Given his inability to consent to admission to hospital himself, any necessary removal and detention in hospital, plus whatever consequent treatment was called for, was lawful in his best interests.

L's carers took his case to the ECtHR and won. L's detention violated Article 5[100] of the Human Rights Convention:

> Everyone has the right to liberty and security of person. No one shall be deprived of his liberty, save in the following cases and in accordance with a procedure prescribed by law.

Article 5(1)(e) permits the lawful detention of 'persons of unsound mind', but Article 5(4) requires that anyone so deprived of their liberty must have the lawfulness of their detention decided speedily by a court. In *HL v United Kingdom*,[101] the ECtHR ruled that L had been deprived of his freedom solely on the basis of clinical judgements and denied the opportunity for a speedy judicial review of his detention, contravening his rights under Article 5. The lack of procedural safeguards breached the Convention. The government was obliged to legislate to close the 'Bournewood gap', a gap that the unamended Mental Capacity Act failed to close.

7.12 Deprivation of Liberty Safeguards (DoLS) and the proposed new Liberty Protection Safeguards

The Mental Health Act 2007 amended the Mental Capacity Act by inserting into the 2005 Act new sections 4A and 4B and Schedules A1 and 1A and so introducing the DoLS. We do no more here than seek to give a broad picture of the controversial DoLS procedure and to outline the defining features of the new Liberty Protection Safeguards system that has recently been enacted to replace it, though at the time of writing the timetable for implementation is uncertain.[102] DoLS do not apply to every instance of restraint imposed to ensure that a patient lacking mental capacity receives proper care and/or medical treatment,[103] but only to levels of restraint that deprive the person of their liberty.[104] Deprivation of liberty is not permitted under the

100 See *Winterwerp v Netherlands* (1979) 2 EHRR 387; *Herczegfalvy v Austria* (1992) 15 EHRR 437.

101 (2004) 40 EHRR 761.

102 A target implementation date of October 2020 was delayed until April 2022, which was then abandoned in December 2021. A consultation – DHSC, *Changes to the MCA Code of Practice and Implementation of the LPS* – was launched in March 2022.

103 See *JE v DE* [2006] EWHC 3459 (Fam).

104 But see *An NHS Trust v A* [2013] EWHC 2442, [56–57].

Act[105] unless either (1) it is authorised under Schedule A1 in relation to deprivations of liberty in hospitals and care homes, or (2) it is authorised by the Court of Protection under section 16(2)(a) if, for example, a person is living in supported accommodation, or (3) it is necessary to give life-sustaining treatment or prevent serious deterioration in health pending a court application.[106]

The rules governing DoLS are exceedingly complex, even in those cases that do not have to go to the Court of Protection. Deprivation of liberty under Schedule A1 relating to patients in hospitals or care homes is currently lawful only if (*inter alia*) the patient is 18 or over,[107] is suffering from a mental disorder within the meaning of the Mental Health Act 1983, is not detained under the Mental Health Acts,[108] lacks capacity, has no advance decision, LPA or deputy refusing the accommodation, and the deprivation of liberty is in their best interests and necessary to protect them from harm. The deprivation of liberty must be authorised by a 'supervisory body' (the commissioning body where a patient is in hospital, or the local authority where the person is in a care home). In defining mental disorder for the purposes of DoLS, the provisions of the Mental Health Act excluding learning disability from the definition of mental disorder should be disregarded. Authorisations could be challenged in the Court of Protection.

The Court of Protection route was impacted by the landmark decision of the Supreme Court in *P v Cheshire West and Chester Council*,[109] which set out a broad definition of what constituted a deprivation of liberty, to include those who in no way objected to their detention. The case involved three applicants with learning difficulties, who lived in comfortable and benevolent living arrangements with a foster mother in one case, and in supported living accommodation in the other two cases. The restrictions placed on them were said by the Court of Appeal to be 'relatively normal' in the context of people with similar disabilities and needs.[110] They were, however, subject to continuous monitoring and control and had they ever sought to leave would have been prevented from doing so. The majority of the Supreme Court held that they were deprived of their liberty. The Court rejected the concept of 'relative normality'. Lady Hale said that being deprived of liberty 'must be the same for everyone, whether or not they have physical or mental disabilities'.[111] The 'acid test' to determine whether there is a deprivation of liberty is (1) whether the person is subject to continuous supervision and control and (2) whether the person is free to leave. The comfort and

105 See s 4(A).

106 See s 4(B).

107 Children of 16 or 17 years old can be detained on the authority of the court under the Children Act 1989 or the Mental Health Act 1983 (as amended).

108 *A NHS Trust v A* [2013] EWHC 2442 (Fam).

109 [2014] UKSC 19. (Hereafter *Cheshire West*). For detailed and insightful analysis of the case, its impacts and potential solutions see L Series, *Deprivation of Liberty in the Shadows of the Institution* (2022) Bristol University Press.

110 [2011] EWCA (Civ) 1257.

111 *Cheshire West*, [46].

even enjoyment of the living arrangements are irrelevant to the analysis. As Lady Hale noted: 'A gilded cage is still a cage'.[112]

The Supreme Court in *Cheshire West* did not rule that the particular arrangements for the care of the applicants and similar people with disabilities were necessarily wrong or not made in their best interests but rather that the vulnerability of such people required that there be a 'periodic independent check on whether the arrangements made for them are in their best interests'.[113]

The decision resulted in an unprecedented increase in applications.[114] Efforts were made by some judges to streamline the process and limit its application.[115] For example, the Court of Appeal in *Ferreira*[116] held that DoLS applications will not usually be required for intensive care patients who lack capacity, even if they have a pre-existing mental disorder impacting on their mental capacity. In December 2021 a Government consultation on human rights questioned whether the Supreme Court in *Cheshire West* had exceeded its powers given the lack of Parliamentary debate on the issue.[117]

Calls for reform of the DoLS[118] were resisted pre-*Cheshire West* but revisited as the case load burgeoned. Following a public consultation, the Law Commission recommended that the DoLS procedure should be replaced by a new scheme called the Liberty Protection Safeguards.[119] A Joint Committee on Human Rights subsequently endorsed the Law Commission's recommendations.[120] The government then enacted the Mental Capacity (Amendment) Act 2019, which inserts a new Schedule AA1 into the 2005 Act in place of the old Schedules A1 and 1A. As we have noted, at the time of writing the timetable for implementation is uncertain.

112 Ibid.

113 Ibid, [57].

114 HSCIC, *Mental Capacity Act 2005, Deprivation of Liberty Safeguards (England) Quarter 3 Return, 2014–15* (February 2015), p 8: In 2014–15 '[o]verall there was a 56 per cent increase in the number of applications (11,700) between quarter 1 and quarter 3'.

115 See for example *Re X and Ors (Deprivation of Liberty)* [2014] EWCOP 25 and *Re X and Ors (Deprivation of Liberty) (Number 2)* [2014] EWCOP 37.

116 *R (Ferreira) v HM Senior Coroner for Inner South London and Ors* [2017] EWCA Civ 31.

117 Ministry of Justice, *Human Rights Act Reform: A Modern Bill of Rights: A Consultation to Reform the Human Rights Act 1998* (December 2021) CP588, paras 159–160.

118 House of Commons Health Committee, Post-legislative Scrutiny of the Mental Health Act 2007 (2013) HC 584, para 106 described them as 'woefully inadequate'; Select Committee on the Mental Capacity Act 2005, *Mental Capacity Act 2005: Post-Legislative Scrutiny* (March 2014) HL Paper 139 said they were 'not fit for purpose'.

119 Law Commission, *Mental Capacity and Deprivation of Liberty*.

120 Joint Committee on Human Rights, *The Right to Freedom and Safety: Reform of the Deprivation of Liberty Safeguards: Seventh Report of Session 2017–19* (2018) HC 890, HL Paper 161.

The new Liberty Protection Safeguards scheme is a streamlined system that will bring forward formal consideration of the justification for a deprivation of liberty so that (except in an emergency) it occurs before any arrangements are made. Rather than applying to individuals from aged 18 it will apply from 16.[121] The process will apply irrespective of the person's living arrangements, and so applications to the Court of Protection will be reduced, though the Court of Protection will continue to assess any disputes and appeals. The new decision-making process requires 'responsible bodies' such as the local authority or NHS decision-makers to confirm that the person lacks capacity to consent to the arrangements, they have a mental disorder, and the arrangements are necessary to prevent harm and proportionate to the likelihood and seriousness of that harm.[122] The responsible body must consult the person and relevant others so that they are as clear as possible as to the person's wishes and feelings.[123] Where the person objects to the living arrangements to proposed treatment, an assessment will be required by an Approved Mental Capacity Professional.[124]

7.13 The role of the family?

Reflecting on the complexity of the law so far, and the immensely difficult process of assessing the welfare of mentally incapacitated adults, why not remove decision-making about patients lacking mental capacity from doctors and 'responsible bodies' and in the first instance entrust decisions to an appropriate 'guardian', often a family member?[125] Intuitively, many people may feel that if a person cannot make decisions for themselves, their family are the best substitute decision-makers. The Law Commission and the government rejected both granting automatic proxy powers to families and a system whereby people lacking mental capacity are routinely subjected to guardianship. Family views are one component of the process for establishing best interests.

Laws granting automatic decision-making powers to 'next of kin' would be fraught with difficulty and danger. Identifying *who* the decision-maker should be is not straightforward, though not impossible: as we explore at 20.9 below, the hierarchy of 'qualifying relatives' in the Human Tissue Act 2004 offers one model. But genetic relationships of themselves may not qualify the person to be the best substitute decision-maker. Envisage A, a widow with three children. The 'next of kin' do not agree how their mother should be treated. Perhaps A has just one son, but he has visited her no more than once or twice a year in the past five decades. He will not be the ideal 'guardian' of his mother's interests. Her interests and his may conflict. He stands to inherit a substantial

121 MCA 2005, Sch AA1, para 2(2)(a).
122 Ibid, para 13.
123 Ibid, para 23.
124 Ibid, Pt 4. This is new role. AMCPs will be independent, trained, registered professionals.
125 See A Grubb, 'Treatment Decisions, Keeping it in the Family' in A Grubb (ed), *Choices and Decisions in Health Care* (1993) Wiley.

sum of money if she dies. If she recovers and enters a nursing home his inheritance may wither away.[126]

Such difficulties might be overcome if laws allowed the express appointment of a guardian, but wholesale appointment of guardians for every person unable to make decisions for themselves is simply impracticable. The courts would sink under a flood of applications. Nor is guardianship necessarily beneficial to patients. It imposes a childlike status on an adult. Given that English law endorses a 'functional' test of capacity, the law's aim is that the person themselves should take as many decisions as they are capable of making. And so, as we will see, the Mental Capacity Act seeks to find means whereby as far as possible the individual now lacking capacity is enabled to contribute to decisions about their future care in advance of the onset of incapacity.

7.14 Advance decisions[127]

An advance decision enables a person to set out their own instructions about any future treatment which they should, or should not, receive, were they to lose mental capacity to make such decisions for themselves. Such decisions need not be restricted to instructions about the continuation of life-sustaining treatment. A woman might, for example, want to give instructions about the management of her pregnancy in advance. A person in the early stages of a neurodegenerative disease might wish to set out their own care plan. Prior to the 2005 Act, the courts had made it clear that advance *refusals* of treatment were legally binding as long as there was unequivocal evidence that the patient's decision was voluntary, competent, and directly relevant to the factual circumstances in question.[128] The threshold for finding an advance refusal to be binding was set high. Advance requests (or demands) were not legally binding. The Court of Appeal in *R (on the application of Burke) v GMC*[129] made it crystal clear that any advance demand (or request) for treatment has no legal force.

> [A] patient cannot demand that a doctor administer a treatment which the doctor considers is adverse to his clinical needs.

So at common law, advance refusals were binding in theory, but exceptionally difficult to execute in practice in order to ensure that the individual's wishes prevailed.[130] The 2005 Act makes the exercise little easier. 'Advance decisions'[131] operate to prohibit specified treatment being carried out. Only

126 For an example of financial self-interest driving a family's defiance of declarations by the Court of Protection see *MASM v MMAM and others* [2015] EWCOP 3.

127 Discussed further below at 22.19 and see A Maclean, 'Advance Directives, Future Selves and Decision Making' (2006) 14 *Med Law Rev* 291.

128 See *Re T (Adult: Refusal of Medical Treatment)* [1992] 4 All ER 649, CA.

129 [2005] EWCA Civ 1003, [35].

130 See, for example, T Thompson, R Barbour and L Schwartz, 'Adherence to Advance Directives in Critical Care Decision Making: Vignette Study' (2003) 327 *BMJ* 1011, demonstrating the divergent attitudes of healthcare professionals when faced with a patient's mock advance directive.

131 See Mental Capacity Act 2005, ss 24–26.

advance *refusals* have legal force.[132] Save for refusals of life-sustaining treatment[133] there is no formal requirement that the advance decision be in writing or witnessed. Evidence that such a decision was made when the patient had capacity to make such a decision, and has not been withdrawn, must still be forthcoming.[134] If there is no written document this may be hard to establish; anecdotal evidence from family and friends may not suffice.[135] And the decision will not have effect if:[136]

- the treatment in question 'is not the treatment specified in the advance decision'; or
- 'any circumstances specified in the advance decision are absent' or
- 'there are reasonable grounds for believing that circumstances exist which [the patient] did not anticipate at the time of his advance decision and which would have affected his decision had he anticipated them'.

These stringent conditions set by the 2005 Act illustrate the difficulty of transforming theory into practice. Imagine this scenario. A is successfully treated for a brain tumour but warned that there is a 20 per cent risk of recurrence and poor prospects of long-term survival if the cancer recurs. Should the tumour return, it will gradually rob them of reasoning powers, memory and capacity for independent living. So A sets out an advance decision that, should the cancer recur, and they are unable to articulate their own wishes, they should not be resuscitated if they suffer a cardiac arrest, and should not be given antibiotics if they develop an infection. The cancer recurs and advances rapidly. A suffers a cerebral haemorrhage. A's advance decision does not cover the treatment in question and so has no force. Or, the cancer does not recur, but A suffers traumatic brain injuries in a road accident. A's advance decision does not apply because it does not relate to the circumstances that materialise. In an attempt to tackle this dilemma, section 24(2) does provide that the 'decision may be regarded as specifying a treatment or circumstance even though expressed in layman's terms'. Perhaps then, the best advice is to express any advance decision in as general terms as possible? But then you may fall foul of section 25(3) because of failure to anticipate circumstances that might have affected your decision. Yet section 25(3) in itself is an important safeguard for

132 Under s 26(1) if P has made an advance decision which is (a) valid and (b) applicable to a treatment, the decision has effect as if he had made it, and had had capacity to make it, at the time when the question arises whether the treatment should be carried out or continued.

133 Which must meet stringent conditions set out in s 25(6) and discussed at 22.19 below.

134 See s 25(1). For some of the difficulties surrounding capacity in respect of advance decisions, see R Heywood, 'Revisiting Advance Decision Making Under the Mental Capacity Act 2005: A Tale of Mixed Messages' (2015) 23 *Med Law Rev* 81.

135 Well illustrated in a pre-2005 Act case; see *W Health Care Trust v H* [2004] EWCA 1324.

136 See s 25(4).

patients. Consider A again. A executes an advance decision in 2018 refusing all treatment should their cancer recur. It recurs in 2023 by which time a new highly effective treatment has been developed.

Some of the rigours of the statutory conditions for a valid advance decision seem to have been abated in recent decisions from the Court of Protection. In both *Nottinghamshire Healthcare NHS Trust v RC*[137] and *Newcastle upon Tyne Hospitals Foundation Trust* v *LM*[138] statements by Jehovah's Witness patients that they would never consent to blood transfusions were in effect treated as advance decisions even though not meeting the exact requirements of the Mental Capacity Act. Moreover, in *Barnsley Hospital NHS Foundation Trust v MSP*, despite the presence of procedural deficiencies in an advance decision, Hayden J accepted that it amounted to clear evidence that the patient would have rejected any treatment designed to artificially prolong his life.[139] Thus, even though the advance decision was not legally binding, it was nonetheless a strong representation of the patient's own expressed wishes, which Hayden J chose to emphasise in his assessment of best interests.[140]

Next, we must consider withdrawal of any advance decision. People must be free to change their minds. What seemed intolerable at 40 may be acceptable at 70. Changes in personal circumstances will alter one's perspective of quality of life. Section 24(4) provides that a withdrawal (or partial withdrawal) need not be in writing. *HE v NHS Trust*[141] (decided prior to the Mental Capacity Act) demonstrates the difficulty of establishing informed withdrawal of an advance decision. When HE was a practising Jehovah's Witness, she executed (in writing) an advance decision prohibiting any blood transfusion. Later she renounced the Witness faith and reverted back to her original Muslim faith, becoming engaged to a fellow Muslim. Her advance decision stated that it could only be revoked in writing. She had taken no formal steps to revoke her original directive. Nonetheless, Munby J found that her conduct offered sufficient evidence that her directive no longer represented her wishes. It was implicitly revoked. He went on to say that 'once there is some real reason for doubt, then it is for those who assert the continuing validity and applicability of the advance directive to prove that it is still operative'.[142] In effect, the facts of each case must be assessed. As Munby J goes on to say:

> [T]he longer the time which has elapsed since an advance directive was made, and the greater the apparent change in circumstance since then, the more doubt there is likely to be as to its continuing validity and applicability.[143]

137 [2014] EWCOP 1317.
138 [2014] EWCOP 454.
139 [2020] EWCOP 26, [19] and [46].
140 Ibid, [46].
141 [2003] 2 FLR 408.
142 Ibid, [43].
143 Ibid, [45].

In its final report on mental capacity and deprivation of liberty, the Law Commission recommended a new provision relating to *advance* consent.[144] This would have allowed an individual, in specific circumstances, to provide an advance consent to a future deprivation of liberty.[145] There would be some dangers associated with this move, not least the potential for abuse if appropriate safeguards were not designed to accompany it. As such, the Government decided not to enact this recommendation in the Mental Capacity (Amendment) Act 2019.[146]

7.15 Lasting powers of attorney

An inevitable difficulty in any form of advance decision is defining in exactly what sorts of circumstances one might lose capacity, and what sorts of diseases lie in wait. Appointing a chosen proxy to act for you may be an option welcome to many people. Before the 2005 Act, it was possible to execute an enduring power of attorney[147] and appoint a proxy to take decisions in relation to property and financial affairs.

Section 9 of the Mental Capacity Act introduced the lasting power of attorney (LPA) whereby a person nominates the chosen donee (or donees) of the power to make decisions for them both in relation to personal welfare (including decisions about medical treatment), and in relation to their property and financial affairs. One person can be selected to manage all your affairs for you. An elderly parent can now authorise a daughter to make any necessary decisions about her intimate welfare and medical care, as much as about her property. The proxy (the donee) may only make decisions about life-sustaining treatment if the donor of the power expressly authorised her to do so. In making any decision on behalf of the donor, the proxy must act in the best interests of the donor and conform fully to the principles underlying the 2005 Act. The proxy's powers are limited by any advance decision made earlier by the donor. A number of formalities are prescribed.[148]

Some people may choose to grant an LPA to a professional adviser. More may prefer to choose a close friend or relative. So is there a risk of conflict of interest again? We think not. LPAs overcome many of the difficulties inherent in automatically entrusting decisions about healthcare to 'next of kin'. The patient actively chooses their preferred 'agent'. If a patient becomes estranged from their daughter, the patient will not grant her power of attorney. If the patient suspects that their daughter is over-anxious to receive an inheritance, the patient will not give the daughter power over their life and death. As long

144 Law Commission, *Mental Capacity and Deprivation of Liberty*, recommendation 43. See also discussion, [15.2]–[15.24].

145 Ibid.

146 DHSC, *Final Government Response to the Law Commission's Review of Deprivation of Liberty Safeguards and Mental Capacity*.

147 See the Enduring Powers of Attorney Act 1985.

148 See the Office of the Public Guardian, which lists recent cases at www.publicguardian.gov.uk.

as the requisite rules about the execution and registration of LPAs ensure that the grant of a LPA is a free and informed decision of the patient, LPAs are an attractive option to people who want to entrust their decisions about future health to relatives, friends or professional advisers chosen by them.

7.16 Deputies

Although guardianship of adults is generally eschewed in the 2005 Act, sections 15–21 make provision for exceptional cases when the Court of Protection may see fit to appoint a deputy authorised to make personal welfare decisions on behalf of the patient. More and more deputies seem to be being appointed sometimes creating serious problems for the Court of Protection. The appointment of a deputy must be shown to be in the patient's best interests and the court has a wide discretion to determine the scope of the powers conferred on the deputy. Where serious questions arise about the continuing treatment and welfare of a patient lacking mental capacity, a deputy may be appointed who will be authorised within strict limits, and for as short a time as possible, to act on the patient's behalf generally. Their powers would not be limited to medical care, but extend to all questions of personal welfare, healthcare, property and finance.

Though family members are often appointed as deputies, not all family members are suitable.[149] In *Re BM*[150] Senior Judge Lush set out guidance. Whilst a family member or friend[151] is generally preferred due to their familiarity with the incapacitated person's affairs and wishes, it will not be appropriate to appoint such a person as deputy where there is evidence of abuse; poor management of the person's own financial affairs; friction between family members; or other conflicts of interest.

7.17 Court of Protection[152]

Central to the Act is the Court of Protection, which enjoys a wide-ranging jurisdiction to oversee the care of adults lacking mental capacity, in both healthcare and welfare matters. It adjudicates on disputes about what form such care should take and can issue declarations about the legality of proposed treatment. The powers of the Court of Protection were considered in *Re MN (Adult)*.[153] Upholding Eleanor King J's ruling,[154] Sir James Munby held that the Court of Protection's powers with respect to an incapacitated person were

149 *G v E and others* [2010] EWHC 2512, [60–61] per Baker J.

150 [2014] EWCOP B20. And see *LB Haringey v CM* [2014] EWCOP B23 on the importance of ensuring that the appointed deputy does not subject the incapacitated person to undue influence.

151 For the appointment of a longstanding friend in preference to a nephew; see *DB v DW* [2015] EWCOP 16.

152 See ss 45–61.

153 [2015] EWCA Civ 411.

154 *ACCG v MN* [2013] EWHC 3859 (COP).

limited to the powers that person would have if they retained capacity. In this case this meant that the best interests declaration was dependent to some extent on practical issues, such as the availability of funding from the local authority. The Court could not compel the authority to allocate additional resources for the care of the person. Any challenge to the legality of resource decisions should be by way of an application for judicial review.

The Court of Protection has extensive powers of enforcement. Like the High Court, it can grant injunctions, summon witnesses and commit those in contempt to prison. Penal notices can be attached to orders making clear the consequences of breach. There has long been uncertainty, however, surrounding the binding nature of a best interests declaration where no injunctive order is made.[155] Will deliberate defiance constitute contempt of court? Hayden J made clear in the case of *In re M* that it will not: 'There cannot be "defiance" of a "declaration" nor can there be an "enforcement" of one. A declaration is ultimately no more than a formal, explicit statement or announcement.'[156]

The court can appoint deputies where appropriate and register and supervise LPAs. But, as we have noted, resort to the court to oversee especially controversial or problematic medical procedures is not mandatory. Does this matter? Can we not trust the good sense of doctors and families to seek judicial oversight of what they propose to do in cases when, and only when, such oversight is truly needed? Doctors and carers are guided by the Code of Practice, which, as we have seen, requires that certain cases are brought before the court. A failure on the part of a health professional to comply with this guidance will be taken into account in any relevant proceedings in any court or tribunal. It would, for example, be relevant to an assessment of a doctor's fitness to practise before the General Medical Council. One difficulty remains. When doctors and families disagree either with each other or among themselves, an application to court is likely to be made. Where there is either consensus among the several people involved with the patient, or perhaps an absence of involved family or friends, resort to court is less likely. The patient, lacking an advocate, is deprived of any voice to speak on their behalf. Two limited safeguards operate. First, under section 37, an IMCA should be appointed where doctors propose serious medical treatment or a patient lacks capacity and does not have a family member or friend to advise as to their best interests. Second, the jurisdiction of the Court of Protection does extend to claims arising from an alleged breach of the Human Rights Act 1998 and can award damages accordingly.[157]

7.18 Mental Health Legislation[158]

This book does not deal in any detail with the provisions of the Mental Health Acts. Brief reference needs to be made here to the Mental Health Acts 1983

155 A question answered in part in *A v A Health Authority* [2002] EWHC 18 (Fam).
156 *MASM v MMAM & Ors* [2015] EWCOP 3 Hayden J at [49].
157 *YA (F) v A Local Authority* [2010] EWHC 2770.
158 See B Hale (Baroness), *Mental Health Law* (6th edn, 2020) Sweet & Maxwell.

and 2007. The 2007 Act makes significant amendments to the earlier statute. For the purposes of this chapter, one of the most crucial provisions of the mental health legislation is that section 63 of the1983 Act grants statutory authority to dispense with detained patients' consent to treatment for mental disorder. A patient's refusal of treatment can thus be overridden, even if they meet the test of mental capacity under the 2005 Act. As we shall see the courts have on occasion interpreted section 63 to sanction treatments that might primarily be seen as treatment for physical illness.

Part II of the 1983 Act (as amended) makes provision for the detention in hospital of certain mentally disordered patients. Only a minority of patients with mental disorder are detained in hospital under the Act. Application for admission for assessment (observation and tests) must be based on the written recommendations of two medical practitioners who testify that (1) the patient is suffering from mental disorder of a nature or degree which warrants their detention in hospital for assessment or assessment followed by medical treatment for at least a limited period; and (2) they ought to be so detained in the interests of their own health or safety, or to protect others.[159] Admission for the assessment authorises the patient's detention for up to twenty-eight days. If they are to be detained longer, an application for admission for treatment must be made.[160] Such an application made under section 3 of the Act must be founded on grounds that:

(a) The patient is suffering from mental disorder of a nature or degree which makes it appropriate for him to receive treatment in a mental hospital; *and*
(b) It is necessary for the health and safety of the patient or for the protection of other persons that he should receive such treatment and it cannot be provided unless he is detained under this section; *and*
(c) Appropriate medical treatment is available for him.

The crucial question becomes how is mental disorder defined? Section 1(2) of the 1983 Act (as amended) adopts a very broad definition; mental disorder means 'any disorder or disability of the mind'. 'Learning disability'[161] will not, however, as such be said to constitute mental disorder. A person with learning disability will be able to be detained under section 3 of the 1983 Act only if their 'disability is associated with abnormally aggressive or seriously irresponsible conduct'.[162]

159 See Mental Health Act 1983, s 2. An emergency application founded on the recommendation of one doctor may be made under s 4 and authorises detention for up to seventy-two hours.

160 A successful application for admission for treatment authorises detention for an initial period of six months.

161 Defined as a 'state of arrested or incomplete development of the mind which includes significant impairment of intelligence and social functioning'; see s 1(4).

162 Section 1(2A), but he could be admitted for assessment under s 2 without establishing such an association.

Note, too, the condition that there should be appropriate medical treatment available for any patient who is to be detained for treatment. Some mental disorders, notably personality disorders, rarely respond to drug therapy as disorders such as schizophrenia may. But section 145 of the Mental Health Act 1983 now defines treatability broadly as 'medical treatment the purpose of which is to alleviate or prevent a worsening of the disorder or one or more of its symptoms or manifestation'.

The effect of sections 2 and 3 of the 1983 Act means that the number of people lacking capacity liable to be detained under the 1983 Act is small:

(1) The many patients who lack capacity as a result of learning disability can be detained only if they become aggressive or seriously irresponsible.
(2) In many cases their disability will not meet the 'treatability' condition. Being shut up in hospital will not do them any good.[163]
(3) A person lacking mental capacity can usually be protected from herself by means other than detention, so condition (b) may not be met.
(4) Government policy for several years was to promote care in the community, and numerous long-stay mental health units were closed down.
(5) Psychiatrists maintain that there are insufficient beds in mental health units even for patients who indubitably meet the criteria set out in the 1983 Act. Only the most dangerously disordered or profoundly disabled patients are detained in hospital under the 1983 Act. When it is deemed necessary to confine a patient lacking capacity with learning or other disabilities for their own safety, the usual route now will be to resort the DoLS (soon to be Liberty Protection Safeguards) introduced into the Mental Capacity Act 2005,[164] though we must re-iterate that the two systems for care and detention have in practice both significant overlap and gaps through which some patients may fall.[165]

The 1983 Act is showing many signs of strain. A review in 2018 took an initial step to changing the law in closer accordance with human rights principles.[166] Worrying evidence has emerged of racial disparities in the use of community treatment orders, and the approach to detaining those with mental capacity against their will conflicts sharply with that taken in the UN Convention on the Rights of Persons with Disabilities, which, amongst other things, requires support of a patient's will and preferences. The review recommended a systemic approach to improving the response of mental health services to a population's ethnic and cultural background. The Government has committed to

163 Even though the Court of Appeal has developed a fairly broad definition of treatment to include group therapy and nursing care in a structured environment; see *R v Canon Park Mental Review Tribunal ex p A* [1994] 2 All ER 659, CA; *R v Mental Health Review Tribunal ex p Macdonald* (1998) Crown Office Digest 205.

164 See 7.12 above.

165 See *A NHS Trust v A* [2013] EWHC 2442 (Fam).

166 DHSC, *Modernising the Mental Health Act – Final Report form the Independent Review* (2018) (Chair: Prof Sir Simon Wessely).

new legislation that will strengthen detention criteria, allow people to nominate an advocate to be involved in decision-making, and allow them to make 'advance choices' about future care and treatment.[167]

7.19 Compulsory treatment under the 1983 Act

Part IV of the Mental Health Act provides for the compulsory treatment of that minority of patients detained under the Act. Section 63 provides that:

> The consent of a patient shall not be required for any medical treatment given to him for the mental disorder from which he is suffering, not being treatment given within section 57, 58 or 58A [of the Act].

Section 63 applies to detained patients only. It cannot be used on voluntary patients, or on an out-patient basis. But that poses a dilemma. A patient may recover in hospital on appropriate medication and be fit to return home if they continue to comply with treatment, but the risk is that when they are out of hospital, they will stop taking their medicine. So, at one hospital doctors admitted patients under section 3, gave them long-term medication, then released them on licence until their next dose of medication was due. That practice was found to be unlawful.[168] Section 63 could be used to dispense with a patient's consent to treatment only where that patient actually needed to be detained; the conditions laid down in section 3 for admission for treatment were not met, and the use of section 3 to enforce treatment was an unlawful fiction. The Court of Appeal, however, later held that as long as some element of hospital treatment was required, 'extended leave' could be used to 'enforce' medicating in the community.[169] Amendments inserting section 17A-G in the 1983 Act now provide for community treatment orders enabling doctors to ensure treatment in the community via the sanction of recall to hospital.

Section 63 on its face authorises psychiatric treatment, not treatment for physical illness. It has been interpreted by judges to extend to allow the forcible feeding of patients with anorexia nervosa[170] and, as we explore in Chapter 13, to justify non-consensual Caesarean surgery on a detained patient. *Tameside and Glossop Acute Services Trust v CH*[171] requires an imaginative approach to section 63. CH suffered from paranoid schizophrenia and was detained in a mental hospital. On admission to hospital, she was discovered to be pregnant. At thirty-seven weeks, the retarded growth of the fetus caused doctors to suspect placental failure and they wanted to deliver the child swiftly by Caesarean section. Wall J held that such surgery

167 DHSC, *White Paper: Reforming the Mental Health Act* (2021). A draft Mental Health Bill was published in June 2022.

168 *R v Hallstrom ex p W (No 2)* [1986] QB 824.

169 *B v Barking, Havering and Brentwood Community NHS Trust* [1999] 1 FLR 106.

170 *B v Croydon District Health Authority* [1995] 1 All ER 683 CA; *Re KB (Adult) (Mental Patient: Medical Treatment)* [1994] 2 FLR 1051. And see *R v Collins and Ashworth Hospital Authority ex p Brady* [2000] Lloyd's Rep Med 355.

171 [1996] 1 FCR 753.

was justified under section 63 as treatment for CH's mental disorder. CH maintained a belief that medical staff were malicious and out to harm her child. She could not be given the medication most appropriate to treat her mental illness while still pregnant. The judge ruled 'a successful outcome of her pregnancy is a necessary part of the overall treatment of her mental disorder'. Whether B or CH should have been compelled to submit to treatment is something reasonable people might disagree on. More recently in *A NHS Trust v A*[172] Baker J expressed concerns about any extended use of section 63 as a device to compel detained patients to accept treatment for essentially physical disorders. Dr A was an Iranian doctor suffering from delusional disorder and detained under the Mental Health Act. He had sought asylum in the UK and been refused on three occasions. His passport was confiscated by the UK Borders Agency and he commenced a hunger strike in protest. The judge held that Dr A lacked capacity both to litigate and in relation to eating and drinking and that it would be in his best interests to be 'force-fed'. But he also held that forcible feeding did not constitute treatment for A's mental disorder, being rather treatment for the physical ills consequent on the hunger strike. Were A detained under the DoLS then treatment for such physical ills could be imposed, but as he was now detained under the Mental Health Act, he was ineligible to be deprived of his liberty under DoLS. The judge fell back on the inherent jurisdiction to protect vulnerable people (discussed at 7.20 below).

In those cases where section 63 may be applicable, it should be noted that sections 57, 58 and 58A provide important safeguards for patients' welfare and autonomy. Section 57 is unusual in that it applies to *all* patients and not just those detained in hospital. Any form of psychosurgery,[173] such as lobotomy, and any surgical implantation of hormones to reduce male sexual drive will be unlawful[174] unless (1) the patient consents *and* (2) a specially appointed and independent doctor certifies that (a) the patient is capable of understanding the nature and purpose of the treatment proposed and its likely effects and (b) the treatment is likely to benefit the patient.

Sections 58 and 58A apply to detained patients only. Any long-term medication (administered for longer than three months[175]) is authorised only if either (a) the patient consents and a doctor certifies that they are competent to do so or (b) an independent doctor certifies that the patient is incapable of giving consent or has refused to do so but that nonetheless 'it is appropriate for the treatment to be given'. Section 58 used to include electroconvulsive therapy (ECT) too, but section 58A now provides that ECT cannot be given without

172 [2013] EWHC 2442 (Fam).

173 See s 57(1).

174 See s 57(2). Section 57(2) empowers the Secretary of State to bring other treatments within the ambit of s 57(2). See also the Mental Health (Hospital, Guardianship and Treatment) (England) Regulations 2008, SI 2008/1184 (amended SIs 2008/2560; 2012/1118), reg 27(1).

175 See s 58(2).

consent (except in emergencies covered by section 62) unless the patient lacks capacity and has not refused ECT via an advance decision.

7.20 Vulnerable patients: the inherent jurisdiction

Should compulsory treatment of a competent patient ever be legally justifiable, outwith any Mental Health Act? Before the Mental Capacity Act came into force the courts had begun to invoke the inherent jurisdiction to protect adults whose health and circumstances made them vulnerable but who may not lack mental capacity. Munby J defined such a vulnerable adult as a person who 'even if not incapacitated, is either under constraint, or subject to coercion or undue influence, or for some other reason deprived of the capacity to make free choice, or disabled from making a free choice, or incapacitated or disabled from giving or expressing a real and genuine consent'.[176] The Court of Appeal has made it clear that such a protective jurisdiction survives the Mental Capacity Act, allowing the courts to intervene to protect the vulnerable individual from abuse or coercion by carers or family members.[177] An injunction could order the 'abusive' relative to cease interfering in the vulnerable person's affairs and even to ban contact altogether. The majority of cases involving such vulnerable adults have involved social care rather than medical treatments. One example that did touch on medical care was *A Local Authority v A*.[178] A local authority feared that a husband was pressuring his wife, who has learning difficulties, to stop contraceptive treatment. The court in the end concluded that for the present no order was needed.

The inherent jurisdiction may also be used in relation to patients who lack capacity where, as in *A NHS Trust v A*,[179] interventions clearly in the best interests of the incapacitated patient fall into the gap between the Mental Capacity Act and the Mental Health Acts.[180] In *Re L (Vulnerable Adults with Capacity: Court's Jurisdiction) (No 2)*, Davis LJ explained that where cases fell clearly within the ambit of the Mental Capacity Act there is no room or need for the inherent jurisdiction but 'even in the case of an adult who lacks capacity within the meaning of the 2005 Act, it appears that the inherent jurisdiction survives, albeit now reinforced by the provisions of the Mental Capacity Act 2005'.[181]

176 *A Local Authority v MA, NA and SA* [2005] EWHC 2942 (Fam), [77].

177 *DL v A Local Authority and others* [2012] EWCA (Civ) 253. Sir James Munby suggests caution in its application: see 'Whither the Inherent Jurisdiction' (2021) 51(Feb) *Family Law* 215 (Part I); (2021) 51(Mar) *Family Law* 365 (Part II); 51(Apr) *Family Law* 508 (Part III). And see discussion of the ambits of the inherent jurisdiction in *Southend-on-Sea Borough Council v Meyers* [2019] EWHC 399 (Fam), [28] (Hayden J quoting Baker LJ when refusing permission to appeal); And see generally the very useful guidance from 39 Essex Chambers, *Mental Capacity Guidance Note – Inherent Jurisdiction* (2022).

178 [2010] EWHC 1549 (Fam); see 13.4 below.

179 [2013] EWHC 2442 (Fam); see 7.19 above.

180 *XCC v A* [2013] 2 All ER 988.

181 [2013] Fam 1.

7.21 Protecting the public

May treatment ever be enforced on an adult with capacity for the benefit of others? In the United Kingdom, unlike the USA,[182] legislation has never enforced sterilisation on those seen as mentally or physically unfit to reproduce. In England, unlike many countries in Europe, childhood vaccination has never been compulsory.[183] Nor in the COVID-19 pandemic was vaccination made mandatory for the general public, though it became a condition of work for care workers in 2021 and was planned but later dropped for patient-facing health professionals in 2022.[184]

The recent COVID-19 pandemic and the outbreak of Ebola in 2014 illustrate that the transmission of infectious diseases across national boundaries can have a devastating effect on public health. The relentless growth of antibiotic resistance also raises the spectre that quite common diseases may again become fatal. The World Health Organisation has said that antibiotic resistance is one of the greatest threats to human health.[185]

The Public Health (Control of Disease) Act 1984 was heavily amended by Part 3 of the Health and Social Care Act 2008, which inserted a new Part 2A in the Public Health (Control of Disease) Act. The Act seeks to implement extensive measures to protect the public from the spread of infection or contamination (including radiation and artificial biological artefacts) which poses or could pose a significant harm to human health. Section 45B–D confers extensive powers on Ministers to make regulations to protect public health from infection or contamination. The scope of such powers is extensive and coercive, enabling government to restrain people, seize property and impose quarantines. By way of example, even though the Coronavirus Act 2020 was introduced as a bespoke piece of legislation to grant the Government a range of policy and financial powers to deal with the virus, it was actually the Public Health (Control of Disease) Act 1984 that was used to give legal force to the range of regulations that were enacted to enforce the first lockdown measures

182 For discussion of compulsory sterilisation laws in the USA see MDA Freeman, 'Sterilising the Mentally Handicapped' in MDA Freeman (ed), *Medicine, Ethics and Law* (1988) Stevens.

183 The European Court of Human Rights held in *Vavřička and Others v the Czech Republic* (App Nos 47621/13, 3867/14, 73094/14, 19306/15, 19298/15 and 43883/15, 8 April 2021), that state-mandated childhood vaccination can be compatible with the European Convention. See D Archard, J Brierley and E Cave, 'Compulsory Childhood Vaccination: Human Rights, Solidarity, and Best Interests' (2021) 29(4) *Med Law Rev* 716.

184 Health and Social Care Act 2008 (Regulated Activities) (Amendment) (Coronavirus) Regulations 2021, No 1 and No 2 (SI 2021/891 and SI 2022/15) amended The Health and Social Care Act 2008 (Regulated Activities) Regulations 2014. Challenges to the policy were dismissed in *R (Peters & Anor) v Secretary of State for Health and Social Care and Anor* [2021] EWHC 3182 (Admin).

185 WHO, *Antibiotic Resistance* (2020) at www.who.int/news-room/fact-sheets/detail/antibiotic-resistance.

in March 2020.[186] The extreme nature of the provisions during the first wave of the virus, which included restrictions on movement, the banning of public gatherings and the closure of a significant number of businesses, demonstrates just how seriously the law treats concerns over public health and the spread of contagious disease and how powerful a tool the Public Health (Control of Disease) Act 1984 can be.

The Health Protection (Notification) Regulations 2010[187] also require doctors to notify the proper authority if they have reasonable grounds to suspect that the patient has a 'notifiable disease', or has some other infection that could present a significant harm to human health, or is contaminated.[188] The list of notifiable diseases includes most major communicable diseases such as tuberculosis, cholera, food poisoning, whooping cough and rubella. But note the doctor must also notify authorities of any other potentially dangerous infection such as a virulent new strain of flu. Such patients lose not only their right to confidential treatment but may also lose their liberty. Magistrates may order such a patient to submit to testing, be subject to restriction on their movements, and in an extreme case be detained in hospital.[189] However there is no power to compel the patient to submit to medical treatment.[190]

Draconian powers to address infectious diseases allowing the detention of the infected person have a long history and many of the original notifiable diseases, such as plague or cholera, carried a high risk of potentially deadly infection to others with little possibility of the patient themselves, whatever they did, of protecting others from infection. Diseases such as HIV and Hepatitis B (and even tuberculosis) do not fit that pattern. A person may be seropositive for HIV or Hepatitis B, but not ill, and certainly not suffering from any mental impairment of confusion. If they amend their lifestyle in conformity with medical advice the risk they pose to others is minimal. Using public health powers to force their compliance with 'safe living' necessarily involves an invasion of their liberty. For how long could society justifiably detain a person with Hepatitis B? That person may never cease to be a carrier of the disease.

The legality of the powers to detain people to prevent the spread of infectious diseases was tested in the ECtHR in 2005. In *Enhorn v Sweden*,[191] an HIV positive man who had unknowingly infected a 19-year-old girl was required under Sweden's Infectious Diseases Act 1988 to attend regular medical appointments. When he failed to do so, he was compulsorily isolated in hospital. Over a period of six years, he spent around eighteen months in compulsory isolation. Did the Swedish courts unlawfully deprive Mr Enhorn of his

[186] See Health Protection (Coronavirus, Restrictions) (England) Regulations 2020, SI 2020/350. Note that these regulations have been amended at various stages of the pandemic.

[187] SI 2010/659.

[188] SI 2010/659, reg 2.

[189] See Public Health (Control of Disease) Act 1984, s 45G.

[190] See s 45E.

[191] [2005] EHHR 34. See R Martin, 'The Exercise of Public Health Powers in Cases of Infectious Disease: Human Rights Implications' (2006) 14(1) *Med Law Rev* 132.

liberty, protected by Article 5, or was the deprivation justified under Article 5(1)(e) for 'the lawful detention of persons for the prevention of spreading of infectious diseases, of persons of unsound mind, alcoholics or drug addicts, or vagrants'? The Court held that the isolation was a disproportionate response to the threat to the public. Mr Enhorn's Article 5 right to liberty had been breached.[192] Compulsory isolation must be used only as a last resort.

7.22 Criminal liability[193]

Does/should a 'patient' who fails to protect other people and recklessly disregards the welfare of others commit a criminal offence?[194] A midwife knows that they are infected by Hepatitis B, conceals their condition and infects several patients; is their conduct significantly different from the train driver who, knowing that they are over the alcohol limit, still takes the controls and endangers their passengers? Identifying a pigeonhole in which to fit criminal liability for spreading diseases used to be tricky. If patients have consented to our hypothetical midwife's ministrations, their consent is unlikely to be vitiated by lack of information about the midwife's infection, so no assault is committed.[195] In one case, a surgeon continued to operate, fraudulently concealing that he had Hepatitis B. Several of his patients contracted Hepatitis. The surgeon was ultimately convicted of the antiquated common law offence of causing a public nuisance.[196]

In *R v Dica*,[197] the Court of Appeal held that reckless transmission of serious disease constituted a criminal offence in English law.[198] *Dica* was convicted on two counts of inflicting grievous bodily harm, contrary to section 20 of the

192 See A Mowbray, 'Compulsory Detention to Prevent the Spreading of Infectious Diseases' (2005) 5 *Human Rights Review* 387.

193 See H Quirk and C Stanton (eds), *The Criminal Law and Contagion* (2016) Cambridge University Press: and see Law Commission, *Reform of Offences against the Person: A Scoping Consultation Paper* (2014) Consultation Paper No 217, ch 6.

194 See SH Bronitt, 'Spreading Disease and the Criminal Law' [1994] *Criminal Law Review* 21; KM Smith, 'Sexual Etiquette, Public Interest and the Criminal Law' (1991) 42 *Northern Ireland Legal Quarterly* 309.

195 *R v Clarence* (1888) 22 QBD 23; *Hegarty v Shine* (1878) 14 Cox CC 124.

196 *R v Gaud* (unreported); analysed in M Mulholland, 'Public Nuisance – A New Use for an Old Tool' (1995) 42 *Professional Negligence* 70. Today a failure to disclose Hepatitis B is likely to provoke a fitness-to-practise investigation. See for example *The Professional Standards Authority for Health and Social Care v The General Dental Council, AB* [2016] EWHC 1539 (Admin).

197 [2004] 3 All ER 593; see M Brazier, 'Do No Harm – Do Patients Have Responsibilities Too?' (2006) 65(2) *CLJ* 397.

198 In *HM Advocate v Kelly* (2001) High Court of Judiciary, Glasgow, a Scottish court convicted a man who infected his lover with HIV of culpably and recklessly endangering her health; see J Chalmers, 'The Criminalisation of HIV Transmission' (2002) 28 *J Med Ethics* 160. And see *R v Konzani* (2005) 2 Cr App R 13; discussed in M Weait, 'Knowledge, Autonomy and Consent: *R v Konzani*' [2005] *Criminal Law Review* 673.

Offences Against the Person Act 1861, on lovers whom he infected with HIV. The trial judge ruled (*inter alia*) that any consent on the part of the victims to the risk of contracting HIV, thus their knowledge or otherwise of the accused's seropositive status, was irrelevant and provided no defence because the women had no capacity to consent to such serious harm.[199] Following the judge's ruling, the accused chose not to give evidence and the question of whether his lovers knew of his HIV positive condition was not left to the jury. The Court of Appeal quashed the conviction and ordered a retrial. Consensual acts of sexual intercourse do not become unlawful 'merely because there may be a known risk to the health of one or other participant'.[200] As Judge LJ said,[201] 'interference of this kind with personal autonomy, and its level and extent, may only be made by Parliament'. The key question was had the victims consented to the risk of contracting HIV? To consent they must first be aware of the accused's condition, though knowledge alone would not normally establish consent. Absence of consent to such a risk did not vitiate consent to intercourse. *Dica* was not guilty of rape. Inflicting serious bodily harm is no longer an offence parasitic on assault.[202] No assault needs to be proven, simply the imposition on the victim of serious harm to which they have not consented.

The decision in *Dica* has met with much criticism.[203] Critics maintain that criminalisation will reinforce stigmatisation of people living with HIV, will deter patients from seeking testing and counselling, and in its operation, discriminate against minority groups such as gay men and drug users.[204] John Spencer lends his voice to a powerful defence of *Dica:*

> To infect an unsuspecting person with a grave disease you know you have, or may have, by behaviour you know involves a risk of transmission, and that you know you could easily modify to reduce or eliminate the risk, is to harm another in a way that is both needless and callous. For that reason criminal liability is justified unless there are strong countervailing reasons.[205]

That *Dica* remains good law is signalled by the Court of Appeal in *R v Golding*.[206] The appellant was convicted of inflicting grievous bodily harm under section 20 of the Offences against the Person Act after he infected his girlfriend with genital herpes. He never warned her about his diagnosis. The appeal court rejected the appeal. One of the grounds of appeal was that genital herpes did not constitute grievous bodily harm. The court held that such harm did not need to be permanent or at the level of danger to life of HIV. The matter was for the jury applying contemporary social standards.

199 Relying on *R v Brown* [1994] 1 AC 212, HL.
200 [2004] 3 All ER 593, 605.
201 Ibid, 606.
202 See *R v Ireland, R v Burstow* [1998] AC 147, HL.
203 See M Weait, 'Criminal Law and Sexual Transmission of HIV: *R v Dica*' (2005) 68 *MLR* 121.
204 Ibid,134.
205 JR Spencer, 'Liability for Reckless Infection – Part 2' (2004) 154 *NLJ* 448, 448.
206 [2014] EWCA (Crim) 899.

There are circumstances where private interests should rightly be subordinated to the public good. This reasoning lies at the heart of public health laws. The basis of enforced treatment under public health legislation is the protection of the public. A person can be removed to hospital if precautions to prevent the infection spreading can be taken, are not being taken, and a 'serious risk of infection is thereby caused to other people'. There is no pretence that the compulsory powers are exercised solely in the 'best interests' of the patient. Where someone, albeit through no fault of their own, poses a threat to the health of others, their interest in autonomy cedes to others' interest in health and safety. Where someone has the capacity to protect others from contracting disease from them and fails to do so, the criminal law is properly engaged.

7.23 The uncooperative patient

What of the patient whose condition or conduct poses a risk of some harm or serious nuisance to others but who refuses to cooperate in measures to minimise that harm or nuisance? In this example, what is in issue is not protecting the individual themselves but protecting others from nuisance or harm they have created. At common law an individual enjoys a right to self-defence. This is a common law right which almost certainly survives the enactment of a public right to use force to prevent crime in section 3 of the Criminal Law Act 1967. If you are attacked by a person so mentally disordered that they could not be found guilty of any crime, you are still lawfully entitled to fend off the attacker using whatever degree of force is necessary. Might there then be circumstances in which treatment of a competent but confused or disturbed patient could be justified because of the harm their untreated condition poses to others? Can a patient who refuses to bathe be washed to prevent them becoming a hazard to hygiene? Such a suggestion sounds like heresy. Apart from the provisions in the Public Health Acts, the Mental Health and Mental Capacity Acts (discussed earlier), treatment of adult patients whose mental capacity is disputed is in theory lawful only if in the patient's 'best interests'. The anomalous provisions of the National Assistance Act 1948[207] that empowered community health doctors to seek to remove from their homes and place in a suitable hospital a person 'suffering from chronic disease, or being aged, infirm or physically incapacitated' and unable to care for themselves either in their own interests or '*to prevent injury to the health of, or serious nuisances to, other persons*' (our emphasis) were at last repealed in 2014.[208]

In practice there can be little doubt that healthcare professionals are imposing 'treatment' on patients which cannot be shown to be exclusively in the patients' interests. We are not suggesting that gynaecologists are sterilising women for eugenic reasons, or that surgeons are experimenting on unfortunate patients. Patients are washed against their will. Patients are sometimes given medication they would rather not have, perhaps disguised in their food. Without such stratagems, nurses struggling to care for wards that cater for

207 National Assistance Act 1948, s 47, as amended by the National Assistance (Amendment) Act 1951.
208 Care Standards Act 2014.

confused geriatric patients, or working in long-stay institutions for voluntary mental patients, might give up the struggle. Should such miscreants be tracked down and prosecuted for assault?

It is dubious whether it is ever possible to divorce the interests of the individual entirely from the interests of the carer. The example that follows is unpleasant but is an instance of a dilemma that doctors have to face, and parents may have to live with. A young woman lives at home with her father. She is physically adult and normal but has profound learning difficulties. She is sexually provocative and fertile. She is incontinent and it is her father who every month has to cope with her periods. None of this distresses her any more than it would a very young child. Sterilisation by hysterectomy could never be said to be in her best interests, even if sterilisation *per se* could. Yet her father may find that he cannot cope much longer. Dealing with menstruation is the straw that breaks the camel's back. Is that young woman better off without a uterus but with her father, or with her uterus intact but in an institution? Her interests and her father's are inextricably intertwined.

The interests of the patient must be the predominant interest to be considered. Perhaps other interests should also be taken into account? Individuals live as part of society. Society has obligations to the individual, especially the vulnerable individual. Individuals, though, have reciprocal obligations to society. Moreover, a careful review of all the decided cases on non-consensual treatment may suggest that courts do in fact take note of interests other than the patient's. If 19-year-old T would never have been properly aware of her pregnancy, or the birth and removal of a child, that experience may at any rate not have harmed her. Her mother and the child would certainly suffer. Would it be wrong to consider their interests? If the interests of others will inevitably be considered, would it not be better to do so openly?

Chapter 8

CLINICAL NEGLIGENCE[1]

8.1 Introduction

The civil law of negligence is designed to provide compensation for one individual injured by another's negligence. Gross negligence resulting in death and wilful neglect of patients may be punished by the criminal courts. We consider possible criminal liability incurred by doctors in Chapter 10. A person seeking compensation for negligence has to establish (1) that the defendant owed them a duty to take care (2) that the defendant was in breach of that duty, that they were careless, and (3) that the harm of which the victim complains was caused by that carelessness. The defendant must satisfy all these tests to succeed. A widow succeeded in establishing that a hospital doctor was careless in not coming down to Casualty to examine her husband. He was admitted to hospital in an appalling state which eventually proved to be caused by arsenical poisoning. He died within hours. She failed to recover any compensation from the hospital in respect of her husband's death because the evidence was that, even had he been properly attended, he would still have died.[2]

The bare bones of the law of negligence outlined above are general to everyone, in the conduct of their everyday activities and in carrying out their job. They are not special to doctors or health professionals more generally. Certain special factors about clinical negligence claims need to be noted. Proving negligence where there is a clash of medical opinion remains difficult. The need to prove 'fault' with its implications of wrongdoing affects the medical profession's reaction to claims against them prompting claims that doctors have become defensive. Patients used to be deferential; historically judges also were unwilling to find against a 'medical man'.[3] A brotherly solidarity bound the ancient professions of law and medicine together. Judicial attitudes have changed.[4] *Claims* against doctors and damages awarded against National

1 See generally, N Poole QC, *Clinical Negligence Made Clear: A Guide for Patients and Professionals* (2019) Bath Publishing.

2 *Barnett v Chelsea and Kensington Hospital Management Committee* [1969] 1 QB 428. And see *Davies v Countess of Chester Hospital* [2014] EWHC 4294 (QB).

3 S Devaney and S Holm, 'The Transmutation of Deference in Medicine: An Ethico-Legal Perspective' (2018) 21 *Med Law Rev* 202.

4 See Lord Woolf, 'Are the Courts Excessively Deferential to the Medical Profession?' (2001) 9 *Med Law Rev* 1.

Health Service (NHS) hospitals have risen dramatically. The medical profession is haunted by the spectre of a malpractice crisis. In the next chapter, we explore whether it is a spectre of any substance.

8.2 Duty of care

A patient claiming against his doctor, or a hospital, generally has little difficulty in establishing that the defendant owes them a duty of care. A general practitioner (GP) accepting a patient on to their list undertakes a duty to the patient. A hospital and its entire staff owe a duty to patients admitted for treatment. If the patient is an NHS patient, the duty derives from the law of tort, which imposes a duty wherever one person can reasonably foresee that his conduct may cause harm to another. Where the patient is a private patient, in addition to the duty in tort, a duty arises from his contract with the doctor or the hospital. It is the same duty regardless of its origins. We look later at the circumstances in which the private patient is owed duties other than that of care.

The relationship between the health professional and the injured party must be sufficiently proximate. Thus, except in very narrowly defined circumstances, a doctor whose actions cause harm to a third party is unlikely to owe them a duty of care.[5] Nor does English law oblige anyone to be a Good Samaritan. If someone has a coronary attack on the TransPennine Express and a doctor fails to respond to the conductor's call, 'Is there a doctor on the train?', the doctor incurs no liability to the victim who dies for lack of medical treatment.[6] Does the law discourage the Good Samaritan? If the doctor comes to the sick person's aid, they undertake a duty to this sick person and in theory may be liable if their skill fails them, but any court ascertaining the standard of care that the Samaritan must attain will take into account the circumstance in which the doctor volunteers their help.[7]

By running a casualty department, an NHS hospital undertakes to treat those who present themselves and will be liable in negligence if any failure on the part of their staff causes the patient to be sent away untreated.[8] In *Darnley v Croydon Health Services NHS Trust*,[9] the Supreme Court held that the Trust was vicariously liable for the negligence of one of its employee receptionists, who carelessly misinformed a patient about A&E waiting times. Based on misleading information, a patient with a head injury left the hospital, which led to him being paralysed. Similarly, a GP currently owes a duty to emergency

5 *ABC v St George's Healthcare NHS Trust* [2020] EWHC 455, discussed at 5.14 above.

6 Though she may be in breach of her professional code of conduct and face professional disciplinary proceedings; see General Medical Council, *Good Medical Practice* (2013), para 26.

7 See K Williams, 'Medical Samaritans: Is There A Duty To Treat?' (2001) 21 *OJLS* 393.

8 *Barnett v Chelsea and Kensington Hospital Management Committee* [1969] 1 QB 428.

9 [2018] UKSC 50.

patients as well as to those on his own list. Their contract with the NHS provides that they will treat visitors to their practice area falling suddenly ill. Like the hospital with the casualty department, the doctor undertakes to treat the genuine emergency as much as their regular patients.

In *Kent v Griffiths*,[10] the duties owed to patients by the ambulance services came before the courts. The claimant was asthmatic. She was also pregnant. She had been exceptionally wheezy on the day in question and called her GP who telephoned for an ambulance using the 999 service. The ambulance took forty minutes to arrive despite two further anxious phone calls from the claimant's husband. On the journey to the hospital, the claimant was given oxygen. Shortly before arrival at the hospital she suffered a respiratory arrest resulting in serious brain damage and a miscarriage. The ambulance service denied negligence. They contended that their only duty to the claimant was not by their own actions to cause her any additional injury. They had no duty to come to her aid, to 'rescue' her from the danger her illness placed her in. Earlier cases[11] involving police and fire services had found that (generally) simply failing to respond to, or respond sufficiently promptly to, a 999 call did not render those services liable in negligence. The Court of Appeal was adamant that the ambulance service was different. It is an NHS service owing equivalent responsibility to patients in need of that service to doctors and nurses. Where an identifiable patient needed and summoned the ambulance service, there was a duty to respond. Due care on the part of an ambulance service demands a reasonably prompt response. There might be cases of conflicting priorities. For example, two major road accidents take place in the same city at the same time as a winter 'flu' epidemic. The elderly 'flu' patient, whose call is given lower priority than the crash victims, is still owed a duty by the ambulance service. In the circumstances, there may be no breach of duty because, confronted by competing demands, the ambulance service responded reasonably.

8.3 Psychiatric harm

Patients may seek to sue, not just in respect of physical harm, such as a perforated bowel in the course of surgery, but also in cases of psychiatric injury. Where additional psychiatric harm ensues directly from bungled treatment of the claimant themselves, such claims have a fair chance of success.[12] In *Farrell*

10 [2000] 2 All ER 74, CA; and see *Taaffe v East of England Ambulance Service NHS Trust* [2012] EWHC 1335 (QB). See K Williams, 'Litigation Against NHS Ambulance Services and The Rule in *Kent v Griffiths*' (2007) 15(2) *Med Law Rev* 153.

11 See, for example, *Capital & Counties plc v Hampshire County Council* [1997] QB 1004, CA. And more recently, *Michael v The Chief Constable of South Wales Police* [2015] UKSC 2. But contrast *Sherratt v Chief Constable of Greater Manchester* [2018] EWHC 1746 where it was held the police owed a duty of care to a woman who was found dead at home having taken an overdose in circumstances where assurances were given to her mother in a 999 call, and the mother then relied on the assurances to her detriment. There were no such assurances in *Michael*.

12 As long as the claimant can prove that the mental illness is related to the defendant's breach of duty; see *Oliver v Williams* [2013] EWHC 600 (QB); P Case, 'Secondary

v Merton, Sutton and Wandsworth Health Authority,[13] the claimant suffered a horrific childbirth. She remained aware during an emergency Caesarean section, she contracted a post-operative infection and her child was born with serious brain damage. News of her child's condition was communicated inadequately and insensitively. She recovered compensation to include the adverse effects on her mental health of all that had happened to her.

Claims where one person alleges that negligent treatment of someone else, a close relative, caused them to suffer mental illness are harder to sustain. The law regards such people as *secondary* victims of psychiatric injury, akin to those who witness some horrific disaster, such as events at Hillsborough Football Stadium when fans were crushed to death as a result of negligence on the part of the police. The tragedy was televised and pictures of the frightened, dying and dead caused untold agony to many. In a claim relating to the Hillsborough incident, the House of Lords set out a series of 'control mechanisms' so that only exceptional claims from secondary victims would succeed.[14] The controls apply to all cases of psychiatric injury, including when it is caused by clinical negligence.

One control mechanism requires that the claimant has a close relationship with the injured person, such as that of a family relative. Another requires that the psychiatric harm occurs through 'shock'. Just because a relative suffers injury from inadequate treatment and the effect of distress and grief make you ill, does not suffice to create a duty owed by the defendant hospital to you. Only if you actually suffer psychiatric injury from the trauma and shock of witnessing or discovering what has happened to your relative are you likely to be owed any duty.[15] Consider *RE (a minor)*.[16] A Trust's negligence led to a baby suffering brain injury in a protracted birth. The mother, who suffered post-traumatic stress disorder, was considered a *primary* victim on the basis that the infant was not legally a separate entity from the mother at the onset of her psychiatric condition. The grandmother, who witnessed the birth with resulting psychiatric injury, succeeded as a secondary victim. Contrast *RE* with the case of *King*.[17] Here, too, an infant was critically ill when negligence resulted in a birthing injury. Mr King suffered psychiatric injury on seeing his critically ill son in the Neonatal Intensive Care Unit. The event was utterly horrifying to Mr King, but not sufficiently horrific in the objective sense required to establish liability to a secondary victim. He had been told what to expect and the baby was sleeping peacefully.

A further control mechanism requires that the claimant must have been close to the incident in time and space. A relative who witnesses a negligently caused

Iatrogenic Harm: Claims for Psychiatric Damage Following a Death Caused By Medical Error' (2004) 67 *MLR* 501.

13 (2001) 57 BMLR 158.

14 *Alcock v Chief Constable of South Yorkshire* [1991] UKHL 5.

15 See *Sion v Hampstead Health Authority* (1994) 5 Med LR 170, CA.

16 *RE (a minor) v Huddersfield and Calderdale NHS Foundation Trust* [2017] EWHC 824 (QB). And see J Lindsey, 'Psychiatric Injury Claims and Pregnancy' (2018) 26(1) *Med Law Rev* 117.

17 [2021] PIQR P20.

accident or its immediate aftermath and suffers psychiatric harm might succeed if the 'relevant event' causing the psychiatric harm is removed in time from the negligence. This is because the requisite proximity is more difficult to establish. The leading case is *Taylor v A Novo (UK) Ltd*[18] in which an accident at work caused racking to fall onto a woman. She died three weeks later from pulmonary emboli related to the incident. Her daughter did not witness the incident but suffered psychiatric illness when she witnessed her mother's death. The Court of Appeal dismissed her claim. The 'relevant event' that was the consequence of the employer's negligence was the accident at work. The daughter did not witness the relevant event or its immediate aftermath.

Taylor involved an accident at work. Should clinical negligence cases be treated differently? Unlike an accident where harm is immediately apparent, in cases of negligent delayed diagnosis, the first manifestation of the harm arguably occurs when symptoms are first displayed. If this is witnessed by relatives and causes them psychiatric harm, can they claim as secondary victims? In *Paul (A Child) v Royal Wolverhampton NHS Trust*, the High Court distinguished *Taylor*. Two children appealed against the striking out of their claims for psychiatric harm that was caused to them as secondary victims. Their father had been subject to a negligent diagnosis by employees of the defendant Trust, which resulted in his death from a heart attack some fourteen and a half months later. The children witnessed their father's sudden collapse and subsequent death and, because that was the first time that the harm had actually crystallised, it was held that the tort occurred at that point. The event would have been horrifying to any close family member who witnessed it, and particularly to young children, so Chamberlain J acknowledged that the claimants had an arguable case and set aside the original order striking out their claim. That the incident occurred so late after the negligent omission that caused it should not automatically rule out liability.[19]

Alas, the case proceeded to the Court of Appeal in a conjoined appeal with two other similar cases,[20] where it was held that *Taylor v A Novo* was binding. The 'relevant event' was the negligent diagnosis rather than the later death and the relatives could not claim as secondary victims. Permission has been granted for the case to be heard by the Supreme Court. The Court of Appeal case turned on the binding nature of *Taylor*. The rationale for linking the requirement of proximity to the initial cause of action warrants deeper inspection. The policy considerations that sought to prevent liability on a mass scale when the shocking events at Hillsborough were televised are blunt and arbitrary tools.

8.4 Medical examinations

A number of cases consider how far doctors examining patients not for the patient's benefit, but on the instruction of a third party, owe a duty to the

[18] [2013] EWCA Civ 194.
[19] [2020] EWHC 1415 (QB).
[20] *Purchase v Ahmed, Polmear v Royal Cornwall Hospital NHS Trust and Paul v Royal Wolverhampton NHS Trust* [2022] EWCA Civ 12.

patient being examined. For example, you have to have a medical examination before a job offer will be confirmed. Two different scenarios must be addressed:

(1) The doctor, had they carried out the examination with due care, would have discovered that you had early signs of cancer. Delay in diagnosis means that your cancer is now inoperable. Did the doctor who performed your 'medical' owe you a duty to alert you to your dangerous condition? A duty may well be found.[21]
(2) The doctor carries out the 'medical' negligently and wrongly concludes that you are unfit for the job. You lose a chance of the job. Does the doctor owe you a duty to protect you from the financial (economic) loss of not getting the job? One case suggests such a duty is owed.[22] A later judgment of the Court of Appeal is to the contrary.[23] The examining doctor owed no duty to the job applicant to protect them from economic loss. The doctor was not responsible for looking after their job prospects.[24]

8.5 Responsibility for harm inflicted by 'dangerous' patients

Patients being treated for some types of mental disorder – in particular personality disorders – are sometimes a danger to themselves. A Trust that fails to take reasonable steps to protect such a patient from harm may be held negligent.[25] What if the patient causes harm to another? As we explain in Chapter 5,[26] English courts are wary of imposing a duty of care in relation to the acts of a third party. It will not be enough to show that an individual doctor or mental health trust was aware their patient posed a risk of harm to the claimant.[27] In *Selwood v Durham County Council*[28] the Court of Appeal upheld an appeal against a trial judge's decision to strike out a claim against two NHS Trusts treating a patient, G, who stabbed and injured the claimant, a social worker working with G and his family in proceedings involving G's children. G had made threats against the claimant, at one stage threatening to 'kill her on the spot'. The claimant was employed by Durham County Council. The Council and the NHS Trusts had signed a protocol on working together that focused in part on protection of staff and sharing information. The Court

21 See DM Kloss, 'Pre-Employment Health Screening' in M Freeman and A Lewis (eds), *Law and Medicine: Current Legal Issues* (2000) Oxford University Press, Vol 3.
22 *Baker v Kaye* (1996) 39 BMLR 12.
23 *Kapfunde v Abbey National Plc* (1998) 46 BMLR 176, CA.
24 For discussion of other circumstances where a medical examination is carried out on the instructions of a third party, see E Jackson, *Medical Law: Text, Cases and Materials* (5th edn, 2019) Oxford University Press, pp 123–131.
25 See for example *Webley v St George's NHS Trust and the Metropolitan Police* [2014] EWHC 299 (QB). And see 3.7 above on claims under Article 2 of the European Convention on Human Rights.
26 See 5.15 above.
27 *Palmer v Tees Health Authority* [1998] 45 BMLR 88 (CA).
28 [2012] EWCA Civ 979.

of Appeal ruled that there was thus sufficient evidence for there to be an arguable case that the defendant Trusts had assumed responsibility for protecting employees of co-signatories, as well as their own employees, from harm by clients where explicit threats had been made.[29]

8.6 The medical standard of care

The second matter that any claimant in negligence has to prove is that the defendant was careless. A warning is called for. The diligent student who searches legal databases for cases on proving clinical negligence will be overwhelmed with hundreds of cases each year. Few will offer more clarity by way of legal principle. What is in dispute will be disagreement about the facts, what happened and how reliable is memory, and/or just how to apply the current law.

The fundamental principles of law are as follows. The onus of proof is on the claimant. They must show that the defendant fell below the required standard of care. The basic standard is that of the reasonable person in the circumstances of the defendant. A professional person must meet the standard of competence of the reasonable professional doing his job. A woman who went to a jeweller's to have her ear pierced developed an abscess because the jeweller's instruments were not aseptically sterile. The jeweller had taken all the precautions that any jeweller could be expected to take. The woman's claim failed. The defendant had done all a jeweller could reasonably be expected to do.[30] If she wanted the standard of care a surgeon could offer, she should have consulted a surgeon.

Before examining the case-law in clinical negligence, we should note briefly section 1 of the Compensation Act 2006. The Act was passed as a knee jerk reaction to much publicised claims of a 'compensation culture'. Supposedly schools were refusing to take children on school trips and local authorities were closing playgrounds to avoid any risk of liability for injury.[31] Section 1 provides:

> A court considering a claim in negligence or breach of statutory duty may, in determining whether the defendant should have taken particular steps to meet a standard of care (whether by taking precautions against a risk or otherwise), have regard to whether a requirement to take those steps might –
> (a) prevent a desirable activity from being undertaken at all, to a particular extent or in a particular way, or
> (b) discourage persons from undertaking functions in connection with a desirable activity.

The Act has had little effect on clinical negligence claims.[32] Unless judges were to decide to accept the wildest claims about defensive medicine and determine that allowing doctors to be sued would damage healthcare, the Compensation

29 But see *Buck v Norfolk and Waveney Mental Health NHS Foundation Trust* [2012] Med LR 266.
30 *Phillips v William Whiteley Ltd* [1938] 1 All ER 566.
31 See S Peyer and R Heywood, 'Walking on Thin Ice: The Perception of Tortious Liability Rules and the Effect on Altruistic Behaviour' (2019) 39 *Legal Studies* 266.
32 See *Uren v Corporate Leisure and Others* [2010] All ER (D) 132 (Jan).

Act need not be treated as a matter of great concern. However, politicians continue to believe that gold digging compensation claims incited by greedy lawyers are damaging public services including the NHS. The principles of law may not be affected by such rhetoric but as we shall see in the next chapter, the process of bringing a claim has become more difficult.

The standard of care demanded of the doctor is the standard of the reasonably skilled and experienced doctor. In *Bolam v Friern Hospital Management Committee*,[33] McNair J said:

> The test is the standard of the ordinary skilled man exercising and professing to have that special skill. A man need not possess the highest expert skill, it is well established law that it is sufficient if he exercises the ordinary skill of an ordinary competent man exercising that particular art.

The defendant doctor will be tested against the standard of the doctor in his particular field of medicine. The GP must meet the standard of the competent GP; the consultant gynaecologist the standard of the competent consultant in that specialty. As Lord Scarman put it: 'a doctor who professes to exercise a special skill must exercise the ordinary skill of his specialty'.[34] A patient who attends their GP complaining of an eye disorder cannot require the doctor to have the skill of a consultant ophthalmologist, but they can complain if the GP fails to refer them to a consultant in a timely fashion[35] when their condition should have alerted a reasonable GP to the need for further advice or treatment. The *Bolam* test in its conventional format usually operates favourably towards defendant health professionals. Yet, it does not always work that way. In *EXP v Barker*, the Court of Appeal confirmed that where two experts disagreed, a trial judge was entitled to treat the evidence presented by an expert who had a previous working relationship with the defendant as suspicious. The trial judge had no obligation to rely on the defendant's expert evidence as establishing that a responsible body of neuroradiologists would not have referred the patient. This was not one of those rare cases where a claimant was driven to show that established medical practice was unreasonable but was one in which negligence could be established by recourse to the conventional *Bolam* test.[36] After weighing up all the expert evidence, the judge was persuaded by the proposition that any responsible properly qualified neuroradiologist should and would have referred the patient for further investigation.[37]

8.7 Junior doctors

No allowance is made for inexperience. The Court of Appeal has consistently rejected arguments that standards of care should vary to allow for the degree of experience possessed by the defendant. They held a learner driver liable

33 [1957] 1 WLR 582, 586.
34 *Maynard v West Midlands Regional Health Authority* [1984] 1 WLR 634, HL, 638.
35 *Wright (A Child) v Cambridge Medical Group* [2011] EWCA Civ 669.
36 [2017] EWCA Civ 63, [55].
37 Ibid.

where, although she had done the best that could be expected of a learner, she fell short of the standard of the reasonably competent and experienced motorist.[38] In *Wilsher v Essex Area Health Authority*,[39] the appeal court considered the liability of junior hospital staff. Martin Wilsher was born nearly three months prematurely. He was admitted to a neonatal unit managed by the defendants where skilled treatment probably saved his life. He needed extra oxygen to survive. Sadly, junior doctors made an error in monitoring the oxygen levels in Martin's blood, and on two occasions, he received an excess of oxygen. It was argued by Martin's lawyers that excess oxygen caused him to develop retrolental fibroplasia (RLF), a retinal condition which left Martin nearly blind. Ultimately, the House of Lords held that the plaintiff had failed to prove that excess oxygen caused RLF in Martin and ordered a retrial.[40] The importance of the Court of Appeal's judgment lies in their exposition of the rules on negligence by junior staff. Argument by the defendants that staff concerned did their best in view of their inexperience was rejected. The law requires all medical staff in such a unit to meet the standard of competence and experience society expects from those filling such demanding posts. This position was confirmed in *FB v Rana*, where the Court of Appeal found that history taking was a basic skill that ought to fall within the range of competencies of an A&E Senior House Officer. Thus, there was no difference in the standard of care required of junior doctors as compared to a more senior doctor in taking a patient's history.[41] Their Lordships in *Wilsher* did, however, recognise the need for medical staff to train 'on the job'. They stressed that a finding of negligence on one occasion did not imply incompetence or any degree of moral culpability, because legal and moral tests of negligence may differ. Doctors may find the distinction hard to understand. To mitigate the harsher effects of the legal position in respect of junior health professionals, it was traditionally thought that a junior doctor, who, recognising his inexperience, calls in his consultant will have discharged his duty, as responsibility in law will at that point move to the consultant.[42] However, some doubt has recently been cast upon this hitherto clear statement of principle. In the Scottish case of *Andrews v Greater Glasgow Health Board* it was suggested that the view that a junior doctor would automatically be immune from liability in negligence simply by virtue of consulting a senior colleague was not an absolute rule.[43]

8.8 Ascertaining the standard of care: *Bolam*

How does a court ascertain the standard of skill which the doctor should have met? Let us consider the case of Mr Bolam again. He was given

[38] *Nettleship v Weston* [1971] 2 QB 691, CA.
[39] [1986] 3 All ER 801, CA.
[40] [1988] 1 All ER 891; see 8.15 below.
[41] *FB v Rana* [2017] EWCA Civ 334.
[42] See *Jones v Manchester Corporation* [1952] 2 QB 852, at 871. Note that in *Wilsher v Essex Area Health Authority* [1986] 3 All ER 801, CA, Dr Wiles, the house officer, was found not negligent.
[43] [2019] CSOH 31; 2019 SLT 727.

electroconvulsive therapy and sustained fractures. He argued that the doctor was negligent (1) in not giving him relaxant drugs, (2) as drugs were not given, in failing to provide adequate physical restraints and (3) in not warning him of the risks involved in the treatment. We have seen that he failed in his argument that he should have been warned, but that today after the decision of the Supreme Court in *Montgomery v Lanarkshire Health Board*[44] he might well have succeeded in this 'informed consent' claim.[45] Indeed, the Supreme Court in *Montgomery* made it clear that the *Bolam* test has no application to the question of what information the doctor must disclose to the patient. As to the absence of relaxant drugs or restraints, the evidence was that while some doctors would have thought them necessary, many did not. The judge found the doctor not guilty of negligence for he acted:[46]

> … in accordance with a practice accepted as proper by a responsible body of medical men skilled in that particular area … a man is not negligent, if he is acting in accordance with such a practice, merely because there is a body of opinion who would take a contrary view.

The *Bolam* test became [in]famous. At first sight, it is unexceptionable. Courts cannot decide whether a doctor was negligent without expert evidence of 'accepted medical practice'.[47] Within any profession, genuine differences of opinion may surface. In obstetrics, doctors have different views about how best to deliver a premature breech baby. Some doctors consider that, in every case, the woman should be strongly advised to agree to an elective Caesarean section. Others believe that a trial of labour should be permitted and that only if complications ensue in labour should surgery be advised as the best 'medical' option. Both sides of the debate advance logical reasons for their respective judgements. Judges are not well placed to resolve such questions. Note, however, in the light of the decision in *Montgomery* (above), the doctor must warn the patients of the risks and pros and cons of both options. The *Bolam* test (responsible professional opinion) will apply to the question whether the doctor has correctly identified the options and the risks and benefits of each, but then she must disclose all the information that a reasonable patient in the circumstances of the claimant would wish to have to make an informed choice.

The *Bolam* test focusing on 'accepted practice' came to be applied to all claims for professional negligence. 'Responsible professional opinion' is the litmus test of liability for solicitors, accountants and architects, just as much as for doctors. There was a crucial difference. In claims against other professionals, the courts rigorously scrutinised expert evidence to ensure that evidence of professional opinion could be demonstrated to be responsible and reasonable.[48] In claims against doctors, it appeared that as long as suitably qualified

44 [2015] UKSC 11.
45 See above at 6.12.
46 *Bolam v Friern HMC* [1957] 1 WLR 582, 587–588.
47 See *Burne v A* [2006] EWCA Civ 24, [10].
48 See, for example, *Edward Wong Finance Co Ltd v Johnson, Stokes & Master* [1984] AC 296, PC.

expert witnesses endorsed the defendant's conduct, English judges simply deferred to the doctors. Providing expert testimony was seen to be truthful, the courts assumed that it must be responsible.[49] The key to successfully defending a claim in negligence was to find expert witnesses who would be impressive in the witness box.[50]

Trial judges who took it upon themselves to scrutinise and evaluate medical evidence faced reprimands from above. In *Maynard v West Midlands Regional Health Authority*,[51] the plaintiff had consulted a consultant physician and a surgeon with symptoms indicating tuberculosis, but she also displayed symptoms which might indicate Hodgkin's disease. The doctors decided on a diagnostic operation, mediastinoscopy. It carried a risk of damage to the vocal cords and Mrs Maynard's vocal cords were in fact damaged. She proved to have tuberculosis. She alleged that the defendants were negligent in subjecting her to the operation. Her expert witness argued that the operation should never have been done. He would have regarded her condition as almost certainly a case of tuberculosis. The defendants called a formidable number of experts who testified that the fatality rate for Hodgkin's disease if treatment was delayed justified the defendants in exposing Mrs Maynard to the risk of the mediastinoscopy. The original judge preferred Dr Hugh-Jones's evidence. The Court of Appeal and the House of Lords overruled him. Lord Scarman said:

> [A] judge's 'preference' for one body of distinguished professional opinion to another also professionally distinguished is not sufficient to establish negligence in a practitioner ...[52]

In *Maynard*, the defendants had numbers on their side. In *De Freitas v O'Brien*,[53] the expert evidence established that only a tiny minority of neurosurgeons endorsed the defendant's practice, just four or five out of two hundred and fifty doctors in that specialty. The Court of Appeal ruled that the body of opinion supporting the defendant need not be large. The perception arose that English judges would not cross swords with the doctors, however thin the evidence advanced in defence of a claim.[54]

Individual judges did on occasion attempt to assert judicial authority over medical evidence. Sir John Donaldson MR[55] emphasised that professional opinion must be '*rightly* accepted as proper by a body of skilled and experienced

49 See the account of the first instance decision in *Bolitho v City & Hackney Health Authority* [1998] AC 232, HL.
50 Graphically illustrated in *Whitehouse v Jordan* [1981] 1 All ER 246, HL.
51 [1984] 1 WLR 634, HL.
52 [1984] 1 WLR 634, HL, 639.
53 [1993] 4 Med LR 281, CA.
54 Michael Jones expressed the state of play as a football score. In six medical negligence claims before the House of Lords between 1980 and 1999, the score stood at *Plaintiffs 0 : Defendants 6*. See MA Jones, 'The *Bolam* Test and the Responsible Expert' (1999) *Tort Law Review* 226.
55 *Sidaway v Royal Bethlem Hospital* [1984] 2 WLR 778, at 752, CA. And see Lord Bridge [1985] 1 All ER 643, HL, 663.

medical men'. In 1968, the Court of Appeal in *Hucks v Cole*[56] rejected expert evidence in the defendant's favour. Evidence that other doctors would have followed the same practice as the defendant was 'a very weighty matter', but not conclusive. Such challenges to the supremacy of medical evidence tended to be ephemeral, apparently forgotten in the next flurry of cases.

8.9 *Bolitho*: a new dawn?

In *Bolitho v City & Hackney Health Authority*,[57] Lord Browne-Wilkinson re-asserted the proper authority of the courts. *Bolitho* involved questions of causation as much as breach of duty. The facts, briefly, were these. Patrick Bolitho, aged 2, was admitted to the defendant's hospital suffering from respiratory difficulties. On the second afternoon of this hospital stay, Patrick was in respiratory distress. A nurse summoned the paediatric registrar. She promised to attend as soon as possible, but did not do so. Patrick appeared to recover. At 2.00 pm, Patrick was once again having breathing problems. The registrar was called a second time, but again failed to attend. At 2.30 pm, the boy collapsed; he stopped breathing and suffered a cardiac arrest causing catastrophic brain damage. The hospital admitted negligence on the part of the paediatric registrar. She should have come to examine the child, or arranged for a suitable deputy to do so. They denied liability, however, arguing that, even if the doctor had attended Patrick prior to 2.30 pm, she would not have intubated him. Intubation offered the only prospect of averting the respiratory distress and cardiac arrest which Patrick suffered at 2.30 pm.

The trial judge accepted the doctor's evidence of fact that *she* would *not* have intubated Patrick. The question then became whether or not a competent doctor who had attended Patrick *should* have intubated the child. The *Bolam* question became the key to resolving causation. The experts were sharply divided. The plaintiff's five experts testified that Patrick's history of breathing problems was such that responsible practice required that he be intubated to prevent just the sort of catastrophe which materialised. The defendants' three experts argued that, apart from the two episodes of respiratory difficulty, Patrick seemed generally well. Intubation was distressing and not risk-free for so young a child. A responsible doctor would not have intubated Patrick prior to 2.30 pm. The judge ruled that, as both sets of experts represented a body of professional opinion espoused by distinguished and truthful experts, he was bound to conclude that Patrick's injury did not result from the defendants' admitted negligence. In effect, the judge asserted that he was disqualified from any form of scrutiny of expert medical evidence.

The Court of Appeal upheld the trial judge. The case proceeded to the House of Lords. Two issues fell to be resolved by their Lordships. The first, whether the *Bolam* test applies to causation, will be addressed later. The second is our

56 Reported [1993] 4 Med LR 393, CA.
57 [1998] AC 232, HL.

present concern. Does the *Bolam* test require a judge to accept without question truthful evidence from eminent experts? Their Lordships, speaking with one voice through Lord Browne-Wilkinson, answered that question with a firm and forceful no. Reviewing precedents relating to claims of negligence against other professionals, his Lordship declared that:

> [T]he court has to be satisfied that the exponents of the body of opinion relied on can demonstrate that such opinion has a logical basis. In particular, in cases involving as they so often do, the weighing up of risks against benefits, the judge before accepting a body of opinion as being reasonable, responsible or respectable, will need to be satisfied that, in forming their views, the experts have directed their minds to the questions of comparative risks and benefits and have reached a defensible conclusion on the matter.[58]

Expert evidence after *Bolitho* remains of the highest importance to the success or failure of clinical negligence claims. Lord Browne-Wilkinson acknowledged that in 'the vast majority of cases the fact that distinguished experts in the field are of a particular opinion will demonstrate the reasonableness of that opinion'. Nonetheless, he went on to say 'if in a rare case, it can be demonstrated that the professional opinion is not capable of withstanding logical analysis, the judge is entitled to hold that the body of opinion is not reasonable or responsible'.[59]

Bolitho returns *Bolam* to its proper limits.[60] Doctors, like solicitors and all other professionals, are subject to legal scrutiny. The courts, not the medical profession, are the ultimate arbiters of the standard of care in clinical negligence claims. *Bolitho* has generated a plethora of academic commentary.[61] How influential has *Bolitho* been? Pessimistic commentators pointed out that Lord Browne-Wilkinson spoke of 'rare' cases and later noted that it will be 'very seldom' that it would be right to conclude that views genuinely held by competent experts were unreasonable. *Bolitho*, they fear, does little to aid patients.[62] Concerns are also expressed that *Bolitho* might stifle innovation and that doctors will be wary of resorting to innovative drugs or techniques even when such measures may offer the last chance of a cure for the patient. So great was this concern for Lord Saatchi whose wife had died of untreated cancer that in 2014 he introduced his Medical Innovation Bill. The Bill was vetoed by the Liberal Democrats and a similar Bill, the Access to Medical Treatments

58 [1998] AC 232, HL, 242.

59 [1998] AC 232, 243.

60 As Andrew Grubb so nicely put it ' "Eureka!" The courts have got it at last. Expert evidence, whether of professional practice or otherwise is not conclusive in a medical negligence case that the defendant has not been careless!' A Grubb, 'Negligence, Causation and Bolam' (1998) 6 *Med Law Rev* 378, 380.

61 See R Heywood, 'The Logic of *Bolitho*' (2006) 22 *Journal of Professional Negligence* 225; H Teff, 'The Standard of Care in Medical Negligence – Moving on from *Bolam*' (1998) 18 *OJLS* 473; J Keown, 'Reining in the Bolam Test' (1998) 57 *CLJ* 248; J Badenoch, 'Brushes With Bolam: Where Will It Lead?' (2005) 72 *Medico-Legal Journal* 127.

62 See N Glover, 'Bolam in the House of Lords' (1999) 15 *Professional Negligence* 42.

(Innovation) Bill, was introduced in 2015. The Bill would provide that it is not negligent to depart from accepted treatments in accordance with a prescribed process, a process that falls well short of the strict regulation of medical research discussed in Chapter 18. The Bill was criticised by doctors and lawyers[63] as opening the doors to allow unregulated research. Fortunately, a much diminished Access to Medical Treatments (Innovation) Act 2016 did no more than give the Secretary of State power to set up an accessible database of innovative treatments. Nothing in *Bolitho* militates against a judicial approach that would allow a well-reasoned and balanced judgement[64] to be held non-negligent in such cases of last ditch choices.[65]

But did *Bolitho* truly herald a new dawn? We would agree with Mulheron that it did even if the day that followed was somewhat cloudy![66] The proclamation of judicial authority over medical practice came at last from the highest court in the UK and came at a time when several other developments in the manner medical practice is regulated and audited were placing limits on unfettered clinical autonomy.[67] Simply asserting that a medical expert considers that there was no negligence is no longer a 'trump card' for defendants. As Laurie, Harmon and Dove put it '*Bolam* can no longer be regarded as impregnable'.[68]

What of the case-law post *Bolitho*? In *Marriott v West Midlands Health Authority*,[69] the plaintiff had suffered head injuries. He was discharged from hospital but remained unwell. Eight days after the fall he was visited by the defendant GP. The GP failed to recognise the severity of his symptoms. Four days later the plaintiff collapsed and was re-admitted to hospital with an extradural haematoma that left him paralysed. In the claim against the GP, there were two conflicting bodies of opinion as to whether a responsible GP would have judged that a full neurological examination was called for and re-admitted the plaintiff to hospital. The trial judge considered that the logically defensible view was that the severity of the repercussions was such that even minimal risk of haematoma should lead to re-admission to hospital.

63 N Hoppe and J Miola 'Innovation in Medicine Through Degeneration in Law? A Critical Perspective on the Medical Innovation Bill' (2015) 14 *Medical Law International* 266.

64 *Duffy v Lanarkshire Health Board* 1998 SCLR 1142: discussed in GT Laurie, S Harmon and E Dove, *Mason and McCall Smith's Law and Medical Ethics* (11th edn, 2019) Oxford University Press, 5.53.

65 And see *Walker-Smith v GMC* [2012] EWHC 503: P Case 'Treading the Line between Clinical Research and Therapy' (2012) 28 *Professional Negligence* 224.

66 R Mulheron argues that there are now recognisable categories which flesh out the requirement that professional peer-opinion must be 'logical', 'responsible' and 'defensible'. She further articulates these categories in the hope that the law further clarifies the ambits of *Bolitho*. See 'Trumping Bolam: A Critical Legal Analysis of "Bolitho's" Gloss' (2010) 69(3) *CLJ* 609.

67 See M Brazier and J Miola, 'Bye-Bye Bolam: A Medical Litigation Revolution' (2000) 8 *Med Law Rev* 85.

68 *Mason and McCall Smith's Law and Medical Ethics*, 5.51.

69 [1999] Lloyd's Rep Med 23.

The Court of Appeal agreed. Beldam LJ endorsed the judge's exercise in risk assessment.[70] In *Burne v A*,[71] Sedley LJ stressed that:

> [J]udges are there to exercise judgment, and their judgment cannot be entirely dictated by expert evidence, even where the evidence is unopposed. The question always remains (provided a party raises it) whether the expert evidence makes sense.

Extra-judicially both the then Lord Chancellor[72] and Lord Chief Justice[73] indicated many years ago that judges should no longer blindly defer to medical opinion. More recently, in *Bradfield-Kay v Cope*[74] Mr Cope performed a metal-on-metal hip replacement on Mr Bradfield-Kay who alleged that Mr Cope was negligent in allowing a part of the hip replacement to remain prominent, resulting in painful tendonitis. Expert evidence suggested that whilst the positioning of the hip so that it protruded could be problematic, it was not a breach of duty in this case. Applying *Bolitho*, that view was rejected by HHJ Sephton QC on the basis that there was no logical basis for it.

However, it has been made clear that *Bolitho* in no sense reverses the burden of proof,[75] and nor was it ever designed to do so. Judges have re-enforced the view that it will seldom be right to reject expert opinion as unreasonable.[76] The Court of Appeal has warned that a judge is 'not entitled to impose his own opinion regardless of the practice of the medical profession'.[77] And a tendency to presume that eminent experts will necessarily give logical evidence can be discerned in *Wisniewski v Central Manchester Health Authority*.[78]

If *Bolitho* offers some assistance to patient-claimants, does it risk damaging medical care? Will doctors simply retreat into defensive practice? Will guidelines and protocols (a tick-box approach) replace a sensitive and imaginative approach to the needs of particular patients? This should not happen. *Bolitho* does not seek to usurp judgements which properly rest with doctors. Judges are not empowered to decide what constitutes good medical practice.[79] What *Bolitho* does is to require expert witnesses to justify and explain the basis of

70 *Penney v East Kent Area Health Authority* [2000] Lloyd's Rep Med 41; *Reynolds v North Tyneside Health Authority* [2002] Lloyd's Rep Med 453; *Lillywhite v University College London Hospital NHS Trust* [2005] EWCA Civ 1466; *Manning v King's College Hospital NHS Trust* [2008] EWHC 1838.

71 [2006] EWCA Civ 24, [10].

72 Lord Irvine of Lairg, 'The Patient, the Doctor their Lawyers and the Judge: Rights and Duties' (1999) 7 *Med Law Rev* 255.

73 See Lord Woolf, 'Are the Courts Excessively Deferential to the Medical Profession?' (2001) 9 *Med Law Rev* 1.

74 [2020] EWHC 1351 (QB).

75 *Smith v West Yorkshire Health Authority* [2004] EWHC 1592 (QB).

76 *Morris v Blackpool Victoria NHS Trust* [2003] EWHC 1744; *Dunn v South Tyneside Health Care NHS Trust* [2003] EWCA Civ 870.

77 *Ministry of Justice v Carter* [2010] EWCA Civ 694.

78 [1998] Lloyd's Rep Med 85; and see *Davies v University Hospital of North Staffordshire NHS Trust* [2014] EWHC 4004 (QB).

79 *Ministry of Justice v Carter* [2010] EWCA Civ 694.

their judgements.[80] It may be noted that expert evidence today is much more based on evidence and literature[81] than simple opinion.

8.10 'Responsible practice' means current practice

It has never been a defence for a doctor to say that a practice was widely accepted when they were at medical school and is therefore accepted practice, once informed medical opinion has rejected the practice.[82] A doctor clearly cannot 'obstinately and pig-headedly carry on with some old technique if it has been proved contrary to what is substantially the whole of informed medical opinion'.[83] Doctors must keep up to date with new developments. But there is an inevitable 'time-lag' between the making of new findings by researchers and the percolation of ideas through to doctors in the field. The doctor will be judged by the standard of awareness and sophistication to be expected of a doctor in their sort of practice. Great emphasis is placed on the professional position and the specialty of the defendant.[84] A patient who suffered from brachial palsy as a result of their arm being extended in a certain position while they were given a blood transfusion in the course of a bladder operation brought a claim against the anaesthetist. Six months before the operation, an article had appeared in the *Lancet* condemning this practice because of the risk of brachial palsy. The claim failed. Failure to read one recent article was not negligent.[85] In 2023 the greater ease of access to medical journals via the Internet may affect judgements about how far doctors must be up to date within their specialty.

The relevant date to judge current practice must be the date of the operation or treatment, not the date the claim comes to trial. In *Roe v Ministry of Health*, a patient had become permanently paralysed after an injection of the spinal anaesthetic Nupercaine, administered in 1947. His claim against the doctors and the hospital came to trial in 1954. Before the operation, the drug had been kept in glass ampoules in a solution of phenol. The accident to the patient occurred because phenol percolated through invisible cracks in the ampoules and contaminated the Nupercaine. No one had ever known this to happen. The claim in negligence failed. Lord Denning said: 'We must not look at the 1947 accident with 1954 spectacles.'[86]

Once a tragic incident of this nature has occurred and has been attended by publicity then of course a further incident would easily be proved to be negligence. Current practice would have been shown to be wanting.

80 Brazier & Miola (2008) 8 *Med Law Rev* 85, 106.
81 See *Newman v Maurice* [2010] EWHC 171.
82 *Hunter v Hanley* (1955) SC 200.
83 *Bolam v Friern HMC* [1957] 1 WLR 582, 587.
84 See *Gascoine v Ian Sheridan & Co* [1994] 5 Med LR 437.
85 *Crawford v Board of Governors of Charing Cross Hospital* (1953) *Times*, 8 December, CA. And see *Whiteford v Hunter* (1950) 94 *Solicitors' Journal* 758, HL.
86 *Roe v Ministry of Health* [1954] 2 KB 66, 84; and see *L (A Child) v West Midlands Strategic Health Authority* [2009] EWHC 259; *Oliver v Williams* [2013] EWHC 600 (QB), [3].

8.11 Protocols and guidelines[87]

Buzz-words in medicine today are evidence-based medicine and clinical governance. Within the NHS, the government has sought to ensure that treatment provided to patients is soundly based on good practice derived from concrete evidence. The National Institute of Health and Care Excellence (NICE) is expressly instructed to investigate medical practice and provide authoritative guidelines on good practice. The Royal Colleges of Medicine, and other doctors' organisations, increasingly draw up protocols for treatment and issue guidelines on good practice.

Evidence of good practice as defined by protocol and guidelines will play a role in any claim for clinical negligence. The considered judgement of NICE, or the profession itself, will be evidence of what constitutes responsible practice. Does this mean any doctor departing from official guidelines will be proven negligent? Some doctors fear guidelines enforced by the courts will lead to a 'tick-box' approach to patient care.[88] Doctors will cease to exercise professional judgement based on the needs and circumstances of the individual patient. This should not happen. Where departure from the guidelines can be justified in the interests of the patient, the doctor discharges his duty of care. In *Price v Cwm Taf University Health Board* it was held that breach of NICE guidelines was not *prima facie* evidence of negligence.[89] Blind adherence to guidelines or protocols would itself be negligent.[90]

One worrying pattern that seems to have emerged is that guidelines are frequently used by judges to justify a more favourable attitude towards defendants, whereas they do not seem to be used in the same way towards claimants.[91] Guidelines should always be considered in the light of the *Bolitho* gloss, which requires that responsible practice be demonstrably logical and defensible. If this is applied appropriately, it may well assist patients in relying on the use of or departure from a guideline to support their case. Guidelines will undoubtedly offer some evidence of what constitutes proper treatment for the patient's condition, but evidence that the patient requires a different mode of care should not be excluded by the presence of such general guidance.[92]

[87] See A Samanta *et al*, 'The Role of Clinical Guidelines in Medical Negligence Litigation: A Shift from the Bolam Standard' (2006) 14 *Med Law Rev* 321; A Samanta *et al*, 'Responsible Practice or Restricted Practice? An Empirical Study of the Use of Clinical Guidelines in Medical Negligence Litigation' (2021) 2 *Med Law Rev* 205.

[88] See J Warden, 'NICE to Sort out Clinical Wheat from Chaff' (1999) 318 *BMJ* 416.

[89] [2019] EWHC 938.

[90] Or for example to textbooks; see *Shortall v Mid Essex Hospital Services NHS Trust* [2014] EWHC 246 (QB).

[91] See R Heywood, 'Reliance on Clinical Guidelines in Contemporary Negligence Litigation: Influential of Determinative?' in J Samanta, A Samanta and J Beswick (eds), *Clinical Guidelines and the Law of Medical Negligence* (2021) Elgar, ch 2.

[92] See Brazier and Miola, 'Bye-Bye Bolam: A Medical Litigation Revolution'; but see B Hurwitz, 'How Does Evidence Based Guidance Influence Determinations of Medical Negligence?' (2004) 329 *BMJ* 1024.

8.12 Diagnosis

A wrong diagnosis is by itself no evidence of negligence on the part of the doctor. As a Scottish judge said:

> In the realm of diagnosis and treatment there is ample scope for a genuine difference of opinion and one man is clearly not negligent merely because his conclusion differs from that of other professional men ...[93]

A patient alleging that a wrong diagnosis was negligent must establish either that the doctor failed to carry out an examination or a test which the patient's symptoms called for, or that his eventual conclusion[94] was one that no competent doctor would have arrived at (the *Bolam* test) or was not 'capable of withstanding logical analysis' (the *Bolitho*[95] test). Not surprisingly, a doctor who failed to diagnose a broken knee-cap in a man who had fallen 12 feet on to a concrete floor was found to be negligent.[96] The courts are readier to find negligence when a patient and his experts can point to a specific failure on the part of the doctor. A casualty doctor, who failed to examine or x-ray a drunken patient admitted with the information that he had been seen under a moving lorry, was found to be negligent when after his death next day he was discovered to have eighteen fractured ribs and extensive damage to his lungs. It was no defence that the patient never complained of pain. The doctor should have known that alcohol would dull the patient's reaction to pain.[97]

In the above examples, the doctors were negligent because they failed to act on information available to them and/or to perform routine tests. Where a diagnostic procedure is not routine or is costly, painful or risky, an additional factor has to be considered. Do the symptoms displayed by the patient justify subjecting them to the procedure? Doctors face a legal as well as a medical dilemma. If they do not arrange for the test and a patient does suffer from some condition which the test would have revealed, the doctor may be sued for that failure. If the doctor does arrange the test and an inherent risk of the test harms the patient, the patient may sue if the test reveals that the doctor's suspicions were groundless. We saw that that is what happened with Staff Nurse Maynard.[98] The defendants were *not* liable to her because they had followed accepted practice in going ahead with the test, despite its dangers. Doctors argue that alacrity to pin liability on them for every diagnostic error may cause patients to be submitted to more expensive and potentially risky procedures than may be strictly medically desirable.

Interpreting screening and diagnostic tests is a difficult skill but failure to act on information that should have alerted the laboratory or the doctor to

93 *Hunter v Hanley* 1955 SLT 213, at 217.
94 See *Lillywhite v University College London Hospitals NHS Trust* [2005] EWCA Civ 1466.
95 See for example *Penney v East Kent Health Authority* [2000] Lloyd's Rep Med 23.
96 *Newton v Newton's New Model Laundry* (1951) *Times*, 3 November.
97 *Wood v Thurston* (1951) *Times*, 25 May.
98 *Maynard v West Midlands Regional Health Authority* [1984] 1 WLR 634; see 8.8 above.

undertake further investigations may give rise to liability. So in *Penney and Others v East Kent Health Authority*,[99] the claimants developed cervical cancer after an erroneous negative report from a screening test. The false negative result itself was no evidence of negligence. It was admitted that abnormalities were present on the patients' slides and that any competent screener would thus have been unable to rule out that the cells were pre-cancerous. Reporting the tests as negative was therefore found by the Court of Appeal to be illogical. Although the defendants' experts sought to argue that the screeners were not negligent in their interpretation of the slides as both set of experts agreed that the standard for a negative report was 'absolute confidence', a negative report in the face of admitted abnormalities failed the *Bolitho* test.[100]

8.13 Treatment

A claim in respect of negligent treatment may be based on an allegation that the treatment chosen was inappropriate, or that while the treatment embarked on was correct, it was negligently carried out. Doctors must ensure that they act on adequate information and supply each other with adequate information. A GP prescribing drugs must check what other medication the patient is on. Doctors must be alert to common drug reactions and actively seek relevant information from patients. A clinic which injected a woman with penicillin was held liable for her death an hour later.[101] Had they inquired of her, or examined her records, they would have been aware of her allergy to penicillin. Doctors must be wary of relying entirely on information supplied by their colleagues. A patient was admitted for a gynaecological operation. The gynaecologist asked a general surgeon to remove what he said was a ganglion from the patient's wrist. Thus the patient would be spared two separate operations. It was not a ganglion. Surgery of that sort was inappropriate and the patient's hand was permanently paralysed. The Medical Defence Union (MDU) settled because the general surgeon should have made his own pre-operative assessment, and not relied on a colleague from another specialty.[102]

Once the doctor is properly informed and has selected his course of treatment, they must ensure that they carry it out properly. They must check the dosage of any drug. Prescribing an overdose will readily be found to be negligent.[103] Electronic records are the norm, but any handwritten instructions must be legible.[104] Care must also be taken always to read drug labelling properly. In

99 [2000] Lloyd's Rep Med 41. Note, too, the discussion as to the applicability of *Bolam* to such screening tests. And see *Farraj v King's Healthcare NHS Trust* [2009] EWCA 1203.

100 See also *Manning v King's College Hospital NHS Trust* [2008] EWHC 1838 (failure to diagnose rare tongue cancer).

101 *Chin Keow v Govt of Malaysia* [1967] 1 WLR 813.

102 MDU, *Annual Report* (1984), p 18.

103 *Dwyer v Roderick* (1983) 127 SJ 806, and see J Finch, 'A Costly Oversight for Pharmacists' (1982) 132 *NLJ* 176.

104 *Prendergast v Sam and Dee* [1989] 1 Med LR 36.

a tragic case,[105] a senior house officer misread a label and administered potassium chloride instead of saline to a newborn infant. The baby died.

Where surgery is called for, the risk of injury is increased. Especially risky is the administration of the anaesthetic. The anaesthetist will be found to be negligent if they failed to make a proper pre-operative assessment of the patient, failed to check their equipment, failed to monitor the patient's blood pressure and/or heartbeat in the course of surgery or if, an inevitable accident having occurred, the anaesthetist fails to invoke adequate resuscitation measures. Some specific failure on the defendant's part must be pinpointed. A disturbing number of claims arose from failure to intubate the patient properly (putting the tube in the wrong place) or attaching tubes to the wrong gas so that the patient failed to receive essential oxygen.[106] Several claims have arisen from failure to anaesthetise the patient completely. Patients are paralysed and unable to communicate but remain awake and feel pain throughout surgery.[107]

An anaesthetic tragedy of itself is generally not evidence of negligence. An anaesthetist who injected cocaine instead of procaine was found negligent,[108] as was the junior doctor who injected pentothal into an anaesthetised patient, causing his death.[109] If the wrong drug, or the wrong dosage, or a contaminated drug, is used, the patient's claim will generally be made good. The exception will be where the error cannot be laid at the anaesthetist's door. So, as we saw in *Roe v Ministry of Health*,[110] a patient who was paralysed because a then unknown risk of phenol percolating into the ampoules of local anaesthetic materialised recovered no compensation.

Surgery must be performed with the utmost care. One judge has suggested that the more skilled the surgeon, the higher the standard of care.[111] Some errors advertise their negligence. Leaving swabs and equipment inside the patient is a good example. And the surgeon must accept responsibility for such matters and not rely on nursing staff.[112] Nor does the surgeon's responsibility end with the careful completion of surgery. They must give their patient proper post-operative care and advice. A surgeon performed a cosmetic operation just below the eye. He told his patient to inform him if bleeding occurred within forty-eight hours. It did and the patient tried to telephone the surgeon and got no reply. The surgeon was held to be negligent.[113]

An especially important issue today concerns the need to protect patients against hospital-acquired (nosocomial) infections such as Methicillin Resistant

105 MDU, *Annual Report* (1989), p 32.
106 MDU, *Annual Report* (1988), pp 28–29; (1989), pp 20–21.
107 For example, *Taylor v Worcester and District Health Authority* (1997) 2 Med LR 215.
108 *Collins v Hertfordshire Corporation* [1947] 1 KB 598.
109 *Jones v Manchester Corporation* [1952] 2 QB 852.
110 [1954] 2 QB 66, CA.
111 *Ashcroft v Mersey Area Health Authority* [1983] 2 All ER 245, 247. And see *Lillywhite v University College London Hospitals NHS Trust* [2005] EWCA Civ 1466.
112 *Urry v Biere* (1955) *Times*, 19 July.
113 *Corder v Banks* (1960) *Times*, 9 April.

Staphyloccus Aureus (MRSA) and Clostridium Difficile (C Diff).[114] In a Scottish case, *Miller v Greater Glasgow NHS Board*,[115] the defendants applied to strike out a claim by a patient who alleged that she had contracted MRSA because staff had not followed an adequate hand hygiene practice. The court refused the application holding that protection from hospital-acquired infection was an integral part of the duty owed to patients by both individual professionals and the Hospital Trust.[116]

8.14 Overtired, overworked doctors

If a doctor makes a mistake because they are intolerably weary, or just having a bad day, will the patient's rights be in any way affected? No, the courts rightly will not accept any argument that the doctor's duty is fulfilled if they provide an adequate service generally and only occasionally falls below the required standard of competence.[117] Judges sympathise with hard-pressed doctors. A doctor who carries on beyond the point when fatigue and overwork impair their judgement remains liable to an injured patient. The fact that the doctor was required by their employer to work such hours will not affect the patient. This issue has been brought more sharply into focus by the recent COVID-19 pandemic. In responding to the spread of the virus, health professionals were required to work long hours, often in fields outside their direct expertise. Everyone on the front line should be applauded for their heroic efforts in regard to the rapidly developing emergency, but there can be no denying that in times where resources are stretched and tiredness takes hold, the potential for error to occur is heightened. Concerned about this, the government provided an indemnity for individual health professionals whose errors caused harm during the course of dealing with the COVID-19 crisis.[118] The MDU argued that this did not go far enough and requested a debate about whether immunity should be granted to health professionals for COVID-related mistakes.[119] Two of us, along with other colleagues, argued against this proposition on the basis that it would send the wrong message about the standard of care patients should be entitled to expect.[120] Quite apart from that, though, immunity is not needed. The indemnity would mean that individual health professionals would never pay damages personally and judges, when determining the question of breach, would remain sensitive to the emergency circumstances. Factors such as stretched resources, inappropriate equipment, the fast-moving nature of the situation and the excessive hours

114 Additionally, hospital-acquired COVID-19 infection was raised as a potential negligence risk by NHS Resolution, *Clinical Negligence and COVID-19* at www.resolution.nhs.uk.

115 [2010] CSIH 40.

116 On the direct liability of Hospital Trusts, see further Chapter 9.

117 *Wilsher v Essex Area Health Authority* [1986] 3 All ER 801, CA.

118 Coronavirus Act 2020, s 11.

119 O Bowcott, 'Union Seeks Legal Immunity for NHS Medics in Pandemic' *Guardian* (2020) 19 April.

120 See C Purshouse *et al*, 'Should Doctors Tackling Covid-19 be Immune from Negligence Liability Claims?' (2020) 370 *BMJ* m2487.

that health professionals were asked to work would naturally mean that the threshold for imposing liability would, quite rightly, remain high.[121] Thus, sufficient measures are already in place to guard against a flood of litigation.

Elsewhere, a patient may also consider proceeding against the doctor's employers, the hospital, on the basis of systemic negligence.[122] The patient would allege that the hospital undertook to provide them with adequate care.[123] Requiring their doctors to work to the point of utter exhaustion, or organising shifts in such a way as to prevent continuity of care, is a breach of that duty. The essence of the patient's claim would become, not that the hospital was vicariously liable for an individual doctor's negligence, but that there was a breach of a primary duty to ensure an adequate and competent service. In *Wilsher v Essex Area Health Authority*,[124] Browne-Wilkinson VC suggested that in many cases this was a more appropriate analysis of clinical negligence claims, avoiding stigmatising overworked doctors for understandable errors. But there is a risk that even fewer patients may obtain compensation if this analysis were accepted. The defendant hospital might plead in its defence the problems it faces arising from lack of resources. If patient A suffers an injury because the surgeon who operated on them was too tired to perform the surgery properly and no other surgeon was available, the hospital may argue that it could not afford to employ more, or more senior, surgeons. It will be contended that, although far from ideal, the level of service was reasonable in the light of the defendant's limited budget. In one judgment, a judge expressly said that lack of resources should be taken into account in medical negligence claims.[125] But in a later case any such argument was vigorously rejected.[126] And it has been made clear that any argument that the conditions of work and need to balance the claims of competing patients for urgent care affects the standard of care owed by the hospital must at the least be supported by cogent evidence. The defendant cannot simply ask the court to assume that an accident and emergency department is so busy that account must be taken of the unusual level of demand.[127]

8.15 Relating the injury to medical negligence: problems of causation[128]

So far, the majority of the cases examined involved something going wrong as a result of a medical mistake. The patient's problem has been to prove that what was done, or not done, amounted to actionable negligence. Proving

121 See *Ball v Wirral Health Authority* [2003] All ER (D) 229; [2003] Lloyd's Rep Med 165 at [32].

122 R Heywood, 'Systemic Negligence and NHS Hospitals: An Underutilised Argument' (2021) 32 *King's Law Journal* 437.

123 *Cassidy v Ministry of Health* [1951] 2 KB 14.

124 [1986] 3 All ER 801, 833–834.

125 *Knight v Home Office* [1990] 3 All ER 237.

126 *Brooks v Home Office* (1999) 48 BMLR 109.

127 *Gardner v Northampton General Hospital NHS Trust* [2014] EWHC 4217 (QB), [32].

128 See generally J Stapleton, 'Unnecessary Causes' (2013) 129 *LQR* 39.

negligence by the doctor does not conclude the case in the patient's favour. The patient must also show that their injury, their worsened or unimproved condition, was caused by the doctor's negligence. They must prove causation. In practice, proving causation is often the most problematic aspect of a patient's claim. The difficulties of causation in medical malpractice cases fall into two main categories. (1) Can the patient convince the court that it was the relevant negligence which caused their injury, rather than the progress of their original disease or condition? (2) How should the courts proceed when the essence of a claim is not that clinical negligence caused any fresh or additional injury to the patient but that that negligence deprived them of a chance of full recovery from their original disease or condition? In each and every case the patient must advance evidence showing that it is more likely than not that the defendant's negligence caused the injury of which they complain.

In *Kay v Ayrshire and Arran Health Board*,[129] a 2-year-old boy, Andrew Kay, was suffering from pneumococcal meningitis. He was negligently given a massive overdose of penicillin and nearly died as a result. Intensive efforts by hospital staff saved Andrew's life and he recovered from both the toxic overdose and from meningitis. But he was found to be profoundly deaf. The board admitted negligence but denied that Andrew's deafness resulted from that negligence. Deafness is often a complication of meningitis even where the disease has been correctly treated. Massive overdoses of the sort that Andrew was given are mercifully rare. So there was little available evidence of whether such an overdose materially increased the risk that Andrew would become deaf as a result of his disease. The trial judge found in Andrew's favour, but his decision was overruled in the appeal courts. In the House of Lords, Lord Keith commented that the lack of recorded cases demonstrating the effect of overdose of penicillin 'cannot in itself make good the lack of appropriate evidence'.[130]

As we have seen, in *Wilsher v Essex Area Health Authority*[131] junior doctors were found to be negligent in administering excess oxygen to a very premature baby, Martin Wilsher. Martin succumbed to RLF, an incurable condition of the retina causing gradual blindness. The question that went to the House of Lords was whether Martin's lawyers could prove that RLF resulted from that negligent administration of excess oxygen. The scientific evidence suggested that RLF *may* result from excess oxygen, but there were five other possible causes of RLF in very sick, very premature infants. The trial judge had held that, as negligence had been proved, the burden of disproving that that negligence caused Martin's injuries moved to the defendants. He said that as the evidence showed that the doctors were in breach of their duty to Martin and failed to take a precaution expressly designed to safeguard Martin from RLF, it was then up to them to prove that Martin's condition resulted from one of the other possible causes. The House of Lords roundly condemned such an approach, and ordered a retrial. The burden of proving causation rests on the claimant alone, and does not move to the defendant even though negligence

129 [1987] 2 All ER 417. And see *Loveday v Renton* [1990] 1 Med L Rep 117.
130 [1987] 2 All ER 417, 421.
131 [1988] 1 All ER 871, HL.

has been proved or admitted. What is crucial for the claimant is the quality of the expert scientific evidence presented on his behalf. That evidence must, at the very least, demonstrate that it is more likely than not that the defendants' negligence materially contributed to the claimant's condition, or materially increased the risk that the claimant would succumb to such a condition.[132] Where the scientific evidence is ambivalent or suggests a variety of competing causes for the claimant's state, the action for negligence will normally fail.

In *Younas v Okeahialam*[133] the court showed 'claimant benevolence' to a patient who had difficulty proving causation in circumstances where the lack of evidence resulted from the defendant's breach of duty. After an abnormal ECG result, the patient suffered spinal cord injury when he fell due to an undiagnosed condition. He alleged that the doctor should have referred him for further investigation in light of the ECG. Relevant further tests would potentially have provided evidence of the condition for which he was not treated. In these circumstances the court will not reverse the burden of proof and nor will it assume evidence that is entirely lacking. But provided there is some relevant, albeit inferior, evidence from which the court can draw an inference, the court may be willing in the circumstances to give the claimant the benefit of the doubt.

Uncertainty about causation is likely to be common in many claims that essentially relate to whether the defendants' negligence caused or exacerbated disease. In *Fairchild v Glenhaven Funeral Services Ltd*,[134] claims were brought by workers who had been exposed to asbestos dust or fibres during their working lives and developed the fatal lung disease mesothelioma. The men had worked for several different employers, so pinpointing which defendant employer was responsible for the onset of the disease was nigh on impossible. Mesothelioma can result from a single asbestos fibre entering the lung. The greater your exposure to asbestos fibres, the more likely it is that this will occur. The Law Lords allowed the claim, holding all the defendant employers liable, as each of them had materially increased the risk of harm to their employees. The judges overtly invoked policy considerations to support their modified approach to, and departure from, the usual strict rules of causation.[135] Might the harsh decision in *Wilsher* thus be reconsidered? It seems unlikely. Lord Hoffmann not only declared *Wilsher* to be correctly decided in principle, but also suggested that policy reasons to protect NHS budgets could play a part in denying patient-claimants a more favourable approach to causation. He said:

> The political and economic arguments involved in the massive increase in the liability of the National Health Service which would have been a consequence of the broad rule favoured by the Court of Appeal in *Wilsher's* case are far more

132 [1988] 1 All ER 871, 882–883, per Lord Bridge.

133 [2019] EWHC 2502 (QB).

134 [2002] UKHL 22; and see *Gardner v Northampton General Hospital Trust* [2014] EWHC 4217 (QB).

135 Subsequently, in *Barker v Corus UK Ltd* [2006] UKHL 22, the Law Lords ruled that each defendant should be liable only to the extent of their relevant contribution to the claimant's exposure to asbestos dust. In the specific context of claims for mesothelioma, s 3 of the Compensation Act 2006 nullified that decision.

> complicated than the reasons ... for imposing liability upon an employer who has failed to take simple precautions.[136]

However, in *Bailey v Ministry of Defence*[137] the Court of Appeal held that in particular circumstances and in relation to cumulative causes a 'material contribution' to the claimant's injury was sufficient to establish causation in a clinical negligence claim. In such cases the 'but for' test could be modified. The claimant was a patient at a hospital managed by the Ministry of Defence. She underwent an unsuccessful procedure to remove a gallstone. The defendants admitted that following the procedure her post-operative care was inadequate, in particular a failure to resuscitate. She became progressively more ill, she was subjected to battery of major medical interventions, and was also diagnosed as suffering from pancreatitis. Her condition deteriorated and she was eventually transferred to the renal unit of an NHS hospital where she aspirated her vomit and suffered a cardiac arrest resulting in brain damage. The issue in dispute was whether the negligent post-operative care caused the cardiac arrest and consequential brain damage. The claimant could not establish that 'but for' that negligence she would not have suffered the arrest. She was a very sick woman and her pancreatitis also contributed to her weakness. The trial judge found that the post-operative negligence contributed to her weakened state and that, but for her weakened state, she would have undergone a further intervention that would have alleviated her condition and spared her some of the later traumatic interventions to which she was subjected. The negligent care thus made a material contribution to her injury. The Court of Appeal upheld his finding. It was sufficient to show that the contribution made by inadequate care was more than negligible. Waller LJ said:

> In a case where medical science cannot establish the probability that 'but for' an act of negligence the injury would not have happened but can establish that the contribution of the negligence was more than negligible, the 'but for' test is modified, and the claimant will succeed.[138]

No distinction was to be drawn between clinical negligence claims and others. *Wilsher* was distinguished on the grounds that it was never established that the excess oxygen, rather than one of the five alternative causes, caused or contributed to the plaintiff developing RLF. Unlike Ms Bailey, Martin Wilsher could not meet the first condition of showing some causal link between the relevant negligence and his injury.

8.16 Modifying the 'strict rules'

In *Chester v Afshar*,[139] an earlier patient-claimant also benefited from judicial willingness to modify strict application of the rules of causation. As we have

136 [2002] UKHL 22, [69].
137 [2008] EWCA Civ 883. And see *Coakley v Rosie* [2014] EWHC 1790 (QB), [118]. (Claimant was able to establish 'but for' causation, but would otherwise have succeeded on the basis of *Bailey*.)
138 Ibid, [46].
139 [2004] UKHL 41, see 6.16 above.

seen, Mr Afshar failed to warn Miss Chester of the one to two per cent risk of nerve damage in the course of spinal surgery. Miss Chester did not contend that, had she been properly warned, she would never have consented to surgery, or that she would have sought a second opinion. All she claimed was that, had she been warned, she would not have gone ahead with surgery that day. The risk of damage on any later occasion would have been just the same. Miss Chester faced the utmost difficulty in proving that, but for Mr Afshar's negligence, she would have avoided injury. The majority (three to two) in the House of Lords invoked policy grounds to assist her. Giving proper legal force to patients' rights to autonomy and dignity justified 'a narrow and modest departure from traditional causation principles'.[140]

Bolitho v City & Hackney Health Authority[141] raised a rather different question of causation. You will recall that Patrick Bolitho stopped breathing and suffered a cardiac arrest resulting in serious brain damage. The hospital admitted negligence in relation to the failure of the paediatric registrar to attend Patrick when she had been summoned to do so earlier. They denied liability because, they said, the registrar would not have intubated Patrick, had she attended him prior to his collapse. Intubation was the only means by which Patrick's respiratory failure and cardiac arrest might have been averted. The plaintiffs argued that, had Patrick been intubated, he would not have suffered injury. The defendants responded that attendance would have made no difference; medical opinion would support not intubating the child. The key question became does the *Bolam* test play a role in causation?

Lord Browne-Wilkinson agreed with counsel for the plaintiff that 'in the generality of cases' *Bolam* plays no role in causation. *Bolitho* exemplifies an unusual problem. How do the courts address causation when the essence of the matter is whether something should have been done which has not been done? The factual inquiry proceeds into the 'realms of hypotheses'.[142] The court has to ask:[143]

(1) What would the defendant have done if she had attended the boy? This is a purely factual question to which *Bolam* has no relevance.
(2) If the answer to that first question is that she would *not* have intubated, would that have been negligent?

In addressing that question, *Bolam* is central. The court had to decide if non-intubation conformed to responsible professional practice applying their

140 Ibid, [24] per Lord Steyn; but see to the contrary, Lord Bingham at [9].
141 [1998] AC 232, HL; see MA Jones, 'The Bolam Test and the Responsible Expert' (1999) *Tort Law Review* 226; A Grubb, 'Negligence Causation and Bolam' (1998) 5 *Med Law Rev* 378. And see *L (A Child) v West Midlands Strategic Health Authority* [2009] EWHC 259.
142 See *Gardner v Northampton General Hospital Trust* [2014] EWHC 4217 (QB) where the judge draws a 'hypothetical time line' to assess what should have happened had there been no breach of duty and thus to assess if that breach caused the damage complained of [31]–[41].
143 [1998] AC 232, 240.

Lordships' *caveat* that responsible practice must be demonstrated 'logical and defensible'. In the event, the evidence of the defendant's experts, that intubation of a child of Patrick's age in his circumstances was itself far from risk-free, convinced their Lordships.

8.17 Loss of a chance

When the unfortunate claimant complains not of some new injury inflicted by the defendants but of a lost chance of recovery, his claim is even more difficult to prove. In *Hotson v East Berkshire Health Authority*,[144] the plaintiff, a schoolboy of 13, fell heavily, from a rope on which he had been swinging, to the ground 12 ft below. He was taken to hospital. His knee was X-rayed and revealed no injury. No further examination was made and the plaintiff was sent home. Five days later, the boy was taken back to the same hospital and an injury to his hip joint was diagnosed and subsequently swiftly and correctly treated. The injury had traumatic consequences. The boy suffered a condition known as avascular necrosis. This condition, caused by a restriction of the blood supply in the region of the original injury, leads to misshapenness of the joint, disability and pain, and later in life almost certainly brings on osteoarthritis in the joint. The plaintiff's disability might have ensued from the accident in any case. But there was a 25 per cent chance that given the correct treatment immediately the plaintiff might have avoided disability and made a nearly full recovery.

The defendant hospital admitted negligence in failing to diagnose and treat the plaintiff's injury on his first visit. Both parties agreed that prompt treatment would have offered a 25 per cent chance of avoiding permanent disability. The trial judge awarded the boy 25 per cent of full compensation for his condition, that is a sum of money to compensate him for a 25 per cent lost chance of full recovery.[145] The House of Lords quashed his judgment.[146] Their Lordships held that the plaintiff had failed to prove that it was more likely than not that avascular necrosis resulted from the negligent delay in treatment, because there was a 75 per cent chance he would have suffered from avascular necrosis, even if the treatment had been given promptly. To recover damages for the avascular necrosis, the plaintiff needed to establish at least a 51:49 likelihood that 'but for' the negligent delay in treatment, he would have made an uncomplicated recovery from his original injury. Had he succeeded in so doing, he would have been entitled to 100 per cent compensation for his disability. Their Lordships declined to say that loss of a less than 50 per cent chance of full recovery was never recoverable in a medical negligence claim. They left that question open.

The claimant in *Gregg v Scott*[147] may have hoped that his case for loss of a chance was stronger. In November 1994, his GP (the defendant) wrongly

144 [1987] 2 All ER 909, HL. See T Hill, 'A Lost Chance for Compensation in the Tort of Negligence in the House of Lords' (1991) 54 *MLR* 111.

145 [1985] 3 All ER 167.

146 [1987] 2 All ER 909, HL.

147 [2005] UKHL 2. Contrast the facts of *Gregg v Scott* with *Manning v King's College Hospital NHS Trust* [2008] EWHC 1838.

diagnosed a lump under Mr Gregg's arm as a benign lipoma. The following August, a different doctor referred him to a consultant, and, in November 1995, a biopsy revealed a malignant lymphoma. The delay in diagnosis reduced Mr Gregg's chance of a 'cure' (defined as ten years in remission) from 42 to 25 per cent. Mr Gregg (unlike the young plaintiff in Hotson) could therefore argue that, as a consequence of the defendant's negligence, he had lost a 17 per cent chance of a 'cure'. But, alas, he could not establish that had the defendant done his job properly, he would have had a better than 50 per cent chance of a 'cure'. He was still more likely than not to face an early death even had his cancer been more promptly diagnosed. The majority of the House of Lords (three to two) applied the rules in causation strictly and found against Mr Gregg. Lord Hoffmann declared:

> [A] wholesale adoption of possible rather than probable causation as the criterion of liability would be so radical a change in our law as to amount to a legislative act. It would have enormous consequences for insurance companies and the National Health Service.[148]

One of the dissenting judges, Lord Nicholls retorted:

> It cannot be right to adopt a procedure having the effect that, in law, a patient's prospects of recovery are treated as non-existent whenever they exist but fall short of 50 per cent. If the law were to proceed in this way it would deserve to be likened to the proverbial ass ...[149]

How may *Gregg v Scott* be distinguished from *Chester v Afshar* and *Fairchild*? Baroness Hale seeks to contend that the latter two decisions were confined to 'problems which could be remedied without altering the principles applicable to the great majority of personal injury cases which give rise to no real injustice or particular problems'.[150] Their Lordships seem deeply divided on causation. Sarah Green argues cogently that distinguishing *Chester* and *Gregg* on grounds of principle cannot be done. Both are hard cases. In her view, it is *Chester* that made bad law.[151] In *Wright v Cambridge Medical Group*[152] the Court of Appeal suggested that while the decision in *Gregg* does not rule out all variations of a loss of chance claim, only the Supreme Court could realistically expand case-law on loss of a chance in the context of clinical negligence claims.

8.18 General practice

Most patients visit their GP on average four or five times a year and make one or two hospital visits in a lifetime. Clinical negligence claims against GPs, whilst comparatively lower than in other areas of medicine, are becoming

148 [2005] UKHL 2, [90].
149 Ibid, [43].
150 Ibid, [192].
151 S Green, 'Coherence of Medical Negligence Cases: A Game of Doctors and Purses' (2006) 14 *Med Law Rev* 1.
152 [2011] EWHC Civ 669, [82], see 8.18 below.

more common.[153] Changes in general practice which alter the more personal relationship between GP and patient may increase the GP's vulnerability to claims for clinical negligence. A claim against a GP may face some particular obstacles. Many common complaints about general practice do not tend to be the kind of grievances that make litigation with its expense, pomp and ceremony worthwhile. Patients object to unhelpful receptionists, difficulty in getting home visits, and often simply sense a lack of sympathy. Rarely do these irritations cause injury serious enough to merit litigation.

Proving negligence, and that the patient's injury resulted from that negligence, is always difficult. Against a GP the problems multiply. How do you prove that a child's sudden deterioration resulted from the GP not seeing the child swiftly? Would immediate referral to hospital have arrested the condition? In *Wright v Cambridge Medical Group*[154] a two-day delay by GPs in referring a baby with a serious bacterial infection back to hospital resulted in permanent damage to the infant's hip, affecting her gait and mobility. Further delays in initiating correct treatment in the hospital contributed to the permanent damage to the hip joint. The hospital was not made a party to the proceedings. The trial judge held that the defendant GP practice was negligent in delaying referral, but that even if the child had been promptly referred to the hospital, it was more likely than not that she would not have been treated properly and would still have suffered the damage to her hip. Thus, the GP practice while negligent did not cause the permanent injury of which the infant claimant complained. The Court of Appeal reversed the decision. The subsequent negligence of the hospital was not so significant as to destroy any causative contribution to the child's injury on the part of the GP.[155] Nor was the judge right to assume that, had she been referred to hospital in a timely manner, the hospital would not have treated her properly. The GP practice as a joint tortfeasor remained liable for the whole of the damage suffered by the claimant, albeit that had the hospital been joined in the proceedings, the practice would have been able to claim a contribution to the damages from the hospital and it was likely that a court would hold that the hospital should bear a greater share of the blame and thus pay a greater share of the damages awarded. Stripping out the complexity of the case, what is clear is that GPs who are negligent in referring a patient to hospital in due time cannot argue that subsequent failures on the part of the hospital wipes out any liability on their part. They deprive the claimant of the opportunity to receive adequate treatment.

153 In its 2020/21 annual reports and accounts, NHS Resolution states that the volume of claims taken on in respect of relatively new general practice indemnity schemes increased from 401 to 1,813 and that it is preparing to take on several hundred more from the Medical Protection Society from 1 April 2021. See NHS Resolution, *Annual Report and Accounts 2020/21* (2021) HC 387, July, p 16. For discussion see R Heywood, '"If the Problem Persists, Come Back to See Me": An Empirical Study of Clinical Negligence Cases against General Practitioners' (2019) 27 *Med Law Rev* 406.

154 [2011] EWCA Civ 669.

155 Ibid, [37].

Every GP must attain that standard of skill and competence to be expected of the reasonably skilled and experienced GP. It is no defence that they have just entered practice or that they are elderly and infirm. Nor, as we have seen, can they be expected to have the skills or qualifications of a consultant specialist. They must exercise their judgement about when to refer a patient to a specialist, or admit the patient to hospital, with due care.[156]

In reported cases where negligence has been proved against GPs, certain danger areas stand out. The maintenance of proper records and ensuring adequate communication with patients,[157] and with hospitals and other doctors sharing the care of a patient is one. A failure to record and pass on to a hospital information on a patient's allergy to certain drugs is a clear case of negligence.[158] Similarly, a failure to check exactly what treatment has been given by the hospital may result in liability. A GP was found liable for a young man's death in this case.[159] The man had gone to a cottage hospital after a lump of coal had fallen on him and crushed his finger. A nurse dressed the wound and instructed him to go to another larger hospital. Either because this was not properly explained to him or because he was in shock, he did not go. He went later to his own doctor, who did not inquire as to his earlier treatment and simply put on a new dressing. At no stage did the patient receive an anti-tetanus injection and he died of toxaemia. The cottage hospital and the GP were both found to be negligent and responsible for the youth's death. The judge made his views emphatically clear:

> [T]he National Health Service had been developed on the basis that a patient might well be transferred for treatment from one person to another so that the responsibility for the patient shifted ... Any system which failed to provide for effective communication was wrong and negligently wrong.

8.19 Prescription errors

Prescribing medicines is another area where GPs must be ultra-cautious, not just out of professional concern for the patient, but also to safeguard themselves. In 1982, a GP prescribed Migril for a Mrs Dwyer. Carelessly he wrote out a prescription for a massive overdose of the drug. A pharmacist dispensed the drug as prescribed. Mrs Dwyer became ill. A partner in the same practice attended her at home. The Migril was on a table in her bedroom, but the second doctor did not notice the bottle. Mrs Dwyer suffered gangrene as a result of the overdose. She sued both doctors and the pharmacist. All were originally found liable.[160] Mrs Dwyer received £100,000 in damages. Eventually the second doctor was exculpated on appeal. At the end of the day, the GP whose slip

156 *Marriott v West Midlands Area Health Authority* [1999] Lloyd's Rep Med 23.
157 See *Langley v Campbell* (1975) *Times*, 6 November.
158 *Chin Keow v Government of Malaysia* [1967] 1 WLR 813.
159 *Coles v Reading and District Hospital Management Committee* (1963) *Times*, 30 January.
160 *Dwyer v Roderick* (1983) 127 SJ 806. Recounted in 'A Costly Oversight for Pharmacists' (1982) 132 *NLJ* 176.

caused the over-prescription paid 45 per cent of the damages, and the pharmacists 55 per cent. Doctors must exercise great care in writing out prescriptions. Pharmacists must exercise even greater care in checking on the doctors.

8.20 Contributory negligence[161]

The Law Reform (Contributory Negligence) Act 1945 provides where a claimant suffers injury partly as a result of his own fault his damages may be reduced to take account of his own responsibility for the damage. How might such a defence apply in a clinical negligence claim? Such a case might arise if a doctor negligently prescribed a moderate overdose of a drug and the claimant exacerbated the injury from the drug by taking twice what the doctor prescribed, or drinking alcohol when they had been correctly instructed to abstain. In one reported case the claimant was wrongly told that her cervical smear test was negative but then over several years failed to attend for further tests which would have identified the cancer more swiftly. She was judged to be two-thirds responsible for her injury.[162] But what of patients whose abuse of drink or drugs, or grossly unhealthy lifestyle, made them need treatment in the first place? So that if they had not neglected their own health they would never have needed treatment and not been at risk of inadequate treatment?

Trevor Horsley was not injured by medical treatment, but by his employers' negligence in exposing him to asbestos. He was found to have contributed to his respiratory disability by having smoked heavily for thirty-five years, having received multiple warnings of the adverse effects it was having on his health.[163] Compare this case with *St George v Home Office*[164] in which the claimant was addicted to drink and drugs. On admission to prison he refused to see a doctor and was assigned to a ward in the hospital wing. He was allocated a top bunk and fell out of the bunk when he suffered a withdrawal seizure. He continued to fit for some time developing a highly dangerous status epilepticus ('status'). He was transferred to an NHS hospital. As a result of his seizures, he suffered permanent brain damage. The judge found that the fall triggered status, the cause of his brain damage. The defendants argued that the claimant's substance abuse contributed to his injury and damages should be proportionately reduced. Noting that this was a case on which there was no direct previous authority the Court of Appeal agreed that the claimant was at fault. But both the judge and the appeal court held that the claimant's conduct in becoming an addict in his teens was too remote from the events in the prison that led to his fall and withdrawal seizures. It could not be said to be a cause of his

161 See J Herring and C Foster, 'Blaming the Patient: Contributory Negligence and Medical Malpractice Litigation' (2009) *Professional Negligence* 76.

162 *Pidgeon v Doncaster Health Authority* [2002] Lloyd's Rep Med 130. Contrast with *Re P* [2011] EWHC 1266 where the appointment letter was sent to the wrong address.

163 *Horsley v Cascade Insulation Services & Others* [2009] EWHC 2945 (QB), applying *Badger v The Ministry of Defence* [2005] EWHC 2941.

164 [2008] EWCA Civ 1068.

negligent treatment by prison hospital staff. Counsel for the defendants had conceded that within the NHS a patient's smoking or drinking could not be invoked to hold him contributorily negligent if he suffered injury in the course of treatment related to those conditions. And it would be an odd result if doctors treating smokers could argue that their responsibility was less because the patient should never have needed their services. However, if a patient were to develop an illness as a result of medical negligence which is unrelated to the treatment – for example a patient with kidney disease is negligently given an overdose which damages his heart – and the injury is indivisible from that caused by, for example, poor weight management which the patient has been warned to address to avoid damage to his heart, it is possible that the claimant might be viewed contributorily negligent.

8.21 Private patients

A patient who pays for treatment enters into a contract with their doctor. They are free to set the terms of that contract, save that the doctor cannot exempt themselves from liability for any injury to the patient arising from their negligence.[165] There is rarely a written contract between them. The terms will be implied from their relationship. This usually means that the doctor undertakes a duty of care to the patient. The doctor's duty of care to their private patient is usually indistinguishable from their duty in tort to their NHS patient.[166] The possibility remains of doctors agreeing to undertake a higher standard of care.

In independent sector practice could a doctor be found to have contracted to guarantee the desired result of treatment? This can never happen in the NHS. The doctor can only be liable in tort for a failure in care. Only rarely will a private doctor be found to have guaranteed a result in contract.[167] Where a patient is ill and seeks a cure, unless the doctor foolishly and expressly promises success in his treatment, no court will infer any term other than that the doctor will exercise skill and care. And, so far, claims by patients who have undergone private sterilisation have ultimately failed in attempts to argue that the surgeon guaranteed permanent sterility.[168]

165 Unfair Contract Terms Act 1977, s 2.
166 *Mary McGill v Royal Group of Hospitals* [2010] NIQB 10.
167 See *Thompson v Sheffield Fertility Clinic* [2001] unreported, Westlaw.
168 *Eyre v Measday* [1986] 1 All ER 488; *Thake v Maurice* [1986] 1 All ER 497, CA.

Chapter 9

MALPRACTICE LITIGATION

9.1 Introduction

In 2020/21, NHS Resolution received 12,629 clinical negligence claims and reported incidents, an increase of 951 (7.5 per cent) compared to 2019/20.[1] Despite the odd spike, a pattern has emerged which indicates that the number of claims is steadily increasing.[2] We have already addressed the doctrinal principles governing liability for clinical negligence, but formidable practical problems also exist for patients in relation to both funding a claim and the complexities associated with the litigation process.[3] In the future, it may become even more difficult to fund a claim by way of a conditional fee agreement. Where funding arrangements are squeezed making it pragmatically more difficult to obtain compensation through a clinical negligence action, it may well be that the number of claims will fall, but there is little evidence to support this contention.[4] Undoubtedly a reduction in the overall number of claims and their associated costs would be welcomed by the National Health Service (NHS), yet we must be careful not to restrict access to justice for patients who have suffered harm as a result of sub-standard medical care but who are not in a position to self-fund a claim. We cannot predict the effect of cumulative reform on clinical negligence claims because it is an area that is constantly under review, so in this chapter we simply provide an overview of the litigation process and discuss what any future changes to the system may look like.

We begin this chapter by focusing on the processes involved in bringing a claim. Then we consider claims that lawsuits against doctors are damaging medicine. The spectre of the malpractice crisis is often invoked but is it a spectre with any substance? Or is the real spectre not the threat to doctors and the NHS of too many claims, but the denial of redress to patients who cannot fund a legitimate claim for compensation and thus a reduction in accountability for medical errors?

1 NHS Resolution, *Annual Report and Accounts 2020/21* (2021) HC 387, July, p 18.
2 Ibid.
3 Lord Justice Jackson, *Review of Civil Litigation Costs: Final Report* (2009).
4 There was a minor reduction in claims between 2014 and 2015.

9.2 Funding a lawsuit: public funding[5]

Few people are rich enough to meet the costs of clinical negligence claims out of their own income and savings. The majority of clinical negligence claims in the past were funded by legal aid. The success rate of such claims was low. The cost to the public purse of legal aid in personal injury claims rose rapidly. Unsurprisingly the government sought to find ways to reduce the legal aid bill. The Access to Justice Act 1999 removed legal aid from most personal injury claims but retained it for clinical negligence claims. The Legal Aid, Sentencing and Punishment of Offenders Act 2012 (hereafter LASPO) abolished legal aid for clinical negligence claims save for 'exceptional cases' where the Director of Legal Aid[6] determines that the claimant qualifies for such services. In the context of clinical negligence, 'exceptional cases' are claims where it is necessary to provide legal aid because not to do so would be a breach of the individual's rights under the European Convention on Human Rights[7] and claims for severe neurological damage to babies injured during pregnancy, labour or the first eight weeks of life.[8]

In the consultation process leading to the enactment of LASPO, the Ministry of Justice took the view that most patient-claimants should be able to access alternative funding primarily via conditional fee agreements (CFAs) and so 'legal aid funding is not justified'.[9] But as we shall see, the same Act (LASPO) made it less likely that solicitors will take on claims that are not both highly likely to succeed and of high value.[10]

In those rare cases where public funding is available, obtaining legal aid 'is no easy task'.[11] Eligible claimants must meet a stringent means test; only adults with a very low income and minimal capital will qualify. Even if the potential claimant passes the means test, their case must be strong on its merits. However, children under 18[12] are assessed on their own rather than their parents' income, so child patients claiming in respect of birth or neonatal injury still qualify for legal aid.

9.3 Conditional fee agreements

The virtual abolition of legal aid for most clinical negligence claims took place in the wake of a major review of the costs of the civil justice system as a whole by Lord Justice Jackson.[13] The government made it clear that it saw a radically

5 See *Legal Aid Handbook 2020/21*, at http:/legalaidhandbook.com.
6 A civil servant appointed by the Lord Chancellor; LASPO, s 4.
7 LASPO, s 10(3); though see also Sch 1, Pt 1, para 22.
8 Schedule 1, Pt 1, para 23.
9 Ministry of Justice, *Proposals for the Reform of Legal Aid in England and Wales* (2010), para 4.165.
10 See M Taddia, 'Medical Negligence: Unkindest Cut' (2013) *Law Society Gazette* 14.
11 Guidance is available at www.gov.uk/legal-aid.
12 LASPO, s 21.
13 *Review of Civil Litigation Costs: Final Report* (2009) (hereafter Jackson Report).

reformed system for CFAs as the primary source of future funding for clinical negligence claims.[14]

Implementing reforms proposed by Lord Justice Jackson, LASPO radically alters CFAs. Section 44 amends the Courts and Legal Services Act 1990 so that claimants will no longer be able to recover the success fee from defendants but will have to pay the success fee and any insurance (after-the-event (ATE)) premium[15] from their own damages. Moreover, the success fee cannot exceed 25 per cent of the claimant's damages, excluding damages for future care and loss. CFAs have therefore become a less attractive option to both solicitors and clients. To meet some of the concerns that claimants would be under-compensated once success fees and ATE premiums were deducted from damages, the Court of Appeal in *Simmons v Castle*[16] announced that there should be a 10 per cent rise in general damages (for pain, suffering and loss of amenity) to compensate successful claimants for loss of the right to recover the success fee from the defendants.

Conditional fees must be distinguished from contingency fees, the system used to fund most claims in the USA. A contingency fee allows the claimant's lawyers to take a proportion of the damages awarded (in some cases up to 50 per cent), but they can claim nothing if the action fails. Until the Jackson Report, contingency fees met little favour in England. The Jackson Report expressed particular concern about the impact of CFAs on the NHS in a chapter dedicated to clinical negligence.[17] Lord Justice Jackson stressed the importance of ensuring that 'the resources of the health service are not being squandered unnecessarily on litigation costs'.[18] As we have seen, his proposals relating to CFAs have been implemented in LASPO. Additionally, Lord Justice Jackson's most radical proposal was that contingency fees should be allowed, renamed damages-based agreements (DBAs), and this proposal was also implemented by section 45 of LASPO. So far few solicitors in personal injury or clinical negligence claims have taken up the option of DBAs.[19]

The Jackson Report also proposed that far more people should be encouraged to take out legal expenses insurance, styled before-the-event (BTE) insurance, to cover them against the costs of claims in the future. Many household insurance policies offer this option. But few people who live lives with little risk of resorting to litigation are likely to consider that a medical accident might create the need for funds to sue their doctor. Moreover, BTE insurance may well be an unaffordable luxury for many families who might before LASPO have qualified for legal aid. Post LASPO, some evidence suggests that risky and

14 Ministry of Justice, *Proposals for Reform of Civil Litigation Funding and Costs in England and Wales* (2010).

15 Save for insurance premiums to cover expert witness fees.

16 [2012] EWCA Civ 1039.

17 Jackson Report, ch 23.

18 Ibid, para 1.4.

19 They may become more popular post *Lexlaw v Zuberi* [2020] EWHC 1855 (Ch), which held that DBAs can contain terms permitting payment upon early termination.

lower-value claims are not being taken on by solicitors and that there seems to be little enthusiasm for DBAs.[20] One consequence of the increased difficulty in obtaining funding for professional legal services is a marked rise in people representing themselves; litigants in person.[21]

9.4 Defending claims[22]

Since 2014, health professionals have been under a statutory obligation to ensure that they have appropriate indemnity cover in place for the clinical work that they undertake.[23] The General Medical Council (GMC) has regulatory powers to check whether doctors have adequate and appropriate cover and can remove a doctor's licence if it is not in place. The GMC can also refuse to grant a licence to a doctor if sufficient cover is not in place.[24]

NHS medical indemnity in England is provided through the Clinical Negligence Scheme for Trusts (CNST). Wales and Scotland have similar schemes and in Northern Ireland, Trusts provide indemnity. Independent sector providers of NHS care were also able to join the CNST from 2013. Membership is conditional on Trusts complying with risk-management procedures prescribed by the CNST. The scheme offers a mutual assurance system so that no individual Trust risks devastation of its service because of a clutch of unfortunate losses in the courts. The Clinical Negligence Scheme for General Practice covers clinical negligence liabilities arising in general practice in relation to incidents that occurred on or after 1 April 2019.[25] Finally, in order to meet clinical negligence liabilities arising from NHS services provided in response to the coronavirus pandemic, NHS Resolution has recently introduced a new scheme called the Clinical Negligence Scheme for Coronavirus.

NHS Resolution now administers these schemes and is the driving force behind the defence of claims against the NHS today. It exercises significant control over all claims seeking to ensure swift resolution of indefensible claims and to minimise the cost to the NHS. Greater efficiency and uniformity should benefit patients as much as hospitals. NHS Resolution plays an active role, not just in advising on defence of individual claims, but also in seeking to ensure that the whole litigation system is regularly kept under review. The medical defence organisations and NHS Trusts were sometimes accused of persisting

20 M Taddia, 'Medical Negligence: Unkindest Cut' [2013] *Law Society Gazette* 14.

21 'Lord Dyson Calls for Simpler Rules' [2015] *Law Society Gazette* 2(1).

22 See generally L Mulcahy, 'The Market for Precedent: Shifting Visions of Clinical Negligence Claims and Trials' (2014) 22 *Med Law Rev* 274.

23 Health Care and Associated Professions (Indemnity Arrangements) Order 2014/1887, schedule 1(1).

24 See GMC, 'Insurance Indemnity and Medico-Legal Support' available at www.gmc-uk.org.

25 An Existing Liabilities for General Practice scheme provides indemnity cover for NHS clinical negligence claims made against current and former GP members of medical defence organisations (MDOs) in respect of liabilities incurred before 1 April 2019.

in defending 'indefensible' cases. NHS Resolution disputes this, claiming that in order to 'resolve claims fairly, reduce the time to resolution, curtail legal costs and reduce the need for formal processes' it tests 'a wide range of innovative dispute resolution techniques'.[26] It also places much greater emphasis on encouraging apologies.[27] Lawyers who act for claimants take a less rosy view of NHS Resolution and Lord Justice Jackson was critical of some of their practices. It should also be noted that the various indemnity schemes in place for both primary and secondary care only cover health professionals for work conducted in the NHS. It follows that most health professionals will choose to take out private indemnity cover with the Medical Defence Union (MDU) or other similar organisations to ensure that they are indemnified for any non-NHS or private work that they undertake. They may also wish to do this to ensure that they are indemnified for such things as inquests, regulatory and disciplinary proceedings, employment and contractual disputes and any non-clinical liabilities.[28]

9.5 Whom should the patient sue?

If funding can be accessed, one of the first practical matters which the patient and his legal advisers must consider is whom they should sue. The legal doctrine of vicarious liability provides that when a person who is an employee commits a tort in the course of his employment, his employer is also responsible to the victim. The employer will often be better able to pay compensation than an individual employee. Let us look first at a claim by a patient who alleges that he suffered injury in the course of treatment as an NHS patient in an NHS Trust or Foundation Trust hospital. If he can identify a particular individual as negligent he may, of course, proceed against him, be he consultant, anaesthetist, junior doctor, nurse, physiotherapist or hospital porter. However, he may also sue the person's employer itself.[29] Insofar as doctors are concerned, where they are defendants in an action, payment of any award of compensation made against them is guaranteed. NHS Indemnity ensures that any liability incurred by an NHS hospital doctor will be met. There is no practical need to bring a claim against the doctor personally. Patients and their lawyers should ponder the wisdom of suing a doctor personally. As their employer will meet any award of compensation in full, there is little to gain other than a very limited form of accountability from naming the doctor in the claim.

The employer to sue, as vicariously liable, in the case of NHS hospital treatment will normally be the NHS Trust or Foundation Trust. Nonetheless, a patient may suffer injury not because any particular doctor or nurse is careless,

26 NHS Resolution, *Annual Report and Accounts 2020/21*, p 21.
27 Ibid, p 65.
28 See GMC, 'Insurance Indemnity and Medico-Legal Support' available at www.gmc-uk.org.
29 A good example of this is the Supreme Court decision in *Darnley v Croydon Health Services NHS Trust* [2018] UKSC 50. See 8.2 above.

but because the system provided by the authority is inadequate. There may be insufficient medical staff to cope swiftly enough with injured patients admitted to the casualty ward. Lack of experienced staff on night duty may cause injury to a patient whose condition deteriorates rapidly, and whom the staff on duty cannot, with the best will in the world, treat sufficiently promptly. For such 'systems errors' an action will lie directly against the hospital.[30] The Court of Appeal has confirmed that hospitals have an 'organisational duty'. An NHS hospital must 'ensure that the hospital staff, facilities and organisation provided are those appropriate to provide a safe and satisfactory service for the patient'.[31]

9.6 Extending direct liability

May direct responsibility to NHS patients go further? When a patient is admitted for hospital treatment under the NHS, the NHS Trust undertakes to provide them with reasonably careful, competent and skilled care. Should their treatment fall below that standard, the hospital is directly, not just vicariously, responsible to the patient.[32] So if an elderly patient falls on a slippery floor, and had proper care been taken that would not have happened, the hospital is liable. It matters not whether a nurse employed by the hospital, an agency nurse or a cleaner employed by a contractor was the individual personally at fault. The hospital undertook to care for the patient. It failed and is directly liable. In *X (Minors) v Bedfordshire County Council*, Lord Browne-Wilkinson said this: 'It is established that those conducting a hospital are under a direct duty of care to those admitted as patients to the hospital.'[33] In *Woodland v Essex County Council*[34] the Supreme Court confirmed that the principle stated *obiter* by Lord Browne-Wilkinson represented the current law.

What of a patient offered a hip replacement on the NHS whose operation is contracted out to a private hospital, or independent treatment centre? This may happen when the NHS Trust to which they are referred contracts with a private sector hospital to carry out surgery on its behalf, often to deal with a backlog of operations. If treatment is carried out negligently, one option is to sue the private provider, but the difficulty here is that the patient is at the mercy of the private provider's financial situation and insurance arrangements. Thus, can they sue the NHS Trust which despatched them to the private sector if, say, the private provider is unable to meet the claim? This requires us to

30 See *Bull v Devon Area Health Authority* [1993] 4 Med LR 117, CA; *Robertson v East Kent Health Authority* [1999] Lloyd's Rep Med 123. See R Heywood, 'Systemic Negligence and NHS Hospitals: An Underutilised Argument' (2021) 32 *King's Law Journal* 437.

31 *Child A v Ministry of Defence* [2004] EWCA Civ 641, [32].

32 See *Cassidy v Ministry of Health* [1951] 2 KB 343, *per* Lord Denning at 359–360; and *Roe v Ministry of Health* [1954] 2 QB 66, at 82.

33 [1995] 2 AC 633, at 740. And see *Miller v Greater Glasgow NHS Board* [2010] CSIH 40.

34 [2013] UKSC 66, [16], [23], [37].

consider what is known as a non-delegable duty of care and the legal position is somewhat unclear.

It is important to recognise from the outset that when we refer to private sector providers, they are equivalent to independent contractors. In this domain, the courts draw a distinction between relationships akin to employment, where vicarious liability will still apply, and relationships with independent contractors that fall outside the ambit of vicarious liability.[35] In terms of the latter, an organisation is usually entitled to delegate certain activities to an independent contractor and, provided any contractor was selected with reasonable care, it will be the contractor who remains liable for any negligently inflicted injury deriving from its carelessness. In certain situations, though, the courts have fixed a particular defendant with a non-delegable duty of care, which renders it directly liable for the acts of independent contractors, effectively transforming the baseline legal position from a duty to take reasonable care into a duty to ensure that care is taken. We are concerned with the situations in which it may be possible to argue that a hospital should be fixed with a non-delegable duty of care, thereby pinning legal responsibility on it for the negligence of independent contractors.

In *M v Calderdale Health Authority*,[36] M became pregnant and consulted an NHS doctor at an NHS Community Health Centre. The doctor arranged an abortion at a private hospital, but it was negligently performed and the woman went on to give birth to a baby boy. The health authority was found liable in negligence to M. Although no NHS employee was negligent, nor was the health authority negligent in selecting the private clinic to which they contracted out abortions, they were in breach of a direct non-delegable duty to their patient. The judge summed up the position.

> [M] never left the care of the first defendant. She was its patient. She never had an opportunity to divert from the route of treatment arranged on her behalf. In these circumstances she is entitled in my view to remain in the same position as a patient who remains in house relying upon the expectation of an effective provision of services.[37]

The judgment in *M* suggested that an NHS patient suffering injury in the private sector could sue an NHS hospital which contracted out her care, but it is only a decision of the county court and in *Child A v Ministry of Defence*[38] the Court of Appeal was dismissive of *M*, stating that the decision does 'not represent the current state of English law'.[39] Very briefly, Child A was born in 1998, in a German hospital while his father was serving with the British Army. Until 1996, the Ministry of Defence had run its own military hospitals in Germany. From 1996, the Ministry (via a complicated set of contracts) contracted out

[35] See *WM Morrison Supermarkets Plc v Various Claimants* [2020] UKSC 12; *Barclays Bank Plc v Various Claimants* [2020] UKSC 13.
[36] [1998] Lloyd's Rep Med 157.
[37] [1998] Lloyd's Rep Med 161.
[38] [2004] EWCA Civ 641, CA.
[39] Ibid, [52].

healthcare for service personnel and their families to German hospitals. Child A suffered brain damage in the course of his delivery. It was not disputed that his injuries were as a result of negligence. A could claim damages in Germany under German law, but his lawyers sought to sue in England and make the Ministry of Defence liable for A's injury, just as Calderdale Health Authority had been liable to M. The Court of Appeal found against him. The Ministry owed a duty to use reasonable care to provide access to suitable hospital care for service personnel and their families.[40] They had a responsibility (an organisational duty) to act reasonably to ensure care provided was on the basis of an adequate system, ie properly equipped hospitals were selected to provide care.[41] There was no 'duty to ensure that the treatment administered ... is administered with reasonable care and skill'. There was no duty 'broken if one of the hospital staff, however competent, commits an isolated act of negligence in the treatment of the patient'. Such a duty (described in *A* as a non-delegable duty) would generally only lie 'in an environment over which the defendant is in control'.[42] An NHS Trust hospital might well owe such a duty to all patients being treated in their hospital. The Ministry of Defence had no control over its German contractors.

Does that mean that NHS hospitals can similarly never be liable for treatment contracted out to the private sector? Not necessarily. Historically, one of us sought to argue that the previously recognised Primary Care Trusts (PCTs) did owe a direct non-delegable duty to those patients for whose care they are responsible.[43] However, Lord Phillips said that even if PCTs did owe such a duty, it would not follow that a similar duty was incumbent on the Ministry of Defence.[44]

The judgment of the Court of Appeal in *Farraj v King's Healthcare NHS Trust*[45] indicated an unwillingness to extend the limits of direct liability. Mrs Farraj knew that she and her husband carried the gene that can cause beta thallassaemia major (BTM), a serious blood disorder. The couple were in the care of an obstetrician in Jordan and a chorionic villus sample was taken from Mrs Farraj and sent for testing at the defendant hospital to determine if the fetus was affected by BTM. The hospital found that the sample was not suitable for DNA testing in its own laboratory and sent it on to an independent specialist cytogenetics laboratory, CSL. CSL were held negligent in wrongly stating that the fetus was not affected by BTM. The issue that concerns us here is could King's Healthcare NHS Trust be held liable for the negligence of CSL on the grounds that they owed a non-delegable duty to the claimants? The appeal court decided no to that question. Dyson LJ was prepared to assume that hospitals owe such a duty to the patient it treats regardless of the employment status of the staff delivering treatment.[46] But he could see no reason in

40 Ibid, [32].
41 Ibid.
42 [2004] EWCA Civ 641, [47].
43 M Brazier and J Beswick, 'Who's Caring For Me?' (2006) 7 *Medical Law International* 183.
44 [2004] EWCA Civ 641, [54].
45 [2009] EWCA Civ 1203. See also 11.12.
46 Ibid, [88].

this case to depart from the usual rule that a defendant can discharge his duty of care by delegating a task to a suitably competent independent contractor. Mrs Farraj was not being treated by King's, but by a hospital in Jordan. King's Healthcare NHS Trust undertook no special duty to her. *Farraj* leaves open the question of whether an NHS patient who undergoes tests organised by the NHS hospital treating them could argue that the hospital owed them a non-delegable duty in respect of tests contracted out to independent laboratories and/or any other form of negligence on the part of the private contractor.

The decision of the Supreme Court in *Woodland v Essex County Council*[47] leaves that possibility open. A pupil at a school for which Essex County Council was responsible suffered serious injuries at a swimming lesson run by a private organisation whose staff were responsible for the negligence that caused the child's injury. The individuals responsible were not employed by the County Council and the Council argued that there was no non-delegable duty owed to the pupils. Lord Sumption reviewed the case-law and crucially 'respectfully' disagreed with Lord Phillips in *Child A v Ministry of Defence*, who had stated that for a non-delegable duty to lie the defendant must have control of the environment in which the injury occurred.[48] The crucial question is whether the defendant has control over the claimant 'for the purpose of performing a function for which the defendant has assumed responsibility'. The injured child was attending a swimming lesson, an integral part of the education for which the defendant assumed responsibility. The parents entrusted the child to the school with no knowledge or influence over when and how the school might contract out some of its functions. The school remained responsible for the child.

Woodland differs markedly from both *Child A* and *Farraj*. Child A's parents had no sound basis for thinking that it was the Ministry of Defence providing healthcare for Mrs A. Mrs Farraj was not a patient of the defendant hospital. *Woodland* may well be applicable to the NHS hospital that contracts out a backlog of operations, or certain sorts of treatments, to private sector organisations.[49] The claimant may well argue that just as the injured child's parents in *Woodland* entrusted their child to the school and had no control over who the school arranged to carry out educational services, where we are referred to Muncaster NHS Trust for a hip replacement we also have no control or choice as to how the hospital discharges the health service provided for us.

Having said that, the argument that a non-delegable duty should be extended to the hospital and patient relationship has been met with criticism.[50] Indeed, in a case that mainly turned on a question of statutory interpretation, the High Court recently declined to recognise that an NHS Primary Care Trust was subject to a non-delegable duty of care for the negligence of a third-party

47 [2013] UKSC 66.

48 Ibid, [24].

49 See P Giliker, 'Non-Delegable Duties and Institutional Liability for the Negligence of Hospital Staff: Fair, Just and Reasonable?' (2017) 33 *Journal of Professional Negligence* 109.

50 C Beuermann, 'Do Hospitals Owe A So-Called "Non-Delegable" Duty of Care to their Patients?' (2018) 26 *Med Law Rev* 1.

provider.[51] Independent sector providers are now able to join CNST and many have done so. The risk for the patient whose care is delegated by the NHS to the private sector in England is that the private provider might go bankrupt, be under-insured or be otherwise unable to meet the claim for compensation. Membership of CNST ensures that the private provider via the NHS Resolution will be 'insured' to meet all claims.

9.7 Private patients

A private patient who engages a private bed in an NHS hospital contracts individually with the surgeon and anaesthetist for the surgery and the administration of the anaesthetic, and he contracts separately with the Hospital Trust for nursing and ancillary care. Even if the surgeon and the anaesthetist are employed by the Trust when caring for NHS patients, when they act for a private patient they are acting on their own behalf, and not in the course of their NHS employment. If an error by surgeon or anaesthetist causes the patient injury, he can sue only the responsible individual. If the carelessness is that of nursing or other medical staff employed by the Trust, he may sue the Trust. As we shall see, this may cause problems of proof of negligence. Identifying who was the responsible individual may be nigh on impossible, leaving surgeon and hospital to blame each other, and the patient to go uncompensated.

A patient entering a private hospital needs to consider the nature and scope of his contract. The usual arrangement is similar to that entered into by a private patient taking a private bed within the NHS. The patient engages his own surgeon and anaesthetist, who will not be employees of the private hospital. The hospital contracts to provide other medical and nursing care. Like the private patient within the NHS, the patient must proceed against the surgeon for any error of theirs, and against the hospital for any error by their staff. Some private hospitals and clinics will contract to provide a whole 'package' of care and treatment. When the hospital undertakes to provide total care – the operation, anaesthetic, post-operative care, etc – then it is liable for any failure to meet the required standard of care. They are in breach of contract.[52] It is irrelevant that the surgeon, anaesthetist or anyone else is not an employee of the hospital. The hospital is not vicariously liable for any fault of a particular person. It is directly responsible for its own breach of contract.

9.8 General practitioners

What of claims against general practitioners (GPs)? First of all, most GPs are not employees of the NHS. A claim relating to negligence by a GP operating a single-doctor practice lies usually against that GP alone.[53] As such, GPs would

51 *Hopkins v Akramy* [2020] EWHC 3445 (QB).
52 Consumer Rights Act 2015, s 49 (service to be performed with reasonable care and skill).
53 But the relevant NHS organisation might be liable if they should have known and acted on information that a GP was not providing appropriate care; see *Godden v Kent & Medway Strategic Health Authority* [2004] Lloyd's Rep Med 521.

commonly take out indemnity cover against potential lawsuits with the MDU or other similar organisations. Note, however, the schemes mentioned earlier that have recently been introduced by NHS Resolution to provide indemnity cover for GPs working under a medical services contract.[54] Despite the introduction of these, it is likely that many GPs will continue to arrange private indemnity, because such policies typically provide a wider range of cover. Where a GP is a member of a partnership, their partners may be sued as jointly responsible for any negligence. If it is not the doctor themselves who is at fault, but a receptionist or nurse employed by the practice, the GP and their partners are vicariously liable as employers. If a receptionist refuses to allow a home visit, or refuses to allow the patient to speak to a doctor, or fails to pass any information on to the doctor with the result that a seriously ill patient becomes sicker or even dies, the doctor, whilst they may be personally blameless, will be vicariously at fault and liable to the patient or their family.

9.9 When must proceedings be started?

A patient contemplating an action for clinical negligence must act relatively promptly. The general rule is that all actions for personal injuries must be brought within three years of the infliction of the relevant injury. This is known as the limitation period and is laid down in the Limitation Act 1980. A claim form must be served no later than three years from the date of the alleged negligence. But sections 11 and 14 of the 1980 Act provide that where the patient originally either (1) was unaware that he had suffered significant injury,[55] or (2) did not know about the negligence which could have caused his injury, the three-year period begins to run only from the time when he did discover, or reasonably should have discovered, the relevant facts. Where the patient knew all the relevant facts, but was ignorant of his legal remedy, the three-year limitation period runs from the time when he was, or should have been, aware of the facts.

All is not quite lost for the patient who delays beyond three years, or who is ignorant of the law. Section 33[56] of the 1980 Act gives the judge discretion to override the three-year limitation period where, in all the circumstances, it is fair to all partics to do so. The courts will examine the effect of allowing the action to go forward on both parties, taking into account, among other things, the effect of delay on the cogency of the evidence, the conduct of the parties, and the advice sought by, and given to, the patient by his lawyers and medical advisers.[57]

One further aspect of the rules on limitation must be noted. Where the injured patient is under a legal disability at the time he suffers injury, that is to say, they are under age (under 18) or lack mental capacity, the limitation period does not begin to run until they reach the age of majority, or cease to lack

54 See 9.4 above.

55 For example, he did not know for some years that he had been given blood infected by CJD; *N v UK Medical Research Council* [1996] BMLR 83.

56 See *Godfrey v Gloucestershire Royal Infirmary NHS Trust* [2003] EWHC 549.

57 See, for example, *Smith v Leicestershire Health Authority* (1996) 36 BMLR 23.

mental capacity. This means that, for example, a baby might be injured at birth and the obstetrician could face an action in respect of the injury up to twenty-one years after the event.

9.10 Civil justice reform: the Woolf and Jackson Reports

Cost, complexity and delay bedevilled not just clinical negligence claims but all actions for compensation in the latter part of the twentieth century. The civil justice system was perceived as inadequate. One of England's most senior judges, Lord Woolf, was commissioned to conduct a comprehensive review of the civil justice system and to recommend radical reform. He issued his Final Report in 1996.[58] Lord Woolf set out a number of admirable objectives for the civil justice system. It should be just in its results, and the operation of the system should be fair to all parties. Costs should be proportionate to the nature of the case. Claims must be dealt with reasonably swiftly. The process should be understandable to everyone using it, including any litigant who chooses not to engage a lawyer but to sue in person. The system should be responsive to the needs of litigants. There should be certainty in the way the process works. Civil justice should be adequately resourced and reasonably funded.

Four features of the Woolf reforms are central to malpractice litigation.

(1) The *Pre-Action Protocol for the Resolution of Clinical Disputes* (hereafter the Clinical Negligence Protocol) sought to find less adversarial and more cost-effective ways of resolving disputes about healthcare.
(2) New Civil Procedure Rules[59] came into force in 1999, introducing a unified set of procedures for claims regardless of whether a claim is heard in the County Court or the High Court.
(3) Integral to the Rules is the concept of case management. Judges are given infinitely greater powers to manage cases.
(4) The rules governing expert witnesses were altered, seeking to limit the misuse of expert evidence.

But by 2009 it was clear that the Woolf reforms had not resulted in total success. Research commissioned by the Ministry of Justice suggested that delay was less of a problem with cases taking less time between issuing a claim and trial or settlement.[60] But costs had risen[61] and thus, as we have seen, Lord Justice Jackson was asked to conduct a further review of civil litigation costs, resulting in radical change to the funding of claims.

58 *Access to Justice: Final Report to the Lord Chancellor on the Civil Justice System in England and Wales* (1996) HMSO. See Chief Medical Officer (CMO), *Making Amends: A Consultation Paper* (2003), pp 86–87.
59 Civil Procedure Rules, SI 1998/3132 (hereafter CPR).
60 Constitutional Affairs, *Civil Justice Reform Evaluation: Further Findings: A Continuing Evaluation of the Civil Justice Reforms* (2002).
61 J Peysner and M Severatne, *The Management of Civil Cases: The Court and the Post-Woolf Landscape* (2005) Department for Constitutional Affairs.

9.11 The Clinical Negligence Protocol and case management

As a result of the Jackson Report and other reviews commissioned by the Ministry of Justice, substantial changes have been made both to the Clinical Negligence Protocol and the Civil Procedure Rules that govern the management of claims that fail to settle. Substantial changes to the Protocol came into force on 6 April 2015.[62] The complexity and detail of the Protocol and the Rules would add several further chapters to this book. Thus we simply outline some of the key points here. The Protocol sets out 'ground rules' for handling disputes at their 'early stages', seeking to encourage a greater climate of openness, to provide guidance how this more open culture can be achieved, and recommend a timed sequence of events when disputes do arise.

The Protocol aims to maintain or restore the relationship between the aggrieved patient and healthcare professionals and providers, and to resolve as many disputes as possible without litigation. Communication between the parties lies at the heart of the Protocol. Cases should be investigated swiftly, and records volunteered to the claimant for a reasonable period of time. Full consideration needs to be given to early settlement and to whether, if agreement between the parties cannot be reached, resort might be had to mediation or some other form of alternative dispute resolution.[63] The Protocol promotes a 'cards on the table' approach. Ideally, when a patient believes that she has a case in clinical negligence, in a matter of months she will be able to judge whether her belief is well founded. The defendant doctor or hospital will be in a position to settle any sustainable claim quickly. Means other than litigation of resolving genuine disputes will be reviewed. Only the truly intractable case should go to court, but more cases still seem to end in court and settlements take too long. Unfortunately the Jackson report found that it was not working well to ensure early settlement in appropriate cases and this was contributing to an escalation of costs.

If attempts to resolve the claim fail, and the patient starts formal proceedings, the conduct of the case will be strictly controlled with an emphasis on enforcing time limits and keeping costs down. The claim will be allocated to a *track*. A clinical negligence claim worth less than £1,000 would theoretically be allocated to the *small claims track*. Most such claims ought never to result in proceedings, but rather be resolved within complaints procedures. Claims worth between £1,000 and £15,000 are allocated to the *fast track*. This means that the case should be resolved within thirty weeks. The actual hearing should take one day or less and oral expert evidence is limited. Claims worth more than £15,000, or where the issues are especially complex, go onto the *multi-track*. Judges control the allocation process. Most clinical negligence claims will be multi-track. At every point, opportunities to resolve the case without further proceedings must be seized. Time-wasting and unnecessary manoeuvres by lawyers will be penalised.

[62] See Ministry of Justice, *Pre-Action Protocol for the Resolution of Clinical Disputes Clinical Disputes Forum* (2015).

[63] See CMO, *Making Amends*, pp 95–96.

The aims of the Protocol and case management are laudable, to settle cases where possible and ensure that cases are handled efficiently. However the system remains complex and if claimants have no access to funding for legal services and are forced to act as litigants in person they will struggle and Lord Dyson has argued that much more needs to be done to simplify procedures.

9.12 Openness, candour and obtaining health records

Where attempts to settle lead to naught, the Protocol aims to ensure that proper disclosure of information facilitates fairness and keeps the costs down. As we shall see in Chapter 11, efforts to engender an NHS culture of openness and learning face significant hurdles. In Chapter 2[64] we considered the duty of candour. A new, statutory duty was introduced in section 81 of the Care Act 2014.[65] When a safety incident occurs, the healthcare provider must inform and support the relevant person and 'provide an account of the incident which, to the best of the health service body's knowledge, is true of all the facts the body knows about the incident as at the date of the notification'.[66]

One of the principal features of the Clinical Negligence Protocol is the provision for voluntary disclosure of records which should normally be provided within forty days. The claimant, too, in setting out their letter of claim must ensure sufficient information is given to enable the defendants to investigate the claim and determine how to proceed. Litigation should not resemble a game of poker. If the Protocol works there should be no need for compulsory disclosure of records. Alas this is not always the case. The patient seeking to compel disclosure of records will rely on section 33[67] of the Senior Courts Act 1981. The court can impose costs and sanctions for unreasonable delay.[68] The claimant can apply for a court order for pre-action disclosure requiring the doctor or hospital whom they plan to sue to disclose any records or notes likely to be relevant in forthcoming proceedings. Section 34[69] goes further. The court may order a person not a party to proceedings to produce relevant documents. So if the patient has started proceedings against a GP, or a private medical practitioner, but believes that the hospital or clinic holds notes of value to his claim, the hospital or clinic can be made to hand over the notes. This will help the private patient in a dilemma of whether he should properly proceed against doctor or hospital. It may also lead to the clinic being brought into the proceedings.

64 See 2.6 above.

65 Brought into force by Health and Social Care Act 2008 (Regulated Activities) Regulations 2014, SI 2014/2936, reg 20: '(1) A health service body must act in an open and transparent way with relevant persons in relation to care and treatment provided to service users in carrying on a regulated activity.'

66 CQC, *Regulation 5 and Regulation 20: Guidance for NHS Bodies* (2014) November, p 16.

67 And see CPR 31.16.

68 Pre-Action Protocol for the Resolution of Clinical Disputes Clinical Disputes Forum (2015), para 3.7.

69 And see CRP 31.7(1).

Three important matters on disclosure need a mention. First, the intention to bring proceedings and the likelihood that they will go ahead must be real before the court will order disclosure. The patient must have some solid ground for thinking he has a claim. He cannot use an application for disclosure as a 'fishing expedition' on the off-chance that some evidence of negligence will come to light.[70] Resort to compulsory disclosure ought to be rare. Relevant documents should have been volunteered under the Protocol. Other avenues to discover records and information may also be pursued. A patient may always apply to see his records under data protection legislation.[71] Or he may use the complaints procedure to explore whether he has any legal entitlement to pursue a compensation claim.[72]

Second, will the patient be able to see notes of any inquiry ordered by the hospital into his misadventure? The Care Quality Commission sets out the information that should be communicated to a relevant person in the event of a 'notifiable safety incident' as part of the statutory duty of candour imposed on healthcare providers.[73] Beyond this, the position is complex. If the inquiry was held mainly to provide the basis of information on which legal advice about the authority's legal liability is based, the records are protected by legal professional privilege. If the dominant purpose of the inquiry was otherwise, for example, to improve hospital procedures or to provide the basis of disciplinary proceedings against staff, then the patient may be allowed access to the notes of the inquiry.[74] That is the legal position. The Court of Appeal long ago expressed its disquiet about the effect such claims of legal professional privilege might have on the patient's claim. Claims of privilege were used to frustrate the patient's attempt to find out what happened, what went wrong, and judges called for a duty of candour.[75] The introduction so many years later of a duty of candour, discussed above, will require the hospital or other health service provider to prepare a report for the family and, married to the emphasis on openness in the Clinical Negligence Protocol, ought to mean that this unsatisfactory state of affairs will not be repeated.

Third, the court retains the power to refuse to order disclosure where to do so would be injurious to the public interest.[76] This is unlikely to be the case where what is asked for is the patient's own medical notes. An attempt by the Secretary of State for Health to plead public interest immunity to avoid disclosure of records in the actions brought by several haemophiliac patients who had contracted HIV from contaminated blood products failed.[77]

70 *Dunning v Liverpool Hospitals' Board of Governors* [1973] 2 All ER 454.
71 See 5.16 above.
72 See Chapter 11 below.
73 CQC, *Regulation 5 and Regulation 20: Guidance for NHS Bodies* (2014) November.
74 *Waugh v BRB* [1980] AC 521.
75 See *Lee v South West Thames Regional Health Authority* [1985] 2 All ER 385 CA; *Naylor v Preston Area Health Authority* 1987] 2 All ER 353 CA.
76 Senior Courts Act 1981, s 35.
77 *Re HIV Haemophilia Litigation* (1990) 41 BMLR 171, CA.

9.13 Proving negligence: the role of the expert

We come now to the heart of the problem. How does the patient prove negligence? How does the claimant discharge the onus of proof laid on them?[78] They will be heavily reliant on expert testimony. They will need to put forward medical evidence to demonstrate (1) that there was negligence on the part of the defendant, or a person for whom the defendant was responsible, and (2) that the relevant negligence caused the harm of which they complain. Obtaining expert evidence used to be a nightmare for patients. Doctors were unhappy about voicing public criticism of a colleague. Doctors in the same hospital may remain unwilling to testify against each other. However, greater openness does mean that today most patients should be able to obtain medical expert advice fairly locally. Before looking further at the rules governing medical expert witnesses, we should distinguish between 'expert' and 'professional' witnesses. The expert witness testifies as to their expert opinion on the facts of the case referred to them, a case that they will not have been involved in personally. The professional witness gives evidence about what occurred in the series of events that led to harm to the claimant on the basis of what they saw and heard.[79]

Until the Civil Procedure Rules came into force, unrestricted freedom for each side to call its own experts sometimes made a mockery of justice.[80] The Civil Procedure Rules are explicit and emphatic that the expert's primary duty is owed to the court to assist the court in matters involving his expertise and this duty to the court 'overrides any obligation to the person from whom instructions were received or by whom the expert is paid'.[81] The Civil Procedure Rules also impose limits on the use of expert evidence. Expert testimony must be restricted to what is reasonably required to resolve the case.[82] The court has power to direct the appointment of a single joint expert rather than each party choosing their own experts.[83] Obviously if a single expert is to be appointed, it makes sense for the parties themselves to agree on such an expert. Lord Woolf saw no reason why, in a straightforward clinical negligence claim up to a value of £10,000, parties should not be able to agree on a single expert. Such cases may necessarily not be all that common. They are likely to be limited to cases where there is no substantial medical dispute about causation or prognosis, and perhaps all that is in issue is the appropriate measure of compensation. Many clinical negligence cases will involve disputes about whether there was negligence at all, whether the negligence caused the injuries

78 In *Laughton v Shalaby* [2014] EWCA Civ 1450, the Court of Appeal ruled that claimants could not invoke bad character evidence about the defendant in order to bolster the case to prove negligence.

79 The line may sometimes be blurred. See *ES v Chesterfield North Derbyshire Royal Hospital NHS Trust* [2003] EWCA Civ 1284, [10].

80 See, for example, *Whitehouse v Jordan* [1981] 1 All ER 287, HL.

81 CPR 35(3).

82 CPR 35(1).

83 CPR 35(7).

of which the claimant complains, and what the likely prognosis for the claimant will be. Such issues may well require separate experts. Imagine a claim that a child was brain-damaged allegedly because of a mismanaged delivery. Obstetric evidence will be needed to establish if the obstetrician was negligent. Neurologists may have to be called to testify to the likely cause of the brain damage. Paediatricians and rehabilitation experts will be required to assess how the child can best be cared for into adulthood. Multiple experts may be unavoidable. Nonetheless, control of proliferation of expert evidence will be asserted by the court. Where practical, a single joint expert must be agreed in relation to any particular issue. So if there is a real and substantive dispute about whether the obstetrician was negligent, each party will probably be allowed to call its own obstetric expert, but, save in the most exceptional case, not more than one expert each. If there is no especial complexity about causation, a single expert should be agreed to address that issue. As much of the expert evidence as possible should be in writing. Oral testimony is allowable only with the permission of the court.

Where there are multiple experts, all letters, documents and instructions must be disclosed to the experts and there must be mutual disclosure of all experts' reports. Experts' meetings are encouraged. The hope may be that, at such a meeting, the experts will resolve the differences between them and promote resolution of the case without proceeding to a hearing. Initially it was envisaged that experts would meet alone and conduct a quasi-scientific seminar. Lawyers and their clients were uncomfortable with such a process, which could be seen as surrendering the judicial process to the doctors. Additionally the objective of resolving proceedings more speedily might well be frustrated. The parties would not accept the experts' conclusions as binding. Consequently it was agreed that the parties' lawyers may be present at experts' meetings.

How expert are the experts? In a number of criminal and family law cases the accuracy and even integrity of some experts of certain experts were challenged. The GMC brought disciplinary proceedings against a very senior paediatrician, Sir Roy Meadow, and found him guilty of serious professional misconduct. He challenged the finding and his erasure from the register. The Court of Appeal ultimately struck down the finding of serious misconduct but held that expert witnesses have no immunity from disciplinary proceeding when giving expert testimony.[84] This and other cases have caused great controversy.[85] In *Jones v Kaney*[86] the Supreme Court ruled that the historical immunity from litigation long enjoyed by expert witnesses should be abolished. The need for better training and accreditation of experts is widely agreed on. The GMC now offers doctors guidance on giving expert evidence.[87]

84 *GMC v Meadow* [2006] EWCA 1390. And see S Devaney 'The Loneliness of the Expert Witness' (2007) 15 *Med Law Rev* 116.

85 See C Williams, 'The Trouble with Paediatricians' (2010) 18 *Med Law Rev* 389.

86 [2011] UKSC 13; and see S Devaney, 'Balancing Duties to the Court and Client; The Removal of Immunity from Suit of Expert Witnesses' (2012) 20 *Med Law Rev* 450.

87 GMC, *Acting as A Witness in Legal Proceedings* (2013).

9.14 May the burden of proof shift to the doctor?

While in the majority of cases the patient must prove negligence and the doctor is not called on to prove their 'innocence', are there ever occasions where an inference of negligence may be drawn from the facts of a case? There is a general rule of the law of negligence that where the defendant is in complete control of the relevant events, and an accident happens which does not ordinarily happen if proper care is taken, then the accident itself affords reasonable evidence of negligence. The defendant will be held liable unless they can advance an explanation of the accident consistent with the exercise of proper care. This derives from the Latin maxim *res ipsa loquitur* (the thing speaks for itself). *Res ipsa loquitur* can apply in clinical negligence cases, but it is limited to only the most obvious of claims, an example of which may be where a swab, or even a pair of forceps, is discovered in the patient's body after an abdominal operation. Without evidence of a quite exceptional nature, it is clear someone has been careless.

Res ipsa loquitur may also help the NHS patient who has undoubtedly suffered because someone was negligent, either in the theatre or in the course of post-operative care, but she cannot identify that someone. If every member of the staff who might be responsible is employed by the hospital, then an inference of negligence is raised against the hospital, who are necessarily vicariously liable for whoever may be the culprit.[88] In *Cassidy v Ministry of Health*,[89] a patient was operated on for Dupuytren's contraction affecting two of his fingers. After the operation, the patient's hand and lower arm had to be kept rigid in a splint for up to fourteen days. When the splints were removed, the plaintiff's whole hand was paralysed. Upon finding that all the staff involved in Mr Cassidy's care were NHS employees, the court held that there was evidence of negligence against their common employer. The onus shifted to the hospital to explain how this disaster might have struck without any of its employees being negligent. From a different angle, would the situation become more complicated if some of the health professionals caring for the patient were not directly employed by the hospital? An example could be where some of the theatre staff on duty when swabs were erroneously left in the abdomen of the patient were agency nurses as opposed to employees of the hospital. Any claim by the hospital that no inference of negligence should be raised against *it* because the negligent actor may well have been one of the nurses for whom it is not responsible would be unlikely to hold sway. As it now seems established that the hospital will be directly liable for any failure to measure up to the required standard of skill and care, it matters not to the patient who actually employs the negligent individual.[90]

Beyond this kind of obvious bungling, *res ipsa loquitur* has limited use in clinical negligence claims and an unexpected outcome in itself will certainly not raise any inference of negligence. Indeed, the Court of Appeal has made it clear

88 *Roe v Ministry of Health* [1954] 2 QB 66.
89 [1951] 2 KB 343.
90 *Woodland v Essex County Council* [2013] UKSC 66.

that *res ipsa loquitur* will rarely be applicable and criticised the phrase itself.[91] This may be one of the reasons why recent cases seek to avoid the language of *res ipsa loquitur*, with judges preferring to take a common sense view of the facts and how far they call for an explanation from the defendants as to any apparent failure in the patient's care. So in *Richards v Swansea NHS Trust*[92] the court held that the length of the delay in moving to carry out a Caesarean section required some explanation as to why the surgery was not performed more expeditiously and when no such evidence was forthcoming, the judge held that the claimant had established the breach of a duty of care. In *Thomas v Curley*,[93] the Court of Appeal held that, even if *res ipsa loquitur* did not apply, the occurrence of injury in an uncomplicated operation and at a site other than where the operation took place called for an explanation and in the absence of a satisfactory explanation negligence could be proven.

The private patient is in a more difficult situation in respect of *res ipsa loquitur*. Whether he enters an NHS or a private hospital, he will usually contract separately with the surgeon and the anaesthetist for surgery and anaesthetic. The surgeon and the anaesthetist will not be acting as employees of the hospital. If something goes wrong in the operating theatre or post-operatively and it is not clear who is to blame, *res ipsa loquitur* probably cannot be invoked. The hospital is not liable for any negligence on the part of the surgeon or anaesthetist. They can raise an inference of negligence against the hospital only if they can trace the relevant negligence to one of the staff. They can raise an inference of negligence against the surgeon or anaesthetist only if they can pin the relevant act on one of them personally.

If the surgeon, anaesthetist and hospital are all sued, none of them can be compelled to testify against each other. The patient will not be able to identify who was negligent. However, hope lies in the following statement made long ago by Lord Denning:

> I do not think that the hospital and [the doctor] can both avoid giving an explanation by the simple expedient of throwing responsibility on to the other. If an injured person shows that one or other or both of two persons injured him, but cannot say which of them it was, then he is not defeated altogether. He can call on each of them for an explanation.[94]

Thus robust common sense would force open any 'conspiracy of silence'.

9.15 Awards of compensation

Once a patient has established that there has been negligence by the defendant as a result of which he suffered harm, what damages will he receive? There are

91 *Ratcliffe v Plymouth & Torbay Health Authority* [1998] Lloyd's Rep Med 162, CA. And see *Lillywhite v University College London Hospitals NHS Trust* [2006] EWCA Civ 1466.
92 [2007] EWHC 487.
93 [2013] EWCA Civ 117. And see *O'Connor v The Pennine Acute Hospitals NHS Trust* [2015] EWCA Civ 1244.
94 *Roe v Ministry of Health* [1954] 2 QB 66, at 82.

no special rules governing clinical negligence awards. The patient's damages will be assessed to compensate them for any actual, or prospective, loss of earnings, and for the pain, suffering and disability which they have endured, and will endure. Their compensation for loss of earnings will include a sum representing any period in which they would have expected to be alive and earning but because of their injuries they will be prematurely dead.[95] Additionally for these sums to represent what they have lost, the patient will be awarded an amount to cover extra expenses which they and their family will incur. If they require intensive nursing care, or their house needs adapting to their invalid needs, or they require constant attendance so that their husband gives up his job, all these expenses will be reflected in the award of damages.[96] It is important to note that the amount of compensation will be tailored to the claimant's actual circumstances and losses. So in *Miller v Imperial College Healthcare NHS Trust*[97] a 63-year-old claimant lost her leg as a result of clinical negligence but she continued to work at least two days a week and so her future loss of earnings still fell to be assessed. If the patient is dead, the damages awarded to her family will reflect the loss to them of the moneys she regularly expended on them. They recover for their loss of dependency.[98] It takes little imagination to see that if the patient dies, the burden of compensation may be reduced. Dead he suffers no pain. Dead he incurs no expenses.

Returning to the living patient, thorny problems bedevil the question of damages. The first is this. The patient must usually sue within three years. At that stage, a prognosis about future health is speculative. All his medical advisers may be able to say is something like this. The patient has a degree of brain damage. He is mildly disabled now. There is a 20 per cent chance he may deteriorate to become paralysed, and totally unable to do anything for himself, in ten years' time. The court can make an award of provisional damages based on the assumption that the prospect of further damage or deterioration will *not* materialise. Should it do so at some later date, the patient may return to court to ask for a further award to compensate him for the consequences of that damage or deterioration.[99]

Until recently, courts had to struggle to assess damages on a once and forever basis. The exercise was particularly difficult when estimating claims for future expenses, especially where the patient is so badly injured as to be unable to manage their own affairs. Large sums of money can be claimed to cover the cost of future care in expensive nursing homes. But there is no guarantee that that money will be so spent. The patient may be consigned to the NHS and the money deposited to grow with interest and eventually, when the patient dies, to form a windfall for relatives. The courts are alert to this danger. They

95 This is known as compensation for the 'lost years'; see *Pickett v BRB* [1980] AC 136, HL. And see the Damages Act 1996, s 3.

96 The complexity of this exercise is well illustrated in *A (A Child) v University Hospitals of Morecambe Bay NHS Foundation Trust* [2015] EWHC 366 (QB).

97 [2014] EWHC 3772 (QB).

98 Fatal Accidents Act 1976, as amended by the Administration of Justice Act 1982.

99 See Senior Courts Act 1981, s 32A and *Chewings v Williams* [2009] EWHC 2490.

will seek to ensure that the sum awarded is such as will be wholly exhausted by care of the patient, aiming at no surplus as a bonus for relatives. Plans for care must be realistic, and section 5 of the Administration of Justice Act 1982 provides that 'any saving to the injured person which is attributable to his maintenance at public expense ... in a hospital ... or other institution shall be set off against any income lost ...'. A further anomaly in the law is that the claimant may be able to claim for the full cost of *any* private medical care regardless of whether such facilities are available free on the NHS.[100] Even where exactly identical surgery to alleviate the patient's condition could have been performed without charge, the claimant may demand the full cost of private care.

Once the patient's monetary losses have been quantified, consideration must then be given to how to compensate pain and suffering. Levels of compensation for those non-monetary losses have traditionally been much lower in this country than in the USA. The sum to be awarded is based on a 'tariff' system with guidance as to what sum each category of injury should attract.[101] In 1986, the Court of Appeal ruled that £75,000 was the 'tariff' to compensate the suffering of a young woman left tetraplegic (paralysed from the neck down).[102] Incrementally that sum crept up to about £100,000. Claimants felt that £100,000 for a lifetime of suffering was ludicrously low. The Law Commission conducted a review of compensation for pain and suffering and recommended that compensation for pain and suffering should be increased dramatically, in some instances of catastrophic injury, by as much as 100 per cent.[103] In *Heil v Rankin*,[104] the Court of Appeal considered the Law Commission's proposals. An especially enlarged court agreed that more generous compensation for suffering and disability was justified. They settled on a lesser increase than that envisaged by the Law Commission. No increase should be offered in claims of less than £10,000. Graduated increases would be allowed thereafter to a maximum of about 50 per cent above prior levels of awards. Their Lordships acknowledged that the impact on the NHS of increased levels of damages played a role in motivating their caution.[105]

Other changes in the law relating to damages have also contributed to the increase in compensation payable in negligence claims against the NHS.[106] Medical skills means patients who suffer injury as a consequence of medical mistakes live much longer. Greater opportunities exist to improve their quality of life. Such benefits escalate costs. The concern generated by spiralling awards

100 Law Reform (Personal Injuries) Act 1948, s 2(4).

101 See Judicial Studies Board, *Guidelines for the Assessment of General Damages in Personal Injuries Cases* (10th edn, 2010) Oxford University Press.

102 *Housecroft v Burnett* [1986] 1 All ER 332, CA.

103 Law Commission, *Damages for Personal Injury: Non-Pecuniary Loss* (1999) Report No 257.

104 [2000] 3 All ER 138.

105 [2000] 3 All ER 138, at 150.

106 See *Wells v Wells* [1999] 1 AC 345, HL; Damages Act 1996.

of damages is exacerbated by the fact that compensating people for injury can never be an exact science.

Claimants and defendants are often unhappy with the level of compensation awarded. For example, when negligence results in a patient's death, compensation for bereavement is only available to parents of children under 18, or to spouses. The level of compensation is set at £15,120.[107] This amount can be seen as an insulting assessment, but can any sum compensate bereavement? Was the old rule that bereavement damages were never available preferable? When a patient survives paralysed from the waist down, will £150,000 heal their pain? Defendants also feel badly done to. Who the patient is may be crucial to the extent of their liability. Should one of us be left paralysed by an anaesthetist's mistake, the defendant hospital will have to cover the cost of future care and of equipment we will need, such as wheelchairs and alterations to our home. Providing that we can still go on lecturing, even if seated, our loss of income will be minimal. Should England's football captain suffer an identical mishap at the height of his career, his claim for loss of income could easily run into the high millions.[108] The lottery element in compensation awards was graphically illustrated by the case of Hollie Calladine.[109] Nine-year-old Hollie was awarded £700,000 in respect of brain damage caused by negligence during her birth. Much of this sum was to cover the expense of her future care. Days after the award was made, Hollie died. The hospital tried unsuccessfully to recover their damages. This sad case must suggest lump sum payments are not accurate or fair. The only equity of the system is that both sides suffer. For every case like Hollie Calladine's, there is another where claimants go grossly under-compensated by any lump sum payment. A young man of 23 is injured in the course of surgery. Doctors estimate he will live a further ten years. He survives for twenty-five years. His compensation will be less than half of what he required.

9.16 Periodical payments – structured settlements[110]

Some of the uncertainties generated by having to assess compensation as a lump sum are avoidable by resort to reviewable periodical payments or, as they used to be described, structured settlements. The claimant receives an initial capital sum to cover actual losses already quantifiable and such matters as compensation for pain and suffering. The remainder of the money is used by the defendant to purchase an annuity for the claimant's benefit.

107 See the Damages for Bereavement (Variation of Sum) (England and Wales) Order 2020, SI 2020/316. This amount only applies to bereaved families who have lost a loved one on or after 1 May 2020.

108 See the compensation claim in 2010 for former Commonwealth Games cyclist Manny Helmot, who was awarded £13.7 million following a road traffic collision which left him with brain injuries, mental health problems and requiring twenty-four-hour care. See www.claimscouncil.org.

109 See 'Legal Moves' (2001) 138 *Liability Risk and Insurance* 19.

110 See C Witting, *Street on Torts* (14th edn, 2015) Oxford University Press, pp 703–704. And see A Sands, 'Periodical Payments – The Development of a Pragmatic Approach' (2006) 74 *Medico-Legal Journal* 69.

The annuity will be flexible to adapt to the changing circumstances of the patient.[111] The income received by the patient is not taxable. The money paid out will be what he requires and no more. Should he die earlier than anticipated, payments will cease. Periodical payments avoid cases like that of Hollie Calladine. In certain cases, the periodical payments agreed or ordered can be reviewed at a later date. In ordinary personal injury claims, the defendant's insurer arranges the settlement and negotiates the purchase of annuities. As we have seen, the NHS does not insure against liability for clinical negligence on the commercial market. NHS structured settlements are usually self-financed.[112] The NHS uses its own income to arrange periodical payments, building the settlement into budgets. Tax concessions aid this process. Periodical payments in large claims may save the NHS some money. Since 2005 the courts have been able to impose a Periodical Payments Order (PPO).[113] Until 2005, structured settlements could only be established with the agreement of both parties. Periodical payments may be efficient and fairer. The overall size of some awards for catastrophic injury is unlikely to drop. In 2018, for example, the NHS agreed to pay a record 19.8 million to a claimant who a suffered catastrophic brain injury as a result of being denied oxygen when she was a baby.[114] The claimant will receive a lump sum of £2.1m, and £203,000 a year for the rest of her life.[115]

9.17 Malpractice crisis: reality or illusion?[116]

Bringing a claim for compensation, in any but the most straightforward of cases, is rarely easy. Yet despite the obvious difficulties associated with funding a claim and proving negligence, critics of the civil justice system have long argued that England has succumbed to a 'compensation culture'. Personal injury claims, it has been said, are stifling ordinary life. 'Gold-diggers' make spurious claims. Schools are afraid to let children engage in any sort of risky activity. Children are barred from conker fights without wearing goggles.[117] Lord Hobhouse suggested:

> The pursuit of an unrestrained culture of blame and compensation has many evil consequences and one is certain interference with the liberty of the citizen.[118]

111 A key issue is indexation to allow for inflation. See *Thompstone v Tameside and Glossop Acute Services NHS Trust* [2008] EWCA Civ 5. And see R Lewis, 'The Indexation of Periodical Payments of Damages in Tort: the Future Assured?' (2010) 30 *Legal Studies* 391.

112 See CMO, *Making Amends*, p 74.

113 See the Damages Act 1996, ss 2–2B (as substituted by the Courts Act 2003) and the Damages (Variation of Periodical Payments) Order 2005, SI 2005/841.

114 See D Campbell, 'NHS Pays Out Record £19.8m Compensation to Brain Injury Teenager' *Guardian* (2018) 1 October.

115 For a discussion of recent periodical payments figures, see NHS Resolution, *Annual Report and Accounts 2020/21*, pp 149 and 157.

116 For a fascinating discussion, see T Baker, *The Medical Malpractice Myth* (2005) University of Chicago Press.

117 See *The Times* (2006) September 18.

118 *Tomlinson v Congleton Borough Council* [2003] UKHL 47, [81].

Nevertheless, the evidence to support the existence of a compensation culture is, at best, equivocal.[119] In May 2010 Lord Young was asked to review the effect of health and safety legislation in particular. While Lord Young acknowledged[120] that there is great deal of exaggeration in the media about a compensation culture, he aroused the wrath of lawyers acting for claimants in personal injury claims by attacking the advertising of lawyers' services and saying that they should be ashamed.[121]

In the context of clinical negligence claims, it has been argued that increased litigation means that doctors may practise 'defensive medicine'.[122] A doctor will choose the treatment for the patient most likely to be 'legally safe' to ensure that he will not be sued by the patient. That treatment may not necessarily be medically best for the patient, and may be unnecessarily expensive and time-consuming.[123] And, it is contended that the NHS is drained of resources because so many people sue.

9.18 Obstetrics and gynaecology: defensive medicine arguments in context

The prospect that doctors will base decisions concerning treatment not on their professional judgement of what is best for the patient but on what is 'legally safest' for the doctor does sound appalling. But is there hard evidence that doctors are being forced to practise defensive medicine?[124] To assist in answering this question, it is worth considering one specific area that speaks to this issue. The field of obstetrics and gynaecology is a notoriously high-risk specialism. Where the health and well-being of a mother and a newborn baby are concerned, the stakes are naturally high. Matters can spiral out of control very quickly in labour and the consequences of adverse incidents can often be catastrophic, resulting in severe lifelong medical conditions for those affected. It follows that this is a 'hot zone' for litigation, both in the sense of it attracting a significant number of claims, and also generating large payments in compensation.[125]

119 For an excellent, balanced discussion, see K Williams, 'State of Fear: Britain's "Compensation Culture" Reviewed' (2005) 3 *Legal Studies* 499.

120 Lord Young, *Common Sense; Common Safety* (2010) HM Govt.

121 See 'News: Lord Young Attacks Personal Injury "Lottery"' (2010) *Law Society Gazette* 7 October 3(1).

122 O Ortashi *et al*, 'The Practice of Defensive Medicine Amongst Hospital Doctors in the UK' (2013) 14 *BMC Med Ethics* 42; N Summerton, 'Positive and Negative Factors of Defensive Medicine: A Questionnaire Study of General Practitioners' (1995) 310 *BMJ* 27.

123 Ibid.

124 See P Case, 'The Jaded Cliché of "Defensive Medical Practice": From Magically Convincing to Empirically (Un)convincing?' (2020) 36 *Journal of Professional Negligence* 49.

125 See NHS Resolution, *Annual Report and Accounts 2020/21*, pp 46 and 59. See also National Health Service Litigation Authority (NHS Resolution), 'Ten Years of Maternity Claims: An Analysis of NHS Litigation Authority Data' (2012) October (hereafter 'Ten Years of Maternity Claims'), at 4.

These concerns have resulted in a number of investigations into the prevalence of maternity claims. In 2012, NHS Resolution published 'Ten Years of Maternity Claims: An Analysis of NHS Litigation Authority Data'.[126] This provided a range of suggested recommendations to reduce the financial and human cost of maternity claims, including the need to: engage with the risk-management processes at all levels; provide suitable learning and training; ensure appropriate supervision and support; produce up-to-date protocols and guidance; and learn lessons from claims.[127] More recently, the NHS has also produced a report entitled *Better Births Four Years On: A Review of Progress*, which concluded that there had been some positive improvements in maternity care since its original report in 2016.[128]

The analysis reported evidence of a steady reduction in stillbirths, combined perinatal mortality and maternal mortality over time. However, some of these improvements, it noted, were likely to be as a result of an increase in clinical interventions such as inductions and Caesarean sections, which were performed with the support of both women and health professionals.[129] This latter point is often given as an example of defensive medicine, with obstetricians voicing a subjective belief that fear of litigation makes them more ready to move swiftly to surgery rather than allow a difficult labour to proceed.[130] This may well be a common perception, but on closer inspection it may prove to be somewhat of a misperception. For a start, the rise in the rate of Caesarean sections has often been found to be explicable by many other factors and the numbers rose in several countries, not all of which experienced rising levels of litigation. Equally, there is the more problematic question of how to define defensive medicine. If we equate a greater inclination amongst obstetricians to perform interventions, might we classify this as over-cautious rather than defensive practice, which is not necessarily a bad thing. The difficulty is to decide when further tests, cross-checks and accelerated interventions cease to be a sensible precaution in the interests of the patient and become a waste of resources.[131]

In any event, should a negligent management of labour claim ever reach court, there is evidence that judges will remain highly sympathetic to the difficult job faced by all the health professionals involved. Not infrequently, cases turn on the interpretation of cardiotocograph traces (CTG traces), which is a technical matter.[132] Where this is so, judges have been seen to afford a wide margin of appreciation to professional judgement in the breach inquiry.[133] It should be remembered that when *Montgomery v Lanarkshire* was heard before the lower Scottish courts, alongside the claim pertaining to inadequate

126 Ibid. And see 11.7 below on rapid resolution and redress.
127 Ibid, 5.
128 NHS, *Better Births Four Years On: A Review of Progress* (2020) March.
129 Ibid, [79].
130 HL Official Report, 10 November 1987, cols 1350–1351.
131 See generally, P Danzon, *Medical Malpractice (* 1985) Harvard University Press.
132 'Ten Years of Maternity Claims', 4.
133 See R Heywood, 'Litigating Labour: Condoning Unreasonable Risk-Taking in Childbirth? (2015) 44 *Common Law World Review* 28.

disclosure, there was also an initial allegation of negligence in the management of the mother's labour.[134] There were a number of signs on a CTG trace that were indicative of the fact that the consultant should have opted for an earlier intervention, but she chose not to.[135] Despite her conduct not being entirely consistent with guidelines that were in existence at the time, Lord Eassie in the Inner House of the Court of Session preferred to view this as a decision that fell within an acceptable range of professional discretion that should be granted to the consultant.[136] Nadine Montgomery thus failed on this branch of her case. The issue was not pursued in the Supreme Court, but it underscores the message that the threshold for imposing liability in childbirth cases remains high, because judges rarely seem to invoke the *Bolitho* risk versus benefit balancing gloss to the advantage of claimants.[137] It follows that health professionals perhaps do not need to fear the threat of the law in this field as much as they do, so arguments about defensive medicine then become more difficult to sustain.

Elsewhere, some of the concerns felt by doctors about defensive medicine may stem from anxiety that this country will see the excesses of malpractice litigation in the USA cross the Atlantic.[138] But we should note first that, in the USA, most medical care is provided by the private sector. If your treatment goes wrong and you suffer a medical accident, you will have to pay out more money for corrective treatment. Naturally, an aggrieved patient is going to be looking to the doctor whom she perceives as responsible for the accident for the money to pay for any necessary corrective treatment. Most patients will carry private health insurance. Their insurers will be as keen as the patient to ensure that any costs arising from medical negligence are recovered from the doctor and his insurers. In a private health system such as that of the USA, healthcare is charged on a fee-for-service basis. The more tests a doctor carries out, the more money he makes. Perhaps some of the apparent evidence for 'defensive medicine' is better explained as 'expensive medicine'?

Note, too, that awards of damages in the USA are decided not by the judge, as is the case in England, but by a jury. Even though the Court of Appeal in *Heil v Rankin*[139] and later *Simmons v Castle*[140] has raised the tariff for compensation for pain and suffering in this country, levels of compensation remain infinitely more generous in the USA. Moreover, currently damages in this country are awarded solely for the purpose of compensating the patient for what he has lost as a result of the defendant doctor's negligence. A US jury is empowered in certain circumstances to double, or even treble,

134 See *KR v Lanarkshire Health Board* [2016] CSOH 133; *Montgomery v Lanarkshire Health Board* [2013] CSIH 3.

135 *Montgomery v Lanarkshire Health Board* [2013] CSIH 3 at [55]–[58].

136 Ibid.

137 See Heywood, 'Litigating Labour: Condoning Unreasonable Risk-Taking in Childbirth?'.

138 See CMO, *Making Amends*, pp 26–27.

139 [2000] 2 WLR 1173, CA.

140 [2012] EWCA Civ 1288.

compensatory damages by making a further award of punitive damages, to punish the defendant for negligence.[141] Combining these factors, the Chief Medical Officer (CMO) found that while malpractice litigation consumed 0.2 per cent of Gross Domestic Product in the USA, that figure was only 0.04 per cent in the United Kingdom.[142]

Finally, lawyers acting for the clients in the USA act on a *contingency* fee basis. If the case fails, the client pays nothing; if the claim succeeds the lawyer takes a percentage of the damages, normally about one third. Such a system gives lawyers a direct interest in the level of damages awarded. With the introduction of a form of contingency fee arrangements, 'damages-based agreements', in LASPO[143] we will have to see what effect this may have in England.

9.19 Financial costs to the NHS

However, the financial effects of litigation on the NHS have generated serious concern for many years now. A study of medical litigation[144] published in 1988 first raised alarm, demonstrating that numbers of claims against doctors doubled between 1983 and 1987. In 2020/21 NHS Resolution received 12,629 clinical negligence claims and reported incidents, compared to 11,678 in 2019/20, an increase of 951 (7.5 per cent).[145] In respect of damages paid for clinical negligence, the amount of expenditure, including personal injury discount rate costs,[146] decreased by £73.4 million (4.4 per cent) from £1,683.2 million in 2019/20 to £1,609.8 million in 2020/21.[147] NHS Resolution attributes this partly to the operational challenges associated with progressing claims during the pandemic.[148] In terms of legal costs for clinical negligence, in 2020/21 claimants' legal costs decreased by £49.4 million (9.9 per cent), from £497.5 million in 2019/20 to £448.1 million, whereas NHS legal costs overall increased from 143.5 million in 2019/20 to 151.4 million in 2020/21, representing an increase of £7.9 million (5.5 per cent).[149]

How do claims fare? NHS Resolution reports that it settled 15,674 clinical and non-clinical claims in 2020/21, 124 more than in 2019/20. Of these, 11,704 (74.7 per cent) claims were settled without formal court proceedings, 3,914 (25 per cent) with proceedings but without trial and 56 (0.3 per cent)

141 Although Law Commission, *Aggravated, Exemplary and Restitutionary Damages* (1997) Report No 247 did propose that, in exceptional cases, punitive damages should be awarded in England.

142 See CMO, *Making Amends*, p 26.

143 See 9.3 above.

144 C Ham *et al*, *Medical Negligence: Compensation and Accountability* (1988) King's Fund Institute/Centre for Socio-Legal Studies.

145 NHS Resolution, *Annual Report and Accounts 2020/21*, p 18.

146 The personal injury discount rate is currently set at minus 0.25 per cent. See The Damages (Personal Injury) Order 2019, SI 2019/1126.

147 NHS Resolution, *Annual Report and Accounts 2020/21*, p 43.

148 Ibid.

149 Ibid.

at trial. This compares to 2019/20 when 71.5 per cent settled without proceedings, 27.9 per cent with proceedings and 0.6 per cent at trial.[150] Based on the 15,674 settled claims in 2020/21, 6,872 (43.8 per cent) settled without damages being paid. This compares to 6,698 (43.1 per cent) out of 15,500 in 2019/20, an increase of 174 (0.7 per cent).[151] The outlay for settling claims in 2020/21 reduced across *all* NHS Resolution schemes by £120 million, to £2.26 billion.[152] NHS Resolution states that its current liabilities arising from claims under *all* its indemnity schemes have decreased by £1.3 billion, from £84.1 billion in 2019/20 to £82.8 billion in 2020/21.[153]

Any judgement about whether the number of clinical negligence claims brought is excessive must be made in the context of estimates of the numbers of medical errors causing harm to patients. In one survey in 2005, 2,081 deaths were attributed to error.[154] It has been estimated that 10 per cent of 'in-patient episodes' result in some injury to patients and that half of these 'adverse events' may be preventable.[155] The figure of 12,629 claims for clinical negligence suggests that many patients or families who could sue do not do so.

Nevertheless, where a claim is made by an NHS patient, money to compensate an injured patient and money to defend claims brought in respect of alleged negligence must come out of NHS funds which might otherwise have been used to employ an extra surgeon, or pay for a new neonatal unit, or support a programme of preventive medicine.[156] When NHS money is used to compensate an injured patient, some benefit to society can be discerned. The disproportion between costs and compensation remains disturbing. John Harris[157] has argued that claimants in clinical negligence should compete for scarce resources with patients in urgent need of treatment. If resources for treatment are rationed, so compensation for medical accidents should be too. Costs arguments must be kept in proportion though. In 2003, the CMO found that just under 1 per cent of the NHS budget was expended on malpractice litigation.[158]

There have been a number of initiatives launched to investigate what can be done about increasing costs and the subsequent impact on the NHS. In 2017, the Department of Health issued a consultation in which it proposed a scheme of fixed recoverable costs for lower-value clinical negligence cases with

150 Ibid, p 18.
151 Ibid.
152 Ibid, p 16.
153 Ibid.
154 See National Audit Office, *A Safer Place for Patients: Learning to Improve Patient Safety* (2005).
155 See CMO, *Making Amends*, pp 31–41.
156 See A Merry and A McCall Smith, *Errors, Medicine and the Law* (2001) Cambridge University Press, p 212.
157 J Harris, 'The Injustice of Compensation for Medical Accidents' (1997) 314 *BMJ* 182.
158 See CMO, *Making Amends*, p 26.

a damages value of no more than £25,000.[159] In the same year, Lord Justice Jackson published a report recommending a general scheme of fixed recoverable costs for all fast track cases and a new 'intermediate track' for cases up to £100,000 in value.[160] However, he concluded that clinical negligence cases were too complex to fall within these proposals and so recommended that the Department of Health and the Civil Justice Council form a working party to develop a solution to dealing with clinical negligence claims up to £25,000.[161] In October 2019, the Civil Justice Council published the findings from its working party.[162] Despite coming close to reaching a compromise on the figures, in the end the various representatives sitting on the working party could not reach an overall agreement for the level of fixed recoverable costs.[163] A number of proposals were thus included from both defendant and claimant representatives and the report concluded that it is now for the Government to decide which fee regime to adopt.[164] At the time of writing, the Government has recently begun exploring different ideas to reform clinical negligence. In September 2021, the Health and Social Care Committee launched an inquiry into NHS litigation reform.[165] In November of the same year, it was announced on the House of Lords Library homepage that the Department of Health and Social Care was looking at the issue of liability costs on the NHS and how they might be reduced, and that the Government would publish a consultation on its next steps shortly.[166] In January 2022, the Department of Health and Social Care launched a further consultation into fixed recoverable costs in lower-value clinical negligence claims, based broadly around its earlier proposal.[167]

9.20 Wider 'costs' to the NHS

Financial costs to the NHS are not the only cause for concern. Critics of the medical litigation process argue that it is unfair to doctors and damaging to the doctor–patient relationship. Are doctors unfairly treated? The evidence does not substantiate such a claim. The majority of claims that actually reach court fail, and of claims settled out of court, many will result in limited compensation to the claimant.[168] Claimants do not seem to be 'winning' disproportionate numbers of cases, and bringing a claim after 2013 is ever more difficult.

159 DHSC, *Introducing Fixed Recoverable Costs in Lower Value Clinical Negligence Claims: Consultation Paper* (2017) January.
160 Sir R Jackson, *Review of Civil Litigation Costs: Supplemental Report – Fixed Recoverable Costs* (2017) July.
161 See Report of the Civil Justice Council Working Group, *Fixed Recoverable Costs in Lower Value Clinical Negligence Claims* (2019) October, at [1.33].
162 See ibid.
163 See ibid, at [8.13].
164 See ibid, at [8.13] and [8.19].
165 UK Parliament, *New Inquiry NHS Litigation Reform* (2021) 22 September.
166 See UK Parliament, *House of Lords Library: Negligence in the NHS* (2021) 29 November.
167 DHSC, Fixed Recoverable Costs in Lower Value Clinical Negligence Claims A Consultation (2022) January.
168 NHS Resolution, *Annual Report and Accounts 2020/21*, p 55.

Nor does an argument that doctors are unjustly judged by lawyers stand up to scrutiny. What is true is that many doctors have become so frightened by the spectre of a malpractice crisis that doctor–patient relationships may be damaged.[169] Evidence of defensive medicine may be disputable; defensiveness in medicine is a sad fact.[170] As we have seen, doctors in 'high-risk' specialties are the worst affected among the profession. Doctors who are sued are concerned about '... the damage to their professional reputation, whether they were found negligent or not: the fact of the case was sufficient for the damage to reputation and morale'.[171] The CMO noted: 'Legal proceedings for medical injury frequently progress in an atmosphere of confrontation, acrimony, misunderstanding and bitterness.'[172]

Clinical negligence litigation is often traumatic for all the parties but unless complaints procedures and other avenues for redress can be seen to be fair and transparent, little is likely to change, save for growing resentment on the part of patient-claimants priced out of the civil litigation system. Before we turn to examine complaints and redress in more specific detail, we first explore the role and impact of the criminal process on medical malpractice.

169 See CMO, *Making Amends*, p 76.

170 Hence Ian Kennedy argued many years ago that what is required to defuse any 'crisis' is better information about the law for doctors so that they will not feel constrained to practise 'defensive medicine': see 'Review of the Year 2: Confidentiality, Competence and Malpractice' in P Byrne (ed), *Medicine in Contemporary Society* (1987) King's Fund.

171 See CMO, *Making Amends*, p 76. And note his estimate that 38 per cent of doctors who have been sued suffer clinical depression (p 43).

172 See *Making Amends*, p 7.

Chapter 10

THE CRIMINAL PROCESS AND MEDICAL MALPRACTICE

10.1 Introduction

In this chapter we examine criminal law and medical negligence, asking when a doctor's malpractice engages criminal liability. Most instances of injury caused by medical error are dealt with under the civil law. However gross or culpable an act of negligence may be, negligence is not generally a crime in England unless made so by statute, as in the case of careless driving. As we have seen in Chapter 9, neither aggrieved patients nor doctors are satisfied with the clinical negligence system. Patients complain of delay, cost and complexity. Fear of litigation creates unease amongst doctors and prompts dire predictions of a malpractice crisis.

Doctors' anxieties become even more pronounced when we consider the role of the criminal law in dealing with medical harm, especially in the light of recent high-profile prosecutions of doctors for manslaughter. Whilst there is a degree of overlap between the aims of civil and criminal law,[1] criminal convictions indicate moral culpability and may result in imprisonment. When in 2022 the Ockenden Report[2] concluded that poor practices at Shrewsbury and Telford Hospital NHS Trust maternity unit had potentially contributed to the deaths of 201 babies and 9 women, West Mercia police made clear that 600 cases were being closely examined.[3] Criminal law has an important role to play. It is the threat of disgrace and harsh penalties coupled with some confusion about the relevant principles of law which has caused doctors concern.[4] Barely even noted not long ago, the role of the criminal process in addressing medical error has provoked a discussion that has gained considerable traction of late and generated extensive literature.[5]

1 See M Allen and I Edwards, *Criminal Law* (16th edn, 2021) Oxford University Press, pp 2–22.

2 DHSC, *Final Report of the Ockenden Review* (2022) HC1219. See 13.1 below.

3 A Gregory, 'Police Examine 600 Cases After Damning NHS Baby Deaths Report' *Guardian* (2022) 30 March.

4 J Vaughan, O Quick and D Griffiths 'Medical Manslaughter: Where Next?' (2018) 100 *Bulletin of the Royal College of Surgeons England* 25.

5 See A Farrell, A Alghrani and M Kazarian, 'Gross Negligence Manslaughter in Healthcare: Time for a Restorative Justice Approach?' (2020) 28 *Med Law Rev* 526.

10.2 The criminal law and medicine: a complex relationship

Doctors in 1695 had reason to fear the criminal law. *Mala praxis* (medical malpractice) was described by Chief Justice Holt as 'a great misdemeanour and offence at common law'.[6] Such a common law offence seems to have fallen into desuetude and for over two hundred years the criminal law played only a background role in dealing with medical harm. While negligence is not usually a crime, the picture changes if the patient dies. Gross negligence causing death can lead to prosecution for gross negligence manslaughter (GNM), which is a difficult crime to prosecute. The central question of what constitutes grossly negligent behaviour is a matter to be determined by a jury, yet judges struggle to construct a direction that usefully assists jurors in identifying when conduct may have transcended ordinary negligence. GNM focuses exclusively on the doctor in the dock. Should a surgeon cause their patient's death having bungled an operation when drunk or under the influence of drugs, the emphasis on the surgeon's misconduct may be appropriate. Case-law and literature on medical error demonstrate that such obviously gross misconduct is rare. Many fatal errors result at least in part from systemic failings which contributed significantly to a patient's death. The hospital might be seen as equally or more at fault than the doctor who made the final fatal mistake. The common law struggled to address corporate criminal liability, and in 2007 Parliament enacted the Corporate Manslaughter and Corporate Homicide Act 2007. The effect of the legislation has been underwhelming.

Given that GNM is only applicable when a patient has died, it has significant limitations as a means of punishing or deterring egregious medical practice. It is arguably unjust to the accused because it depends on 'moral luck'.[7] Imagine that Dr A, an anaesthetist, carelessly failed to monitor patient B undergoing surgery and as a result B died. Dr C made exactly the same gross error, but her patient, D, survived with brain damage. Where a patient survives, we need to consider other criminal offences that address non-fatal gross negligence. Charges for causing grievous bodily harm under the Offences Against the Person Act 1861 may be considered. Convictions have been rare due to the difficulties associated with the concept of consent and what has been termed the 'medical exception', issues addressed later in this chapter.

In the next section, we focus on GNM. It is not only doctors who have faced prosecution. Nurses and other health workers, including an optometrist, have featured in recent cases. We explore the legal principles deriving from the main

See, more generally, A Alghrani, R Bennett and S Ost (eds), *Bioethics, Medicine and the Criminal Law: Volume 1 – The Criminal Law and Bioethical Conflict: Walking the Tightrope* (2012) Cambridge University Press; D Griffiths and A Sanders (eds), *Bioethics, Medicine and the Criminal Law: Volume 2 – Medicine, Crime and Society* (2013) Cambridge University Press; M Brazier and S Ost (eds), *Bioethics, Medicine and the Criminal Law: Volume 3 – Medicine and Bioethics in the Theatre of the Criminal Process* (2013) Cambridge University Press (hereafter Brazier and Ost).

6 *Dr Groenvelt's Case* (1695) 91 English Reports 1038, 1039.

7 Brazier and Ost, pp 79–80.

judgments and then discuss some controversial recent cases. After considering the possible impact that fear of criminal liability may have on health professionals, we reflect upon situations where a patient has died as a result of systemic fault. Finally, we examine offences relevant where a patient has been injured but survived.

10.3 Gross negligence manslaughter (GNM)

For a successful prosecution in GNM, much more than ordinary negligence must be proved. In older cases, the negligence was seen to derive from morally disgraceful conduct – a doctor operating while drunk or under the influence of drugs. In *R v Bateman*, the Court of Appeal overruled a conviction for manslaughter of a doctor whose ignorance and failure to send a woman to hospital resulted in his patient's death. The judge at the trial had failed to direct the jury properly. Criminal liability required more than the degree of negligence needed to establish civil liability. The doctor must be proved to have shown 'such disregard for the life and safety of others as to amount to a crime against the State and conduct deserving punishment'.[8] The language of disregard of the life and safety of the patient might suggest that only recklessness on the part of the doctor would engage liability for GNM. Not so – the Court of Appeal and the House of Lords have made it clear that the test of gross negligence is objective.

In *R v Prentice*, *R v Adomako* and *R v Holloway*,[9] the Court of Appeal considered two[10] appeals by doctors against conviction for manslaughter. In the first case, two junior doctors, Drs Prentice and Sulman, were convicted of manslaughter after they had wrongly injected a potent chemotherapeutic drug (vincristine) into the patient's spine, when it should have been administered intravenously. Their 16-year-old patient was suffering from leukaemia. Every month he received an intravenous injection of vincristine. Every other month he received a spinal injection of another powerful drug, methotextrate. The drug came down to the ward on the same trolley. Neither Dr Prentice nor Dr Sulman had ever administered such drugs before, and they were left unsupervised.

The second case involved Dr Adomako, an anaesthetist. During surgery to re-attach a detached retina, Dr Adomako failed to notice, for over four minutes, that the tube administering oxygen to his patient had become disconnected. He neither noticed the evidence before his eyes that the tube was no longer in place, nor did he respond to the alarm raised by the operating theatre's monitoring system. One prosecution expert described his standard of care as abysmal. The appeal court quashed the convictions of Drs Prentice and Sulman, but upheld Dr Adomako's conviction. The Court of Appeal set the following test for GNM:

8 [1925] All ER Rep 45, 49.

9 [1993] 4 All ER 935, CA.

10 The third appeal, *R v Holloway*, involved an electrician whose faulty wiring caused a death.

(1) Did the doctor show obvious indifference to the risk of injury to his patient?
(2) Was he aware of the risk but nonetheless (for no good reason) decided to run the risk?
(3) Was an attempt to avoid a known risk so grossly negligent to deserve punishment?
(4) Was there a degree of inattention or failure to have regard to risk, going beyond mere inadvertence?

Only if at least one of these questions could be answered affirmatively should a doctor be convicted of manslaughter. In the case of Dr Prentice and Dr Sulman, there was insufficient evidence of gross negligence deserving punishment. Dr Adomako, the Court of Appeal declared, failed to perform:

> ... his essential and in effect sole duty to see that his patient was breathing satisfactorily and to cope with the breathing emergency ... his failure was more than mere inadvertence and constituted gross negligence of the degree necessary for manslaughter.

Dr Adomako appealed to the House of Lords without success. His conviction was upheld.[11] The Law Lords offered no precise definition of 'medical manslaughter'. Lord Mackay endorsed the trial judge's warning to the jury: 'You should only convict a doctor of causing death by negligence if you think he did something which no reasonably skilled doctor would have done.'[12]

The lack of clarity about what degree of negligence constitutes 'gross' medical negligence was challenged in the Court of Appeal in *R v Misra and Srivistava*.[13] Drs Misra and Srivistava were convicted of manslaughter after a patient died because of a failure to treat a post-operative infection. The evidence established that, over a period of forty-eight hours, the doctors failed to act on information that their patient was critically ill. They did not chase up blood tests and ignored warnings from nurses and another doctor. Part of the grounds for their appeal was that the ill-defined boundaries of GNM contravened Article 7 of the Human Rights Convention. Article 7 requires that criminal offences must be defined in clear enough terms so that people are aware what constitutes criminal conduct. The appeal failed.[14] The Court of Appeal said that to be convicted of GNM, the doctor must have failed to avert a risk of death. Other risks of lesser harm were not sufficient. Once a risk of death was established, it was for the jury to determine if the relevant negligence was gross. The citizen seeking to understand his potential criminal liability should be advised that, if he negligently breaches a duty of care, so as to endanger life,

11 *R v Adomako* [1995] 1 AC 171, HL.
12 Ibid, 188.
13 [2004] EWCA Crim 2375; note that subsequently the Trust employing the two doctors was convicted of offences contravening health and safety legislation in respect of the same events: *R v Southampton University Hospitals NHS Trust* [2006] EWCA Crim 341.
14 Leave to appeal to the House of Lords was refused; *R v Misra* [2004] All ER (D).

he may be convicted of manslaughter if a jury is satisfied that his negligence is gross. The appeal court judges acknowledged an element of circularity in their own arguments. The definition of what constitutes gross negligence remains vague and vulnerable to the subjective interpretations of juries.

Later cases address the requirement that to convict a defendant for GNM, there must have been a serious and obvious risk of death at the time of the breach. In *R v Rudling*, the Crown appealed against the trial judge's ruling that a general practitioner (GP) had no case to answer in respect of a charge of GNM for failing to put in place suitable arrangements to assess the severity of a child's reported illness, either by a visiting the child herself or calling for an ambulance if that was not possible.[15] A telephone conversation with the child's mother, which was the point the alleged breach of duty was said to have occurred, may have indicated the child was seriously ill, but that did not mean that a serious and obvious risk of death was foreseeable to the GP at that point.[16] In *R v Rose*, the defendant, an optometrist, failed *inter alia* to examine her child patient's internal eye structure. Had she done so a competent optometrist would have seen signs of swelling of the optic nerve and the condition that resulted in the boy's death five months later. She appealed against her original conviction for GNM on the grounds that a serious and obvious risk of death would not have been reasonably foreseeable at the time she conducted the inadequate examination of the victim's eyes, which was the point at which she was alleged to have breached her duty of care.[17] The Court of Appeal confirmed that the test of reasonable foreseeability was objective and requires the notional objective exercise of putting a reasonably prudent professional in the shoes of the person whose conduct is under scrutiny and asking whether, at the moment of breach of the duty on which the prosecution rely, that person ought reasonably to have foreseen an obvious and serious risk of death.[18]

As Alexandra Mullock put it:

> While the court in *Rose* asserted that the test remains objective, the objective/subjective dichotomy appears to have become blurred. Indeed, generally the distinction is not always necessarily clear.[19]

Although a reasonably competent optometrist would or should have known that it was possible that signs of potentially life-threatening conditions may go undetected if she failed to carry out a satisfactory examination of a patient's eyes, that did not amount to reasonable foresight of a serious and obvious risk of death. The conviction in *Rose* was therefore quashed. *Rose* is a puzzling decision. A reasonably competent optometrist would have conducted the

15 *R v Rudling* [2016] EWCA Crim 741, at [16] and [17].
16 Ibid, [39].
17 *R v Rose* [2017] EWCA Crim 1168, [83]–[86].
18 Ibid, [84].
19 A Mullock 'Gross Negligence (Medical) Manslaughter and the Puzzling Implications of Negligent Ignorance: *Rose v R* [2017] EWCA Crim 1168' (2018) 26 *Med Law Rev* 346, 352; A Samanta and J Samanta, 'Death Caused by Negligent Medical Care: Reconsidering the Role of Gross Negligence Manslaughter in the Aftermath of Bawa-Garba' (2021) 21 (4) *Medical Law International* 293, 302.

requisite examination. An optometrist 'in a state of negligent ignorance' is not acting as a competent professional.[20]

Finally, to convict the accused health professional for GNM, the prosecution must establish causation. It must be shown that the defendant's gross negligence caused or made a significant – that is more than minimal – contribution to the patient's death.[21] In medical manslaughter cases applying this test can be complicated.[22] The patient may be very ill and at risk of dying even if treated without any negligence. It seems that in such cases it must be proved beyond reasonable doubt that, absent the negligence, the patient's life would have been saved or prolonged. Or put slightly differently the defendant's negligence made a significant contribution to the patient dying *as* and *when* he did.[23]

10.4 *R v Sellu; R v Bawa-Garba*

Two high-profile cases intensified the spotlight on GNM in medical settings. David Sellu, a colorectal surgeon, was convicted of GNM in November 2013, and sentenced to thirty months' imprisonment.[24] Mr Sellu was called to attend a 66-year-old man who had developed an abdominal infection after knee surgery. The patient subsequently died as a result of a perforated colon. It was argued that Mr Sellu was grossly negligent in, *inter alia*, failing to ensure antibiotics were administered, failing to chase up test results and delaying surgery to repair the colon beyond the 'window of opportunity' within which the patient might have survived. After his release from prison having served fifteen months of his sentence, Mr Sellu appealed and the Court of Appeal quashed his conviction as unsafe, holding that the judge's direction as to what amounts to grossly negligent behaviour was sub-standard. Even though a specific formula of words was not required, some assistance had to be provided to enable jurors to recognise the dividing line between serious mistakes and conduct that was so 'truly exceptionally bad' that it consequently amounted to being criminal.[25] This decision left the door open for a second trial. The Crown Prosecution Service (CPS) decided not to seek a retrial as Mr Sellu had already served several months in prison.

The second case concerned Dr Bawa-Garba, a Registrar working in paediatrics. A 6-year-old patient, Jack Adcock, died whilst under her care and Dr Bawa-Garba was found guilty of GNM and given a suspended sentence.[26] Subsequently she faced disciplinary proceedings. A Medical Practitioners Tribunal found that her fitness to practise was impaired and she was suspended from practice for a year. The General Medical Council (GMC) felt that her punishment was insufficient to match the gravity of her conduct and

20 Mullock ibid, 353.
21 *R v Broughton* [2020] EWCA 1093.
22 Samanta and Samanta, 'Death Caused by Negligent Medical Care', 297–300.
23 *R v Bawa-Garba* [2016] EWCA Crim 1841, [33].
24 *R v Sellu* [2016] EWCA Crim 1716.
25 Ibid, [152].
26 *Bawa-Garba*, [17] and [18].

successfully appealed that decision, seeking her erasure from the Medical Register. Dr Bawa-Garba, in turn, appealed against the decision to remove her entirely from the Medical Register and the Court of Appeal ruled in her favour.[27] The chain of events surrounding the case aroused significant concern in healthcare practice, not least because there was evidence that Dr Bawa-Garba had been let down by the system in which she worked.[28] She was a junior doctor having just returned to work after maternity leave.[29] Suspicions that she was overworked, inappropriately supervised and constrained by limited resources raised questions about whether she had been made a scapegoat to conceal wider systemic failings that were the main contributing factor to the child's death.

10.5 Impact of the criminal process on healthcare practice

Despite David Sellu's conviction being deemed unsafe, and Hadiza Bawa-Garba's success in contesting erasure from the Medical Register, both cases provoked acute concern within the medical profession. Health professionals, observing a surgeon in his sixties who had fought his way to become a consultant from abject poverty in the country of his birth, Sierra Leone, sent to gaol, were fearful of the prospect of exposure to the criminal justice system and convinced that the CPS were keen to put doctors in the dock.[30] Hadiza Bawa-Garba faced the prospect of never again being able to work in the profession that she had studied and trained for extensively. Add to this the intense media coverage that both cases generated,[31] and the acute pressure that both practitioners would have felt as a consequence of being very much in the public eye, it is apparent that the stigma that attaches to a GNM charge brought against a health professional can profoundly affect not just their career but every aspect of life.

It is unsurprising that health professionals are concerned about the risk that a professional error could result in criminal charges, even imprisonment. The immediate custodial sentence handed down to Mr Sellu shocked his colleagues. While there is no evidence that the threshold for prosecution has been lowered, a change in the general law relating to sentencing means that a doctor convicted of GNM is today more likely to face gaol instead of a suspended sentence. Section 63 of the Sentencing Act 2020 expressly directs judges to take account of the harm caused as well as the culpability of the defendant.[32]

27 Ibid, [98].

28 See Samanta and Samanta, 'Death Caused by Negligent Medical Care'; L Hamilton, *The Final Report of the Independent Review of Gross Negligence Manslaughter and Culpable Homicide* (2019) GMC at [19] (hereafter Hamilton Review).

29 *Bawa-Garba v General Medical Council* [2018] EWCA Civ 1879, [4].

30 J Moorhead, 'They Look for a Scapegoat: A Surgeon's Battle to Clear his Name' *Guardian* (2019) 16 June.

31 Ibid, and see S Boseley, 'Doctor Struck Off Over Boy's Death Allowed to Return to Work' *Guardian* (2019) 9 April.

32 And see H Quirk, 'Sentencing White Coat Crime: The Need for Guidance in Medical Manslaughter Cases' (2013) *Criminal Law Review* 871: *R v Bala Subrahmanyam*

Even if a case does not result in conviction, or never goes to trial, publicity triggered by a police investigation, possible arrest, and the stigma being accused of 'killing' a patient could discourage people from pursuing a medical career, especially in surgery or anaesthetics. But we must not forget that anyone whose gross negligence causes death can be charged with GNM. Some doctors argue that the pressures of practice and the inevitable risks of many treatments make them different. Echoing claims of a malpractice crisis in relation to civil litigation, the spectre of defensive medicine is summoned.[33]

A particular matter which concerns health professionals is fear that the CPS is too ready to prosecute doctors; a fear reinforced by Ferner and McDowell, who in 2006 reported rising rates of prosecution and suggested that the CPS saw prosecuting doctors for GNM as 'an emotionally satisfying way of exacting retribution'.[34] Griffiths and Sanders, who surveyed CPS files from 2004–2009, found no evidence of a rise in the number of prosecutions, rather the contrary might be the case and the CPS were too reluctant to prosecute 'without – to put it crudely – evidence of "badness" on the part of the suspect'.[35] Griffiths and Sanders, however, did observe an increase in police investigations and inquests into medical deaths.[36]

Consternation amongst health professionals about the potential impact of prosecutions for GNM led to the Government ordering a review of the offence in the healthcare environment. The findings highlighted that, even though prosecutions for GNM were infrequent, there was an 'increased sense of fear and trepidation, creating great unease within the healthcare professions'.[37] A perceived randomness and lack of consistency in investigations and prosecutions of GNM exacerbated these fears, and investigations can cause excessive levels of stress.[38] A sense of fear then sets in amongst health professionals and they become cautious about being open and transparent, which adversely affects the capacity for lessons to be learned.[39] The review panel noted that GNM only arises in the most serious cases of a 'truly exceptionally bad' breach of duty resulting in death. In such cases families, the public and health

Kovvali [2013] EWCA Crim 1056. See also S Boseley, 'Doctors Sign Letter Expressing Worry Over Criminalisation of Surgeon' *Guardian* (2015) 6 August.

33 See 9.18 for further discussion.

34 R Ferner and S McDowell, 'Doctors Charged with Manslaughter in the Courts of Medical Practice' (2006) 99 *Journal of RSM* 309; O Quick, 'Prosecuting "Gross" Medical Negligence: Manslaughter, Discretion and the Crown Prosecution Service' (2006) 33 *Journal of Law and Society* 421.

35 D Griffiths and A Sanders, 'The Road to the Dock: Prosecution Decision-Making in Medical Manslaughter Cases' in D Griffiths and A Sanders (eds), *Medicine, Crime and Society* (2013) Cambridge University Press, p 117.

36 Ibid, p 118.

37 Professor Sir Norman Williams, *Gross Negligence Manslaughter in Healthcare: The Report of a Rapid Policy Review* (2018) June, at 5 (hereafter Williams Review).

38 Ibid.

39 Ibid.

professionals themselves rightly expect individuals or their organisations to be held to account. 'No-one is above the law.'[40]

In the aftermath of the *Bawa-Garba* case, the GMC also commissioned an independent review of GNM, the aim of which was to explore how the criminal justice system functions and how it is perceived in healthcare practice.[41] The final report produced twenty-nine recommendations, which were broadly aimed at improving methods of redress for medical mistakes by finding a fair balance between personal and system accountability and learning from errors to safeguard against future adverse events.[42] One consequence of the *Bawa-Garba* case was that it caused tension between the GMC and the doctors it regulates.[43] In an effort to rebuild trust that had been lost between the medical profession and its regulator, both the Government and GMC reviews into GNM recommended that the GMC's right to appeal decisions of the Medical Practitioners Tribunal Service to the High Court should be abolished.[44] Both reviews also recognised that where fatalities occur in health settings, adequate consideration needs to be given to any organisational responsibility that may have contributed to the death.[45]

10.6 Systemic error in the NHS: The Corporate Manslaughter and Corporate Homicide Act 2007 and other offences

Historically, the criminal law was rather ineffectual in addressing systemic fault. A series of high-profile disasters resulting in significant loss of life in the late 1980s highlighted the problem of institutional culpability.[46] These incidents gave rise to the question of whether companies could be guilty of GNM. Judges answered this in the affirmative and so notionally the offence of corporate manslaughter was recognised.[47] The problem was that in order for a prosecution to be successful, the 'identification doctrine' needed to be satisfied, which rested on the ability to locate the senior directing minds of a corporation.[48] Once identified, the guilty minds of a company's senior executives were regarded as the guilty mind of the company itself for the purposes of imputing criminal liability to the organisation. The extent to which this truly focused on systemic as opposed to individual fault though was questionable, as it often caused attention to be placed on pinpointing an individual who represented *the* senior and directing mind of the company, instead of

40 Ibid, [7.2].
41 Hamilton Review.
42 Ibid, [4].
43 Ibid, [188].
44 Williams Review, [6.1]; Hamilton Review, rec 21, p 76. At the time of writing, the recommendations have not yet been implemented.
45 Williams Review, p 9; Hamilton Review, pp 32–35.
46 See, amongst others, the Zeebrugge ferry disaster (1987); the explosion on the Piper Alpha oil rig (1988); the sinking of the Marchioness pleasure boat (1989); and the Hillsborough stadium disaster (1989).
47 *R v P&O European Ferries (Dover) Ltd* [1990] 6 WLUK 21.
48 *Tesco Supermarkets Ltd v Nattrass* [1972] AC 153.

considering collective thought processes. It also created the perverse situation in which it was easier to prosecute smaller companies, but more difficult to prosecute larger companies, because in the latter, management structures were often more diffuse.[49] The Corporate Manslaughter and Corporate Homicide Act 2007 ('the 2007 Act') was introduced to help remedy this problem.

The 2007 Act stipulates that an organisation is guilty of an offence if the way in which its activities are managed or organised causes a person's death, and amounts to a gross breach of a relevant duty of care owed by the organisation to the deceased.[50] It further provides that an organisation is guilty of an offence under this section only if the way in which its activities are managed or organised by its senior management is a substantial element in the breach.[51] An individual cannot be charged with the offence, so organisational fault remains the essential element, with emphasis placed on the way in which senior managers have arranged corporate activities.[52] The role played by senior management in the design, implementation and supervision of systems is crucially important to how the offence created by the Act operates.

Despite its title, the Act applies to a range of Government departments, including National Health Service (NHS) institutions.[53] The applicability of the Act to NHS organisations is significant, recognising that individuals (as with Dr Bawa-Garba and Mr Sellu) are rarely solely responsible for fatal medical errors.[54] Mistakes are more likely to happen because of flaws in the systems in which health professionals operate, such as sub-standard interview procedures leading to improper appointments, inappropriate training, unsuitable supervision, hazardous shift patterns and unsafe premises.[55]

At the time of writing, only one prosecution has been brought against an NHS Trust. In *R v Dr Errol Cornish and Maidstone and Tunbridge Wells NHS Trust*, Coulson J held that there was insufficient evidence for a jury establishing that the Trust had acted in breach of duty in respect of the systems it had in place for interviews and appointments to post, and in relation to its arrangements for conducting appraisals and maintaining an ongoing general level of staff supervision.[56] Although there was at least sufficient evidence for a jury to consider a breach of duty pertaining to the management and organisation of anaesthetic supervision on the specific labour unit at the actual time of the adverse event, it was still insufficient to be characterised as a *gross breach*

49 For example, the case against P&O European Ferries for the role the company played in the Zeebrugge ferry disaster collapsed, whereas in the case of *Kite v OLL and Others* [1994] *Independent* (1994) 9 December, a much smaller company was successfully prosecuted for corporate manslaughter.

50 Corporate Manslaughter and Corporate Homicide Act 2007, s 1(1)(a) and (b).

51 Ibid, s 1(3).

52 Ibid, s 18.

53 Ibid, Sch 1. See also *R v Cornish and Maidstone and Tunbridge Wells NHS Trust* (2016) unreported, ruling by Coulson J on 26 January 2016, [12].

54 *R v Sellu* [2016] EWCA Crim 1716; *R v Bawa-Garba* [2016] EWCA Crim 1841.

55 *Cornish*, [81].

56 Ibid, [93] and [101].

of duty for the purposes of satisfying the Act.[57] There was evidence of some confusion as to precisely who the defendant's designated supervisor was at the relevant time, but it had no direct bearing on the outcome of the case, because a number of different colleagues attended at various stages who were all suitably qualified to provide appropriate supervision and who indeed did so. The charge was accordingly dismissed on the basis that the defendant Trust had no case to answer.[58]

The liberal interpretation given in *Cornish* to the definition of senior management within an NHS organisation means that it was unnecessary to identify the precise tier or the precise individuals involved in the Trust's management.[59] A major obstacle was proving whether the alleged breach constituted a *gross breach*, which will always be difficult to overcome in respect of large NHS organisations.[60] Alongside that, prosecutors will also encounter problems of causation in proving that the systemic failure caused the death of a patient.[61] Any prosecution requires the consent of the Director of Public Prosecutions, and Trusts convicted of corporate manslaughter face unlimited fines and/or a publicity order.[62] Although it has been acknowledged that the 2007 Act is unlikely to result in many prosecutions,[63] its implementation has prompted disquiet about the potential impact of the legislation on NHS Trusts.[64]

Health and Safety laws can also be invoked to address systemic error in healthcare. For example, section 3(1) of the Health and Safety at Work Act 1974 imposes a duty on an employer to conduct his undertaking in such a way as to ensure, so far as is reasonably practicable, that persons not in his employment are not exposed to risks to their health or safety. Mid Staffordshire NHS Trust was prosecuted by the Health Service Executive under this section for several systemic deficiencies that resulted in several patient deaths. The Trust pleaded guilty and was fined £500,000. In 2021, East Kent Hospitals University Trust was charged by the Care Quality Commission over the death of a seven-day-old baby, Harry Richford.[65] In the first prosecution of its kind, the regulator charged the Trust with a breach of regulation 12 of the Health and Social Care Act 2008 (Regulated Activities) Regulations 2014, which compels Trusts to provide safe care and treatment.[66] In exposing the child to a significant risk

57 Ibid, [108].
58 Ibid, [113].
59 Ibid, [79].
60 Ibid, [106]–[108].
61 Ibid, [106]–[109].
62 Corporate Manslaughter and Corporate Homicide Act 2007, s 1(6), s 10 and s 17.
63 V Roper, 'The Corporate Manslaughter and Corporate Homicide Act 2007—A 10-Year Review' (2018) 82 *Journal of Criminal Law* 48, 64–70.
64 S O'Malley, 'Corporate Manslaughter and Corporate Homicide Act 2007: Implications for Healthcare Providers' (2008) 3 *Journal of Management & Marketing in Healthcare* 297; C Dyer, 'New Law Puts NHS Trusts at Risk of Charges of Corporate Manslaughter' (2008) 336 *BMJ* 741.
65 D Campbell, 'NHS Trust Pleads Guilty After "Wholly Avoidable" Death of Week-Old Baby' *Guardian* (2021), 19 April.
66 Ibid.

of avoidable harm, the Trust admitted that it failed to provide safe care and treatment for the child and so pleaded guilty to the offence.[67]

10.7 Non-fatal medical injury

Given that GNM only applies if the patient dies, doctors who were grossly negligent showing no regard for their patient's welfare and causing serious injury short of death faced little risk of criminal liability. Such 'immunity' could be a thing of the past.[68]

Parliament has created a new offence. You may have read reports of investigations into appalling care at some hospitals, recounting how patients were left to lie in filthy beds, with dressings left unchanged and not being fed.[69] The conduct of some staff appears more morally culpable than that of some doctors convicted of manslaughter. Under the Mental Health[70] and Mental Capacity[71] Acts, wilful neglect of a mentally ill or mentally incapacitated patient has long been a crime. Sections 20–25 of the Criminal Justice and Courts Act 2015 extends the offence of ill treatment or wilful neglect to cover such misconduct by all paid care workers, which includes doctors and nurses. Care providers too are made subject to the Act. Wilful neglect, unlike GNM, focuses on the culpability of the health professional's conduct, not on the chance of outcome.[72]

More generally, the conviction of surgeon Ian Paterson under sections 18 and 20 of the Offences Against the Person Act 1861 marks a possible new direction, expanding the role of criminal law and medical malpractice.[73] Over many years, Paterson had *inter alia* performed so-called 'cleavage sparing' (partial) mastectomies, mutilating patients while leading them to believe they were receiving appropriate treatment for breast cancer. Paterson told some patients that they had breast cancer when they did not.[74]

Section 20 of the 1861 Act establishes a crime of unlawfully and maliciously wounding or inflicting grievous bodily harm. No intent to harm need be proved, nor need any assault be proved.[75] Section 18 establishes the more serious offence; causing grievous bodily harm *with intent*. Read literally almost all surgery would amount to a crime. Nor will patient consent alone justify the

67 Ibid.

68 For an interesting progressive analysis, see A Farrell, A Alghrani and M Kazarian, 'Gross Negligence Manslaughter in Healthcare: Time for a Restorative Justice Approach?' (2020) 28 *Med Law Rev* 526.

69 A shocking example is the *Independent Inquiry into Care Provided by Mid Staffordshire NHS Foundation Trust January 2005–March 2009* (2010) HC 375–I.

70 Mental Health Act 1983, s 127.

71 Mental Capacity Act 2005, s 44.

72 A Alghrani *et al*, 'Healthcare Scandals in the NHS' (2011) 37 *J Med Ethics* 230.

73 A Mullock, 'Surgical Harm, Consent, and English Criminal Law: When Should "Bad-Apple" Surgeons Be Prosecuted?' (2021) 21(4) *Medical Law International* 343.

74 For other examples of prosecutions see Mullock, ibid, 352–355.

75 Section 47 creates the crime of causing actual bodily harm.

surgery. In its controversial decision in *R v Brown*[76] the House of Lords held that consent is no defence where a person inflicts actual or serious bodily harm on another.[77] Consent is necessary but not sufficient. The bodily invasion must be justified as in the public interest. Their Lordships confirmed the existence of the 'medical exception'. As Lord Mustill put it: '[S]urgical treatment which requires a degree of bodily invasion well on the upper side of the critical level will nevertheless be legitimate *if performed in accordance and with good medical practice and with the consent of the patient*.'[78] Thus normally surgery such as mastectomy carried out in accordance with good practice and informed consent falls within the 'medical exception'.[79] As Mullock says, this means that 'in order to establish criminal liability in a situation where a surgeon appears to have harmed a patient in a way that might be criminal, the surgery must sit outwith the medical exception'.[80] This could occur where a patient has not provided a valid consent to a procedure,[81] or, even where she has, that the procedure in question falls outside the definition of reasonable surgery.[82] In *Paterson*, the prosecution focused on the absence of valid consent rather than the more difficult question of whether the surgery itself was reasonable.[83] While Paterson's patients had signed consent forms, their consent was invalidated by the false information given to them by Paterson.[84]

10.8 What next?

The role of the criminal law in addressing medical malpractice is contested. The decision in *Paterson* opens the door to an increased possibility that non-fatal malpractice may result in prosecution, eliminating the element of moral luck inherent in GNM. But that might mean more health professionals end up in the dock. Improving patient safety is a common objective. Arguments that, save in the most blatant case of disregard for patient welfare, resorting to the criminal process does little to advance patient safety and can be unjust

76 *R v Brown* [1993] UKHL 19.

77 Ibid, 213.

78 Ibid, 258–259.

79 To qualify for the medical exception the procedure must be performed by a licensed medical practitioner. See *R v BM* [2018] EWCA Crim 560. Note that legislation may expressly limit or ban certain controversial 'surgeries', such as the Female Genital Mutilation Act 2003, and the Health and Care Act 2022, Part 5 (hymenoplasty).

80 Mullock, 'Surgical Harm', 7.

81 Simon Bramhall was convicted of assault by beating as a result of his practice of liver branding during surgery (*R (Bramhall) v GMC* [2019] EWHC 3525). A five-month suspension order was imposed by the Medical Practitioners Tribunal in 2020. The GMC successfully appealed on the ground that it was too lenient in *GMC v Bramhall* [2021] EWHC 2109 (Admin). At a fresh hearing of the tribunal in 2022 he was struck off the register. See 2.15 above.

82 Mullock, 'Surgical Harm', 349.

83 See M Brazier and S Fovargue, 'Transforming Wrong into Right: What is 'Proper Medical Treatment'? in S Fovargue and A Mullock, *The Legitimacy of Medical Treatment: What Role le for the Medical Exception?* (2016) Routledge, pp 12–31.

84 Mullock 'Surgical Harm', 349.

to doctors attract support.[85] Addressing patient safety *Merry and McCall Smith* distinguish between *errors* and *violations*, the latter involving deliberate wrongdoing, including deliberate risk-taking. They contend that criminalising error and an emphasis on blame is counterproductive, likely to inhibit learning from errors reducing the occurrence of error.[86] Fear of the criminal process may make doctors less ready to acknowledge error.[87] *Merry and McCall Smith* advance a strong case that in the context of deterrence and prevention, the criminal law is ineffective.

This chapter does no more than introduce the principal issues in relation to the criminal law and medical malpractice, issues which form part of a broader debate about whether English law should (contrary to the common law tradition)[88] criminalise negligence generally. Any case that health professionals should be treated more favourably than, say, electricians or building site managers needs powerful argument, if it is not to be seen as simply privileging doctors. Notably *Merry and McCall Smith* contend that their diagnosis of, and prescription for, the prevention of errors applies in all the many settings in which life or limb are at risk.

85 See M Brazier and A Alghrani, 'Fatal Medical Malpractice and Criminal Liability' (2009) 25 *Professional Negligence* 49.

86 A Merry and W Brookbanks (eds), *Merry and McCall Smith's, Errors, Medicine and the Law* (2nd edn, 2017) Cambridge University Press. And see O Quick, *Regulating Patient Safety: The End of Professional Dominance?* (2017) Cambridge University Press.

87 But see now the statutory duty of candour at 2.6 above.

88 For a comparative perspective, see M Kazarian, *Criminalising Medical Malpractice: A Comparative Perspective* (2020) Routledge.

Chapter 11

COMPLAINTS AND REDRESS

11.1 Introduction

In this chapter we consider the schemes by which patients seek accountability when things go wrong with their or their relatives' treatment. We consider the interaction between mechanisms designed to provide answers and redress for patients and those that seek to ensure learning to improve patient safety. In the second part of the chapter, we consider criticisms of the tort system and alternative proposals.

11.2 Raising complaints and concerns

When injury results from medical treatment, patients or their relatives seek accountability. Such cases are not limited to the kinds of injury that would give rise to a claim for clinical negligence, but may include poor care, rudeness and a failure to have regard for the welfare of the patient. In these and other instances, patients may seek redress when they feel that health professionals have let them down, or they might simply want assurance that lessons have been learned and mistakes will not be repeated. Patients and relatives in this position have a bewildering array of options beyond the possibility of taking legal action:

(1) Complain to the appropriate professional regulator. Some may wish the responsible health professionals to be disciplined and raise a concern with a professional regulator such as the General Medical Council (GMC). We examined in Chapter 2 ways in which that might be achieved.
(2) Complain to the Care Quality Commission (CQC). In Chapter 2 we discussed the role of the CQC, the independent regulator of health and adult social care in England, which registers providers and monitors, inspects and rates services. The CQC will not take up complaints from individual patients and relatives but does encourage 'feedback' about poor care to be reported to them and will consider how well organisations handle complaints as part of its inspections.
(3) Complain locally to the organisation that provided the care. National Health Service (NHS) complaints guidance sets out mechanisms to provide feedback on treatment and care, or to raise a formal

complaint.[1] Regulations introduced in 2009 launched a single complaints system across health and social care, with two stages.[2] The first stage is to complain locally. All providers are required to have an NHS complaints procedure. The aim is to provide patients with an explanation and, where appropriate, an apology, remedial action and financial compensation for direct and indirect loss.[3] The NHS receives around 80,000 complaints a year.[4] As we explore below, the system is much criticised. There is inconsistency in how organisations handle complaints and they are too often seen negatively rather than as a learning tool.[5]

(4) Complain to the Ombudsman. Final decisions on complaints that have not been resolved locally can progress to the Health Service Commissioner for England (the Ombudsman), which is supported by an independent organisation of around 400 staff called the Parliamentary and Health Service Ombudsman (PHSO).[6] From 1996, the Ombudsman was empowered to investigate all aspects of NHS treatment and care, including action taken as a result of the exercise of the clinical judgement of doctors or nurses.[7] The PHSO conducts initial checks to see if it can deal with the complaint, and will not usually investigate complaints that could be resolved through legal action.

If it decides to investigate, information is gathered. Dealing with complaints about clinical matters is not easy. Identifying if a complaint has substance is time-consuming. Records must be obtained with the complainant's consent. Clinical advice is required and often must be sought from specialists outside the Ombudsman's office. The Ombudsman's powers of inquiry are extensive. He and his staff investigate in private.

1 See DHSC, *NHS Complaints Guidance* (updated 2021). The right to complain is set out in the NHS Constitution (updated 2021), provided for under the Health Act 2009, s 1.

2 The Local Authority Social Services and National Health Service Complaints (England) Regulations 2009, SI 2009/309. The 2009 Regulations have been amended several times. Most recently, the Provision of Integrated Care Regulations 2019, SI 2019/248, Pt 3 extended complaints processes to new bodies to reflect provision under Integrated Care Provider contracts.

3 See Parliamentary and Health Service Ombudsman (hereafter PHSO), *Service Model Policy and Guidance* (v 19, 2021), Annex P. The PHSO guidance provides a scale by which financial redress might be recommended. For example, at level 1, a one-off event that causes frustration or worry would usually attract an apology. At level 6 a devastating irreversible impact or avoidable death might attract a payment of £10,000 or more.

4 NHS Digital, *Data on Written Complaints in the NHS 2020–21* (2021).

5 PHSO, *Making Complaints Count* (2020) HC 390, p 8.

6 The Ombudsman makes final decisions on complaints that have not been resolved by the NHS. The post was created in the National Health Service Reorganisation Act 1973. The Ombudsman's powers are set out in the Health Service Commissioners Act 1993 (as amended).

7 The Health Service Commissioners (Amendment) Act 1996.

They will contact all hospital or primary care staff involved in the complaint and seek their comments. The Ombudsman has complete control of the investigation. If cooperation from hospital staff or administrators is not forthcoming, the production of records and documents may be ordered and staff may be compelled to testify to the Ombudsman.[8] Investigations must generally be concluded within twelve months[9] after which, if a complaint is upheld, the PHSO makes recommendations as to how to put matters right.

The PHSO has faced criticism for being too slow and for communication failures.[10] Cases are published on the PHSO website. One tells of Mrs W, whose husband died of COVID-19. She complained about nursing care, poor communication, and the disposal of her husband's belongings after his death. The Ombudsman recommended that the Trust should apologise and explain how it would ensure that mistakes were not repeated in future. It was recommended that the Trust should pay £500 to Mrs W in recognition of the distress the failings caused.[11]

The Ombudsman deals with NHS cases. Private cases can generally be escalated to the Independent Sector Complaints Adjudication Service.

(5) Raise a safety issue with the Healthcare Services Safety Investigations Body (HSSIB). As we discussed in Chapter 2, patient safety has, at last, moved up the political agenda.[12] For safety issues that occurred after 2017,[13] a new Healthcare Safety Investigation Branch (HSIB) could initiate an investigation. The HSIB was renamed the Healthcare Services Safety Investigations Body (HSSIB) and put on a statutory footing in Part 4 of the Health and Care Act 2022. There are two programmes: a national programme and a dedicated maternity programme. The aim is not to attribute blame or liability.[14] In the interests of openness, patients, relatives and staff come together with the sole purpose of learning in order to improve safety.

(6) Petition for a public inquiry. In particularly serious cases of repeated error or bad practice, patients and families may demand a formal public inquiry. Several different procedures exist within the NHS. An NHS

8 Health Service Commissioners Act 1993, ss 11, 12.

9 Health Service Commissioner for England (Complaint Handling) Act 2015 amends the Health Service Commissioners Act 1993, s 14.

10 See, for example PHSO, *Report of a Review into the Parliamentary and Health Service Ombudsman's Handling of Mr Nic Hart's case from August 2014 to December 2017* (2020).

11 PHSO, *Mid and South Essex NHS FT* (Ref P-001137) (2021) 14 October.

12 See 2.6 and 2.19 above. And see NHS England and NHS Improvement, *The NHS Patient Safety Strategy* (2019).

13 Set up in response to DHSC, *Learning not Blaming: Response to 3 Reports on Patient Safety* (2015).

14 Health and Social Care Act 2022, s 110(4).

inquiry may be established under section 2 of the National Health Service Act 2006,[15] whereby the Health Minister has a general power to do anything calculated to facilitate the discharge of his duty. In serious cases, an independent team will be drafted in to conduct the investigation. Such an inquiry will be conducted by a small committee, usually consisting of a legally qualified chairman and two medical practitioners, one from the same specialty as the person whose competence is in issue. The complainant and the subjects of the complaint may be legally represented, and cross-examination of witnesses is allowed. The committee's findings of fact are then submitted to the staff concerned for further comment. Finally, the committee reports its findings and recommendations. The inquiry procedure can be effective, but if hospital staff refuse cooperation the procedure may break down altogether. No one can be compelled to attend the inquiry. NHS inquiries of this kind are relatively informal and lack coercive powers. The Morecambe Bay Investigation, chaired by Dr Bill Kirkup, looked at maternity and neonatal services between 2004 and 2013. It made forty-four recommendations for the Trust and NHS.[16]

At the other end of the spectrum, the Department of Health and Social Care may set up a formal, independent inquiry under the Inquiries Act 2005[17] where the matter is of sufficient public concern. A public inquiry report into the regulatory failures at Mid Staffordshire (the 2013 Francis Inquiry), referred to in Chapter 2, made 290 recommendations designed to effect culture change.[18] The Infected Blood Inquiry referred to in Chapter 12 is ongoing at the time of writing. Its brief is to investigate the cases in which NHS patients were given infected blood and inflected blood products.[19]

Inquiry principles have sought to ensure transparency, as patients will have less confidence in inquiries held behind closed doors. Government fears the cost of public inquiries both in cash and to the reputation of the NHS. Claims that they do not offer good value for money[20] are forcefully rebutted by arguments that, without them, the state will not be held accountable.[21]

15 Formerly NHS Act 1977, s 2.

16 DHSC, *Morecambe Bay Investigation Report* (2015) March. See 2.1 above.

17 Previously, formal statutory NHS inquiries of this kind were conducted (publicly or privately) under the National Health Service Act 1977, s 84. One famous example is the public inquiry into children's heart surgery at the Bristol Royal Infirmary. See *Learning from Bristol – The Report of the Public Inquiry into Children's Heart Surgery at the Bristol Royal Infirmary* 1984–1995 (2001) CM 5207 (1) (hereafter Bristol Inquiry Report).

18 *Report of the Mid Staffordshire NHS Foundation Trust Public Inquiry*, chaired by Robert Francis QC (2013) HC 947, February.

19 See Infected Blood Inquiry website www.infectedbloodinquiry.org.uk/.

20 See S Jenkins, 'Public Inquiries are Institutionally Corrupt, We Should Just Give the Money to Victims' *Guardian* (2021) 17 June.

21 See D Johnson MP, 'Simon Jenkins is Wrong about the NHS Infected Blood Inquiry' *Guardian* (2021) 21 June.

The Inquiries Act gives Ministers the power to convert other types of inquiry, both statutory and non-statutory, into an Inquiry Act inquiry[22] at which point the Minister can change the terms of reference. The findings of an inquiry are not determinative of liability.[23] Instead the aim is to restore public confidence and ensure that mistakes are not repeated. Under section 19(4)(d) of the Inquiries Act, wide-ranging restrictions on public access may be applied according to the requirements of the particular inquiry.

11.3 Conflicting goals?

Of the methods briefly outlined in the previous section, there are stark contrasts in ethos and purpose.[24] Whereas the HSSIB and inquiries focus on learning to enhance patient safety, clinical negligence attributes blame and promotes financial redress. The NHS Constitution[25] sets out a patient right to have complaints properly investigated and to compensation where harm is caused by negligent treatment. But the array of complaints mechanisms is bewildering and potentially overlapping. Some mechanisms can take years to resolve, leading to terrible pressures on patients, families and health professionals.

The impact of complaints in their various forms on health professionals is often underemphasised. And yet Black, Asian and minority ethnic staff groups have been shown to suffer disproportionate levels of disciplinary action.[26] For all health professionals, when 'human factors' – environmental, organisation and human characteristics that can impact on safety – lead to something going wrong, the sense of personal responsibility if often acute. Slow and unsupportive investigations into concerns and complaints can exacerbate the adverse effects. Between 2005 and 2013, twenty-eight doctors were reported to have died from suicide or suspected suicide whilst under investigation by the GMC.[27] Complaints, inquests and negligence litigation can be equally

22 See s 15.

23 Inquiries Act 2005, s 2.

24 On the importance of the various mechanisms for redress being 'joined-up' see E Cave, 'Redress in the NHS' (2011) 27 *Journal of Professional Negligence* 139.

25 DHSC, *The NHS Constitution for England* (updated 2021).

26 See NHS Equality and Diversity Council, *Data Analysis Report for NHS Trusts* (2018): It is around 1.24 times more likely that BAME staff will face disciplinary action than white counterparts in NHS Trusts in England; NHS England, *A Fair Experience for All: Closing the Ethnicity Gap in Rates of Disciplinary Action Across the NHS Workforce* (2019). And in relation to the GMC, see GMC, 'GMC Targets Elimination of Disproportionate Complaints and Training Inequalities' (2021) 18 May.

27 GMC, *Doctors who Commit Suicide While Under GMC Fitness to Practise Investigation* (2014). The GMC improved support of doctors under investigation in the GMC, *Supporting Vulnerable Doctors Programme* (2020). But see C Dyer,

traumatising. This in turn can lead to defensiveness, to emphasis on protecting colleagues and to distrust of investigating organisations. Health professionals need to know that they will be supported appropriately whilst investigations are underway.

11.4 Reforming the complaints process

The two-stage complaints process requires that complaints are made locally and that a final decision can be made by the Ombudsman. The process has come under fire repeatedly in public inquiries[28] and Health Select Committee reports.[29] A good complaints process has two key goals. The first one is to enhance system learning to promote patient safety. This requires openness and candour on the part of health professionals. But some are fearful of admitting wrong lest it should result in litigation with the stress and reputational damage it can bring. Reforms have attempted to effect culture change by stressing the appropriateness of apologies when errors and mistakes are made. Section 2 of the Compensation Act 2006 states that '[a]n apology, or offer of treatment or other redress, shall not of itself amount to an admission of negligence or breach of statutory duty',[30] and a duty of candour is now set out in statute[31] and professional guidance.[32] The second goal is to deliver suitable and timely redress to patients and families. Yet there is evidence that some litigate simply to find out what really happened,[33] or complain to the GMC that a doctor is not fit to practise because they do not get the answers they need by raising a complaint locally.[34]

'GMC and Trust Facing Legal Action Over Case of Doctor Who Took His Own Life' (2021) 373 *BMJ* n1525.

28 *The Independent Inquiry into Care provided by Mid Staffordshire NHS Foundation Trust* (2010) (Chair: Robert Francis QC); *Report of the Mid Staffordshire NHS Foundation Trust Public Inquiry* (2013).

29 Health Select Committee, *Complaints and Litigation*, HC 786-I 2010–12 (2011); *Complaints and Raising Concerns*, HC 350 2014–15 (2015).

30 But see P Vines, 'Apologies and Civil Liability in the UK: A View from Elsewhere' (2008) 12(2) *Edinburgh Law Review* 200 commenting on the brevity of the provision which does not define 'apology' and seems to add little to existing law.

31 Health and Social Care Act 2008 (Regulated Activities) Regulations 2014, reg 20. Discussed at 2.6 above.

32 NHS Resolution, *Saying Sorry* (2018); GMC, *Good Clinical Practice* (2013), para 55; GMC, *Openness and Honesty When Things Go Wrong: The Professional Duty of Candour* (2015) July, discussed at 2.6 above.

33 See NHS Resolution and The Behavioural Insights Team, *Behavioural Insights into Patient Motivation to Make a Claim for Clinical Negligence* (2018) https://resolution.nhs.uk/resources/behavioural-insights-into-patient-motivation-to-make-a-claim-for-clinical-negligence/.

34 There is evidence that many complaints put to the GMC are from patients who feel there is nowhere else to complain effectively: see Baroness Julia Cumberlege (Chair), *First Do No Harm – The Report of the Independent Medicines and Medical Devices Safety Review* (2020) (hereafter Cumberlege Review), para 2.45.

The 2009 Complaints Regulations have been amended several times. In 2019 the Health Select Committee considered that, notwithstanding repeated calls for change, the will to improve local NHS complaints handling had 'fizzled out'.[35] A further view promulgated in the 2020 report of the Independent Medicines and Medical Devices Safety Review, chaired by Baroness Julia Cumberlege (hereafter the Cumberlege Review), noted that patients struggle to navigate the complaints system.[36] The Cumberlege Review recommended that all organisations who take complaints from the public should designate a non-executive member of the board to oversee processes and outcomes and ensure that appropriate action is taken. Its ultimate aim would be to provide a more streamlined model for complaints that would provide faster resolution for patients.[37] The Government promised a Patient Safety Action Plan to set out ways to improve the complaints process.[38]

The second stage of the complaints process has also come under fire. The Government committed to a speedier and more transparent process but a draft Public Services Ombudsman Bill in 2016 did not proceed to parliamentary scrutiny. A 2019 report showed that the Ombudsman 'completed fewer investigations, more slowly'.[39] During the COVID-19 crisis a backlog of 2,500 complaints developed and the Ombudsman decided to look only at the most serious complaints.[40]

11.5 An attack on tort

Amending the complaints process is necessary, but it is not sufficient to address problems associated with redress and patient safety. Clinical negligence litigation has come under sustained attack for many years.[41] The Bristol Inquiry Report[42] called for the 'abolition of clinical negligence litigation, taking clinical error out of the courts and the tort system'.[43] Litigation should be replaced by effective systems for identifying and addressing errors. Complaints and redress, including financial redress, should be aligned.

In 1997, Professor Atiyah called for the abolition of recovery in tort for personal injuries, highlighting that the system was inefficient and expensive and

35 *PHSO Annual Scrutiny 2017/18: Towards a Modern and Effective Ombudsman Service* (2019).
36 Cumberlege Review, para 2.45.
37 Ibid, paras 2.37–2.38.
38 DHSC, *Government Response to the Report of the Independent Medicines and Medical Devices Safety Review* (2021).
39 *PHSO Annual Scrutiny 2017/18: Towards a Modern and Effective Ombudsman Service* (2019).
40 See PHSO, 'Changes to the Way we Handle Complaints About the NHS' (2021) 4 August.
41 See in particular, P Cane and PS Atiyah, *Atiyah's Accidents, Compensation and the Law* (8th edn, 2013) Cambridge University Press.
42 See Bristol Inquiry Report, p 367.
43 Ibid, ch 26; and see DH Expert Group, *An Organisation with a Memory* (2000).

that the defendant wrongdoer rarely paid damages out of their own pocket.[44] As such, the moral premise on which the tort is predicated – the notion that a careless person who has caused harm to another by their actions should make good any loss suffered – becomes questionable.[45] In response, Professor Burrows (now Lord Burrows of the Supreme Court) made the counter point that the benefit of tortious liability derives from the fact that the tort system pins legal responsibility on the defendant and, even though they are unlikely to ever pay damages themselves, they are fixed with an obligation to ensure that payment is made.[46] Notwithstanding this, Atiyah's view remained that the tort system for compensating personal injuries should be replaced by a system of compulsory, no-fault first-party insurance for road accidents, and for all other injuries people should be encouraged, but not required, to take out first-party insurance.[47] These ideas were not acted upon, but they have recently been given a new lease of life by Lord Sumption, who, writing extra-judicially, reiterated the inefficiencies of the tort system as a compensation scheme.[48] Four problems with the torts system are worthy of elaboration:

(1) It is unpredictable. The injured claimant, on whom the burden of proving negligence falls, cannot know in advance whether they will receive any monetary compensation. Lord Sumption noted that one problem with negligence is that it 'often misses the target, or hits the wrong target'.[49]
(2) It is unfair. What is the justification for giving X, who can attribute his injury to human error, full compensation, and leaving Y, whose injury has some other cause, to struggle on state benefits?
(3) It is not conducive to patient safety. Litigation generates distrust and defensiveness. The blame culture has been perceived as adverse to the promotion of patient safety and proper accountability for error.[50] As we discussed in Chapter 9, the litigation system has generated dissatisfaction on the part of patients and led to claims of defensiveness,[51] concealment and low morale on the part of health professionals. Solicitors and claims management companies tout for business, inviting claims with advertising campaigns. The Constitutional Affairs Committee reported in 2006 that the compensation culture is a myth but that the *cost* of the belief, in terms of risk aversion, is real.[52]

44 PS Atiyah, *The Damages Lottery* (1997) Bloomsbury.
45 Ibid.
46 Andrew Burrows, *Understanding the Law of Obligations: Essays on Contract, Law and Restitution* (1998) Hart, p 123.
47 Discussed by Lord Sumption, 'Abolishing Personal Injuries Law – A Project' (2018) 34 *Journal of Professional Negligence* 113, 113.
48 Ibid, at 118.
49 Ibid.
50 See A Merry and A McCall Smith, *Errors, Medicine and the Law* (2001) Cambridge University Press, p 217.
51 See for example O Ortashi *et al*, 'The Practice of Defensive Medicine Among Hospital Doctors in the United Kingdom' (2013) 42 *BMC Medical Ethics* 14.
52 House of Commons, Constitutional Affairs Committee, *Compensation Culture Third Report of Session 2005–06*, HC 754–I, para 111. And see Lord Young,

(4) It is costly. In 2022 the pressure for reform is exacerbated by unsustainable costs. As we discussed in Chapter 9, cash payments have quadrupled over the last fifteen years to £2.2 billion in 2020–1,[53] which in turn impacts severely on Trust finances.[54]

11.6 Speedy redress schemes

Despite a searching critique of its problems, Lord Sumption concluded that the fault-based negligence system would survive in England, mainly because of problems perceived with viable alternatives.[55] He suggested that concentrated benefits but diffused costs would allow tort to maintain its appeal, and that predominantly public notions about personal responsibility and the function of the law would cause the tort system to survive. Lord Sumption's suggested improvements therefore focused on some statutory intervention, and indeed some additional judicial control, in order to restrain the problems associated with the rising costs.[56]

A statutory scheme was suggested by Sir Liam Donaldson, then Chief Medical Officer (CMO), in his report *Making Amends*.[57] Sir Liam condemned the tort system in terms of its financial and emotional ramifications, especially in relation to low-value claims. He proposed reform of the existing negligence system, incorporating four main elements:

(1) an investigation of the incident which is alleged to have caused harm and of the harm that has resulted;
(2) provision of an explanation to the patient and of the action proposed to prevent repetition;
(3) development and delivery of a package of care providing remedial treatment, therapy and arrangements for continuing care where needed;
(4) payments for pain and suffering, out of pocket expenses and care or treatment which the NHS could provide.[58]

The report provided the basis for the NHS Redress Act 2006. The Act provided an alternative to litigation in the form of a broad structure for a new

Common Sense, Common Safety (2010); J Hyde, 'Compensation Culture is "Media-Created" Myth – Dyson' (2013) *Law Society Gazette* 25 March referring to a lecture on the topic by Lord Dyson MR.

53 NHS Resolution, *Annual Statistics (Supplementary Annual Statistics, Table 1A)* (2021).

54 NAO, *Managing the Costs of Clinical Negligence in Trusts* (2017), p 6.

55 Lord Sumption, 'Abolishing Personal Injuries Law – A Project' (2018) 34 *Journal of Professional Negligence* 113, 120. We consider alternatives to tort in the next section.

56 Ibid, 120–121. And see J Morgan, 'Abolishing Personal Injuries Law? A Response to Lord Sumption' (2018) 34 *Journal of Professional Negligence* 122.

57 CMO, *Making Amends: A Consultation Paper* (2003), p 7.

58 CMO, *Making Amends*, p 16.

fast-track scheme for claims under £20,000. However, it requires secondary legislation which, in England, now seems unlikely.[59]

Section 17 of the Act gave the National Assembly for Wales power to introduce an NHS Redress Scheme. Wales has been operating a successful[60] optional Speedy Resolution Scheme for low-value claims since 2005. The NHS Redress (Wales) Measure 2008 is designed to align complaints and redress. The NHS (Concerns, Complaints and Redress Arrangements) (Wales) Regulations[61] introduce a single portal for 'concerns' which include 'a complaint, a notification of an incident concerning patient safety or, save in respect of concerns notified in respect of primary care providers or independent providers, a claim for compensation [under £25,000]'.[62] When a concern is raised, a responsible body generally has thirty days to investigate the issue and make a written response. This might incorporate an apology or action taken, and include a right to take the case to the NHS Ombudsman or request further information. The relevant body considers whether there is a 'qualifying liability in tort' in which case the redress process is activated. Unlike the proposed English scheme, it attempts to bring together a fragmented system of redress and constitutes a credible attempt to offer a just and unified approach to redress.[63]

In England, calls for a redress scheme were renewed in 2020 in the report of the Cumberlege Review.[64] The Review recognised the difficulties faced by patients seeking to prove negligence, but did not call for the route to litigation to be closed, as some find value in it. Instead, the Review called for a new Redress Agency operating a non-adversarial process for anyone harmed by medicines or medical devices, with a focus on systemic as opposed to individual failings. Like the complaints system, it would provide financial and non-monetary redress and support. Its ultimate aim would be to provide a more streamlined model to provide a faster resolution for patients.[65] However, the Government rejected calls for a Redress Agency in 2021, saying: 'We do not believe that a redress agency would make products safer and support our commitment to patient safety.'[66]

59 See A-M Farrell and S Devaney, 'Making Amends or Making Things Worse? Clinical Negligence Reform and Patient Redress in England' (2007) 27(4) *Legal Studies* 630.

60 See M Rosser, 'The Changing Face of Clinical Negligence in Wales' (2010) 3 *Journal of Personal Injury Law* 162, at 169.

61 SI 2011/704 (amended SI 2011/1706).

62 SI 2011/704 – Explanatory note.

63 An alternative timely resolution scheme was proposed by Lord Young, *Common Sense, Common Safety* (2010) based on extension of the Road Traffic Accident Personal Injury Scheme. But though the fast track web portal was extended to cover Public and Employers' Liability personal injury claims in 2013, clinical negligence was excluded due to its complex nature.

64 Cumberlege Review, recommendation 3.

65 Cumberlege Review, paras 2.37–2.38.

66 DHSC, *Government Response to the Report of the Independent Medicines and Medical Devices Safety Review* (2021), 3.1.

11.7 Birth injuries[67]

Pressure to introduce a redress scheme is particularly intense in relation to birth injury cases, which are typically high value. NHS Resolution's Early Notification scheme[68] requires hospitals to report cases of severe brain injury in newborn babies so that NHS Resolution can communicate with the parents swiftly in order to better support them and to improve learning. Early Notification can facilitate redress without either litigation or a complaint. There is potential for NHS Resolution to roll this out more widely.

Additionally, in 2017 the Government consulted on a new fast-track insurance-based compensation scheme for children suffering neurological injury at birth called the Rapid Resolution and Redress scheme (RRR).[69] It would be administered by NHS Resolution and provide a viable alternative to litigation. There would be two stages to the scheme: the first stage investigates potentially avoidable cases of neurological birth injury and the second stage provides support and compensation to families. The scheme would provide a one-off payment of around £50,000–£100,000 when the child is around the age of 4 and then annual in-kind payments to support care. Elements of the proposal have since been initiated, but the 2021 *Report into the Safety of Maternity Care* recommendation that it be fully implemented seems increasingly unlikely to be acted upon.[70]

11.8 Alternatives to tort

So should we abolish clinical negligence litigation? Tort is not the only means of providing compensation to victims of misadventure. An alternative is no-fault compensation. In *Making Amends*[71] Sir Liam Donaldson rejected a no-fault medical injury scheme, but in the light of escalating costs and the failure to set out a comprehensive NHS Redress scheme, has the time come to revisit this recommendation?

In 1974 New Zealand introduced a publicly funded accident compensation scheme, which covers medical injury within comprehensive provision for compensation for personal injury from all causes. Whilst the scheme has been commended for providing timely compensation and effective complaints resolution, there remain concerns surrounding patient safety.[72] But the provision of a no-fault scheme does not necessarily render health professionals unaccountable. A Patient Safety team was introduced to address systemic

67 And see 9.18 above.

68 See NHS Resolution, *The Early Notification Scheme Progress Report* (2019).

69 DHSC, *Rapid Resolution and Redress Scheme for Severe Birth Injury* (2017).

70 House of Commons Health and Social Care Committee, *The Safety of Maternity Services in England* (2021) HC 19, paras 98, 102, rec 18.

71 CMO, *Making Amends*, p 7.

72 See M Bismark and R Paterson, 'No-fault Compensation in New Zealand: Harmonizing Injury Compensation, Provider Accountability and Patient Safety' (2006) 25(1) *Health Affairs* 278.

problems and an independent health ombudsman, the Health and Disability Commissioner,[73] mediates, resolves complaints and promulgates lessons for the health service.

Another favoured model is the Swedish Patients' Insurance Scheme,[74] which is expressly designed to provide compensation for medical injuries. Compensation is payable in respect of any injury or illness resulting from any procedure related to healthcare. Injury arising from any diagnostic procedure, inappropriate medication, medical treatment or surgery falls within the ambit of the Swedish scheme. But compensation for such injury is subject to three important provisos. First, the injury must be proved to result from the procedure in issue, and not from the original disease. Second, injury resulting from a risk taken by the doctor to save life or prevent permanent disability is excluded. Third, and most crucially, the claimant has to show that the procedure causing their injury was *not medically justified*. The test of whether the procedure was medically justified often re-introduces the question of negligence. Nevertheless, certain claimants who lose in England will obtain compensation in Sweden. Mrs Ashcroft, who suffered injury to a facial nerve when the surgeon accidentally cut the nerve, would recover in Sweden. The surgeon was not to blame, but cutting the nerve was not medically indicated.[75]

In the UK, there are various no-fault schemes including the Industrial Injuries Scheme, the Criminal Injuries Compensation Scheme and the Vaccine Damage Payment Scheme. The latter includes damage that might flow from COVID-19 vaccination.[76] Sir Robert Francis KC was recently appointed[77] to undertake an independent study on a framework for compensation for victims of the infected blood tragedy that is the subject of an ongoing public inquiry discussed at 11.2 above. Still, the UK schemes are piecemeal and incomprehensive.

11.9 The rejection of no-fault compensation in England

As long ago as 1978, the Pearson Commission[78] advised against abolition of tort as a means of compensating personal injuries. The Commission decided

73 Created by the Health and Disability Commissioner Act 1994 (NZ). The Act was passed to implement the recommendations of Judge Cartwright: *The Report of the Committee of Inquiry into Allegations Concerning the Treatment of Cervical Cancer at National Women's Hospital and Into Other Related Matters* (1988) Government Printing Office.

74 Patient Injury Act 1996 (Sweden). LH Fallberg and B Borgenhammar, 'The Swedish No-fault Patient Insurance Scheme' (1997) 4 *European Journal of Health Law* 279; Patient Claims Panel (Sweden), *Patient Injury Compensation for Healthcare-Related Injuries* (2007) accessible at www.patientforsakring.se.

75 *Ashcroft v Mersey Regional Health Authority* [1983] 2 All ER 245.

76 The Vaccine Damage Payments (Specified Disease) Order 2020, SI 2020/1411.

77 Cabinet Office, 'Appointment of Sir Robert Francis QC to Undertake the Infected Blood Compensation Framework Study' (2021) 20 May.

78 Royal Commission on Civil Liability and Compensation for Personal Injury (1978) Cmnd 7054, vols 1–3.

against recommending a no-fault scheme for all medical injuries.[79] Following its recommendations, the Vaccine Damage Payment Scheme was introduced. Strict liability for defective drugs was introduced by the Consumer Protection Act 1987.[80] That reform came not as a result of the Pearson Report but because of pressure from Europe. The Commission's report gathered dust. Many of their proposals went unheeded.

Since 1978 the costs of malpractice litigation have grown exponentially and pressure has increased to reform malpractice litigation in favour of a no-fault system. Sir Ian Kennedy supported such a scheme in the Bristol Inquiry Report. In Scotland, a review group led by Sheila McLean recommended in 2011 that a no-fault scheme based on the Swedish model should be introduced.[81] Early estimates considered that the increase in expenditure would be relatively modest when compared with the costs of instituting such a scheme in England.[82] But a consultation in 2014 was more cautious about the projected costs and recommended further work.[83] A 2016 consultation[84] was more supportive, and the Scottish Government has expressed an intention to bring primary legislation to Scottish Parliament, though, at the time of writing, this has yet to occur.

11.10 Renewed calls for reform

At the time of writing, however, no-fault compensation is once again on the political agenda. Firstly, NHS Litigation is the subject of a Health and Social Care Committee inquiry.[85] Secondly, when giving oral evidence to the Health and Social Care Committee in 2021 Nadine Dorries (then Health Minister) said that a review was underway, 'looking across the NHS in the round ... at how issues of no-blame, no-fault compensation and clinical negligence are treated'.[86] Do we need a no-fault scheme?

11.11 The case for a no-fault scheme

The case for a no-fault scheme is made out in part by the manifest deficiencies of the present system. It is beyond the scope of this book to consider whether a

79 Ibid, paras 1304–1371.

80 See 12.1 below.

81 No-fault Compensation Review Group, *Report and Recommendations: Volume 1* (February 2011).

82 Discussed in *Mason and McCall Smith's Law and Medical Ethics*, 5.05.

83 The Scottish Government, *Consultation Report – Consultation on Recommendations for No-Fault Compensation in Scotland for Injuries Resulting from Clinical Treatment* (2014) April.

84 Scottish Government, *Draft proposals for a 'No-Blame' Redress Scheme in Scotland for Harm Resulting from Clinical Treatment* (2016).

85 House of Commons Health and Social Care Committee, *NHS Litigation Reform* (2021). As we go to press, we note that the report was published in April 2022.

86 House of Commons Health and Social Care Committee, *Oral Evidence Safety of Maternity Services in England* (2021) HC 677.

comprehensive no-fault scheme for all types of accidents should be introduced. In a perfect society, any person suffering from disability from whatever cause would receive appropriate financial support. The person paralysed by a stroke has identical needs to the person paralysed by a fall from a ladder or a bungled operation. That ideal would require not an accident compensation scheme, but provision of a general disability income.[87] Radical reform can never be expected to happen instantly. It must be approached incrementally. Previous editions of this book have put forward a scheme of no-fault compensation embracing two categories of medical injury:

(1) Injury or illness arising from an absence of, or delay in, appropriate medical treatment[88] provided that
   (i) treatment would have prevented that injury or illness, and
   (ii) a reasonable request for medical care from a person or authority under an obligation to provide care has been made by the patient or some other person acting on his behalf.

(2) Injury or illness resulting from medical treatment provided that
   (i) the injury or illness is not caused by the natural progression of disease or the ageing process, and
   (ii) the injury or illness is not the consequence of an unavoidable risk inherent in the treatment, of which the patient has received proper warning.

Category 1 would cover injury arising from failure to treat both in circumstances where the present tort of negligence would operate, and where it would not. For example, a request for treatment might be made and not acted on by a general practitioner because at the time they acted reasonably in thinking an immediate appointment was not necessary. Events prove them wrong. This would not render the doctor negligent. Under our proposed no-fault scheme, the patient would recover because they did in fact suffer as a result of lack of treatment, albeit no one was to blame.

Category 2 is more difficult to define. The intention of category 2 is that it should extend to any damage to the patient, which is neither the result of the natural progression of his original disease or condition nor a consequence inherent in that treatment and unavoidable if that treatment is to be successful. Under that last limitation, the side-effects of certain surgery and therapy would be excluded. At one level, the patient could obviously not recover compensation for pain and suffering ordinarily attendant on surgery. At another level, unpleasant and dangerous side-effects, for example the

[87] See C Ham *et al*, *Medical Negligence: Compensation and Accountability* (1988) King's Fund Institute/Centre for Socio-Legal Studies.

[88] Treatment would be defined to include treatment given to the mother and injuring the child. Consideration of the implications of ante-natal treatment would be required, for example (1) would treatment necessary for the mother but injuring the child be excluded? (2) what about pre-conception injury to either parent?

patient's hair falling out during chemotherapy or the risk of a stroke in some forms of brain surgery, would have to be excluded if they were inescapable in the pursuit of proper treatment. One important proviso is attached to the exclusion of unavoidable side-effects from compensation. The patient must have been properly warned. Failure to give proper warning, which results in injury unexpected and unconsidered by the patient, would remain a ground for compensation.

Avoiding definitions and drafting points may well be criticised as cowardice. The scheme above operates in a presumption of entitlement when injury follows medical treatment and ensues from lack of treatment. It seeks to avoid the linguistic complications of concepts of error or mishap. Ken Oliphant[89] has argued that experience from New Zealand should make us cautious. Initially at least, a compensation scheme should be based on evidence of 'medical error'. Where investigation and hindsight indicate that the patient receives less than the optimum treatment and with such treatment their injury could have been avoided, they would receive compensation. Simple evidence of an unexpected outcome of treatment would not suffice however serious that outcome. If a previously healthy patient suffers a cardiac arrest in the course of minor surgery, they will recover compensation if, for example, a defect is found in the anaesthetic equipment or some error was made by the anaesthetist. They will not have to show blameworthiness. If no reason for the sudden heart failure can be discovered, they have no claim in relation to that mishap.

The 'Oliphant solution' would, as he says, provide 'consistency and ease of application'. It might provoke awkward questions of causation and make it difficult to cast off the shackles of negligence. It is a notable attempt to put substance into the defining of 'medical misadventure'.

Counter arguments tend to focus on matters of causation, deterrence and accountability, and the financial implications of a no-fault scheme. Let us examine these criticisms more carefully.

11.12 Causation

The difficulty of distinguishing between an injury arising from treatment given and the natural progression of disease or inescapable side-effects of treatment is a valid concern. But is it enough to rule out a change to no-fault compensation? Causation presents just as much of a problem within the present system. Reform of the law introducing a no-fault principle would have the following benefits. A greater number of claimants would obtain compensation to help them adapt their lives to their disabilities, or to meet financial loss resulting from death of a breadwinner. The damage done to relations between the medical profession and the public by bitter and protracted litigation would be removed. The patient would obtain compensation because they suffered

[89] K Oliphant, 'Defining "Medical Misadventure": Lessons from New Zealand' (1996) 1 *Med Law Rev* 30–31.

injury as a result of treatment going wrong. The issue of *why* it went wrong and the health professional's competence would be for completely separate investigatory procedures. The problem of causation would still be present. Distinguishing between injury and the progression of disease (or whatever) would be made easier. The issue of causation would be investigated. It would not be part of a battle between the patient and the NHS, with the NHS having a vested interest in finding experts to deny that the patient's condition was caused by the treatment. Consideration could be given to whether the burden of proof of causation might be alleviated by requiring only proof of a reasonable possibility of causation.

11.13 Deterrence and accountability

Arguably tort serves a valuable purpose in emphasising the accountability and responsibility of individual medical staff. It may be costly and inefficient, and it may be inequitable in whom it compensates, but if it deters medical malpractice, can we afford to abandon it? Holm, Stanton and Bartlett point out that in future the deterrent effect of tort will be limited by the increasing prevalence of artificial intelligence (AI) systems that advise health professionals.[90] AI errors are challenging to deal with in a tort-based system because, where there is no attributable human error, it will often be impossible to explain how the error happened. They argue that no-fault compensation provides a viable alternative to tort and would help future proof redress as AI becomes increasingly prevalent.

Even outside the realm of AI, we remain unconvinced that the tort system has much systematic deterrent effect in healthcare insofar as individual health professionals are concerned. Moreover, that the alleged deterrent impact of tort often obscures the crucial question of accountability.

(1) The tort system is capricious in its operation. Obstetricians are at high risk of a law suit. Geriatricians are hardly ever sued. This is not because obstetricians are more likely to be negligent than their colleagues in geriatrics. It is because if Granny dies as a result of a negligent overdose so little could be claimed by way of damages that it is not worth suing the responsible doctor.

(2) Even where NHS doctors are sued, the deterrent effect of tort is not direct. The damages will not come out of the doctor's pocket. The deterrent function of tort normally operates via the insurance system. Poor drivers are deterred from carelessness and encouraged to improve because 'carelessness costs money'. NHS Indemnity means that NHS doctors do not pay any sort of insurance or indemnity. There is the emotional impact of litigation. Does the worry of being sued deter the

[90] S Holm, C Stanton and B Bartlett, 'A New Argument for No-Fault Compensation in Health Care: The Introduction of Artificial Intelligence Systems' (2021) 29 *Health Care Analysis* 171.

incompetent doctor? We doubt it. Where negligence is gross and obvious, claims are settled swiftly to avoid adverse publicity. It is the cases where there truly is doubt about whether an error is negligent that drag on in the public eye. We suspect 'good' doctors worry about litigation and 'bad' doctors rarely give the possibility much thought.

(3) Finally, there are a number of cases where, albeit there was actionable negligence, there is no moral culpability. Health professionals who make mistakes after hours without sleep in under-resourced hospitals should not be blamed for their error. The tort system could operate to deter such 'negligence' only by either encouraging such a doctor to refuse to treat patients at all, once they suspected they could not do so entirely competently, which would prompt more patient suffering, or by shifting the focus to the liability of organisations for systemic failures.

One *caveat* must be issued before dismissing the impact of deterrence via the tort system. Health providers are encouraged to be cost-conscious. The fear of litigation might operate on the collective mind of the Trust to deter economy measures that prejudice patients' safety. The impact of tort on providers must not be overlooked in the no-fault debate. Evaluating the extent to which providers may be influenced by the deterrent function of tort is difficult. Risk-management has a high profile within the NHS now. That is good. Hospitals review their practice and investigate adverse outcomes to try and prevent medical accidents.

Crucial to risk-management processes within the modern NHS are the various indemnity schemes administered by NHS Resolution. The manner in which these schemes operate means that NHS Resolution is effectively the enforcer of risk-management. It operates a strategy embedded in the tort system. Put simply, NHS hospitals and other bodies are obliged to comply with risk-management or face financial disaster. Risk-management could and should survive a no-fault compensation scheme. But what would replace the various indemnity schemes and would it have the same 'teeth'?

Returning to accountability, does the tort system ensure that health professionals and providers are made to account for their conduct? Tort's role in ensuring accountability is minimal. Adversarial litigation does not encourage an open and honest account of an incident from which institutions can learn. Doctors and nurses in the shadow of litigation clam up; they are naturally wary of admitting any doubts they may have as to what they did or did not do. If the patient fails to prove negligence within the tort system that is the end of the matter. Accountability is crucial. The tort system provides only token accountability. It is organisations such as the CQC and HSSIB which should help ensure the NHS learns from its mistakes.

11.14 Cost

Picking up on some of Lord Sumption's earlier points, for Laurie, Harmon and Dove, cost is a major reason for the government's rejection of no-fault compensation in England.[91] The overall cost of a no-fault scheme is difficult to judge. It is not a cheap option. But as Sir Robert Francis KC recently pointed out, 'those points are decreasingly significant because we only have to look at how much it is costing now'.[92]

No-fault compensation can be cost-effective in some respects. The ultimate cost of a no-fault scheme will depend on the level of payments made to victims. Several hard questions need to be addressed. It would seem obvious that the payment of compensation for loss of income and cost of care should generally be by way of periodical payments rather than as a lump sum. Payments can then be adjusted to meet the claimant's current needs. Should there be a ceiling on payments? Under the tort system, a high-earning solicitor rendered unable to work obtains money to make up their actual loss of income. Should no-fault compensation be limited to sufficient to provide for the claimant's needs arising from their disability up to the 'average' standard of living?[93] What about compensation for pain and suffering? The harder a no-fault scheme tries to offer generous compensation, the harder it is to fund a scheme to meet the needs of the widest possible range of claimants. An affordable no-fault scheme will necessarily have to limit compensation payments. Typically, no-fault compensation schemes do not compensate non-pecuniary loss. Previously wealthy victims of medical accidents will not receive full compensation for their monetary loss. Their loss of income will be capped. Medical and rehabilitation costs which could be met from other sources will not be included in compensation payments.

Proponents of social justice will argue then it is better to offer some recompense to more people than award lottery-type damages to winners in the tort system. The problem is this. If a no-fault compensation scheme exists side by side with access to the tort system, some patients will still opt for the tort system. Two options could be explored.

(1) Claimants who opt to sue in tort do so at their peril. If their claim fails they are excluded from the no-fault scheme. That might radically lower the cost of tort claims because only the most clear-cut claims will be brought and they should be swiftly settled.

(2) Or, as in New Zealand, if a claimant is entitled to claim under the no-fault scheme a tort claim is barred altogether. No-fault becomes the exclusive route to compensation for medical accidents. Financially, and to achieve the objective of a no-fault scheme, the second option makes

91 GT Laurie, SHE Harmon and ES Dove, *Mason and McCall Smith's Law and Medical Ethics* (11th edn, 2019) Oxford University Press, 5.09. And see CMO, *Making Amends*, p 15. And see T Douglas, 'Medical Injury Compensation: Beyond No-fault' (2009) 17 *Med Law Rev* 30 who argues that, given the limited resources available, a fairer scheme might require abandoning medical injury compensation altogether, in favour of better social security and public healthcare systems and a safer NHS.

92 House of Commons Health and Social Care Committee, *Oral Evidence: NHS Litigation Reform* (2021) HC 740, Q32.

93 In New Zealand, a maximum limit of 80 per cent of actual earnings. CMO, *Making Amends*, p 98.

> pre-eminent sense. But in barring access to the courts, would it violate Article 6 of the European Convention on Human Rights entitling everyone to a fair trial in determination of his civil rights and obligations?

We have examined several reasons why the system of redress needs to be reformed. Most pressing is perhaps the unsustainable costs of NHS litigation. Yet equally important is the elevation of patient safety up the political agenda, thanks to successive public inquiries. If the current tort system is not conducive to openness and the culture of learning that patient safety requires it must be amended or replaced. Progress is slow. When giving evidence to the Health and Social Care Committee in 2021, Sir Robert Francis KC commented that he and Sir Ian Kennedy were 'used to making recommendations that are welcomed and then perhaps, when they are particularly awkward or challenging, buried'.[94]

[94] House of Commons Health and Social Care Committee, *Oral Evidence: NHS Litigation Reform* (2021) HC 740, Q32.

Chapter 12

MEDICAL PRODUCTS LIABILITY[1]

12.1 Introduction

During the COVID-19 pandemic, the pharmaceutical industry made unprecedented efforts to collaborate and work in the public interest to develop novel treatments, diagnostics and vaccines. But a long history of opacity, competitiveness and catastrophes mean there is much ground to make up. Starting with the thalidomide tragedy, a series of disasters taught us the painful lesson that drugs can be dangerous and their use must be paid for. The list of drugs enthusiastically promoted in the first place and withdrawn from the market a few years later, amid bitter allegations that the drug in question caused injury and even death, is long. Opren,[2] human growth hormone,[3] the Pill itself,[4] the painkiller Vioxx[5] and the Type 2 diabetes drug Avandia[6] are but a random sample of the better-known cases. Allegations of gross profit-making by multi-national drug companies have proliferated.[7] Pharmaceutical companies have been criticised for testing products destined for the West on patients in developing countries.[8] Concern about the safety of drugs has extended today to anxiety about the safety of vaccinations,[9] medical

1 See generally E Jackson, *Law and the Regulation of Medicines* (2012) Hart; R Goldberg, *Medicinal Product Liability and Regulation* (2013) Hart; D Fairgrieve and R Goldberg, *Product Liability* (3rd edn, 2019) Oxford University Press.

2 *Nash v Eli Lilly and Co* [1993] 4 All ER 383. For a full analysis of the Opren litigation, see PR Ferguson, *Drug Injuries and the Pursuit of Compensation* (1996) Sweet & Maxwell, 14.

3 *The CJD Litigation, Newman v Secretary of State for Health* (1997) 54 BMLR 85.

4 See *XYZ v Schering Health Care Limited and Ors* [2002] EWHC 1420 (QB). See 12.13 below.

5 See 12.14 below.

6 'GlaxoSmithKline: £2.2bn Charge over Avandia and Legal Case' (2011) *BBC News*, 17 January.

7 R Anderson, 'Pharmaceutical Industry gets High on Fat Profits' *BBC News* (2014) 6 November.

8 See S Shah, *The Body Hunters: How the Drug Industry Tests its Products on the World's Poorest Patients* (2006) The New Press.

9 See 12.15 below.

devices[10] (such as breast implants[11] and pelvic mesh[12]) and the risks posed by contaminated blood supplies[13] and other body parts.

Commissioned in 2018 after extensive patient campaigns, the Cumberlege Review[14] investigated the safety of two medications and one device. Hormone pregnancy tests were withdrawn in the 1970s for fear of an association with birth defects and miscarriage; sodium valproate is an anti-epileptic drug which, if used during pregnancy, is associated with developmental delay and physical malformations; pelvic floor implants manage urinary incontinence and have been linked to life-changing complications. The 2020 report noted patient concerns over several other medications and devices and emphasised the need to carry over conclusions to other products.

The report disparaged 'a healthcare system that cannot be relied upon to identify and respond promptly to healthcare concerns'. Themes emerged that are pertinent to other chapters in this book such as failures regarding patient safety (Chapter 2) and informed consent (Chapter 6). The Review called for an immediate apology from government[15] and the formation of a new Patient Safety Commissioner to 'champion the patient voice'.[16] It concluded that litigation has not served patients sufficiently and recommended a new Redress Agency to reduce blame, encourage reporting and provide non-adversarial resolution. We considered redress in Chapter 11 and focus in this chapter on the potential for litigation.

Thalidomide was developed originally by West German manufacturers, Chemie Grünenthal. A British company, Distillers, bought the formula and manufactured and marketed the drug here under licence from Chemie Grünenthal. The drug was promoted as a safer alternative to existing sedatives and was expressly claimed to be suitable for pregnant and nursing mothers. Thalidomide was alleged to be the cause of gross fetal deformity. All over Europe, wherever thalidomide had been available, babies began to be born suffering from startlingly similar deformities, notably phocomelia (deformities

10 We do not look at the regulation of medical devices in any detail. Medical devices are regulated by EU Directives implemented into domestic legislation and preserved as 'retained EU law' via the European Union (Withdrawal) Act 2018. The Medicines and Medical Devices Act 2021, Pt 4 provides a general power to amend the regulations, consolidate the enforcement regime for medical devices, and impose sanctions.

11 See R Watson, 'Europe Launches Investigation into Health Risks of Faulty Breast Implants' (2012) 233 *BMJ* e939.

12 See Australian class action *Gill v Ethicon Sàrl & Ors* (No 5) [2019] FCA 1905 finding that certain polypropylene mesh medical devices were defective and instructions and marketing materials were misleading.

13 See 12.6–12.9 below.

14 Baroness Julia Cumberlege (Chair), *First Do No Harm: The report of the Independent Medicines and Medical Devices Safety Review* (2020) (hereafter Cumberlege Review).

15 See Minister for Patient Safety (Ms Nadine Dorries), HC Deb 9 July 2020, vol 678, col 1147.

16 Established in the Medicines and Medical Devices Act 2021, s 1.

of the limbs). After a bitter campaign, Distillers and the children's parents reached a settlement to provide compensation for children recognised as damaged by thalidomide.[17] But as they got older and their needs changed, the compensation proved inadequate. In 2010 the British Government issued a formal apology and set up a £20 million support package.[18]

In 1987, Parliament enacted the Consumer Protection Act. Part 1 imposed on all producers of goods strict liability for unsafe products. This Act was based on a European Community Directive[19] which required all Member States to introduce strict liability for products. In part the intention of the Directive was to ensure fair competition between businesses in the Community. If France required French producers to meet more stringent safety laws than other Member States, French businesses competed at a disadvantage to their rivals. However, much of the impetus for strict liability for unsafe goods in Europe and the United Kingdom arose from a desire to give more effective protection and remedies to people who suffered injury as a result of defects in goods. Withdrawal from the EU in 2020 has weakened that protection. Regulations were passed to amend the 1987 Act and make it workable post-EU Exit.[20] UK consumers buying from UK businesses are largely unaffected by EU Exit, but now that the UK is classified as a non-EU country, in cross-border disputes patients may need to seek international enforcement where previously they could have brought their claim domestically.[21]

Hopes that the Consumer Protection Act might make the law on drug-induced injury straightforward were unfounded.[22] A drug which causes kidney damage or fetal abnormality would be perceived by most lay observers as 'unsafe'. Defining 'defective' under the Act will be seen to be more problematical. The damage caused by some drugs takes years to manifest itself. No action under the Act is allowed more than ten years after the drug in question was put on the market.[23] Nor is a drug company's liability under the Act wholly strict, for the Act permits producers to plead a 'development risks' defence and so escape liability. Victims of drug-induced injury may still resort to prior common law remedies in contract and the tort of negligence. And negligence liability for drug-induced injury needs to be understood to evaluate how far strict liability

[17] For a full and lively history of the events surrounding the thalidomide tragedy, see H Teff and C Munro, *Thalidomide: The Legal Aftermath* (1976) Saxon House.

[18] See Parliamentary Statement, 'Government Money for Thalidomide Survivors' (2010) 15 January.

[19] EU Product Liability Directive 85/374/EEC.

[20] Amendments required in light of EU Exit are contained in the Product Safety and Metrology etc. (Amendment etc) (EU Exit) Regulations 2019, SI 2019/696, Sch 3.

[21] See House of Commons Research Briefing, *Brexit: UK Consumer Protection Law* (2021).

[22] But see M Mildred, 'Pitfalls of Product Liability' (2007) 2 *Journal of Personal Injury Law* 141.

[23] For definition of 'put into circulation' see Case C-127/04, *O'Byrne v Sanofi Pasteur MSD Ltd (formerly Aventis Pasteur MSD Ltd)* [2006] ECR I-01313; [2010] UKSC 23, discussed at 12.5 below.

under the Act is a real advance on the bad old rules under which thalidomide victims had to play.[24]

12.2 Product liability and drugs

Whatever scheme for compensation is in operation there are problems relating to drug-induced injury which will not go away. English law purports to treat drugs (and body products such as blood) as just another product. For legal purposes a defective drug is (in theory) little different from a defective electric blanket or kettle. In practice there are vital distinctions affecting both user and manufacturer if litigation is started. Defects in products can be of two sorts; in *design*, which means that every example of the product will prove defective, or in *construction*, which means that some but not all of the eventual products will be faulty simply because they have not been put together properly.[25] Faults in electric blankets, kettles, or even aircraft are usually construction faults.

Defects in drugs are mostly design defects. That means that a drug company facing a claim alleging their product to be defective is facing a disaster. There are going to be not just one or two claimants but a host of embittered and injured users. The cost to the company may put it out of business. The company fights back with equal vigour.

From the user's viewpoint, changes to legal aid eligibility in the Legal Aid, Sentencing and Punishment of Offenders Act 2012 made it increasingly difficult to claim against pharmaceutical companies, especially given the poor record of success which makes 'no win, no fee' arrangements unattractive.[26] The greatest difficulty in any claim against the drug company is proving that the drug caused her injury. Should a new brand of electric blanket suffer a design defect, and within a week of purchase 5 per cent of users suffer an electric shock, the link between cause and effect is clear. With a new drug the process will be nothing like so swift or sure. Consider the case of diethylstilboestrol, a drug prescribed over fifty years ago to women threatening to miscarry. Evidence has emerged that women, *in utero* when their mothers took the drug, were affected in disproportionate numbers by vaginal and cervical cancer.[27] Delay in effect is only one of the problems. There may be uncertainty whether injury resulted from the drug taken, the original disease or some other

24 *Richardson v LRC Products Ltd* [2000] Lloyd's Law Reports; *Abouzaid v Mothercare (UK) Ltd* [2000] EWCA Civ 348; *A v National Blood Authority* [2001] Lloyd's Rep Med 187.

25 In *A v National Blood Authority* [2001] Lloyd's Rep Med 187, Burton J prefers the terminology *standard* and *non-standard* products.

26 E Jackson, *Law and the Regulation of Medicines* (2012) Hart, p 119; R Goldberg, *Medicinal Product Liability and Regulation* (2013) Hart, p 9. And see 11.2 above.

27 A particular difficulty here has been establishing which manufacturer made the actual drug taken by the mother. There were several brands of the same drug on the market; see *Sindell v Abbott Laboratories* (1980) 26 Cal 3d 588, *Mindy Hymowitz v Eli Lilly & Co* (1989) 541 NYS 2d 941 (NY, CA). See discussion of *Fairchild v Glenhaven Funeral Services Ltd* [2002] UKHL 22, *Barker v Corus* [2006] UKHL 20 and the Compensation Act 2006 below at 12.10.

natural cause. When a drug is alleged to cause fetal deformity this is a particular difficulty. Was the child's disability the result of the drug, or of some inherited disorder or disease in the mother, or one of a number of other possible causes? Then in all claims there is the problem of proving that the drug was taken by the patient in the proper dosage, and as often the same drug is manufactured under different brand names, it must be shown which brand the patient actually used.[28] Medical records are often far from perfect; memory is fallible. Finally, there is the intractable difficulty of personal idiosyncrasy. A drug beneficial to 99.9 per cent of us may be lethal to 0.1 per cent. Is that drug defective? Should the company, or anyone else, compensate the 0.1 per cent who suffers injury?

The pharmaceutical industry argues that laws which weigh too onerously on it may inhibit research.[29] Medicine would be held back and British companies would suffer loss of competitiveness. Some view this claim sceptically. Much of the competition appears aimed at producing new brands of the same basic drugs. The pace of innovation has been impacted by poor investment[30] though the life sciences are increasingly central to the Government's innovation strategy.[31] Any decline in the pharmaceutical industry is as likely to be due to this factor as it is to be the result of law reform to help drug-injured patients.

12.3 Consumer-buyers: most favoured claimants

A victim of drug-induced injury who bought the offending drug himself, or acquired the drug in the course of a contract, has a more effective remedy than any of his fellow sufferers. Despite the Consumer Protection Act, consumer-buyers remain the most favoured claimants in England.

The Consumer Rights Act 2015 was enacted to simplify the law.[32] It sets out conditions implied in every contract for the sale of goods.[33] The goods must be of satisfactory quality.[34] This means they must meet the standard that a reasonable person would regard as satisfactory. The goods must be reasonably fit for the purpose for which they are sold.[35] And the good must match the description.[36] When drugs are bought over the counter, they must meet these conditions just like any other goods. To take a simple example, a patient

28 See *Sindell v Abbott Laboratories* (1980) 26 Cal 3d 588.

29 See, for example, RA Epstein, *Overdose: How Excessive Government Regulation Stifles Pharmaceutical Innovation* (2006) Yale University Press.

30 Institute for Public Policy Research, *A Lost Decade* (2019).

31 Dept for Business, Energy & Industrial Strategy, *UK Innovation Strategy* (2021).

32 And to implement provisions of Directive 2011/83/EU of the European Parliament and of the Council on consumer rights.

33 Consumer Rights Act 2015, ss 9–18.

34 Ibid, s 9. For contracts made before 1 October 2015, see Sale of Goods Act 1979, s 14(2) (as amended by the Sale and Supply of Goods Act 1999).

35 Consumer Rights Act 2015, s 10. For contracts made before 1 October 2015 see Sale of Goods Act 1979 s 14(3).

36 Consumer Rights Act 2015, s 11.

buying a bottle of cough mixture suffers internal injury because the medicine is contaminated by powdered glass. That patient recovers full compensation for their injuries from the pharmacist who sold them the medicine. The pharmacist may be entirely without fault. The medicine may have been supplied by the manufacturer in a sealed, opaque container. That does not matter; the medicine is neither of satisfactory quality nor fit to be sold, and the pharmacist is in breach of contract. This simple and effective remedy has a defect, however. It is normally available only when the person suffering injury from the defective drug bought it themselves. Had the contaminated medicine in our example been purchased by a husband and taken by his wife, she may well have had no remedy in contract.[37] She cannot benefit from a contract to which she is not a party.

How useful is the contractual remedy in practice? A growing range of medicines are no longer available by prescription only. They have been reclassified to allow sale in pharmacies, or in many cases just in ordinary shops. Antihistamines to alleviate hayfever, similar drugs to aid sleep, emergency contraception and a host of medicines to help digestive problems can now be bought over the counter. These 'deregulated' drugs are more likely to carry inherent risks of harm than the sort of cough and cold remedies available over the counter historically. More patients may look to their pharmacist or local supermarket for redress. Patients prescribed their medicines on the National Health Service (NHS) remain less favoured. Such medicines will not attract conditions of satisfactory quality and fitness for purpose because there is no contract between the pharmacist and the patient into which such conditions can be implied, even though the patient will often pay for his prescription.[38] The pharmacist dispenses the drug as part of his obligation under his contract with local NHS commissioners to provide pharmaceutical services in the area. The patient pays a statutory charge. He does not buy the drug; he pays a tax for NHS services.

By contrast, when drugs are dispensed under a private prescription, a contract does exist between the pharmacist and the patient. The patient pays the full cost of the drug directly to the pharmacist. It matters not whether the contract is one of simple sale or a contract of service under which the pharmacist provides a skilled service and incidentally supplies the drug. Quality conditions are imposed in identical terms regardless of whether goods are supplied in the course of a service or in an ordinary sale transaction.[39] The pharmacist is exposed on the front line of liability for defective drugs. When more potent drugs become the subject of conditions of fitness for purpose, whether by private prescription or an over-the-counter sale, problems of applying those conditions are likely. The question may arise as to whether a drug perfectly safe for all but pregnant women is fit to be supplied. If it is specifically aimed at pregnant women, for example a morning sickness preparation, clearly if

37 Unless she can show that her husband bought the medicine for her as her agent.
38 *Pfizer v Ministry of Health* [1965] AC 512; *Appleby v Sleep* [1968] 1 WLR 948.
39 See Consumer Rights Act 2015 and, for contracts made before 1 October 2015, the Supply of Goods and Service Act 1982.

it damages the woman or her baby it is not fit for the purpose for which it is supplied. If it is a general medicine, such as a hayfever remedy, it could be argued that if it carries risk to a substantial section of the community, pregnant women, then it is not of satisfactory quality, nor fit to be on general sale. This immediately raises further questions. Did the manufacturer warn of the risk to pregnant women? Is such a warning sufficient? Should the woman herself be aware of the dangers of taking drugs and avoid drugs while pregnant?

These sorts of problems inevitably plague questions of liability for defective drugs. Where a remedy lies in contract, once a court finds the drug unsafe, the claim for compensation is established. It is no defence for the retailer of the drug, or the pharmacist dispensing the drug, to argue that he personally was blameless. Nor is it any answer to the patient's claim that the state of scientific and technical knowledge at the time when the drug was produced was such that the defect could not have been discovered. There is no 'development risks' defence against a claim in contract. The liability imposed on the retailer or supplier is truly strict.

12.4 The remedy in negligence

Patients who suffer injury as a result of drugs prescribed within the NHS must look outside contract for a remedy. Prior to the Consumer Protection Act 1987 that remedy would have to be found in the tort of negligence. Gaps in the Consumer Protection Act mean that victims of drug-induced injury cannot ignore the tort of negligence.

An action in negligence arises where one person suffers injury as a result of the breach of a duty of care owed him by another. The doctor may be the first person to whom the patient turns for a remedy when they believe a drug prescribed by that doctor has harmed them. The doctor will be liable for drug-induced injury if the drug caused damage because they prescribed an incorrect dosage, or because they ought to have appreciated that that drug posed a risk to a particular patient in the light of his medical history, or where drugs have been prescribed in inappropriate and harmful combination. Similarly, if the injury to the patient results from a negligent error by the pharmacist in, for example, dispensing the wrong drug, or indicating the wrong dosage, an action in negligence lies against the pharmacist. The problem for the patient is that all they know is that they are ill and they believe the drug to be the cause. They will have no means of knowing whether an inherently 'safe' drug was prescribed for them in an unsafe and careless fashion, or whether the drug is inherently defective and harmful, however careful their doctor may be. Hence patients contemplating litigation for drug-induced injury often have to start by considering suing the doctor, the pharmacist *and* the manufacturer, and hope that evidence of who was actually to blame will emerge in the course of the litigation.

Turning now to the liability in negligence of drug companies manufacturing drugs, the manufacturer of any product:

> ... which he sells in such a form as to show that he intends them to reach the ultimate consumer in the form in which they left him with no reasonable possibility of intermediate examination, and with the knowledge that the absence of care in

> the preparation or putting up of the products will result in injury to the consumer's life or property, owes a duty to the consumer to take that reasonable care.[40]

There is no doubt that this duty to take care attaches as much to the manufacturer of drugs as to the manufacturer of ginger beer or any other product. The duty covers the design and formulation of the drug as well as its construction. Nor is the duty limited to the original manufacturer.[41] Establishing a duty to avoid negligence is not the problem. Determining what amounts to negligence is a formidable task. The potential harm caused by a defective drug is such that a very high standard of care will be imposed on the manufacturer. This is generally acknowledged. However, in England no action for personal injuries against a drug company has yet resulted in an award of damages by a court although a claim against the National Blood Authority has, as we shall see, succeeded. What are the obstacles confronting claimants? First, the drug company must be judged by the standards for drug safety pertaining at the date when the drug was put on the market, not at the date proceedings are taken against them. Second, the claimant must obtain the evidence he will need to prove the company careless. Such evidence would need to be given by experts and might not be conclusive. The burden of proof lies on the claimant. The contents of adverse reports on a drug, the sequence and exact dates on which those reports are received, are of crucial importance to a claimant. No drug company is likely to hand the reports over voluntarily. The process of discovery, of compelling a defendant to hand over documents, was seen to be complex enough in a malpractice claim against an individual doctor. In claims against a drug company the process often became an insuperable obstacle race.

It may ultimately prove to be the case that there is insufficient evidence that the company was negligent when it originally marketed the drug. There may be evidence, however hard to come by, that it was negligent in failing to act on adverse reports and recall the drug. Is that a breach of the manufacturer's duty? Two separate situations must be examined. If it could be proved that harm resulted from a drug marketed *after* a date by which the manufacturer should have known it to be dangerous, there is no problem. The drug was negligently put into circulation. Difficulty would arise where the drug was put into circulation before the manufacturer should have known it was dangerous, but was actually prescribed and taken after that date. There is a strong case that a manufacturer owes a further duty to monitor its product and to take reasonable steps to withdraw it if it proves unsafe.[42] Proving breach of the duty could be a nightmare. Stories of doctors continuing to prescribe, and pharmacists retaining stocks of, withdrawn drugs recur. The patient bringing such a claim may falter and sink in a sea of allegation and counter-allegation between drug company, doctor and pharmacist.

40 *Donoghue v Stevenson* [1932] AC 562, at 599, HL.

41 *Watson v Buckley and Osborne, Garrett & Co Ltd* [1940] 1 All ER 174 (duty imposed on distributors of hair dye).

42 *Wright v Dunlop Rubber Co. Ltd* [1972] 13 KIR 255; *Hollis v Dow Corning Corporation* (1995) 129 DLR (4th) 609 (Canada).

The inadequacy of negligence as an effective means of compensating victims of drug-induced injury has been demonstrated time and time again. Successive reviews of negligence as a means of remedying personal injuries resulting from any unsafe product concluded that the reform of product liability laws was essential.[43] What must now be evaluated is how effective reform by way of the Consumer Protection Act 1987 has proved to be.

12.5 Strict liability: the Consumer Protection Act

The concept of strict liability is simple.[44] A claimant seeking compensation from the manufacturer of a product need prove only (1) that the product was defective *and* (2) that the defect in the product caused his injury. Strict liability is fairer to claimants because it establishes that responsibility for an injury caused by a defective product is borne by the person creating the risk and benefiting financially from the product; that is the manufacturer. The manufacturer is in the best position to exercise control over the safety and quality of the product and can more conveniently insure against the risk of injury posed by the product. Prolonged, expensive and complex litigation should be less common with a strict liability regime.

The Act imposes liability for personal injury arising from defective products on all *producers* of goods. 'Producers' embraces a wider category of businesses involved in the marketing of drugs than simply the companies manufacturing the finished products.[45] Manufacturers of components are liable for any defect in the components. A company that brands a drug is a producer within the Act. Companies cannot use their name to claim the credit and the profit for a drug and, when something goes badly wrong, disclaim any responsibility for that drug. Any supplier[46] of a drug will be deemed to be a producer unless he identifies the source of his supply. This provision is crucial for patients. The patient may well receive his prescription or injection in a form such that he cannot possibly identify the original producer of the drug. The community pharmacist or hospital pharmacy supplying the drug must identify the producer or bear liability for the patient's injuries themselves.[47] The intention of

43 Notably the Law Commission in their report *Liability for Defective Products* (1977) Law Com No 82, Cmnd 6831 (hereafter Law Com), and the Royal Commission on Civil Liability and Compensation for Personal Injury (1978) Cmnd 7054 (hereafter Pearson Report).

44 The pharmaceutical industry repeatedly argued that drugs should remain exempt from any regime of strict liability, mainly on the grounds that (1) scientific research and innovation would be adversely affected; (2) the nature of drug disasters meant that strict liability could have catastrophic results for the industry; (3) the difficulty of defining defect in a drug. These arguments have been consistently rejected: see Law Com, pp 19–21; Pearson Report, para 1274.

45 Consumer Protection Act 1987, ss 1–2.

46 This includes pharmacists dispensing NHS drugs even though they do not sell NHS drugs to patients.

47 See, for example, C Langley, 'Pharmacy Legislation: Public Protector or Professional Hindrance?' (2014) 22(1) *Med Law Rev* 87.

the European Directive,[48] on which the Act is based, and of the Act itself is that there should, as far as humanly possible, always be an identifiable producer on whom liability must rest. No company should be able to hide behind a smokescreen.

Procedural problems can arise if the producer cannot be identified in a timely manner. A Haemophilus influenzae type b ('Hib') vaccine produced by a French company, Aventis Pasteur SA ('SA'), was sold to an English subsidiary company, Aventis Pasteur MSD Ltd ('MSD'), who supplied it to the Department of Health, who provided it to a medical centre, which then vaccinated 1-year-old O'Byrne. O'Byrne suffered brain damage and alleged that the vaccine had caused it. His claim was mistakenly brought against MSD, the supplier of the vaccine, rather than the producer, SA. By the time the mistake became apparent, O'Byrne could no longer bring a claim against the producer due to a time limit imposed by the Act – claims must be brought within ten years of the product being put into circulation.[49] The Supreme Court held that the claim against the supplier (which was brought within the time limit) could not be substituted for a claim against the producer. After extensive litigation, O'Byrne's claim failed.[50]

Assuming the claimant has identified the right defendant, how do you establish that the drug is defective?[51] Section 3(1) provides that:

> [T]here is a defect in a product … if the safety of the product is not such as persons generally are entitled to expect;

Section 3(2) goes on to direct the judge to take into account all relevant circumstances pertaining to the safety of a product including:

> (a) the manner in which, and purposes for which, the product has been marketed, its get-up, the use of any mark in relation to the product and any instructions for, or warnings with respect to, the doing of anything with or in relation to the product;
> (b) what might reasonably be expected to be done with or in relation to the product; and
> (c) the time when the product was supplied by its producer to another;
>
> and nothing in this section shall require a defect to be inferred from the fact alone that the safety of a product which is supplied after that time is greater than the safety of the product in question.

48 Council Directive of 25 July 1985 *Products Liability* 85/374/EC.

49 Consumer Protection Act 1987, s 22A.

50 [2010] UKSC 23. See H Preston, 'The End of the Decade' (2010) 33 *Commercial Litigation Journal* 5.

51 See D Fairgrieve and G Howells, 'Rethinking Product Liability: A Missing Element in the European Commission's Third Review of European Product Liability Directive' (2007) 70(6) *Modern Law Review* 962 which suggests that there is a lack of consistency in Europe on the concept of defectiveness.

Determining when a drug falls within the definition is far from easy.[52] Drugs are by their nature dangerous. They are designed to do damage to the bacteria or diseased cell or whatever caused the original disease. How much safety are persons generally entitled to expect? Side-effects are often unavoidable. The court has to try to balance the potential benefit against the risk when deciding if an unwanted side-effect renders a drug defective. Distinctions may be drawn based on the condition that the drug was designed to combat. A minor tranquilliser which carried an unforeseen 5 per cent risk of liver damage could be deemed defective when an anti-cancer drug carrying identical risk would not. Relief of moderate anxiety may be seen as insufficient to warrant the risk, whereas the battle against cancer may justify that degree of inherent danger.

Anticipated risks raise different issues. An anticipated risk must be warned against. Of course, there must be some determination as to the seriousness of the anticipated risk. Consider a drug used to treat schizophrenia which may cause weight gain. Must the pharmaceutical company warn of this relatively benign potential side-effect? Class actions in the USA were brought against AstraZeneca on the ground that they should have warned that weight gain might occur in patients using Seroquel, particularly in view of the links between weight gain and type-two diabetes.[53]

What if the risk is acknowledged? Will the tranquilliser be deemed not defective if its potential danger is outlined to doctors and patients, leaving the choice to them? What if the risk is made clear to doctors but not passed on to the patients? In *Wilkes v DePuy International Limited*,[54] warnings to surgeons were taken into account by the court as part of the broad circumstances considered in determining whether a replacement hip was defective. Where detailed information was provided to the surgeon, a failure to pass it on to the patient did not render the product defective. The patient could potentially claim against the intermediary in negligence for failure to warn of a material risk, as we discuss in Chapter 6 above.

Guidance on defining 'defective' is to be found in a series of judgments. In *Abouzaid v Mothercare Ltd*[55] a 12-year-old boy was trying to attach a fleece-lined sleeping bag to his baby brother's pushchair. The sleeping bag had to be clipped on to the pushchair by passing elasticated straps round the back of the chair joined by a metal buckle. There were no instructions provided. As the boy struggled to fasten the sleeping bag to the chair, one of the straps slipped from his grasp and the metal buckle flew up and hit him in his left eye. The injury caused him to lose significant vision in that eye. The Court of Appeal found that the product was defective. There was a failure to provide instructions and the design of the product was unsafe because it could not be secured without risk. Consumers would properly expect that such a product could be

52 See the thorough and excellent discussion of this problem in C Newdick, 'Strict Liability for Defective Drugs in the Pharmaceutical Industry' (1985) 101 *LQR* 405, 409–420.

53 'AstraZeneca in $198m Claim Payout' *BBC News* (2010) 9 August.

54 [2016] EWHC 3096 (QB) discussed at 12.6 below.

55 [2000] EWCA Civ 348, CA.

used without that degree of risk. Relatively minor alterations in design would eliminate that risk.

The *Mothercare* judgment can be applied to make two key points about liability for drugs. (1) Instructions about the use of and warnings concerning possible adverse effects of drugs are crucial. Failure to warn of a known risk will, as argued earlier, render a drug defective. (2) Common sense will play its part in determining what 'people generally' may expect from a product.[56] That latter point is reinforced in *Richardson v LRC Products Ltd*.[57] The plaintiff became pregnant after a condom split. She sued the manufacturers arguing that the condom failure demonstrated that the product was defective. She was unable to identify any particular construction defect in the condom or point to a risk of damage which the manufacturers should have avoided. The judge found no evidence of unsatisfactory testing of the product. The evidence was simply that, in actual use, an inexplicable number of condoms fail. Dismissing the plaintiff's claim, the judge held that the manufacturers made no claims that their (or any) method of contraception was 100 per cent safe. The fallibility of contraception is well known.

12.6 Defining defect: The rise and fall of *A v National Blood Authority*[58]

A v National Blood Authority (hereafter *A v NBA*) breathed new life into strict liability, but seventeen years later the court in *Gee v De Puy*[59] all but snuffed it out. *A v NBA* addressed claims by patients infected with hepatitis C from blood and blood products through blood transfusions after 1 March 1988. Two important points must be made. First, the defendants (rightly) conceded that blood and body parts fell within the regime of strict liability imposed by the Consumer Protection Act. Secondly, the judge ruled (pre-EU Exit) that the provisions of the UK legislation (the 1987 Act) must be interpreted in the light of the European Product Liability Directive. Where there were apparent inconsistencies between the two, the Directive should be preferred. The importance of this will be highlighted later.

Moving to the substance of the claims, the judge held that in determining whether the contaminated blood products were defective what must be decided is what the *legitimate expectations* of the public were in relation to that product. People expected blood to be 100 per cent clean. Whether the relevant 'defect' in the product was *avoidable* was not the issue. The judge marked a clear boundary between negligence and strict liability. He went on to say a

56 See also *Tesco Stores v Pollard (A Minor)* [2006] EWCA 393 where the child resistant top on a bottle of dishwasher powder was more difficult to open than an ordinary top and therefore fell in line with reasonable expectations.

57 [2000] Lloyd's Law Report 280. And see *Worsley v Tambrands* [2000] PIQR P 95; *Foster v Biosil* (2000) 59 BMLR 178.

58 [2001] Lloyd's Rep Med 187.

59 *Gee and others v DePuy International Limited* [2018] EWHC 1208 (QB), building on *Wilkes v DePuy International Limited* [2016] EWHC 3096 (QB).

distinction needs to be made between *standard* and *non-standard* products, a distinction analogous to design and construction defects. Establishing that a standard product was defective would continue to be difficult. The infected batches of blood were non-standard. They could only not be defective if it could be shown the public were made aware of the risks. In this instance, this was not the case. Unlike condoms, which most people know do and can split for no apparent reason, most of us assume that blood will not cause us to succumb to serious, even fatal, disease.

In *Wilkes v DePuy International*,[60] Hickinbottom J revisited *A v NBA*. DePuy had produced a stainless-steel prosthetic hip joint which the claimant received as part of a total hip replacement in 2007. When the stem fractured, the claimant alleged that he had a legitimate expectation that this would not occur. The defendant claimed that the surgeons had been warned of the risk of fatigue and argued that the stem was not defective. Finding for the manufacturer, Hickinbottom J held that the first step should not be to identify 'the harmful characteristic which caused the injury', but rather to determine whether the product is defective: the 'legitimate expectations' test set out in *A v NBA* was an unnecessary gloss on the Act which in fact requires only consideration of what people are generally 'entitled to expect'. Hickinbottom J's approach was affirmed in *Gee v DePuy International Ltd*,[61] which considered whether DePuy was liable in respect of its prosthesis, subject to any development risk defence.

The approach to determining whether a product is defective post-*Gee* and -*Wilkes* is *holistic*, including all relevant considerations such as cost, avoidability of harm, approvals sought, warnings given[62] and risk–benefit profile.[63] With regard to the latter, expectations around safety will depend on the risks and benefits of avoiding the alleged defect. The benefits of some products, such as cancer drugs, for example, might be such that even severe side-effects could be tolerated. The relevant risk–benefit profile might also extend beyond the particular patient. Several COVID-19 vaccines were fast-tracked and given temporary authorisation, and the long-term risks are, at the time of writing, unknown. If cases emerge and liability is alleged, arguably the assessment of risk and benefit should take into consideration the public health context of their development. Thus, Richard Goldberg has argued that assessment of benefits might justifiably take into consideration immunity conferred not just on the individual but also on the community.[64]

As *A v NBA*, *Gee* and *Wilkes* were all heard in the High Court, *Gee* does not overrule *A v NBA*, but it does signal the onset of a more holistic approach to

60 *Wilkes v DePuy International Limited* [2016] EWHC 3096 (QB).

61 [2018] EWHC 1208 (QB).

62 But see Scottish case, *Hastings v Finsbury Orthopaedics Ltd and Stryker UK Ltd* [2019] CSOH 96, [120]: warnings in very small type were thought to be of limited value and significance.

63 D Fairgrieve and R Goldberg, *Product Liability* (3rd edn, 2019) Oxford University Press, 10.43, 10.45.

64 R Goldberg, 'Vaccine Liability in the Light of Covid-19: A Defence of Risk–Benefit' (2022) 30(2) *Med Law Rev* 243. And see 12.15 below.

defining 'defect', as has been confirmed in subsequent cases.[65] Fairgrieve and Goldberg welcome the clarifications in *Wilkes*, which could open the way for 'an indication of the importance of categories of product, such as whether the product is a prescription-only medicine'.[66] But for consumers, the rejection of the 'legitimate expectations' test shifts away from their protection.

12.7 Development risks[67]

In *A v NBA*,[68] the Blood Authority had another weapon. If the contaminated blood was defective, they argued, they were not liable because they could invoke the development risks defence.[69] A 'development risks' defence amounts to this. The manufacturer will not be liable if he can prove that the state of scientific and technical knowledge at the time when he put the product into circulation was not such as to enable the existence of the defect to be discovered.[70]

The scope of the development risks defence in the United Kingdom looked broad. The European Directive on Products Liability framed the defence in terms of the scientific and technical knowledge generally available. Section 4(1)(e) of the Consumer Protection Act provides:

> ... the state of scientific and technical knowledge was not such that a producer of products of the same description as the product in question might be expected to have discovered the defect.

The test in the Act appears to be what was the knowledge and practice of the pharmaceutical industry at the time. The European Commission challenged the British Act alleging that the UK had improperly sought to broaden the defence allowed by the Directive. The challenge failed.[71] The European Court of Justice allowed the UK interpretation of the Directive. The result might have been

65 See *Bailey v GlaxoSmithKline UK Ltd* [2019] EWCA Civ 1924, [8]. Note the Scottish case *Hastings v Finsbury Orthopaedics Ltd and Stryker UK Ltd* [2019] CSOH 96 (appeal dismissed [2021] CSOH 6) applied *Wilkes* and *Gee* but subject to a more claimant-friendly approach. Whereas in *Gee* it was held that a person is entitled to expect a product not to be worse than those it replaced, in *Hastings* a person could expect it to be at least as good as alternatives. Mr Hastings lost his claim against the manufacturer of a metal-on-metal hip replacement, but in Scotland at least, the case signals a more permissive approach.

66 Fairgrieve and Goldberg, *Product Liability*, 10.43.

67 The Consumer Protection Act, s 4 outlines a number of defences that will only rarely be relevant in claims for drug-related injuries. For example, in *Piper v JRI (Manufacturing)* [2006] EWCA (Civ) 1344 a replacement hip sheared into two, but the manufacturer was not liable because 'the defect did not exist in the product at the relevant time'.

68 [2001] Lloyd's Rep Med 187.

69 See s 4(1)(e).

70 The European Directive Article 7(e) permitted states to incorporate a development risks defence.

71 Case C-300/95, *Commission v UK* [1997] All ER (EC) 481.

depressing.[72] Academic research may reveal significant concerns about the safety of a novel drug. If that research has not permeated industry, the 'development risks' defence could still avail the drug companies creating a test little different from 'old' negligence rules. So, in *A v NBA* the defendants argued (1) that as at the relevant time there was no effective test to screen blood for Hepatitis C the development risks defence applied, and (2) that the 1987 Act provided that producers of analogous products must at the relevant time have been aware of and able to eliminate the relevant risk. Construing the Act in the light of the Directive, the judge dismissed both arguments. The defence applies only where the very existence of the defect was unknown and undiscoverable.[73] Authorities responsible for blood supplies at the relevant time were aware of the risks of contamination. That no method of screening for Hepatitis C had yet been developed was irrelevant. The wording of section 4(1)(e) of the 1987 Act was inappropriate. The Directive made it clear that once knowledge of a risk was accessible to manufacturers, the risk was known. A single article in an obscure journal ('the Manchurian exception') might not suffice.[74] General knowledge accessible to the academic and commercial communities would.[75] Since 2001, however, digital searching has rendered previously obscure journals more readily accessible. It may be increasingly difficult to claim lack of accessibility to published research. A more pressing difficulty is differentiating the relevant from the irrelevant or poor-quality research.

Were this aspect of *A v NBA* to be followed in the higher courts, there would be potential for the Consumer Protection Act to make a difference.[76] A producer invoking the development risks defence would have to establish that the defect in the drug, or device, or bodily product, was undiscoverable and the onus would lie on him to prove this.

12.8 Collective actions

Class or 'collective' actions where members of a larger faction sue on behalf of the whole group, are common in the USA, but rarer and more limited[77] in the UK. The most common procedural method for a collective action is the Group Litigation Order,[78] but this is more a method of case management

[72] Discussed in C Hodges, 'Developing Risks: Unanswered Questions' (1998) 61 *Modern Law Review* 560; M Mildred and G Howells, 'Comment on Development Risks: "Unanswered Questions"' (1998) 61 *Modern Law Review* 570.

[73] And see *Richardson v LRC Products Ltd* [2000] Lloyd's Rep Med 280.

[74] [2001] Lloyd's Rep Med 187, at 220–221.

[75] See G Howells and M Mildred, 'Infected Blood: Defect and Discoverability: A First Exposition of the EC Product Liability Directive' (2002) 65 *Modern Law Review* 95.

[76] For a contrary view, see J Stapleton (1999) 34 *Texas International Law Journal* 45 and J Stapleton, 'Bugs in the Anglo-American Products Liability' (2002) 53 *South Carolina Law Review* 1225.

[77] See, for example, *Emerald Supplies Ltd v British Airways Plc* [2010] EWCA Civ 1284.

[78] Civil Procedure Rules, 19.10: A Group Litigation Order (GLO) means an order made under rule 19.11 to provide for the case management of claims which give rise to common or related issues of fact or law (the 'GLO issues').

rather than a representative action. At the time of writing, there are several current GLOs relating to medicinal products and devices.[79] One example is the Contaminated Blood Products Group Litigation which, pending the outcome of the Infected Blood Inquiry, focuses on infection of blood products with Hepatitis C and HIV. There are also GLOs relating to medicines and devices at the heart of the Cumberlege Review, referred to at 12.1 above. The review considered some of the failed group litigation attempts and difficulties in establishing negligence and recommended new *ex gratia* schemes for each of the three interventions (hormone pregnancy tests, sodium valproate and pelvic mesh), to provide need-based payment, funded by the state and relevant manufacturers.[80] This recommendation was rejected on the basis that the government's focus is on funding improvements to safety and in improving the welfare system so that it better meets the needs of disabled people, rather than improving redress through *ex gratia* schemes.[81]

12.9 CJD contaminated blood products

When bovine spongiform encephalopathy (BSE) was linked to new variant Creutzfeldt-Jakob Disease (vCJD), a fatal neurological disease, a class action was mounted against the Government.[82] It petered out when, without admission of liability, a no-fault compensation scheme, run by the national CJD Surveillance Unit, was put in place in 2001 in the wake of the BSE Inquiry. The scheme has been criticised for its complexity and the extensive discretion given to Trustees, but an application for judicial review of the Department of Health's decision to reject radical amendment failed.[83]

In 2004, the Secretary of State announced a similar *ex gratia* payment scheme for people infected with Hepatitis C from NHS blood or blood products.[84] In *R (Moore) v Skipton Fund Ltd*[85] M applied for judicial review of the terms of the scheme. During the course of medical treatment, M was infected with Hepatitis C in 1987. Very occasionally, the immune system clears the body of the disease. In the vast majority of this small number of cases, this occurs in the early, acute stage of the disease, in which case, no compensation is payable. M's body was clear of the disease and, according to the scheme, she bore the burden of proving, with 'robust medical evidence', that this occurred in the later chronic stage of the disease if she were to be paid compensation. M could not prove this and complained that such proof was, in her case, scientifically impossible. Her application failed. Parker J held that, given the

[79] Since 2015 the government has published a list of ongoing GLOs. See GOV.UK, 'Group Litigation Orders' www.gov.uk/guidance/group-litigation-orders.

[80] Cumberlege Review, recommendation 4.

[81] *Government Response to the Report of the Independent Medicines and Medical Devices Safety Review* (2021), 3.6–3.8.

[82] See, for example, 'Families of CJD Victims Will Sue for Millions' *Telegraph* (2001) 19 June.

[83] See *R (McVey) v Secretary of State for Health* [2010] EWHC 437 (Admin).

[84] DH, 'Details of Hepatitis C Ex-Gratia Payment Scheme Announced' 2004/0025.

[85] [2010] EWHC 3070 (Admin).

statistical improbability of the disease clearing after six months, and the low risks of long-term problems if it cleared before that time, it was right that M must demonstrate that she had suffered the chronic stage of the disease. As we have seen, the Infected Blood Inquiry, chaired by Sir Brian Langstaff, was set up to investigate the infection of up to 30,000 people with infected blood in what has been hailed the biggest treatment disaster in NHS history. Part of its focus is the financial assistance provided to those infected and affected.[86]

Fears have also arisen surrounding the contamination of blood products with vCJD. In 2003, it was found that a blood donor may have transmitted vCJD to a patient who underwent a blood transfusion.[87] The National Blood Service[88] now asks anyone who has received blood products since 1980 not to donate blood. A donor history is taken from potential or definite vCJD cases, and their blood products recalled. Plasma is imported from countries with few or no cases of BSE. All children born after 1996 receive this plasma.[89] Since 2005, donors and donees who are identified as being 'at risk' for public health purposes are informed of the public health precautions they and their healthcare staff should take. Around six thousand patients, many of them haemophiliacs, were told they are 'at risk'. For them the uncertainty had the potential to blight their lives. There is no test and no cure for this fatal disease. Today, there remain considerable uncertainties about vCJD, but the estimated risk is decreasing as time goes on and few clinical cases emerge.[90]

In the case of vCJD, acceptance of compensation does not preclude legal action.[91] For those infected, group litigation is conceivable if it can be demonstrated that the Government was aware of the potential risk but took no action because of the cost of alternative synthetic products.[92]

12.10 Causation

The claimants in *A v NBA* were lucky in one respect. They knew who had supplied the 'defective' blood. Where a claim relates to a drug, a potential claimant may well have taken the drug over several years and not be able to trace which of several drug companies manufactured the drug that caused his

86 See Cabinet Office, *Compensation and Redress for the Victims of Infected Blood: Recommendations for a Framework* (2022) conducted by Sir Robert Francis KC, which led to interim payments. See Cabinet Office, *Infected Blood Interim Compensation Payment Scheme* (2022).

87 See, for example, CA Llewelyn *et al*, 'Possible Transmission of Variant Creutzfeldt-Jakob Disease by Blood Transfusion' (2004) 363 *Lancet* 417.

88 Part of NHS Blood and Transplant, a Special Health Authority established by the NHS Blood and Transplant Order, SI 2005/2529.

89 *UK Blood Services Joint Statement on Blood Safety*, August 2011.

90 DHSC, *Risk Assessment of the Transmission of vCJD by Blood Components* (2019).

91 *vCJD Main Trust Deed* (2002), para B.

92 For an examination of product liability for pathogenically infected products, see J Stapleton (2002) 53 *South Carolina Law Review* 1225. For tortious liability arising from public health initiatives see R Martin, 'Public Health and the Scope of Potential Liability in Tort' (2005) 21 *Professional Negligence* 39.

injury. An analogous problem arose in *Fairchild v Glenhaven Funeral Services Ltd*[93] facing workers who contracted the industrial disease, mesothelioma. They could show that their illness was caused by exposure to asbestos dust or fibres. They established that their employers were negligent in exposing them to asbestos. However, as they had worked for several companies during their working life, they could not pinpoint which employer was actually responsible for their disease, which can be caused by a single fibre entering the lung. The Law Lords ruled that as each defendant employer had increased the risk to the affected workers, causation was established against all of them. In the USA, in *Sindell v Abbott Laboratories*,[94] it has been held that where patients are exposed to risk from a defective drug manufactured by several different companies, each company is held liable in proportion to its market share. Lord Hoffmann in *Fairchild* did not consider that the industrial disease claims before the Law Lords and claims against drug companies were the same. He said that the risk from consuming a drug bought in one shop is not increased by the fact it can be bought in another shop. With respect, he overlooks the possibility of drug-induced injury caused by prolonged or incremental use of a medicine. However, more importantly, he signalled that, even if *Fairchild* does not conclusively determine that the *Sindell* rule prevails in England, he looked at the possibility with some favour.[95]

Lord Hoffmann implemented this approach in *Barker v Corus*,[96] which also involved a mesothelioma victim employed by a number of employers who had breached their duty of care and exposed the employee to asbestos. Lord Hoffmann stated:

> In my opinion, the attribution of liability according to the relative degree of contribution to the chance of the disease being contracted would smooth the roughness of the justice which a rule of joint and several liability creates. The defendant was a wrongdoer, it is true, and should not be allowed to escape liability altogether, but he should not be liable for more than the damage which he caused and, since this is a case in which science can deal only in probabilities, the law should accept that position and attribute liability according to probabilities.[97]

Consequently, Corus was liable according to the probability of risk it created. Corus was not liable for the probability of risk created by the first, insolvent employer. This meant that Mr Barker went under-compensated. Those employed by a single solvent employer, however, could be assured of 100 per cent compensation. The Government responded with the Compensation Act 2006, section 3 of which reverses the effect of Barker for mesothelioma victims and provides that compensation will be joint and several. Victims of mesothelioma can seek full compensation from any solvent negligent employer. The negligent employer will then be able to claim back contributions from other

93 [2002] UKHL 22. See also *Gregg v Scott* [2005] UKHL 2. These cases are discussed in Chapter 8.
94 (1980) 607 P 2d 924.
95 [2006] UKHL 20, [74].
96 Ibid. Examined in 8.15 above.
97 Ibid, [43].

responsible persons under the Civil Liability (Contribution) Act 1978. *Barker* remains an authoritative decision in non-mesothelioma cases.[98] The case was applied in *Heneghan v Manchester Dry Docks Limited and others*[99] in a case of asbestos lung cancer.

Problems proving causation are not confined to those cases where there are multiple defendants. The toxicity of medicinal products and the health of patients render a causal link between the product and the alleged harm particularly hard to prove.[100] Does the *Fairchild* exception to the normal causation principles extend to cases involving a single defendant? The Supreme Court in *Sienkiewicz v Greif*[101] held that it can. Enid Costello died of mesothelioma in 2006 having been exposed to asbestos in the course of her employment as well as low levels of asbestos in the environment. Overturning the Court of Appeal decision, the claim succeeded on the basis of the *Fairchild* exception.

Sienkiewicz raises another issue in relation to causation in product liability cases. The claim failed in the Court of Appeal on the basis that the employers had not doubled the relative risk of the claimant contracting mesothelioma.[102] The 'doubles the risk' approach involves a statistical risk analysis based on epidemiological evidence. In other words, it looks at the effect of the drug on the population as a whole. If the analysis reveals more than double the chances of injury, it is considered on the balance of probabilities to have caused the injury. This approach has proved problematic in the US but has found favour in some cases in the UK.[103] In *Sienkiewicz*, the Supreme Court, however, deemed the 'doubles the risk' approach unsuited to mesothelioma cases, because science cannot pinpoint the precise origin of the disease. For non-mesothelioma cases, on the other hand, it seems that the 'doubles the risk' approach survives *Sienkiewicz*, at least where there are competing alternative (rather than cumulative) causes of disease.[104] Could the 'doubles the risk' approach be used in product liability litigation? Whilst possible, it seems unlikely. In Australia, a claim that the painkiller Vioxx[105] doubled the risk

98 The Court of Appeal in *IEG Ltd v Zurich Insurance Plc* [2013] EWCA Civ 39 held that the common law decision of *Barker* was effectively overruled by the Compensation Act 2006. However, the Supreme Court allowed the appeal: Neither the 2006 Act nor *Durham v BAI (Run Off) Ltd* [2012] UKSC 14 (*Trigger* litigation) undermines the decision in Barker. See *Zurich Insurance Plc v IEG Ltd* [2015] UKSC 33.

99 [2014] EWHC 4190; [2016] EWCA Civ 86.

100 R Goldberg, 'Epidemiological Uncertainty, Causation and Drug Product Liability' (2014) 59(4) *McGill law Journal* 777.

101 [2011] UKSC 10I.

102 [2009] EWCA Civ 1159.

103 See *XYZ v Schering Health Care Ltd* [2002] EWHC 1420 (QB) discussed at 12.13 below and see R Goldberg, *Medical Product Liability and Regulation* (2013) Hart, pp 90–95.

104 *Jones v Secretary of State for Energy and Climate Change* [2012] EWHC 2936 (QB), [42], [53]. See E O'Leary, 'Double or Nothing' (2013) 163(7553) *NLJ* 22 March.

105 See further at 12.14 below.

of heart attack across the population and thus materially contributed to the claimant's heart attack was accepted at first instance but rejected on appeal.[106] Whilst a relative doubled risk shows an association in the general population, other factors, such as the individual's obesity and history of smoking, indicated a lack of causality in the individual case.

In Chapter 6, we examined a causation case which had potentially wider implications for product liability. In *Chester v Afshar*[107] Miss Chester underwent surgery on the advice of Mr Afshar, her surgeon, during which she suffered nerve damage to her legs. The operation was performed with due care but, even so, there was a one–two per cent risk of nerve damage. Miss Chester was not warned of the risk. Had she been so warned, she would have deferred the operation, but on the balance of probabilities, it could not be said that she would have withheld consent. Did the lack of causation defeat her claim? The majority held that it did not.[108] If the same practical justice is applied to product liability could a failure by the manufacturer or supplier to warn a patient of side-effects or adverse reactions result in liability, even if the claimant cannot prove that they would not have used the product if they had been properly warned?[109] It now seems unlikely. Recent case-law has sought to confine *Chester* or avoid its application.[110]

12.11 Prevention better than cure?[111]

The thalidomide tragedy prompted new laws to vet drugs before they could be marketed in the UK. The Medicines Act 1968 provided for the licensing and monitoring of drugs. In 1998 a similar system was set up to regulate medical devices (for example diagnostic tests or intra-uterine devices) and in 2003 both systems were brought under a single agency: the Medicines and Healthcare products Regulatory Agency (MHRA), an executive agency of the Department of Health and Social Care (DHSC), based in London. With a staff of around 1,200, the MHRA supports expert advisory bodies, such as the Devices Expert Advisory Committee,[112] and the Commission on Human

106 *Merck Sharp & Dohme (Australia) Pty Ltd v Peterson* [2011] FCAFC 128, [2012] HCA Trans 105, discussed in R Goldberg *Medical Product Liability and Regulation* (2013) Hart, pp 94–95.

107 [2004] UKHL 41. For a critique, see T Clark and D Nolan, 'A Critique of *Chester v Afshar*' (2014) 34 *OJLS* 659, exploring an alternative position taken in the High Court of Australia in *Wallace v Kam* [2013] HCA 19 (2013) 87 ALJR 648.

108 [2004] UKHL 41, [87].

109 See L Jones, '*Chester v Afshar*: Effect of Product Liability' (2005) 5(1) *Health and Safety Law* 12.

110 See for example *Correia v University Hospital of North Staffordshire NHS Trust* [2017] EWCA Civ 356; *Duce v Worcestershire Acute Hospitals NHS Trust* [2018] EWCA Civ 1307.

111 We deal predominantly with medicines here.

112 Which replaced the Committee on the Safety of Devices in 2015 following recommendations in Professor T Stephenson's report: *Expert Clinical Advice – MHRA Medical Devices* (April 2014).

Medicines (CHM),[113] which advises ministers on the safety, efficacy and quality of medicinal products.

UK laws (including over 200 statutory instruments) are consolidated in the Human Medicines Regulations 2012.[114] The licensing process (described below) evolved to take into consideration European regulations that applied before EU Exit. The 2012 Regulations implemented EU Directive 2001/83/EC relating to medicinal products for human use[115] and also EC Regulation 726/2004 on the authorisation of medicinal products[116] and EU Directive 2010/84/EU on pharmacovigilance (safety-monitoring) in the EU market. In 2020, the UK became a non-EU country and the MHRA became the UK's standalone medicinal products regulator. The 2012 Regulations were amended in 2019 and 2020 to allow continued sale of and access to medicines post-EU Exit, and to implement the Northern Ireland Protocol, where new EU pharmaceutical laws remain relevant.[117]

No medicine[118] may be manufactured, imported or marketed without a licence. There are three different types of licence in the development of an investigational medicinal product. First, the companies manufacturing and distributing the medicines are required to have 'manufacturer's and wholesale dealer's licences'; second, 'clinical trial authorisations' are required in order to develop new products; and third a 'marketing authorisation' is required before the product can be marketed.[119]

There are various routes to marketing authorisation. The European Medicines Agency (EMA) gives centralised authorisation valid in all European Union (EU) and European Economic Area (EEA) states. The EMA was based in London until EU Exit and is now based in Amsterdam. One of its committees is called the Committee for Medicinal Products for Human Use (CHMP),[120] which licenses human medicinal products for distribution across the EU. Some drugs must be authorised by this route. Post-EU Exit, centrally granted marketing authorisations in Great Britain were converted to UK marketing authorisations. For two

113 Established under the Medicines Act 1968, s 2. The terms of reference are set out in s 3 as amended by the Medicines (Advisory Bodies) Regulations 2005, SI 2005/1094.

114 SI 2012/1916 (as amended).

115 Directive 2001/83/EC, as amended by Directives 2002/98/EC, 2003/63/EC, 2004/24/EC, 2004/27/EC, 2006/1901/EC, 2007/1394/EC, 2008/29/EC, 2009/53/EC, 2009/120/EC, 2010/84/EU, 2011/62/EU and 2012/26/EU.

116 As amended by Regulation (EU) 2019/5.

117 Human Medicines (Amendment etc) (EU Exit) Regulations 2019 and 2020, SI 2019/775, 2020/1488.

118 As to what constitutes a medicine, see MHRA, *A Guide to What is a Medicinal Product* (March 2020) MHRA Guidance Note 8.

119 Note that the COVID-19 vaccines were rolled out via a special route allowing temporary approval to respond to a public health crisis: Human Medicines Regulations 2012, SI 2012/1916, reg 174, as amended by the Human Medicines (Coronavirus and Influenza) (Amendment) Regulations 2020, SI 2020/1125, reg 6.

120 Established by Regulation 726/2004, replacing the Committee for Proprietary Medicinal Products (CPMP).

years from 1 January 2021, decisions taken by the European Commission to approve new marketing authorisations were adopted in Great Britain. An alternative route is the decentralised / mutual recognition procedure whereby drugs licensed in a specific member state are recognised in other EU and EEA member states. The MHRA can recognise marketing authorisations approved in those states with a view to granting marketing authorisation in the UK or Great Britain.

A product can also be licensed in the UK only, via the MHRA. To improve the attractiveness of UK-based approvals, new assessment routes were introduced in 2021. The Accelerated Assessment Procedure promises a decision within 150 days and applies to both new and existing drugs. A Rolling Review route applies to novel medicines and facilitates input and feedback from the regulator.

Once marketing authorisation is obtained, the product manufacturer must show that the product is cost-effective before the NHS will make it available.[121] The MHRA then subject the product to a lifetime of checks and inspections, operating systems to control product information, advertising,[122] pharmacovigilance and potentially reclassification (for example, if a prescription drug is made available in pharmacies or ordinary shops). Marketing authorisations are granted for periods of up to five years after which they must be renewed.

The CHM 'promote the collection and investigation of information relating to adverse reactions for human medicines'.[123] Post-marketing surveillance systems include the 'yellow card scheme', which concerns adverse reactions to medicines and Adverse Incidence Reports regarding devices. On the basis of these systems the CHM makes recommendations regarding safety issues and the minimisation of risk and less urgent issues are communicated via a regular bulletin.

Section 28 of the Medicines Act 1968 empowers the Minister to revoke an existing licence. Several grounds for revocation are established, of which the most important is where:

> ... medicinal products of any description to which the licence relates can no longer be regarded as products which can safely be administered for the purposes indicated in the licence, or can no longer be regarded as efficacious for those purposes ...

The decision to withdraw a drug from the market is no longer solely a matter for the manufacturer. A manufacturer aggrieved by the refusal or revocation of a product licence may seek a review by the CHM. No product licence can be refused or revoked without consultation with the CHM. A manufacturer

121 The 'Transparency Directive' 89/105 EEC governs transparency of measures designed to regulate pricing. Proposals for a new directive were withdrawn in 2014.

122 Prescription drugs cannot be advertised directly to the public. Human Medicines Regulations 2012, SI 2012/1916, Pt 14, implementing European Directive 2001/83/EC as amended.

123 As do the Advisory Board on the Registration of Homeopathic Products and the Herbal Medicines Advisory Committee.

whose product has been approved by the CHM, but who is refused a licence by the Minister, has a right to a further hearing. If the Minister chooses, as they may, to reject the CHM's advice, they must set up an independent inquiry before which the manufacturer may state their case.[124]

Does post-market surveillance work? The Cumberlege Review found it to be flawed, stating:

> It is clear that there is gross under-reporting, and our complaints systems are both too complex and too diffuse to allow early signal detection.[125]

Manufacturers were too motivated by sales, evidence gathering was insufficient, negative results of research projects were sometimes buried. The review pointed to systemic failings and a dangerous and unsafe system. Litigation has proved insufficient to bring about either justice or change. Dame Cumberlege recommended a new Patient Safety Commissioner to 'champion the value of listening to patients and a new independent Redress Agency to address patient needs'. A duty to appoint such a commissioner was established in section 1 of the Medicines and Medical Devices Act 2021. But the Cumberlege Report's recommendation to set up a new non-adversarial Redress Agency that would focus on systemic failings rather than apportioning individual blame fell on deaf ears.[126]

12.12 Off-label drug use[127]

Drugs are sometimes used 'off-label' – that is, in an unapproved form or dosage. For example, a drug licensed for use in adults might be used 'off-label' to treat a child with a related illness when no licensed treatment exists.[128] The alternative would be to refuse the child treatment until a clinical trial can be carried out and marketing authorisation received.[129] Clearly this would be too late for the patient. In other cases a patient might suffer a rare disease and a trial would not be financially viable. As a result, some 'off-label' drug use is sanctioned, but the lack of regulation and limited recourse to redress can expose (sometimes vulnerable) patients to risk.[130]

124 Medicines Act 1968, s 21(5).
125 Cumberlege Review, 1.20.
126 Ibid, recommendation 3; DHSC, *Government Response to the Report of the Independent Medicines and Medical Devices Safety Review* (2021), p 8. See 11.6 above.
127 For a description of off-label use in the EU see: EU, *Study on Off-label Use of Medicinal Products in the European Union* (2017). The report indicated that off-label use is particularly prolific in paediatrics.
128 See Royal College of Paediatrics and Child Health, *The Use of Unlicensed Medicines or Licensed Medicines for Unlicensed Applications in Paediatric Practice* (2013) (last modified in 2019).
129 See 8.9 above for discussion of the Access to Medical Treatments (Innovation) Act 2016.
130 See for example R Harding and E Peel, '"He was Like a Zombie": Off-Label Prescription of Antipsychotic Drugs in Dementia' (2013) 21(2) *Med Law Rev* 243.

The drug company should not actively market the drug for this use. However, it has been alleged that the profits attainable by marketing a drug for unlicensed use might justify the fines imposed upon the company if they are caught.[131] A lacuna in the law relating to off-label drug use was revealed in 2008. The anti-depressant drug, Seroxat, was licensed for use in adults, but frequently used off-label to treat teenagers. GlaxoSmithKline were alleged to have withheld clinical trial data showing that Seroxat was ineffective and potentially unsafe for those under the age of 18.[132] However, the regulations controlling safety information did not extend to off-label drug use and as a result the case against the drug company was weak. Nevertheless, the MHRA was much criticised for its decision not to prosecute, especially as other countries responded far more harshly.[133] In 2009 the Medicines for Human Use (Marketing Authorisations Etc) Amendment Regulations 2009[134] extended the requirement to provide safety information to encompass off-label drug use.

12.13 Holding regulators to account

The MHRA authorises, inspects, surveys and enforces the use of medicines and devices, aiming to protect, promote and improve public health. But does the system adequately represent patient's interests? Critics fear that drug regulators lack transparency and favour efficacy over patient safety. The Cumberlege Review recommended reform of the MHRA to strengthen adverse event reporting and improve engagement with patients.[135]

Can aggrieved patients sue the regulators? The possibility of governmental liability for drug-induced injury was aired even in the thalidomide days. The Health Minister, Sir Keith Joseph, dismissed suggestions that the Government could be liable. He argued further that, even when the elaborate licensing provisions of the 1968 Act were in force, the legal liability for any defect in the drug rested on the manufacturers alone.[136] The Infected Blood Inquiry is,

131 D Evans, 'When Drug Makers' Profits Outweigh Penalties' *The Washington Post* (2010) 21 March. Though see report of 'unprecedented' $3bn (£1.9bn) settlement in 2012: 'GlaxoSmithKline to pay $3bn in US Drug Fraud Scandal' *BBC News* (2012) 2 July.

132 L McGoey and E Jackson, 'Seroxat and the Suppression of Clinical Trial Data: Regulatory Failure and the Uses of Legal Ambiguity' (2009) 35 *J Med Ethics* 107. For a comparable US case see US Department of Justice, 'Pharmaceutical Giant AstraZeneca to Pay $520 Million for Off-label Drug Marketing' (2010) April 27.

133 D Batty, 'Seroxat' *The Times* (2008) 6 March; 'Critics of the MHRA and the pharmaceutical industry point to the tougher penalties faced by firms overseas. In the US, GSK was sued by the New York state attorney general, Eliot Spitzer, and settled for $2.5m (£1.25m) and an agreement to publish all its trial results – negative or positive – on a publicly available database.'

134 SI 2009/2820, consolidated with minor amendments in the Human Medicines Regulations 2012, SI 2012/1916.

135 Cumberlege Review, recommendation 6.

136 HC Deb, vol 847, col 440–441, 29 November 1972.

at the time of writing, considering whether the government could have done more to ensure self-sufficiency in the UK rather than relying on commercial products from abroad, and will consider what was or ought to have been known by the government about the risks.

A claim was mounted against the Committee on Safety of Medicines (CSM) (which was replaced by the CHM in 2005) in *Smith v Secretary of State for Health (on behalf of the Committee for Safety of Medicines)*.[137] In May 1986, 7-year-old Amanda Smith caught chickenpox and was given one aspirin tablet on two consecutive days by her mother, who followed the advice on the label. Amanda's condition worsened. She developed spastic tetraplegia and was eventually diagnosed with Reye's Syndrome. In June 1986, the CSM issued a warning that aspirin should not be given to children under the age of 12 except on medical advice because it could trigger Reye's Syndrome. They had met in March 1986, but delayed the warning so as to cooperate with the drug companies. No interim warning was made. Was the CSM negligent? Morland J held that it was not. There was no breach of statutory duty or common law duty of care. The decision by the CSM was a discretionary policy decision which is not, Morland J held, justiciable in private law, even if there was fault in the timetabling of the warning.[138]

In *XYZ and Others v Schering Health Care Ltd*,[139] the CSM was once again under fire, but this time from the drug companies. The case involved a group action by claimants alleged to have suffered cardiovascular injuries as a result of taking certain brands of the Combined Oral Contraceptive ('the Pill'). In 1995, the CSM circulated a warning to prescribers of the Pill that three as yet unpublished articles indicated a twofold increase in risk of venous-thromboembolism. The defendants argued that the letter was ill-considered and that the ensuing 'pill scare' was a public health disaster. Mackay J held that there was not in fact a twofold increase in risk and on that basis the claimants lost their case. Nor was the advisability of the CSM's letter under review in this case. Regulators have the unenviable task of deciding when it is appropriate to 'act as though a given association were causal rather than to continue to assume that it is not'.[140]

In *R (Roche Registration Limited) v Secretary of State for Health*[141] the MHRA supplied a pre-inspection report on Roche's pharmacovigilance systems (monitoring the effects of licensed drugs) to the EMA, which then used it for penalty proceedings. It was not clear that the EMA had the requisite power to request the report. Had the MHRA acted unfairly in collating the information and passing it on? Carr J held that the MHRA acted appropriately. Roche was not misled about the purpose of the inspection or the use of the report.

137 [2002] EWHC 200 (QB).
138 Ibid, [93] per Morland J.
139 [2002] EWHC 1420 (QB).
140 [2002] EWHC 200 (QB), [19] per Mackay J.
141 [2014] EWHC 2256.

Could a claim against the CHM, in effect for negligently monitoring drugs and/or blood products, succeed? In *Smith*, Morland J did not rule out the possibility. Neither the Secretary of State nor the CHM enjoys blanket immunity from a common law suit.[142] Improper exercise of a duty, such as the postponing of a meeting 'because it clashed with the Epsom Derby meeting',[143] would clearly be considered negligent. Beyond that, claimants would have to persuade the court that it was 'just, fair and reasonable' for the CHM to be subjected to a duty of care to individual patients and that the decision was not discretionary or policy-based. Two particular questions will pose problems for claimants. The court will seek to ask whether the scheme of regulation established by the Medicines Act and now heavily influenced by European legislation was designed to provide a right to compensation to those injured by unsafe drugs. And given that the primary responsibility for the medicine still rests with the drug company, should the government be liable for their wrongdoing?

12.14 Claims brought abroad

The majority of drug companies are multinationals. Drugs are not confined within national borders. British women who suffered injury as a result of suing the Dalkon Shield IUD sued the manufacturers in the USA and recovered compensation from a settlement fund set up when the company went bankrupt.[144] When can an injured patient resort to a foreign court and why should they want to?

When a claim has a foreign element a set of rules known as private international law, or conflict of laws, comes into play. These are excessively complex and we give only the barest outline of the relevant law. Essentially, when a claim for negligence is brought, the claimant can sue in any country where a relevant act of negligence occurred, or in the country where the drug company is based. There may be more than one such country. So, in the case of a defective drug, negligence may have occurred both in the country where it was carelessly manufactured and in the country where it was carelessly marketed as safe[145] and injured the claimant. It is on the basis of the careless manufacture of the device in the USA that the women suing over the Dalkon Shield were able to go to Court in USA. Where there is a dispute over whether an action should be allowed to go ahead, the law of the country where the claimant is trying to sue determines whether it should do so.

Why should anyone want to sue abroad? After all, if they took the drug here and were injured here they can bring their claim in their homeland on the

142 *Stovin v Wise* [1996] AC 923, HL, at 937–941, per Lord Nicholls.

143 *Smith v Secretary of State for Health* [2002] EWHC 200 (QB), [95].

144 See Ferguson, *Drug Injuries and the Pursuit of Compensation*, pp 6–8.

145 *Distillers Co (Biochemicals) Ltd v Thompson* [1971] AC 458. Where a New Zealand mother was allowed to sue the British company Distillers in New Zealand over thalidomide manufactured here; the essence of the negligence alleged was failure to warn her, in New Zealand, of the danger to her baby.

basis that it was here the drug caused them harm. There are three reasons why claimants may opt for the hassle of a foreign lawsuit. First, the procedural rules in the foreign courts may be more favourable to claimants. They may be able to conduct a 'collective (or class) action' more effectively than in England. Second, there remain financial incentives to sue in the USA if you can. Not only is liability for drugs strict, but awards of damages are made by juries, and are generally much higher than English judge-made awards. The contingency fee system may offer more favourable access to the courts than conditional fees do here. And finally, a threat to sue in the USA may prompt the defendants into offering a more generous settlement than would otherwise have been the case.

However legal action abroad is fraught with difficulties. When the pharmaceutical giant, Merck, withdrew the drug Vioxx from the market because of links to cardiovascular problems such as heart attacks,[146] successful claims were brought in Australia and the USA. However, legal aid was refused in England and Wales,[147] and law firms were unwilling to risk action based on a conditional fee arrangement.[148] As a result, UK citizens took their case to the American courts, but this too was unsuccessful.[149]

12.15 Vaccine damage: a special case?

Vaccine damage has received special treatment because of the distinction in social effect between vaccines and other drugs.[150] Generally the benefit and risk of taking a drug rests with the individual patient alone. No one else suffers directly if he does not take the drug. No one else benefits directly if he does. With a vaccine the position is different. If an individual is immunised, the person himself benefits from the immunity conferred and his friends, schoolfellows or colleagues benefit from the reduction or elimination of the risk of that disease being passed on to them. Consequently, vaccines have been approved in emergency situations such as swine flu and COVID-19, and routine vaccination of young children against diseases such as tetanus, diphtheria, polio, measles, meningitis C and whooping cough is actively promoted by the DHSC. The whooping cough vaccine initially caused outcry and distress, and concerns about the MMR vaccine generated similar controversy. A number of children healthy before vaccination have, their parents claim, suffered severe and lasting brain damage as a consequence of receiving the vaccine. More recently however, the scientific claims that

146 See, for example, T Nesi, *Poison Pills: The Untold Story of the Vioxx Drug Scandal* (2008) Thomas Dunne Books.

147 But not in Scotland: *Cooper v Merck Sharp & Dohme* [2012] CSOH 48; *Hamilton and Others v Merck Sharp & Dohme Ltd* [2012] CSOH 144, discussed in R Goldberg, *Medical Product Liability and Regulation* (2013) Hart, p 8.

148 J Dreaper, 'UK Vioxx Cases Await Court Hearing' *BBC News* (2006) 11 April.

149 *In re Vioxx Litigation*, 395 NJ Super 358, 373–374 (Sup Ct NJ, App Div, 2007): See J Robins, 'Stars and Gripes' (2006) 46 *Litigation Funding* 4–6 discussing a New Jersey Court decision to reject UK class action for alleged injuries suffered as a result of using Vioxx.

150 See in particular, the Pearson Report, ch 25.

MMR vaccine had such an effect have been largely discredited and the doctor who led the research was found guilty of serious professional misconduct by the General Medical Council.[151]

What remedies have the parents of a vaccine-damaged child? First they may, as a number of parents of children allegedly damaged by whooping cough vaccine have done, seek to use the tort of negligence to obtain compensation. The advantage of this course is that, if the claim were successful, their children would receive full compensation for any disability caused by the vaccine. One problem is whom to sue. The crux of the question is often whether the risk of the vaccine to a child is greater than the risks posed by contracting the disease itself. An action against a doctor for negligently using a reputable vaccine is likely to fail because, even if some doctors and experts condemn its use, a substantial body of informed opinion still backs the vaccine. A negligence action is usually only viable if some special feature of the child's history should have ruled out routine vaccination, or if symptoms at a first vaccination, indicating that further vaccination was unwise, were missed. Suing the manufacturers will run into the problem of the risk–benefit ratio of the product. The manufacturers dispute the level of risk from the vaccine and will argue that the overwhelming benefit to the community of vaccination outweighs any risk to a very few. They will contend that, properly used, the vaccine is not defective. In relation to the whooping cough vaccine the companies deny that the vaccine does indeed cause brain damage. In *Loveday v Renton*[152] a judge held that the claimants failed to prove that the pertussis (whooping cough) vaccine caused the child's brain damage. Attempts to recover compensation for vaccine injuries through claims in negligence have generally proved unsuccessful in England.[153] The MMR litigation cost in the region of £15 million. In 2004, the High Court rejected an application for a judicial review of an earlier decision to withdraw legal aid on the basis that the claims were unlikely to succeed and would cost the public a further £10 million.[154] Today legal aid would not be accessible for such a claim. Unless there is a very good chance that the case will succeed and unless the claim is based on solid research, group actions such as the MMR Vaccine Group Litigation are unlikely to attract funding via a conditional fee or damages-based agreement.[155]

151 GMC, *Dr Andrew Wakefield: Determination on Serious Professional Misconduct and Sanction*, May 2010. Accessible at www.gmc-uk.org. A finding of serious professional misconduct against Professor John Walker-Smith, who had carried out tests on children later used by Dr Wakefield, was quashed in *Walker-Smith v General Medical Council* [2012] EWHC 503 (Admin).

152 [1990] 1 Med LR 117.

153 Though parents in Ireland succeeded, see *Best v Wellcome Foundation* [1993] 2 IR 421.

154 See C Dyer, 'Commission Withdraws Legal Aid for Parents Suing over MMR Vaccine' (2003) 327 *BMJ* 641. And see 'MMR Vaccine: Lawyers Sued for Pursuing Claim Based on Link to Autism' *BBC News* (2014) 26 June, detailing legal action against lawyers for pursuing a 'hopeless claim'.

155 See 9.2 above.

The problems of litigation deter many parents from going to court. Successive reviews of the issue of compensation for vaccine damage recognised that it is an example of injury where compensation via the tort of negligence, or the Consumer Protection Act, may be inappropriate. There may prove to be no negligence on anyone's part because the benefit to the majority is held to justify the risk to a small minority. Yet it is scarcely fair that those who suffer damage should bear the whole burden of disability alone. On the recommendation of the Pearson Commission, Parliament enacted the Vaccine Damage Payments Act 1979 to provide for a no-fault compensation scheme for vaccine-damaged individuals. The current amount payable is £120,000.[156] The making of a payment under the 1979 Act does not debar a claimant from also suing for negligence in respect of the vaccination.

The Act remains a target of criticism.[157] Successful cases are rare. £120,000 may sound a substantial amount. If a child is so damaged that he will never be able to care for himself and earn his own living, it falls far short of his needs. A successful tort claim would result in a multi-million-pound award. The Act remains a compromise. It has not replaced tort with an adequate compensation mechanism. Critics complain that the ever-present problem of causation of drug-induced injury is simply ignored in the Act. The claimant must establish on the balance of probability that his disablement resulted from the vaccine.[158]

The emergence of new pandemic diseases such as swine flu, Ebola and COVID-19 have led to collaboration and financing to develop vaccines. The question of how inevitable (if rare) vaccine damage is compensated is one of the ethical considerations relevant to its use. In October 2020 the Human Medicine Regulations were amended[159] to allow temporary authorisation of batches of COVID-19 vaccines and to extend immunity from healthcare workers and manufacturers to companies producing them. Because longitudinal studies had not been conducted, the long-term effects of the vaccines were unclear.[160] Early cases of anaphylactoid reaction to the Pfizer vaccine in people with pre-existing allergies and then rare blood clot reactions to the Astra-Zeneca and Johnson & Johnson vaccines led to pauses, warnings and restrictions. COVID-19 vaccinations were added to the no-fault scheme in 2020.[161] Given

156 The Vaccine Damage Payments Act 1979 Statutory Sum Order 2007, SI 2007/1931.

157 See S Pywell, 'The Vaccine Damage Payment Scheme – A Proposal for Radical Reform' (2002) 9 *Journal of Social Security Law* 73.

158 See *Re John (A Minor: Vaccine Damage Payments scheme)* [2017] EWCA Civ 61: establishing that the determination of the severity of disablement can take account of prognosis.

159 Human Medicines (Coronavirus and Influenza) (Amendment) Regulations 2020, SI 2020/1125, amending the Human Medicines Regulations 2012, SI 2012/1916.

160 See 12.6 above.

161 Vaccine Damage Payments (Specified Disease) Order 2015, SI 2015/47 as amended by SI 2020/1411.

the scheme's serious limitations, Fairgrieve *et al* have convincingly argued that a bespoke COVID-19 vaccines compensation scheme should make eligibility automatic and cover loss of livelihood as well as medical costs.[162] Such claims are accentuated by the subsequent decision to mandate COVID-19 vaccination amongst certain populations. The Health and Social Care Act 2008 (Regulated Activities) Regulations 2014 were amended[163] to require that care home workers are 'vaccinated with the complete course of doses' unless they should not be vaccinated for clinical reasons. The aim was initially to extend the mandate to all healthcare workers with patient contact,[164] until a U-turn in January 2022 when two doses became less effective to infection with a new variant. The availability of effective redress when things go wrong is pertinent to the assessment of the proportionality of vaccine mandate.

162 D Fairgrieve *et al*, 'In Favour of a Bespoke COVID-19 Vaccines Compensation Scheme' (2021) 21(4) *The Lancet* P448. And see R Goldberg, 'Vaccine Damage Schemes in the US and UK Reappraised: Making Them Fit for Purpose in The Light of Covid-19' (2022) 42(4) *Legal Studies* 576.

163 The Health and Social Care Act 2008 (Regulated Activities) (Amendment) (Coronavirus) Regulations 2021, SI 2021/891, reg 5 amends reg 12 on 'safe care and treatment'.

164 DHSC, Press Release: *Government to Introduce COVID-19 Vaccination as a Condition of Deployment for all Frontline Health and Social Care Workers* (2021) 9 November.

Part III

MATTERS OF LIFE AND DEATH

Chapter 13

CONTRACEPTION, PREGNANCY AND CHILDBIRTH

13.1 Reproductive autonomy and reproductive health

> Gone are the days when it was thought that, on becoming pregnant, a woman lost, not only her capacity, but also her right to act as a genuinely autonomous human being.

So concluded Lady Hale in the 2015 Supreme Court decision of *Montgomery v Lanarkshire Health Board*.[1]

But we shall see in this chapter that choices in pregnancy spanning conception, pregnancy and childbirth are not always well protected by health professionals or the law. The Ockenden Review of Maternity Care[2] issued its final report into failings at Shrewsbury and Telford Hospital NHS Trust maternity unit in 2022. What started with a focus on twenty-three cases led to a total of 1,486 families coming forwards. Problems with governance and leadership and a failure to listen to women potentially contributed to the deaths of 201 babies and nine women and many others suffered physical and mental injuries. Two of the three products investigated in the 2020 Cumberlege Review[3] discussed at 12.1 above affected women in pregnancy and their children. Patient complaints about life-changing consequences were met with dismissive attitudes. The report highlighted a theme of misinformation and failures to warn patients of the risks: patients were not in a position to make informed decisions about their treatment in pregnancy.

The domestic courts have made efforts to resist a professional monopoly on choice. In *Rees v Darlington Memorial Hospital NHS Trust*[4] a woman who gave birth to a child after a failed sterilisation was said to have suffered a legal wrong – 'the denial of an important aspect of their personal autonomy,

1 [2015] UKSC 11.
2 DHSC, *Final Report of the Ockenden Review* (2022) HC1219. See 2.1 and 10.1 above. As we go to press, we also note concerns raised in the Kirkup report regarding performance, compassion and honesty: DHSC, *Maternity and Neonatal Services in East Kent: 'Reading the Signals' Report* (2022) HC681.
3 Baroness Julia Cumberlege (Chair), *First Do No Harm: The Report of the Independent Medicines and Medical Devices Safety Review* (2020).
4 [2003] UKHL 52.

viz the right to limit the size of their family.'[5] The majority of the House of Lords concurred with Lord Millett in *McFarlane v Tayside Health Board*[6] in his endorsement of a legal right of reproductive autonomy. English law today leaves such matters to personal choice.[7]

This chapter will examine several aspects of how the law implements or fails to implement broad notions of reproductive autonomy, embracing choices about whether or not to conceive or beget a child, and choices that may face women in the course of pregnancy. We also look at practical legal questions relating to contraception, pregnancy and childbirth.

13.2 Contraceptives: patients' rights

An infallible contraceptive has yet to be invented. Contraceptives, such as the Pill and the IUD (intra-uterine device), carry a price-tag. They pose some risk to women's health. Contraception is a medical as well as a social issue. And it largely concerns women for, except for the still-experimental male 'Pill', men must choose between the condom and vasectomy. The more sophisticated contraceptives which pose medical risk are used by women. A doctor advising a woman on contraception owes her the same duties as in any other area of medicine. They must offer competent and careful advice and must perform any technical procedure, for example inserting an IUD, skilfully.[8] The doctor must obtain consent to any invasive procedure and ensure that the patient is competent to give it.

Modern contraceptive treatments have resulted in litigation where they have resulted in adverse effects for women.[9] Several million dollars in compensation were paid out to women who suffered injury through use of the Dalkon shield, an IUD which caused substantial pelvic injuries to patients.[10] And the injectable contraceptive Depo-Provera led to a number of lawsuits in the United Kingdom. The use of Depo-Provera in its early years offers a classic example of how not to approach contraceptive advice and treatment.

Depo-Provera is a synthetic form of a natural hormone, which acts like most brands of the Pill to prevent eggs developing and makes the womb hostile to any fertilised embryo. One injection is effective for three months. Depo-Provera can produce unpredictable and unpleasant side-effects, including severe and irregular bleeding. Complaints were made that (1) some women

5 Ibid, [123].

6 [1999] 4 All ER 961, HL. Discussed at 13.8 below.

7 *R (on the application of SPUC) v Secretary of State for Health* [2002] 2 FLR 146. For attitudes in days gone by see Lord Denning in *Bravery v Bravery* [1954] 3 All ER 59, at 67–68.

8 For example, making a 20 cm incision to perform a hysterectomy when a 15 cm incision was appropriate constituted negligence: *Brown v Scarborough and North East Yorkshire Healthcare NHS Trust* [2009] EWHC 3103 (QB).

9 See for example *JS v Morey* [2020] 6 WLUK 628. (A 16-year-old suffered a large DVT in her leg after being prescribed the combined contraceptive pill despite a family history of vascular disease. An out-of-court settlement was approved.)

10 See above at 12.14.

were injected with the drug without ever being told of its nature, and (2) even where Depo-Provera was expressly prescribed and described as a contraceptive, inadequate explanation of its potential side-effects was given. Fears were voiced that Depo-Provera might be 'forced' on inarticulate, or not particularly intelligent, woman.[11]

A Salford woman, Mrs Potts, won £3,000 damages[12] after she was injected with Depo-Provera concurrently with a vaccination against rubella. She suffered severe bleeding. The aim of her doctor was laudable, to protect her from pregnancy while the vaccine might harm any unborn child. He had no right to deprive her of her choice of whether or not to accept or decline it. Women must be told the nature of the drug offered to them, and if their right to choose is to be effective they must have its advantages and disadvantages explained to them.[13]

A doctor prescribing contraception must be properly informed about the current stage of research and knowledge about different types and brands and their risks to particular patients. What information is the user entitled to? We would argue that in the light of *Bolitho v City & Hackney Health Authority*,[14] *Pearce v United Bristol Healthcare NHS Trust*[15] and *Montgomery v Lanarkshire Health Board*,[16] women must be advised of any risk that the contraception poses to them which a woman of sound mind would consider material to a reasonable decision about what sort of contraception to use.[17]

What about contraceptives which simply fail? We shall see later that parents cannot recover compensation for the cost of bringing up a normal, healthy child.[18] Might a failed contraceptive method be viewed as 'defective' under the Consumer Protection Act 1987? In *Richardson v LRC Products Ltd*[19] it was held that evidence a condom split was not by itself sufficient to prove that product defective. The fallibility of condoms was well known. The manufacturer never guaranteed 100 per cent success.

11 When Depo-Provera and Norplant (a slow-release capsule injected into the arm) were first licensed in the USA, they were used as sentencing alternatives as a pregnancy restriction for addicts and child abusers, though most cases were overturned on appeal. See J Mertus and S Heller, 'Norplant Meets the New Eugenicists: The Impermissibility of Coerced Contraception' (1992) 11 *St Louis University Public Law Review* 359.

12 See *The Guardian* (1983) 23 July, p 4.

13 See for example *A Local Authority v A* [2010] EWHC 1549 (Fam), discussed at 7.20 above.

14 [1997] 4 All ER 771.

15 [1999] PIQR P 53; see above 6.10.

16 [2015] UKSC 11, at [87].

17 But see *Vadera v Shaw* (1999) 45 BMLR 172, CA. Discussed in R Goldberg, 'The Contraceptive Pill Negligence and Causation: Views on *Vadera v Shaw*' (2001) 8(3) *Med Law Rev* 316.

18 See *McFarlane v Tayside Health Board* [1999] 4 All ER 961, HL.

19 [2000] Lloyd's Law Reports 280.

13.3 Sterilisation

When a further pregnancy or the burden of caring for more children may endanger a woman's health, therapeutic sterilisation may be advised. Non-therapeutic sterilisation is increasingly sought as a method of permanent birth control,[20] both by older people who feel that their family is complete and by younger people adamant that they never wish to reproduce.

A doctor undertaking sterilisation must ensure that the patient understands and agrees to what is to be done. Operating without any consent is obviously a battery. Nor should sterilisation be automatically performed concurrently with some other gynaecological operation to which the patient has consented. The doctor may correctly judge, in the course of some other form of surgery, that a woman should not risk pregnancy again. They cannot act 'in her best interests' without her agreement. In *Devi v West Midlands Area Health Authority*,[21] a married woman of 33, who already had four children, entered hospital for a minor gynaecological operation. Her religion outlawed sterilisation or contraception. In the course of the operation the surgeon discovered her womb to be ruptured and sterilised her there and then. She received £4,000 damages for the loss of her ability to conceive again and £2,700 damages for the 'neurosis' caused by the knowledge of what had been done to her. The choice whether to accept sterilisation is the patient's. It may be more convenient to sterilise the patient on the spot. It is unlikely to be so immediately necessary as to justify acting in an emergency without consent.

A doctor who has obtained consent may still be liable for negligence if they fail to discuss properly with the patient the implications of the operation in a manner consistent with good medical practice. The doctor must not only give the patient sufficient information on which to make up their mind but do so at a time when they are in a fit state to make a reasoned decision.[22] In *Thake v Maurice*, Mr Thake decided to have a vasectomy and paid £20 for the operation. The judge found that the defendant never warned Mr and Mrs Thake of the small but real risk that nature would reverse the surgery. She did not discover her pregnancy until it was nearly five months advanced. The couple sought compensation from the defendant surgeon. As Mr Thake had paid for his vasectomy, unlike an National Health Service (NHS) patient he had a contract with the surgeon. The trial judge held[23] that Mr Thake had agreed to an operation that he understood would render him irreversibly infertile. That is what he contracted for. The defendant was in breach of contract if he failed to achieve that aim. By failing to warn Mr Thake of the risk of natural reversal of the vasectomy, he *guaranteed* to make him sterile. He was responsible for the financial loss to the family occasioned by the birth of the unplanned infant.

20 See also NICE, *Guideline CG30: Long-Acting Reversible Contraception* (2005, updated 2019).
21 [1980] 7 *Current Law* 44.
22 *Wells v Surrey Area Health Authority* (1978) *Times*, 29 July.
23 [1984] 2 All ER 513.

The Court of Appeal[24] held by a majority that the surgeon never guaranteed to make Mr Thake sterile. Neill LJ found that no reasonable person would have understood the defendant as giving a binding promise that the operation would achieve its purpose. They nevertheless unanimously found for Mr Thake on grounds enabling NHS patients as well as private patients to sue if they are not warned of the risk of nature reversing sterilisation of either sex. They held that failure to warn of this risk was negligent.

If sterilisation is proposed on therapeutic grounds the patient's consent must necessarily be based on adequate and careful advice as to the medical need for sterilisation. In *Biles v Barking Health Authority*[25] a woman was advised to undergo sterilisation on the grounds that she was suffering from a severe and probably fatal kidney complaint. That diagnosis was proved later to be mistaken and negligent. Mrs Biles recovered damages of £45,000, which included the cost of a failed attempt to reverse the sterilisation and the cost of IVF (*in vitro* fertilisation) treatment to try to enable her to have a child of her own, despite her surgically blocked Fallopian tubes.

13.4 Involuntary sterilisation and contraception[26]

No statute in England ever provided for the compulsory sterilisation of patients with physical or mental disability.[27] In 1989, in *F v West Berkshire Health Authority*,[28] their Lordships ruled that sterilisation of an adult woman with mental disability was not unlawful if that operation was in her 'best interests'. In theory, a woman may not be sterilised in the interests of society or of her potential children, or on eugenic grounds[29,30] She may be sterilised only where she lacks the capacity to make decisions on childbearing for herself, and to protect her health and welfare.

The Mental Capacity Act 2005 governs the law surrounding adults and young persons who lack mental capacity. It is examined in detail in Chapter 7. Much of the Act and the accompanying Code of Practice[31] enshrine principles

24 [1986] 1 All ER 497; and see *Eyre v Measday* [1986] 1 All ER 488.

25 See M Puxon and A Buchan, 'Damages for Sterility' (1988) 138 *NLJ* 80.

26 See further 7.6–7.7 above.

27 We note that, in some countries, sterilisation was a requirement for legal gender recognition but this requirement was challenged in *AP v France* App No 79885/12 (ECHR, 2017). See P Dunne, 'Transgender Sterilisation Requirements in Europe' (2017) 25(4) *Med Law Rev* 554.

28 [1989] 2 All ER 545, HL.

29 See *Mental Health Trust v DD* [2015] EWCOP 4, [8] per Cobb J: 'This case is not about eugenics. This outcome has been driven by the bleak yet undisputed evidence that a further pregnancy would be a significantly life-threatening event for DD.' And see [114].

30 To do so may breach Articles 3 and 8 of the ECHR: see *VC v Slovakia* (2014) 59 EHRR 29 on forced sterilisation of a Roma woman.

31 Mental Capacity Act 2005 Code of Practice, updated 2020. And see (at time of writing) Draft MCA Code of Practice (2022).

developed by the common law. In *F v West Berkshire HA*[32] protection from liability to carers and health professionals was granted through the application of the doctrine of necessity. Section 5 of the Mental Capacity Act 2005 performs a similar role, granting a 'general authority' to act in the best interests of the patient lacking mental capacity and setting conditions that must be satisfied before liability can be avoided. The Act defines what constitutes a lack of capacity in section 2(1):

> [A] person lacks capacity in relation to a matter if at the material time he is unable to make a decision for himself in relation to the matter because of an impairment of, or a disturbance in the functioning of, the mind or brain.

The Code of Practice gives guidance on how to make that judgement. The requirement of an 'impairment or disturbance' sets the 'diagnostic threshold' for lack of capacity. In addition to this, it must be demonstrated that the person is 'unable to make a decision'; the test is decision-specific.[33]

Where a person lacks capacity, the Act requires that the 'act done, or decision made ... must be done, or made, in his best interests'.[34] In *Oxford University Hospitals NHS FT v Z*,[35] for example, the court found it was in the best interests of a 22-year-old woman who lacked capacity to implant an intra-uterine contraceptive device against her wishes. Future pregnancies would have carried a significant risk to her and her baby's health. And in *Mental Health Trust v DD*,[36] sterilisation was authorised in the best interests of a 36-year-old woman with Autistic Spectrum Disorder who lacked capacity. The decision was based on the stark expert evidence that: 'The risk to [DD] of a future pregnancy, especially if concealed, is highly likely to lead to her death.'[37] *Z* and *DD* were exceptional cases on their facts. As Cobb J summarised in *DD*:

> Any proposal for significant, life-changing surgery in respect of a person who lacks capacity will ... only [be] authorised where it is clearly demonstrated to be necessary, proportionate and 'best' for the individual involved. In this exercise, the views of the person concerned, of those close to them, and of the professionals will be considered with care; steps will be taken to assist the vulnerable person to make the decision for themselves. The court should ... always have regard to the less restrictive way of achieving the ultimate objective.[38]

The Mental Capacity Act requirement that consideration is given to the least restrictive means by which the best interests of an individual lacking capacity

32 [1989] 2 All ER 545, HL.

33 See *Re A (Capacity: refusal of contraception)* [2011] Fam 61.

34 Section 1(5). See also s 4 which lists factors relevant to the determination of an individual's best interests. See 7.9 above.

35 [2020] EWCOP 20. See DM O'Connor, 'A Mother on Trial: Best Interests and the Conflict of Maternal Instincts' (2021) 29(3) *Med Law Rev* 562.

36 [2015] EWCOP 4, discussed at 7.4 above.

37 Ibid, [8] per Cobb J. This was the fifth Court of Protection judgment concerning DD. See [2014] EWCOP 8; [2014] EWCOP 11; [2014] EWCOP 13; [2014] EWCOP 44; The administration of short-term contraception pending the 2015 hearing (December 2014).

38 Ibid, [6].

can be met[39] was relevant in the case of *A Local Authority v K*.[40] K had learning difficulties associated with Down's syndrome. Having received medical advice about contraception for their daughter, K's parents sought sterilisation. The Court of Protection held that sterilisation would not achieve a proportionate balance between K's protection and empowerment.[41]

For men, the choice of contraceptive methods is limited. In *An NHS Trust v DE*,[42] a 37-year-old man with learning difficulties had capacity to consent to sexual relations but lacked capacity to make decisions about contraception. He already had one child and did not want another. His female partner was thought to be unreliable in using the contraceptive pill and had a needle phobia which ruled out contraceptive injections. In light of the limited options, Eleanor King J authorised a vasectomy.

Contraception is less restrictive than sterilisation, but the courts are rightfully reluctant to compel its use. In *A Local Authority v A*[43] Bodey J refused to make an order requiring Mrs A to have contraception. Mrs A had learning difficulties and had previously had two children taken away at birth. Her refusal of contraception was involuntary on account of pressure bought to bear by her husband. Bodey J held that efforts should be made to achieve a capacitated decision from Mrs A, 'through "ability-appropriate" help and discussion without undue contrary pressure from Mr A'.[44] More controversially, in *A Local Authority v P*[45] it was found to be in the best interests of a woman with learning difficulties that the existence of a contraceptive device implanted some years ago without her consent should remain unknown to her, though when it was time for it to be replaced she should be involved in the decision-making process about future contraception.

Must all sterilisation cases come before the court? The Code of Practice on the Mental Capacity Act 2005 advises that a court order be sought in cases of non-therapeutic sterilisation.[46] The Act also gives authority to the decision-maker to act when there is a therapeutic necessity. Thus, the Code of Practice acknowledges that there may be situations when treatment should be given without delay[47] and the duties incumbent on the decision-maker under sections 4(6) and 4(7) to consult others when determining whether treatment is in the best interests of the person lacking capacity exist only 'if it is practicable

39 Mental Capacity Act 2005, s 1(6). There is evidence that, even before the Act came into force, judges were already endorsing this principle: *Re S (Medical Treatment: Adult Sterilisation)* [1998] 1 FLR 944.
40 [2013] EWCOP 242.
41 Ibid, [33] per Cobb J.
42 [2013] EWHC 2562 (Fam).
43 [2010] EWHC 1549 (Fam).
44 Ibid, [75].
45 [2018] EWCOP 10.
46 Mental Capacity Act 2005 Code of Practice, 8.18; *Serious Medical Treatment, Guidance* [2020] EWCOP 2, [11] operates pending a revised MCA Code; Draft MCA Code of Practice (2022), 6.37.
47 Mental Capacity Act 2005 Code of Practice, para 6.35; Draft MCA Code of Practice (2022), 2.13.

and appropriate'. Where the procedure is therapeutic but not urgent, the waters remain murky. The definition of best interests under the Act is not synonymous with non-negligent care. The decision-maker is required to look beyond the clinical need of the person lacking capacity, to her wider welfare issues. Consequently, it is likely doctors and carers will seek reassurance from the Court of Protection that any therapeutic (but not urgent) sterilisation they propose for an adult lacking capacity is in her best interests.

13.5 Actions for injury sustained before birth

Medical care begins long before a baby is born. In the next sections we explore whether a parent or child can claim for injury sustained before birth.

The terminology is confusing and is often interchanged. In the sections that follow we begin by looking at possible claims from parents. Parents may allege 'wrongful birth' if conception was desired, but they were denied an opportunity to end the pregnancy. This might happen if ante-natal screening is performed negligently, and they are denied information that would have led them to terminate the pregnancy. 'Wrongful conception' is an action where a parent who intended to avoid pregnancy has conceived. This might flow from a botched sterilisation, for example.

Children might seek to claim in their own right or someone might claim on their behalf. They might claim for 'wrongful disability': injury sustained prenatally as a result of someone's negligence. Alternatively, they might seek to argue that they should not have been conceived or born at all in which case their claim is one of 'wrongful life'. As we shall see, the barriers to wrongful life actions are considerable.

13.6 Can parents sue?

The parents of a child injured before birth may be able to recover for their loss at common law. The doctor caring for the woman in pregnancy owes her a duty in relation to her own health and in respect of the health of the developing fetus. The damage which she will suffer if she bears a disabled child, the emotional trauma[48] *and* the financial burden of the extra expense such a child entails, are readily foreseeable and recoverable. But will she be able (1) to prove negligence, and (2) to prove that the child's disability resulted from that negligence? One rare success occurred in a 2009 Group Litigation,[49] where Akenhead J found a local authority to have been negligent in allowing harmful dust to contaminate the environment during their reclamation of a British Steel complex. The dust contained heavy metals and dioxins and was found to be teratogenic – exposed to pregnant women, it caused some babies to suffer birth defects.[50]

48 *S v Distillers Co* [1970] 1 WLR 114.

49 *Corby Group Litigation v Corby DC* [2009] EWHC 1944 (TCC). The contamination was also found to constitute a public nuisance.

50 An out of court settlement was reached in 2010: S Adams, 'Council to Pay Out Millions to Birth Defect Children' *Telegraph* (2010) 17 April.

Proving negligence is no easy task in any malpractice claim. A claim in relation to the birth of a disabled child has two special problems. First, if the claim lies against the doctor, it has to be established that they should have been aware of the risk posed to the fetus by drugs they prescribed or treatment they gave. Second, where a woman becomes ill in pregnancy, or the pregnancy itself is complicated, the interests of the woman and the fetus may conflict. For example, a woman injured in an accident may need surgery which can only be carried out under general anaesthetic. The anaesthetic may harm the fetus. The doctor's duty to the woman is to give her sufficient information about her needs and the risk to the fetus. If she chooses to reject treatment for the sake of the baby, the doctor cannot impose it. The doctor must in any case aim at a course of action which will benefit the woman with minimum risk to the fetus. Even if it can be shown that the doctor has failed in their duty to the mother, that they were negligent, establishing that the infant's disability resulted from that negligence is likely to be even more difficult.[51] Despite immense advances in knowledge concerning the development of the fetus, pinpointing the exact cause of the birth defect remains extremely difficult. Success in a claim for negligence depends on proof that it is more likely than not that the relevant negligence caused the injury. All a claimant with an injured child is likely to be able to prove is that a drug they took or treatment they received *may* have caused the harm to the baby. However, the cause may be inherited disease, a problem that the parent suffered in pregnancy, or some unknown cause. The parents may well fail to satisfy the burden of proof.

13.7 Pre-pregnancy advice and genetic counselling

Women planning a child often seek advice before conception. For a healthy woman, this may simply constitute a check that she is immune from rubella. Another may seek reassurance that pregnancy will not damage her own health, for example, if she has a history of cardiac disease. Couples in whose family genetic disease is prevalent, or couples who already have a child with a genetic disease, may need specialised genetic counselling.[52]

In all these cases, those counselling the individual or couple undertake a duty to them in relation not only to their own health and welfare, but also in relation to the birth of a healthy child. If they are given the green light to go ahead with a pregnancy and suffer at the end of it the trauma and additional financial burden of a disabled child, they may have a claim in negligence.[53] They will be

[51] On the difficulties in proving causation of birth defects, see the Royal Commission on Civil Liability and Compensation for Personal Injury (1978) Cmnd 7054, paras 1441–1452.

[52] And see 14.20 below on pre-implantation genetic testing.

[53] See *Parkinson v St James and Seacroft University Hospital NHS Trust* [2001] EWCA Civ 530, CA; *Hardman v Amin* [2000] Lloyd's Rep Med 458; *Enright v Blackpool Victoria Hospital NHS Trust* [2003] EWHC 100 (QB); *Farraj v King's Healthcare NHS Trust* [2006] EWHC 1228; *FP v Taunton and Somerset NHS Trust* [2009] EWHC 1965 (QB) (interim payment) with an additional award in [2011] EWHC 3380 (QB).

able to claim the additional cost to them of caring for a disabled child. Proving negligence may not be easy. Not only must they show that the doctor failed to take into account factors relating to medical history or genetic background or failed to conduct tests that would have alerted them to the danger, but they must also show that a reasonably competent doctor would have discovered the risk.[54] If a woman requests a test for immunity from rubella, is brushed aside, and subsequently contracts the disease in pregnancy, her claim should succeed. If the sister of a haemophiliac consults her doctor and explains her brother's condition, and the doctor fails to refer her for counselling with the result that she bears a haemophiliac son, she too should succeed.[55] Finally, the claimant must also establish that had she received proper advice she would not have allowed herself to become pregnant when she did.

13.8 Wrongful conception[56]

In *Udale v Bloomsbury Health Authority*[57] Jupp J held that the birth of a healthy child could not be allowed to create a claim in damages. He argued that the child, when he came to know of the award, might feel unwanted and the family's relationship be disrupted. Doctors might put pressure on women to have abortions. Children were a blessing, and any financial loss was offset by the joy of their birth.

A series of judgments from the Court of Appeal firmly rejected Jupp J's invocation of policy to refuse parents compensation in such a case.[58] Damages amounting to the cost to the family of raising an unplanned child appeared to be readily endorsed in claims for wrongful conception. Two decisions of the House of Lords restored English and Scottish law to the position declared by Jupp J in *Udale*, albeit on different grounds. It was held in *McFarlane v Tayside Health Board*[59] that compensation for the cost of bringing up a healthy child would not be awarded. Such a loss is categorised now as irrecoverable economic loss. *McFarlane* is difficult to analyse.[60] Five Law Lords

54 See for example *Constable v Salford and Trafford HA and Kerr* [2005] EWHC 2967 (QB) (failure to re-test a woman for Chlamydia which allegedly caused her son to be born prematurely was not shown to have caused or materially contributed to his prematurity).

55 See *Anderson v Forth Valley Health Board* (1998) 44 BMLR 108. And see discussion of wrongful birth case *Khan v Meadows* [2021] UKSC 21 at 13.9 below.

56 See JK Mason, *The Troubled Pregnancy: Legal Rights and Wrongs in Reproduction* (2007) Cambridge University Press.

57 [1983] 2 All ER 522.

58 See *Emeh v Kensington & Chelsea Health Authority* [1984] 3 All ER 1044, CA; *Thake v Maurice* [1986] 1 All ER 479, CA, see 13.3 above.

59 [1999] 4 All ER 961, HL. See also *Greenfield v Irwin (A Firm)* [2001] 1 FLR 899.

60 Se JK Mason, 'Unwanted Pregnancy: A Case of Retroversion?' (2000) 4 *Edinburgh Law Journal* 191; J Weir 'The Unwanted Child' (2000) 59 *CLJ* 238; L Hogano, 'Misconceptions about Wrongful Conception' (2002) 65 *MLR* 883; JK Mason, *The Troubled Pregnancy* (2007) Cambridge University Press, ch 4; N Priaulx, *The Harm Paradox: Tort Law and the Unwanted Child in an Era of Choice* (2007) Routledge Cavendish.

rejected the parents' claim. Five sets of very different reasons are advanced by their Lordships.

The facts of the case are straightforward. Mr and Mrs McFarlane had four children. Mr McFarlane had a vasectomy. Six months after his operation, the surgeon told him that his sperm count was negative and he and his wife could dispense with contraception. The couple relied on that advice. Mrs McFarlane became pregnant. They alleged that the surgeon was negligent and sought compensation (1) for Mrs McFarlane's pain and distress in pregnancy and labour and (2) for the costs of bringing up their healthy daughter, Catherine.

Four out of the five Law Lords[61] held that Mrs McFarlane could recover damages for the pain and discomfort of pregnancy and any immediately consequential financial loss to her. All agreed that the more substantial claim for the cost of raising Catherine should fail. All tried to avoid Jupp J's forthright reliance on policy to categorise such claims as repugnant to the public interest.[62] Lord Slynn appeared to accept that the blessings conferred by healthy children come in tandem with substantial burdens. He rejected the argument that courts should regard the financial costs of raising a child as offset by the joys of parenting. He claimed not to be concerned by possible psychological consequences to a child of learning that she is unwanted because her parents received damages for her wrongful conception. His speech focused on his finding that doctors are not responsible for the economic loss entailed in child rearing. Doctors owe a duty of care to prevent pregnancy and the consequential physical effects on the mother. It is not fair, just or reasonable to extend that responsibility to the costs of rearing the child.[63] Lord Hope took a somewhat similar approach. He appeared exercised by the potential scale of claims for wrongful conception. If such a claim is allowable it would relate to the actual costs to particular parents of raising that child. Thus a claim by wealthy aristocrats might extend to the cost of nannies, ponies, public school and so on. The extent of liability would be disproportionate to the negligence.[64]

Lord Hope and Lord Steyn both, unlike Lord Slynn, adverted to the benefits of parenthood. Lord Hope declared:

> [I]t would not be fair, just or reasonable, in any assessment of the loss caused by the birth of a child, to leave these benefits out of account. Otherwise the [claimant] would be paid far too much. They would be relieved of the costs of rearing the child. They would not be giving anything back to the wrongdoer for the benefits. But the value attached to their benefits is incalculable. The costs can be calculated but the benefit, which must in fairness be set against them, cannot. The logical conclusion, as a matter of law, is that the cost to the [claimant] of meeting their obligations to their child during her childhood are not recoverable as damages.[65]

61 Lord Millett dissented on this point.

62 And for commentary on a related Irish High Court case, see C Craven, 'Recoverability of Damages for Pregnancy and Children: Variations on the Theme of Byrne v Ryan' (2008) 3(1) *Quarterly Review of Tort Law* 8.

63 [1999] 4 All ER 961, at 978, HL.

64 Ibid.

65 Ibid.

Lord Steyn contended that his rejection of the parents' claim was not on policy grounds. He 'would avoid those quicksands'.[66] He saw the question as one of distributive justice. He stated that he was 'firmly of the view that an overwhelming number of ordinary men and women' would reject claims such as the McFarlanes'. He argued that if claims by a child for wrongful life should be rejected as repugnant to the value of human life, so should a claim by parents for its wrongful conception.[67] Lord Steyn may have sought to avoid the quick sands of public policy but became immersed in them none the less.

Lord Clyde treated the claim as one of *quantum* of damages. Like Lord Hope, he was exercised by questions of proportionality. There could be significant differences in the level of awards depending on parental lifestyle. The expense of bringing up the child would be disproportionate to any wrongdoing and go beyond reasonable restitution.[68] Lord Millett, uniquely, sought to reject both claims by the parents, the claim for the mother's pain and suffering in pregnancy, as well as the claim for the cost of raising Catherine. Lord Millett was forthright in his views:

> In my opinion, the law must take the birth of a normal healthy baby to be a blessing, not a detriment. ... It is morally offensive to regard a normal, healthy baby as more trouble and expense than it is worth.[69]

The only damages Lord Millett would allow was a nominal sum to represent the loss of the parental freedom to limit the size of their family. He proposed £5,000. Lord Millett stands alone in the openness of his opinion that it is just unacceptable to society to compensate parents for having a child, however hard they had tried to avoid further pregnancies. His honesty should be commended. The reasons advanced by his colleagues are not convincing.

In private treatment, could there be a claim in contract? In *ARB v IVF Hammersmith*[70] a couple (R and ARB) contracted with an IVF clinic for the provision of fertility services. Five embryos were frozen and one was successfully used in IVF. The couple subsequently separated, and R returned to the clinic, which thawed and implanted another embryo, resulting in the birth of a second child. The clinic required the consent of both partners, but R had forged ARB's signature. ARB sought damages for the breach of contract that had resulted in a second child he would be morally obliged to support financially. Jay J held that there was a breach of contract but ARB could not recover damages for the cost of the child's upbringing for the same policy reasons articulated in *McFarlane*. The Court of Appeal dismissed ARB's appeal.

The Law Lords in *McFarlane* expressly restricted their decision to claims concerning healthy infants. The Court of Appeal endorsed such a distinction in *Parkinson v St James and Seacroft NHS Hospital Trust*[71] ruling that where a

66 Ibid, at 998.
67 Ibid.
68 Ibid.
69 Ibid, 1005.
70 [2017] EWHC 2438 (QB); [2018] EWCA Civ 2803 (permission to appeal denied).
71 [2001] Lloyd's Rep Med 309, CA.

disabled child is born as a consequence of clinical negligence his parents may recover the additional costs occasioned by his disability. The relevant negligence in *Parkinson* ensued from a bungled operation to sterilise the mother. The surgeon failed to secure a clip effectively to Mrs Parkinson's left fallopian tube. She conceived again ten months after the operation. The case for compensation covering the costs resulting from a child's disability when the alleged 'wrong' is a failure to prevent the conception and birth of a disabled infant looks stronger. Doctors expressly advising potential parents about the risks of conception, and screening women in pregnancy, undertake that responsibility expressly to avoid the birth of a disabled child. The 'harm' to the parents of the conception and birth of a child with spina bifida, or damaged by rubella,[72] is just what the doctors seek to prevent. Only a limited group of people (parents whose children were unfortunately born disabled) could bring a claim and Brooke LJ saw no difficulty with the proposition that the doctor assumed responsibility for the disastrous economic consequences of the birth of such a child. '[O]rdinary people would consider that it would be fair for the law to make an award in such a case provided that it is limited to the extra expenses associated with the child's disability'.[73] Both Brooke LJ and Hale LJ[74] constructed elegant examples to distinguish the case of the disabled child from *McFarlane*. Hale LJ proposed a model of 'deemed equilibrium' whereby the costs and benefits of a healthy child balance each other out. The reader may ponder whether the appeal court did not in reality simply regard *McFarlane* as wrongly decided.[75] Unable to say so forthrightly, the judges sought to mitigate its worst effects. The parents' damages, however, will be limited to the additional costs of raising a child with his particular disability.[76] Before *McFarlane*, English courts awarded such parents the whole cost of childrearing.[77] Compensation in such cases of wrongful conception and birth will now relate only to the additional cost of caring for the disabled child.[78] Compensation may still be considerable.[79] Compensation can and

72 As in *Hardman v Amin* [2000] Lloyd's Rep Med 498.

73 [2001] EWCA Civ 530, [50]; and see Hale LJ, [82].

74 Note Hale LJ's analysis of the nature of the loss and injury. Are the costs consequent on the birth of an unplanned child, disabled or not, truly pure economic loss?

75 The Australian High Court rejected *McFarlane* in *Cattanach v Melchior* [2003] HCA 38. Queensland and New South Wales have legislated to counteract the effects of this case. For analysis see JK Mason, *The Troubled Pregnancy: Legal Rights and Wrongs in Reproduction* (2007) Cambridge University Press, p 125.

76 For guidance on what constitutes 'disability', see [2001] EWCA Civ 530, [91] per Hale LJ.

77 *Salih v Enfield Health Authority* [1991] All ER 400 (though note that, if the parents would in any case have gone on to have a healthy child, the damage would be restricted to the costs incurred by the child's disability).

78 *Rand v East Dorset HA* [2000] Lloyd's Rep Med 181; and see *Anderson v Forth Valley Health Board* (1997) 44 BMLR 108 (Scotland).

79 See NHSLA, *Ten Years of Maternity Claims an Analysis of NHS Litigation Authority Data* (2012), including an analysis of wrongful birth claims made on the basis of alleged negligence in ante-natal screening. NHS Resolution FOI 5031 (2021) lists thirteen wrongful birth and seventeen unwanted pregnancy cases closed / settled with damages paid in 2019–20 with a total payout of £34,790,330.

should include cost of care beyond the child's minority.[80] 'Good' parents will seek to provide for their disabled children into adulthood.

The tangled web of case-law following *McFarlane* may be morally disturbing to some people. Refusing to compensate parents for the unplanned birth of a healthy child, Lord Millett said in *McFarlane*: 'There is something distasteful, if not morally offensive, in treating the birth of a normal healthy child as a matter of compensation.'[81] He regarded childbirth as akin to a balance sheet. The joys of parenthood offset financial costs. Mutual support of parent and child, the support perhaps of the parent in old age, offset the burdens of parenting. Distinguishing the healthy and disabled child might seem to suggest the latter is a 'curse' not a 'blessing'. In *Parkinson*, Hale LJ took a pragmatic approach. She said of the disabled child that: 'This analysis treats a disabled child as having exactly the same worth as a non-disabled child. It affords him the same dignity and status. It simply acknowledges that he costs more.'[82]

If cost is key, then what of the wrongful conception of a healthy baby to a disabled parent? In *Rees v Darlington Memorial Hospital NHS Trust*,[83] the Court of Appeal allowed the claim of a visually impaired woman whose negligent sterilisation led to the birth of a healthy child. The claimant suffered from retinitis pigmentosa. She had only very limited vision in one eye. She elected to be sterilised because she did not want children and judged that her virtual blindness would prevent her looking after a child. Hale LJ[84] distinguished *McFarlane* on a number of grounds, relying on the pragmatic 'deemed equilibrium' model she first set down in *Parkinson*. Unlike the healthy parent of a healthy child, but like the parent of any disabled child, the claimant incurred extra costs in bringing up a child. The compensation awarded to her was not compensation for the cost of the child *per se*, but the costs occasioned by her own disability. *McFarlane*, it was held, applied only to healthy parents.

80 *Nunnerley v Warrington Health Authority* [2000] Lloyd's Rep Med 170; and see R Glancy, 'Damages for Wrongful Birth: Where Do They End?' (2006) 3 *Journal of Personal Injury Law* 271.

81 [1999] 4 All ER 961, at 1003, HL.

82 *Parkinson v St James and Seacroft NHS Hospital Trust* [2001] Lloyd's Rep Med 309, at 325, CA. It should be noted Hale LJ seems less than convinced of Lord Millett's general reasoning that the joys of a healthy child outweigh the costs. And see *Hardman v Amin* [2000] Lloyd's Rep Med 498. GT Laurie, SHE Harmon and ES Dove, *Mason and McCall Smith's Law and Medical Ethics* (11th edn, 2019) Oxford University Press, 11.25 argue that Lady Hale's opinion, which is based on bodily integrity, can be applied equally to the disabled and healthy child. 'The feeling remains that one or other decision [*McFarlane* or *Parkinson*] must be wrong.'

83 [2002] 2 All ER 177.

84 Note the difference in reasoning between Hale and Robert Walker LJJ. Consider whether poverty is a 'disability' deserving at least some compensation for an unplanned child. Waller LJ dissented, comparing a hypothetical woman driven to 'crisis in health terms' by the birth of a fifth child following a negligent sterilisation, with a similar crisis on the part of a disabled parent. For both, the recovery of the costs of caring for the healthy child might alleviate the crisis. Why should the law treat the two differently?

The case proceeded to the House of Lords,[85] where the Law Lords had an opportunity to revisit their judgment in *McFarlane*. They refused to do so. By a four–three majority, they overturned the decision of the Court of Appeal. Though, for reasons of public policy, it is unacceptable to view a healthy child as a financial liability, the Law Lords put a 'gloss' on the *McFarlane* ruling. As we noted at the start of this chapter, the Law Lords in *Rees* belatedly endorsed Lord Millett's proposal in *McFarlane* that an award of general damages was appropriate to mark the injury to the claimant. Lord Bingham proposed that, in addition to the award for pregnancy and birth, a conventional figure of £15,000 should be awarded to reflect that the defendant's negligence constituted a legal wrong causing the parents to suffer a loss of autonomy.[86] The majority agreed. Elevated costs of rearing a healthy child as a result of parental disability are not recoverable. 'General damages' are all such parents can hope for.[87]

Hale LJ's 'deemed equilibrium' was rejected on the basis that the costs and benefits associated with the birth of a child were unquantifiable and consequently impossible to balance. But this raises questions as to the legal basis for the 'gloss' on *McFarlane*.[88] Whilst there may be public policy grounds for the avoidance of general negligence principles in wrongful conception cases, even after two House of Lords decisions, sound legal reasoning remains elusive. Perhaps, as Emily Jackson suggests,[89] the Law Lords in *Rees* were simply creating their own novel scheme of compensation to acknowledge the legal wrong whilst limiting the payout. On the other hand the 'gloss' may be viewed, as Lord Steyn suggested in his dissenting judgement, as 'a radical and most important development which should only be embarked on after rigorous examination of competing arguments'.[90] On this view, the majority in *Rees* overstepped the limits of judicial discretion.[91]

85 [2003] UKHL 53.

86 Note that no damages for loss of autonomy are awarded under *Rees* if the child is not born alive: See *Less and Carter v Hussain* [2012] EWHC 3513.

87 But see V Chico, 'Wrongful Conception: Policy, Inconsistency and the Conventional Award' (2007) 8 *Medical Law International* 139 and A Mulligan, 'A Vindicatory Approach to Tortious Liability for Mistakes in Assisted Human Reproduction' (2020) 40(1) LS 55, arguing that errors in assisted reproduction should be compensated through an award of damages to vindicate parental rights to reproductive autonomy, preferably through a separate strict liability tort focusing on vindication rather than compensation.

88 See P Cane, 'Another Failed Sterilisation' (2004) 120 *LQR* 181.

89 E Jackson, *Medical Law: Text, Cases and Materials* (2019) Oxford University Press, p 161.

90 Per Lord Steyn (dissenting), *Rees v Darlington Memorial Hospital NHS Trust* [2003] UKHL 52, [43]. See also Lord Hope's Judgment. Note that the decision in *Rees* is referred to in the landmark decision *Montgomery v Lanarkshire* [2015] UKSC 11, [108] per Lady Hale, who went on to say: '[T]he interest which the law of negligence protects is a person's interest in their own physical and psychiatric integrity, an important feature of which is their autonomy, their freedom to decide what shall and shall not be done with their body.'

91 The *Rees* decision has since been cited by the Supreme Court to justify a conventional award of damages serving a vindicatory purpose: see *Lumba (WL) v Secretary*

Rees has implications for the status of *Parkinson*. Though Lord Hutton approved of the decision,[92] Lord Bingham was critical of it.[93] The refusal of the majority to make a calculation of costs based on benefits and detriments in the case of a healthy child is arguably equally applicable to the disabled child.

13.9 Wrongful birth

Wrongful birth cases focus on events post conception that negligently deny the mother an opportunity to terminate the pregnancy. Will *McFarlane* affect a claim by parents of a disabled child who can establish that, had the child's disability been diagnosed *in utero*, the mother would have terminated the pregnancy? In *Groom v Selby*,[94] a general practitioner (GP) failed to diagnose Ms Groom's pregnancy. Megan was born prematurely having contracted meningitis salmonella which led to neurological disability. Applying the same principles developed in relation to wrongful conception, the Court of Appeal held that Ms Groom could recover the costs associated with Megan's disability.

In *Khan v Meadows*[95] the Supreme Court confirmed that compensation for the cost of bringing up a disabled child is in principle available in wrongful birth cases. Ms Meadows had a family history of haemophilia, which is inherited in an X-linked recessive pattern. She was wrongly advised by her GP that she was not at risk of being a carrier for the gene. Had she known that she was at risk she would have undergone fetal testing for haemophilia when she became pregnant. She later discovered that she was indeed a carrier of the haemophilia gene, which was passed on to her son. As we discussed at 6.16 above, Ms Meadows was able to claim damages with respect to the child's haemophilia. She was not able to claim additional costs for the child's autism, which was an unrelated condition. Dr Khan was not liable for all the consequences of the birth.

Nor is there a duty to advise on negligible risks. There must be a material risk to which the claimant should have been alerted. In *Mrs A v East Kent Hospitals University NHS Foundation Trust*,[96] Mrs A sought damages for costs suffered when her baby was born with a chromosomal abnormality. She alleged that she would, if aware of the risk, have had amniocentesis and terminated the pregnancy. Dingemans J recognised a 'background risk' of about 1 in 1,000 of chromosomal abnormality, but considered that this was not 'a risk to which a reasonable patient … would have attached any significance'.[97]

of State for the Home Department [2011] UKSC 12, [179]–[180], [216]–[217], [236]–[237].

92 [2003] UKHL 53, [96].

93 Ibid, [9].

94 [2001] EWCA Civ 1522.

95 [2021] UKSC 21, [74], [86]. See CP McGrath, 'A Khan of Worms: The Scope of Medical Advice' (2021) 80(3) *CLJ* 440.

96 [2015] EWHC 1038 (QB).

97 Ibid, [101].

Wrongful birth cases are often associated with sub-standard ante-natal screening during pregnancy. For example, in *Mordel v Royal Berkshire NHS FT*[98] there was a miscommunication around ante-natal screening for Down's syndrome. Ms Mordel's first language was Polish. She thought she had requested testing for Down's syndrome and the sonographer thought it had been declined. Finding for Ms Mordel, Jay J acknowledged that clinicians are not required to 'delve into the reasoning processes and motivations' of patients, but stressed the importance of ensuring that information can be understood in order to establish informed consent.

13.10 Actions by or on behalf of children: The Congenital Disabilities (Civil Liability) Act 1976

The Congenital Disabilities (Civil Liability) Act 1976, passed to give rights and a remedy to children born disabled because of human fault, is ambitious, complex and largely irrelevant. It is ambitious in that it sought to provide a scheme to protect children, not just against injury in the womb, but against any act at any stage of either parent's life which might ultimately result in a disability affecting a child. Its complexity we outline in succeeding sections. It is largely irrelevant because it fails to address the central problem in this type of claim. How do you prove that the disability resulted from an identified act of negligence? Just as his mother's claim is likely to founder for lack of proof of the cause of the disability so is the child's. If Parliament intends and desires to give children disabled by human act a remedy, it must consider whether retaining the normal burden of proof in actions by mother and child is practical.

The Act applies to all births after 1976 and purports to provide a comprehensive code of liability for disabled children in respect of damage caused to them before birth. Under the Act the child's mother[99] is generally exempt from any liability to her child. The father is offered no such immunity. The Act entirely replaces the common law, and it would not be possible for a child unable to recover under the Act to argue that liability exists at common law. So, for example, a child seeking to sue his mother, exempt under the Act, must fail, however reckless her conduct in pregnancy and however clear it might be that she caused him to be born disabled.

The scheme of the Act is this. The child must be born alive[100] and establish that their disabilities resulted from an 'occurrence' which either (1) affected either parent in their ability to have a normal healthy child (pre-conception event), as per section 1(2)(a), or (2) affected the mother during

98 [2019] EWHC 2591 (QB).

99 Under s 2, she is liable for injuries caused through negligent driving of a vehicle on the road.

100 Where the child is not born alive, the mother may be able to claim for the pain and suffering of miscarriage or stillbirth.

her pregnancy, or (3) affected mother or child in the course of its birth, as per section 1(2)(b).

At this first hurdle, proving the cause of the disability, many claims will fail. Where proof of cause is forthcoming the child faces further obstacles. It is not enough to show that the person responsible for the occurrence was negligent. The child must prove that the person responsible for the occurrence was liable to the affected parent. The child's rights are derivative only. The likelihood is that the occurrence at the time caused the parent no harm. The Act provides that it is no answer that the parent affected suffered no visible injury at the time of the occurrence providing there was 'a breach of legal duty which, accompanied by injury, would have given rise to the liability'. The breach of duty is the negligence of the defendant in relation to the affected parent's reproductive capacity.

13.11 Wrongful disability

Let us take move on now to what appears to be a simple case. A pregnant woman takes a drug prescribed for her by her GP that damages her baby causing it to be born disabled. The child can prove that their disability results from the effect of the drug on the fetus. They will have to show that the doctor was negligent towards their mother.

It must be proven that (1) the doctor knew or ought to have known that she was pregnant, and therefore was in breach of duty to her in prescribing a drug which might damage her baby, and (2) that the doctor ought to have been aware of the risk posed by the drug. It will be no defence for the doctor to answer that, far from injuring the mother, the primary effect of the drug benefited her by ameliorating the symptoms of some common ailment or helping her to relax or sleep. The doctor's responsibility to her embraces taking care to avoid harm to the child she carries.

Two difficulties arise. First, a GP is judged by the standard of the reasonable, average GP. They are not expected to be an expert on embryology or drug-related damage. Proving that they ought to have been aware of the risk of the drug may be awkward. Second, the doctor may be aware of the risk to the baby but argue that the risk to mother and child of not prescribing the drug is greater. Perhaps the mother might argue that given the uncertainty surrounding the effect of medicines on fetal development only exceptionally should *any* drug be prescribed to a pregnant woman by her GP. Advice should be sought from the specialist obstetrician. However, is it reasonable to deny pregnant women basic medicine for minor ailments and is the cost to the NHS of multiple referrals to obstetricians justifiable? The focus ought to lie on ensuring that all doctors give women adequate advice about the potential risks of drugs in pregnancy.

Doctors are not the only potential source of compensation for a drug-damaged child. Could the child sue the drug company? The company's liability is governed by the Consumer Protection Act 1987, which we examined in Chapter 12. The crucial questions will be is the drug defective, and did it cause the relevant injury to the fetus? There can be little doubt that if the company can be shown to be aware of a risk of fetal damage, yet still marketed the drug with *no* warning of that risk, the drug is defective. The unborn baby is most vulnerable to harm in the earliest stages of pregnancy. The woman may not know that she is pregnant. Warnings about the use of many non-prescription medicines in pregnancy are routine, but futile if a woman is unaware of her pregnancy. Might a drug be defective simply because it poses a risk of fetal harm? Clearly that cannot generally be the case with many prescription drugs. The benefit such drugs offer when properly prescribed outweigh the remote chance of unwitting fetal harm. Over-the-counter, non-prescription medicines might be looked at differently. If a cough remedy poses a substantial risk of harm, greater than other similar products, for relatively small benefit, that product might be found to be defective.[101]

13.12 Suing a doctor

We have already mentioned the potential liability of the mother's GP in prescribing drugs for her. She will meet other doctors during ante-natal visits. One special feature of suing a doctor under the Act needs note: section 1(5) of the 1976 Act, 'the doctors' defence'. Section 1(5) of the Act provides:

> The defendant is not answerable to the child, for anything he did or omitted to do when responsible in a professional capacity for treating or advising the parent, if he took reasonable care having due regard to the then received professional opinion applicable to the particular class of case; but this does not mean that he is answerable only because he departed from received opinion.

The aims of those who sought the inclusion of those words 'then received professional opinion' were probably twofold. First, they quite reasonably wanted it made clear that hindsight as to the effect of a drug or course of treatment should not prejudice a doctor, and second, less reasonably, they did not want the courts to adjudicate on the adequacy of received opinion. As the defendant's standard of care will always be tested by what was expected of the competent practitioner at the time of the alleged breach of duty, that first objective was met at common law. Second, perhaps doctors sought to ensure courts would not seek to evaluate 'received professional opinion'. In 1976, it is likely that no court would have done so. The judgment of the House of Lords in *Bolitho v City & Hackney Health Authority*[102] now requires that responsible professional opinion be demonstrably 'logical and defensible'. We see no reason why section 1(5) should not be susceptible to similar judicial scrutiny.

13.13 Wrongful life

What if the essence of the child's claim is that but for the negligent act she would not have been born at all? As we have seen, a parent might seek a

101 See 12.3 above.
102 [1997] 4 All ER 771.

remedy for wrongful birth or conception, but can the child sue in respect of wrongful life, a life, her counsel argues, she would have chosen not to endure?

A classic claim for wrongful life is recounted in *McKay v Essex AHA*.[103] The plaintiffs in *McKay* were a little girl, born disabled as a result of the effect of rubella suffered by her mother early in pregnancy, and her mother. When Mrs McKay suspected that she had contracted rubella in the early weeks of her pregnancy, her doctor arranged for blood tests to establish whether she had been infected. As a result of negligence by either her doctor or laboratory staff, Mrs McKay was wrongly informed that she had not been infected by rubella. She continued with the pregnancy. Had she known the truth she would, as her doctor was well aware, have requested an abortion under the Abortion Act 1967. The little girl was born in 1975, before the Congenital Disabilities Act was passed. The Court of Appeal had to decide the position at common law. They said that no action lay where the essence of the child's claim was that but for the negligence of the defendant she would never have been born at all. The child's claim was thrown out, although her mother's claim was allowed to proceed. The case is not solely of historical interest. The judges further said that under the Act no child born after its passing could pursue such a claim.

Ackner LJ, considering section 1(2)(b) of the Act, said that the relevant 'occurrence' has to be one that affected the mother in pregnancy 'so that the child *is born* with disabilities which would not otherwise have been present'. Clearly under the Act, then, where the breach of duty consists of carelessness in the conduct of the pregnancy or the birth, the claim must relate to disabilities inflicted as a result of the breach of duty by the defendants. Where the essence of the claim is that the child should never have been born at all, it lies outside the scope of section 1(2)(b). A claim by the child that amniocentesis should have been performed or that subsequent tests were negligently conducted so that the pregnancy continued, and they were born disabled, will fail.

The effect of the judgment in *McKay* was that in England a child injured post-conception and before birth could claim only compensation for *wrongful disability* against a defendant whose conduct actually caused their disability. They could not sue for *wrongful life*. The Court of Appeal gave three main reasons for ruling out such claims. (1) It was not possible to arrive at a proper measure of damages representing the difference between the child's disabled existence and non-existence.[104] (2) The law should not impose a duty on doctors to abort, to terminate life *in utero*.[105] (3) To impose any duty to abort would be to violate the sanctity of life and to devalue the life of handicapped persons.[106] The second and third reasons are difficult to sustain in the light of the fact that the court did allow Mrs McKay to pursue her *wrongful birth* action.

103 Ibid.
104 Ibid, at 782, 787 and 790.
105 Ibid, at 787.
106 Ibid, at 781.

13.14 Children damaged by pre-conception events

The Congenital Disabilities (Civil Liability) Act 1976 purports to protect children against pre-conception injury,[107] not just injury *in utero*. This could happen where the father or mother is affected by radiation or drugs so that the sperm or egg carries a serious defect. Or the child may be damaged if doctors mismanage a previous pregnancy, for example if they fail to take note of and treat Rhesus incompatibility in the mother and the second child is born brain-damaged.[108] The Act intended to cover such cases, providing as it does that the relevant occurrence may be one which affected either parent in his or her ability to have a healthy child. But it may be argued that, if the claim is that the child was born disabled because one of their parents is incapable of creating a healthy infant, their claim is essentially that they should never have been born at all, and that it is an action for 'wrongful life' and is barred under the Act. We think this is a mistaken view of the Act. The child's claim in the case of a pre-conception occurrence rests on the hypothesis that *but for* that occurrence they would have been born normal and healthy, and that their actionable injury is therefore the difference between the life they might have had and the life they must now perforce endure. In *McKay*,[109] the child sought to maintain that her actionable injury was life itself, and as such her claim was not and would not be sustainable. What *McKay* does clarify in cases of *pre-conception* injury is that a doctor who is not responsible for that original injury cannot be liable under the Act if they fail to diagnose the disabilities in pregnancy and fail to perform an abortion in such circumstances.

13.15 What if a parent realises the risk?

Alas, further problems confront the child whose claim is based on pre-conception injury. Section 1(4) of the 1976 Act provides that in such cases if the affected parent is aware of the risk of the child being born disabled the defendant is not liable to that child. Responsibility for knowingly running the risk of creating a disabled baby rests with the child's parents, and whatever the degree of fault, the original creator of the risk is relieved of liability to the child. There is one exception to this rule. Where the child sues their father, the fact that the father is aware of the risk of begetting an abnormal child will not defeat the child's claim as long as the mother is ignorant of the danger. This raises a nice question. A young man suffers contamination by toxic chemicals at work through the negligence of his employers. He is warned that his reproductive capacity has been damaged, that he is likely to beget abnormal offspring and is advised never to have children. He ignores the warning, marries and tells his wife nothing. A disabled child is born.

107 Including injury caused by infertility treatment: see Congenital Disabilities (Civil Liability) Act 1976, s 1A, as amended by the Human Fertilisation and Embryology Act 1990, s 44(1).

108 See American cases: *Yeager v Bloomington Obstetrics and Gynaecology, Inc* 585 NW2d 696 (Ind, 1992); *Lazenvnick v General Hospital of Munro City Inc* F Supp 146 (Md, 1980).

109 *McKay v Essex Area Health Authority* [1982] 2 All ER 771.

The child cannot sue his father's original employers. Even if they were in breach of duty to his father, 'the affected parent', the father's knowledge of the risk is a defence. Can the child sue her father? The answer has to be no. This child, like the plaintiff in *McKay*,[110] can only claim against her father that she should never have been born at all. His father's condition at the time of the relevant 'negligence', begetting the child, was such that he could not beget a normal child. The father's 'negligence' was in creating him, not in inflicting a disability which but for some act or omission on his part would not have been present.

13.16 Must a mother consider abortion?

Section 1(7) of the 1976 Act offers a partial defence whereby, if the affected parent shared responsibility for the child being born disabled, the child's damages may be reduced. For example, the child's disabilities may be diagnosed when the mother has an ultra-sound scan, or amniocentesis, before his birth. Once the mother knows of the potential damage to her child, she will under the 1967 Abortion Act be entitled to an abortion on the grounds that there is substantial risk that the child if born would be seriously handicapped. Assuming that it is the mother who is the affected parent, does she share responsibility for the child being born disabled, if she refuses an abortion? In *McKay v Essex Area Health Authority*, refusing to allow the child's claim that she should have been aborted, Ackner LJ said that he could not accept:

> ... that the common law duty of care to a person can involve, without specific legislation to achieve this end, the legal obligation to that person, whether or not in utero, to terminate his existence. Such a proportion runs wholly contrary to the concept of the sanctity of human life.[111]

Applying Ackner LJ's proportion to a submission that a mother should have accepted abortion advanced by the defendant responsible for inflicting the disabilities suffered by the child, such a submission must fail. To impose an *obligation* on a mother to undergo an abortion is more repugnant to the concept of the sanctity of human life than to impose an obligation to abort on a doctor.

In *Emeh v Kensington, Chelsea and Fulham Area Health Authority*,[112] the plaintiff brought a wrongful conception claim, long before *McFarlane*.[113] An operation to sterilise her was carried out negligently by the first defendant and she became pregnant again. She was offered but refused an abortion. The trial judge held that once she elected to continue the pregnancy, the pregnancy ceased to be unwanted, and that the birth of the child was the result of her own actions and not a consequence of the defendant's negligence. Her refusal to consider an abortion was so unreasonable as to eclipse the defendant's wrongdoing. The Court of Appeal overruled him.[114] Mrs Emeh did not become aware of her pregnancy until it was about seventeen to eighteen weeks

110 Ibid.
111 [1982] 2 All ER 771, at 787.
112 *Times* (1983) 3 January.
113 *McFarlane v Tayside Health Board* [1999] 4 All ER 961, HL.
114 [1984] 3 All ER 1044.

advanced. Refusing an abortion at that stage in pregnancy could not be considered unreasonable. Whether the Court would have taken a different view had the pregnancy been less advanced remains open to question. Waller LJ laid great stress on the increased risk, discomfort and hospitalisation entailed in abortion at twelve weeks plus.[115] Slade LJ was emphatic that abortion should generally never be forced upon a woman. He said:

> Save in the most exceptional circumstances, I cannot think it right that the court should ever declare it unreasonable for a woman to decline to have an abortion in a case where there is no evidence that there were any medical or psychiatric grounds for terminating the particular pregnancy.[116]

Slade LJ's condemnation of judicially enforced abortion is endorsed in *McFarlane* by Lords Slynn,[117] Steyn[118] and Millett. Lord Millett declares[119] that it is morally repugnant to suggest that it is unreasonable not to have an abortion.

Some slight doubt, however, lurks in the kind of cases we are currently considering. If a fetal abnormality is diagnosed in pregnancy, and caused by the defendants' prior negligence, does this constitute *medical* grounds to terminate the pregnancy, and constitute the sort of exceptional circumstances Slade LJ refers to? Certainly, the fetal injury would entitle the mother to choose to abort the child. We cannot see that it could require her to do so or risk a reduction to her child's compensation for the disability the child suffers. Section 1(7) of the 1976 Act envisages the sort of case where a pregnant woman ignores medical advice and exacerbates her child's disability by drinking, smoking or failing to take precautions advised by her doctors. The mother actively contributes to the disability. That is very different from refusing abortion. Assume a court was prepared to entertain this defence, how will they assess the mother's decision? Is it some totally objective test? Or must the woman's own moral views and religious affiliation be considered? Given that the Court of Appeal has finally confirmed that no woman can be forced to undergo a Caesarean section to protect the life or health of the fetus, to 'force' a woman to 'kill' her fetus would be illogical.[120] Maternal autonomy demands that pregnant women's choices in this delicate arena of moral controversy should be respected.

13.17 Maternal immunity: discriminating against fathers?

We noted earlier that, save in respect of road accidents on public roads, mothers remain immune from claims under the 1976 Act.[121] Fathers enjoy no such formal immunity. A pregnant woman who drinks so heavily that her child is

115 Ibid, 1048.
116 Ibid, 1053.
117 [1999] 4 All ER 961, HL, at 970.
118 Ibid, 976.
119 Ibid, 1004.
120 *St George's Healthcare NHS Trust v S* [1998] 3 All ER 673, CA.
121 See above at 13.10.

born with fetal alcohol syndrome or whose drug habit is such that her baby is born addicted to opioids cannot be sued by her child. The Law Commission,[122] recommending that mothers be exempted from claims for pre-natal injury, offered a number of reasons for maternal privilege. They considered that a claim against the mother would have little practical utility. She, unlike the father, was unlikely to have funds to meet an award of damages. Suing 'mum' would disturb the parental bond and in practice would only happen where a father used his child's claim as a weapon in parental dispute. The first of these two reasons looks rather outdated now when many more women have independent means. The second applies equally to fathers. Other reasons remain more compelling.[123]

How could an equitable standard of reasonable pregnancy conduct be set? Women are beset by contradictory advice about what they should and should not eat, drink or do. Though, objectively, one might agree that the reasonable mother-to-be should give up smoking, for example, achieving that standard is more difficult for some than others. The harassed mother of four struggling alone in poverty may know that she ought to quit smoking but struggles to do so. Most importantly, potential liability for fetal injury would in practice constitute a significant invasion of pregnant women's liberty and privacy. The threat of possible redress by the child could be used by partners and doctors to impose their judgement of fetal welfare. Given evidence of the fetus's vulnerability in early pregnancy, when a woman may not know she is pregnant, as Sheila McLean has said, the law would in effect demand that 'fertile, sexually active women of childbearing age should act at all times as if they were pregnant'.[124] Finally, pragmatically, we should remind ourselves that a claim under the 1976 Act can only arise if a child is born alive. Maternal liability under the 1976 Act could simply provide an incentive to abort. A woman fearing, perhaps for little reason, that she has harmed her child could ensure that the child was never born at all.

If there remains a case for maternal immunity, consideration must at least be given to paternal immunity. In 1976, the kind of harms men might do their unborn children were perceived as crude and obvious wrongdoing. A father who beats his partner up so badly that he injures both her and the child in the womb elicits little sympathy. What science can now tell us about how lifestyle from an early age may affect human gametes is cause for concern. Studies have shown that heavy smoking in teenage years could increase the risk of a man's child born years later succumbing to certain cancers. Whether fathers ought to be constrained by law in their pre-conception conduct must be questionable. Paternal liability unearths a further quirk of the 1976 Act. Even absent maternal immunity, in what sort of circumstances could either parent be liable for pre-conception injury? Liability under the Act is derivative only. The defendant must be liable in tort to the affected parent. Consider this example. A man

122 Discussed in P Pace, 'Civil Liability for Pre-Natal Injuries' (1977) 40 *MLR* 193.

123 See M Brazier, 'Parental Responsibilities, Foetal Welfare and Children's Health' in C Bridge (ed), *Family Law: Towards the Millennium* (1997) Butterworths, p 263.

124 See SAM McLean, *Old Law, New Medicine* (1999) Pandora Press, p 66.

is a heavy drug user in his youth in an era when such drug use is known to damage sperm. Later he begets a child born disabled because of his damaged gametes. To be liable to the child, he must be liable to her mother. To be liable to the mother, the courts would have to find that men have a duty of care to their future partners to ensure that they protect those partners' reproductive health. Imagine the outcry if the law declared that women must order their lives to safeguard their husbands' right to have healthy children.

13.18 Criminal liability[125]

Before concluding that pregnancy conduct can never be subjected to legal redress, the decision of the House of Lords in *Attorney General's Reference (No 3 of 1994)*[126] must be considered. A father attacked his pregnant girlfriend and injured his child in the womb. The baby was born alive but subsequently died of her pre-natal injuries. The father was charged with his daughter's murder. Following his acquittal, the Attorney General referred the case to the Court of Appeal to determine whether murder or manslaughter can be committed where a fetus is injured *in utero*, but is subsequently born alive only to die later of pre-natal injuries. In a convoluted judgment, the Court of Appeal answered yes to both questions.[127] The House of Lords partially upheld their judgment on very different grounds. The Law Lords endorsed earlier judgments[128] that a charge of murder or manslaughter can be sustained where a fetus injured *in utero* is born alive and later dies as a consequence of those injuries. On the facts of this case, their Lordships held that a charge of murder could not be sustained, but that a charge of manslaughter could. Murder could not be committed in this case because there was no express design to harm the fetus 'or the human person which it would become'.[129] However, manslaughter could be established in this instance. In his assault on the mother, the father committed an unlawful and dangerous act which inadvertently caused death. The implications of *Attorney General's Reference (No 3 of 1994)* are that:

(a) a person whose unlawful and dangerous conduct results in fetal injury followed by the birth of a child 'doomed to die' commits manslaughter;
(b) gross and culpable negligence in relation to the fetus may similarly, where the child is born alive and subsequently dies, constitute manslaughter;
(c) a deliberate attempt to harm or kill the fetus directly could in such cases amount to murder.

125 See E Cave, *The Mother of All Crimes: Human Rights, Criminalization and the Child Born Alive* (2004) Routledge.
126 [1997] 3 All ER 936. See S Fovargue and J Miola, 'Policing Pregnancy: Implications of the *Attorney-General's Reference (No 3 of 1994)*' (1998) 6 *Med Law Rev* 265; Cave, ibid.
127 [1996] 2 All ER 10, CA. Discussed in M Seneviratne, 'Pre-Natal Injury and Transferred Malice: The Invented Other' (1996) 59 *MLR* 884.
128 *R v West* (1848) 175 ER 329; *R v Senior* (1832) 168 ER 1298.
129 [1997] 3 All ER 936, 949 (Lord Mustill).

Finally, Lord Mustill[130] suggested that any violence against the fetus resulting in harm short of death may engage criminal responsibility.

At no point did any of the Law Lords in the Attorney General's Reference consider maternal criminal responsibility. Their reasoning left pregnant women open to such liability in a range of scenarios. Could the pregnant woman who continues to abuse illegal drugs so that her child is born damaged by those substances and dies of their effect be said to commit unlawful act type manslaughter? Could the woman whose heavy abuse of alcohol results in a child so dreadfully harmed by fetal alcohol syndrome that he lives only a short while be seen as criminally negligent? And even if her child does not die, might the mother be charged with causing them grievous bodily harm?[131]

In 2014, the Court of Appeal in *CP (A Child) v Criminal Injuries Compensation Authority* tackled the latter question.[132] CP was a 7-year-old girl with fetal alcohol spectrum disorder whose mother had drunk excessive amounts of alcohol during pregnancy. She appealed against a decision of the Administrative Upper Tribunal that she was not entitled to compensation from the Criminal Injuries Compensation Scheme. CP needed to show that there had been a 'crime of violence' to claim under the Scheme. But the Court of Appeal held that there was no offence under section 23 of the Offences Against the Person Act 1861, which criminalises 'maliciously administering poison so as to endanger life or inflict grievous bodily harm'. The judges reasoned that CP was harmed in utero, and the fetus is not recognised in law as a person. This position can be contrasted with the *Attorney General's Reference*, where the harm started in utero and continued after the child's birth.

Had CP succeeded in her appeal it would have created a precedent that would lead inexorably to criminalisation for acts in pregnancy that harm the fetus born alive. The moral obligation to have due regard for the welfare of a child whom a mother elects to bring to term is incontrovertible.[133] Whether the invocation of the criminal law would in practice enhance fetal welfare and not simply offer means of coercing pregnant women and stigmatising unfortunate mothers is to be doubted.[134] The decision in *CP* brings a measure of clarity but leaves open the possibility, raised by the *Attorney General's Reference*, that a

130 Ibid, 942.

131 C Stanton, 'Maternal Transmission of HIV Infection: A Crime Against my Child?' (2015) 41(5) *J Med Ethics* 375.

132 [2014] EWCA Civ 1554. Permission to appeal to the Supreme Court was refused. For commentary see E Cave and C Stanton, 'Maternal Responsibility to the Child Not Yet Born' in C Stanton *et al* (eds), *Pioneering Healthcare Law: Essays in Honour of Margaret Brazier* (2015) Routledge; N Priaulx, 'Pre (Natal) Crime: Pregnant Women, Substance Abuse and the Law' (2015) 83 *Medico-Legal Journal* 43.

133 M Brazier, 'Liberty, Responsibility, Maternity' (1999) 52 *Current Legal Problems* 359.

134 M Brazier 'Parental Responsibilities, Foetal Welfare and Children's Health' in C Bridge (ed), *Family Law: Towards the Millennium* (1997) Butterworths; Brazier, 'Liberty, Responsibility, Maternity'.

woman could be prosecuted for an unlawful act in pregnancy which causes the subsequent death of her child.

Once the baby is born alive, a mother who deliberately kills her baby will not necessarily have committed murder or manslaughter. Section 1(1) of the Infanticide Act 1938 provides a partial defence if 'the balance of her mind was disturbed by reason of her not having fully recovered from the effect of giving birth to the child.'[135] In *R v Gore*,[136] G hid her pregnancy and abandoned her baby which sadly died due to lack of medical attention. At the time section 1 stipulated that '... notwithstanding that the circumstances were such that but for this Act the offence would have amounted to *murder*, she shall be guilty of felony, to wit of infanticide' (our emphasis).[137] Her parents argued[138] that the elements of murder (including the requisite *mens rea*) must be proved, but the Court of Appeal held not. There is no requirement in the Act of proof of intention to kill. In 2006 the Law Commission expressed concern that a negligent act which falls short of gross negligence manslaughter might lead to prosecution.[139] Section 57 of the Coroners and Justice Act 2009[140] made minor amendments to section 1 of the Infanticide Act.[141] Now no one can be convicted of infanticide unless a homicide is committed.

In *R v Tunstill*[142] the requirement that 'the balance of her mind was disturbed by reason of her not having fully recovered from the effect of giving birth to the child' was broadly interpreted in order to provide merciful treatment of a vulnerable woman. Ms Tunstill gave birth to her daughter alone at home and killed the baby with scissors before wrapping it and putting it in the kitchen bin. She told others that she had suffered a miscarriage and the baby had been stillborn. She had a history of mental illness and psychosis. At first instance

135 Infanticide Act 1938, s 1(1), as amended. But see E Milne, *Criminal Justice Responses to Maternal Filicide: Judging the Failed Mother* (2021) Emerald Publishing Limited.

136 [2007] EWCA Crim 2789. See A Ashworth, 'Infanticide' (2008) *Criminal Law Review* 388.

137 Infanticide Act 1938, s 1(1) prior to amendment.

138 G was deceased and her parents appealed on her behalf.

139 See Law Commission, *Murder, Manslaughter and Infanticide No 304 (*2006); and Ministry of Justice, *Murder, Manslaughter and Infanticide: Proposals for Reform of the Law* (2008).

140 Which came into force October 2010. See A Samuels, 'The Coroners and Justice Act 2009' (2010) 174 *Criminal Law and Justice Weekly* 250.

141 Infanticide Act 1938, s 1(1), as amended: where a woman by any wilful act or omission causes the death of her child being a child under the age of twelve months, but at the time of the act or omission the balance of her mind was disturbed by reason of her not having fully recovered from the effect of giving birth to the child or by reason of the effect of lactation consequent upon the birth of the child, then, if the circumstances were such that but for this Act the offence would have amounted to murder or manslaughter, she shall be guilty of felony, to wit of infanticide, and may for such offence be dealt with and punished as if she had been guilty of the offence of manslaughter of the child.

142 [2018] EWCA Crim 1696. See K Brennan and E Milne, 'Infanticide: Guarding Against Harshness' (2019) 7824 *NLJ* 13.

it was held that the partial defence of diminished responsibility was relevant but that the Infanticide Act would not apply because disturbance of mind was not solely caused by the effects of childbirth: Ms Tunstill's mental disturbance was pre-existing. The Court of Appeal disagreed: the purpose of the Act was to limit the harshness of the law of murder, and it should be interpreted with that in mind.

13.19 Pre-pregnancy advice and the child

Has the disabled child a remedy if the parent is given negligent pre-pregnancy advice? We must distinguish three types of cases where negligent pre-pregnancy advice results in the birth of a disabled child. In the first case, the relevant negligence may be that the woman was encouraged to become pregnant when, had proper care been taken, she could have been advised never to contemplate pregnancy because of the risk to *any* child she might bear. The child's action in such a case will fail because the essence of their claim is that they should never have been born at all. It is a claim for 'wrongful life'.

In the second instance, at the opposite end of the spectrum, there is a class of case where the child's action based on allegedly careless pre-pregnancy advice may succeed. That is where adequate counselling advice would have enabled that very child to be born hale and hearty. Realistic examples are difficult to think of. Perhaps one example concerns the relationship between maternal diet before conception and spina bifida. There is evidence that folic acid supplements may reduce the likelihood of spina bifida. The child could contend that, had their mother been advised to follow that regime, their disability would not have developed. They would have been born, but not born disabled. Such a child claims for their disabilities, not wrongful life. They overcome the first problem in their claim against medical staff, but will they be able to prove that the treatment if given would have prevented their disability?

Finally, the negligence may have been in failing to counsel the mother properly on precautions to take, or the timing of pregnancy. Such a claim raises an awkward problem. A woman is not tested for immunity to rubella, or the test is negligently conducted. She is wrongly told that she has immunity. She becomes pregnant, contracts the disease and the child is born disabled. Had she been properly advised, she would have been vaccinated against the disease and advised in the strongest of terms to delay pregnancy for three months after the vaccination. The actual child born would never have been born. The particular set of genes in the egg and sperm that went to create them would never have met. A strict interpretation of *McKay* would seem to deny the child a remedy on the ground that that unique individual would never have been born had the mother had proper advice. It would seem a harsh result.

The 1976 Act gives cause for hope. It allows a claim if a child is born disabled as a result of an 'occurrence' before its birth. According to section 1(2) an occurrence is one which:

(a) affected either parent of the child in his or her ability to have a normal, healthy child; or

(b) affected the mother during her pregnancy, or affected her or the child in the course of its birth, so that the child is born with disabilities which would not otherwise have been present.

The 1976 Act requires under sub-section 1(2)(b) on post-conception injury that the effects are such 'that the child is born with disabilities which would not otherwise have been present' but adds no such rider in the case of section 1(2)(a) on pre-conception events. Arguably then section 1(2)(b) prevents actions based on the argument that the child would not have been born at all, in a way which 1(2)(a) does not. Under 1(2)(a) it is conceivable that a claim that a child should not have been born disabled might succeed even if the child would not have been born but for the negligent act. Arguably, that fact becomes irrelevant if the disability is regarded as 'damage' as per section 1(1) of the 1976 Act. The compensation sought is for the disability rather than being born.

This argument was recently accepted in *Toombes v Mitchell*.[143] The decision involved a trial of a preliminary issue in 2020 and a subsequent hearing in 2021. In the preliminary issue decision, Lambert J concluded that there was a cause of action under the 1976 Act. Mrs Evie Toombes was born in 2001 with spinal cord tethering which led to double incontinence and limited mobility. She claimed that her mother was not advised to take folic acid by the defendant GP, Dr Mitchell, and had her mother been so advised she would have delayed pregnancy in which case the claimant would not have been born. Mrs Toombes' mother had a potential claim for wrongful conception but had chosen not to pursue it. Could Mrs Toombes claim in her own right? Lambert J noted that the 'occurrence' required to satisfy the 1976 Act was not a *post*-conception event affecting the mother invoking section 1(2)(b) as occurred in *McKay*. Rather it was a *pre*-conception event, which fell squarely within section 1(2)(a) as it 'affected either parent of the child in his or her ability to have a normal, healthy child'. She found that the three components of section 1(2) were satisfied. There was: (1) a wrongful act (the failure to advise the mother about the relevance of folic acid); (2) an occurrence (widely interpreted to include sexual intercourse before starting folic acid); and (3) a disabled child being born as a result. This preliminary issue determined, Mrs Toombes was required to prove the alleged facts in order to establish breach and causation. This she did successfully in 2021 when HHJ Coe KC accepted that Mrs Toombes' mother was not pregnant at the consultation and that she followed the flawed advice given and became pregnant shortly afterwards. Had she had the correct advice, conception would have been delayed whilst she took a course of folic acid and on the balance of probabilities she would have had a healthy baby.[144]

On the alleged facts in *Toombes*, a causative link was established between the act, the occurrence and the disability. In the trial of the preliminary issue,

143 [2020] EWHC 3506 (QB); [2021] EWHC 3234 (QB).
144 *Toombes v Mitchell* [2021] EWHC 3234 (QB).

Lambert J was clear that this link was essential to a cause of action, which would not lie 'if the mother would not have been able to have a healthy child whatever the circumstances of the intercourse'. She gave the example of negligent advice about parental genetic status. If the parents relied on this advice and conceived and gave birth to a child with an inherited genetic disability, they would not be able to claim under the Act because there 'would be no circumstances affecting the intercourse in which a healthy child could have been conceived and no causal connection between the occurrence and the disability'.

Toombes advances the law by making a clear distinction between pre-conception and post-conception negligence, but it begs several questions. One relates to the breadth of the definition of 'occurrence' under section 1(2), which may be subject to challenge according to the argument that the occurrence must cause the claimant's parent injury. Another relates to the strength of the required causative link. A parent is undergoing treatment for venereal disease. They are carelessly advised that pregnancy is now safe. It is not. Treatment was not complete. The particular child born disabled would not have been born had proper advice been given. They would have waited and had a healthy child. There is a clear link between the act and the disability but is the link between the occurrence (sexual intercourse before being given a reliable 'all clear') and the disability sufficient if the parent's condition was pre-existing? A woman knows a little of a family history of genetic disease affecting some members of her family. She seeks counselling. She should have been advised of the availability of pre-implantation genetic testing (PGT) so that she could if she wished have ensured she did not give birth to an affected child. Lambert J said there would be no case if the mother could not have had a healthy child, but access to PGT would have enabled just that possibility.

13.20 Childbirth: how much choice?[145]

In future, artificial wombs may allow the fetus to be gestated outside the pregnant person.[146] Today medical technology offers a whole range of sophisticated devices to monitor mother and baby and ensure safe delivery. For a number of women the ideal is delivery at home in the comfort of familiar surroundings. Others seek delivery by Caesarean section for a variety of reasons including the safety of the baby, fear of natural delivery or simple convenience.[147]

145 See guidance from Royal College of Obstetrics and Gynaecology, *Obtaining Valid Consent* (2015).

146 See A Alghrani, *Regulating Assisted Reproductive Technologies: New Horizons* (2018) Cambridge University Press; EC Romanis, 'Challenging the "Born Alive" Threshold: Fetal Surgery, Artificial Wombs, and the English Approach to Legal Personhood' (2020) 28(1) *Med Law Rev* 93; A Nelson, 'Should Delivery by Partial Ectogenesis be Available on Request of the Pregnant Person?' (2022) 15(1) *International Journal of Feminist Approaches to Bioethics* 1. And see 15.6 on the developments of artificial embryos called 'blastoids'.

147 See EC Romanis 'Addressing Rising Caesarean Rates: Maternal Request Caesareans, Defensive Practice, and the Power of Choice in Childbirth' 13(1) (2020) *International Journal of Feminist Approaches to Bioethics* 1.

For those that seek a home birth, it is only relatively recently that the NHS Choice Framework has said that there should be a choice to give birth at home with the support of a midwife.[148] Those seeking a Caesarean section have also faced significant barriers.[149] Increased rates of Caesarean sections raised concerns about complications and longer recovery times compared to vaginal birth. This was thought to justify restrictions on choice. The Supreme Court decision of *Montgomery v Lanarkshire Health Board*[150] is a powerful assertion of reproductive autonomy. Nadine Montgomery was awarded £5.25m in damages when her son sustained cerebral palsy when he was deprived of oxygen during childbirth. She was not advised of the possibility of an elective Caesarean section, despite her small stature and the fact that her baby would be bigger than average. Nor was the operation offered during the difficult labour. The Supreme Court affirmed that doctors have a duty to ensure patients are aware of any material risk of injury, whether or not they question the doctor about the risk.

The first Ockenden Report[151] on maternity services in Shrewsbury and Telford Hospital NHS Trust found that that one of the reasons for appalling avoidable deaths and injury to babies and mothers was a failure to listen to women. The Caesarean section rate at Shrewsbury was particularly low and women 'appeared to have little or no freedom to express a preference for caesarean section or any choice on their mode of delivery'.[152] The report lists essential actions to improve safety in maternity units and 'ensure that women and their families are listened to and their voices heard'. With regard to Caesarean sections, recent research shows little increased absolute risk over vaginal birth.[153] The Department of Health and Social Care is now clear that women can choose a Caesarean even for non-medical reasons and 'If your doctor is unwilling to perform the operation, they should refer you to a doctor who will.'[154]

148 DHSC, *The NHS Choice Framework: What Choices are Available to Me in the NHS?* (2020).

149 The ECtHR ruled in 2020 that three complaints by Irish women who were given symphysiotomies (cutting the cartilage of the pubic symphysis to widen the pelvis) without consent were inadmissible in *LF v Ireland, KO'S v Ireland* and *WM v Ireland* (App Nos 62007/17, 61836/17 and 61872/17). The practice was attributed to 'attitudes of an earlier age, when medical paternalism was more widely accepted'. It has been alleged that symphysiotomies, which continued in Ireland long after the practice had been abandoned elsewhere, was to avoid the need for Caesarean section, which may limit the ability to have further children.

150 [2015] UKSC 11. See 6.12 above.

151 D Ockenden (Chair), *The Independent Review of Maternity Services at Shrewsbury and Telford Hospital NHS Trust*, First Report following 250 Clinical Reviews (2020) HC1081. See 2.1 above.

152 Ibid, 4.43.

153 L Herstad *et al*, 'Elective Caesarean Section or Not? Maternal Age and Risk of Adverse Outcomes at Term: A Population-Based Registry Study of Low-Risk Primiparous women' (2016) 16 *BMC Pregnancy Childbirth* 230.

154 NHS, *Caesarean Section*. See www.nhs.uk/conditions/caesarean-section/.

13.21 Hospital birth

How far does a woman retain control of her labour? Save in an emergency, explicit consent is required for any invasive examination or procedure in labour.[155] That does not mean that the midwife must obtain a written consent for every vaginal examination, or that explicit consent to wiping the woman's brow is called for. Any significant procedure must where possible proceed with the woman's agreement.

Childbirth can be an unpredictable process. Midwives and obstetricians sometimes have to respond swiftly to an unforeseen emergency. The woman may be in acute pain, or significantly affected by doses of painkilling drugs which can cause some mental confusion. Doubts may surface about her decision-making capacity, and/or time to seek consent may truly be limited. The Court of Appeal[156] has suggested that if the woman temporarily lacks capacity to make decisions for herself, health professionals may do whatever is required in her best interests. Defining the borderline between capacity and mental incapacity in such cases is tricky.[157] It is too easy to assume women are incompetent. 'Birth plans' offer a partial solution to such dilemmas. Women, ideally in consultation with their midwives, outline how they wish to be treated if certain emergencies materialise. 'Advance decisions'[158] should have just as great force and authority at childbirth as in the life-threatening circumstances in which they are more usually invoked. The controversy over whether the law should compel medical attendance in childbirth would be much less substantial if the woman's rights in hospital were fully protected.

It goes without saying that a mother suffering injury as a result of carelessness in the management of childbirth is entitled to compensation for negligence. She will recover compensation for her pain and suffering and for the shock and grief consequent on the death of a baby, or the birth of a disabled child. Her damages may also include any effect of the mismanaged delivery on her prospects of future childbearing.[159] Where obstetric negligence results in the birth of a disabled infant, the child too has a claim. The most common case centres on allegations that the baby suffered brain damage as a consequence of oxygen starvation during delivery. The parents argue that the obstetric team failed to act on signs of fetal distress and perform a Caesarean section as swiftly as the circumstances required. The child is born with cerebral palsy. Very often the core of the dispute is not whether clinical negligence can be proven, but whether causation can be established. Such cases are expensive, slow and worryingly common. Little

155 But see C Pickles and J Herring (eds), *Childbirth, Vulnerability and the Law: Exploring Issues of Violence and Control* (2021) Routledge, and C Pickles and J Herring (eds), *Women's Birthing Bodies and the Law* (2020) Hart, on unauthorised intimate examinations in childbirth.

156 *Re MB (An Adult) (Medical Treatment)* [1997] 2 FCR 541, CA.

157 See *A NHS FT v An Expectant Mother* [2021] EWCOP 33 discussed at 13.23 below.

158 See 7.14 above.

159 *Kralj v McGrath* [1986] 1 All ER 54.

wonder the government has given serious consideration to a special redress system for birth injuries.[160]

13.22 Giving birth during the COVID-19 pandemic

As the pandemic took hold in 2019–2020, some Trusts withdrew home birth services and others closed midwife-led birth centres or restricted access to Caesarean sections. Scans, appointments and sometimes birth had to be negotiated without the support of a partner or friend. Difficult as this would be if birth proceeded normally, negotiating fear and grief alone in the event that birth did not go as planned could be catastrophic. Recognising the importance of a birth partner to the pregnant woman's safety and well-being, in December 2020 the NHS set out guidance saying that pregnant women should be allowed to have someone with them 'at all stages of her maternity journey'.[161] Romanis and Nelson have argued that the restrictive approach in the pandemic is indicative of an insufficient focus on choice in maternity care.[162]

13.23 Maternal autonomy

In 1998, the Court of Appeal in *St George's Healthcare NHS Trust v S*[163] finally ruled that in English law no mentally competent woman could be required to submit to a Caesarean section or any other form of obstetric intervention to which she objected. Neither pregnancy nor labour diminished the woman's rights of self-determination. Judge LJ put the position succinctly: '[W]hile pregnancy increases the personal responsibilities of the pregnant woman it does not diminish her entitlement to decide whether or not to undergo medical treatment.'[164]

Six years of uncertainty were apparently ended. In 1992, in *Re S*,[165] the then President of the Family Division had ruled doctors could carry out a Caesarean on a woman whose own life and whose child's life were imminently imperilled by an obstructed labour. Several other cases[166] followed where courts, often

160 DHSC, *A Rapid Resolution and Redress Scheme for Severe Avoidable Birth Injury: Government Summary Consultation Response* (2017). See 11.7 above.

161 NHS, *Supporting Pregnant Women using Maternity Services during the Coronavirus Pandemic: Actions for NHS Providers* (2020). There were several such guidelines issued during the course of the pandemic, revealing a bewildering and changeable environment for pregnant people.

162 See EC Romanis and A Nelson, 'Homebirthing in the United Kingdom During COVID-19' (2020) 20(3) *Medical Law International* 183; EC Romanis and A Nelson, 'The Medicalisation of Childbirth and Access to Homebirth in the UK: Covid-19 and Beyond' (2021) 29(4) *Med Law Rev* 661.

163 [1998] 3 All ER 673.

164 Ibid, 692.

165 [1992] 4 All ER 671.

166 *Rochdale Healthcare NHS Trust v C* [1997] 1 FCR 274; *Norfolk and Norwich (NHS) Trust v W* [1996] 2 FLR 613; *Re L (An Adult: Non-Consensual Treatment)* [1997] 1 FCR 609; *Tameside & Glossop Acute Services Trust v CH* [1996] 1 FLR 762.

in hurried hearings in circumstances of dire emergency, ordered Caesarean surgery despite maternal objections. In a number, but not all, of these cases the mother's mental capacity was questionable. In 1997, in *Re MB (Adult: Medical Treatment)*[167] the Court of Appeal said that if a woman retained mental capacity she retained the right to make decisions about surgery for herself but found on the facts that MB's needle phobia rendered her temporarily incompetent.

In practice, the temptation to seek grounds to find her capacity to be impaired is great.[168] Judge LJ in *St George's* is emphatic in his endorsement of maternal autonomy. The mother's wishes should be respected even if her thinking process is 'apparently bizarre and irrational and contrary to the views of the overwhelming majority of the community at large'. Yet in *Re MB*, Butler-Sloss LJ suggested a woman might suffer temporary incapacity induced by confusion, shock, pain or drugs. Or fear might paralyse the will.[169] Finding any of these factors in childbirth will not be hard.

The situation is altered little by the Mental Capacity Act 2005.[170] The Act codifies the test for capacity in section 2. Capacity is judged at the 'relevant time'. Its temporary nature is irrelevant. However, neither a condition (such as pregnancy) nor an aspect of the person's behaviour (such as irrationality) can establish a lack of capacity under the Act.[171]

In the case of a pregnant woman, it must be demonstrated that she is unable to make the particular decision as a result of an impairment or disturbance of the mind. The Code of Practice on the Mental Capacity Act recognises a wide range of factors which can lead to such impairment, including drugs and delirium.[172] Consequently, it will remain the case that doctors may have little difficulty in demonstrating a temporary lack of capacity during labour.

Where it is established that a patient lacks capacity, an assessment of her best interests must be undertaken under section 4 of the Act. This too can be highly controversial. There have been several recent cases where the Court of Protection has authorised Caesarean sections in cases where women have serious mental disorders and either lack capacity or have fluctuating capacity in which case an anticipatory declaration may be warranted.[173] Halliday has

167 [1997] 2 FLR 426.

168 See *Bolton Hospitals NHS Trust v O* [2003] 1 FLR 824.

169 The DH, *Reference Guide to Consent for Examination or Treatment* (2009), ch 1, para 46 recognises that withdrawal of consent during a procedure may be non-capacitous (and therefore not valid) if brought on by 'pain, panic and shock'. And see *Connolly v Croydon Health Service NHS Trust* [2015] EWHC 1339 (QB), discussed at 6.1 above, where a claimant consented to angiogram which, due to complications, led to a (probably life-sustaining) angioplasty. C's claim to have withdrawn consent during the procedure was rejected on the basis that she lacked capacity.

170 See Chapter 7.

171 Mental Capacity Act 2005, s 2(3)(b).

172 *Mental Capacity Act 2005 Code of Practice*, updated 2020, para 4.12.

173 See, for example, *Re AA* [2012] EWHC 4378 (COP); *In the Matter of P* [2013] EWCOP 4581; *Great Western Hospitals NHS Foundation Trust v AA* & Ors

argued in relation to two 2016 cases that the existence of a mental disorder can problematise the woman herself as a source of danger to both the fetus and health professionals and lead to a risk averse approach which leaves little room for patient choice.[174]

Planning is essential if the pregnant person's views are to be properly represented and the court is to be presented with all the relevant evidence. In *NHS Trust & Ors v FG (Rev 1)*,[175] Keehan J said: 'Save in a case of genuine medical emergency, any application should be made no later than four weeks before the expected date of delivery.' But all too often applications are left to the last minute.[176]

Anticipatory declarations pose risks of their own, especially if they are made about women with serious mental health disorders who currently have capacity, as occurred in *Guys and St Thomas NHS Foundation Trust & Anor v R*.[177] R had polyhydramnios – an excess of amniotic fluid round the baby – which created a significant risk that a Caesarean section would be clinically indicated. R, who had capacity, had told medical staff that would be 'the last thing she would want'. The matter came before Hayden J when R was thirty-nine weeks and six days pregnant. Staff feared that a psychotic episode resulting from her bipolar disorder could lead to a deterioration in her mental health and potentially a loss of capacity. Granting the 'draconian' order that in such circumstances a Caesarean would be in her best interests, Hayden J noted that this was the first time he had decided a serious medical treatment issue contrary to the person's wishes and feelings.[178] He said:

> 63. The caselaw has emphasised the right of a capacitous woman, in these circumstances, to behave in a way which many might regard as unreasonable … This includes the right to jeopardise the life and welfare of her foetus. When the

[2014] EWHC 132 (Fam); *Royal Free NHS Foundation Trust v AB* [2014] EWCOP 50; *The Mental Health Trust v DD* [2014] EWCOP 11; *Wakefield MDC and Wakefield CCG v DN and MN* [2019] EWHC 2306 (Fam); *X NHS Foundation Trust v Ms A* [2021] EWCOP 17; East Lancashire Hospitals NHS Trust v GH [2021] EWCOP 18. And see discussion: S Fovargue and J Miola, 'Are we Still "Policing Pregnancy"?' in C Stanton *et al* (eds), *Pioneering Healthcare Law: Essays in Honour of Margaret Brazier* (2016) Routledge, ch 21.

174 S Halliday, 'Court-Authorised Obstetric Intervention: Insight and Capacity, A Tale of Loss' in Pickles and Herring (eds), *Childbirth, Vulnerability and Law* pp 178–203 referring to *The NHS Acute Trust & The NHS Mental Health Trust v C* [2016] EWCOP 17 and *A University Hospital NHS Trust v CA* [2016] EWCOP 51.

175 *NHS Trust & Ors v FG (Rev 1)* [2014] EWCOP 30.

176 See for example *University Hospitals Dorset NHS Fdn Trust & Anor v Miss K* [2021] EWCOP 40 where Lieven J said at [2]: 'it was incumbent upon the Trusts to have made this application significantly earlier than today'.

177 [2020] EWCOP 4I. This and *United Lincolnshire Hospitals NHS Trust v CD* [2019] EWCOP 24 are discussed in: S Fovargue, 'Anticipating Issues with Capacitous Pregnant Women' (2020) 28(4) *Med Law Rev* 781. See also *North Middlesex University Hospital NHS Trust v SR* [2021] EWCOP 58.

178 [2020] EWCOP 4I, [66].

> Court has the responsibility for taking the decision, I do not consider it has the same latitude. It should not sanction that which it objectively considers to be contrary to P's best interests. The statute prohibits this by its specific insistence on 'reasonable belief' as to where P's best interests truly lie. It is important that respect for P's autonomy remains in focus but it will rarely be the case, in my judgement, that P's best interests will be promoted by permitting the death of, or brain injury to, an otherwise viable and healthy foetus.

Anticipatory decisions can be equally contentious if the person lacks capacity, but the risk of complications in childbirth is low. Consider *A NHS FT v An Expectant Mother*.[179] Holman J made an anticipatory judgment that a 21-year-old woman with severe agoraphobia lacked capacity to decide whether to attend hospital for the birth. She wanted to give birth at home and the birth was progressing normally. Nevertheless, in disagreement with the Official Solicitor acting for the pregnant woman, it was held to be in her best interests to give birth in hospital. Given her strong desire to have a healthy child, Holman J was concerned at what would happen if a transfer to hospital became urgent, as occurs in around 1–2 per cent of home births. A planned hospital birth was considered preferable to the low risk of complications and potential delay to hospital care, even if some force or restrain should be required to get her to and from the transport and into hospital.

Women with a serious mental disorder who want to ensure that their choice not to have a Caesarean section is protected could make an advance decision compliant with sections 24–26 of the 2005 Act (see 7.14 above). They have at least two limitations. First, many people in R's situation will be unaware that their choices are so limited or that the option of an advance decision exists. Second, advance decisions should be made with caution: valid and applicable advance decisions are as binding as a contemporaneous refusal and the advance decision-maker loses the right to change her mind if she loses capacity.

In an insightful analysis of the recent case-law, Sara Fovargue fears:

> there will only ever be one answer to questions about the mode of childbirth framed around best interests: that women must deliver in the way deemed medically 'best', regardless of their wishes. This may sometimes be appropriate, but it ought not to be the universal and automatic approach. If it is, it renders best interests assessments redundant.[180]

13.24 Protecting fetal interests?

Is the theory right? Or ought the fetus at the point of birth to be more highly valued? The difficulty of using law to enforce a duty to the fetus is well

179 [2021] EWCOP 33.

180 S Fovargue, 'In Whose Best Interests? Childbirth Choices and Other Health Decisions' (2021) 137(Oct) *LQR* 604, 604.

illustrated in *Re F (In Utero)*,[181] where a local authority unsuccessfully tried to make a fetus a ward of court. The mother was a 36-year-old woman who suffered from severe mental disturbance, but she was not 'sectionable' under the Mental Health Act 1983. She refused ante-natal care and had disappeared by the time the local authority started proceedings to make the fetus a ward of court. There was concern for the child's welfare. Refusing to extend the wardship jurisdiction to unborn children, the court advanced the following reasons for their decision.

(1) In English law the fetus has no legal personality until it is born, and has an existence independent of the mother.
(2) To extend the wardship jurisdiction to the fetus with its predominant principle that the interests of the ward are paramount would create inevitable conflict between the existing legal interests of the mother and her child. Is the mother to be 'sacrificed' for the child?
(3) There are immense practical difficulties in enforcing any order against the mother. If she is, for example, refusing to consent to an elective Caesarean and is not already in hospital, will the police be called on to go and arrest her?
(4) There would be problems with the limit of such a jurisdiction. Mothers can do most harm to their unborn children early in pregnancy by, for example, alcohol and drug abuse. Yet up to twenty-four weeks in pregnancy a mother may well be able to obtain a legal abortion. Would a woman who wants her baby be subject to coercive measures in the baby's interests, yet free to destroy it should she change her mind? May LJ concluded that in the light of these problems any such radical extension of the wardship jurisdiction was a matter for Parliament and not for the courts themselves. In the event, and unbeknownst to the court, while they were hearing the action the mother had already safely given birth to a healthy child.

Parliament should reject any proposal to extend the wardship jurisdiction to unborn children or to endorse non-consensual obstetric interventions.[182] Over and above those reasons given by the Court of Appeal, such a proposal should be thrown out on the grounds of the damage it would do to antenatal care generally. Obstetricians, knowing that they could in the end coerce their patients, would become less willing to inform and persuade, to rely on patience rather than compulsion. Women, knowing that they could be forced against their will to submit to blood transfusion or surgery, may opt out of formal obstetric care and far more babies could be born damaged as a result. The law must continue to recognise the pregnant woman's autonomy and her sovereignty over her own body. In no other circumstances can one person

181 [1989] 2 All ER 193.

182 As the Royal College of Obstetricians and Gynaecologists itself has done; see RCOG, *Law and Ethics in Relation to Court-Ordered Obstetric Intervention* (2006). And see RCOG, *Obtaining Valid Consent* (2015).

be required to submit to any medical procedure to benefit another's welfare. Once a child is born neither of his parents could be forced to donate even a drop of blood to him however trivial the discomfort to them or great the child's need. Caesarean surgery remains major invasive surgery with significant risks and pain for the patient.[183]

183 See L Miller, 'Two Patients or One? A Problem of Consent in Obstetrics' (1993) *Medical Law International* 97.

Chapter 14

ASSISTED CONCEPTION[1]

14.1 Introduction

About one in seven couples have difficulty conceiving naturally. The birth of the first 'test-tube' baby, Louise Brown,[2] in 1978 gave hope to many childless couples. Since then *in vitro* fertilisation (IVF) success rates have improved year on year.[3] The pace of development in the reproductive technologies has been relentless. Reproductive medicine no longer focuses exclusively on the management of infertility. Single women can be assisted to have a child without resort to sexual intercourse. Same sex couples can be helped to have a child. Couples who are fertile but know that one or both of them is a carrier of a genetic disease can be helped to have a healthy child, by way of pre-implantation genetic testing (PGT) whereby embryos are screened to avoid implanting any embryos with the defective gene. Those who already have one sick child can seek PGT together with tissue typing, to attempt to create a 'saviour sibling' for their sick child. And in 2015 the United Kingdom became the first country in the world to permit the use of mitochondrial donation in fertility treatment to vastly reduce the risk of a woman passing serious mitochondrial disease on to the child. Each and every development in the reproductive technologies attracts controversy. For everyone who rejoices at what doctors can now do, there are those who condemn the advances in medicine as unnatural, contrary to the will of God, or destructive of 'normal family life'.

Louise Brown's birth did not only generate moral controversy. Concerns arose about the safety of the 'new' technologies. Fears grew about the competence of practitioners and basic issues, such as hygienic storage of human gametes.[4] In response, the government established a Committee under Dame Mary Warnock which reported in 1984 and recommended legislation to regulate

1 See E Jackson, *Regulating Reproduction: Law Technology and Autonomy* (2001) Hart. And on the legacy of this impactful book see J Bridgeman, 'Emily Jackson, Regulating Reproduction: Law, Technology and Autonomy' in S Fovargue and C Purshouse, *Leading Works in Health Law and Ethics* (2023) Routledge, ch 2.

2 Who gave birth to her own first child without fertility treatment in 2006.

3 HFEA, *Fertility Treatment: Trends and Figures 2019* (2021). In 2019 birth rates were three times higher than in 1991.

4 There is a (possibly apocryphal) story about one clinic storing sperm in the same fridge as milk for staff coffee breaks.

these emerging reproductive technologies.[5] Parliament eventually enacted the Human Fertilisation and Embryology Act 1990. That Act entrusted the primary responsibility for regulating the reproductive technologies in the United Kingdom to the Human Fertilisation and Embryology Authority (HFEA).

The 1990 Act and the HFEA were once seen as the model for effective regulation of assisted conception and embryo research but the 1990 Act, and the HFEA, became the subject of increasingly intense criticism.[6] It is scarcely surprising that a statute enacted in 1990 no longer meets the needs of scientific developments, undreamed of thirty years before. The 1990 Act generated prolific litigation.[7] It was heavily amended by the Human Fertilisation and Embryology Act 2008 and that Act also introduced new rules relating to parenthood, allowing female same sex couples to achieve the status of legal parents when they seek fertility treatment together. The amended 1990 Act[8] and the self-standing parts of the 2008 Act continue to generate case-law especially in the context of surrogacy, parental status and contact with children born as a result of assisted conception. The Law Commission consulted on outdated surrogacy laws in 2019 and plans to publish a draft bill in 2023. Further reform is proposed by the HFEA, which in 2021 marked its thirtieth birthday with a call for change to better protect patients and to address scientific developments. But will further tweaks of the 1990 Act suffice or is root and branch reform required?

14.2 Regulating human fertilisation and embryology

The primary responsibility for regulating the reproductive technologies in the United Kingdom is vested in the Human Fertilisation and Embryology Authority (HFEA), operating as a statutory licensing authority, and established by section 5 of the Human Fertilisation and Embryology Act 1990. Schedule 1 of the Act prescribes the authority's membership with a strong emphasis on a partnership between lay representation and expert input. Neither the chair nor the deputy chair may be a medical practitioner, or professionally involved in

5 *Report of the Committee of Inquiry into Human Fertilisation and Embryology* (1984) Cm 9314 (the Warnock Report). See E Jackson, 'The Legacy of the Warnock Report' in E Dove and N Shuibhne, *Law and Legacy in Medical Jurisprudence* (2021) Cambridge University Press, ch 11 and E Cave, 'Report of the Committee of Inquiry into Human Fertilisation and Embryology' in S Fovargue and C Purshouse, *Leading Works in Health Law and Ethics* (2023) Routledge, ch 4.

6 See in particular, the House of Commons Science and Technology Committee Fifth Report of Session 2004–5, *Human Reproductive Technologies and the Law*, HC 7–1, vol 1.

7 See, for example, *R (Quintavalle) v Human Fertilisation and Embryology Authority* [2003] 2 All ER 105; *R (Quintavalle) v Human Fertilisation and Embryology Authority* [2005] UKHL 28.

8 New technical amendments to the Act were made by Regulations under the European Union (Withdrawal) Act 2018, s 8(1) to ensure that retained EU law operated effectively post-EU Exit. See the Human Fertilisation and Embryology (Amendment) (EU Exit) Regulations 2019, SI 2019/482; SI 2020/1307.

embryo research or assisted conception. At least one third, but fewer than half, of the members must be persons involved in research or infertility treatment.

The HFEA is granted impressive powers, many focusing on the power to license clinics to undertake fertility treatments. Section 3 of the Act makes it a criminal offence to bring about the creation of an embryo outside the human body, or keep or use such an embryo,[9] except in pursuance of a licence granted by the HFEA. Any infertility treatment requiring the creation of an embryo by means of IVF, that is the creation of a 'test-tube' embryo, must be licensed. An embryo *in vitro* is defined to include embryos where the process of fertilisation started outside the woman's body.[10]

Section 4 prohibits storage of gametes (sperm or eggs), and the use of donor sperm or eggs, without a licence from the HFEA. Any infertility treatment involving artificial insemination by donor (DI) or egg donation is unlawful unless licensed by the HFEA. There is a limited exception to the rule relating to sperm. DI can be undertaken outside a licensed clinic if the sperm is 'partner-donated sperm which has neither been processed nor stored'.[11] The amendments to the 1990 Act introduced much stricter controls on DI designed to control the growing number of 'businesses' offering both access to fresh donated sperm and 'sperm sorting', a crude form of primary sex selection. Often based on Internet sites, sperm was advertised to women who wanted a child but no relationship with a man. Given that the sperm was fresh and the sites were not based in any form of medical environment, health risks were high, as are the risks of later disputes about parentage of a resulting child.[12] Any such enterprise must now be licensed in the new category of 'non-medical fertility services'. One question that arises is whether the new law effectively bans self-insemination in such cases as a lesbian woman asking a friend to donate sperm to her with which she inseminates herself, or an intended father providing sperm for self-insemination by a surrogate mother. A literal reading of the Act might suggest that it does for in such cases the sperm is not partner-donated. Laurie, Harmon and Dove[13] argue that the man providing sperm on the basis of a private agreement with a woman who is a friend or a potential surrogate falls outside the ban in section 4 as he is not 'providing treatment services'. We tend to agree but wonder about the case of a man who widely advertises his own services as a sperm donor?[14]

Sections 3 and 4 outlaw a number of specific procedures, for example, keeping an embryo after the appearance of the primitive streak (fourteen days),

9 See *Attorney General's Reference (No 2 of 2003)* [2004] EWCA Crim 785.
10 Section 1(2).
11 See s 4(1)(b)(i). And see s 1(5): sperm to be treated as partner-donated if the donor and the recipient declare that they have an 'intimate physical relationship'.
12 See *M v F* [2013] EWHC 1901 (Fam). See discussion in E Jackson, 'The Law and DIY Assisted Conception' in K Horsey (ed), *Revisiting the Regulation of Human Fertilisation and Embryology* (2015) Routledge, pp 31–49.
13 GT Laurie, SHE Harmon and ES Dove, *Mason and McCall Smith's Law and Medical Ethics* (11th edn, 2019) Oxford University Press, 8.27.
14 See for example the activities of Mr F in *M v F* [2013] EWHC 1901 (Fam).

placing an embryo in an animal and the use of embryos for reproductive cloning, which we discuss in the next chapter. One point must be made here. Only 'permitted' embryos and gametes may be placed in a woman in the course of fertility treatment.[15] Permitted gametes must have been produced or extracted from a human male or female and the nuclear or mitochondrial DNA of the gamete must not have been altered.[16] Permitted embryos must be created from permitted gametes. No embryo created from the mixing of human and animal material may be used in fertility treatment. The Act, however, provided for Parliament to make Regulations to amend the definitions of permitted embryos and eggs to allow for the licensing of treatment to prevent the transmission of serious mitochondrial disease,[17] and this Parliament has now done.[18] We discuss this development later in the chapter.

14.3 Licensing fertility treatment

Any clinic that offers IVF or artificial insemination is subject to the control of the HFEA. A clinic cannot operate lawfully without a licence and its staff and procedures are strictly monitored and controlled. Failure to comply with HFEA guidelines about, for example, safety procedures, numbers of embryos to be implanted,[19] selection of donors or assessment of patients may lead to forfeiture of that licence.

The 1990 Act only provided a basic framework of rules governing assisted conception in the United Kingdom. The Act entrusted to the HFEA extensive powers to fill in the details of those rules and to regulate both the ethical and practical problems of assisted conception. So, the HFEA has had to consider – should ovarian tissue be harvested from fetuses, should sister-to-sister egg donation be banned, should egg sharing be permitted? And these were examples of the HFEA's less contentious business. Developments in techniques of assisted conception continually posed novel problems for the HFEA. The controversy relating to pre-implantation genetic testing (PGT) exposed the HFEA to attack on several fronts. Other ethical dilemmas facing the HFEA fade almost into insignificance in comparison with the debate surrounding human cloning. The HFEA found itself making policy in relation to deeply divisive social questions generated by the rapid developments in reproductive medicine. The rewards for its efforts were charges that the unelected Authority has usurped the role of Parliament.[20]

15 Section 3(2).

16 Section 3ZA.

17 Section 3ZA(5).

18 The Human Fertilisation and Embryology (Mitochondrial Donation) Regulations 2015, SI 2015/572.

19 See *R (Assisted Reproduction and Gynaecology Centre) v HFEA* [2002] EWCA Civ 20; But see *The Assisted Reproduction and Gynaecology Centre and The Reproductive Genetics Institute v HFEA* [2013] EWHC 3087 (Admin), discussed below.

20 See in particular, the Report of the House of Commons Science and Technology Committee.

Crucial to the role played by the HFEA is its Code of Practice setting out the general 'rules' within which clinics must work. Clinics that violate the Code may lose their licence.[21] The ninth edition of the Code was published in 2018 but is subject to a continuous process of revision and updating. Grand ethical issues have faced the HFEA. Their everyday difficulties are apparently more mundane. How often should gametes from one donor be used? The more often sperm from one donor is used, the higher the risk of unwitting incest. No single donor is to be used for more than ten inseminations.[22] The HFEA has led a successful campaign to reduce the number of multiple births resulting from IVF.[23] The more embryos replaced in the woman, the greater the risk of multiple pregnancies. Such pregnancies increase the risk of premature labour with adverse consequences for mother, babies and overstretched neonatal units within the National Health Service (NHS). The current guidance requires all clinics to consider when it might be appropriate to move to Single Embryo Transplants. Some fertility specialists vehemently opposed what they saw as paternalistic interference with clinical freedom. If the woman considers that increased chances of pregnancy outweigh the risk of multiple pregnancy, those doctors argued that the number of embryos replaced is none of the HFEA's business. An attempt to strike down this policy by way of judicial review failed.[24] In 2011 the emboldened HFEA made it a condition of clinics' treatment and storage licences not to exceed the 10 per cent multiple birth rate target. This time judicial review sought by disgruntled clinics was successful.[25] They argued that the decision about how many embryos to implant is a medical one in which the individual circumstances of each patient should be considered. Patterson J held that the HFEA did not have the power to impose a licence condition before the appeals process initiated by the clinics had been completed. In 2014, the HFEA withdrew the maximum multiple birth rate condition from licences, but the target rate and policy stand.

Another dilemma for the HFEA relates to ensuring that patients are properly informed. Patients anxious for success may be easily swayed by advertising and manipulated claims of success. The HFEA publishes information to help patients choose a clinic, including information about patient feedback and success rates.[26] Ensuring patients receive information designed to help them to determine whether and where to seek treatment might seem uncontroversial. Alas for the HFEA, neither the Warnock Committee nor the framers of the 1990 Act could have anticipated how competitive the fertility market would become.[27] The HFEA lacks powers to control advertising, but a

21 *X v St Bartholomew's Hospital Centre for Reproductive Medicine* [2015] EWFC 13.

22 See HFEA, *Code of Practice* (9th edn, 2018), paras 11.56–11.62.

23 HFEA, *Fertility Treatment 2019: Trends and Figures* (2021).

24 *R (Assisted Reproduction and Gynaecology Centre) v HFEA* [2002] EWCA Civ 20.

25 *The Assisted Reproduction and Gynaecology Centre and The Reproductive Genetics Institute v HFEA* [2013] EWHC 3087 (Admin).

26 See HFEA, Choose a Fertility Clinic at www.hfea.gov.uk/choose-a-clinic/.

27 See 14.7 below.

recent collaboration with the Competition and Markets Authority (CMA)[28] and Advertising Standards Authority (ASA)[29] aims to improve the accuracy of advertised services and reduce misleading practices around success rates, costs and so-called 'add-ons': optional treatments, techniques and tests, some of which have limited evidence of efficacy.

The ethical decisions entrusted to the HFEA go to the heart of differences in our society and those who disagree with the HFEA may incline to perceive the Authority as remote and undemocratic. The role of the HFEA as an everyday regulator of fertility practice is sometimes overlooked. The HFEA received little credit for the job it did in ensuring 'quality control' of reproductive medicine at a time when in some other European countries assisted conception was wholly unregulated. British patients could be reasonably assured that they would be treated by competent practitioners and protected by standards enforced by the HFEA.[30]

Some serious errors in fertility clinics contributed to the HFEA coming under attack. In one incident, evidence emerged that the sole embryologist who was working for two clinics had engaged in a range of malpractice. A number of frozen embryos had been allowed to thaw. The embryologist knew this but did not disclose this disaster to his colleagues. Several women underwent procedures which they believed involved implanting 'their' embryos. In fact, no embryo was within the substances inserted in the women. The embryologist was convicted of assault as well as several charges of fraud.[31] Another mistake came to light in *Leeds Teaching Hospital NHS Trust v A*.[32] A white couple, Mr and Mrs A, were receiving IVF treatment. Mrs A gave birth to mixed race twins. It emerged that failure to monitor the sperm used to create the embryos implanted in Mrs A led to the use of sperm from Mr B who was black. Mr and Mrs B were also undergoing treatment at the same clinic. And in *ARB v IVF Hammersmith*,[33] procedures were insufficient to prevent a woman from forging her ex-partner's signature on the consent forms, leading to the birth of a child through IVF without his consent.

Failures in procedures have led to confusion over parental status. Sir James Munby, in one of 'a long line of such applications'[34] held that an order should be given to correct a clinic's administrative error which had resulted in a critical section of a form being unsigned. This lapse resulted in the unmarried partner

[28] See Gov.uk, *Self-funded IVF: Consumer Law Guidance* (2020) at www.gov.uk/cma-cases/self-funded-ivf-consumer-law-guidance.

[29] See ASA, *The UK Code of Non-broadcast Advertising and Direct & Promotional Marketing* (12th edn, 2021).

[30] See M Brazier, 'Regulating the Reproduction Business?' (1999) 7 *Med Law Rev* 166.

[31] See O Bowcott, 'IVF Fraudster Gets 18 Months in Jail' *Guardian* (2003) 16 January. And see *Attorney General's Reference (No 2 of 2003)* [2004] EWCA Crim 785.

[32] [2003] 1 FLR 1091.

[33] [2017] EWHC 2438 (QB); [2018] EWCA Civ 2803 (permission to appeal denied). Discussed at 13.8 above.

[34] *Re AM* [2018] EWHC 3178 (Fam). This was the thirty-ninth of similar cases in which Sir James gave judgment. See 14.10 below.

of a woman whose child had been born as a result of IVF not being considered the child's legal parent. In another such case Sir James recognised that 'joy but also, sadly, much misery has been caused by the medical brilliance, unhappily allied with the administrative incompetence, of various fertility clinics'.[35] Judges have shown a willingness to seek where possible to give effect to the wishes of prospective parents and to adopt a 'rights-based' approach to the law governing assisted conception.[36] Such errors are not directly attributable to the HFEA but in detracting from its reputation for quality control render the Authority more vulnerable to attack from those who dislike its ethical decisions.

14.4 *In vitro* fertilisation (IVF): opening Pandora's box?

Before the birth of Louise Brown, doctors were limited in what they could offer couples who could not have a child. Women might be offered drugs to help them ovulate or undergo surgical investigations and procedures. Where the man was infertile, DI had been practised for decades. IVF created a whole new range of possibilities for those who seek to have a child. IVF of itself provokes relatively few ethical[37] or legal dilemmas. The original context for resort to IVF related to women who ovulate normally, but whose Fallopian tubes are absent or damaged, and so cannot conceive naturally because the eggs they produce cannot travel to meet sperm and be fertilised. Eggs are removed from the woman and fertilised in the laboratory with sperm taken from her husband, or partner or a donor. The embryo, or embryos, are carefully tested and implanted in the mother's womb.

IVF is now used in several other instances including cases of 'unexplained infertility'. The woman ovulates, her Fallopian tubes are clear and her partner provides healthy sperm, yet no pregnancy results. Male infertility may be addressed via IVF in that if the male partner produces very few or poor-quality sperm, a single spermatozoon can be injected directly into an egg taken from the woman, creating an embryo that is then implanted in the woman's womb. Intra-cytoplasmic sperm injection (ICSI) is the most common treatment for male infertility. No questions of family law normally arise from IVF where a couple use their own gametes. That child has the same relationship to her parents as if they were naturally conceived.

The ability to fertilise eggs outside the woman opened Pandora's Box. No longer was it only sperm that could be donated, eggs could be too. As reproductive medicine developed, social attitudes changed. Individuals who were not infertile, single women and same sex couples sought treatment as did women past the normal age of childbearing. The difficult questions posed by IVF relate to whom should have access to 'fertility' treatment, how to define

35 *A and Ors (Human Fertilisation and Embryology Act 2008)* [2015] EWHC 2602 (Fam).

36 See for example *Warren v Care Fertility* [2014] EWHC 602 (Fam).

37 IVF is still opposed by the Roman Catholic Church on the grounds that it separates the conjugal act and the creation of a child: see E Jackson, *Medical Law: Text, Cases and Materials* (5th edn, 2019) Oxford University Press, p 694.

parenthood once donor gametes are used, and if, when and which embryos should be selected.

Before looking at access to treatment we ask what happens even in a straightforward IVF if a mistake is made, and the woman's eggs are inseminated by the 'wrong' sperm from someone else's husband or partner, as occurred in *Leeds Teaching Hospital NHS Trust v A*.[38] As we noted earlier, sperm from Mr B (intended for treatment of his wife, Mrs B) was in error used to fertilise eggs from Mrs A (who was undergoing treatment with her husband, Mr A). The mistake became apparent only when Mrs A gave birth to mixed race twins. Who was the twins' father? Which couple should bring up the children? Section 28(2) of the 1990 Act deemed a husband to be the legal father of his wife's child born as a result of sperm donation if he consented to her undergoing donor insemination. This was of no help to Mr A as he patently did not consent to donor insemination of his wife. Nothing in the 1990 Act assisted Mr A in his claim to become the legal father of his wife's children. Mr B was their genetic father. Dame Elizabeth Butler-Sloss P held that, although he had not consented to the use of his sperm to fertilise Mrs A's eggs, Mr B as the genetic father should be treated as the legal father of the twins. Nonetheless, she ruled that Mr and Mrs A should retain 'custody' of the children. The twins should stay with the 'parents' who had settled them in a loving home. Mr A could apply for a parental responsibility order or the couple could apply to adopt the twins. At some point when they were older, their origins should be explained to them and contact with Mr B arranged. In this case and in many others where the complexity of the law and the actions of others leave a child's status unclear, judges focus on the child[39] and its needs, sometimes resorting to imaginative interpretations of the law.

14.5 Access to fertility treatment: the welfare of the child

Women who have no male partner may want to have a child. They plan to raise the child alone or be part of a same sex couple wanting a family. During the passage of the first Human Fertilisation and Embryology Act, attempts were made in Parliament to outlaw fertility treatment, IVF or DI, for women without a male partner. A compromise was embodied in section 13(5) of the Act, which provided, apparently innocuously, that a licence holder treating a woman must take into account the welfare of any child who may be born as a result of treatment, *including the need of that child for a father*.[40]

Section 13(5) was viewed by many commentators as outdated and unnecessary.[41] The House of Commons Select Committee on Science and Technology

38 [2003] 1 FLR 1091. And see A Bainham, 'Whose Sperm Is It Anyway?' [2003] *CLJ* 566.

39 *M v F* [2013] EWHC 1901 (Fam), [9].

40 A number of MPs and peers (in 1990) hoped that the HFEA would ban DI, and other forms of assisted conception, for all single women, save in the most exceptional circumstances.

41 See, for example, E Jackson, 'Conception and the Irrelevance of the Welfare Principle' (2002) 65 *MLR* 176.

concluded that the requirement to consider the need for a father was 'offensive to many' and constituted 'unjustified discrimination against unconventional families'.[42] The Select Committee went further and recommended abolition of the welfare principle. In the event the welfare principle survives in an amended form now requiring that clinics must still take account of the 'welfare of any child who may be born as a result of the treatment (*including the need of that child for supportive parenting*) and of any other child who may be affected by its birth' (our emphasis). Section 13(5) as amended would seem to look more favourably on any couple seeking treatment, heterosexual or not, than a single woman. The HFEA Code of Practice that had long sought to attenuate the effect of the provision when it focused on the need for a father, now seeks to limit the impact of the current wording. Clinics must assess each patient individually and gauge whether 'there is a risk of significant harm or neglect to any child'.[43] Clinics should operate on a presumption of providing treatment to those seeking help to conceive whether they be heterosexual couples, lesbian couples or single women. Only if there is evidence of risk of serious harm to a future child should treatment be refused. In considering the statutory need for supportive parenting, clinics should regard this as a commitment to the health and well-being of the child that all prospective parents may be presumed to have. The HFEA has de facto virtually eliminated the need to demonstrate any specific family structure before being granted access to fertility treatment. Lacking a partner is of itself no bar.

14.6 Access to fertility treatment: post-menopausal mothers

The menopause no longer marks the end of a woman's chance to bear a child. Eggs are collected from a donor and implanted in the post-menopausal woman whose womb has been restored to a pre-menopausal state by hormone treatment. In 2006, a British woman of 62 gave birth as a result of such treatment in Russia, and in Germany a woman of 65 had quadruplets.[44] Many UK clinics have an upper age limit of 50. The crux of the question should not be the post-menopausal state of the woman. Some women suffer a premature menopause in their twenties. Few argue that they should be denied help. The question is whether women over 50, or even 60, should be assisted to have a child. Those opposed to treating older women focus on the child. If a woman gives birth at 62, she will be 80 before her child is legally an adult. Others point out that men fairly often beget children in their fifties and later. Is it discriminatory to prohibit helping women to do what nature permits men to do?

In *R and S v T*,[45] a British couple (both in their early sixties) sought a parental order in respect of twins born to a Ukrainian surrogate. Addressing briefly the

42 See House of Commons Science and Technology Committee, *Human Reproductive Technologies and the Law*, para 101.
43 HFEA, *Code of Practice* (9th edn, 2018), para 8.3.
44 'German Woman aged 65 Gives Birth to Quadruplets After IVF Treatment' *Guardian* (2015) 23 May.
45 [2015] EWFC 22.

welfare of the children, who by this stage were born and living with the couple, the judge noted that both parents seemed to be in good health and that the father's niece had agreed to be the guardian of the children should the couple either die or become incapacitated. Given the reality of two infants settled in their home, the judge had little choice but to ensure that the legal status of the twins was secured.

14.7 Access to treatment on the NHS

The liberal guidance from the HFEA, and in particular their advice that only a risk of significant harm or neglect to a potential child should 'disqualify' patients from receiving treatment, grants clinics a broad discretion about whom to treat. Courts have shown reluctant to interfere.[46] Mrs Harriott was refused IVF because of a criminal record for prostitution offences and because she and her husband had been rejected as prospective adoptive or foster parents by Manchester social services department. The judge found that the grounds for regarding her to be an unsuitable parent were reasonable.[47]

Private treatment costs a great deal of money and many prospective parents are unable to pay such sums, or nearly bankrupt themselves to do so. For them the real problem is not access to any clinic but access to treatment funded by the NHS. In 2019 only 32 per cent of cycles in England were funded by the NHS. Scotland does considerably better with 62 per cent of cycles being NHS funded.[48] Decisions about who gets access to treatment on the NHS rest with those who fund NHS care. NICE currently recommend that women aged under 40 years who have not conceived after two years of regular unprotected intercourse or twelve cycles of artificial insemination are offered three full cycles of IVF.[49] Women aged 40–42 should generally be offered one cycle. Commissioners may set additional conditions, such as childlessness or smoking cessation. By no means all commissioners comply with NICE guidance and some do not fund IVF at all.[50] Private fertility treatment remains the only viable option for many.

14.8 A right to reproduce?

Issues surrounding access to fertility treatment go beyond questions of funding. At the heart of the matter lies the intractable problem of whether individuals enjoy a right to reproduce, and just what such a right entails. Articles 8, 12

[46] But note at the time of writing judicial review proceedings have been initiated against a clinical commissioning group over its fertility treatment policy: see A Rimmer, 'Same Sex couple Take Commissioners to Court Over "Discriminatory" IVF Policy' (2021) 375 *BMJ* n2769.

[47] *R v Ethical Advisory Committee of St Mary's Hospital ex p Harriott* [1998] 1 FLR 512. And see *R v Sheffield Area Health Authority ex p Seale* [1994] 25 BMLR 1.

[48] HFEA, *Fertility Treatment 2019* (2021), 8.

[49] NICE, *Fertility Assessment and Treatment for People with Fertility Problems* CG156 (2013, updated 2017), 1.11.1.3.

[50] HFEA, *Fertility Treatment 2018: Trends and Figures* (2020).

and 14 of the European Convention on Human Rights (ECHR) all touch on this problem. The European Court of Human Rights (ECtHR) in *Evans*[51] and *Dickson*[52] has acknowledged that Article 8 rights to private life are engaged in laws regulating reproductive medicine and access to treatment. Article 12 speaks of a 'right to marry and found a family'.[53] Article 14 prohibits unjustifiable discrimination, so a woman denied fertility treatment might argue that barriers to treatment discriminate against her just because she is infertile. The first difficulty of a rights-based argument in the context of fertility treatment is this. As Wall J noted in his first instance judgment in *Evans*:

> The right to found a family through IVF can only, put at its highest, amount to a right to have IVF treatment. Self-evidently it cannot be a right to be treated successfully.[54]

What would a right to procreate entail? Does it manifest a right to reproductive autonomy ie to reproductive choice? Would that include a right to abortion? Is it a positive as well as a negative obligation?[55] The ECtHR seems at present to go little further than this. Article 8 is engaged in claims touching on reproduction and the right to respect for decisions 'to become and not become a parent'.[56] But any such claim must be weighed against the countervailing public interests in Article 8(2) and in the stormy waters of debates on reproduction the Court will allow states a more than generous margin of appreciation.[57]

14.9 Access and prisoners

A particular issue of access arises in the context of couples where the man is serving a prison sentence. English law does not permit conjugal visits. If a couple wish to have a child while the male partner remains in gaol, he has to be able to access the facilities to 'donate' sperm to his wife or partner. The Home Office placed substantial restrictions on any attempt to facilitate artificial insemination (AI) by prisoners and two prisoners refused permission to access AI challenged the Secretary of State, contending that this violated their rights to family life (Article 8) and to found a family (Article 12). The first case failed in the Court of Appeal, the court holding that such restrictions were justifiable in the public interest under Article 8(2). The Court noted that the wife would in this case still be of childbearing age when her

51 *Evans v United Kingdom* (2008) 46 EHRR 34. See 14.19 below.

52 *Dickson v United Kingdom* (2007) 46 EHRR 41, discussed at 14.9 below; but see *SH and Others v Austria*, App No 57813/00 (ECHR, 3 November 2011) (Grand Chamber).

53 But Article 12 has seemingly been relegated to the sidelines by the ECtHR: see M Eijkholt, 'The Right to Found a Family as a Stillborn Right to Procreate?' (2010) 18 *Med Law Rev* 127.

54 [2003] EWHC 2161 (Fam), [263].

55 A question skilfully ducked in *Dickson v United Kingdom* [2008] 46 EHRR 41.

56 Ibid, [71].

57 *See A, B and C v Ireland* [2010] ECHR 25579/05.

husband was eligible for parole.[58] Founding a family was merely delayed and not prevented. In the second case, Mrs Dickson would be past childbearing age before her husband would be free. Her husband's challenge to the refusal of AI succeeded before the Grand Chamber of the ECtHR.[59] The UK government argued that as Mr and Mrs Dickson had married while he was in prison and had never lived together, the relationship had never been tested in a normal environment and there were concerns about the welfare of any child. Moreover, the public had a legitimate concern that the punitive element in the prison sentence would be circumvented by allowing him to father a child. The ECtHR was unimpressed. Mr Dickson's conviction deprived him of some of his rights to private life, but rules, rules made by the Minister and not sanctioned by Parliament, that effectively denied him and his wife any prospect of conception did not represent a fair balance between the public and private interests involved.

14.10 Gamete donation and parental status: meaning of 'father'

The capacity to fertilise eggs outside the womb and the expansion of those who can access treatment has generated a host of legal questions, many relating to gamete donation when IVF involves the use of donated gametes, for example where the woman cannot ovulate and/or her partner produces no sperm. The use of donor eggs and sperm has rapidly increased in the last thirty years and birth rates where donor eggs are used are above 30 per cent for all age groups.[60] If a woman is treated with donated eggs, who is the child's legal mother? If a woman is treated with donated sperm who is the father? Where the man is infertile, couples have long had the opportunity to have a child using sperm from another man, by DI. In its most basic form, DI is so simple that it can be, and often is, performed without medical assistance. There are many instances when donor sperm will now be used in conjunction with IVF. In any such a case who is the child's legal father? Two sets of rules now operate. If the woman was treated using donor sperm before April 2009, section 28 of the 1990 Act still applies. If the couple were married, were treated in a licensed clinic and the husband fully and freely consented, section 28(2) deems the child to be the husband's child[61] and gives the husband all the usual privileges of fatherhood, including an entitlement to contact with his child should the marriage break down.[62]

Section 28(3) of the 1990 Act related to unmarried heterosexual couples who sought DI together because the male partner was infertile. Whenever donor sperm were used in the treatment of a woman and a man together by a person to whom a licence applies, the man was to be treated as the father of the

[58] *R v Secretary of State for the Home Department ex p Mellor* [2001] EWCA Civ 472.
[59] *Dickson v United Kingdom* (2007) 46 EHRR 41.
[60] HFEA, *Fertility Treatment 2019* (2021).
[61] In cases where the husband's consent is disputed, it would be for him to prove that he did not consent.
[62] *Re CH (Contact: Parentage)* [1996] 1FCR 768.

child.[63] The intent of sections 28(2) and (3) was to bestow the legal rights and responsibilities of fatherhood on the social father, the man who seeks a child with his wife or partner. The apparent simplicity of these provisions about legal paternity is misleading. The notion of the couple treated together posed endless points of tricky interpretation. Evidence that at the time the mother received DI she was living with a male partner was not sufficient. The social father himself was unlikely to receive any treatment, though he would have undergone fertility tests at an earlier date.[64] Several legal cases ensued that are dealt with fully in the fourth edition of this work.[65] What was clear was the law was not satisfactory.[66]

Sections 35 to 41 of the 2008 Act provide new rules on the meaning of 'father' whenever a woman is treated with donor sperm after April 2009. The position of a married couple has changed little. Section 35 provides that if a married woman is treated with donor sperm as part of IVF or simple DI, her husband will be the legal father of the child unless he did not consent to the use of donor sperm or DI. The section applies regardless of whether fresh or frozen sperm is used, whether the woman is treated in a licensed clinic or elsewhere or simply self-inseminates,[67] and whether the woman is treated in the UK or abroad. The position is more complicated when a couple are unmarried. The 'agreed fatherhood conditions' in sections 36 and 37 apply. If the woman is treated in a licensed clinic in the UK and no man is deemed to be the father by virtue of section 35, nor any female civil partner deemed to be parent by virtue of section 42, fatherhood is conferred by agreement. A man will be deemed to be the legal father of the child if he has given notice in writing to the clinic that he consents to be treated as the father and the woman has given notice in writing that she agrees that he shall be the father of her child, and neither party has withdrawn such consent.

Problems have arisen when clinics have failed to use or record the requisite information demanded by the legislation. Such failure runs the risk of invalidating the clinic's licence and thus threatening to deprive the 'agreed father' of his status as the legal father. Judges seek to avoid such an outcome where

63 This means that if he and the mother register the birth of the child together, they share parental responsibility for the child. Should they not do so, to gain parental responsibility for the child, the 'social' father must either enter into a formal agreement with the mother to do so, or seek a court order to share parental responsibility with the mother; see the Children Act 1989, s 4 as amended by the Adoption and Children Act 2002.

64 *Re B (Parentage)* [1996] FLR 15; *In Re Q (Parental Order)* [1996] 1 FLR 369.

65 See for example *U v W (Attorney General Intervening)* [1998] Fam 29: *Re R (A Child) (IVF: Paternity of a Child)* [2003] 2 AC 621, HL.

66 See C Lind, 'In Re R (Paternity of IVF Baby) – Unmarried Paternity under the Human Fertilisation and Embryology Act 1990' (2003) 15 *Child and Family Law Quarterly* 327.

67 But not to any case where the pregnancy is established by sexual intercourse even if the man and the woman perceive the man as acting merely as a 'sperm donor'. In such a case the biological father will be the legal father of the child. See the strange and troubling case of *M v F* [2013] EWHC 1901 (Fam).

possible.[68] In *Re A, B, C, D, E, F, G and H*[69] Sir James Munby acknowledged the issue at stake:

> The issue which confronts me here … is, as a moment's reflection will make obvious, a question of the most fundamental gravity and importance. What, after all, to any child, to any parent, never mind to future generations and indeed to society at large, can be more important, emotionally, psychologically, socially and legally, than the answer to the question: Who is my parent? Is this my child?

In 2015 the HFEA required clinics to carry out an audit of cases where the patients receiving treatment were not married or in a civil partnership and several more administrative errors necessitating court declarations came to light.[70]

There does not seem to be any requirement as such that the man and the woman must be living together or be partners. So a single woman planning to bring her child up largely alone could, if she so wished and he agreed, nominate a friend to act as the child's legal father. When sections 35 and 36 apply, the sperm donor need fear no parental responsibility to his genetic offspring for the husband or the agreed father and no other man is to be treated as the father. But we should note that if DI is conducted outside the UK, or outside a licensed clinic within the UK, and the woman is not married or a civil partner, the donor will remain the legal father of the child. So if X agrees to help out a friend and gives her sperm for her to self-inseminate, he remains as much the legal father of the child as if the child were conceived naturally.

14.11 Gamete donation: the meaning of 'mother'[71]

IVF created the possibility to treat women who do not ovulate, with donated eggs. A woman could have eggs implanted that were donated by another and fertilised with her husband or partner's or donor sperm enabling her to bear a child. Who is the child's legal mother – the donor or the woman who gives birth? Section 27 of the 1990 Act applying to a woman treated before April 2009 and section 33 applying to women treated after that date both set out a simple rule: the woman who carries the child 'as the result of the placing in her of an embryo or sperm and eggs; and no other woman' is the legal mother. If a woman is treated with donor eggs the donor has no claim on or responsibility to the child. That also means that if a surrogate carries a child, even using eggs provided from the intended mother, it is the surrogate and not the woman who seeks to have the child via surrogacy who is in law the mother. A court order is needed to make the intended parent/s the legal parent/s. In 2019 the

68 See *X v Y (St Bartholomew's Hospital Centre for Reproductive Medicine (CRM) intervening)* [2015] EWFC 13; but contrast with the sad outcome in *AB v CD* [2015] EWHC 1418 (Fam).

69 [2015] EWHC 2602 (Fam), [3].

70 See for example *Re P, Q, E, S, T, U, W and X* [2017] EWHC 49 (Fam) and *Re AM* [2018] EWHC 3178 (Fam), discussed at 14.3 above.

71 See R D'alton-Harrison, 'Mater Semper Incertus Est: Who's Your Mummy?' (2014) 22 *Med Law Rev* 357.

Law Commission consulted on proposals that would allow intended parents to become legal parents on the birth of the child, subject to a short period where the surrogate retains a right to object.[72]

14.12 Gamete donation: same sex couples

The 1990 Act made no express provision for the growing number of cases where a same sex couple sought fertility treatment to have a child together. One partner in a lesbian couple might seek DI or IVF with donated sperm with a view to bringing up the child with her partner. The partner would have no legal status in relation to the child unless she later sought to adopt the child. The 2008 Act makes express provision for such couples. The provisions are modelled as closely as possible on those applying to heterosexual couples. Section 42 provides that when two women are in a civil partnership or marriage[73] and one becomes pregnant via IVF or DI, the other partner will be treated as parent of the child unless she did not consent to the treatment of her partner. Section 42 applies whether in the UK or abroad, and to self-insemination, as much as treatment in a licensed clinic. Sections 43 and 44 deal with unmarried lesbian couples not party to a civil partnership and provide that a second woman can be treated as a parent of the child by virtue of 'agreed female parenthood conditions'. The prospective 'second' parent and the woman being treated must both give notice in writing that they consent to the second woman being treated as a parent of the child. The parenthood provisions only apply if the woman is treated in a licensed clinic in the UK.[74] As with heterosexual couples, when a second woman is treated as the other parent by virtue of the Act, the sperm donor has no legal relationship with his genetic child. If the couple are not in a civil partnership and perhaps ask a male friend to provide sperm for self-insemination, once again the 'partner' obtains no parental status and the sperm donor is in law the father of the child.

A number of problems have beset the provisions for female same sex parents. The complexity of the legislation and conditions which must be met in relation to consents, information, counselling and record keeping may mean that if the 'parental relationship' breaks down, the second parent may find herself deprived of the parental status that she thought that she had secured. In *Re E and F (Children) (Assisted Conception)*[75] CD gave birth to twins after IVF. She was the legal mother and her partner, AB, believed she had the status of a second female parent. When their relationship broke down and AB sought

[72] Law Commission, Scottish Law Commission, *Building Families Through Surrogacy: A New Law A Joint Consultation Paper* (2019). See further 14.33 below.

[73] See Marriage (Same Sex Couples) Act 2013, Sch 7, para 40.

[74] On problems of record keeping and process see *AB v CD* [2013] EWHC 1418 (Fam).

[75] [2013] EWHC 1418 (Fam). And see *Re G (Children) (Shared Residence Order: Biological Mother of Donor Egg Children)* [2014] EWCA Civ 336, discussed in C Bridge, 'Parental Responsibility' (2014) 44(Jul) *Family Law* 970; and *Re G (A Child)(Sperm Donor: Contact Order); Re Z (A Child)(Sperm Donor: Contact Order)* [2013] EWHC 134 (Fam), discussed in A Brown, 'Essential "Biological Fathers" and Invisible "Legal Parents"' (2014) 26(2) *Child and Family Law Quarterly* 237.

a contact order, CD opposed it on the ground that AB was not a legal parent. Cobb J found with great reluctance that a series of errors on the part of the clinic meant that treatment was not provided within the terms of the clinic's licence and the consents given by the parties were not effective. He granted the order that AB was not a legal parent while seeking to assure her that this did not mean she had no parental role to play in the boys' lives and listing her application for contact to be heard later.

14.13 On the horizon?

Despite the breadth of the provisions in the 2008 Act, they do not cover all the permutations of parenthood that modern medicine can or may soon facilitate.[76] They address only female same sex couples and make no provision for trans parents.[77] In *R (McConnell and YY) v Registrar General for England and Wales*[78] the Court of Appeal considered whether a trans man was a mother or father to the child he had conceived and given birth to. He was in receipt of a gender recognition certificate conferring status of his gender for all purposes including his sex.[79] According to the court's interpretation of the Gender Recognition Act 2004, the Registrar General was correct to register Mr McConnell as the mother on his son's birth certificate. His gender and his status as a parent were distinct. Any interference with Article 8(1) of the ECHR was proportionate and justified under Article 8(2). Any change to address the disjunct will need to come from Parliament.

Male couples have to navigate the murky waters of the law governing surrogacy. If two men agree with a surrogate that she will bear a child for them created by the fertilisation of her eggs with sperm from one of them, the latter will, until the law is reformed,[80] be the father of the child and the surrogate the mother. The other partner will, as we shall see later, have to seek an adoption or parental order. If it becomes possible to transplant a womb into a man so he could gestate his own child, or if artificial wombs become reality, then the very notion of 'mother' and 'father' will be turned on its head.[81]

14.14 Artificial insemination by partner (AIP)

There are cases where, although a woman's husband or partner is fertile, he cannot beget a child because he is incapable of normal intercourse. His sperm may

76 See S McGuinness and A Alghrani, 'Gender and Parenthood: The Case for Realignment' (2008) 16 *Med Law Rev* 261.

77 See *R (JK) v Registrar General for England and Wales* [2015] EWHC 990 (Admin). J, a transgender woman who was born male, objected to being recorded as the father on her children's birth certificates. Her application for judicial review was refused. Hickinbottom J held there was no breach of articles 8 or 14 of the ECHR.

78 [2020] EWCA Civ 559. See A Brown, 'Trans Parenthood and the Meaning of "Mother", "Father" and "Parent"' (2021) *Med Law Rev* 157.

79 Gender Recognition Act 2004, s 9.

80 See 14.27 below.

81 See 16.15 below.

be used to impregnate his wife or partner by artificial means.[82] Or the man may produce some sperm, but not sufficient healthy and mobile sperm to achieve fertilisation in the usual way. Such a couple may be helped by intra-cytoplasmic sperm injection (ICSI). A single sperm is injected into the cytoplasm (outer casing) of the woman's egg. IVF is combined with AIP. The child's legal status will be just the same as if she were conceived naturally. Where normal intercourse was not possible so that a marriage has never been consummated, AIP will not prevent the wife from petitioning the court to annul the marriage,[83] although on policy grounds, the court may refuse a decree if they consider that in having the child the wife approbated the marriage.

AIP may also be resorted to when a man has banked sperm for example in advance of chemotherapy for cancer. If he survives and the couple agree to treatment using the stored sperm no problems arise, but what if he dies and the woman seeks treatment with his sperm? Or she asks a doctor to take sperm from a dying or just dead partner?

14.15 Gamete donation and consent

The issue of posthumous donation made headlines in the case of Diane Blood. Diane and Stephen Blood had been married for four years before Mr Blood was struck down with meningitis. He lapsed into a coma and died. Shortly before his death, at Mrs Blood's request, doctors used electro-ejaculation to take sperm from her dying husband which was then stored at a licensed fertility clinic. The HFEA instructed the clinic not to treat Mrs Blood, nor to release her husband's sperm to her so that she could seek treatment abroad. The HFEA ruled that the storage and use of Stephen Blood's sperm was unlawful under the 1990 Act. The storage of sperm did not comply with Schedule 3 of the 1990 Act which imposed a mandatory requirement for written 'effective' consent. No such written consent had ever been given by Mr Blood, although his widow argued that they had planned to start a family, and that Stephen had told her that in the kind of tragic circumstances which ultimately overtook him she should do just as she did.

Mrs Blood challenged the HFEA by way of an application for judicial review, alleging that it was the HFEA who were acting unlawfully. The High Court upheld the HFEA, but Mrs Blood succeeded in the Court of Appeal.[84] That Court agreed that the storage of sperm without Mr Blood's written consent was unlawful. It contravened the 1990 Act.[85] The Court expressed sympathy

82 And see *Dickson v United Kingdom* [2008] 46 EHRR 41, at 14.8 above.

83 *L v L* [1949] P 211.

84 [1997] 2 All ER 687, CA. See D Morgan and R Lee, 'In the Name of the Father? Ex parte Blood Dealing with Novelty and Anomaly' (1997) 60 *MLR* 84.

85 But note *R (AB) v HFEA* [2014] EWHC 1528 (Admin), where a woman seeking recovery of sperm from her partner, who was said to be in a permanent vegetative state after a cardiac arrest, sought to argue that the recovery of sperm was in his best interests and thus would be lawful by virtue of s 4 of the Mental Capacity Act 2005. Even were that argument to succeed and the process of recovery itself be deemed not to be an assault, further storage and use of the gametes would contravene the

with Mrs Blood. She had acted in good faith. Nonetheless, treatment in the United Kingdom would be unlawful. However, the Court of Appeal held that the HFEA had failed to give sufficient consideration to EU law that applied pre-EU Exit. Section 24(4) of the 1990 Act permitted the HFEA to issue directions authorising the export of sperm. Articles 59 and 60 of the Treaty of Rome guaranteed fundamental freedoms, which included a right to receive services. Such a right was not absolute, but any limitations on that right had to be justified. Given its ruling that storing sperm without written consent was unlawful, the Court said that the circumstances of Mrs Blood's case would not be repeated. It directed the HFEA to reconsider Mrs Blood's request to export sperm. They did so and granted her permission to take her husband's sperm to Belgium where she finally received treatment and gave birth to a healthy son, Liam, followed some years later by a second son. The narrow grounds of the appeal court's ruling in Mrs Blood's favour left domestic law unchanged. No woman in a similar position would benefit. Unless the deceased then had given formal written consent to storing and use of his sperm,[86] no British clinic could treat his widow or former partner.

Judicial optimism that there would be no repeat of the *Blood* case proved ill founded. In *L v HFEA*,[87] L's husband died suddenly in the course of a minor operation. L obtained an order that it was lawful to retrieve sperm from his body and the sperm was then stored at a licensed clinic. L sought to argue that the absolute rule that prevented her using the sperm contravened both EU law and Article 8 of the ECHR. She failed. The judge found that while the retrieval of the sperm fell outside the Act and indeed immediate use of the sperm might have done so too, he had no power to declare that continued storage of the sperm was lawful. The power vested in the HFEA to allow the sperm to be exported meant that EU treaty rights were not violated and later the HFEA authorised the export of the sperm retrieved from L's husband so that she like Mrs Blood could seek treatment abroad.

Post-EU Exit, Articles 56 and 57 of the Treaty on the Functioning of the European Union, which set out rights for EU citizens to obtain services, including medical treatment services, no longer apply.[88] But the importance of the *Blood* case lies in its approach to consent as much as its application of EU law. Consider *Y v A Healthcare NHS Trust*.[89] A husband and wife had one child and had started IVF to try for another when the husband suffered a traumatic brain injury in a car crash. Would it be lawful to retrieve and store his gametes before he died and use them after his death? The court held that it

Human Fertilisation and Embryology Act in the absence of the requisite effective consents in writing.

86 A number of children have been born after posthumous AIP where the requisite written consent had been given.

87 [2008] EWHC 2149.

88 Freedom of Establishment and Free Movement of Services (EU Exit) Regulations 2019, SI 2019/1401, reg 3.

89 [2018] EWCOP 18.

was. Taking a broad interpretation of sub-paragraph 1(2) of Schedule 3 of the 1990 Act, Knowles J held that his relative could sign on his behalf. In *Jennings v HFEA*[90] Ted Jennings and his wife, Ms Choya, had undergone fertility treatment but she tragically died during pregnancy. He sought to use a remaining frozen embryo created with his sperm and his deceased wife's egg, to have a family with a surrogate. Ms Choya had not given the necessary written consent, and the HFEA had concluded that the use of the embryo would therefore be unlawful. Theis J criticised the unclear forms used by the HFEA which limited the opportunity for Ms Choya to provide consent and found that the Authority's decision breached Mr Jennings' Article 8 rights. Theis J held that it was appropriate to 'dispense with the requirement for written and signed consent in this limited situation'.[91] Consent was inferred.

After the *Blood* case, Professor Sheila McLean conducted an extensive review of the law on consent and removal of gametes, but recommended only limited changes in the law.[92] One change did, however, result from the review and Mrs Blood's campaign to have her dead husband recognised as her sons' father. The Human Fertilisation and Embryology (Deceased Father) Act 2003 amended section 28(6) of the 1990 Act to allow the name of the deceased (genetic) father to be entered on the child's birth certificate. That Act has now been repealed and sections 28(5)A–I of the 1990 Act as amended by the 2008 Act address questions of post-mortem fatherhood in relation to women treated before April 2009 and sections 39–41 address children born as a result of treatment after that date. Under both Acts the written consent of the husband or partner remains a pre-condition to lawful treatment. Assuming that such consent is present and the woman is successfully treated and bears a child, she has forty-two days to elect to have her deceased husband or partner treated as the father of the child in the sense that his name will be entered into the Register of Births. However, the child born in such circumstances remains ineligible to inherit from his genetic father's estate.

The 2008 Act has not substantially changed the law and the *Blood* case leaves more questions unanswered that it resolves. If Stephen Blood's sperm had been lawfully stored, could Diane Blood have demanded treatment? It seems unlikely; the ultimate decision remains with the clinician. In the context of private treatment a widow might seek to argue that she has a contractual right to AI by husband. The possibility remains of attempts to contend that the frozen sperm form part of the deceased husband's partner's estate. Should a court accept that sperm can be classified as 'property' and 'inherited' by the wife, it would logically follow that she could demand 'her' sperm, but she could still not require a licensed clinic to inseminate her. In the light of the underlying philosophy of the 1990 and 2008 Acts, it seems at first sight unlikely that such a 'property' argument would succeed. But consider the judgment of the

90 [2022] EWHC 1619 (Fam).

91 Ibid, [104].

92 *Review of Common Law Provision Relating to the Removal of Gametes and of the Consent Provision in the Human Fertilisation and Embryology Act 1990* (1998).

Court of Appeal in *Yearworth v North Bristol NHS Trust*.[93] The claimants sued in negligence after sperm banked in advance of treatment for cancer was negligently allowed to thaw. The appeal court held that for the purposes of a claim in negligence the men enjoyed property rights in that sperm and could be awarded damages for the damage to their property.

Might anyone other than a spouse or partner seek access to stored gametes? In *R (M) v HFEA*[94] a mother (M) sought access to her deceased daughter's eggs stored before the young woman underwent chemotherapy for the bowel cancer that killed her. M wanted her daughter's eggs to be fertilised by an anonymous sperm donor and implanted in her. She and her husband would bring up their 'grandchild'. The couple advanced evidence of their daughter's passionate desire to have a child, that she had asked her mother to carry 'my babies' and 'wanted her genes to be carried forward after her death'.[95] The deceased daughter had never executed the necessary effective consents under the 1990 Act. The applicants therefore sought special directions from the Authority authorising export of the eggs to New York where M would receive the fertility treatment that would allow her to give birth to the deceased daughter's child. The Authority's Statutory Approvals Committee considered all the evidence and finally rejected the application. The Committee expressly stated that M's age and her relationship to her daughter and any child whom she might bear were not a factor in their decision-making. The Committee were not satisfied that prior to her death the daughter was fully informed of the process that would be needed to allow her mother to bear 'her' child, that she would have agreed to the use of an anonymous donor, or that she explicitly expressed a wish for her mother to carry her child after her death. M and her husband's judicial review failed at first instance but was successful on appeal. The court found that there was sufficient evidence that the daughter had wished treatment to occur and that she had consented to the use of her eggs after her death. Note that both the HFEA Committee and the court based their decisions wholly on the scope and validity of any consent given by the daughter to posthumous use of her eggs and avoided any moral judgements on whether 'grandparents' should be allowed to bring to birth a dead child's child and eschewed any consideration of M and her husband's ages.

14.16 Gamete donation: what should the child be told?

Does a child born after the use of donor gametes have a right to know the identity of his genetic parents? An adopted child has, at 18, a right of

[93] [2009] EWCA Civ 37; discussed at 21.10 below.

[94] [2015] EWHC 1706 (Admin); [2016] EWCA Civ 611. Contrast *Re X (Catastrophic Injury: Collection and Storage of Sperm)* [2022] EWCOP 48: X suffered catastrophic brain injury with no prospect of recovery. X's parents sought to retrieve X's gametes and store them after his death. Their application was dismissed: X had not consented and there was insufficient evidence of his intentions. It was not in X's best interests (including his autonomy interests) to make the declarations sought.

[95] [2015] EWHC 1706, [33].

access to his original birth certificate and so has the opportunity to trace his natural parents.[96] If an adopted child may trace his birth mother and genetic father, should children born from gamete donation be afforded a similar right?[97] Or would loss of prospective anonymity exacerbate the shortage of gamete donors? Until 2005, anonymity protected all gamete donors, while affording some limited rights to children born as a result of donation. Regulations removing anonymity from gamete donors[98] are now consolidated in the heavily amended section 31 of the 1990 Act. The 'new' section 31 provides that a person will, at the age of 18, acquire the right to information about the identity of donor parents.[99] An offer of counselling must be made to the applicant before any information is released. Anyone in the UK donating now is aware that his or her offspring may be able to trace them and make contact and the HFEA has a power to warn donors when requests for information are made.[100] In 2023, eighteen years after the lifting of anonymity, the first cohort of donor-conceived adults will be able to seek access to the register.

14.17 Gamete donation: supply and demand

For many prospective parents seeking fertility treatment, access to suitable donated gametes is crucial to their treatment. Both eggs and sperm are in short supply and so there have been several proposals to increase supply. Egg donors are especially hard to recruit. Unlike sperm donation, egg donation is attended by some risk to the donor. Payments for eggs, sperm or embryos are currently unlawful in the UK unless authorised by directions from the HFEA.[101] In 2012 the HFEA introduced new limits for what is described as 'donor compensation' allowing payments of £35 per clinic visit for sperm donors and a fixed sum of £750 per cycle for egg donors. Payments for eggs still fall well short of offering significant incentives to young women to sell their eggs. The HFEA uses cautious language speaking only of expenses, compensation and benefits in kind. One such benefit in kind is 'egg sharing'. Women who are undergoing egg collection as part of their own IVF treatment agree to donate a proportion of their eggs to others. In return, they receive reduced cost or even free IVF. Counselling is offered to egg donors to help them think through the implications.

96 Adoption Act 1976, s 51(2).

97 See *R (Rose) v Secretary of State for Health* [2002] EWHC 1593: Article 8 of the Human Rights Convention was relevant to the question of what access to information children born via assisted conception should enjoy.

98 HFE (Disclosure of Donor Information) Regulations 2004, SI 2004/1511.

99 And about possible half siblings.

100 In light of the rise of consumer genetic testing websites, which can undermine donor anonymity, the HFEA announced in May 2022 that it is considering recommending lifting anonymity requirements from birth. See H Devlin, 'UK Fertility Watchdog could Recommend Scrapping Donor Anonymity Law' *Guardian* (2022) 20 May.

101 See Human Fertilisation and Embryology Act 1990, s 12(e).

14.18 Storing gametes and embryos

The capacity to freeze and store gametes and embryos has been crucial to the improvement of success rates in fertility treatment. In 2019, nearly half of IVF cycles used frozen embryo transfer.[102] Storage of gametes and embryos is lawful only if licensed by the HFEA.[103] Women who have to undergo medical treatment that may compromise their fertility, or women who simply want to preserve and freeze eggs to allow them to delay motherhood, can store their own eggs for future use. Increasing numbers of clinics offer egg freezing to women worried about the decline of their fertility as they get older. Egg and embryo storage increased fivefold between 2013 and 2018.[104] Emily Jackson warned in 2018 that due to a lack of evidence, it is not yet clear that 'social' egg freezing is a positive development for women.[105] She points out that many will not use their frozen eggs and that, whilst enhancing choice, it is not necessarily an adequate solution to the mismatch between optimal fertility and today's social preferences regarding the timing for having children.[106]

Storage has generated its own ethical and legal conundrums. The 1990 Act (as amended) prescribed a maximum statutory storage period of ten years for both gametes and embryos,[107] subject to regulations that can in certain circumstances alter the storage periods prescribed in the Act.[108] Regulations in 2009 allowed storage for up to fifty-five years if the individual suffers or is likely[109] to suffer from premature fertility.[110] And Regulations in 2020 extended the ten-year storage limit by two years to account for disruptions to treatment in the COVID-19 pandemic.[111] Though welcome, these amendments did not address social and scientific developments. There has been a significant rise in the number of women freezing eggs for whom the ten-year limit is proving too restrictive. In 2019, around 2,000 women aged 40 or under froze eggs.[112] After a consultation, the Health and Care Act 2022 increased the maximum storage period from ten years to fifty-five years.[113]

102 HFEA, *Fertility Treatment 2019* (2021).
103 Section 4.
104 HFEA, *Fertility Treatment 2018* (2020).
105 E Jackson 'The Ambiguities of "Social" Egg Freezing and the Challenges of Informed Consent (2018) 13(1) *BioSocieties* 21.
106 E Jackson '"Social" Egg Freezing and the UK's Statutory Storage Time Limits' (2016) 42(11) *J Med Ethics* 738.
107 See s 14(3)(4).
108 See s 14(5).
109 For example, some treatments for cancer can impact on reproductive ability.
110 Human Fertilisation and Embryology (Statutory Storage Period for Embryos and Gametes) Regulations 2009, SI 2009/1582, amended SI 2009/2581. In *Warren v Care Fertility* [2014] EWHC 602 (Fam) Mrs Warren sought a declaration that it was lawful for her deceased husband's sperm to be stored for up to fifty-five years even though he had not provided the requisite written consent. Granting the declaration, it was held that the Regulations must be read in light of Article 8 ECHR.
111 The Human Fertilisation and Embryology (Statutory Storage Period for Embryos and Gametes) (Coronavirus) Regulations 2020, SI 2020/566.
112 HFEA, *Fertility Treatment 2017: Trends and Figures* (2019).
113 Health and Care Act 2022, s 171.

Some cancer treatment can affect fertility in which case sperm or eggs – or ovarian or testicular tissue if the patient is pre-pubertal – may be harvested and frozen. Legal and ethical dilemmas arise in the case of children. If a child of 7 is about to undergo chemotherapy, can her parents authorise surgical removal of ovarian tissue in case their daughter, once she is an adult, wants to have children?[114] Is such a procedure in the child's interests? Perhaps that will depend on the extent of the immediate risk and distress posed to the child by additional surgery balanced against the long-term benefit of preserving some hope of fertility. Storing eggs and sperm when a patient faces the loss of fertility as a result of medical treatment is coming to be seen as routine medical care. Egg storage may be simply a matter of choice.

14.19 Disputes and stored embryos

What about embryos in storage prior to their expiry date? The Act requires anyone storing gametes or embryos to decide what may or may not be done with those embryos before any treatment begins. The donors of the genetic material jointly decide its fate in foreseeable circumstances. In *Evans v Amicus Healthcare Ltd*,[115] Natalie Evans wanted to be able to have 'her' frozen embryos implanted to establish a pregnancy. Her former partner, Howard Johnson, refused to agree and sought to have the embryos destroyed. Some years earlier, Ms Evans had been diagnosed with pre-cancerous tumours in both ovaries. She was advised to have her ovaries removed. As the cancer was growing slowly, there was time for her and her partner to undergo IVF and freeze embryos for future use. Ms Evans enquired about the possibility of freezing her eggs and was told that success rates using frozen eggs were much lower than where frozen embryos were used. Her partner reassured her that they would not split up, but would go on to have children together when she was recovered and clear of cancer. Both partners signed the necessary forms consenting to storage of the embryos. A year later, the relationship broke down and Mr Johnson notified the clinic that he withdrew his consent to storage of the embryos and asked that they be destroyed. Ms Evans was prepared to undertake that she would never make a financial claim for child support and argued that the stored embryos offered her her only chance to have a child genetically related to her.

The obstacle confronting Ms Evans, when persuasion failed to change her former partner's mind, lay in Schedule 3 of the 1990 Act. To summarise, any continuing storage of the embryos and any use (ie implantation) of the embryos required the 'effective consent' of both the parties who had contributed the gametes creating the embryos. Mr Johnson had withdrawn his consent to continued storage of the embryos and never gave any consent to Ms Evans to use the embryos on her own. Wall J held that Schedule 3 made it clear that the continuing consent of both parties was required and that either party was free

114 See 'Baby Born from Ovary Frozen in Mother's Childhood' *BBC News* (2015) 10 June.

115 [2004] EWCA Civ 727.

to withdraw that consent.[116] The Court of Appeal upheld his judgment.[117] Throughout the litigation in England, Ms Evans argued that if Schedule 3 was interpreted to require Mr Johnson's continuing consent, the 1990 Act was incompatible with Ms Evans's rights under Articles 8, 12 and 14 of the European Convention. Her rights to family life and to found a family were violated by an absolute rule that denied her her only chance to have a genetically related child. The Court of Appeal held (*inter alia*) that any interference with Ms Evans's right to private and family life under Article 8(1) was justifiable within the terms of Article 8(2). Permitting implantation without Mr Johnson's consent would violate his Article 8 rights.

Ms Evans took her case to the ECtHR. She lost again in both the European court of first instance[118] and the Grand Chamber.[119] The Court noted that there is no consensus among Convention states, or internationally, as to how to regulate consent to implantation of embryos. Despite sympathy from the European judges, the Court held that the UK regime was based on a clear and principled rule and fell within the margin of appreciation. The Grand Chamber concurred.

The 2008 Act made one small change to help anyone finding themselves in the same position as Natalie Evans, amending Schedule 3 of the 1990 Act to provide that if one party withdraws consent to storage of embryos, a one year 'cooling off' period should be introduced before the embryos have to be destroyed.[120] Within that year, the hope is that the parties can reach some agreement about the future of the embryos.

14.20 Pre-implantation genetic testing for monogenic disorders (PGT-M)

Advances in reproductive medicine have helped not only infertile couples, but also couples who risked transmitting a genetic disease to their children. Initially a woman who was a haemophilia carrier could avoid giving birth to an affected son by opting for egg donation. Pre-implantation testing offers such a woman the chance to have her own genetic child. Embryos are created by IVF, and PGT is used to screen out embryos affected by the relevant genetic disease. Only healthy embryos are selected for implantation. Previous editions of this book referred to 'pre-implantation genetic diagnosis' (PGD). However, a change in terminology was necessary as new types

116 [2003] EWHC 2161 (Fam).

117 [2004] EWCA Civ 727; see A Alghrani, 'Deciding the Fate of Frozen Embryos' (2005) 15 *Med Law Rev* 244.

118 [2006] 1 FCR 585 (ECtHR). The House of Lords declined to hear Ms Evans's appeal. See T Annett, 'Balancing Competing Interests Over Frozen Embryos: The Judgment of Solomon' (2006) 14 *Med Law Rev* 425; C Lind, 'Evans v United Kingdom – Judgments of Solomon: Power, Gender and Procreation' (2006) 18 *Child and Family Law Quarterly* 576.

119 [2008] 46 EHRR 34.

120 See Sch 3, para 4A(4).

of genetic testing on embryos emerged. They are now known collectively as 'pre-implantation genetic testing' and testing for single gene disorders is now called 'pre-implantation genetic testing for monogenic disorders' or PGT-M.

The 1990 Act made no express provision for PGT-M and it was the HFEA that developed the framework within which it could lawfully be offered to couples at risk of transmitting a genetic disease. Not everybody applauded this development and PGT-M has been criticised both on the grounds that it involves deliberate destruction of embryos and that in screening out disabled embryos it discriminates against disabled people and reinforces negative images of disability.[121] Pro-life groups challenged the legality of PGT-M arguing that the HFEA had no power to license a treatment for couples who could have children without assistance. The Court of Appeal[122] confirmed that HFEA policy permitting PGT-M (then called PGD) was lawful under the Act in that for couples affected by a risk of transmitting such disease PGT-M constituted treatment 'for the purpose of assisting women to carry children'. A process that enabled the woman to become pregnant free from the fear that her child would be affected by a serious genetic disease was one that assisted her to carry a child. Amendments to the 1990 Act now set out a statutory framework for PGT-M modelled on HFEA policy. The provisions are lengthy and complex and we do no more than set out the basics here. Schedule 2 1ZA of the Act now provides that PGT-M may be licensed for certain genetic conditions to establish if the embryo has a defect affecting its capacity to result in live birth, in any case where there is a particular risk that the embryo may have a gene, chromosomal or mitochondrion abnormality, or to establish gender where there is a particular risk of a serious gender-related condition. In cases where PGT-M is licensed in relation to an abnormality in the embryo it must further be shown that there is significant risk that if born the person would have or develop a serious disability or illness. Not every genetic anomaly will qualify as 'serious'. The ends of the spectrum are easy to discern. You could not license PGT-M to screen out red hair. Dreadful diseases – for example Tay Sachs, where the child born is condemned to early disability and death while little more than an infant – clearly meet the test. Other conditions provoke debate and prospective parents may have different perceptions about both risk and seriousness.[123] At the time of writing, the HFEA has licenced PGT-M for around 600 genetic conditions.

14.21 Pre-implantation tissue typing (PTT) and 'saviour siblings'

It was the development of the ability to use pre-implantation genetic testing as the first step to offering treatment to a sick child that provoked especial

121 See R Scott, 'Choosing Between Possible Lives: Legal and Ethical Issues in Pre-Implantation Genetic Diagnosis' (2006) *OJLS* 153.

122 *R (Quintavalle) v Human Fertilisation and Embryology Authority* [2003] EWCA Civ 667.

123 The HFEA's *Code of Practice* (9th edn, 2018), para 10.6 notes that, once a condition is licensed, 'The perception of the level of risk for those seeking treatment will also be an important factor for the centre to consider.'

controversy, what is popularly described as the creation of 'saviour siblings'. Parents who have a child already afflicted by a potentially fatal genetic disorder can seek to have another baby whose stem cells, taken from her umbilical cord, could 'cure' her brother or sister. PGT-M is combined with pre-implantation tissue typing (PTT) so that a baby is created who is both unaffected by the genetic disorder in question[124] and an exact tissue match for the sick sibling. Opponents of PGT-M/PTT argued that it was wrong to create a baby purely as a means to an end. But desperate parents often make several attempts to have a baby naturally to achieve just that end – a tissue match for a sick child. Nothing in the original 1990 Act addressed this question. The HFEA struggled to deal with the dilemma. The Authority gave a clinic permission to treat Zain Hashmi. Zain suffered from *beta thallasaemia* (BT), a genetic disease. His family could provide no compatible stem cell donor, so his parents sought PGT-M with PTT. Charlie Whitaker suffered from Diamond Blackfan Anaemia (DBA). His parents also wanted to use PGT-M with PTT to create a 'saviour sibling' for Charlie. The HFEA said no. The Hashmi embryo was itself at risk of BT. DBA is not thought to be a genetic disease, so the HFEA initially argued that Whitaker embryos could not be screened as they would obtain no benefit. The distinction between the two cases met vigorous criticism.[125] The HFEA changed its mind.

Meanwhile pro-life groups challenged the legality of the HFEA decision to allow PGT-M/PTT in the Hashmi case. Ultimately, the House of Lords[126] ruled in favour of the HFEA, confining themselves to an exercise in statutory interpretation and seeking to side-step moral controversy. Amendments to the 1990 Act give statutory backing to the use of PGT-M/PTT to create saviour siblings. Schedule 2, paragraph 1ZA expressly allows testing on the embryo to ascertain if the tissue of the embryo would be compatible with an existing sibling who suffers from a serious illness that could be treated by umbilical cord cells, bone marrow or other tissue from the child to be born. Other tissue is expressly defined to exclude solid organs. But while this prohibition would mean that tissue typing could not go ahead were there an intent to resort to organ donation at the time of the creation of the savour embryo, it would not of itself make it unlawful to authorise organ donation later if all other measures had failed. A living transplant from a minor would, however, require approval under the Human Tissue Act 2004 and that would be unlikely to be forthcoming.[127]

14.22 PGT-M: selecting for 'disability'

As the 2008 Act made its way through Parliament a new controversy erupted. PGT-M is normally used to screen out certain sorts of serious

124 Note that PTT might be used without PGT-M to create a saviour sibling if the existing child does not suffer from a heritable condition. Applications are made to the HFEA on a case-by-case basis.

125 See S Sheldon and S Wilkinson, 'Hashmi and Whitaker: An Unjustifiable and Misguided Distinction' (2004) 12 *Med Law Rev* 137.

126 *R (Quintavalle v Human Fertilisation and Embryology Authority* [2005] UKHL 28.

127 See 20.5 below.

disease or disability. What if a couple wanted to screen *in* a particular condition, for example a deaf couple wanted to ensure that their child was also deaf?[128] They want their child to be part of their community and challenge society's notion of deafness as disability. Section 13(8)–(10) of the 1990 Act as amended now provides that embryos known to have a serious abnormality 'must not be preferred to those not known to have such an abnormality'. Nor must a gamete donor known to carry such an abnormality be preferred to one who is not. Note the limits of the statute. First, is it clear that deafness would qualify as sufficiently serious under the Act? If it did, note that the Act does not ban implantation of the 'deaf embryo' but just states that it cannot be selected if there are unaffected embryos created at the same treatment.

14.23 PGT-M: social sex selection

It may be that at the root of concerns about PGT-M lies discomfort with the notion of parents having a free choice of what kind of children they have, the prospect of 'designer babies'. The UK legislation as it relates to PGT-M is heavily based on a medical model so testing an embryo to establish its gender is allowed to avoid the birth of a child with a sex-linked genetic disease. Should the law allow sex selection for non-medical reasons? A couple with three sons want a daughter to 'balance' their family.[129] A single woman wants only female children. Despite strong support for lifting any ban on social sex selection, the law is now clear. It is unlawful to use PGT-M to test for gender save in the context of gender-linked disease.[130] Nor can techniques be used based on sperm sorting, that is separating X and Y sperm and using only Y sperm to inseminate the woman wanting a son and vice versa. The legislation now prohibits any use of sperm without a licence save as we have seen for partner-donated sperm that has not been processed. Sorting will constitute processing. The debate will continue.[131]

14.24 Mitochondrial donation

As we have noted above, only permitted eggs and embryos may be implanted in a woman and used for fertility treatment. All forms of animal–human hybrids fall outside the definition of permitted eggs or embryos, as does any egg or embryo where the genetic structure of the egg or embryo has been altered *unless* Parliament makes regulations to confer permitted status on such eggs or embryos. The germ line should not be tampered with.

128 See J Savulescu, 'Deaf Lesbians, "Designer Disability" and the Future of Medicine' (2002) 325 *BMJ* 771.

129 S Wilkinson, 'Racism and Sexism in Medically Assisted Conception' (1998) 12 *Bioethics* 25.

130 Schedule 2, para 1ZB.

131 Some intended parents might be able to select the sex of their child by accessing services abroad: see H Mays, 'UK Doctors Accused of Helping Couples Choose the Sex of Their Babies' *Guardian* (2018) 8 October.

In the face of much controversy, Parliament approved regulations[132] to allow alteration of the genetic structure of eggs and embryos, and to confer on them the status of 'permitted', in the case of treatment for mitochondrial disease. Ninety-nine per cent of our DNA is to be found in the nuclei of our cells and in the case of an egg or embryo the same holds good. The remainder lies in the mitochondria from the outer layer of the egg (rather like the 'egg shell') and inherited from the mother and acting so to speak as the battery for the egg, embryo or cells of the born individual. In a few women, defects in the mitochondria can result in serious disease affecting any children they may bear, sometimes resulting in early death and/or terrible suffering. Mitochondrial donation involves taking an egg from woman A (the woman affected by mitochondrial disease), or an embryo created from one of her eggs, and removing the nucleus of the egg or embryo. An egg or embryo is also taken from woman B, a woman unaffected by mitochondrial disease, and the nucleus removed. The nucleus from A is then inserted in the egg or embryo from B and the resultant embryo implanted in A. A will carry a child unlikely to be affected by the curse of mitochondrial disease but sharing 99 per cent of its genetic heritage with her and the father. The defective mitochondria will have been practically eliminated from the matrilineal line. Some of the media and opponents of such treatment (that inevitably does alter the genetic structure of the egg or embryo) argued first that this was creating 'three parent' families and second that it opened the doors to wholesale genetic manipulation of embryos. The notion of 'three parent' families is somewhat exaggerated, and we would argue that the donor of the egg (or egg shell) is much more akin to the donor of bone marrow than either a biological mother or indeed a conventional egg donor.[133]

14.25 Liability for disability[134]

What if fertility treatment results in the birth of a disabled infant? This could happen for several reasons. In DI, the donor may turn out to be the carrier of some disease or genetic disorder. Babies have been born abroad suffering from HIV contracted from donor sperm. An error may be made in the laboratory, damaging an IVF embryo. Or treatment, such as mitochondrial donation, might in years to come be shown to produce abnormalities manifesting themselves only when the children reach maturity.

Parents will be able to maintain an action against the doctors and the clinic if mother or child is injured by negligence. Clearly if the mother herself suffers

132 The Human Fertilisation and Embryology (Mitochondrial Donation) Regulations 2015, SI 2015/572.

133 See Nuffield Council on Bioethics, *Novel Technologies for the Prevention of Mitochondrial Disorders: An Ethical Review* (2012).

134 Note *ARB v IVF Hammersmith* [2018] EWCA Civ 2803 discussed at 13.8 above: an unsuccessful claim for damages in respect of the cost of bringing up a healthy child born after IVF, the clinic having failed to ensure the father's proper consent in circumstances when the mother forged his signature.

any injury, for example in the course of collecting eggs, she may recover compensation for that injury. The woman accepted for treatment expects care, not only in relation to herself, but also in the 'production' of a healthy infant. If, by negligence, the child is born disabled, damage to the parents is readily foreseeable. Both mother and father will suffer emotional trauma and face the added expense of bringing up a disabled child.[135] Is there a problem if the parents cannot pinpoint exactly who was negligent? It may be impossible for them to know if the embryo was damaged by the gynaecologist removing the eggs and implanting the embryo, or by the scientists in the laboratory. In NHS clinics, the NHS Trust owes a direct duty to the parents and is responsible for negligently failing to discharge that duty. In the private sector, patients should ensure that the clinic similarly undertakes a contractual duty to provide and underwrite the whole course of treatment. One final point relating to actions by parents is that, while they may have legal redress if a damaged baby is born, there will be no legal remedy if no baby is born. Neither NHS nor private clinics undertake more than to attempt to assist conception using all due skill and care.

What of an action by the child? They will need to rely on the right of action in respect of pre-natal injuries enacted in the Congenital Disabilities (Civil Liability) Act 1976.[136] The Human Fertilisation and Embryology Act 1990 amended the 1976 Act to allow for an action arising out of negligence in the process of assisted conception. Section 44 inserts into the 1976 Act section 1A, which provides for an action if a child carried by a woman as a result of the placing in her of an embryo, or sperm and eggs, or DI, is born disabled, and the disability results from negligence in the selection, or keeping or use outside the body, of the relevant embryo or gametes. Providing the defendant is answerable in tort to one or both parents, he is liable to the child. The sorts of cases envisaged by section 1A are just the sort of examples mentioned earlier – the child born HIV positive because doctors failed to screen donors adequately, the child born damaged by some technical error in his creation, and the child born disabled because a defective embryo was negligently implanted in the mother. A further extension to the rights of the child is made in section 35(4) of the 1990 Act, again amending the 1976 Act, to provide that injury to the reproductive capacity of the genetic parent gives rise to a derivative action under the 1976 Act for the child. Sections 34 and 35 of the 1990 Act make extensive provision for disclosure of information necessary to any action by parent or child for damages occasioned by assisted conception.

Both parents and children seeking compensation for disability will face problems proving negligence where it is difficult to isolate the cause of the damage to the child. A baby resulting from DI born HIV positive, or afflicted by a genetic disease carried by the father, poses no legal problem in a claim by his parents. Competent screening should have discovered the disease or defect

135 See *Parkinson v St James and Seacroft University Hospital NHS Trust* [2001] 3 All ER 97, CA. See 13.8 above.

136 See 13.10 above.

and that sperm should never have been used to inseminate the mother. Linking a defect to an error in the laboratory will be less easy. An action based on abnormalities manifesting themselves later in life is almost bound to fail. If in 2025 it is shown that freezing embryos produces cancer in a person's thirties, the defence to any claim in negligence will be that responsible professional opinion, endorsed by countless official reports, believed freezing to be safe in 1995 when the child was born.

Finally, if parent or child has a right to sue and proves negligence, are there defences open to the doctor based on the parents having agreed to run the risk of a damaged child? Section 44(3) provides that an action by the child shall fail if either or both parents knew of the risk of their child being born disabled 'that is to say, the particular risk created by the act of omission'. So if the mother is known to carry a genetic disease herself and is counselled that it would be better to use donor eggs for an IVF pregnancy, yet insists on a child who is genetically hers, she cannot turn round and sue the doctors who carried out her wishes, if her genetic problem is inherited by her child. However, it would be no defence for a defendant simply to say: 'Well, parents know that this is a relatively new and risky process, so I am not liable.' The parents must be aware of the particular risk of harming their child.

14.26 Reproductive cloning

Human reproductive cloning is illegal in the United Kingdom. It does not matter how the 'clone' is created. When Parliament enacted the Human Fertilisation and Embryology Act 1990, the intent was to ban any form of reproductive cloning and the assumption was that section 3(1)(d) outlawed any form of human cloning. Replacing the nucleus of an embryo with the nucleus of a cell taken from any other person or embryo was prohibited. The development of cell nuclear replacement (CNR), heralded by the birth of Dolly the Sheep, highlighted the inadequacy of section 3(1)(d). Placing the donated nucleus into an emptied egg still fell outside the prohibition. As we shall see in the next chapter, the government sought to permit the HFEA to license the use of CNR in developing stem cell therapies, often referred to as therapeutic cloning.[137] Reproductive cloning was condemned.[138] Pro-life groups, however, challenged the regulations arguing that CNR embryos fell outside the 1990 Act altogether because the embryos were not created by fertilisation. Their victory at first instance[139] led to the Human Reproductive Cloning Act 2001 prohibiting the implantation in a woman of an embryo 'created otherwise than by fertilisation'.[140] That Act has now been repealed. The amendments to the 1990 Act made by the 2008 Act make it clear that embryo is defined to include embryos created by fertilisation or 'any other process capable of

137 See Human Fertilisation and Embryology (Research Purposes) Regulations 2001, SI 2001/188.

138 HFEA/HGAC, *Cloning Issues in Reproduction, Science and Medicine* (1998).

139 *R (Quintavalle) v Secretary of State for Health* [2001] EWHC Admin 918.

140 And see *R (Quintavalle) v Secretary of State for Health* [2003] UKHL 13.

resulting in an embryo'.[141] Only 'permitted embryos' may be implanted in a woman and that excludes any cloned embryo.[142]

Several arguments are advanced for,[143] and against, reproductive cloning.[144] Safety is a concern that all parties in the debate share. Mammalian cloning has shown a high rate of birth defects and miscarriage. Research might overcome this hurdle to permitting cloning. Other arguments centre on the impact on the cloned child of her means of production. She will (it is said) lack a unique genetic identity, but so does any identical twin. If she is a clone of her mother, she will see her genetic future mapped out from birth. Moreover, she may be condemned to live more generally in her creator's shadow – a copy, not a daughter. If she is a clone of a dead sibling, her parent(s) may not value her, but rather the ghost of her sister. Yet environment shapes us as much as our DNA. A clone of one of the authors would grow up in different times and with different parents. Confusion about relationships is another problem for a clone. Would a clone of Emma Cave have Emma for her mother? Or would Emma's mother be mother to the clone? The Emma clone would be truly fatherless. The debate goes on. Yet Laurie, Harmon and Dove 'suspect that the days of the outright prohibition on reproductive cloning are numbered'.[145]

14.27 Surrogacy

Where a woman is unable to carry a child herself, perhaps because she has undergone a hysterectomy or has endured several miscarriages, surrogacy may be her only hope for a child. Increasingly surrogacy is also used to enable a male couple or indeed a single man to found a family. In *B v C and others*[146] B's mother acted as surrogate bearing his child (her grandchild) created from a donor egg fertilised with B's sperm. Surrogacy has become an accepted form of assisted reproduction, but its regulation has long been out of touch with the needs of surrogates, intended parents and children. Proposals for reform in 1997[147] fell on deaf ears, and Horsey and Neofytou argue that the 2008 Act was a missed opportunity to debate the issue.[148] The Law Commission in 2019 reiterated the call for reform and will produce a draft bill in 2023.

Surrogacy can take a number of forms. In *traditional surrogacy* (sometimes called 'partial' surrogacy), a surrogate agrees with the intended parent/s

141 Section 1(1).

142 Section 3(2).

143 See, notably, J Harris, *On Cloning* (2004) Routledge.

144 Summed up in Jackson, *Medical Law: Text, Cases and Materials* (2010), pp 831–835.

145 *Mason and McCall Smith's Law and Medical Ethics*, 7.95.

146 [2015] EWFC 17.

147 M Brazier, A Campbell and S Golombok, *Surrogacy: Review for Health Ministers of Current Arrangements for Payments and Regulation* (1998) Cm 4068 (hereafter Surrogacy Review).

148 K Horsey and K Neofytou, 'The Fertility Treatment Time Forgot: What Should be Done about Surrogacy in the UK?' in K Horsey (ed), *Revisiting the Regulation of Human Fertilisation and Embryology* (2017) Routledge.

(sometimes called the 'commissioning parent/s') to undergo artificial insemination with the man's sperm. Traditional surrogacy accounts for about a third of surrogacy cases in the UK.[149] The surrogate agrees to carry any resulting child, and to hand the child over to the genetic father and, where there is such a person, his wife or partner, immediately she is born. In the past, many surrogates practised self-insemination privately,[150] and although amendments to the 1990 Act have imposed stricter controls on the use of fresh sperm, self-insemination (sometimes described as home-insemination) persists. It would appear that a purely private arrangement between the intended father and the surrogate still falls outside the need for a licence and note that, even if that were not the case, a pregnancy could still be established via normal sexual relations.[151] As we shall see, traditional surrogacy is not wholly unregulated. The ban on commercial surrogacy arrangements applies and couples who seek to acquire parental status for both partners are subject to the regulations governing parental orders. The attraction of traditional surrogacy using self-insemination, however, may be that its initiation is private. There is no need to seek treatment at a licensed fertility clinic and thus no intrusive questions to answer about the welfare of the child. Alas a plethora of cases now demonstrate how easily such private arrangements entered into without advice on the law and parental status can go wrong.

IVF offers a couple where the woman ovulates, but cannot safely carry a child to term, the chance of a baby who is genetically theirs. Eggs are taken from the woman, fertilised in the laboratory with sperm from the man, and the embryo implanted in the surrogate. The surrogate once again carries the child and agrees to hand her over at birth. The surrogate is literally a 'hostess' for the embryo. This practice may be styled *gestational* (sometimes called 'full' or 'complete') *surrogacy*. It accounts for around two thirds of surrogacy cases in the UK.

14.28 Who are the parents?

The first legal question is who in English law are the mother and father of a child born as a result of a surrogacy arrangement? As will become clear, in both traditional and gestational surrogacy intended parents currently need to seek a parental order or adopt the child if they are both to become the legal parents of the child, and, moreover, to obtain a parental order the couple will need to establish that the legal parents consent to the granting of the order. Until recently, only couples could seek parental orders. As we shall see, the law changed in 2018 to allow a single intended parent to become a legal parent.

149 Surrogacy UK, *Surrogacy in the UK: Further Evidence for Reform – Second Report of the Surrogacy UK Working Group on Surrogacy Law Reform* (2018).

150 See Surrogacy Review.

151 As was the case in *M v F and another* [2013] EWHC 1901 (Fam).

In relation to both traditional and gestational surrogacy the surrogate who carries the child is the legal mother[152] and the wife or female intended parent has no legal relationship with the child,[153] even if her eggs are used and she is the genetic mother of that child. If the surrogate is married and her husband consented[154] to her participation in the surrogacy arrangement the surrogate's husband will be the legal father of the child, whenever and wherever the surrogate was inseminated or the embryo implanted in her body.[155] If the surrogate is not married and practised self-insemination using donor sperm from the intended father, he will be the legal as well as the biological father of the child. If the surrogate was treated in a licensed clinic before April 2009 then it may be that her partner, if she has one, will be the legal father or the child will be legally fatherless.[156] After April 2009 theoretically the agreed fatherhood conditions could apply and the surrogate could nominate her partner as the 'father'.[157] Note that the surrogate cannot give notice that the intended father be the legal father of the child as the agreed fatherhood conditions exclude the donor of the sperm.[158]

The complexity of the provisions on parenthood and the mistaken belief by many intended parents that biological parenthood will confer legal status on them has resulted in a raft of cases before the Family Division, many (but by no means all) relating to surrogacy arrangements entered into abroad. Obtaining a parental order is crucial not simply to confer parental status on the intended parent/s but also to ensure that the surrogate ceases to be the legal mother of the child. All too often couples who access surrogacy outside licensed clinics have little or poor advice on the need to and how to obtain an order. In *JP v LP and others (Surrogacy Arrangement: Wardship)*[159] the problems are well illustrated and we give only a brief overview of a most complicated case. A couple arranged with a friend of the woman that she would carry a child for them as part of a traditional surrogacy arrangement, and the friend became pregnant after self-insemination with the father's sperm. The baby was born and handed over to the couple. A few months later the marriage broke

152 See Human Fertilisation and Embryology Act 1990 (as amended), s 27; and Human Fertilisation and Embryology 2008, s 33. See R D'alton-Harrison (above n 71).

153 And so if her relationship with the biological father breaks down before a parental order is obtained she may have no legal claim in relation to the child: see *JP v LP and others (Surrogacy Arrangement: Wardship)* [2014] EWHC 595 (Fam).

154 So it may be that the intended parent/s will want to try and show that the husband did not consent; see *Re G (Surrogacy: Foreign Domicile)* [2007] EWHC 2814.

155 See Human Fertilisation and Embryology Act 1990 (as amended), s 28; and Human Fertilisation and Embryology Act 2008, s 35. And see *R (H) v Secretary of State for Health and Social Care* [2019] EWHC 2095 (Admin); *H v UK*, App No 32185/20 (ECHR, 2022) where a child's claim to have her biological father named as her father on her birth certificate in place of the husband of her surrogate mother was ruled inadmissible.

156 Human Fertilisation and Embryology Act 1990 (as amended), s 28.

157 See Human Fertilisation and Embryology Act 2008, ss 36–38.

158 Ibid, s 36(d).

159 [2014] EWHC 595 (Fam).

down and the woman (JP) left the marital home with the child. A whole series of legal applications followed but were changed or abandoned and this case came before Eleanor King J when the child was 3 years and 8 months old. The judge found, as she had to, that the legal mother remained the surrogate and the legal father the husband. JP, who had cared for the child all his life, had no legal relationship with 'her' son, though interestingly the judge chose to refer to JP as the mother. She found that given the six-month time limit to apply for a parental order and the fact that the couple were no longer living together so that the child had his home with the applicants no such order could be granted. Granting an adoption order to JP was inappropriate as that would extinguish the father's parental responsibility and as the couple were no longer together they could not adopt together. A shared residence order granted JP parental responsibility but not legal motherhood and the surrogate remained the legal mother with parental responsibility for the child. In the end the parties agreed to a complex solution. The child became a ward of court. The couple were granted a joint residence order and the surrogate prohibited from exercising any parental responsibility without leave of the court.[160] The couple had sought legal advice and a wholly inadequate agreement had been drawn up by a firm of solicitors. Perhaps more worrying than this case, where in the end the couple did agree a way forward to care for the child well, is the evidence that a number of surrogacy arrangements are effected without any attempt by the 'parents' to seek a parental order or other legal means to assure the parental status of both parties.

14.29 Parental orders and adoption

Prior to the 1990 Act the only way that intended parents could both acquire parental responsibility for 'their' child was to adopt the child. Intended parents, especially in gestational surrogacy arrangements, were unhappy at being obliged to adopt their own genetic child and so section 30 introducing 'parental orders' was inserted in the 1990 Act to help some intended parents in surrogacy cases.[161] It provided for a simpler and faster procedure, other than adoption,[162] by which some couples could acquire parental rights over 'their' child. Parental orders are now governed by section 54 of the Human Fertilisation and Embryology Act 2008, which empowers the court to order that the intended parents be treated in law as the parents of the child, but *only* in a limited number of circumstances. In the past few years virtually every condition for the grant of a parental order has proved problematic and judges have engaged in some imaginative interpretations of the law to secure the legal status of a child living with the intended parent/s whose legal parents

160 And see *Re D (A Child)* [2014] EWHC 2121 (Fam).

161 See *Re W (Minors Surrogacy)* [1991] 1 FLR 385.

162 See *AB v CD (Surrogacy: Time Limit and Consent)* [2015] EWFC 12, [71] for the view that a parental order is much to be preferred to adoption in that the former recognises the reality of the child's identity and biological relationship to at least one of the intended parents.

may have no interest, no capacity to raise, or are untraceable. Section 54 of the 2008 Act originally required applications to be made by 'two people'. To achieve sole parental responsibility for the child and relieve the surrogate of her status as the legal mother, a single man establishing a family via surrogacy had to adopt his child.[163] This position was challenged in *Re Z*[164] and found to breach the human rights of a biological father under Articles 8 and 14. In 2019 a new section 54A was duly added, setting out conditions for a parental order from a single intended parent.[165] To obtain an order:

(1) Where the applicants are a couple, they must be married, or civil partners, or 'living as partners in an enduring family relationship'. Until the passing of the 2008 Act, only married couples could apply for parental orders. Where the applicant is a single intended parent, the child must have been carried by a woman who is not the intended parent using the gametes of the applicant.[166]
(2) The child must have been conceived either from the placing of the embryo, or sperm and eggs, in the woman, or by DI. And the eggs or sperm or both must come from at least one of the applicants. Children conceived by natural intercourse between the surrogate and a male intended parent are not within the ambit of section 54.[167]
(3) Normally the application must be made within six months of the birth of the child. Exceptionally an application may be made beyond the time limit where there were grounds to explain the delay and the welfare of the child or children required that an order be made.[168]
(4) At the time of the making of the order, the child's home[169] must be with the applicant/s, one or both of whom are domiciled[170] in the United Kingdom.
(5) The surrogate (and the 'legal father' if he is not the intended 'father')[171] must have given full and free consent not less than six weeks after

163 *B v C and others* [2015] EWFC 17.
164 [2016] EWHC 1191 (Fam). See also *Re B v C (Surrogacy Adoption)* ibid, where a single man adopted his biological child who was his legal brother: and see discussion in K Horsey, 'Fraying at the Edges: UK Surrogacy Law in 2015' (2016) 24(4) *Med Law Rev* 608.
165 Human Fertilisation and Embryology Act 2008 (Remedial) Order 2018, SI 2018/1413.
166 Human Fertilisation and Embryology Act 2008, s 54A.
167 As was the case in *Re an Adoption Application (Surrogacy)* [1987] 2 All ER 826; and see *M v F* [2013] EWHC 1901 (Fam).
168 *X (A Child) (Surrogacy: Time Limit)* [2014] EWHC 3135; *AB v CD (Surrogacy: Time Limit and Consent)* [2015] EWFC 12; *Re A (A Child: Surrogacy: S.54 Criteria)* [2020] EWHC 1426 (Fam).
169 See *Re A* ibid, discussed below.
170 See *A and B (Parental Order: Domicile)* [2013] EWHC 426 (Fam); *JV and OV v AR* [2014] EWHC 4756 (Fam).
171 On which see *Re Q (Parental Order)* [1996] 2 FCR 345.

the birth.[172] Sections 54 and 54A are of no relevance if the surrogate changes her mind and is not willing to hand over the child. Nor is it a backdoor route to enforcing a surrogacy contract. Unlike adoption the court cannot dispense with the consent of a legal parent on the grounds that it is unreasonably withheld but sections 54(7) and 54A(6) do provide that consent is not required from a legal parent who cannot be found or is incapable of giving consent. In several cases relating to foreign surrogacy arrangements the courts have found themselves in effect 'forced' to conclude that either the surrogate or her partner cannot be located and that the applicants had taken all reasonable measures to locate them and seek consent.[173]

(6) No payments (other than for expenses reasonably incurred)[174] must have been made to the surrogate unless authorised by the court. As we shall see the ban on overt payments and the interpretation of expenses has become a challenging part of many applications for parental orders.

The courts' interpretation and application of section 54 recognises the transformative effect of a parental order on the welfare of the child that engages the child's rights under Article 8.[175] In *Re A*[176] Keehan J made a parental order notwithstanding concerns over three of the section 54 requirements. The facts were complex and we present but a synopsis. A was born by a surrogacy arrangement. His intended parents, M and F, were his biological parents. Though separated, they made a joint application for a parental order as they both wanted to play a parental role in A's life. They were more than two years beyond the time limit, but section 54(3) was 'read down' in light of the obligation in section 3 of the Human Rights Act 1998 to, so far as possible, interpret legislation in a manner that is compatible with Convention rights.[177] The intended parents lived separately, but section 54(4) was given a 'wide and purposive interpretation' and the child had a 'home' with each of his parents. And nor did their separation prevent them being considered to be 'living as partners in an enduring family relationship' as required by section 54(2)(c).

172 In *AB v CD (Surrogacy: Time Limit and Consent)* [2015] EWFC 12, the couple set out to seek a single surrogate in India so that AB would be the legal father but in the event it appeared that the surrogate was still married. The judge, however, held that the husband would not have consented to his 'wife's' treatment and so was not the legal father.

173 See again *AB v CD*, ibid.

174 But note payments of £12,000 and more have been deemed reasonable expenses; *Re C (Application by Mr and Mrs X under s 30 of the Human Fertilisation and Embryology Act)* [2002] EWHC 157.

175 Note though that the ECtHR found no violation of Article 8 in *Valdís Fjölnisdóttir and Others v Iceland*, App No 71552/17 (ECHR, 2021) where the domestic court refused to recognise a parental link between intended parents and X born to them via a surrogate mother in the USA and in circumstances where neither of the intended parents were genetically related to him and where surrogacy is illegal.

176 *Re A (A Child: Surrogacy: S.54 Criteria)* [2020] EWHC 1426 (Fam).

177 Ibid, [28] and see *Re X (A Child) (Surrogacy: Time Limit)* [2014] EWHC 3135 (Fam).

14.30 Prohibiting 'commercial' surrogacy

Surrogacy where no money changes hands is lawful in the sense that no crime is committed. The Surrogacy Arrangements Act 1985 made it a criminal offence for anyone to play any part in setting up a surrogacy arrangement on a commercial basis, and advertising or compiling information to promote or assist surrogacy arrangements was also made criminal. The ban applied equally to traditional and gestational surrogacy. Section 59 of the 2008 Act amended the Surrogacy Arrangements Act to allow reasonable payments to be made to non-profit-making bodies and for such non-profit agencies to place advertisements. Under the Act, no offence is committed by a woman herself seeking to become, or becoming, a surrogate, nor is any offence committed by the person or the couple who persuade her to carry a child. The 1985 Act (as amended) is limited to banning the activities of any commercial agencies or individuals aiming to make a profit out of arranging surrogacy. A fertility specialist who helps in establishing a gestational surrogacy even in the private sector incurs no criminal liability, so long as they do not involve themselves in arranging the introduction of couple and surrogate. Lawyers, however, who draw up agreements for profit may contravene the law and this of itself contributes to the problems of surrogacy, acting as a disincentive to firms to provide advice.[178]

Although the surrogate and the couple engaging her services do not commit any offence under the 1985 Act even if she is paid for what she does, the law still seeks to prevent any payment suggesting that the child has been bought. As we have seen the intended parent/s need either to adopt the child or obtain a parental order. It is a criminal offence to give or receive any payment in relation to the adoption of a child, the grant of consent to adoption, or the handing over of a child with a view to its adoption, unless that payment is authorised by a court.[179] Any payment beyond 'reasonable expenses' (again unless authorised by the court) will debar the couple from obtaining a parental order.[180] And if barred from obtaining a parental order the couple's only option is to adopt, but if they try to adopt the child, and money paid to the surrogate is found to include a sum in payment for her agreement to the adoption and handing over the child, the surrogate and the couple may all face prosecution.

Judicial responses to 'commercial surrogacy' have been pragmatic and rightly focused on the needs of the child. In 1985, Kim Cotton had agreed to carry a child for a childless couple from abroad. She was artificially inseminated with the husband's sperm. The arrangements were made through an agency that was paid £13,000 by the father, of which the surrogate received £6,500. At the relevant time, the Surrogacy Arrangements Act had not yet been enacted. The baby was born and the mother prepared to hand her over. Barnet Social

178 *JP v LP and others (Surrogacy Arrangement: Wardship)* [2015] EWHC 595 (Fam), [41].

179 See Adoption and Children Act 2002, s 95.

180 Section 54(8).

Services stepped in. The child was made a ward of court. Latey J[181] set the precedent for pragmatic compassion that his judicial colleagues have followed since. He said that the crucial issue before him was what was best for this baby. The methods used to create the child and the commercial aspects of the case raised delicate problems of ethics, morality and social desirability. They were not for him to decide. Careful inquiries showed that the father and his wife were eminently suitable parents. The judge granted them custody of the baby and permission to take her abroad with them to their home. The question of adoption, and the illegality of any payment under the Adoption Act 1976, did not arise in that case.

The problem of payments to the surrogate remains a source of difficulty. In *Re L (A Minor)*[182] Hedley J faced a case where there could be no doubt that the payments made exceeded even the most generous interpretation of reasonable expenses. The commercial surrogacy arrangement entered into by a British couple in Illinois was lawful under the law of Illinois and unlawful under the 2008 Act in the UK. Nonetheless the judge used his powers under section 54(8) of the 2008 Act to authorise the payment retrospectively and grant the parental order. He was careful to stress that the couple acted in good faith unaware of the law here. He described the authorised payment as 'compensation' and stressed that each case must be scrutinised on its own facts. But when the welfare of the child was at stake, Hedley J stressed that the good of the child must be accorded priority and that 'if it is desired to control commercial surrogacy arrangements, those controls need to operate before the court process is initiated'.[183] In *J v G*[184] payments to a surrogate in California of £35,650 plus expenses were authorised. Reading the case-law it may seem that the courts are re-writing the law, but what can a judge do, especially given that the Human Fertilisation and Embryology (Parental Orders) Regulations (2010)[185] require that the child's welfare be the paramount consideration? More worrying perhaps than payments to the surrogate may be the payments made to agencies overseas. In *P-M (Parental Order; Payments to Surrogacy Agency)*[186] a couple paid $17,700 to the surrogate and $48,000 to the agency, including sums described as a 'gift' to jump the queue.

Public and judicial attitudes to commercial surrogacy have softened. In *Whittington Hospital NHS Trust v XX*[187] the Supreme Court held that it was 'no longer contrary to public policy' to award damages for foreign commercial surrogacy. The claimant had negligently been given negative cervical smear

181 *Re C (A Minor)* [1985] FLR 846 and see *Re an Adoption Application (Surrogacy)* [1987] 2 All ER 826.
182 [2010] EWHC 3146 (Fam).
183 Ibid, [10].
184 [2013] EWHC 1432 (Fam).
185 SI 2010/985 and The Human Fertilisation and Embryology (Parental Orders) (Consequential, Transitional and Saving Provisions) Order 2010, SI 2010/986.
186 [2013] EWHC 1561 (Fam).
187 [2020] UKSC 14. See K Horsey, A Powell, 'A Step Too Far? Whittington Hospital NHS Trust v XX [2020] UKSC' (2021) 29(1) *Med Law Rev* 172; E O'Callaghan, 'Surrogacy and Public Policy' (2021) 72(3) *Northern Ireland Legal Quarterly* 7.

test results. When cancer was detected, it was not possible to preserve her ability to bear children. She had eight eggs collected and frozen and sought to use them and donor eggs to create a family. The hospital admitted liability, but should damages extend to commercial surrogacy in California? By a majority the Supreme Court held that, subject to a reasonableness criterion, it should.[188] As we shall see, efforts to reduce the potentially harmful financial and welfare impacts of commercial surrogacy abroad focus on providing an easier and safer pathway to legal parenthood in the UK.

14.31 'Custody' of the baby

If the surrogate is content to hand the baby over, the courts will help the intended parent/s to become the legal parent/s of the baby. What if she changes her mind? First, it is absolutely clear in England that surrogacy agreements are not enforceable as contracts. The intended parent/s cannot sue the surrogate for breach of contract or ask a court to order performance of a contract. Nor can the surrogate sue if she does not receive any agreed payments. Section 1A in the Surrogacy Arrangements Act 1985 provides quite simply that: 'No surrogacy arrangement is enforceable by or against any of the persons making it.' It does not matter by what means the child was created, be it sexual intercourse, DI or IVF, the arrangement is not an enforceable contract.

That still leaves open the question of what happens if the surrogate wants to keep the baby. In England, if the surrogate changes her mind and refuses to surrender the child, she will usually be allowed to keep the child. In *A v C*[189] as long ago as 1978, a young woman agreed to have a baby by DI and hand over the child to the wealthy father and his partner. When the child was born she refused to give him up. The father sought care and control. The trial judge found that the mother should be allowed to keep the child but granted the father limited access. The Court of Appeal removed his rights of access, condemning the whole arrangement as 'irresponsible, bizarre and unnatural'. Nor does it seem that greater tolerance of surrogacy has altered judicial policy where surrogates change their minds. In *Re T (A Child) (Surrogacy: Residence Order)*,[190] Baker J refused to make a residence order in favour of the intended father after a surrogacy agreement broke down in acrimony.

But there are exceptions. If the surrogate hands over the child, who is settled into the couple's home, but later changes her mind about consent to adoption or a parental order, the court has on two occasions at least overruled the surrogate's refusal of consent.[191] The welfare of the child once established in a 'new' family will override any claims of the surrogate. The case of *H v S (Surrogacy Agreement)*[192] was presented in the media as a judge enforcing a surrogacy

188 Lady Hale gave the majority judgment with which Lords Kerr and Wilson agreed. Lord Carnwath gave a dissenting judgment with which Lord Reed agreed.

189 [1985] FLR 445 (FD and CA).

190 [2011] EWHC F 33 (Fam).

191 *Re MW (Adoption: Surrogacy)* [1995] 2 FLR 759; *C v S* (1996) SLT 1387.

192 [2015] EWHC 36 (Fam).

agreement against the surrogate in favour of a gay couple. Russell J was, however, explicit stating that she was not enforcing the agreement but acting in the best interests of the child when she granted a shared residence order in favour of the couple. The facts were extraordinary. The surrogate agreed with the two men (H and B) that she would carry a child and was inseminated with H's sperm. She later denied any such agreement and claimed that in effect H agreed to act as sperm donor. She did all she could to keep H out of the child's life. She had the child baptised in breach of a prohibited steps order, adopted a highly possessive parenting style and was obstructive and untruthful in court proceedings. The mother was unable to put the child's needs first or to meet her emotional needs. The judge decided that despite the fact the child had lived with her mother for over a year, her interests were better served by moving her to live with her father and his partner.

14.32 Cross-border surrogacy arrangements

Many cases reaching the courts relate to couples who go abroad to find a surrogate in a jurisdiction where more young women may be prepared to act as surrogates, or the rules on parenthood may be more favourable to the couple and controls on payment less rigorous.[193] In particular, the rule that makes a surrogate's husband the legal father has proved problematic. The couple may be told that the surrogate is single (perhaps divorced) only to discover later that she probably remained married.[194] When couples seek to gain the requisite consent there may even be uncertainty about the literacy[195] or even the identity of the surrogate.[196]

We have also seen that judges will take a fairly lenient view of payments so as not to disrupt an established relationship between intended parents and the child.[197] Other couples have faced more serious problems. If the child is born abroad and intended parents are not in law her parents how can they lawfully bring her home to the UK? Can they only apply for such an order when the child has a home with them in this country? The immigration authorities will grant exceptional leave to allow the child into the UK if at least one partner has a genetic link to the child and it is likely that a parental order will be granted.[198]

Problems also arise when couples come from abroad to seek a surrogacy arrangement in the UK. A Turkish couple made such an arrangement and the

193 See E Jackson *et al*, 'Learning from cross-border reproduction' (2017) 25(1) *Med Law Rev* 23 on the motivations and experiences of those accessing cross-border services.

194 *Re D (A Child)* [2014] EWHC 2121 (Fam).

195 *Re WT (Foreign Surrogacy)* [2014] EWHC 1303 (Fam).

196 *Re D (A Child)* [2014] EWHC 2121 (Fam). And see *R v T* [2015] EWFC 22.

197 As in *Re L (A Minor)* [2010] EWHC 3146 (Fam). On the issue of judicial leniency in relation to a host of reproduction services abroad, see B van Beers, 'Is Europe "Giving in to Baby Markets"? Reproductive Tourism in Europe and the Gradual Erosion of Existing Legal Limits to Reproductive Markets' (2015) 23(1) *Med Law Rev* 103.

198 But see *Re K (Minors)* [2010] EWHC 1180 (Fam).

child was handed over to them but they were not domiciled in the UK and so ineligible to apply for a parental order. The judge was able to exercise a power under the Adoption and Children Act 2002 to confer parental responsibility on the couple to permit them to take the child home to Turkey and adopt the child there.[199]

14.33 Surrogacy in need of reform[200]

The cases discussed, a small sample of the many decisions on surrogacy, demonstrate that the law is sorely in need of reform. Many couples are unaware of the law governing surrogacy arrangements and the potential exists for exploitation of parties. How serious is the problem? The number of surrogacy arrangements is impossible to ascertain accurately. In 2019 the Law Commission (discussed below) pointed to a growing number of parental orders: from 117 in 2011 to 367 in 2018.[201] The number of surrogacy arrangements is likely to be higher given that not all intended parents seek parental orders.

In 1996 the government set up a review of the law relating to surrogacy.[202] The Surrogacy Review made a number of recommendations, which included maintaining the prohibition on paying surrogates for their services. A new Surrogacy Act should define expenses to exclude covert payments. Any agency which introduced couples and surrogates or offered advice on surrogacy would have to be registered with the Department of Health and Social Care (DHSC). A Code of Practice would be developed which agencies must abide by, setting out a model of good practice for couples and surrogates. The Code would seek to ensure frank exchanges of information and offer independent counselling to all involved. Prohibition on payments was vigorously opposed by the major surrogacy agency COTS (Childlessness Overcome Through Surrogacy) and a number of eminent scholars. The most telling criticism of the Surrogacy Review came from Michael Freeman,[203] who argued, first, that surrogates are entitled to payment and, second, that a ban on payment will drive surrogacy underground increasing risks of exploitation and harm the children. In the event, the report of the Surrogacy Review has simply mouldered on the shelves of the DHSC.

In 2022 the pressing need for more effective regulation of surrogacy is patent. In 2015 Surrogacy UK published a report recommending legal reform governing

199 *Re G (Surrogacy: Foreign Domicile)* [2007] EWHC 2814 (Fam).

200 See A Alghrani, D Griffiths and M Brazier, 'Surrogacy Law: From Piecemeal Tweaks to Sustained Review and Reform' in A Diduck, N Peleg and H Reece (eds), *Law In Society: Reflections on Children, Family, Culture and Philosophy: Essays in Honour of Michael Freeman* (2014) Brill Publishers, 425–453.

201 Law Commission, Scottish Law Commission, *Building Families Through Surrogacy: A New Law A Joint Consultation Paper* (2019).

202 Surrogacy Review.

203 M Freeman, 'Does Surrogacy Have a Future after Brazier?' (1999) 7 *Med Law Rev* 1.

issues such as attribution of parenthood and the payment of expenses.[204] In 2019 a joint Law Commission consultation was launched.[205] A response and draft bill is expected in 2023.[206] The consultation proposed a new pathway to legal parenthood which would in most cases make the intended parents the legal parents at birth unless the surrogate objects. Parental orders would be retained, but only as an alternative route for those who do not or cannot follow the new pathway. The welfare of the child would be assessed pre-conception in a manner akin to section 13(5) of the Human Fertilisation and Embryology Act 1990 discussed at 14.5 above. Non-profit surrogacy organisations would provide matching and facilitation services and they would potentially be regulated by the HFEA. The section 54 and 54A criteria currently used to determine whether a parental order can be granted would change. The Law Commission provisionally propose the removal of the requirement for the child to have a genetic link to one of the intended parents. Double donation would be accepted, allowing single people and couples where both are infertile to become legal parents. The proposals also intend to enhance openness and transparency so that the right that children have to know their heritage is better protected.

The form of regulation will not be settled, however, until the vexed question of payment is resolved. The Law Commission set out possible categories of payment that the law could allow intended parents to pay, from an allowance, to lost earnings, to compensation, to gifts. The arguments are finely balanced. We expect and receive payment for the use of our brains. Why should a surrogate not be paid for the use of her uterus? But should bodily services or body parts be traded? Can you buy children?[207] Proponents of payment argue that paying a surrogate for reproductive labour is not buying a child. Yet what couple would pay if the child is not surrendered? Most pro-payment campaigners argue that surrogacy contracts should remain unenforceable.[208] Is that logical? If the use of the uterus is no different from manual or intellectual labour, why should the surrogate not be obliged to honour her contract?

204 Surrogacy UK Working Group on Surrogacy Law Reform, *Surrogacy in the UK: Myth Busting and Reform – Report of the Surrogacy UK Working Group on Surrogacy Law* Reform (2015) and subsequently their *Surrogacy in the UK: Further Evidence for Reform – Second Report of the Surrogacy UK Working Group on Surrogacy Law Reform* (2018).

205 Law Commission, Scottish Law Commission, *Building Families Through Surrogacy: A New Law A Joint Consultation Paper* (2019). And see APPG, *Report on Understandings of the Law and Practice of Surrogacy* (2020).

206 Not every Law Commission report is implemented but the government has indicated support in this case.

207 See M Brazier, 'Can You Buy Children?' (1999) 11 *Child and Family Law Quarterly* 345.

208 With the honourable exceptions of COTS and *Mason and McCall Smith's Law and Medical Ethics*, at 8.116. And see Jackson, *Medical Law: Text, Cases and Materials*, pp 866–869.

Given the growth of surrogacy here and abroad, a ban on payments no longer looks feasible even to those who, like the first named author, might wish to affirm a gift relationship. If there is to be a market it needs to be overt and regulated. The provision for parenthood must be revisited and the option of pre-natal approvals considered. The task will be immense as surrogacy is now an international business.

Chapter 15

EMBRYO RESEARCH

15.1 The status of the embryo and embryo research[1]

The legal and moral status of the human embryo continues to attract controversy. For the devout Roman Catholic and many others, life is given by God and begins at conception, thus the deliberate destruction of an embryo, be it in the course of embryo research, or by abortion (which we discuss in Chapter 16), is the equivalent of killing you or us. Others contend that the human embryo has no greater moral status than a mouse embryo, and so neither research nor abortion is morally wrong. 'Gradualists' argue that the embryo acquires increasing moral claims as it develops in the womb.

The present English laws on embryo research attempt to reach a compromise in a debate in which there is no consensus. In 1990, Parliament, in the first Human Fertilisation and Embryology Act, sanctioned embryo research up to fourteen days when the primitive streak appears. Sections 3 and 4 also prohibit placing an embryo in an animal and the use of embryos for reproductive cloning. 'Pro-life' campaigners continue to fight to ban research. Others argue that the 14-day rule is arbitrary and could safely be extended.[2] Allowing an extension beyond fourteen days could aid research into the early development of the embryo and improve the safety of techniques such as mitochondrial donation which, as we saw in Chapter 14, aims to prevent maternal transmission of mitochondrial DNA diseases.

15.2 The ethical debate

The development of *in vitro* fertilisation (IVF) offered not just new means to overcome infertility, but also the capacity to develop medicine via research on embryos in the laboratory. The process of IVF generates far more embryos than will ever be implanted in a maternal womb. What should happen to the 'spare embryos'? John Harris argued that it cannot 'be morally worse to end

1 See generally, A Dyson and J Harris (eds), *Experiments on Embryos* (1999) Routledge.

2 I Hyun *et al*, 'Human Embryo Research Beyond the Primitive Streak' (2021) 371(6533) *Science* 998 and see ISSCR, *Guidelines for Stem Cell Research and Clinical Translation* (2021).

the life of an embryo *in vivo* than it is to do so *in vitro*'.[3] The law regulating abortion in England sanctioned the destruction of 210,860 fetuses in 2020.[4] Advocates of embryo research asked how society can logically accept abortion yet ban research. Both camps in the debate on embryo experiments link the questions of abortion and research.[5]

At the heart of the debate lies the question of the moral status of the developing embryo. When does it acquire the same right to protection as we enjoy? We will for the moment assume that the embryo is created the 'old-fashioned' way via fertilisation (even if fertilisation takes place in a Petri dish) rather than cell nuclear replacement (CNR). Is it at fertilisation, when a new unique genetic entity comes into being?[6] Or is it at some later stage in embryonic development? This might be at fourteen days, when the primitive streak forms,[7] or when brain activity is first discernible at eight to ten weeks.[8] Or is it much, much later, after birth? One school of philosophy argues thus:[9] Humanity is just another species of animal and as such has no greater moral status than any other animal. What gives rise to moral rights is not being a human animal but being a *person*. It is the capacity to value your own existence which gives a person rights, including the right to life. Embryos, and newborn infants, lack that capacity and so are *not* persons. So at no stage of embryonic or fetal development, inside or outside the womb, does the embryo or fetus have moral status.

Each ethical school of thought marshals impressive arguments in support of its thesis. Argument that the embryo enjoys full human status from fertilisation is an argument often resting on theological grounds. If you believe that human life is divinely created in the image of God, and that human beings possess an immortal immaterial soul, you are unlikely to find any argument based on personhood acceptable. Any concept of human life as special *per se* is irrelevant to those who support the personhood thesis. JK Mason advanced a rather different argument, one which allows a clearer demarcation between abortion and embryo research. Mason argued that the embryo in the Petri dish can be viewed as either a human being or as no more than a 'laboratory artefact'. Arguably, the crucial factor that brings an embryo within the moral

3 JM Harris, *The Value of Life* (1985) Routledge & Kegan Paul, p 117.
4 DHSC, *Abortion Statistics, England and Wales: 2020* (2021).
5 See M Brazier, 'Embryos' "Rights": Abortion and Research' in MDA Freeman (ed), *Medicine, Ethics and Law* (1988) Stevens, pp 9–23.
6 See O O'Donovan, *Begotten Not Made* (1984) Oxford University Press; A Holland 'A Fortnight of My Life is Missing: A Discussion of the Status of the Pre-embryo' (1990) 7 *Journal of Applied Philosophy* 25.
7 As concluded in the *Report of the Committee of Inquiry into Human Fertilisation and Embryology* (hereafter Warnock Report), pp 63–64.
8 See in particular, M Lockwood, 'When Does a Life Begin?' in M Lockwood (ed), *Moral Dilemmas in Medicine* (1988) Oxford University Press.
9 See Harris, *The Value of Life*, pp 18–25; and 'Embryos and Hedgehogs: On the Moral Status of the Embryo' in Dyson and Harris (eds), *Experiments on Embryos*, p 65; and see J Glover, *Causing Death and Saving Lives* (1977) Penguin.

community of humankind, and so entitles it to protection, is implantation.[10] Implantation in the womb connects the embryo to its mother and grants it capacity for meaningful development.[11]

How should the law respond to such a divergence of moral opinion? Consensus is impossible to attain. Proponents of embryo research argue that no one is compelled to participate in research. A liberal democracy should respect divergent moral views. But that is anathema to 'pro-life' groups. It is rather like saying that if a sufficient number of people decide redheads are not human and have no moral claim on society, anyone who holds that belief may kill off any redhead he meets. Of course, no 'pro-redhead' will be required to join in the slaughter! So what is the difference between redheaded adults and embryos? On any analysis, the redhead enjoys moral and legal rights. She is without doubt a person. The embryo's true nature is unprovable. One of the authors of this work happens to believe that from fertilisation the embryo is *very probably* of the same moral value as herself. It is a unique being created in the image of God, in whom she believes. She cannot prove that belief. But then nor can those who maintain that humanity is just another animal species prove their contention. The verdict on the nature of the embryo must be 'not proven'.

What consequences should the 'not-proven' nature of the embryo have for its legal status? It must be accorded recognition and respect. If its claims to rights conflict with the claims of an entity whose status is beyond doubt, its claims may be subordinated to that entity's. Thus, if there is a conflict between the claims of the embryo and the rights of the mother, indubitably a legal person, the mother's rights take precedence. A belief that the embryo must be respected as fully human from fertilisation requires that a woman rejects abortion as an option for herself. As that belief is unprovable, she cannot legitimately enforce it on other women.[12] Embryo research, by contrast, gives rise to no such direct conflict of rights. The question becomes whether society can legitimately destroy an entity which may be fully human in nature and status. The embryo should be given the benefit of the doubt. Justifications have always been advanced for permitting the killing of indubitably human persons in certain cases. It might be argued that the public 'good' expected from embryo research justifies destruction of these 'maybe' human persons. The onus of proof lies on those who advocate research.

What are the goods which may flow from research? They include developments in medicine for which we already have evidence of proven effect such as improvement in fertility treatments[13] and the detection and 'cure' of genetic

10 JK Mason, *Medico-Legal Aspects of Reproduction and Parenthood* (2nd edn, 1998) Routledge, p 234; GT Laurie, SHE Harmon and ES Dove, *Mason and McCall Smith's Law and Medical Ethics* (11th edn, 2019) Oxford University Press, at 8.74.

11 JK Mason, *Human Life and Medical Practice* (1988) Edinburgh University Press, p 94.

12 For a powerful argument that even if the embryo is presumed to enjoy full human status, abortion remains defensible, see J Jarvis Thompson, 'A Defence of Abortion' in RM Dworkin (ed), *The Philosophy of Law* (1977) Oxford University Press, p 112. But note the response by JM Finnis, 'The Rights and Wrongs of Abortion' in the same book, p 129.

13 See Chapter 14 above.

defects and disease.[14] Most notably at present we should note the potential for the development of stem cell therapies, 'therapeutic cloning', the use of pluripotent stem cells retrieved from early embryonic tissue to transplant into sick adults and children.[15] Embryonic stem cells extracted from the blastocyst have the potential both to multiply endlessly and can be manipulated to form different cells within the body: they are pluripotent at that stage of development and not confined to becoming say a brain cell or a kidney cell. Stem cell therapies offer the hope that regenerative medicine will produce radical new ways of treating a range of diseases, in particular neurodegenerative conditions such as Parkinson's and injuries to the spinal cord. The benefit of such therapies is not disputed. How much could be achieved without research on human embryos is. At the heart of the dispute lies evidence derived from research on *induced* pluripotent stem (iPS) cells. It is suggested that the need for stem cells harvested from embryos could be eliminated by retrieving adult stem cells and manipulating those cells to operate like embryonic stem cells. There would then be no need for embryonic stem cells.[16] Some predicted that iPS cells would oust embryonic stem cell research but that has not (yet) happened due in part to concerns about safety and cost.[17] It is difficult for a layperson to evaluate the scientific debate, partly because scientific opinion on the merits of research seems to depend on what stance the scientist takes on the ethics of research. However, if the 'pro-research' camp confronts some difficulty establishing that the manifest benefit of research justifies the destruction of arguably human embryos, the 'anti-research' camp has a fundamental problem of its own. If an embryo is arguably human, it is wrong to destroy it, to experiment on it for a purpose not designed to benefit it, so that it must ultimately perish. If it is wrong to destroy embryos for research purposes, it must also be wrong to destroy them in the course of infertility treatments using IVF. As long as 'spare' embryos are created, surplus embryos are doomed to die. To return to a practice of harvesting only one egg from the woman, and so creating and implanting just one embryo, was thought to be a fatal blow to IVF.[18]

It is difficult to argue that it is ethical to destroy embryos to alleviate infertility and yet unethical to destroy embryos in order to improve our knowledge and treatment of genetic disease. Opponents of research should logically also have opposed the creation of multiple embryos for IVF.[19]

14 Notably the development of Pre-Implantation Genetic Testing: see 14.21 above.

15 The science and the ethical issues are lucidly explained in *Mason and McCall Smith's Law and Medical Ethics*, 10.78–10.86.

16 See E Jackson, *Medical Law: Text, Cases and Materials* (5th edn, 2019) Oxford University Press, pp 707–708.

17 D Cyranoski, 'How Human Embryonic Stem Cells Sparked a Revolution' (2018) 555 *Nature* 428.

18 Clinicians are now suggesting that modern treatment may achieve much greater success with single embryo transplant (SET) at less risk to the woman. However, even with SET, multiple embryos will be created and stored and so the issue of the fate of the 'spare' embryo remains moot.

19 See M Brazier, 'The Challenge for Parliament: A Critique of the White Paper on Human Fertilisation and Embryology' in Dyson and Harris, *Experiments on Embryos*, p 142.

15.3 Embryo research: the Human Fertilisation and Embryology Act 1990 (as amended)

At this point the reader is advised to apply a cold flannel to their head! To begin to understand the regulation of embryo research in the UK, we need to examine the Human Fertilisation and Embryology Act 1990 as amended by the later 2008 Act. We can do little more than introduce the legislation. One initial point should be made. The UK legislation now distinguishes sharply between those 'permitted' embryos, eggs and sperm that can be used in fertility treatment and those embryos and gametes which must not be implanted in a human but may be used in research and the development of stem cell therapies.

The 1990 Act was, and even as amended remains, based on a compromise advanced in the Warnock Report of 1984.[20] The human embryo should be accorded special status and treated with respect[21] but that 'status' is far short of the status to be accorded to any born human. Legislation currently permits research on embryos but only if licensed by the Human Fertilisation and Embryology Authority (HFEA),[22] subject to a strict limit of fourteen days ('not counting any time during which the embryo was stored'),[23] and a number of other prohibitions. The 1990 Act expressly prohibited certain activities, seeking to ban both reproductive cloning and attempts to create human–animal hybrids. Amendments in the 2008 Act provide for both stem cell therapies ('therapeutic cloning') and for what are now called 'human admixed embryos'. But while the HFEA may now license research in these fields, the Act in its rules on permitted embryos ensures that no cloned or hybrid embryo may be implanted in a woman.[24] Other restrictions apply. Human embryos or gametes may not be implanted in animals, nor may animal embryos be inserted in humans.[25] A non-human primate could not be used as a surrogate to gestate a human embryo. The genetic structure of an embryo may not be altered 'except in such circumstances (if any) as may be specified in' regulations to be made by the Human Fertilisation and Embryology Authority (HFEA).[26] Such regulations have now been made to allow for mitochondrial treatment, discussed at 14.24 above.

The original rules governing embryo research in the Act centred on two principles. We suggest that the 2008 amendments changed the application but not the premise of those principles:

(1) The Act implicitly accords respect to the embryo from fertilisation, but up until the development of the primitive streak, the 'goods' to be expected from research outweigh the interests of the embryo.

20 Warnock Report and see 14.1 above.
21 Baroness Warnock subsequently regretted that her committee endorsed any notion of respect for the embryo; see Jackson, *Medical Law: Text, Cases and Materials*, p 697.
22 See s 3(1). Breach is a criminal offence, punishable by up to ten years' imprisonment. Any prosecution under the Act will require the consent of the DPP; s 42.
23 s 3(3)(a).
24 See ss 3 and 3ZA.
25 See s 3(2) and s 3(3)(b).
26 Schedule 2, para 3(4).

(2) The Act sought to allay fears of a science-fiction nightmare in which scientists freely create all sorts of clones, hybrids and other monsters. It should be noted that until the enactment of the Human Fertilisation and Embryology Act 1990 embryos *in vitro* enjoyed no legal protection at all. The wording of abortion legislation prohibiting 'procurement of miscarriage' meant that in theory 'test-tube' embryos could then be grown and destroyed at will.

Subject to the express prohibitions above, the HFEA was given a remarkably free hand by the Act. Legislation allows embryos to be created solely for research purposes. Schedule 2 outlines what a research licence may authorise. First the HFEA must be satisfied that the proposed research is necessary and desirable for an authorised purpose. Five specific purposes were originally set out in 1990:

(1) promoting advances in the treatment of infertility;
(2) increasing knowledge about the causes of congenital disease;
(3) increasing knowledge about the causes of miscarriage;
(4) developing more effective techniques of contraception;
(5) developing methods for detecting the presence of gene or chromosomal abnormalities in embryos before implantation.

Those five specific purposes may be regarded as justification for the destruction of embryos, aimed at improving medicine and increasing human happiness, designed to re-assure those who were doubtful about, but not adamantly opposed to, research. To those named purposes was added an apparently innocuous phrase 'or for such other purposes as may be specified in regulations'.

15.4 Embryo research and 'cloning'

For a short while from 1990 to about 1998 the fury of the embryo research debate abated. The birth of Dolly, the cloned sheep, changed all that. Dolly was created by a process of CNR. The nucleus of an unfertilised egg was removed ('enucleated') and a stem cell introduced to the empty cell and fused by applying an electrical impulse. The egg cell then began to divide and develop as an embryo. The embryo was implanted in a surrogate 'mother'. CNR replacement has been successful in creating (cloning) many other species of mammals albeit with a high failure rate and incidence of abnormalities.[27] There is no scientific reason why this process could not (in theory) be replicated in humans. Two principal and very different purposes could drive the development of CNR in humans.

[27] Department of Environment, Food and Rural Affairs, *Commission Report on Animal Cloning for Food Production* (2010) COM(10) 585, para 1.2: 'The overall success rate for cloning procedures is less than 10% in bovine animals and between 5 and 17% in pigs ...'

(1) Obviously attempts could be made to create a child, a copy of its lone parent sharing most of his or her DNA. Many British scientists abhor the notion of 'reproductive cloning'. A number of eminent ethicists argue no case has been made out sufficient to justify banning 'reproductive cloning'.[28] As we saw in Chapter 14, reproductive cloning is prohibited in the UK.

(2) Stem cells could be collected from the cloned embryo. As we have noted above, embryonic stem cells retain their pluripotency and can be cultured to develop into different sorts of tissue, or even potentially grown into organs. 'Therapeutic cloning', or stem cell therapy as it is more usually styled today, offers a tantalising range of scientific benefits. In the case of a patient with a neurodegenerative disease, an embryo could be created by CNR using DNA from one of the patient's own cells and stem cells taken from the resulting embryo could be used to create tissue to repair their damaged brain. As the cells used were 'theirs' there would be no risk of rejection.

In 1998, the HFEA joined the Human Genetic Advisory Commission (HGAC) to consider the ethics of cloning in both its guises. Their report[29] recommended that regulations under the 1990 Act should be extended to ban reproductive cloning and allow the HFEA to authorise procedures:

(a) to extract embryonic stem cells for research on the possible treatment benefits in a wide range of disorders by replacing cells which have become damaged or diseased; and

(b) to conduct research into the treatment of some rare but serious inherited disorders carried in maternal mitochondria.

Regulations to permit stem cell therapy were approved by Parliament in January 2001.[30] These regulations purported to authorise the following additional research purposes:

- increasing knowledge about development of embryos;
- increasing knowledge about serious disease;
- enabling such knowledge to be applied in developing treatment for serious disease.

The regulations were made on an assumption that CNR fell within the 1990 Act. Pro-life groups challenged the regulations, arguing that embryos created

[28] See, for example, J Harris, 'Goodbye Dolly? – The Ethics of Human Cloning' (1997) 23 *J Med Ethics* 353.

[29] HFEA/HGAC, *Cloning Issues in Reproduction, Science and Medicine* (1998). And see J Harris, *Clones, Genes and Immortality* (1998) Oxford University Press. And see Expert Group of the CMO, *Stem Cell Research: Medical Progress and Responsibility* (2000) DH. See also House of Lords, *Stem Cell Research* (2002) HL 83(i); Nuffield Council on Bioethics, *Stem Cell Therapy: A Discussion* (2000).

[30] The Human Fertilisation and Embryology (Research Purposes) Regulations 2001, SI 2001/188. Such was the public concern about their regulations that they were immediately reviewed (and in the event approved) by a Select Committee of the House of Lords; see ibid House of Lords, *Stem Cell Research*.

by CNR fell wholly outside the 1990 Act and were not covered by section 3(3)(d), which had been intended to ban cloning. Section 3(3)(d) only barred replacing a nucleus of a cell taken from an embryo with a nucleus taken from any person or an embryo. CNR removes the nucleus from an egg cell, not an embryo. The government argued that nonetheless reproductive cloning was effectively outlawed because the HFEA would never license any attempt at reproductive cloning and creating an embryo without an HFEA licence is a crime. But 'embryo', for the purpose of the unamended 1990 Act, was defined as follows: 'embryo means a live human embryo where fertilisation is complete.'[31] If CNR is used to create the embryo, *fertilisation* never takes place.[32] CNR involves propagation not fertilisation. Did it fall outside the 1990 Act and so CNR 'cloning' (for either therapeutic or reproductive purposes) could take place without a licence?

The All-Party Pro-Life Alliance challenged the regulations allowing stem cell therapy. They argued that the regulations were *ultra vires* because an embryo created by CNR was not an embryo within the definition provided in the 1990 Act. Crane J agreed that an embryo created otherwise than by fertilisation fell outside the Act.[33] The government rushed through the Human Reproductive Cloning Act 2001. That Act made implanting a CNR embryo in a woman a criminal offence. The status of the regulations governing stem cell therapy remained in limbo. The Court of Appeal came to the government's rescue.[34] The House of Lords upheld the Court of Appeal.[35] In both courts, moral controversy was translated into an exercise in statutory interpretation. Lord Bingham declared[36] that the 'basic task of the court is to ascertain and give effect to the true meaning of what Parliament has said in the enactment to be construed'. The 1990 Act must 'be read in the historical context of the situation which led to its enactment'. Parliament, their Lordships concluded, never intended to distinguish between live embryos produced by fertilisation, and embryos produced without fertilisation. Parliament, in 1990, would have been unaware that the latter process was possible. The fundamental purpose of section 3(1)(a) of the Act was to provide protection for embryos created outside the human body: 'The protective purpose was plainly not intended to be tied to the particular way in which an embryo might be created.'[37]

Amendments made by the 2008 Act, give statutory endorsement to the earlier regulations allowing and controlling stem cell therapies. What of the moral arguments? Does it follow that anyone who in 1990 was sceptical about the legitimacy of embryo research should be outraged by developments allowing

31 Section 1(1)(a).
32 See M Brazier, 'Regulating the Reproduction Business?' (1999) 8 *Med Law Rev* 166.
33 *R (Quintavalle) v Secretary of State for Health* [2001] EWHC 918 (Admin).
34 *R (Quintaville) v Secretary of State for Health* [2002] 2 All ER 625, CA.
35 [2003] 2 All ER 113. The House of Lords, however, did also confirm that s 3(3)(a) of the Act did not impose an absolute prohibition on CNR.
36 [2003] 2 All ER 113, at 118.
37 Ibid, at 126 per Lord Steyn.

stem cell therapies, 'therapeutic cloning'? It is no more than a logical outcome of permitting research at all. If the 'goods' of more successful fertility treatments justified destroying embryos, it is difficult to say that the 'good' of helping seriously ill patients does not. The argument may be raised that use of embryos is not essential to achieve that end. We have seen that adult stem cells could be treated to recover pluripotency. It might just take longer to do the research. But CNR forces some reconsideration of the basis of opposition for embryo research. Embryos created from fertilisation of egg by sperm result (normally) in the creation of a unique new genetic entity. What is the nature of an embryo created by CNR using our nuclei, our DNA? If used solely for stem cell therapy, is it different from taking a skin graft from a leg to treat burns on an arm?

Amendments to the 1990 Act clarify the status of CNR embryos and give statutory endorsement to the development of stem cell therapies. First, section 1(b) re-defines an embryo as 'an egg that is in the process of fertilisation *or is undergoing any other process capable of resulting in an embryo*' (our emphasis). Thus CNR embryos are 'captured' by the Act and so would be embryos created by any other process as yet unknown. Schedule 2, paragraph 3A of the 1990 Act (as amended) formally extends the list of purposes for which the HFEA may grant a research licence adding to the original five:

(a) increasing knowledge about serious disease or other serious medical conditions,[38]
(b) developing treatments for serious disease or other serious medical condition
(c) increasing knowledge about the cause of any congenital disease or other congenital condition that does not fall within paragraph (a).

But it is crucial to remember that for a licence to be granted for any of these purposes (and/or for the use of human admixed embryos), the applicant must establish that the use of embryos is necessary.[39] Those opposed to embryo research will no doubt seek to argue that it is not necessary, as the objectives above could be met by using iPS cells.

15.5 Hybrid and chimera embryos

Before the amendments to the 1990 Act, once the regulations to permit stem cell therapies had been declared lawful by the courts under the unamended Act, the HFEA granted licences to allow the use of embryos to develop stem cell therapies, but scientists immediately faced a resource problem. Developing CNR embryos needs a plentiful supply of eggs to 'empty' and into which the nucleus cell can be inserted to create embryos, from which embryonic stem cells can then be cultured. Human eggs for the purposes of egg donation in

[38] The addition of serious conditions to serious diseases in the Act is to cover research into treatment for such conditions as spinal injury.
[39] Human Fertilisation and Embryology Act, Sch 3A.

fertility treatment are in short supply, never mind human eggs for research such as this. However, human eggs are not necessary for the purpose. A cow or rabbit egg will do just as well; sometimes referred to as cytoplasmic hybrid embryos, the resulting embryo remains more than 99.9 per cent 'human'. Only the mitochondrial DNA from the animal egg remains and any stem cells retrieved are 100 per cent human.

The 2008 Act amended the 1990 Act to permit the HFEA to license research on what the Act now terms human admixed embryos. It is worth repeating that the Act still prohibits implanting any such embryo in a woman (because they are not permitted embryos) and equally bans implanting a human admixed embryo in any animal.[40] Section 4A defines human admixed embryos to include not only the cytoplasmic hybrids described above but a range of other embryos created by mixing animal and human gametes. So human–animal hybrids mixing human and animal gametes are allowed as are transgenic embryos in which animal DNA has been introduced, and chimeras where a human embryo has been altered by the addition of animal cells. And finally provision is made for other hybrids/chimeras subject to the condition that the animal DNA is not predominant.[41]

It may soon be possible to create targeted organs for transplant in humans through 'interspecies blastocyst complementation'.[42] The idea is this. An animal embryo is created which lacks a gene for the production of a particular organ. Human iPS cells are then injected into the animal embryo which are used to generate a functional human organ matched to a particular individual. The iPS cells contribute to the organ but only minimally elsewhere in the chimera embryo. The hope is that eventually (and subject to reform of the 1990 Act) organs could be harvested from chimera animals. In contrast to transplantation from another human, there would be no need for the organ recipient to take immunosuppressants for the rest of their life. In contrast to xenotransplantation, discussed at 20.17 below, the organ produced would have the profile of a human organ rather than an animal organ genetically modified to reduce the chances of rejection in humans. The International Society for Stem Cell Research recommended that more research is needed before genes of human embryos or gametes intended for implantation are edited.[43]

15.6 Artificial gametes and embryos

Developments in stem cell research open up the possibility that scientists may be able to manipulate stem cells to create artificial gametes. That is to say that stem cells taken from an infertile man or woman could be used to create

40 Section 4A(4).

41 See *Mason and McCall Smith's Law and Medical Ethics*, 8.05–8.07.

42 For an analysis of the ethical implications see JJ Koplin and J Savulescu, 'Time to Rethink the Law on Part-Human Chimeras' (2019) 6(1) *Journal of Law and Biosciences* 37.

43 ISSCR, *Guidelines for Stem Cell Research and Clinical Translation* (2021).

functioning sperm and eggs, even that stem cells from a male could be used to create artificial eggs and vice versa. Research into the development of artificial gametes remains lawful in the UK but section 3ZA of the Act prohibits the use of any artificial gametes in treatment by providing that only permitted sperm and eggs may be so used and defining such gametes as extracted from the testes of a man or ovaries of a woman with no alteration of the nuclear or mitochondrial DNA of sperm or eggs.

In 2021 scientists created early embryo growth (termed 'blastoids') from human stem cells.[44] Creating cell clusters that mimic the function of human blastocysts holds promise for scientific innovation but raises ethical questions as to how far the rules that apply to human embryo research (such as the 14-day rule) will apply to blastoids. In conjunction with artificial womb technology[45] it raises the potential of artificial reproduction.

15.7 Genome editing

Emmanuelle Charpentier and Jennifer Doudna won the 2020 Nobel Prize in Chemistry for their development of CRISPR-Cas9, a tool that can cut away strands of DNA and removes, adds to or otherwise alters sections of the DNA sequence. CRISPR, which emerged in 2012 and has since developed rapidly, can potentially correct genetic defects. It also has potential to engineer mutations into human embryos, which could be passed on to future generations. CRISPR has been injected into the body of patients to correct degenerative eye disorders. Genome editing human embryos intended for fertility treatment is currently unlawful in the United Kingdom, and the International Society for Stem Cell Research (ISSCR) in 2021 recommended that this position be maintained until research has advanced sufficiently to reduce the risks. It can, however, be utilised in research, subject to the 14-day rule.

We saw in Chapter 14 that, from 2015, Regulations allowed mitochondrial donation treatment, where embryos or eggs are made from nuclear genetic material (which controls the future child's traits) and donated mitochondria (which provides the power for cells).[46] Further Regulations could in theory amend the Human Fertilisation and Embryology Act 1990 to permit modification of the *nuclear* DNA. In 2018, the Nuffield Council on Bioethics considered that heritable genome editing *could* one day be ethically acceptable subject to two provisos. First, the intention must be to secure the welfare of children born as a consequence, whether by preventing the child developing a serious disease or otherwise. Second it should be consistent with principles of social justice and solidarity, which means it must not marginalise groups

[44] See for example G Guo *et al*, 'Human Naive Epiblast Cells Possess Unrestricted Lineage Potential' (2021) 28(6) *Cell Stem Cell* 1040; L Yu *et al*, 'Blastocyst-like Structures Generated from Human Pluripotent Stem Cells' (2021) 591 *Nature* 620.

[45] See 16.15 below.

[46] Human Fertilisation and Embryology (Mitochondrial Donation) Regulations 2015, SI 2015/572. See 14.24 above.

within society.[47] In contravention of these principles, in a world first in 2019, Chinese biophysicist He Jiankui announced the birth of twin girls dubbed Lulu and Nana, whose genomes had been edited, ostensibly to protect them from HIV. The application of genome editing in living patients was experimental and widely condemned as premature and unethical. A Chinese court sentenced him to three years in prison for illegal medical practices.[48]

In 2020 evidence emerged that CRISPR can risk undesirable and unwanted changes to the genome.[49] A 2020 international report[50] has, like the Nuffield Council, argued that heritable genome editing *could* be ethically appropriate. However, the report argues that several restrictions should apply, including its limitation to the treatment of serious monogenic diseases causing premature death where pre-implantation genetic testing (discussed 14.20 above) would not be appropriate or sufficient. He Jiankui's experiment did not satisfy these criteria.

15.8 Calls for reform

The 14-day rule, recommended in the Warnock Report and adopted in the 1990 Act, set out a somewhat arbitrary line that coincides with the development of the 'primitive streak' marking the onset of the process by which the neural tube and nervous system develop. It constituted a regulatory compromise which was sufficient to build public trust whilst allowing scope for scientific development. Many other countries adopted the same approach. Sophie McCully argues that the time has come for change. Extending it to twenty-eight days would facilitate research into what she terms the 'black box period' of development when germ cells are developed and from which the nervous system, placenta and heart emerge.[51] She argues that such an extension would retain the bright-line approach that has worked so well. Arguably the extension would not need to go beyond this point given that embryonic tissue from twenty-eight days could be obtained from fetal tissue, such as aborted fetuses. In 2021 the ISSCR paved the way for the lifting of the widely adopted 14-day rule, subject to robust review.[52]

Embryo research brings with it the possibility of children inheriting genomes in multiple ways. In Chapter 14 we considered regulated and broadly accepted practices of donated gametes, surrogacy, pre-implantation genetic testing and

47 Nuffield Council on Bioethics, *Genome Editing and Human Reproduction* (2018).

48 I Sample, 'Chinese Scientist who Edited Babies' Genes Jailed for Three Years' *Guardian* (2019) 31 Dec. And see discussion in S Pattinson, *Law at the Frontiers of Biomedicine* (2023) Hart, chapter 3.

49 See MV Zuccaro *et al*, 'Allele-Specific Chromosome Removal after Cas9 Cleavage in Human Embryos' (2020) 183(6) *Cell* P1650; H Ledford, 'CRISPR Gene Editing in Human Embryos Wreaks Chromosomal Mayhem' *Nature* (2020) 25 June.

50 National Academy of Medicine *et al*, *Heritable Human Genome Editing* (2020).

51 S McCully, 'The Time has Come to Extend the 14-day Limit' (2021) 47 *J Med Ethics* e66.

52 ISSCR, *Guidelines for Stem Cell Research and Clinical Translation* (2021).

mitochondrial donation. In this chapter we have looked at emergent biotechnologies such as reproductive cloning, chimera and hybrid embryos, artificial gametes and genome editing. Some methods offer solutions for people who cannot have a child of their own and some present opportunities to bear a child that will be less likely to carry genetic disease. In all cases the welfare of the child should be a driving force for change. This should include consideration of the child's interest in knowing their genetic heritage.

Chapter 16

ABORTION[1]

16.1 Embryo to fetus: fetus to baby

An embryo *in vitro* will not be allowed to develop beyond fourteen days from fertilisation. What of the embryo *in vivo*, growing and developing in the pregnant woman's womb? By twelve weeks, the embryo will, if seen on an ultrasound scan, bear a distinct resemblance to a baby[2] and from then on will usually be termed a fetus. In many legal systems, the protection given to the embryo/fetus is extended as the pregnancy progresses, and the fetus develops. Thus, in France, abortion is allowed on demand up to fourteen weeks' gestation, and from then is permissible only on the ground of risk to the pregnant woman's health. In the USA, the Supreme Court in *Roe v Wade*[3] declared that any restriction on abortion in the first twelve weeks of pregnancy was unconstitutional, as a violation of the pregnant woman's right to privacy. States could regulate abortion to protect maternal health from twelve to twenty-four weeks, and from viability (between twenty and twenty-eight weeks) the interests of the fetus took precedence over the interests of the pregnant woman. *Roe v Wade* adopted an openly gradualist approach to the conflict of rights between the pregnant woman and fetus.

For some states, the destruction of the fetus can only be justifiable, if at all, where the pregnant woman's life is at risk. Even in such a case, abortion is still not lawful in some countries. A near-total ban on abortion came into force in Poland in 2020.[4] A shift in the ideological leanings of the US Supreme Court followed the appointment of conservative Justices under Donald Trump's

1 We are grateful to Dr Chloe E Romanis for helpful comments on a draft of this chapter.

2 D Kirklin, 'The Role of Medical Imaging in the Abortion Debate' (2004) 30 *J Med Ethics* 426.

3 (1973) 93 S Ct 705. Though since *Roe v Wade*, anti-abortion campaigners have ceaselessly sought to reverse the decision or limit its impact; see GT Laurie, SHE Harmon and ES Dove, *Mason and McCall Smith's Law and Medical Ethics* (11th edn, 2019) Oxford University Press, pp 341–343.

4 A Gliszczynska-Grabias and W Sadurski, 'The Judgment That Wasn't (but which Nearly Brought Poland to a Standstill) (2021) 17(1) *European Constitutional Law Review* 130.

presidency. States passed legislation to limit abortion rights only for appeals courts to strike them down on the basis that they conflicted with *Roe v Wade*. However, in 2022 an attempt by the single abortion provider in Mississippi to challenge a law banning most abortions after 15 weeks' gestation as unconstitutional failed. In the landmark decision of *Dobbs v Jackson Women's Health Organization*[5] the Supreme Court overruled *Roe* by six votes to three. It found that the US Constitution does not explicitly or implicitly confer a right to abortion. Notwithstanding public protests, several states subsequently placed restrictions on abortion.

In Europe, the majority of the European Court of Human Rights (ECtHR) in *Vo v France*[6] dodged the central question of fetal status.[7] They held that the question of when a right of life accrued fell within the margin of appreciation allowed to contracting states. This was a question unresolved among European countries, and there was no European consensus on scientific and legal definitions of the beginning of life. In 2010, three women went to the ECtHR to challenge Irish laws that failed to provide access to safe and lawful abortion for women whose health was imperilled by pregnancy. The ECtHR allowed one of the three claims but stopped well short of ruling that draconian restrictions on abortion in Ireland violated Article 8 of the Convention.[8] Eight years later, a referendum in Ireland voted to repeal the Eighth Amendment of the Constitution Act 1983, which had recognised the equal right to life of the unborn child and the pregnant woman. Subsequently the Health (Regulation of Termination of Pregnancy) Act 2018 legalised abortion on request up to twelve weeks of pregnancy, subject to a mandatory waiting period.[9]

In subsequent sections we will set out the Abortion Act 1967 that applies in England, Wales and Scotland. It does not apply in Northern Ireland,[10] where, until recently, it was a criminal offence to have or perform an abortion in most circumstances. In 2017 the British government decided to fund women who travelled from Northern Ireland to seek abortion in England, though a Supreme Court majority judgment had concluded there was no legal duty to do so.[11] A year later, another majority in the Supreme Court held that the law in Northern Ireland, insofar as it prohibited abortion in cases of rape, incest and fatal fetal abnormality, was incompatible with the right in Article

5 No 19-1382, 597 US (2022).

6 [2004] 2 FLR 577; see JK Mason, 'What's in a Name?: The Vagaries of *Vo v France*' [2005] *Child and Family Law Quarterly* 97. And see *Evans v United Kingdom* (2008) 46 EHRR 34.

7 See K O'Donovan, 'Taking a Neutral Stance on the Legal Protection of the Fetus' (2006) 14 *Med Law Rev* 115.

8 *A, B and C v Ireland* [2010] ECHR 2032, ECHR 25579/05.

9 Shortly afterwards, the Isle of Man Abortion Reform Act 2019 decriminalised abortion in the first fourteen weeks of pregnancy.

10 On which see S Sheldon *et al*, '"Too Much, Too Indigestible, Too Fast"? The Decades of Struggle for Abortion Law Reform in Northern Ireland' (2020) 83(4) MLR 761.

11 *R (A and B) v Secretary of State for Health* [2017] UKSC 41. On appeal from [2015] EWCA Civ 771. See H Dindjer, 'Devolution, Abortion, and Respect' (2018) 134 *LQR* 187.

8 of the European Convention on Human Rights (ECHR) to respect for private and family life.[12] The appeal was dismissed, however, on a procedural issue as to legal standing. Subsequently, the Abortion (Northern Ireland) Regulations 2020[13] decriminalised abortion. The reception of the Regulations was mixed, and commissioning of services slow to come about, particularly when the COVID-19 pandemic disrupted services. In 2021, Regulations[14] were laid before Parliament to implement recommendations from a 2018 UN Committee on the Elimination of Discrimination Against Women (CEDAW) report to operationalise the new approach.[15]

16.2 Criminal abortion[16]

The Abortion Act 1967 applies in Scotland, England and Wales. In Scotland, abortion was governed by the common law until the 1967 Act. The matter was reserved to the UK Parliament until devolution to the Scottish Parliament in the Scotland Act 2016. In England and Wales, the law relating to criminal abortion is still to be found in sections 58 and 59 of the Offences against the Person Act 1861. Strictly speaking, all that the Abortion Act 1967 does is create defences to charges under the 1861 Act. Section 58 of that Act makes it a criminal offence punishable by a maximum of life imprisonment (1) for any woman, being with child, unlawfully to do any act with intent to procure a miscarriage,[17] and (2) for any other person unlawfully to do an act with intent to procure the miscarriage of any woman.[18] Self-induced abortion by the woman herself is criminal only if the woman is in fact pregnant. Any act by a third party is criminal regardless of whether or not the woman can be proved to be pregnant. This limited protection afforded to the woman extends

12 *Northern Ireland Human Rights Commission for Judicial Review (Northern Ireland: Abortion* [2018] UKSC 27. On appeal from [2017] NICA 42. See also *Re Ewarts' Application* [2019] NIQB 8.

13 SI 2020/503, following the repeal, by s 9 of the Northern Ireland (Executive Formation etc) Act 2019, of ss 58 and 59 of the Offences against the Person Act 1861. Replacing SI 2020/345 which were revoked to correct drafting errors.

14 SI 2021/365, conferring power to the Secretary of State to direct the NI Ministers regarding actions to implement the recommendations in paragraphs 85 and 86 of the 'Report of the Inquiry concerning the United Kingdom of Great Britain and Northern Ireland under Article 8 of the Optional Protocol to the Convention on the Elimination of All Forms of Discrimination against Women', CEDAW/C/OP.8/GBR/1 (2018) and CEDAW/C/OP.8/GBR/3 (2019) (hereafter CEDAW Report).

15 CEDAW Report, paras 85 and 86.

16 See, generally, S Sheldon, *Beyond Control: Medical Power and Abortion Law* (1997) Pluto; E Lee (ed), *Abortion: Whose Right?* (2002) Hodder and Stoughton.

17 Sarah Catt was convicted under s 58 after she took poison to abort her own child at close to full term. Her original prison sentence of eight years was reduced to three and a half years on appeal; *R v Catt (Sarah Louise)* [2013] EWCA (Crim) 1187. And see A Kindred 'Boyfriend Force-Feeds Abortion Pill to Pregnant Partner After Nurse Steals Drug' *Mirror* (2021) 22 September.

18 See *R v Fletcher (Matthew)* [2014] EWCA (Crim) 1876: a man obtained pills on the Internet to induce his girlfriend to miscarry despite her settled wish to keep the child.

only to cases where she acts entirely alone. If she seeks help from a doctor, or any other person, she may be charged with aiding and abetting that person to commit the offence of criminal abortion[19] or of conspiracy with them to commit that offence.[20] Section 59 makes it an offence to 'unlawfully supply or procure any poison or other noxious thing, or any instrument or thing whatsoever, knowing that the same is intended to be unlawfully used or employed with intent to procure the miscarriage of any woman'.

A possible lacuna in the law is to be seen in the extraordinary case of *R v A*.[21] Mr A set up a deliberate scheme of deception to seek to ensure that his young wife (to whom he was unhappily married) underwent an abortion without her consent or even her knowledge. Mrs A spoke no English and he took her to two clinics attempting to deceive doctors into believing that his wife wanted a termination. Both attempts failed and the wife was very upset when she discovered on the second occasion that she was booked into an abortion clinic. She finally managed to escape from her husband who was convicted under section 59 of the Offences Against the Person Act. His conviction was, however, overturned in the Court of Appeal. The appeal court rejected the argument that A had sought to procure a 'thing', ie surgery, contrary to section 59 and found many of the grounds for the prosecution to be unsustainable. Additionally, the court noted that on the information available to them, the doctors, had the deception succeeded, might have acted lawfully in terminating the pregnancy. So A walked free after trying to terminate his wife's pregnancy against her will.

The rigour of the law has always been tempered by a defence to a charge of criminal abortion by a doctor that they acted to preserve the life or health of the pregnant woman.[22] At no time in England was abortion absolutely prohibited so as to require the woman to be sacrificed for her fetus.[23] In the 1939 case of *R v Bourne*,[24] acquitting a doctor of a charge of criminal abortion, the judge suggested that there might be a *duty* to abort to save the 'yet more precious' life of the woman. The extent of the defence available to doctors was unclear. Some doctors interpreted this defence liberally to include the woman's mental health and even happiness. Others would intervene only to prevent a life-threatening complication of pregnancy. Abortion on the ground that the fetus suffered from some serious disability was not lawful. Illegal abortion flourished. Several thousand women were admitted to hospital for treatment after back-street abortions. The Abortion Act 1967 was introduced to bring

19 *R v Sockett* (1908) 72 JP 428. In 1927, a girl of 13 was prosecuted for attempting to induce an abortion on herself by taking laxative tablets and sitting in a hot bath.

20 *R v Whitchurch* (1890) 24 QBD 420.

21 [2010] EWCA Crim 1949.

22 *R v Bourne* [1939] 1 KB 687.

23 See M Brazier, 'Can the Common Law Accommodate Moral Controversy in Medicine: The Case of Abortion' in A Alghrani, R Bennett and S Ost, *The Criminal Law and Bioethical Conflict; Walking the Tightrope* (2012) Cambridge University Press, p 191.

24 *R v Bourne* [1939] 1 KB 687, at 693.

uniformity into the law, to clarify the law for the doctors, and to stem the misery and injury resulting from unhygienic, risky, illegal abortions.

16.3 Background to the Abortion Act 1967

In England and Wales, the Abortion Act 1967 originally set no limit to the time when an abortion might lawfully be performed. Section 5(1) provided instead that nothing in the Act should affect the provisions of the Infant Life (Preservation) Act 1929 protecting the viable fetus. Under that Act any person who with intent to destroy the life of a child capable of being born alive causes the child to die before it has an existence independent of the mother is guilty of child destruction. The fetus was deemed to be capable of being born alive at twenty-eight weeks.[25] The objective of the 1929 law was to protect the fetus in the course of delivery,[26] and to safeguard any fetus who, but for improper intervention, could have been born alive.

But what was meant by 'capable of being born alive'? In *C v S*,[27] a young man, seeking to stop his girlfriend aborting their child at eighteen weeks, argued that at eighteen weeks a fetus was 'capable of being born alive'. It is fully formed and its heart may beat for a second or so after expulsion from the mother. At eighteen weeks there is no prospect of a baby breathing independently of its mother even with the aid of a ventilator. The Court of Appeal found that to be 'capable of being born alive' a fetus must be able, on delivery, to breathe either naturally or with mechanical aid. The fight to limit late abortions returned to Parliament. Anti-abortion campaigners persuaded the government to agree to the introduction of an amendment to what was to become the Human Fertilisation and Embryology Act 1990, an amendment designed to reduce the time limit for abortions. Their attempt misfired, and after a night of confusion, section 37 of the Human Fertilisation and Embryology Act emerged. Section 37 produced a liberalisation, rather than restriction, of abortion laws in England.

16.4 The Abortion Act 1967

The Abortion Act 1967, as amended by section 37 of the Human Fertilisation and Embryology Act 1990, provides that abortion may be lawfully performed under certain conditions.[28] A pregnancy may be terminated by a registered medical practitioner if two registered medical practitioners[29] are of the

[25] Although at twenty-eight weeks the fetus was deemed to be capable of being born alive, that did *not* mean an earlier abortion was necessarily lawful. It would be for the prosecution to prove *that* fetus was capable of being born alive.

[26] Closing a lacuna in the abortion laws.

[27] [1987] 1 All ER 1230. A somewhat different interpretation was offered in *Rance v Mid-Downs Health Authority* [1991] 1 All ER 801.

[28] See s 1 as amended by Human Fertilisation and Embryology Act 1990, s 37.

[29] An attempt to amend the Abortion Act 1967 to require only one medical practitioner to certify that one of the grounds specified in the Act was met failed; see Abortion Act 1967 (Amendment) Bill 2014 HL Bill 26.

opinion, formed in good faith, that one of four grounds specified in the Act are met. They are:

(1) The pregnancy has not exceeded its twenty-fourth week[30] and the continuance of the pregnancy would involve risk to the life of the pregnant woman, or of injury to her physical or mental health, or that of the existing children of her family, greater than if the pregnancy were terminated. This is sometimes described as the 'social' ground for abortion.
(2) The termination is necessary to prevent grave permanent injury to the physical or mental health of the woman.
(3) The continuance of the pregnancy would involve risk to the life of the pregnant woman, greater than if the pregnancy were terminated.
(4) There is a substantial risk that if the child were born it would suffer such physical or mental abnormalities as to be seriously handicapped.

Section 37 amended the Abortion Act 1967 to provide that the time limit for lawful abortions carried out on grounds of risk to the physical or mental health of the woman or her existing children (so-called 'social abortions') is twenty-four weeks. No time limit restricts termination of pregnancy on any of these latter three grounds, ie an abortion may be performed right up to the end of the pregnancy. In assessing any risk to the health of the woman or her children, account may be taken of the woman's actual or reasonably foreseeable environment. Exceptionally, one registered medical practitioner may act alone when they are of the opinion that an abortion is immediately necessary to save the life of the woman, or to prevent grave permanent injury to her physical or mental health. Save in an emergency any termination of pregnancy must be carried out in a National Health Service (NHS) hospital or a place approved by the Secretary of State.[31] Section 4 of the Act provides that no person shall be under any duty to participate in the performance of an abortion if they have a conscientious objection to abortion, save where immediate treatment is necessary to save the life of the woman or to prevent grave permanent damage to her health.[32]

It is the fourth of these categories, set out in section 1(1)(d), which has proved most controversial. The Infant Life (Preservation) Act permitted action necessary to save the woman's life, even if doing so inevitably entailed the destruction of the fetus; preventing grave permanent injury to her health was also almost certainly permissible.[33] Such cases of a stark choice between woman

30 In *R (on the application of British Pregnancy Advisory Service) v Secretary of State for Health and Social Care* [2020] EWCA Civ 355 the correct interpretation of the words 'the pregnancy has not exceeded its twenty-fourth week' was twenty-four weeks + zero days (which occurs from midnight on the day that the woman is twenty-three weeks + six days pregnant) rather than twenty-four weeks + one day as argued by the appellants.

31 Abortion Act 1967, s 1(3), as amended by the Health and Social Care Act 2022, s 178 discussed at 16.9 below.

32 See *Greater Glasgow and Clyde Health Board v Doogan* [2014] UKSC 68 discussed at 16.11 below.

33 See *R v Bourne* [1939] 1 KB 687.

and fetus are few and far between in modern medicine. Permitting abortion up to forty weeks on grounds of fetal disability was novel.

16.5 Defining serious fetal disability

In debate in Parliament, section 1(1)(d) seemed to be regarded as covering only the most grave of disabilities, perhaps where a woman was found late in pregnancy to be carrying an anencephalic child incapable of surviving more than a few hours after birth. However, the wording of section 37 of the Human Fertilisation and Embryology Act 1990 is identical to the general fetal disability ground provided for in the 1967 Act. So, if Down's syndrome or spina bifida is diagnosed, however late into pregnancy, may the fetus lawfully be destroyed? The wording of the Act is vague.[34] The Royal College of Obstetricians and Gynaecologists (RCOG) offer doctors further guidance.[35] They shy away from prescription, considering that 'it would be unrealistic to produce a definitive list of conditions that constitute serous handicap'. The RCOG emphasises the need for the parents and the doctor to weigh the potential suffering of the child, the suffering of the woman, the burden on the family, and the severity of the disability affecting the fetus. The 2010 report does set a minimum threshold, advising that the child must have a physical or mental disability which would cause 'significant suffering or long term impairment of their ability to function in society'. The RCOG acknowledges that in applying these criteria to actual cases, fetal medicine specialists take different moral views.[36]

In 2004, the Reverend Joanna Jepson challenged the decision by West Mercia Police not to investigate a complaint that doctors had authorised the termination of a pregnancy at twenty-eight weeks of a fetus with bilateral cleft lip and palate. She obtained leave to apply for judicial review.[37] The Crown Prosecution Service (CPS) reviewed the evidence and decided not to pursue a prosecution. Reverend Jepson took no further action.[38] The CPS found that

34 See E Wicks, M Wyldes and M Kilby, 'Late Termination of Pregnancy for Fetal Abnormality: Medical and Legal Perspectives' (2004) 12 *Med Law Rev* 285; S Sheldon and S Wilkinson, 'Termination of Pregnancy for Reasons of Foetal Disability: Are there Grounds for a Special Exception in Law?' (2001) 9 *Med Law Rev* 85.

35 Royal College of Obstetricians and Gynaecologists, *Termination of Pregnancy for Fetal Abnormality in England, Scotland and Wales* (2010).

36 Evidence of under-reporting of abortions on grounds of fetal disability resulted in guidance from the DH: *Matching Department of Health Abortion Notifications and Data from the National Down's Syndrome Cytogenetic Register and Recommendations for Improving Notification Compliance* (May 2014).

37 *Jepson v The Chief Constable of West Mercia Police Constabulary* [2003] EWHC 3318.

38 C Dyer, 'Doctor Who Performed Late Abortion will Not be Prosecuted' (2005) 330 *BMJ* 668.

doctors acted in good faith on the basis of appropriate expert opinion. Much was made of the importance of consultation in the absence of a precise definition of 'serious fetal handicap'.[39] It seems that in effect, serious handicap may come to be defined subjectively – do the parents and the doctors consider the relevant handicap to be serious? The impact of section 37 of the Human Fertilisation and Embryology Act is that in England children capable of being born alive may be killed, providing they are disabled.[40] The protection afforded to the viable fetus by the Infant Life (Preservation) Act is withdrawn from the disabled fetus. A medical practitioner acting within the provisions of the amended and extended Abortion Act cannot be convicted of child destruction. The 1929 Act remains in force, but applicable only to *unlawful* late abortions, and those cases where a violent attack on a pregnant woman kills the child within her.

An unsuccessful challenge to late abortion on grounds of serious disability in 2021 sought to argue that it was incompatible with human rights. Heidi Crowter, the first claimant, has Down's syndrome and campaigns for disability rights. In *R (Crowter & Ors) v Secretary of State for Health and Social Care*[41] she argued that the provision breaches Article 2 by endangering the life of a disabled unborn viable child. The High Court, however, recognised that the ECtHR has never found that a fetus, even if viable, has human rights. Another argument alleged breach of Article 8 (protecting family life) in conjunction with Article 14 (protecting against discrimination). This, too, failed. Even non-fatal disabilities can be very severe. Section 1(1)(d) is not responsible for discriminatory attitudes to people with disabilities. A more restrictive approach would have potential to violate the human rights of the pregnant woman. Section 1(1)(d) was thus found to be compatible with human rights and 'within the margin afforded to Parliament'.[42]

16.6 'Social abortions'

Late abortions on grounds of fetal disability are not the only source of controversy in relation to time limits to termination of pregnancy. As we shall see in Chapter 17, developments in the care of extremely premature babies mean that a small number of babies born before twenty-four weeks' gestation survive. The twenty-four-week limit for 'social abortions' is under attack. It is argued that it is not ethically justifiable to destroy a fetus which may have the

39 See R Scott, 'The Uncertain Scope of Reproductive Autonomy in Pre-implantation Genetic Diagnosis and Selective Abortion' (2005) 13 *Med Law Rev* 291; R Scott, 'Interpreting the Disability Ground of the Abortion Act' (2005) 64 *CLJ* 388.

40 See S McGuinness, 'Law, Reproduction and Disability: Fatally Handicapped' (2013) 21 *Med Law Rev* 213.

41 [2021] EWHC 2536 (Admin). See Z Tongue, 'Discrimination, Disability, and Access to Abortion' (2022) 30(1) *Med Law Rev* 177. The appeal was dismissed in *R (Crowter & Ors) v Secretary of State for Health and Social Care* [2022] EWCA Civ 1559.

42 [2021] EWHC 2536 (Admin), [144].

capacity to survive independently outside its mother's womb. A 'viable' fetus should acquire a right to survive.[43]

Conversely, Rosamund Scott has questioned whether section 1(1)(a) may be too prohibitive, at least insofar as it operates to impose conditions and restrictions on abortion in the first trimester. She argues that the conditions requiring that there must be a risk to the woman's mental and physical health may conflict with the negative obligations under Article 8 of the ECHR.[44]

16.7 Feticide

The issue of feticide brings the debate on late abortions into a sharp focus. Doctors aborting a fetus late on in pregnancy will seek to ensure that they use means that will destroy the fetus before it emerges from the woman. For if a child is born alive, nothing in the Abortion Act authorises their destruction. Accounts are given of premature infants left to die in the sluice room adjacent to the operating theatre where an abortion was attempted.[45] What are the legal rules applicable when an attempted abortion results not in a dead fetus but in a living, albeit sick infant? The child, once born alive, is protected by the law. Any positive act to destroy it is murder. Failure to offer the child proper care *with the intention that it shall die* on the part of persons with an obligation to care for the child is equally murder.[46] Failure to offer the child proper care out of incompetence or carelessness is manslaughter.

Unsurprisingly, obstetricians try to avoid entering that minefield. Advice from the RCOG recommends feticide in all terminations of pregnancy at a gestational age of more than twenty-one weeks and six days, unless the fetal abnormality is such that early neonatal death is inevitable.[47] In practice, this means that fetal medicine specialists administer a fatal injection of potassium chloride into the fetal heart before beginning the process of terminating the pregnancy. Feticide has become a routine part of late termination of pregnancy. It is performed not only to ensure that the fetus is born dead, but also to ensure

43 See M Brazier and J Harris, 'Fetal Infants: At the Edge of Life' in P Ferguson and GT Laurie (eds), *Inspiring a Medico-Legal Revolution: Essays in Honour of Sheila McLean* (2015) Ashgate, ch 4.

44 See R Scott, Risks, Reasons and Rights: The European Convention on Human Rights and English Abortion Law (2016) 24(1) *Med Law Rev* 1.

45 See SK Templeton and L Rogers, 'Babies that Live after Abortions are Left to Die' *Sunday Times* (2004) 20 June.

46 *R v Hamilton* (1983) *Times*, 16 September. In 1983, a consultant gynaecologist was charged with attempted murder. Police had been informed that a baby had been left on a slab to die for some time before being transferred to a paediatric unit. The allegation against the doctor was that he performed an abortion on the basis of an estimate of twenty-three weeks' pregnancy and, when the baby proved to be of thirty-four weeks' gestation, left it without attention intending it to die. The prosecution was dismissed by magistrates for lack of evidence.

47 RCOG, *Termination of Pregnancy for Fetal Abnormality* (2010), pp 29–31.

that the fetus suffers no pain in the course of the termination.[48] Not all women agreeing to termination of pregnancy for a serious abnormality want also to agree to feticide. The RCOG recognises that in cases where a lethal abnormality is present, feticide may not be appropriate.

16.8 Abortion on demand or request?

The total number of abortions carried out in England and Wales in 2020 was 209,917; the highest number since the Act was introduced. Ninety-nine per cent were funded by the NHS with 77 per cent taking place in the independent sector. Eighty-eight per cent were carried out before ten weeks.[49] Critics claim that abortion is available on demand, and that the Act is not being properly applied. Gynaecologists prepared to perform an abortion on the request of the pregnant woman rely on statistics which appear to show that statistically the risk of abortion in the first twelve weeks of pregnancy is less than the risk of childbirth. Therefore, any abortion performed in that period meets the requirement of the Act that the continuance of the pregnancy poses a greater risk to the health of the woman than does termination. Such statistics include women for whom pregnancy poses exceptional risk, such as very young girls, or older women. The individual patient's risk will often be much less than any statistical 'average'. The issue has never been tested in court.

A successful prosecution against a doctor performing an abortion on demand would have to establish (a) that the statistics indicating that abortion posed less risk than childbirth were invalid, and (b) that the doctor on trial did not believe them to be applicable and so failed to act in good faith. Because only one successful prosecution has ever been brought against a doctor for performing an abortion purportedly under the 1967 Act in bad faith,[50] such a course would appear a clumsy means of regulating or eliminating abortion on demand or request. However, the Abortion Act confers on women no right to abortion. By making doctors the 'gatekeepers' for the Act, abortion in England is a privilege granted or withheld at the doctors' discretion.[51]

Many doctors, however, will comply with the woman's request at least before the twenty-four-week limit for so-called 'social abortions'. They do not question the woman's reasons for ending her pregnancy. One reason, however, that generates huge controversy is sex selective abortion, ending a pregnancy

[48] See RCOG, *Fetal Awareness: Review of Research and Recommendations for Practice* (2010).

[49] DHSC, *Abortion Statistics, England and Wales 2020* (2021).

[50] *R v Smith (John)* [1974] 1 WLR 1510, CA. In 2013 the CPS decided not to prosecute two doctors investigated for certifying abortions based on the gender of the fetus. In response, the DH produced *Guidance in Relation to Requirements of the Abortion Act 1967* (May 2014).

[51] The history of abortion in England from well before the 1967 Act is marked by 'medicalisation'; see J Keown, *Abortion, Doctors and the Law* (1988) Cambridge University Press.

because the fetus is not of the preferred sex. In 2012, media reports alleged that two doctors were offering tests to determine fetal sex and agreeing to abort female fetuses.[52] Claims were made that sex selective abortions are illegal under the Abortion Act. That is not so. Such abortion might well not be carried out until after twenty-four weeks and in such cases must meet one of the grounds for late termination. But even then, there might be a case where a woman is under such pressure to have a son that her mental health is at risk. We loathe the notion that one would abort a fetus for not being the 'right' sex but sex selective abortion of itself is not at present illegal. Fiona Bruce MP unsuccessfully sought to introduce a Bill to make it so and section 84 of the Serious Crime Act 2015 commits the government to investigate and report on the incidence of sex selective abortion.[53] The issue is challenging. If abortions should be refused for one reason, however good, should a more rigorous test of motivation for all abortions be carried out?

16.9 From post-coital birth control to early medical abortion at home

The Abortion Act 1967 envisaged that once a diagnosis of pregnancy had been made, the doctor faced with a request for an abortion would consider and weigh any risk to the woman or the child. Post-coital contraceptive drugs (emergency hormonal contraception), if taken by a woman within seventy-two hours of intercourse, ensure that any fertilised egg will not implant in the womb. This, inaptly named, 'morning-after' pill is not the only means by which a fertilised egg may be disposed of at a stage before pregnancy can be confirmed. An intra-uterine device (IUD) fitted within a similar time after intercourse will have the same effect.[54] Post-coital contraception raised the question of where the line is drawn between contraception and abortion. Post-coital contraception works before the fertilised egg can implant in the womb. The crucial legal issue, in relation to the use of the post-coital contraception, is whether a drug or a procedure which prevents implantation is an act done to procure a miscarriage.[55]

52 See CPS, *Statement from Director of Public Prosecutions on Abortion Related Cases* (2013) 7 October. And more recently, see A Forrest, 'Early Gender Tests Leading to Selective Abortions of Girls in UK' *Independent* (2018) 17 September.

53 DHSC, *Assessment of Termination of Pregnancy on Grounds of the Sex of the Foetus* (2015) 'found no substantiated concerns of gender abortions occurring in England, Wales and Scotland' (p 6).

54 In *R v Price* [1969] 1 QB 541, a prosecution for criminal abortion was brought against a doctor who inserted an IUD into a woman who was some months pregnant. The prosecution failed because it was not proved that he knew her to be pregnant.

55 As long ago as 1983, the Attorney General expressed his opinion that prior to implantation there is no pregnancy and so means used to prevent implantation do *not* constitute procuring miscarriage. HC Official Report, 10 May 1983, col 238–239. In 1991, a judge dismissed a prosecution for criminal abortion based on the insertion of an IUD agreeing with the Attorney General that until implantation there is no pregnancy; *R v Dhingra* (1991) unreported.

In 2000, a version of the 'morning-after' pill (Levonelle) was deregulated to allow sale over the counter in pharmacies. Women no longer need a prescription to obtain post-coital birth control.[56] The Pro-Life Alliance unsuccessfully sought judicial review, arguing that the free availability of such a drug contravened the 1861 Act because the drug procures miscarriage. Munby J poured scorn on their case, and forcefully held that no pregnancy is established until the fertilised egg implanted in the uterus.[57] 'Miscarriage' today means the termination of an established pregnancy, whatever it may have meant in 1861.

Emergency hormonal contraception must not be confused with early 'medical abortion'[58] and the 'abortion pill'. Mifepristone (RU-486) and misoprostol (prostaglandin) are drugs which are administered orally in the first ten weeks of pregnancy and will, in most women, induce a complete miscarriage. A small percentage of women require a surgical abortion to complete the evacuation of the uterus.[59] The use of mifepristone is lawful only within the conditions laid down in the 1967 Act. Section 37(3) of the Human Fertilisation and Embryology Act permitted its routine use in England by authorising the Secretary of State for Health to approve clinics prescribing the drug. Section 1(3) of the Abortion Act requires that treatment is carried out either in a specified type of hospital or in a place approved by the Secretary of State.

Until the COVID-19 pandemic (which we will discuss shortly), women needed to attend an approved clinic to take mifepristone, which blocks the hormones necessary to maintain pregnancy. In the past, she had to return two days later to receive misoprostol, which causes the uterus to contract. 'Miscarriage' usually occurs four to six hours after taking misoprostol. Some women feared that contractions would start on the journey home, whilst others objected to the inconvenience and stress of having to attend the clinic twice and lose control over the timing of their termination. The British Pregnancy Advisory Service (BPAS) challenged the Department of Health's interpretation of section 1(3) of the Abortion Act 1967, which requires that 'any treatment for the termination of pregnancy' is carried out in an approved clinic or hospital. BPAS branded the rule 'medically unnecessary' and called for women to be allowed to take the second part of the treatment, the misoprostol, at home. Their application for judicial review failed.[60] In 2018, however, the Secretary of State in England

56 See Prescription Only Medicines (Human Use) Amendment (No 3) Order 2000, SI 2000/3231.

57 *R (on the Application of Smeaton) v Secretary of State for Health and Others* [2002] 2 FLR 146. See J Keown, 'Morning After Pills, Miscarriage and Muddle' (2005) 25 *Legal Studies* 302.

58 In England and Wales, 85 per cent of abortions are now 'medical abortions'; see DHSC, *Abortion Statistics, England and Wales 2020* (2021).

59 The woman will be asked to agree to undergo surgical abortion should the drug fail to work before being given mifepristone. She cannot be forced to go through with the surgical procedure should she later change her mind. But, providing she has been properly warned of the risk of failure and possible adverse effect on the embryo, neither she nor any child damaged by the drug could sue in respect of their injuries. See RP Jansen, 'Unfinished Feticide' (1990) 16 *J Med Ethics* 61.

60 *British Pregnancy Advisory Service v Secretary of State for Health* [2011] 3 All ER 1012.

gave approval for the second drug to be taken at home, provided that the woman had previously attended an appointment with a doctor at an approved place and taken the first drug, mifepristone, there.

From 2018 women could take the misoprostol at home, but during the COVID-19 pandemic it became apparent that the requirement to take the first drug, mifepristone, at a clinic was disrupting services and limiting access to early medical abortion.[61] After a false start when approvals were set out and then revoked hours later, the Secretary of State temporarily allowed women to take both mifepristone and misoprostol at home after a phone conference.[62] A proposed judicial review initiated by Christian Concern was rejected.[63] The rule was set to expire with coronavirus legislation, but – following forceful arguments from academics,[64] charities and advocacy groups that telemedical abortion services are safe and preferred by women – Parliament voted in 2022 to make telemedicine provision of early medical abortion (TEMA) permanent in England.[65]

Laurie, Harmon and Dove, who for the most part support lawful abortion, express concerns that link emergency hormonal contraception and the 'abortion pill'. They fear both 'will inevitably come to be regarded as a safe form of contraceptive back-up', blurring the distinction between preventing new life and taking life.[66] We are less pessimistic. Early medical abortion at home places responsibility for ending her pregnancy on the woman taking the drugs. She cannot evade responsibility by seeing the abortion as something done to her. The loss of the embryo will be very evident to her. It is no more likely to be used lightly than recourse to surgical abortion.[67]

16.10 Fetal reduction: selective feticide

So far, discussion of the legality of abortion has proceeded on the basis that the procedure used terminates the woman's pregnancy completely. There are cases where only selected fetuses in a multiple pregnancy are destroyed, and

61 EC Romanis and JA Parsons, 'Legal and Policy Responses to the Delivery of Abortion Care during COVID-19' 151(3) (2020) *Int J of Gynecology and Obstetrics* 479 and JA Parsons and EC Romanis, *Early Medical Abortion, Equality of Access and the Telemedical Imperative* (2022) Oxford University Press.

62 DHSC, *The Abortion Act 1967 – Approval of a Class of Places* (March 2020). The approval was made under the Abortion Act 1967, ss 1(3) and 1(3A), as amended.

63 *R (on the application of Christian Concern) v Secretary of State for Health and Social Care* [2020] EWCA Civ 1239. And see *Judicial Review of a Decision of the Scottish Ministers* [2019] CSIH 31.

64 See JA Parsons and EC Romanis, *Early Medical Abortion, Equality of Access, and the Telemedical Imperative* (2021) Oxford University Press.

65 Health and Care Act 2022, s 178, amending Abortion Act, s 1. Discussed in ALM Wilson, 'The Health and Care Act 2022: Inserting Telemedicine into the Abortion Act 1967' (2022) *Med Law Rev* fwac046.

66 *Mason and McCall Smith's Law and Medical Ethics*, at 9.100.

67 For a personal account of early medical abortion see L Burns, *Larger than an Orange* (2021) Penguin.

the pregnancy continues to term when the woman delivers her surviving children. Selective reduction, or selective feticide, may be advised either when the woman has a multiple pregnancy and is unlikely to carry all the fetuses safely to term, or when one of two or more fetuses is disabled. The 'surplus' or disabled fetuses will, using fetoscopically directed procedures, be killed. The dead fetuses are not expelled from the uterus, but become 'foetus papyraceous', and emerge on delivery of its healthy brothers and sisters. Selective reduction to destroy a disabled twin was quietly practised for years. The development of *in vitro* fertilisation (IVF) and consequent increase in multiple pregnancies brought the procedure to public attention. Until quite recently, in a number of fertility clinics, to maximise the woman's chances of pregnancy, several embryos were implanted. If she conceived quadruplets or more, the risk was that the babies would be delivered prematurely and in the worst-case scenario *all* might fail to survive. Selective reduction offered the prospect of one or two healthy children being born safely. The Human Fertilisation and Embryology Authority's 'one at a time policy' has vastly reduced the problem. In 2007, one in four IVF births were multiple births, which was twenty times higher than in natural conception. Multiple births constituted 24 per cent of IVF births in 2008 but are now reduced to around 6 per cent.[68]

The deliberate destruction of selected fetuses raised ethical[69] and legal problems. Legal debate focused on whether selective reduction was lawful.[70] Section 37(5) of the Human Fertilisation and Embryology Act legalises selective reduction, if performed for one of the grounds on which termination of the whole pregnancy is lawful. Thus, if fetuses are destroyed on grounds of fetal disability, or because a multiple pregnancy poses a risk to the woman's health, selective reduction is as lawful as ending the pregnancy altogether would be. The anomalous situation is this. Where multiple pregnancy occurs, the underlying reason for wanting to destroy fetus A and B is to maximise the prospects of a healthy birth for fetuses C and D. The ground that would need to be invoked is that permitting abortion to safeguard the health of any 'existing children' of the pregnant woman. Can fetuses C and D be regarded as 'existing children'? The whole philosophy of English law relating to the status of the fetus is that a fetus is not for legal purposes a child.

Section 37(5) grants legal recognition to a much disputed procedure.[71] If fetuses can be selected and destroyed in effect as part and parcel of infertility

[68] HFEA, Our Campaign to Reduce Multiple Births at www.hfea.gov.uk/about-us/our-campaign-to-reduce-multiple-births/ and see HFEA, *Fertility Treatment 2019: Trends and Figures* (2021) discussed at 14.3 above.

[69] On which see J Räsänen, 'Twin Pregnancy, Fetal Reduction and the "All or Nothing Problem"' (2020) 48 *J Med Ethics* 101 and D Begović, EC Romanis and EJ Verweij, 'A Response to Räsänen' (2022) 48 *J Med Ethics* 139.

[70] See J Keown, 'Selective Reduction of Multiple Pregnancy' (1987) 137 *NLJ* 1165; DPT Price, 'Selective Reduction and Feticide: The Parameters of Abortion' [1988] *Criminal Law Review* 199.

[71] R Lee and D Morgan, *Human Fertilisation and Embryology: Regulating the Reproductive Revolution* (2000) Blackstone, pp 252–256.

treatment, the message from Parliament seems to be that unborn life is little more than a means to an end. The fetus itself counts for little. The parents' desire for children justifies its destruction. Does selective killing of disabled fetuses with legal blessing reinforce the second-class status of the disabled fetus?

16.11 Conscientious objection[72]

A vital component of the compromise on which the Abortion Act 1967 was based was the right of conscientious objection.[73] Section 4 provides that no person shall be under any duty 'to participate in any treatment authorised by this Act to which he has a conscientious objection'.[74] It is for the person objecting to prove that their objection rests on grounds of conscience. The professional's conscience does not relieve them of any duty to intervene to save the life of the woman or to prevent grave permanent injury to her health.

In *Janaway v Salford Area Health Authority*,[75] the House of Lords was asked to determine *who* was entitled to rely on the right of conscientious objection. Mrs Janaway was a devout Roman Catholic employed as a secretary. She refused to type abortion referral letters and the authority dismissed her. She challenged her dismissal as unlawful because, she argued, she was entitled to rely on the right of conscientious objection provided for by section 4. Her action failed. The Law Lords ruled that the term 'participate' in section 4 meant actually taking part in treatment designed to terminate a pregnancy. Mrs Janaway was not asked to do anything that involved her personally in the process of abortion. Yet she was an essential cog in the wheel. Abortion was as repugnant to her as murder. For Mrs Janaway, however irrational others might perceive her views to be, her employers were asking her to type out a death warrant.

The scope of section 4 and conscientious objection was revisited by the Supreme Court in *Greater Glasgow and Clyde Health Board v Doogan*.[76] Two Roman Catholic midwives working as ward managers in the labour ward sought to avoid any involvement with women who were admitted to the labour ward for medically induced abortions. They were not asked to take any direct part in the process of terminating pregnancies. But they sought to argue that they

[72] See S McGuinness and M Thomson, 'Conscience, Abortion and Jurisdiction' (2020) 40 *OJLS* 819.

[73] *Greater Glasgow and Clyde Health Board v Doogan* [2014] UKSC 68, [27] per Lady Hale.

[74] The Human Fertilisation and Embryology Act, s 38 confers a similar right to refuse to participate in embryo research or any of the infertility treatments regulated by that Act.

[75] [1988] 3 All ER 1051, HL.

[76] [2014] UKSC 68. And see *Grimmark v Sweden* (App No 43726/17) [2020] IRLR 554 (ECHR); *Steen v Sweden*, App No 62309/17 (ECHR, 11 February 2020): two cases arguing that midwives have a right to conscientious objection to abortion under Article 9 of the ECHR. Both were found to be 'manifestly ill-founded'.

were entitled to refuse to undertake a number of administrative tasks, too, such as booking patients in, allocating staff to duties, briefing staff coming on shift. The Supreme Court held that the question was one of simple statutory construction and took a narrow view of section 4. Section 4 in effect allowed an objector to refuse to take part in any 'hands-on' role in terminating a pregnancy, to refuse to undertake any task that but for the defences provided by the Abortion Act would have been unlawful. Thus administrative duties such as booking patients in, allocating staff to duties in the ward and ensuring staff took breaks fell beyond section 4 whereas supporting any medical intervention or fetching the drugs came within the scope of conscientious objection.[77] However a key point in the judgment that must not be overlooked is this. Lady Hale made it clear that, even if they were not protected by section 4, the midwives could still claim that under the Human Rights Act or the Equality Act their employers should have made reasonable adjustments to accommodate the objectors' religious beliefs.[78]

The right to conscientious objection is thus limited in scope and in practice difficult to exercise. Hospitals are wary of staff who will not participate in what has become a common procedure. It is said that nurses face greater risk to their career prospects if they declare their conscientious objection to abortion.[79] Paradoxically, there remain areas of England where abortion within the NHS is difficult to obtain. Is that a violation of women's rights caused by giving undue precedence to the professional's right to their conscience? If the doctor is a consultant or a general practitioner (GP), no one can order them to participate in an abortion.[80]

16.12 Fathers and abortion[81]

Has the genetic father of the fetus any say in whether or not it is aborted? In 1978, in *Paton v British Pregnancy Advisory Service*,[82] a husband tried to prevent his wife having an abortion. She had been concerned about her pregnancy and consulted her doctor, but did not consult her husband. She obtained a certificate from two registered medical practitioners that the continuance of the pregnancy would involve risk to her health. So an abortion could lawfully proceed. Her husband intervened. He went to court to ask for an injunction (an order) to prevent the abortion from being carried out without his consent. The court refused an injunction. The judge said that the 1967 Act gave no right to the husband to be consulted. In the absence of such

77 See Lady Hale's helpful list of examples: *Doogan*, ibid, [39].
78 Ibid, [24]. See J Montgomery, 'Conscientious Objection: Personal and Professional Objections in the Public Square' (2015) 23 *Med Law Rev* 200, 219–220.
79 See *Greater Glasgow and Clyde Health Board v Doogan* [2014] UKSC 68, [25]–[27].
80 Montgomery, 'Conscientious Objection', 206.
81 See M Fox, 'Abortion Decision-Making – Taking Men's Needs Seriously' in E Lee (ed), *Abortion Law and Politics Today* (1998) Macmillan, p 198; S Sheldon, 'Unwilling Fathers and Abortion: Terminating Men's Child Support Obligations' (2003) 66 *MLR* 175.
82 [1979] QB 276.

a right under the Act, the husband had 'no legal right enforceable at law or in equity to stop his wife having this abortion or to stop the doctors from carrying out the abortion'.

The abortion went ahead. The husband went to the European Commission of Human Rights, arguing that the Act and the judge's decision infringed the ECHR. He argued that his right to family life and the unborn child's right to life had been infringed. The Commission dismissed his claim.[83] They said that where an abortion was carried out on medical grounds, the husband's right to family life must necessarily be subordinated to the need to protect the rights and health of the woman. The fetal right to life was similarly subordinate to the rights of the pregnant woman, at least in the initial months of pregnancy. In *C v S*,[84] the Court of Appeal, having held that the abortion of a fetus at eighteen weeks did not contravene the Infant Life (Prevention) Act 1929, refused the father any right *qua* father or a guardian of the fetus to challenge the proposed abortion. In England, husbands have no standing to oppose an abortion agreed to by the wife, nor has a genetic father any right to intervene to 'save' the fetus, nor can anyone argue that the fetus itself has legal personality so enabling them to act as its 'guardian' and stop an abortion.

One issue remains open. The father in *Paton* reluctantly accepted that the doctors' certificate as to the need for the abortion was issued in good faith. Had he challenged the certificate, could he have asked for an injunction to prevent an unlawful abortion taking place? The judge in *Paton* did not have to decide this point. He expressed the view that an injunction would not be granted. The supervision of abortion and the issue of the doctors' good faith is left to the criminal law and a jury. The Court of Appeal in *C v S*[85] endorsed that opinion.

16.13 Girls under 16

The Abortion Act made no special provision for abortion involving girls under 16. In 1981, a 15-year-old girl who already had one child became pregnant again while in local authority care. She wanted an abortion. Her doctors believed that the birth of a second child would damage her mental health and endanger her existing child. The girl's father objected. Abortion was contrary to his religion. The local authority applied to have the girl made a ward of court and thereby seek the consent of the court to the operation. Butler-Sloss J authorised the abortion.[86] She said that while she took into account the feelings of the parents she was satisfied that the girl's best interests required that her pregnancy be ended. Her decision was approved by the House of Lords in *Gillick v West Norfolk and Wisbeck Area Health Authority*.[87] *Gillick* would suggest that as long as the girl is mature enough to understand what abortion entails physically and emotionally, the doctor may go ahead on the basis of her

83 [1980] 3 EHRR 408.
84 [1987] 1 All ER 1230. And see *Kelly v Kelly* 1997 SLT 896 (Scotland).
85 [1987] 1 All ER 1230, 1243.
86 *Re P (A Minor)* (1981) 80 LGR 301.
87 [1985] 3 All ER 402, HL.

consent alone.[88] Nor are doctors under any obligation to inform her parents. The *Gillick* competent girl is as entitled to confidential treatment as the adult woman.[89] If the girl is insufficiently mature to make a decision for herself, the doctor must act in her best interests. Should her parents refuse consent to abortion, doctors and social workers may seek to go to court[90] and ask a judge to decide on the conflict between medical and parental opinion. Her wishes will be considered, but not treated as decisive.[91] A doctor who ignores parental views will not be guilty of an offence of criminal abortion. He may face legal action by the girl's parents in the civil courts, or, in an extreme case, prosecution for an assault on her.

What of a case where parents want their daughter to have an abortion but she refuses? The Court of Appeal in *Re W (A Minor) (Medical Treatment)*[92] ruled that a doctor may lawfully proceed with treatment of any young person under 18 with parental consent. The doctor simply needs a valid consent either from the young patient herself, or from her parents. *Gillick* competent children and minors under 18 can authorise their own treatment, but not necessarily veto treatment. In theory, a gynaecologist could elect to override their patient's refusal to terminate her pregnancy as long as her parents endorsed the abortion. In *Re W*, Lord Donaldson, considering the implications of his judgment, said:

> Hair-raising possibilities were canvassed of abortions being carried out by doctors in reliance upon the consent of parents and despite the refusal of consent by 16- and 17-year-olds. Whilst this may be possible as a matter of law, I do not see any likelihood taking account of medical ethics, unless the abortion was truly in the best interests of the child. This is not to say that it could not happen.[93]

To force an abortion on a girl must question whether either doctor or parents act in her interests. Lord Donaldson considered it unthinkable that doctors would use the law to coerce young girls into abortion.[94]

In *An NHS Trust v A, B, C and a Local Authority*[95] a grandmother noticed a change in her 13-year-old granddaughter, A, and took her to the GP. A was uncommunicative and there was some doubt as to her competence. She was found to be at least twenty-one weeks pregnant. Mostyn J held that she had

88 See *An NHS Trust v ABC and a Local Authority* [2014] EWHC 1445 Fam, where Mostyn J held that a girl aged 13 was *Gillick* competent and could consent to an abortion; but see KL Moreton, 'Gillick Reinstated: Judging Mid-Childhood Competence in Healthcare Law' (2015) 23 *Med Law Rev* 303.

89 *Axon v Secretary of State for Health* [2006] EWHC 37.

90 See *Re B (A Minor) (Wardship: Abortion)* [1990] 3 All ER 927 (Hollis J authorised abortion for a 12-year-old girl).

91 Though they may be given considerable weight; see *X (A Child) (Capacity to Consent to Termination)* [2014] EWHC 1871 (Fam).

92 [1992] 4 All ER 627, discussed below at 17.27.

93 [1992] 4 All ER 627, at 635.

94 Ibid.

95 [2014] EWHC 1445 (Fam). See K Moreton, 'Gillick Reinstated: Judging Mid-Childhood Competence in Healthcare Law' (2015) 23(2) *Med Law Rev* 303.

'sufficient understanding and intelligence'[96] and was therefore *Gillick* competent to decide whether to continue or terminate her pregnancy.

The courts are loath to force termination of pregnancy on a young person, even if they lack competence. In *Re X (A Child)*,[97] 13-year-old X, who had an IQ of 54, was fourteen weeks pregnant to a 14-year-old boy. X lacked *Gillick* competence and so could not consent. Moreover, she initially objected to the termination. Sir James Munby concluded that termination was in her best interests, but that she should not be subjected to termination unless she was 'accepting'. By the end of the proceedings she was compliant and the order was made.

16.14 Mentally incapacitated women

Termination of pregnancy where the pregnant woman may lack capacity is governed by the Mental Capacity Act 2005, discussed earlier in Chapter 7. In *S v Birmingham Women's and Children's NHS Trust*,[98] the Court of Protection considered whether 38-year-old S had capacity to consent to a termination of pregnancy. She brought the proceedings herself, with no litigation friend. She had come off medication to treat her bipolar disorder having conceived through IVF. When her mental health deteriorated, she was sectioned under the Mental Health Act 1983 and voiced doubts about continuing the pregnancy. Her clinicians considered that she lacked capacity and that termination of pregnancy would be contrary to her best interests. Judge Hilder criticised the Trusts for not bringing the matter before the Court more promptly, necessitating urgent consideration, for failing to refer the matter to court themselves and for their inadequate assessments of her capacity. She held that the presumption of capacity was not rebutted: 'How S chooses to exercise her capacity is a matter for her and her alone'.[99]

Where the pregnant woman is shown to lack capacity, the fundamental test is whether, in all the circumstances, abortion is in her best interests. Regard must be had for any views or feelings the woman herself expresses, or has expressed, in the past. The impact on her must be fully evaluated. The timing of the proposed abortion may be crucial. In 2002, a judge refused to authorise an abortion close to the 24-week limit for 'social abortions'.[100]

In *Re AB*[101] 24-year-old AB was nearly twenty-three weeks pregnant when Lieven J authorised an abortion. AB had moderate learning disabilities and functioned at the level of a 6- to 9-year-old. She lacked capacity to decide but wanted to proceed with the pregnancy. Lieven J heard evidence that AB would

96 [2014] EWHC 1445 (Fam), [15].
97 [2014] EWHC 1871.
98 [2022] EWCOP 10.
99 Ibid, [60].
100 *Re SS (Medical Treatment: Late Termination)* [2002] 1 FLR 445. Contrast with *D v An NHS Trust (Medical Treatment: Consent: Termination)* [2003] EWHC 2793.
101 [2019] EWCOP 26; [2019] EWCA Civ 1215. See L Cherkassky, '"Wishes and Feelings" Under the Mental Capacity Act 2005' (2020) 28(3) *Med Law Rev* 605.

be unable to care for the child and was concerned about the risks posed to AB if the child were to be taken into care. AB's mother appealed and the Court of Appeal came to a different conclusion about AB's best interests. Eleanor King LJ acknowledged that the invasion of AB's Article 8 rights would be legitimate and proportionate if the procedure were in her best interests. She found that insufficient account had been taken of AB's wishes and feelings. Best interests decisions under the 2005 Act 'must respect and maximise that person's individuality and autonomy to the greatest possible extent'.

16.15 Fetal status: research and ectogenesis[102]

Both in England and in the ECtHR the question of the status of the fetus is fudged whenever possible. Most (though not all) decisions about the fate of the fetus are entrusted to the woman and her doctors to the exclusion of the father. The reason for such a state of affairs is simple. For so long as the fetus is within the woman, her claims to bodily integrity conflict with any claim of the fetus to survive or of the father to intervene on his putative child's behalf. Biology grants women control over access to the fetus in her womb.[103] As we have seen, too, she cannot be compelled to undergo a Caesarean section or other intervention to which she objects, however great the potential benefit to the fetus.[104]

But does this mean that the woman has untrammelled rights to do as she wishes to the fetus? Consider this scenario. Sue is twenty weeks pregnant when doctors advise her that the fetus has a minor cardiac defect. Research on animals has resulted in a procedure that in 80 per cent of cases cures the defect but with a 20 per cent risk of severe brain damage which will not be apparent until sometime after birth. Sue is happy to consent and take the risk. Her husband and putative father of the child, Tom, is not. Does it follow from the case-law denying Tom any say about whether his wife can terminate a pregnancy or deliver by Caesarean section that he equally has no say about a decision to intervene that may affect the child-to-be adversely?

What though if the fetus were not located in a human womb but rather in an artificial womb, ectogenesis? Evading the question of fetal status would no longer be an option and maternal priority would be hard to defend. Ectogenesis could in theory be complete in that the embryo is fertilised in a Petrie dish and immediately transferred to an ectogenic chamber. At present such a course of action would be unlawful under the Human Fertilisation and Embryology Act 1990, which prohibits the keeping of an embryo beyond the 14-day limit.[105]

102 A Alghrani and M Brazier, 'What is it? Whose is it? Re-Positioning the Fetus in the Context of Research' (2011) 70 *CLJ* 51. And see 13.9 above on choice in childbirth.

103 R Scott 'The English Fetus and the Right to Life' (2004) 11 *European Journal of Health Law* 347.

104 See 7.9 and 13.23 above.

105 A Alghrani, 'Regulating the Reproductive Revolution: Ectogenesis: A Regulatory Minefield' in M Freeman (ed), *Law and Bioethics* (2008) Oxford University Press, p 303.

Were that ban to be lifted so a fetus could be gestated for the whole term of 'pregnancy' in the artificial chamber, what then of fetal status? Is the fetus 'capable of being born alive' from its insertion in the artificial womb? How does such a machine differ from the apparatus that now keeps very premature babies alive in neonatal intensive care? If the law is to allow the fetus to be destroyed and disconnected from the ectogenic chamber, must both gamete donors (parents) agree? Paradoxically it is perhaps the case that as the law stands today, the embryo in the ectogenic chamber has no protection at all. Remember that sections 58 and 59 of the Offences Against the Person Act prohibit the procuring of a miscarriage in a woman. The embryo in the artificial womb is never carried in a woman.

Complete ectogenesis may be many decades away. Partial ectogenesis may be closer to reality whereby a fetus could be transferred part way through pregnancy from the uterus to an ectogenic chamber. In those cases where pregnancy threatens a woman's health forcing her to choose between her own health and the birth of a wanted child, partial ectogenesis may be welcomed. Some commentators have gone further, presenting partial ectogenesis as the solution to the battles over abortion. Sheila McLean[106] has argued that women have the right to be free of pregnancy but it does not follow that they have the right to kill the fetus. Thus if partial ectogenesis becomes feasible after say eighteen weeks of gestation a woman wishing to end her pregnancy would be obliged to agree to the fetal transfer. Alas such a possibility is more likely to ignite than calm the 'abortion wars'. The argument rests on an assumption that a woman seeking to abort seeks only to be free of pregnancy rather than to avoid becoming a mother even if the law were to free her of any legal parental responsibility.[107] Surgery to remove the fetus from the human womb would be complex and probably more intrusive than a Caesarean section and so a woman could not be compelled to consent. Finally, in removing the fetus might doctors contravene section 58 of the Offences Against the Person Act 1861 in that they are procuring a miscarriage?[108]

If medical progress comes close to making ectogenesis in any form feasible, the compromise on which abortion laws rest in England will be severely challenged and evading the thorny question of fetal status and father's rights will become impossible. Chloe Romanis[109] has argued that the term 'fetus' should be avoided altogether for human beings in artificial wombs. They are neither babies nor fetuses and are 'unique in behaviour, location and the process they are undergoing'. She suggests a new, value-neutral term, 'gestateling'.

106 S McLean, 'Abortion Law: Is Consensual Reform Possible?' (1990) 17 *Journal of Law and Society* 106.

107 See Brazier and Harris, 'Fetal Infants: At the Edge of Life'.

108 See EC Romanis, 'Artificial Womb Technology and the Choice to Gestate ex utero: Is Partial Ectogenesis the Business of the Criminal Law?' (2020) 28(2) *Med Law Rev* 342.

109 EC Romanis, 'Artificial Womb Technology and the Frontiers of Human Reproduction: Conceptual Differences and Potential Implications' (2018) 44 *J Med Ethics* 751.

16.16 Safe access

Much of this chapter has been devoted to the issue of who can access abortion and in what circumstances. In this final section we note that the debate on abortion policy can reach a level of vitriol that can put women at risk. Some councils and local authorities in England have resorted to Public Spaces Protection Orders (PSPO) to limit protests (whether pro-life or pro-choice) in the immediate vicinity of abortion clinics. Do such orders offend protesters' rights of freedom of expression protected by Article 10 of the ECHR? The thin line between legitimate protest and anti-social behaviour was negotiated by the Court of Appeal in *Dulgheriu and Ors v London Borough of Ealing*.[110] The court found that a PSPO made by the London Borough of Ealing to protect women accessing the Marie Stopes West London Centre was compatible with Articles 8, 10 and 11 of the ECHR.

Another issue relates to the quality of abortion care. In 2016 a Care Quality Commission report monitoring Marie Stopes International found governance issues and poor practices taking informed consent. The safety of women was not assured, incident reporting was not effective and not all staff were appropriately trained.[111] Abortion care extends beyond matters of access and legality.

110 [2019] EWCA Civ 1490. And see the Public Order Bill 2022, which, at the time of writing, proposes to enforce buffer zones around abortion clinics in England and Wales.

111 CQC, *Marie Stopes International Quality Report* (2016) 20 December.

Chapter 17

DOCTORS AND CHILDREN

17.1 Introduction

In this chapter, we examine the law governing doctors' relationships with child patients. The courts are often asked to determine the fate of sick children when doctors and parents[1] disagree about how best to care for the child. Several cases attracted publicity when parents and the medical team disagreed about whether to withdraw or maintain life support for young children. Donald Trump, the President of the United States, tweeted his support for baby Charlie Gard who was born with a rare mitochondrial disease. His parents fought to access experimental treatment in the USA which UK doctors and then the courts considered to be contrary to Charlie's best interests.[2] And in 2018 protesters blocked the road outside the hospital when the European Court of Human Rights (ECtHR) ruled that an application by the parents of baby Alfie Evans was inadmissible. He had a neurodegenerative disorder and doctors, and the English courts did not consider treatment abroad to be in his best interests.

Some cases involve, not disagreement between doctors and parents, but disputes between parents themselves. Should a little boy be circumcised as his Muslim father wishes, when his mother vehemently opposes circumcision? On the opposite side of the coin, are there limits to treatment to which a parent may agree on behalf of the child? For instance, may a mother, learning that her 4-year-old daughter is a likely carrier of haemophilia, have the child subjected to genetic testing for carrier status? As a child matures, common sense dictates that she be allowed to take more decisions for herself. *Gillick*[3] appeared to establish a right to adolescent autonomy. It proved to be an odd sort of 'right', a right to say yes but not to say no.[4]

We begin by looking at the legal position where everyone would agree that the child is too young to make any sort of decision about medical treatment for herself. Then we explore the vexed issues surrounding adolescents.

1 Or others with parental responsibility.
2 See 17.15 below.
3 *Gillick v West Norfolk and Wisbech Area Health Authority* [1985] 3 All ER 402, HL.
4 See *Re R (A Minor)* [1991] 4 All ER 177, CA; *Re W (A Minor)* [1992] 4 All ER 627, CA; *Re X (a child)(No 2)* [2021] EWHC 65 (Fam).

17.2 Treating babies

The birth of a very sick baby is a tragedy. The joy of normal childbirth is replaced by fear for the baby's and the family's future. There are special features surrounding any discussion of the care of sick babies. The conscious adult patient can speak for themselves. The decision about any continuation of treatment may be theirs. Even if unconscious, they may earlier have expressed their wishes should the question arise. The baby cannot express any preference. The parents may give their views. Should parental wishes be decisive? Parents' views are crucial, but children have interests too. The baby's plight is different from that of a newly disabled adult. The baby does not move from full health to disability. A life of disability is all that they can know. Nor will their parents be as able to speak for them as for an older child. The older child (even at 2 or 3 years old) will have indicated what gives them pleasure and what causes them pain. Questions about how to treat newborn babies raise somewhat different issues to the more general questions about when to give priority to prolonging life.

For doctors, one critical factor has been the evidence that certain kinds of intervention have poor long-term results. While some parents will want doctors to do everything possible to keep their baby alive, others who discover at birth that their baby is severely disabled may be perplexed by suggestions that their newborn baby must now be subjected to aggressive measures to keep the baby alive. The Abortion Act permits the termination of pregnancy when there is a substantial risk that the child, if born, will be severely disabled. Some people ask why a child who could have been actively destroyed if their disability had been diagnosed in pregnancy must be the subject of intensive life-saving measures if their disability goes unnoticed until birth. Some philosophers argue that it is irrational that the law should allow the killing of a fetus at thirty-eight weeks into pregnancy but insist on saving the baby prematurely delivered at twenty-four weeks. What moral difference does the journey though the birth canal make? The concept of the sanctity of each and every human life is under attack. Forceful arguments are advanced[5] that the value of life lies in its quality and its contribution to society, rather than in any intrinsic merit in life itself. The newborn baby is no more a 'person' than the embryo or the fetus. Such arguments are equally forcefully rebutted.[6]

Debate about whether the law should make special provision in relation to newborn babies is not new. The prosecution of Dr Leonard Arthur for murder prompted calls for new legislation as long ago as 1981.[7] Broadly similar proposals were made by Mason and McCall Smith in the first edition of *Law and Medical Ethics*,[8] and survived with amendments to the sixth edition of that work.[9] Legislation aimed solely at clarifying the law concerning

5 See J Glover, *Causing Death and Saving Lives* (1977) Penguin, ch 12. And see 4.10–4.13 above.

6 A McGee, 'The Moral Status of Babies' (2013) 39 *J Med Ethics* 345.

7 See, for example, the draft 'Limitation of Treatment Bill' discussed by D Brahams (1981) 78 *Law Society Gazette* 1342.

8 JK Mason and RA McCall Smith, *Law and Medical Ethics* (1985) Butterworths, p 89.

9 At p 390.

withholding and withdrawing treatment may be of limited utility. What is meant by 'worthwhile quality of life'? What degree of pain and suffering renders life unbearable?

17.3 Neonatal euthanasia

Another question in relation to changing the law to try to clarify when doctors may lawfully withhold or withdraw treatment is this. If it is lawful to withhold life support from a baby, 'allowing her to die', should it also be lawful to take active steps to end her life swiftly and painlessly? Is there any moral difference between the two? What of the baby whose condition is agonising and likely to be fatal who hangs on to life?

In the Netherlands, the Groeningen Protocol[10] permits doctors to act to end the life of a baby in the most exceptional circumstances. To put it crudely, the Protocol allows neonatal euthanasia. It is not formally part of Dutch law. A team of physicians, including a doctor who is not directly involved in the care of the baby, must confirm that the baby's condition is such that he is subjected to unbearable suffering, and that the condition is untreatable. If the parents consent, high doses of opiates such as morphine are used to induce the death of the baby gently over one to two days. After the baby's death, a report should be made to the coroner, and a committee of five members, including an ethicist and a lawyer, who scrutinise the decision to check that the treatment of the baby meets the conditions set out in the Protocol. The 'killing' of the baby remains a criminal offence, but if the Protocol is followed, doctors will not be prosecuted.

If legislation allowing active neonatal euthanasia were to be enacted in England,[11] a series of difficult decisions would need to be taken. Do we accept some distinction in the value of the life of the newborn baby, and the older child or adult? If so, where is the line to be drawn? Is it seventy-two hours, or twenty-eight days, or later? Debate has ebbed and flowed for centuries as to the moral status of the fetus. Abortion, although severely punished, was never equated with murder in England. Birth is a relatively clear dividing line. No other distinction can be as clear. So how (if at all) could legislation, expressly and exclusively designed to allow ending the lives of newborn babies, be justified? Do we regard the parents as standing proxy for their child in any decision as to treatment? If so, why draw the line at twenty-eight days? Older children develop chronic disease, are disabled in accidents, or are discovered to suffer from severe disabilities later in childhood.

One other possibility to be considered is whether, without changing the law, guidelines relating to the resuscitation of extremely premature babies would be

[10] See AAE Verhagen, 'The Groningen Protocol for Newborn Euthanasia; Which Way did the Slippery Slope Tilt?' (2013) 39 *J Med Ethics* 293.

[11] As we shall see in Chapter 22, some countries have allowed assisted dying in adults. Belgium removed the age restriction in 2014. In the Netherlands children over 12 can request euthanasia and there are proposals to extend that to younger children.

helpful. Resuscitation of a very premature baby raises questions of the ethics of attempting to resuscitate a baby who is highly likely to die whatever is done for her. And when a baby does survive on a ventilator, but the long-term prognosis is dire, decisions to withdraw intensive care may be even more painful than decisions to institute care. The Nuffield Council on Bioethics[12] proposed guidelines for deciding whether to institute neonatal intensive care. The guidelines suggest that below twenty-two weeks no baby should be resuscitated, except within an approved clinical research study. Between twenty-two and twenty-three weeks, the general practice would be not to institute intensive care unless the parents, fully informed, re-iterate requests for resuscitation. Between twenty-three and twenty-four weeks, precedence should be given to parental wishes, and from twenty-four weeks, the presumption should be that full intensive care for the baby should be instituted. In 2015 the Royal College of Paediatrics and Child Health issued guidance on decision-making in life-limiting and life-threatening conditions in children, including those resulting from extreme prematurity.[13] And in 2019 the British Association of Perinatal Medicine issued a Framework for Practice outlining a risk-based approach to decision-making, considering gestational age and other factors.[14]

Finally, the question of use of resources raises its ugly head. Should money spent on intensive care of babies unlikely to survive be spent elsewhere, say on treatment for early breast cancer? Would money spent on Baby A born at twenty-two weeks be better spent on B, born a little later? The limited number of places in neonatal units means that doctors sometimes have to arrange for a baby to be transported hundreds of miles to a neonatal unit far away because there is no capacity to care for the infant nearer the family home. Flessas and Jackson counsel that resource decisions for neonates should turn on the same principles that apply to other individuals: namely a consideration of their best interests. Models that seek to consider the costs of the child's special needs as they grow up, aligning the premature infant with a fetus, construct the neonatal intensive care unit 'as a space in which children are not really children, and, as a result, parents are not really parents'.[15]

17.4 The emergence of the 'best interests' test

For the present, legal principles governing the medical care of newborn babies and small children must be discerned from the judgments of the courts. The

[12] Nuffield Council on Bioethics, *Critical Care Decisions in Fetal and Neonatal Medicine* (2006). For commentary see G Birchley and R Huxtable, 'Critical Decisions for Critically Ill Infants' in C Stanton *et al* (eds), *Pioneering Healthcare Law: Essays in Honour of Margaret Brazier* (2016) Routledge, ch 10.

[13] Royal College of Paediatrics and Child Health, *Making Decisions to Limit Treatment in Life-Limiting and Life-Threatening Conditions in Children: A Framework for Practice* (2015).

[14] British Association of Perinatal Medicine, *Perinatal Management of Extreme Preterm Birth Before 27 weeks of Gestation* (2019).

[15] T Flessas and E Jackson, 'Too Expensive to Treat? Non-Treatment Decisions at the Margins of Viability' (2019) 27(3) *Med Law Rev* 461.

focus in any case referred to court is the individual baby.[16] The fundamental principle governing withholding life-saving treatment from young children was settled in *Re B* in 1981. An infant girl, Alexandra, was born with Down's syndrome and an intestinal obstruction. Without surgery, the baby would die within a few days. Her parents refused to authorise the operation. They argued that God or nature had given their child a way out. The doctors contacted the local authority, and the child was made a ward of court. A judge was asked to authorise the operation. He refused to do so. The authority appealed, and the Court of Appeal[17] ordered that the operation go ahead. Counsel for the parents submitted that in this kind of decision, the views of responsible and caring parents must be respected and that their decision should decide the issue. The Court of Appeal rejected the submission, holding that the decision must be made in the best interests of the child.

In the same year that the Court of Appeal held that Alexandra must be treated and live, Dr Arthur faced trial for murder.[18] A baby was born in the hospital where Dr Arthur was consultant paediatrician. The baby suffered from Down's syndrome. His parents did not wish him to survive. He died sixty-nine hours after his birth. The prosecution alleged that Dr Arthur ordered nursing care only and prescribed a drug to suppress the baby's appetite and so starve him to death. They claimed that, apart from Down's syndrome, the baby was otherwise healthy, and that his death resulted from starvation and the effect of the drug causing him to succumb to bronchopneumonia. Defence evidence established that (1) the baby suffered from severe brain and lung damage, (2) Dr Arthur followed established practice in the management of such an infant, and (3) that in the first three days of life, normal babies take in little or no sustenance and usually lose weight (which the dead baby had not done). The baby patently did not starve to death. The judge directed that the charge be altered to attempted murder. Summing up, the judge stressed that there is 'no special law in this country that places doctors in a separate category and gives them special protection over the rest of us'. He emphasised that, however severely disabled a child may be, if the doctor gives it drugs in an excessive amount so that the drugs will cause death, then the doctor commits murder. He highlighted the distinction between doing something active to kill the child and electing not to follow a particular course of treatment which might have saved the infant. Considering the ethical arguments on terminating newborn life, the judge reminded the jury that if ethics and the law conflict, the law must prevail. Nonetheless his Lordship concluded:

16 See GMC, *Treatment and Care Towards the End of Life: Good Practice in Decision Making* (2010), para 90: 'You must also consider the role and responsibilities of parents and others close to them, but your primary duty is to the child or young person who is your patient.'

17 *Re B (A Minor) (Wardship: Medical Treatment)* [1981] 1 WLR 1421, CA.

18 (1981) 12 BMLR 1. See also 'Dr Leonard Arthur: His Trial and Its Implications' (1981) 283 *BMJ* 1340; H Benyon, 'Doctors as Murderers' [1982] *Criminal Law Review* 17; M Gunn and JC Smith, 'Arthur's Case and the Right to Life of a Down's Syndrome Child' [1985] *Criminal Law Review* 705.

> I imagine that you [the jury] will think long and hard before deciding that doctors of the eminence we have heard in representing to you what medical ethics are and apparently have been over a period of time, you would think long and hard before concluding that they in that great profession have evolved standards which amount to committing crime.

The jury acquitted Dr Arthur.

A confused picture emerged. A baby with Down's syndrome was ordered to be saved, yet Dr Arthur was not guilty of a crime in relation to his treatment of a severely damaged infant with Down's syndrome. The acquittal of Dr Arthur tells us little about the law. The confusion over the pathological evidence may have irretrievably prejudiced the jury against the prosecution's case. The baby's multiple abnormalities should have been irrelevant to the reduced charge of attempted murder. When Dr Arthur ordered nursing care only, he thought that he was dealing with a baby as entitled to survive as Alexandra. Did the jury see it that way? As Mason puts it: 'Murder, in the popular sense of the word, was the one thing of which Dr Arthur was certainly innocent.'[19]

17.5 Deliberate killing

In all but one exceptional instance illustrated by the case of the Manchester conjoined twins, it is indisputable that neither doctor, nor parents, nor anyone else may do any *act* intended *solely* to hasten the death of the disabled baby. The deliberate killing of any human being is murder. The moment that the child has an existence separate from his mother,[20] the moment he has independent circulation, even though the afterbirth may not yet fully have been expelled from the mother's body, he is protected by the law of homicide. It has on occasion been faintly argued that a grossly malformed child, 'a monstrous birth', should not be regarded in law as human. We shall see that this argument was advanced unsuccessfully in the conjoined twins case.[21] Defining humanity, other than by virtue of human parentage, is an impossible and unacceptable task. Does 'monstrous' refer to appearance, in which case an intelligent infant of appalling mien could legitimately be destroyed? Does it cover lack of intelligence, or lack of a brain?[22] Both are almost impossible to measure at birth.

In *Re A (Children) (Conjoined Twins: Surgical Separation)*,[23] the Court of Appeal authorised the killing of the weaker of two conjoined twins. Jodie

19 JK Mason, *Human Life and Medical Practice* (1988) Edinburgh University Press, p 63.

20 Some dispute exists as to the moment in childbirth when this occurs. The child need not have breathed apparently. See *R v Poulton* (1832) 5 C & P 329, and *R v Brain* (1834) 6 C & P 349; *Attorney General's Reference (No3 of 1994)* [1997] 3 All ER 936, HL.

21 *Re A (Children) (Conjoined Twins: Surgical Separation)* [2000] Lloyd's Rep Med 425, at 464–465.

22 How would you classify the status of a baby born with anencephaly?

23 [2000] Lloyd's Rep Med 425. The names were given to the girls to preserve their anonymity, but the ban on identifying the family was later lifted.

and Mary were born in Manchester after a scan in their native Malta revealed their condition. Their parents came to this country in the hope of surgery to separate and save both children. The girls were joined at the pelvis. Each had her own arms and legs as well as a brain, heart and lungs. Mary's brain was said to be 'primitive', her heart was defective, and she had no functioning lung tissue. Mary remained alive only because a common artery allowed Jodie's heart to circulate oxygenated blood to both infants. Left conjoined, the strain on Jodie's organs would result in the death of both children within three to six months. Surgery to separate the girls would result in Mary's death within minutes of separation. Surgery would kill Mary.[24] Doing nothing would result in the death of both girls. The parents were devout Roman Catholics. They refused to consent to surgery because they believed that it would be a sin to 'murder' Mary and that their children's fate must be subject to God's will. The hospital applied to the court for authority to overrule the parents' objections.

The Court of Appeal ruled that surgery should go ahead. What follows can only be a summary of their Lordship's complex, and not always unanimous, reasoning. Let us deal first with the question of how it could be said to be lawful to kill Mary. Mary, the judges agreed, was in law a person whose right to life was entitled to respect. She was not to be regarded as non-human, a monster or, as some had suggested, a 'tumour' attached to Jodie's body.[25] Ward LJ and Brooke LJJ[26] accepted that surgery to separate the twins constituted killing Mary. However much their doctors wished the case to be different, in cutting off Mary's blood supply by clamping the common artery, they 'intended' Mary's death. Unless some lawful excuse justified their conduct, the doctors were exposed to liability for murder. The Court found that excuse in the doctrine of necessity.[27] Brooke LJ cited the analogy of the captain of a ship about to capsize. He had to choose who entered the lifeboats. The judge continued:

> He would not be guilty even though he kept some of the passengers back from the boat at revolver-point and he would not be guilty even though he had to fire the revolver.[28]

Doctors caring for the conjoined twins had duties to both girls. Surgery would involve an assault, a fatal assault on Mary. To save Jodie, it was justifiable. It was necessary to avoid an inevitable and irreparable evil. Given Mary, too, would die without surgery, the evil of her inevitable death was

24 For an eloquent discussion of the issues raised by surgery to separate conjoined twins prior to *Re A*, *see* S Sheldon and S Wilkinson, 'Conjoined Twins: The Legality and Ethics of Sacrifice' (1997) 2 *Med Law Rev* 149.

25 Though note Mason's interesting argument that as Mary had no independent lung function she should have been classified as stillborn; JK Mason 'Conjoined Twins: A Diagnostic Conundrum' (2001) 5 *Edinburgh Law Review* 226.

26 [2000] Lloyd's Rep Med 425, at 456, 466–467. Robert Walker LJ sought to argue that Mary's death resulted not from surgery but her own inability to sustain life (at 510).

27 Ward LJ advanced, and preferred, a doctrine of quasi-self-defence.

28 [2000] Lloyd's Rep Med, at 474.

not disproportionate. A finding that surgery did not constitute murder did not conclude the question of the twins' fate. The more important question revolved around who had the right to make the crucial decision. Doctors wanted to operate. The parents objected. Before going on to look at the question of who decides,[29] we must first consider the more common case, where what is at stake is not actively killing a child, but withholding treatment from her.

17.6 Can withholding and withdrawing treatment be in an infant's best interests?

To what extent does the law require parents and doctors to provide treatment to prolong the baby's life? Before any failure to treat a child can engage *criminal* liability, it must be established that a duty to act was imposed on the accused. Parents are under a duty to care and provide for their dependent children. Failing to provide proper care, including medical aid where necessary, will result in a conviction for wilful neglect of the child, provided that the parent was aware of the risk to the child's health.[30] Should the child die, the parents may be convicted of manslaughter.[31] Parents who are aware of the danger to a child's health, but who do not seek medical aid because of religious or other conscientious objection to conventional medicine, have no defence to criminal prosecutions for neglect or manslaughter.[32] Parents who deliberately withhold sustenance and care from a child intending him to die may be guilty of murder.[33] Finally, a range of other legal remedies is available to local authorities. Failure to provide medical aid, risking significant harm to the child, is a ground for taking a child into care.[34]

What of the doctor? If they are under a duty to treat a baby then, like the parent, should the child die, they could be prosecuted for manslaughter if their omission resulted from neglect, or for murder if they intended the infant to die. Once the doctor accepts the baby as a patient, they assume a duty to that baby to give them proper medical care. Nor is it likely that a paediatrician could, should anyone ever want to, evade responsibility by refusing to accept a child as a patient after birth. Their contract with the National Health Service (NHS) imposes on them an obligation towards the children born in their hospital, giving rise to a duty to the individual infant.[35]

Parents and doctors have a duty to provide medical aid, but what is the scope of that duty? Where a child is suffering from severe abnormalities, may proper medical care be defined as keeping the child comfortable, but withholding life-prolonging treatment? Two factors play a vital role in the decision as to

29 We revisit *Re A* at 17.5 and 17.9 below.
30 Children and Young Persons Act 1933, s 1(1).
31 *R v Lowe* [1973] QB 702.
32 *R v Senior* [1899] 1 QB, 823.
33 *R v Gibbins and Proctor* (1918) 13 Cr App Rep 134.
34 Children Act 1989, s 31(2).
35 See H Beynon, 'Doctors as Murderers' [1982] *Criminal Law Review* 17, at 27–28.

whether to treat an acutely ill child. (1) What do her parents desire? (2) What is the practice of the medical profession in the management of her kind of illness or disability?[36] The answer to the second question is that in many instances, doctors will explain the treatment available, give a prognosis as to the child's future, and accept the decision taken by the parents. Yet, as we have seen, the Court of Appeal in the case of Alexandra ordered surgery to remove an intestinal blockage against her parents' wishes. The baby would be affected by the mental and physical disabilities attendant on Down's syndrome. If treated, she could expect the same quality of life as any one of the many other Down's babies born each year. She would suffer no pain from her disability, and the evidence suggests that, properly cared for, Down's children lead happy lives. The surgery needed to save Alexandra was simple and without risk. Her proposed treatment had a purpose, the baby was not inevitably dying, and the treatment was in no way unduly burdensome.

Re B[37] signalled that the legality of withholding treatment is dependent on the degree of a child's disability and the degree of suffering continued life may cause her. Some sort of balance between the pain of prolonged life and the finality of death has to be struck.[38] In striking that balance, the law, in appropriate cases, allows doctors and parents to conclude that it is not in the best interests of the baby to intervene to prolong her life.

In *Re C (A Minor) (Wardship: Medical Treatment)*,[39] a baby had been made a ward of court shortly after birth on grounds of her parents' inability to care for her. C suffered from an exceptionally severe degree of hydrocephalus, and the brain itself was poorly formed. It was said to be inevitable that she would die in a matter of months at most. The judge made an order that leave be given to 'treat the ward to die'. This infelicitous phrase caused an outcry, being wrongly interpreted by some of the media as sanction for active euthanasia. The Court of Appeal affirmed his judgment, deleting the unfortunate phrase. Lord Donaldson MR saw C's case as very different from that of the baby in *Re B*. C was inevitably dying. Her life appeared to offer her no pleasures.

Re J (A Minor) (Wardship: Medical Treatment)[40] is a more difficult case. J was born thirteen weeks prematurely at a birth weight of 1.1 kg and was found to have severe brain damage: 'A large area of fluid filled cavities where there ought to have been brain tissue.' Unlike baby C, his life expectancy might extend to his late teens. If he developed an infection, must he be treated? If he suffered a further episode of cyanosis and collapse, must he be resuscitated? The Court of Appeal found that he need not. Lord Donaldson regarded *Re B* as near to binding authority that a balancing exercise should be performed in assessing the course to be adopted in the best interests of the child.

36 See GMC, *Treatment and Care Towards the End of Life*, para 106; Royal College of Paediatrics and Child Health, *Making Decisions to Limit Treatment*.
37 *Re B (A Minor) (Wardship: Medical Treatment)* [1981] 1 WLR 1421, CA.
38 In GMC, *Treatment and Care Towards the End of Life*, para 93.
39 [1989] 2 All ER 782, CA.
40 [1990] 3 All ER 930, CA.

Note that in *Re J* there was no disagreement between J's parents and doctors. The application to court was undertaken to ensure that any decision to withhold treatment was lawful so neither parents nor doctors would risk prosecution.

English judges have shown themselves prepared to accept that appropriate care for a terribly sick child is not always to prolong his life. Does the Human Rights Act 1998 make any difference, enforcing as it does the right to life enshrined in Article 2 of the Human Rights Convention? In *A National Health Service Trust v D*,[41] a baby was born with irreversible lung disease and multi-organ failure. D was in the process of dying and the Trust sought a declaration that it would be lawful not to resuscitate him if he stopped breathing. The judge held that provided any decision not to resuscitate D was made in his best interests, there was no violation of Article 2. Article 3 which prohibits cruel or inhuman treatment entails a right to be allowed to die with dignity.

What, though, of withdrawing treatment already instituted? A baby may be resuscitated at birth, or an older child put on a ventilator after a traumatic injury, but tests later show that the child is never likely to leave hospital, or even to survive off the ventilator. It is thought his best interests are best served by allowing him to die peacefully in his parents' arms. Can doctors lawfully switch off the ventilator? Or is that an act hastening death and so murder? We shall see later that the House of Lords[42] has ruled that switching off a ventilator or withdrawing life-sustaining treatment from a patient of any age does not constitute an act hastening death. Discontinuing life support is 'no different from not initiating it in the first place'.[43] In a case directly concerned with the care of a baby in intensive care, the judge stressed that 'there is no legal distinction between withholding or withdrawing life support ... the best interests test applies equally to both situations'.[44] Where withdrawal of treatment includes the withdrawal of artificial nutrition and hydration, the General Medical Council (GMC) advise that a second medical opinion is sought.[45] The Royal College of Paediatrics and Child Health advises that treatment limitation be considered where it cannot provide overall benefit, either because it is unlikely to prolong life significantly (for example in cases of brain stem death and imminent or inevitable death) or due to the unlikelihood that treatment will alleviate burdens associated with illness or treatment.[46]

17.7 'Best interests': a balancing exercise

Since *Re B*, the case-law has evolved to give a fuller picture of the balancing exercise required. Medical treatment cases involve 'the upbringing of the

41 (2000) 2 FLR 677.

42 *Airedale NHS Trust v Bland* [1993] AC 789, HL. See 22.4 and 22.15 below.

43 Ibid, 866, per Lord Goff.

44 *An NHS Trust v MB* [2006] EWHC 507 (Fam), [20].

45 See GMC, *Treatment and Care Towards the End of Life*, para 106.

46 Royal College of Paediatrics and Child Health, *Making Decisions to Limit Treatment*, exec summary.

child', which brings into play section 1 of the Children Act 1989 requiring that 'the child's welfare shall be the court's paramount consideration'. Domestic law has been influenced by internationally agreed principles of human rights, in particular the European Convention on Human Rights (ECHR) and the United Nations Convention on the Rights of the Child (CRC), which was ratified by the UK in 1991.[47] Wales has set out a duty to have regard to the CRC[48] and Scotland voted in 2021 to incorporate it into domestic law. The CRC protects children's inherent right to life and, by virtue of Article 3, it requires that 'in all actions concerning children … the best interests of the child shall be a primary consideration'.

The case-law on best interests is voluminous, but in 2018 MacDonald J helpfully reviewed it and set out a tenfold summation.[49] An abridged version is repeated here:

(i) The paramount consideration is the best interests of the child. The role of the court when exercising its jurisdiction is to take over the parents' duty to give or withhold consent in the best interests of the child. It is the role and duty of the court to do so and to exercise its own independent and objective judgement.

(ii) The starting point is to consider the matter from the assumed point of view of the patient. …

(iii) … The term 'best interests' is used in its widest sense, to include every kind of consideration capable of bearing on the decision, this will include, but is not limited to, medical, emotional, sensory and instinctive considerations. …

(iv) In reaching its decision the court is not bound to follow the clinical assessment of the doctors but must form its own view as to the child's best interests.

(v) There is a strong presumption in favour of taking all steps to preserve life … The presumption, however, is not irrebuttable. …

(vi) Within this context, the court must consider the nature of the medical treatment in question, what it involves and its prospects of success, including the likely outcome for the patient of that treatment.

(vii) There will be cases where it is not in the best interests of the child to subject him or her to treatment that will cause increased suffering and produce no commensurate benefit, giving the fullest possible weight to the child's and mankind's desire to survive.

(viii) Each case is fact specific and will turn entirely on the facts of the particular case. …

47 See 3.1 above.

48 Rights of Children and Young Persons (Wales) Measure 2011.

49 *Kings College Hospital NHS FT v Haastrup and* Ors [2018] EWHC 127 (Fam), [69], building on Holman J's tenfold summation in *An NHS Trust v MB* [2006] EWHC 507 (Fam), [16]. See also Peel J's tenfold summation in *GOSH for Children NHS FT v MK* [2020] EWHC 3476 (Fam), [18].

(ix) The views and opinions of both the doctors and the parents must be considered. ... However, the court must also be mindful that the views of the parents may, understandably, be coloured by emotion or sentiment. ...
(x) The views of the child must be considered and be given appropriate weight in light of the child's age and understanding.

In exercising its 'independent and objective judgement' as per point (i), the court must perform a balancing exercise. It has become popular to utilise a 'balance sheet' approach to demonstrate how the various factors are weighted by the court but Holman J, who has himself used the balance sheet approach,[50] has warned:

> I do caution against over reliance upon a balance sheet approach. A true accountancy balance sheet is based upon precise and arithmetical figures or values, even if some are estimates. However, ... it is impossible in cases [of this nature] ... to weigh all the considerations mathematically.[51]

The weight ascribed to relevant factors is not subject to a mathematical calculation.

The weight to be given to parental views is particularly controversial, especially in disputes about treatment sustaining a child's life. Parents can consent to or refuse treatment but where disagreements about what is best for the child cannot be resolved, the court will apply the best interests test.[52] Parents will usually know their child best and can therefore give valuable insight into the child's assumed position. But parents do not by virtue of their status gain a legal right to decide. If a parental decision is considered by doctors to be contrary to the child's best interests and the matter comes before the court, Holman J has stated:

> Their own wishes, however understandable in human terms, are wholly irrelevant to consideration of the objective best interests of the child save to the extent in any given case that they may illuminate the quality and value to the child of the child/parent relationship.[53]

As we shall see in the next sections, parents have attempted to gain more control over treatment decisions about their children. One attempt was to argue that the threshold for judicial intervention should be based on the significant harm test rather than the best interests test.[54] In a different context, when care orders are made under section 31 of the Children Act 1989, the court can only intervene if 'the child concerned is suffering, or is likely to suffer, significant harm'. In 2017 the Court of Appeal rejected the notion that this

50 See for example *An NHS Trust v MB* [2006] EWHC 507 (Fam), [60].
51 *Cambridge University Hospitals NHS Foundation Trust v Mother of E & Anor* [2021] EWHC 126 (Fam), [41].
52 *Gillick v West Norfolk and Wisbech Area Health Authority* [1985] 3 All ER 402, at 432, Lord Templeman.
53 *An NHS Trust v MB* [2006] EWHC 507 (Fam), [16], endorsed in *Re A (A Child)* [2016] EWCA Civ 759 and *Haastrup* [2018] EWHC 127 (Fam), [69].
54 See D Diekema, 'Parental Refusals of Medical Treatment: The Harm Principle as Threshold for State Intervention' (2004) 25 *Theor Med Bioeth* 243. And see *Re King*

threshold is applicable to medical treatment cases.[55] A significant harm threshold would require proof of a significant risk of a serious and preventable harm. It could potentially allow parents to insist on futile treatment that cannot benefit the child. Another attempt to strengthen parental rights was proposed in the Access to Palliative Care and Treatment of Children Bill 2019–21.[56] It sought to impose on the courts an assumption that any treatment proposal made by parents is in the child's best interests. But adoption of this position could constrain judges in exercising their 'independent and objective judgement' and potentially constrain older children who want their views to be considered. A proposed amendment to the Health and Care Bill in 2022 was also unsuccessful.[57] An uncomfortable truth is that parents who very understandably want to keep their child alive may not always be in the best position to judge if this course of action is in their child's best interests.[58] For now, the best interest test remains the gold standard.[59]

17.8 When parents and doctors disagree

When parents and doctors disagree about the best interests of a baby or child, professional guidelines place great emphasis on working in partnership with parents.[60] In some cases a decision can be postponed until consensus between doctors and parents is reached. In other cases, an application is made to the High Court to establish the child's best interests. The GMC hails this a 'constructive way of thoroughly exploring the issues and providing reassurance for the child and parents that the child's interests have been properly considered in the decision',[61] though sadly the court's involvement sometimes signifies a breakdown in the relationship between parents and doctors. Independent mediation, dispute resolution, and consultation of clinical ethics committees are increasingly utilised to find common ground and avoid court.[62]

[2014] EWHC 2964 (Fam), [31], which gives some support to the view that the significant harm threshold is relevant to medical treatment cases.

55 *Yates & Gard v Great Ormond Street Hospital* [2017] EWCA Civ 410, [104]–[105].

56 HL Bill 13, clause 2. The Bill ran out of time.

57 Health and Care Bill: Dispute resolution in children's palliative care, HC Deb, 20 March 2022, col 955.

58 See *Yates & Gard v Great Ormond Street Hospital* [2017] EWCA Civ 410, [112], McFarlane LJ.

59 See W Seagrim, 'Best Interests: The "Gold Standard" or a Gold Plating? Should Significant Harm be a Threshold Criterion in Paediatric Cases?' in KA Choong (ed), *Medical Futility in Paediatrics: Interdisciplinary and International Perspectives* (2019) Trivent, pp 51–77; and I Goold, J Herring and C Auckland (eds), *Parental Rights, Best Interests and Significant Harms: Medical Decision-Making on Behalf of Children Post-Great Ormond Street Hospital v Gard* (2019) Hart.

60 GMC, *Treatment and Care Towards the End of Life*, paras 95, 107; Royal College of Paediatrics and Child Health, *Making Decisions to Limit Treatment*, para 2.4.3.

61 GMC, *Treatment and Care Towards the End of Life*, para 108.

62 On the potential role of clinical ethics committees, see *Great Ormond Street Hospital for Children NHS Foundation Trust v MX & Ors* [2020] EWHC 1958 (Fam) discussed: J Brierley *et al*, 'Challenging Misconceptions about Clinical Ethics Support

Clearly judicial intervention cannot always be avoided. As Jo Bridgeman has eloquently argued, where the course of action favoured by parents conflicts with professional obligations to their patient, doctors may be unable to compromise.[63] Trusts will usually be willing to treat if a court considers it in the best interests of a child to do so, but the courts will not order doctors to treat in contravention of their judgement of the patient's clinical needs.[64]

17.9 Parental treatment refusals

Disagreement was present in the case of the conjoined twins, *Re A*.[65] Having decided that ending Mary's life was not unlawful, the court had to address whose judgement on the interests of the two little girls should determine their fate. Their Lordships stressed that while the decisions of devoted and responsible parents should be treated with respect, the court retained power to intervene to protect the paramount welfare of the child. The conjoined twins' case was unique because Jodie's welfare depended on Mary's demise. The parents, however, had other separate concerns about Jodie. They feared[66] that she would be profoundly disabled, unable to walk, likely to have to undergo several more operations during her infancy and possibly doubly incontinent. Their view was that it was not in the interests of either child to operate. The Court of Appeal disagreed. There was a reasonable prospect that Jodie could lead a relatively normal life. Mary, Ward LJ said, was 'beyond help'. Surgery might shorten her brief life. Without surgery she would still die. '[The] least detrimental choice, balancing the interests of Mary against Jodie and Jodie against Mary permit the operation to be performed.'[67]

Will the courts always rule in favour of continuing a child's life unless it is either likely to involve unbearable suffering, or will be such that the child will have virtually no ability to enjoy any of the senses, or use any of her abilities? In *Re T* (1997),[68] T was born with biliary atresia, a life-threatening liver disease. Earlier surgery when he was 3½ weeks old had failed, and the baby suffered great pain and distress. His parents, both health professionals, adamantly opposed liver transplant surgery. Fearing intervention by social services, the parents fled abroad. The local authority intervened seeking a court order requiring the family's return to England and that the transplant go ahead. The parents argued that if their son had the transplant, even if the operation was successful, he would

During Covid-19 and Beyond: Role, Remit And Representation' (2021) 47(8) *J Med Ethics* 549. And see J Brierley *et al*, 'Ethical Advice in Paediatric Care' (2022) 107 *Archives of Disease in Childhood* e18.

63 J Bridgeman, *Medical Treatment of Children and the Law: Beyond Parental Responsibilities* (2020) Ashgate.

64 *R (Burke) v GMC* [2005] EWCA Civ 1003, [50].

65 [2000] Lloyd's Rep Med 425, discussed above at 17.5.

66 These fears have not materialised. Surgeons expected 'Jodie' to be able to walk, to avoid incontinency and even to be able to bear children. S Laville, 'Siamese Twin Jodie is Making Progress' *Telegraph* (2000) 9 November.

67 [2000] Lloyd's Rep Med 425, 455.

68 *Re T (A Minor) (Wardship: Medical Treatment)* [1997] 1 All ER 906, CA, discussed in M Fox and J McHale, 'In Whose Best Interests?' (1997) 60 MLR 600.

be subjected to further pain and distress, he would have to take anti-rejection drugs for the rest of his life and might face repeated surgery. They thought that his best interests were better served by a short, happy life and a peaceful death. The Court of Appeal ruled that the parental views should prevail. The parents in *Re T* were entitled to withhold life-saving treatment from their child. The essence of the court's ruling in *Re T* was that, on the 'unusual facts' of the case, any presumption that the best interests of the child are to prolong his life was rebutted. The trial judge, ordering the transplant, had given insufficient weight to the mother's views. Best interests are not limited to clinical considerations.[69] If the operation was ordered against her will, her son's welfare would be compromised. Her commitment to his care was an integral part of any successful recovery post-transplant. Deprived of her care (ie taken into care) he would suffer. If she reluctantly complied with the court order, family problems would beset child and parents. The mother would have to return to, and remain in, England reluctantly. It was not clear whether the father would give up his job and return with her. If not, problems would arise in terms of financial and emotional support for mother and son. Butler-Sloss LJ, finding that the mother's view could not be considered unreasonable, said this:

> The mother and child are one for the purposes of this unusual case and the decision of the court to consent to the operation jointly affects the mother and it also affects the father. The welfare of the child depends on his mother.[70]

Is *Re T* an aberration?[71] Consider Butler-Sloss LJ's language. She says 'mother and child are one' and that the child's welfare depends on his mother. Where the child remains with loving parents, is this not usual rather than unusual? A sick child always requires extra parental commitment. All the judges emphasise that the parents were themselves health professionals. Did this give their views extra weight? More importantly, what is truly unusual about *Re T* is that any court order would also have needed to drag the family back from the other side of the world. Would *Re T* have had the same outcome if the parents had never left England?[72]

17.10 Scruple or dogma?[73]

Re T is an unusual case where parents refuse to consent to treatment for their child because of their judgements about the medical outcome. As parents turn increasingly to the internet for information such cases have grown in number. Some cases involve parents who are Jehovah's Witnesses refusing to consent

69 See GMC, *Treatment and Care Towards the End of Life*, para 90.

70 [1997] 1 All ER 906, at 914–915.

71 Note that *Re T* was affirmed in *LA v SB* [2010] EWCA Civ 1744, [2] per Wall P.

72 This seems to be the tenor of Roch LJ's judgment. See also discussion of *Re Ashya King* [2014] EWHC 2964 (Fam) at 17.11 below.

73 See C Bridge, 'Religion, Culture and Conviction – the Medical Treatment of Young Children' (1999) 11 *Child and Family Law Quarterly* 1; J McHale, 'Health and Health Care Law, Faith(s) and Beliefs: New Perspectives and Dilemmas' (2009) 9(4) *Medical Law International* 279.

to blood transfusions. Transfusions violate a fundamental tenet of Witnesses' faith.[74] The kinds of case which reach the courts are well illustrated by *Re S* (1993).[75] S was 4½ and suffering from T-cell leukaemia. His parents agreed to intensive chemotherapy. Doctors argued that transfusion of blood products was essential to maximise the prospects of successful treatment and saving S's life. His parents objected not just on religious grounds. They raised concerns about the safety of blood products. Their lawyers argued that S's relationship with his family might suffer, for his parents would believe that his life had been prolonged by an 'ungodly act'. Thorpe J dismissed the parental objection. The child's welfare required he be given the best chance of prolonged life. He was unimpressed by talk of problems in the family later in life. Reconciling *Re S* and *Re T* is nigh on impossible. In a series of cases, while judges now show some understanding of the dilemma confronting Jehovah's Witness parents, in the end the courts endorse the child's interest in survival and overrule parental objections.[76]

Perhaps part of the key to apparently contradictory decisions about parents' rights to determine the treatment of their young children can be found in the judgment of Waite LJ in *Re T* (1997).[77] He contrasts cases where parental opposition to treatment is 'prompted by scruple or dogma of a kind which is patently irreconcilable with principles of health and welfare widely accepted by the generality of mankind' and 'highly problematic cases where there is a genuine scope for a difference of opinion'. Ward LJ, in the conjoined twins' case, says[78] that that was not a case where the parents' opposition to surgery to separate the girls was 'prompted by scruple or dogma'. How much weight should parents' religious beliefs carry? Parents will argue that Article 8 of the Human Rights Convention (endorsing their right to family life) and Article 9 (guaranteeing religious freedom) mean that their views should be conclusive. Both Articles are qualified. The parents' 'rights' must be balanced against the children's interests. Caroline Bridge has argued that in delaying treatment (so prolonging a child's suffering), in attempts to meet parents' convictions, the child's interests are undervalued.[79]

17.11 Responsibilities not rights?

A consistent message can be elicited from English case-law about the medical treatment of young children. The common law only confers on parents those

74 Although the Council of Elders does seem to have softened slightly its opposition to transfusions, leaving the matter more to the conscience of the believer.

75 *Re S (A Minor) (Medical Treatment)* [1993] 1 FLR 376.

76 *Re E (A Minor)* (1990) 9 BMLR 1 (see 17.26 below); *Re R (A Minor)* [1993] 2 FLR 757. Though note that not all such cases reach the courts. See, for example, L Roberts, 'Teenage Jehovah's Witness Refuses Blood Transfusion and Dies' *Telegraph* (2000) 18 May.

77 *Re T (A Minor) (Wardship: Medical Treatment)* [1997] 1 All ER 906.

78 *Re A* [2000] Lloyd's Rep Med 425, at 454.

79 See C Bridge, 'Parental Powers and the Medical Treatment of Children' in C Bridge (ed), *Family Law: Towards the Millennium* (1997) Butterworths, p 321. Note that in *An NHS Trust v MB* and *Barts NHS Foundation Trust v Begum, Raqeeb & Raqeeb* [2019] EWHC 2530 (Fam) (discussed at 17.15 below) some weight was given to the parents' religious beliefs.

rights they need to fulfil their responsibilities to provide adequate medical care for their children. Parents can consent to or refuse treatment but where there is disagreement as to what is best for the child, the court will exercise its independent judgement applying the best interests test.[80]

In *An NHS Trust v SR*,[81] doctors recommended chemotherapy and radiotherapy for a 7-year-old suffering from a medulloblastoma; a cancer affecting the brain and spinal cord. The father consented but the mother objected to radiotherapy which could impact the child's quality of life. Authorising the treatment, Bodey J concluded:

> The balance of advantage and disadvantage tilts well in favour of radiotherapy and chemotherapy, notwithstanding the detrimental side-effects. One cannot enjoy even a diminished quality of life if one is not alive.[82]

What if the parent seeks an alternative that doctors do not consider optimal? A parental preference for Chinese medicine was overridden in the case of a 10-year-old boy with craniofacial osteosarcoma (jaw cancer). The evidence suggested that a failure to remove the cancer would result in 'a brutal and agonising death'.[83] *Re King*[84] was a more difficult decision. It concerned a 5-year-old boy, Ashya King, who had a medulloblastoma. The parents agreed that both radiotherapy and chemotherapy were required but disagreed with the hospital's plan for conventional radiotherapy to target the head and neck. They sought more-targeted proton therapy, not generally available in the UK at the time, but available in Prague. Relations broke down and Mr and Mrs King took Ashya from the hospital without informing the staff. The hospital, concerned about Ashya's health, successfully applied for Ashya to be made a ward of court, following which a European Arrest Warrant was issued and the parents were arrested in Spain. Baker J considered evidence that the travel arrangements and treatment options favoured by the parents were satisfactory. The hospital's fears that the parents would not be able to feed and care for Ashya were not substantiated and it was thus in Ashya's best interests to follow the course of treatment chosen by his parents.

17.12 Emergency treatment

In a genuine emergency,[85] doctors may proceed without parental consent or court authority. So if a child is brought into casualty bleeding to death after

[80] *Gillick v West Norfolk and Wisbech Area Health Authority* [1985] 3 All ER 402, at 432, Lord Templeman.
[81] *An NHS Trust v SR* [2012] EWHC 3842 (Fam).
[82] Ibid, [23]. And see *Cambridge University Hospitals NHS Foundation Trust v Mother of E & Anor* [2021] EWHC 126 (Fam).
[83] *Re JM (A Child)* [2015] EWHC 2832 (Fam), [2] per Mostyn J.
[84] [2014] EWHC 2964 (Fam). See J Bridgeman, 'Misunderstanding, Threats, and Fear of the Law in Conflicts over Children's Healthcare' 23(3) *Med Law Rev* 477.
[85] As Lord Scarman put it in *Gillick v West Norfolk and Wisbech Area Health Authority* [1985] 3 All ER 402 at 410, HL: 'Emergency, parental neglect, abandonment of the child, or inability to find the parent are examples of exceptional situations justifying the doctor proceeding to treat the child without parental knowledge or consent.'

a road accident and his Jehovah's Witness parents refuse to agree to a blood transfusion, the hospital can overrule them if delay threatens the child's life. Dire necessity justifies their action.

The decision of the ECtHR in *Glass v United Kingdom*[86] issues a warning to doctors not to stretch the definition of emergency and places a strong emphasis on a presumption of the parents' right to make decisions about the treatment of their young children. David Glass suffered from multiple disabilities. In 1998, he suffered a series of infections after a tonsillectomy. Doctors believed that David had little awareness of, or pleasure in, his surroundings, and that he was dying. They decided that if David stopped breathing, he would not be resuscitated, and administered diamorphine to relieve any distress. His mother vehemently objected both to the administration of diamorphine, and the doctors' decision not to resuscitate David. On one occasion she successfully resuscitated David herself. The relationship between David's family and doctors deteriorated into acrimony and violence. Mrs Glass unsuccessfully challenged her son's treatment in the English courts.[87] She eventually took his case to the Human Rights Court in Strasbourg and won. The Court ruled that administering diamorphine to David against the wishes of his mother violated Article 8 of the Human Rights Convention. Doctors violated David's right to respect for his privacy, notably his bodily integrity. Where children are too young, or otherwise unable, to make their own decisions about medical treatment, doctors must normally seek consent from the parents who speak on their child's behalf. Where doctors considered that parents were not acting in the child's interests, they must seek authority from a court before overruling the parents, except where intervention was immediately necessary to save the child's life.

17.13 Disputing best interests: parental demands

Glass v United Kingdom[88] reiterated that doctors may not unilaterally override the wishes of a child's parents. Courts retain the authority to do so. We have seen that courts will rarely endorse a parental refusal of treatment offering to a child a realistic prospect of continued life. Other cases present the reverse scenario. Parents want doctors to continue treating a child for whom the doctors judge there is little (if any) hope of meaningful survival. In these cases, as Holman J has pointed out, 'the approach of the law is the same whether it is the doctor or the parents who wish or do not wish to give the treatment involved'.[89]

In *Re C (A Minor) (Medical Treatment)*,[90] Orthodox Jewish parents argued that their 16-month-old daughter with spinal muscular atrophy should continue to

[86] [2004] 1 FLR 1019, ECtHR. Contrast *Re OT (a baby)* [2009] EWHC 635 (Fam) (an emergency application was considered procedurally fair).

[87] *R v Portsmouth NHS Trust v Glass* (1999) 50 BMLR 269, CA.

[88] [2004] 1 FLR 1019, ECtHR.

[89] *Cambridge University Hospitals NHS Foundation Trust v Mother of E & Anor* [2021] EWHC 126 (Fam), [38].

[90] [1998] 1 FLR 384. And see *Royal Wolverhampton Hospitals NHS Trusts v B* [2000] 2 FLR 953; *Re MM (Medical Treatment)* [2000] 1 FLR 224.

be ventilated. Doctors argued that continued ventilation was futile. The child was dying. Ventilation would only prolong her life by a few days. The parents' faith dictated that every effort be made to preserve the spark of life. The court declined to interfere with the doctors' clinical judgement. *Re C* can be explained in several ways. English Courts have on several occasions refused to order doctors to carry out treatment which in their clinical judgement they consider inappropriate.[91] It can persuasively be argued that prolonging a child's suffering cannot be in their interests.[92]

Charlotte Wyatt's parents received a sympathetic hearing from Hedley J. Their religious faith and determination to prolong their daughter's life were given careful consideration. Charlotte was born at twenty-six weeks' gestation. She needed to be ventilated for most of her first three months of life. She was believed at the first hearing to be blind and deaf and incapable of voluntary movement. On five occasions, Hedley J was asked to adjudicate in disputes between her parents and her doctors,[93] and on one occasion, the case went to the Court of Appeal.[94] The dispute concerned not the current care of the child, but a contingency that might arise. Should Charlotte stop breathing, must she be re-ventilated? Her fundamentalist Christian parents were adamant that everything be done to prolong her life. They sought a miracle. Her doctors considered that the pain and distress likely to ensue from ventilation would only prolong the process of her dying. The Trust sought a declaration that doctors were not obliged to re-ventilate Charlotte. Rejecting her parents' views, Hedley J acknowledged that her parents knew her best. He had to regard their 'intuitive feelings', but he reminded himself 'they may project those on Charlotte'. So in three hearings, the judge granted and continued the declaration sought by the Trust.

Charlotte survived, and in October 2005, the judge lifted his declaration.[95] The judge found that given her improved condition, it could no longer be said that ventilation would inevitably be futile or wholly inappropriate. Whether ventilation was in Charlotte's best interests would depend on her condition at the relevant time when a decision must be made. Charlotte's improved condition was such that one would expect that decisions about her care would fall to be determined by normal principles of law and clinical practice. However, the relationship between her parents and the hospital had been, at times, openly hostile. Professionals feared retribution if they made a decision opposed by the Wyatts. The Trust sought a declaration that in the event of irreconcilable disagreement, the professionals' decision would be lawful and final. This wide declaration, Hedley J refused to grant. Instead, he sought to reinforce that the usual principles relating to the medical care of infants must apply. If a decision whether or not to intubate (or provide other treatment) arose, her parents and

91 *R (Burke) v GMC* [2005] EWCA Civ 1003.
92 See *Superintendent of Family and Child Services and Dawson* (1983) DLR (3d) 610.
93 *Re Wyatt* [2004] EWHC 2247; [2005] EWHC 117; [2005] EWHC 693; [2005] EWHC 1181; [2005] EWHC 2902; [2006] EWHC 319.
94 *Wyatt v Portsmouth NHS Trust* [2005] EWCA Civ 1181.
95 *Portsmouth NHS Trust v Wyatt* [2005] EWHC 2293 (Fam).

doctors must seek to agree on what constitutes her best interests. They must seek to work in partnership. No doctor was compelled to administer treatment they considered not to be in the child's best interests or an affront to their conscience, though they should not prevent other clinicians from so doing. Hedley J concluded by urging the parties to work together. In 2006, the case returned to court. Charlotte developed an infection and her condition had worsened again. The judge re-affirmed that doctors have no obligation to intubate or ventilate her, should she stop breathing.

The protracted litigation relating to Charlotte Wyatt highlighted three rather different issues about the role of the law. (1) Hedley J declined to replace the best interests test with any test of 'intolerability' or 'significant harm' that might give more force to parental judgements. Nor is it the role of the court to rubber stamp medical opinion of the child's best interests. In reaching an independent assessment, he preferred to retain the traditional 'balancing exercise' of best interests. (2) The length and bitterness of the litigation spelled out a cruel lesson concerning the consequences of a breakdown in trust between families and professionals. (3) Medical prognosis is not always accurate. Charlotte defied medical expectations and improved, but the converse can also happen. Court declarations sought by Hospital Trusts may vary in their specificity and may need to be revisited.

17.14 Independent and objective judgement

That judicial best interest decision-making will not necessarily follow the parental or clinical view is reiterated in *An NHS Trust v MB*.[96] Whilst the courts do not have powers to require doctors to carry out a medical procedure against their medical judgement, they can declare that the best interests of the child are served by continuation of treatment.[97] Thus, Holman J refused to authorise doctors to withdraw life support from baby MB, against the strongly voiced objections of his parents. MB was 18 months old; he had the most severe form of spinal muscular atrophy and breathed only with the aid of a ventilator. He would inevitably die within the next twelve months or so. His parents refused to consent to switching off the ventilator except as a test to see if he could breathe independently. They also wanted MB to have a tracheotomy to allow the baby to be ventilated outside hospital. The doctors sought to withdraw the endo-tracheal tube and, with the aid of sedatives, allow MB a pain-free dignified death. The medical evidence unanimously supported this course of action, as did the guardian appointed by the court to represent the baby. His parents gave evidence that MB responded to them, that he enjoyed stories and songs. The Muslim father believed that the decision about when, or if, his son dies must be left to God. The judge refused the parents' request for an order for further invasive treatment to prolong MB's life. He refused the

96 [2006] EWHC 507 (Fam).

97 See E Cave, 'Selecting Treatment Options and Choosing Between Them: Delineating Patient and Professional Autonomy in Shared Decision-Making' (2020) 28 *Health Care Analysis* 4.

doctors' request to withdraw ventilation. He attempted a balancing exercise in which the crucial feature was that MB retained some significant cognitive function. MB was (or might be) still able to function at some level like any other infant, recognising his mother and taking simple pleasures from touch, light and sound. The suffering he might endure because of all the invasive, intrusive treatments keeping him alive was in the judge's view balanced by these benefits.

The judgment in *An NHS Trust v MB* poses difficult questions. If MB's cognitive function is the *key* factor tipping the balance in favour of continuing to ventilate him, those questions include the following. MB's parents fought to keep him alive. What of a baby whose medical condition is identical to MB, but whose parents want him to be allowed to die – does that tip the balancing exercise the other way?[98] If MB does have the cognitive function to distinguish him from earlier cases where ventilation was withdrawn, is his suffering maybe all the greater? What weight do we put on cognitive function? Does mental disability make a life less worth living than even grave physical abnormalities? Why was this case decided differently from Baby C who was also dying of spinal muscular atrophy?[99]

17.15 The limits of parental rights to demand treatment

In a series of recent high-profile cases, the limits of parental rights to demand treatment have been tested. When Charlie Gard[100] was a few weeks old, his parents grew concerned about his development. He was diagnosed with infantile onset encephalomyopathic mitochondrial DNA depletion syndrome (MDDS), a rare mitochondrial disease that affected the energy produced within his cells and with it his ability to move, think and breathe. Great Ormond Street Hospital considered the potential for nucleoside therapy abroad to extend Charlie's life. Nucleoside therapy had been used in the USA to help children with a similar condition but never used on children with MDDS. It would be experimental. However, Charlie's health declined, and the team took the view that travelling to the USA was not in his best interests and that ventilation should be withdrawn. Second opinions supported this conclusion, except for the 'lone voice' of Professor Hirano in the USA, who maintained his willingness to treat Charlie there, even though the chance of any improvement was very low.[101] Charlie's parents wanted to take this chance. The High Court concluded, however, that on the available evidence further treatment was futile and experimental treatment was not in Charlie's best interests. The

98 Consider *Re RB (A Child* [2009] EWHC 3269 (Fam). After a six-day hearing, RB's father accepted the views of the medical team that withdrawal of treatment was in his son's best interests. The ten-paragraph judgment endorses the parental decision. See further G Douglas, 'Medical Treatment' (2010) 40 *Family Law* 139.

99 [1998] 1 FLR 384.

100 See E Cave and E Nottingham, 'Who Knows Best (Interests)? The Case of Charlie Gard' (2018) 26(3) *Med Law Rev* 500.

101 *GOSH v Yates & Gard* [2017] EWHC 972, [16], [75], [127].

case went to appeal, and ultimately to the Strasbourg Court,[102] and back to the High Court[103] when his parents unsuccessfully argued that new evidence suggested the therapy might be beneficial. Quite amazingly, at this point, Professor Hirano had neither examined Charlie nor seen his most recent medical records. With legal avenues exhausted, ventilation was withdrawn and, aged 11 months, Charlie died.

In *Gard*, as in *MB*, the judges reaffirmed the applicability of the best interests test and rejected a test based on significant harm. Three factors contrast with the situation in *MB*. (1) The appeal process relating to Charlie's treatment lasted several months. This raises questions as to how well the system protects the interests of patients from futile and harmful treatment, and how well it protects health professionals from the moral distress they can incur when they continue to treat contrary to their view of what is ethically appropriate. On the other hand, Cressida Auckland and Imogen Goold celebrate the clear procedures which ensure that parental views are fully considered.[104] As we saw in the case of Charlotte Wyatt, the judicial process is responsive to the potential for the medical prognosis to improve as well as decline. (2) The search for suitable treatment can now be global rather than national or even regional as once might have been the case. If doctors in the UK agree that treatment is not clinically appropriate, then parents can search for doctors across the world who might disagree. (3) The case demonstrates the power of social media. A vast network supported the Gard family. They demonstrated outside the hospital and the courts, they elicited the support of US President Trump, they raised over £1m in a crowdfunding campaign. A small number directed abusive messages to hospital staff, lawyers and the NHS and it has been argued that some of those were less concerned about Charlie's treatment and more focused on the campaign's potential to further their political ideals.[105]

A shocking feature of cases where parents challenge doctors over treatment withdrawal is that legal aid is not always available. This can increase reliance on crowd funding and on interest groups with their own agendas. Charlie's parents, Chris Gard and Connie Yates, were represented pro bono. At the time of writing, the Government has undertaken to provide free legal representation for all under-18s and parents in this position.[106]

102 *Yates & Gard v Great Ormond Street Hospital* [2017] EWCA Civ 410 – the Supreme Court declined permission to appeal, 8 June 2017; *Gard and Ors v the UK*, App No 39793/17 (ECHR, 27 June 2017) (Commission Decision) 605.

103 *GOSH v Gard, Yates and Gard* [2017] EWHC 1909.

104 C Auckland and I Goold, 'Resolving Disagreement: A Multi-Jurisdictional Comparative Analysis of Disputes About Children's Medical Care' (2020) 28(4) *Med Law Rev* 643.

105 See eg 'Charlie's Army: The People Fighting for Charlie Gard' *This Week* (2017) 26 July. And see in relation to a case discussed below, *Evans v Alder Hey Children's NHS Foundation Trust* [2018] EWCA Civ 984, [40], McFarlane LJ: '[I]t has become apparent … that the representation of the parents may have been infiltrated or compromised by others who purport to act on their behalf.'

106 Ministry of Justice, 'Legal Aid Sector put on Sustainable Footing for Years to Come' (2022) 15 March.

A year after Charlie's death, baby Isaiah Haastrup[107] suffered brain injury when he was deprived of oxygen at birth. The Trust sought a declaration that it would be in Isaiah's best interests to withdraw ventilation and to restrict care to palliation. Isaiah's parents are Pentecostal Christians and believed that, even on life support, Isaiah's life was worth living. They suspected that the hospital had caused the birth injuries through negligence[108] and they trusted neither the hospital's reasoning nor its motives. They arranged for a Polish doctor to examine him, without permission of the court and, it is alleged by the hospital, without identifying the doctor's role or intent. Balancing the relevant considerations, MacDonald J made the declarations sought by the Trust. The evidence suggested that Isaiah's brain injury was profound and irreversible, and that treatment was futile and burdensome.

Two-year-old Alfie Evans had a progressive brain disorder that had destroyed the thalami, which regulates the brain's pathways. His parents wanted to take him to Italy for treatment and to keep him alive in accordance with their Roman Catholic faith, but the hospital considered this to be contrary to his best interests and argued that treatment should be withdrawn. Alfie's parents made three legal attempts to prolong treatment. In the first application[109] the argument that the significant harm test should apply was rejected and ruled inadmissible by the ECtHR. The second application[110] was an application for habeas corpus: an ancient writ demanding release from unlawful detention. But the Supreme Court refused permission to appeal stating that the writ of habeas corpus cannot be used in a manner that is not in the child's best interests: 'The release to which he is entitled … is release from the imposition of treatment which is not in his best interests'.[111] The third application[112] was brought when ventilation was withdrawn and Alfie was unexpectedly able to breathe spontaneously, with only modest access to oxygen. Alfie had by this time been declared by Italy an Italian citizen and a military plane was made available to fly him to hospital in Rome. The appeal was refused. Alfie was not under the Italian jurisdiction and his breathing did not amount to a change in circumstances. Alfie died in April 2018, just before his second birthday.

The High Court was more sympathetic to the views of Tafida Raqeeb's parents. Tafida was 4 when she suffered a sudden rupture of an arteriovenous malformation causing catastrophic brain injury and leaving her with minimal, if any,

107 *Kings College Hospital Foundation Trust v Haastrup* [2018] EWHC 127 (Fam).

108 On which see 'Isaiah Haastrup: Hospital "Admits Liability" in Brain Damaged Baby Case' *BBC News* (2021) 4 February.

109 *Alder Hey Children's NHS Foundation Trust v Evans* [2018] EWHC 308 (Fam); *E (A Child) (Rev 1)* [2018] EWCA Civ 550; *Evans v UK* (App No 14238/18) [2018] ECHR 297 (inadmissible).

110 *Alder Hey Children's NHS Foundation Trust v Evans* [2018] EWHC 818 (Fam); *Evans v Alder Hey Children's NHS Foundation Trust* [2018] EWCA Civ 805.

111 *Re Alfie Evans No 2* (2018) 20 April: www.supremecourt.uk/docs/in-the-matter-of-alfie-evans-court-order.pdf.

112 *Alder Hey Children's NHS Foundation Trust v Evans* [2018] EWHC 953 (Fam); *Evans v Alder Hey Children's NHS Foundation Trust* [2018] EWCA Civ 984.

awareness. It was unlikely that she could feel pain and clinicians agreed that she could not substantially recover. Her parents sought to transfer her to Italy whereupon, with mechanical ventilation, she could live ten to twenty years. Royal London Hospital sought a declaration that it was in her best interests for life-sustaining treatment to be withdrawn.[113] MacDonald J refused the declarations sought by the Trust having found that on the balance of probabilities Tafida was not in pain, that ongoing treatment would not be a burden to her and that at 4 'she would not reject out of hand a situation in which she continued to live'.

Raqeeb raised questions that were addressed in subsequent cases.[114] Firstly, provided a child is not in pain, is continued treatment sought by parents ever capable of causing the child harm? In *Re Pippa Knight*[115] Baker LJ in the Court of Appeal opined that the judgment in *Raqeeb* did not proceed on the basis that no pain would mean there would be no harm, but rather that the debilitating physical symptoms Tafida would suffer did not tip the balance in favour of granting the declarations sought by the Trust.[116] Pippa Knight had developed acute necrotising encephalopathy at 20 months and, by the time of the hearing when she was 6, was in a persistent vegetative state. The evidence suggested she had no awareness or capacity to feel pain. In the High Court, Poole J granted the Trust's application that mechanical ventilation should be withdrawn. The Court of Appeal concurred. Pippa could be physically harmed notwithstanding her incapacity to feel pain.

A second question concerns references in the *Raqeeb* judgment to 'medical best interests' which ostensibly separated *medical* best interests assessments by clinicians and the *overall* assessment made by the court. In *Fixsler* (discussed imminently), MacDonald J clarified that clinicians should not sever medical best interests from the overall evaluation of children's best interests.[117]

17.16 The assumed point of view of the patient

A child's assumed point of view attracts considerable weight, but they are but one of the relevant factors to consider when the court makes an independent and objective assessment of best interests. In *Raqeeb*, MacDonald J rejected

113 *Barts Health NHS Trust v Raqeeb & Raqeeb* [2019] EWHC 2530 (Fam); *Raqeeb and Barts Health NHS Trust* [2019] EWHC 2531 (Admin). Two cases were heard together by Mr Justice MacDonald: a best interests determination sought by the Trust and a judicial review brought by the parents. On the latter see B van Leeuwen, 'Free Movement of Life? The Interaction Between the Best Interests Test and the Right to Freely Receive Services in *Tafida Raqeeb*' (2020) July *Public Law* 398.

114 See E Cave *et al*, 'Making Decisions for Children – Accommodating Parental Choice in Best Interests Determinations' (2020) 28(1) *Med Law Rev* 183.

115 [2021] EWHC 25 (Fam); [2021] EWCA Civ 362; *Parfitt v Guy's and St Thomas' Children's NHS FT*, UKSC 2021/0077 (permission to appeal refused); *Parfitt v UK*, App No 18533/21 (ECHR, 2021) (inadmissible).

116 [2021] EWCA Civ 362, [61], Baker LJ.

117 [2021] EWHC 1426 (Fam), [61].

the argument that the assumed point of view of the child *must* be given preferential weight.[118] This conclusion was endorsed by the Court of Appeal in *Fixsler v Manchester University NHS FT*.[119] Alta Fixsler was born prematurely and suffered hypoxic ischaemic brain injury, which would lead to her death in infancy. Aged 2, her doctors were of the view that she was in pain and that treatment should be withdrawn. Her parents were Hasidic Jews and they wanted to take her abroad so that her treatment could be continued in accordance with their religious beliefs. At first instance, MacDonald J's assessment of her overall best interests led to the conclusion that she was likely to be experiencing pain which was a significant burden to her. Whereas in *Raqeeb* there was sufficient evidence that Tafida might share her parent's values, such evidence, MacDonald J concluded, was lacking in this case: 'it is more likely than not that Alta's point of view would be that continued life-sustaining treatment would not be acceptable to her.'[120] The Court of Appeal agreed that treatment should be withdrawn, with the proviso that it was not possible to say what Alta's views would be given her age and lack of understanding.

17.17 Not just life or death

Difficult decisions about the medical care of young children are not exclusively confined to decisions relating to life-sustaining treatment. In *Re C (HIV test)*,[121] a baby was born to an HIV positive mother. She had declined conventional treatment for HIV, rejected treatment in pregnancy which might have diminished the risk of transmitting HIV to the child, and intended to breastfeed. Both parents refused to agree to an HIV test for their baby. They argued that any possible treatment for the child (were she HIV positive) could be more toxic than beneficial, and that sero-positive status would stigmatise the child. The local authority, applying for an order to test the child, relied on medical opinion that the child was at a 25 per cent risk of having contracted HIV and that effective medical care of the child required knowledge of her HIV status. The Court of Appeal upheld the trial judge's view that it was in the child's best interests to allow the HIV test. The parents sought to assert their right to respect for family life enshrined in Article 8 of the ECHR. As the trial judge noted, such a claim is swiftly countered by consideration of the child's own rights and the needs of his health and welfare expressly recognised in Article 8(2).[122]

Resolving 'conflicts of rights' is not easy. Disputes between parents can be just as complex as disagreements between doctors and parents. In *Re J (Child's Religious Upbringing and Circumcision)*,[123] a devout Muslim father sought a

118 [2019] EWHC 2530 (Fam), [122]–[124].
119 [2021] EWCA Civ 1018.
120 [2021] EWHC 1426 (Fam), [96].
121 [2000] Fam 48, CA.
122 See L Haggar, 'Some Implications of the Human Rights Act 1998 for the Medical Treatment of Children' (2003) 6 *Medical Law International* 25.
123 [2000] 1 FRC 307. *Re J* concerned a young child. On the relevance of older children's views see M Fox and M Thomson, 'Older Minors and Circumcision: Questioning the Limits of Religious Actions' (2009) 9(4) *Medical law International* 283.

court order to circumcise his 5-year-old son. The child's non-Muslim mother objected. The couple were estranged. The father argued that circumcision would identify child with father and establish the boy within the Muslim community. He invoked his right under Article 9 of the ECHR to freedom of religion. The mother's religious adherence to Christianity was said to be notional only. There were no medical grounds for circumcision. The courts found for the mother, influenced by the pain and distress circumcision might cause the boy.[124]

The balance is more complex when the dispute concerns preventive action. In *Re C (Welfare of the Child: Immunisation)*,[125] two fathers applied for court orders that their daughters should receive the MMR vaccine. Both girls lived with their mothers who considered the MMR vaccine to be unsafe. The Court of Appeal upheld the trial judge's ruling that vaccination was in the girls' best interests. The judges considered that the medical evidence of both the efficacy and safety of the MMR vaccine was overwhelming. They dismissed the contrary evidence out of hand. In *F (Mother) v F (Father)*[126] Theis J considered the differing perspectives of a father who wanted his 15- and 11-year-olds to receive the MMR and the mother and children who disagreed. Despite the opposition of the children and the fact that the older child had already had the first of two MMR vaccines (and thus heightened immunity) the vaccinations were considered to be in the girls' best interests.[127]

Where a parent objects to vaccination to a child in care, there has been conflict in the High Court as to the appropriate procedural route. If vaccination is characterised as preventive care, then the local authority might be able to consent to it under section 33(3) of the Children Act 1989, notwithstanding the objections of parents. This route would not be considered appropriate in relation to serious medical treatment. The matter came to the Court of Appeal in *Re H*,[128] which held that the categorisation of vaccination as either preventive care or treatment was unhelpful. What was important was whether vaccination was a grave or serious decision. Provided there are no contraindications and given that the link between MMR and autism has been disproved, Lady Justice King, giving the leading judgment, held that it is not grave.[129] As a result, not all parental objections need to come before the court.

Compulsory vaccination offends the right of individuals to exercise choice, but this must be balanced against public health considerations in

124 But see *SS (Malaysia) v Secretary of State for the Home Department* [2013] EWCA Civ 888, where an asylum seeker challenged expulsion on the ground that the son was likely to be circumcised in Malaysia. Moore-Bick LJ (at [14]) found it 'difficult to see how C's circumcision would involve any infringement of the appellant's Convention rights'.

125 [2003] 2 FLR 1095, CA.

126 [2013] EWHC 2683.

127 E Cave, 'Adolescent Refusal of MMR inoculation' (2014) 77(4) *MLR* 630.

128 *Re H (A Child) (Parental Responsibility: Vaccination)* [2020] EWCA Civ 664. In *C (Looked After Child) (Covid-19 Vaccination)* [2021] EWHC 2993 (Fam), [20] it was held that the principles also apply to COVID-19 vaccination.

129 *Re H*, ibid, King LJ, [85].

vaccine-preventable pandemic diseases and the interests of children.[130] In *Vavřička and Others v the Czech Republic*[131] the Grand Chamber of the Strasbourg Court held that the Czech Republic's policy of fining parents who refused routine childhood vaccinations was proportionate and did not violate Article 8 of the Convention. It is questionable whether the same approach would apply if more draconian methods of compulsion were utilised, or if there were legitimate concerns as to safety. Would compulsion have been necessary and proportionate to combat COVID-19? A novel vaccine that has not had the benefit of post-market surveillance may pose additional risks but might conversely more readily satisfy the requirement of necessity if the alternative had been mass quarantine.

As parental rights to determine medical treatment of their child derive from the parental duty to obtain adequate medical care for them, those rights cannot be unfettered. In Skegg's words, a parent may give 'a legally effective consent to a procedure which is likely to be for the benefit of the child, in the sense of being in the child's best interests'.[132] Routine treatment or surgery for an existing physical condition, diagnostic procedures or preventive measures, such as vaccination, pose no problem. The benefit is there for all to see. More intricate and even risky procedures cause little difficulty. Not all parents might agree to complex heart surgery on a baby, but if doctors and parents weigh risk and benefit, and conclude in favour of going ahead, they have exercised their respective duties properly. Problems surface in relation to medical or surgical procedures not immediately called for to treat or prevent ill health. Two classic issues are dealt with later – whether a child can donate organs or tissue (in Chapter 20), and when children can be used for medical research purposes (in Chapter 18).

17.18 The limits of the best interests test

The best interests test will not apply if the child is clinically dead. As we discuss at 19.3 below, a patient who is brain-stem-dead is considered dead by neurological criteria, even though the heart and lungs are supported artificially. Baby Midrar's parents had been advised by their Imam that as long as his heart continued to beat, there was hope of improvement. Sadly, the clinical evidence suggested there was no prospect of recovery. The Court of Appeal dismissed an appeal of the High Court decision to grant declarations sought by a Manchester Trust that mechanical ventilation could be removed. Whereas the best interest test will determine disputes as to medical treatment in the living, 'where a person is dead, the question of best interests is, tragically, no longer relevant'.[133]

130 E Cave, 'Voluntary Vaccination: The Pandemic Effect' (2016) 37 *LS* 279.

131 App no 47621/13 (ECHR, 2021). See D Archard, J Brierley and E Cave, 'Compulsory Childhood Vaccination: Human Rights, Solidarity, and Best Interests' (2021) 28(1) *Med Law Rev* 183.

132 See PDG Skegg, 'Consent to Medical Procedures on Minors' (1973) 36 *MLR* 370, at 377.

133 *Re M (declaration of death of child)* [2020] EWCA Civ 164, [24].

As the book goes to press, we briefly note a subsequent tragic case. Archie Battersbee was found unconscious with a ligature round his neck. Doctors were unable to apply the standard brain stem test due to aspects of his clinical presentation, but other tests, including scans, and consultation with other hospitals led them to conclude that on the balance of probabilities he was dead. The High Court initially accepted this evidence,[134] but on appeal, counsel from both sides agreed that in circumstances where the standard brain stem test could not be administered a child's best interests should be evaluated.[135] In a series of appeals to the Court of Appeal, Supreme Court and the ECtHR it was found that treatment was not in Archie's best interests. In August 2022 life support was withdrawn.

17.19 Procedures to protect children

We do not examine in any detail the procedural means by which disputes about the care or treatment of a child come before the courts. One or two brief points about parental responsibility and family law procedures are noted here.[136] When a child's parents are married or in a civil partnership, both parents share parental responsibility. When the parents are unmarried, they share parental responsibility if either they jointly register the child's birth, or they subsequently enter into a formal agreement to share parental responsibility. Or a father may seek a court order conferring parental responsibility on him where the mother is not voluntarily prepared to share legal responsibility for the child.[137] Normally, in relation to medical treatment, the consent of one parent to the treatment of their young child suffices.[138] If a mother takes her 5-year-old for a booster vaccination, the doctor does not need to delay matters by ensuring that the father also agrees to vaccination. The courts have, however, made it clear that where some major or irreversible decision needs to be made about a child's treatment, or where there is disagreement between the parents sharing parental responsibility, both parents' consent is required and/or the case must be referred to the court.[139]

Should a father without parental responsibility, other relatives (such as grandparents), local social services, or any other third party have concerns about a child's medical treatment, a number of means exist by which a dispute concerning the child's welfare can be adjudicated by a court. The child could be taken into care or made a ward of court,[140] but that is rare these days. The inherent jurisdiction of the Court can be invoked, or an order sought under

134 *Barts Health NHS Trust v Dance* [2022] EWHC 1435 (Fam).

135 *Barts Health NHS Trust v Dance* [2022] EWCA Civ 935. See also *Re A (A Child)* [2022] EWHC 1873 (Fam); [2022] EWCA Civ 1221 and discussion at 19.3 below.

136 See S Gilmore, *Parental Rights and Responsibilities* (2017) Routledge.

137 See the Children Act 1989, s 4 as amended by the Adoption and Children Act 2002.

138 GMC, *Treatment and Care Towards the End of Life*, para 104.

139 See *Re J (Child's Religious Upbringing and Circumcision)* [1999] 2 FLR 1004 CA.

140 In which case the court will acquire control over all aspects of the child's life and upbringing.

section 8 of the Children Act 1989.[141] Section 8 orders are diverse in kind. Of particular relevance here are 'specific issue orders' and 'prohibited steps orders'. If an unmarried father (who does not have parental responsibility) strongly believes that surgery to correct a birthmark is in his child's interests and her mother opposes surgery solely because she believes that her child's abnormality was 'God's will – a punishment for being born out of wedlock', he may seek a 'specific issue order'.[142] Should he seek to prevent the performance of purely cosmetic surgery which his child's mother wants because she wants the child to be a model, he could apply for a 'prohibited steps order' to prevent surgery.

17.20 The views of the child

What of a child's own wishes? Once a child can communicate, they will in many cases have an opinion of their own. The Children Act 1989 includes a 'welfare checklist' that requires consideration of the 'ascertainable wishes and feelings of the child concerned (considered in the light of his age and understanding)'.[143] Most 4-year-olds object robustly to injections and anything likely to cause them discomfort. At 4 years, the case that the child cannot form any sensible judgement about the pros and cons of treatment may well be made out. At 8, 10 and 12 years, the child acquires greater maturity, albeit most doctors and parents would be reluctant to bow to the child's judgement. What must be remembered, however, is that the balance of the child's best interests will be (radically) affected by his willingness or otherwise to participate in treatment. Obtaining assent even from very young children is good practice.[144] Forcible treatment, which may involve restraining, even detaining, the child, requires strong justification. And as the child reaches their teens, becoming what is rather pompously called a 'mature minor', the legal picture changes. GMC guidance states: 'Parents are usually the best judges of their children's best interests and should make important decisions up until children are able to make their own decisions.'[145]

141 Where the child is 16 and over and the issue does not concern an aspect of parental responsibility, the inherent jurisdiction is preferred to an order under s 8: *Re JM (a child)* [2015] EWHC 2832 (Fam). And see *GOSH for Children NHS FT v MK* [2020] EWHC 3476 (Fam) (concerning authorisation of medical treatment where no one with parental responsibility can give lawful consent).

142 As the fathers did in *Re B (Welfare of the Child: Immunisation)* [2003] EWCA Civ 1148.

143 Section 1(3)(a).

144 See United Nations Convention on the Rights of the Child Article 1989, Art 12(1): 'States Parties shall assure to the child who is capable of forming his or her own views the right to express those views freely in all matters affecting the child, the views of the child being given due weight in accordance with the age and maturity of the child.' And see Royal College of Paediatrics and Child Health, *Making Decisions to Limit Treatment*, para 2.4.5.

145 GMC, *0–18 Guidance for all Doctors* (2007), para 21.

The Mental Capacity Act 2005, discussed in Chapter 7 above, applies from the age of 16. A functional test for capacity is set out in sections 2 and 3. Where a patient is found to lack capacity, a decision must be made in their best interests, as set out in section 4. Great weight is given to the patient's points of view. William Verden was a 17-year-old patient in end-stage kidney failure. He had complex learning difficulties, ADHD and autism and was prone to outbursts. He lacked capacity to decide for himself. The Court of Protection considered whether it was in William's best interests to undergo a kidney transplant. Clinicians feared that he would not tolerate the post-operative treatment well and that there were significant risks around extended sedation and ventilation. His mother felt that he could tolerate the treatment and cited expert evidence that it would give him a reasonable change of a good outcome. Arbuthnot J considered the case from William's point of view. William wanted to continue the activities he enjoyed and to experience the company of his loving family. She found that it would be in William's best interests to have the kidney transplant.[146]

17.21 Family Law Reform Act 1969

The Mental Capacity Act deals with *mental* capacity; person-specific decision-making abilities. The Family Law Reform Act 1969 concerns *legal* capacity; the ability to hold and exercise rights. It reduced the age of majority from 21 to 18. Section 8 of the 1969 Act empowered 16- and 17-year-olds to consent to their own medical treatment. Sub-sections (1) and (2) of section 8 provide:

> (1) The consent of a minor who has attained the age of 16 years to any surgical, medical or dental treatment which, in the absence of consent, would constitute a trespass to his person shall be as effective as it would be if he were of full age: and where a minor has by virtue of this section given an effective consent it shall not be necessary to obtain any consent for it from his parent or guardian.
>
> (2) In this section 'surgical, medical or dental treatment' includes any procedure undertaken for the purposes of diagnosis, and this section applies to any procedure (including, in particular, the administration of an anaesthetic) which is ancillary to any treatment as it applies to that treatment.

So far, so good; once a person is 16 they can consent to treatment themselves. That does not mean that any parental consent relating to their children under 18 is always ineffective. If the child of 16 or 17 is incapable of giving consent, for example because they lack mental capacity, their parents may still act on their behalf until they come of age. Section 8 went on in sub-section (3) to provide:

146 *Manchester University NHS Trust v Verdon* [2022] EWCOP 9. See D Archard *et al*, 'Involving Parents in Paediatric Clinical Ethics Committee Deliberations: A Current Controversy' (2022) *J Med Ethics* DOI:10.1136/jme-2022-108460.

(3) Nothing in this section shall be construed as making ineffective any consent which would have been effective if this section had not been enacted.

The majority of lawyers and doctors interpreted section 8(3) in this way. The common law had never directly determined when, if at all, a child could give effective consent to medical treatment. The assumption was that the law gave effect to consent by a minor provided they were sufficiently mature to understand the proposed treatment or surgery;[147] 16 was the average age at which doctors judged patients to be old enough to give consent without consulting parents on every occasion. Many doctors also regarded themselves as free to treat children under 16 without parental approval, if the individual child appeared sufficiently intelligent and grown up to take the decision on treatment alone. Before 1969, every case turned on the doctor's assessment of the particular minor in their surgery. The 1969 Act freed the doctor from doubt and risk where the patient was over 16. Doctors no longer had to consider the maturity of a patient over 16. They could assume adult status and capability. Sub-section (3), it was argued, simply preserved the *status quo* for the under-16s. Doctors could continue to treat a child under 16 as long as that child was mature enough to make their own judgement. This assumption, that there had always been a limited freedom to treat children under 16 without parental consent, and that what sub-section (3) did was preserve that freedom, was at the heart of the *Gillick* saga and its sequels in *Re R* and *Re W*.

17.22 The *Gillick* case

The *Gillick* saga has its origins in a circular issued by the Department of Health and Social Security (DHSS) in 1974, outlining arrangements for a comprehensive family planning service within the NHS. Statistics on the number of births and induced abortions among girls under 16 led the DHSS to conclude that contraceptive services should be made more readily available to that age group. The essence of their advice was that the decision to provide contraception to a girl under 16 was one for the doctor. They might lawfully treat, and prescribe for, the girl without contacting her parents. They should not contact parents without the girl's agreement. In 1980, the DHSS revised its advice. The revised version stressed that every effort should be made to involve parents. If the girl was adamant that her parents should not know of her request for contraception, the principle of confidentiality between doctor and patient should be preserved. This amended advice from the DHSS did not satisfy critics. Victoria Gillick sought assurances that none of her daughters would be given contraceptive or abortion advice or treatment without her prior knowledge and consent until they were 16. Those assurances were refused, and Mrs Gillick went to court seeking declarations (1) against her health authority and the DHSS to the effect that their advice that children under 16 could be treated without parental consent was unlawful and wrong, and (2) against her health authority to the effect that medical personnel employed by them should not give contraceptive and/or abortion advice

[147] See Skegg (1973) 36 *MLR* 370, 370–375.

and/or treatment to any child of Mrs Gillick's under 16 without her prior knowledge and consent. Mrs Gillick's concern was with contraception and abortion for under-16s. She had no axe to grind in respect of other forms of medical treatment. The trouble is that contraception cannot be isolated from more general questions. Mrs Gillick's counsel challenged the assumption that the common law permitted medical treatment of children under 16 in the absence of parental consent.

17.23 Children under 16 and consent to treatment: *Gillick* competence

At first instance, Woolf J[148] endorsed the view that once a child was able to understand what was entailed in proposed treatment, they could consent to such treatment. Any physical contact involved in treatment would not constitute battery. Mrs Gillick appealed and, in a complex judgment, the Court of Appeal[149] found for her. Not only was any treatment of a child under 16 potentially battery unless authorised by a parent, but giving children advice or information about contraception without parental knowledge could constitute an infringement of parental rights. After the Court of Appeal decision, no doctor could (save in emergency) safely see a child under 16 in her clinic or surgery without parental knowledge. The DHSS appealed to the House of Lords. By a majority, the House of Lords held that the original advice circulated by the DHSS was not unlawful and that a child under 16 could in certain circumstances give a valid consent to medical treatment, including contraception or abortion treatment, without parental knowledge or agreement.[150]

17.24 The general problem of consent

The majority of their Lordships rejected the Court of Appeal's finding that consent given by a child under 16 was of no effect. Like Woolf J, they accepted the view that the Family Law Reform Act had left that question open. The matter was for the common law to determine. The common law was not static, fossilised in eighteenth-century notions of the inviolable rights of the *paterfamilias*. Judge-made law must meet the needs of the times. Parental rights derived from parental duties to protect the person and property of the child. Modern legislation qualified and limited parental rights by placing the welfare of the child as its first priority. Parental rights being dependent on the duty to care for and maintain the child, they endured only so long as necessary to achieve their end. As Lord Scarman put it:

> [T]he parental right yields to the child's right to make his own decisions when he reaches a sufficient understanding and intelligence to be capable of making up his own mind on the matter requiring decision.[151]

148 [1984] 1 All ER 365.
149 [1985] 1 All ER 533.
150 [1985] 3 All ER 402.
151 Ibid, at 422.

Their Lordships argued that the common law had never regarded the consent of a child as a complete nullity. Were that the case, intercourse with a girl aged under 16 would inevitably be rape. That is not so. Provided the girl is old enough to understand what she is agreeing to, intercourse with her consent will not be rape. Parliament, to protect girls under 16 from the consequences of their own folly, enacted a separate offence of unlawful sexual intercourse with girls under 16 in the commission of which the girl's consent is irrelevant. If the girl validly consented, that is the only offence committed, and not the more serious crime of rape.[152]

Moving from the general issue of consent by children to the problem of consent to medical treatment, the House of Lords saw no reason to depart from the general rule. Lord Fraser thought it would be ludicrous to say that a boy or girl of 15 could not agree to examination or treatment for a trivial injury. Importantly, Lord Templeman, who dissented on the specific issue of contraceptive treatment, agreed that there were circumstances where a doctor could properly treat a child under 16 without parental agreement. He concurred that the effect of the consent of the child depended on the nature of the treatment and the age and understanding of the child. A doctor, he thought, could safely remove tonsils or a troublesome appendix from a boy or girl of 15 without express parental agreement. *Gillick* establishes that a child below 16 may lawfully be given general medical advice and treatment without parental agreement, provided that child has achieved sufficient maturity to understand fully what is proposed. The doctor treating such a child on the basis of her consent alone will not be at risk of either a civil action for battery or criminal prosecution.

17.25 The special problem of contraception[153]

Lord Templeman, however, dissented on the specific issue of contraception. He did not accept that a girl under 16 has sufficient maturity and understanding of the emotional and physical consequences of sexual intercourse to consent to contraceptive treatment. His Lordship put it thus:[154]

> I doubt whether a girl under the age of 16 is capable of a balanced judgement to embark on frequent, regular or casual sexual intercourse fortified by the illusion that medical science can protect her in mind and body and ignoring the danger of leaping from childhood to adulthood without the difficult formative transitional experiences of adolescence. There are many things a girl under 16 needs to practise but sex is not one of them.

The majority of his colleagues disagreed. They conceded that a request by a girl under 16 for contraception, coupled with an insistence that her parents not be told, posed a problem for the doctor. Assessing whether she was mature

152 See Sexual Offences Act 2003, s 5 (rape of a child under 13) and s 9 (sexual activity with a child).
153 And see further 16.14 above on the related issue of abortion.
154 [1985] 3 All ER 402, HL, 432.

enough to consider the emotional and physical consequences of the course she had embarked on was not easy. But that question should be left to the clinical judgement of the doctor. Lord Fraser set out five matters the doctor should satisfy themselves on before giving contraceptive treatment to a girl below 16 without parental agreement. They are:

(1) that the girl ... will understand his advice;
(2) that he cannot persuade her to inform her parents ...;
(3) that she is very likely to begin or continue having sexual intercourse with or without contraceptive treatment;
(4) that unless she receives contraceptive advice or treatment her physical or mental health or both are likely to suffer;
(5) that her best interests require him to give her contraceptive advice or treatment or both without the parental consent.[155]

Lord Fraser's formula failed to satisfy Mrs Gillick. She regarded it as inadequate in two respects. (1) In a busy surgery or clinic has any doctor sufficient time to embark on the investigation and counselling of the girl necessary to fulfil the criteria laid down? (2) Underlying the judgments of the majority is acceptance of the view that, as significant numbers of young girls under 16 are going to continue having sexual intercourse regardless of whether they have lawful access to contraception, it may be in their best interests to protect them from pregnancy by contraceptive treatment. Mrs Gillick disagreed. She contended that if access to contraception without parental agreement were stopped, at least the majority of young girls would (a) be deterred from starting to have intercourse so young by fear of pregnancy and/or parental disapproval, and (b) would have a defence against pressure from their peers to 'grow up' and sleep with someone. Both sides in the debate on 'under-age' contraception agree that early sexual intercourse increases the danger of disease to the child, be it cervical cancer or venereal disease. Most agree about the emotional damage the child risks. They are no nearer agreement on how girls under 16 may best be protected than on the day Mrs Gillick first went to court.

Mrs Gillick had, however, a second line of attack. The Sexual Offences Act 1956 made it a criminal offence 'to cause or encourage ... the commission of unlawful sexual intercourse with ... a girl for whom [the] accused is responsible'. So, Mrs Gillick argued that providing contraception for a girl under 16 amounted to 'encouraging' that crime. The Law Lords dismissed this second claim too. The Sexual Offences Act 2003 replaces the 1956 Act. It creates a raft of new criminal offences and toughens up the law relating to unlawful sexual relations with people under 16. But sections 14 and 73 of the Act provide express protection for doctors and nurses providing contraceptive advice or treatment, abortions, or indeed any healthcare relating to the young person's sexual health. No offence of facilitating a child sex offence or aiding and abetting unlawful sexual intercourse is committed if the person acts either (1) to protect the child from sexually transmitted diseases; (2) to protect the

155 Ibid, 413.

child's physical safety; (3) to prevent a child from becoming pregnant; or (4) to promote the child's emotional well-being by the giving of advice.

17.26 The threshold of *Gillick* competence

The requirement that a child 'understands fully' what is proposed in order to be considered *Gillick* competent can lead to the imposition of a high threshold for competence. Consider *Re E.*[156] E was 15 and shared his parents' Jehovah's Witness faith. He was seriously ill with leukaemia. Doctors advised that to maximise the prospects of successful chemotherapy, E should receive transfusions of blood products. E, like his parents, refused to agree to transfusions. The boy was made a ward of court. The judge authorised transfusion. He acknowledged that E was highly intelligent, mature for his age and well informed about his illness. Nonetheless, he held that E was not *Gillick* competent. He lacked insight into the process of dying. He could not turn his mind to the effect of the manner of his death or its effect on his family. How many adults enjoy such insight? Understandably, courts seek to protect young people from decisions that may endanger their life. In E's case, the outcome is tragic. Treatment at 15 resulted in a temporary remission. At 18 he relapsed, refused treatment and died believing that he had participated in an ungodly act. Then in *Re M (Child: Refusal of Medical Treatment)*,[157] a girl of 15½ refused to consent to a heart transplant. Her refusal was overridden by Johnson J whereupon M complied with the treatment. One of M's reasons for refusing surgery was said to be the prospect of lifelong medication. Were her reasons for refusing a transplant much different from those of T's parents in *Re T (A Minor) (Wardship: Medical Treatment)*?[158]

Attempts by the courts to flesh out the vague threshold for *Gillick* competence have been controversial. Keira Bell was diagnosed with gender dysphoria and as a late teen transitioned to male before later de-transitioning, claiming that the treatment had been harmful and should not be offered to children. The Divisional Court in the judicial review case of *Bell & Anor v The Tavistock and Portman NHS Foundation Trust (Bell)*[159] cited evidence of a significant rise in referrals to the Gender Identity Development Service: from 97 in 2009 to 2,519 in 2018.[160] The Court sought to identify precisely what must be fully understood in the context of treatment for gender dysphoria. Sharp P, Lewis LJ and Lieven J found that *Gillick* set out the appropriate test, but that eight factors must be complied with in order to establish that children were *Gillick* competent to consent to puberty-blocking treatment. For example, they would

156 *Re E (A Minor)* (1990) 9 BMLR 1.
157 [1999] 2 FLR 1097.
158 [1997] 1 All ER 906, CA.
159 [2020] EWHC 3274 (Admin); [2021] EWCA Civ 1363. See E Cave, 'Adolescent Consent to Treatment for Gender Dysphoria in England and Wales' in L Austin and J Miola, *Research Handbook on Informed Consent* (forthcoming) Edward Elgar.
160 On which see the Cass Review: Hilary Cass (Chair), *Independent Review of Gender Identity Services for Children and Young People: Interim Report* (2022).

need to understand that the treatment would usually progress to additional treatment with cross-sex hormones, and potentially then to surgery. They should understand that the later treatments could lead to loss of fertility and could impact on future relationships. Furthermore, they would need to understand that the physical consequences of taking puberty blockers in this context were poorly evidenced. The Court did not duck the issue that this would leave most children unable to consent:

> It is highly unlikely that a child aged 13 or under would be competent to give consent to the administration of puberty blockers. It is doubtful that a child aged 14 or 15 could understand and weigh the long-term risks and consequences of the administration of puberty blockers.[161]

On appeal this approach was firmly rejected. Lord Burnett of Maldon CJ giving the leading Court of Appeal judgment said the Divisional Court had improperly restricted the *Gillick* test by requiring 'clinicians to suspend or at least to temper their clinical judgement and defer to what amounts to the clinical judgement of the court'.[162] Whilst in theory the Court of Appeal opened the way for competent decisions of children with gender dysphoria to be determinative, policy controls will determine the circumstances in which children and young people can access treatment.[163]

In an adoption case, *In re S*,[164] Cobb J applied aspects of the Mental Capacity Act 2005 test, to determine competence in an under-16-year-old. This position found favour with the Divisional Court in *Bell*,[165] but was not considered helpful 'in this case' by the Court of Appeal in *Bell*.[166] It was scorned by Sir James Munby in *Re X (A Child) (No 2)*.[167]

17.27 A right to say no?

For several years, *Gillick* was assumed to have established that once young people acquired the necessary maturity to consent to treatment, what Lord Donaldson was later to style *Gillick* competence,[168] they acquired a right to determine what medical treatment they received. One might assume that competent minors would have a right to say no, as much as a right to say yes. Recall Lord Scarman's words in *Gillick*,[169] '... the parental right yields to the child's right to make his own decision when he reaches a sufficient understanding and intelligence to be capable of making up his own mind on the matter requiring a decision'. Subsequent judgments of the Court of Appeal rejected that apparently

161 [2020] EWHC 3274 (Admin), [51].
162 Ibid, [74].
163 See (ongoing at time of writing) Hilary Cass (Chair), *Independent Review of Gender Identity Services for Children and Young People*.
164 [2020] EWHC 3274 (Admin), [116]–[118]. *In re S (A Child) (Child Parent: Adoption Consent)* [2017] EWHC 2729 (Fam).
165 [2020] EWHC 3274 (Admin), [126], [131].
166 [2021] EWCA Civ 1363, [83].
167 [2021] EWHC 65 (Fam), [73]–[75] (see 17.27 below).
168 See *Re R (A Minor)* [1991] 4 All ER 177, CA.
169 [1985] 3 All ER 402, HL, 422.

logical conclusion. Adolescent autonomy is little more than myth, for no young person under 18 – no minor – has a right to refuse treatment, at least if the treatment is life sustaining and in their best interests.[170] Parental powers to authorise treatment against their offspring's will were endorsed concurrently with extensive judicial powers to order minors to submit to treatment others deem necessary for their welfare.

In *Re R*, R[171] was a 15-year-old girl suffering from acute psychiatric problems. Her condition fluctuated. At times she appeared rational and lucid. However, she lacked insight into her illness. During her lucid phases she refused medication and became psychotic once again. R was in care, and the local authority responsible for her sought judicial guidance seeking authority to administer anti-psychotic drugs without R's consent. The Court of Appeal agreed with the trial judge that R was not *Gillick* competent. Her illness prevented her from fully understanding the need for drugs to control her condition. R could lawfully be treated against her will. In this particular case, the court authorised her treatment via its wardship jurisdiction. But the local authority as her legal guardian could equally have provided a proxy consent on R's behalf. The interest of *Re R* lies in Lord Donaldson's *dicta*. He went on to say that even were R *Gillick* competent, she would still have no power to veto treatment. A *Gillick* competent minor could consent to, but not refuse, treatment. Consent was akin to a key which 'unlocked the door to treatment' making the doctor's action lawful, but not obligatory. Once a young person became *Gillick* competent she became a keyholder. Her parents remained keyholders until she reached 18. They could still authorise treatment on her behalf. Doctors faced with willing parents but unwilling children were not obliged to treat the child, indeed might choose not to. They could, however, lawfully elect to act on the basis of the parents' consent alone. The problem was one of ethical and clinical judgement for the physician.[172]

Re R was not well received.[173] In *Re W*,[174] Lord Donaldson was unphased by his critics. W was a 16-year-old girl. She was critically ill with anorexia nervosa and had had a tragic childhood. The local authority sought guidance whether W could, if it proved necessary, be moved to a specialist unit and force-fed. As W was 16, she was empowered to consent to treatment by virtue of section 8 of the Family Law Reform Act 1969. The Court of Appeal ruled that section 8 on its wording solely empowered a minor over 16 to give an 'effective consent' to treatment. Section 8(3)[175] preserved the concurrent parental power to authorise treatment and the inherent powers of the courts to act to protect a minor's welfare. Lord Donaldson regretted only one part of

170 See C Bridge and M Brazier, 'Coercion or Caring: Analysing Adolescent Autonomy' (1996) 15 *LS* 84.
171 *Re R (A Minor)* [1991] 4 All ER 177, CA.
172 Ibid, 184.
173 See, for example, A Bainham, 'The Judge and the Competent Minor' (1992) 108 *LQR* 104.
174 [1992] 4 All ER 627.
175 Ibid, 639 (Balcombe LJ).

his *dicta* in *Re R* – his use of the keyholder metaphor. For as he acknowledged, keys can lock as readily as unlock. In *Re W* he preferred to compare consent to a flak jacket, saying pithily:

> ... I now prefer the analogy of the legal 'flak jacket' which protects from claims by the litigious whether [the doctor] acquires it from his patient who may be a minor over the age of 16, or a '*Gillick competent*' child under that age or from another person having parental responsibilities which include a right to consent to treatment of the minor. Anyone who gives him a flak jacket (i.e. consent) may take it back, but the doctor only needs one and so long as he continues to have one he has the legal right to proceed.[176]

Re R and *Re W* make a nonsense of *Gillick*. They are explicable on their facts. There are powerful grounds to argue that both R and W lacked mental capacity regardless of their age. Their illness deprived them of the understanding and capacity to decide about treatment. Were they adults, they might be found to lack capacity applying sections 2 and 3 of the Mental Capacity Act. The same is arguably true of the young people involved in several similar cases where judges ruled that an adolescent could not veto treatment.[177]

The cases left the law in a contradictory and unsatisfactory state and subject to challenge.[178] Guidance from the Department of Health called for a test case[179] and we still await a definitive Supreme Court ruling on the matter. Is it consistent with children's rights and interests that parents should be able to provide the consent their competent child withholds? Lady Hale referred to this as a 'controversial question' in *Re D*, which 'fortunately' did not arise on the facts of the case.[180] The court's inherent jurisdiction to authorise coercive treatment in the best interests of the child is more readily justifiable. Though Article 8(1) is engaged, the breach is likely to be permissible if the child's life depends on it, both under Article 8(2) and Article 2, which protects the right to life.[181]

A common feature of such cases is the emergency nature of the decision and the lack of time to consider the issues. In *An NHS Foundation Hospital v P*[182] Baker J, in an emergency hearing, authorised treatment of a non-consenting 17-year-old who had a history of self-harming behaviour and had taken an overdose of paracetamol. P's wishes and feelings were considered but were not decisive. Her Article 8 rights to privacy were trumped by the positive obligation to protect life under Article 2. In *University Hospitals Plymouth NHS*

176 Ibid, 635.

177 For example, *South Glamorgan County Council v B & W* [1998] 1 FLR 574; *Re S (A Minor) (Consent to Medical Treatment)* [1994] 2 FLR 1065; *An NHS Foundation Hospital v P* [2014] EWHC 1650 and see Bridge and Brazier (1996) 15 *LS* 84.

178 See R Taylor, 'Reversing the Retreat from Gillick?' (2007) 19(1) *CHLQ* 81 and E Cave, 'Adolescent Consent and Confidentiality in the UK' (2009) 16(4) *EJHL* 309.

179 DH, *Reference Guide to Consent to Examination or Treatment* (August 2009), para 8.1.

180 *Re D* [2019] UKSC 42, [26].

181 *An NHS Foundation Hospital v P* [2014] EWHC 165, [15] per Baker J.

182 [2014] EWHC 1650.

Trust v B[183] MacDonald J overrode the refusal of insulin by a 16-year-old suffering from diabetic ketoacidosis. B had stated that she wished to die and there was no evidence that she lacked capacity.

Two cases involving a young Jehovah's Witness[184] gave rise to an important case in 2021. X had sickle cell syndrome which led to crises where blood transfusion was needed to keep her alive, which she refused on religious grounds. On the first occasion, treatment was authorised without consideration of her competence, but on the second occasion Sir James Munby considered X, by now aged 15, to be *Gillick* competent. Applying *Re W*, he authorised the treatment in her best interests. In common with many of the cases highlighted in this section, the urgent nature of the cases left no time for a full consideration of a potential challenge to *Re R* and *Re W* on the basis that they do not accord with societal and human rights developments. An opportunity arose in *Re X (No 2)*[185] when the Trust made a less urgent application involving *Gillick* competent X. It sought an anticipatory declaration authorising further blood transfusions if they were life-sustaining up until X's eighteenth birthday. Sir James Munby refused the declaration, preferring judicial consideration of each case on its facts to running 'the risk of privileging "medical paternalism" '. He also affirmed *Re R* and *Re W*, concluding that any 'change … is a matter for Parliament, not the courts' and refused permission to appeal. Notwithstanding developments departing from medical paternalism, promoting patient choice and upholding patient rights, competent children remain subject to a strongly protectionist stance.[186] The courts have distorted common sense and ethics in attempts to avoid the implications of *Gillick*,[187] but *Re R* and *Re W* are now settled law.

Re W was confirmed again in the Court of Appeal decision of *E & F (Minors: Blood Transfusion)*.[188] Two young Jehovah's Witnesses, E and F, appealed against decisions at first instance that blood transfusions could be

183 *(a minor) (urgent medical treatment)* [2019] EWHC 1670. See RA Limb, 'According Appropriate Weight to Children's Wishes and Feelings' (2021) 29(3) *Med Law Rev* 524.

184 *Re X* [2020] EWHC 1630 (Fam); *Re X* [2020] EWHC 3003 (Fam).

185 [2021] EWHC 65 (Fam).

186 See E Cave, 'Confirmation of the High Court's Power to Override a Child's Treatment Decision' (2021) 29(2) *Med Law Rev* 408.

187 Resulting in an incoherent set of children's rights and liberties. See for example S Fovargue and S Ost, 'Does the Theoretical Framework Change the Legal End Result for Mature Minors Refusing Medical Treatment or Creating Self-generated Pornography? (2013) 13(1) *Medical Law International* 6; E Cave, 'Competence and Authority: Adolescent Treatment Refusals for Physical and Mental Health Conditions' (2013) 8(2) *Contemporary Social Science* 92; B Lyons, 'Dying to be Responsible: Adolescence, Autonomy and Responsibility' (2010) 20(2) *LS* 257; E Cave, 'Goodbye Gillick? Identifying and Resolving Problems with the Concept of Child Competence' (2014) 34(1) *LS* 103; E Cave, 'Skeleton Keys to Hospital Doors: Adolescent Adults who Refuse Life-Sustaining Medical Treatment' (2023) *MLR*, forthcoming.

188 [2021] EWCA Civ 1888.

administered to them in the course of an operation if necessary, notwithstanding their capacitous refusals. They complained that the orders were unnecessary in their cases as clinical need for transfusion was statistically unlikely. They argued therefore that their rights under Article 8 of the European Convention were breached because the interference with their autonomy was not justified as necessary. The Court of Appeal disagreed: whilst with hindsight the transfusion was not necessary, had a crisis occurred the order could have sustained their lives.

Can the Trust treat in a medical emergency without a court order? The Court of Appeal is clear that they can provided there is an urgent medical need and the patient is unable to express a view; 'However, we very much doubt that such a power exists in respect of treatment that has been foreseen and refused by a capacitous patient.'[189]

Emergency hearings carry risks of error. In E's case at first instance, heard urgently by video link whilst E awaited an operation to remove her appendix, a list of cases cited in support of the order included cases that did not concern capacitous older children. The Court of Appeal warned that 'an undifferentiated list [of cases] does not help'.[190] Moreover, the order itself was erroneous, referring as it did to E's lack of capacity and competence 'by reason of her age and minority', notwithstanding acceptance in the hearing that 16-year-old E had capacity. The Court of Appeal advised, however, that the error with the order could have been amended informally rather than used as grounds for allowing an appeal.

Not all best interests assessments lead to a decision in favour of treatment. In *DV (A Child)*[191] a 17-year-old Jehovah's Witness with cancer had previously been transfused against his will, leading to post-traumatic stress disorder. When a further operation was required, clinicians felt that his refusal should not be respected if transfusion was once again clinically indicated. The Court of Appeal in *E & F* is clear that:

> Welfare assessments in medical treatment cases concerning young persons with decision-making capacity involve the balancing of two transcendent factors: the preservation of life and personal autonomy.[192]

In some cases, the impact of treatment without consent is such that the personal autonomy of the minor will prevail.

17.28 Confidentiality and children under 16

Do young people seeking treatment independently of their parents have any right to confidentiality? A young girl, embarking on a sexual relationship and

189 Ibid, [24].
190 Ibid, [71].
191 *A Teaching Hospitals NHS Trust v DV (a child)* [2021] EWHC 1037 (Fam). And see BBC Sounds, Podcast: *Inside the Ethics Committee*, Series 11, Teenager Refuses Chemotherapy.
192 [2021] EWCA Civ 1888, [53].

considering seeking contraception, probably does not think so much about her capacity to give consent to treatment as 'Will the doctor tell my mum?' The thought that a doctor may be free to give contraceptive advice to a child without the parents even knowing of what is proposed was perhaps at the heart of Mrs Gillick's concern. The disruption of family life, and the danger that the girl might omit to give the doctor information on other drugs she might be taking, worried many caring parents. The Law Lords' decision in *Gillick* did not expressly address confidentiality. The assumption on which most doctors[193] and lawyers proceeded was that a *Gillick* competent minor had as much of a claim to a right of confidentiality as he had a right to grant an independent consent to any treatment proposed by his doctor. Twenty years after *Gillick*, Mrs Axon challenged this assumption.[194] She argued that the parent of a child under 16 had a right to be notified if a health professional proposed to offer advice or treatment relating to abortion or contraception to a child under 16. The parents' responsibility for the welfare of their children justified a limited exception to the usual duty of confidentiality to patients. The parents' right to respect for their privacy and family life under Article 8 of the ECHR granted them a right to such information about their child. Silber J[195] rejected Mrs Axon's case: A *Gillick* competent minor has the same right to confidentiality as any adult patient. This is reflected in guidance from the Department of Health.[196] Nevertheless it remains good practice to involve parents, 'unless the young person specifically wishes to exclude them'.[197] If the doctor considers that their young patient is not *Gillick* competent, the GMC advises that the doctor first seek to persuade her to involve her family, but ultimately, they may disclose information to an appropriate person (usually the girl's parents). Could a doctor justify disclosure without consent in relation to a *Gillick* competent young patient? A difficult dilemma arises if the doctor suspects that the girl is being subjected to sexual abuse. Might public interest justify their action, especially if they suspected that other children might also be at risk from abuse?

Gillick champions the right of competent minors to make decisions for themselves and in confidence but aligning minors' decisions with the obligation to protect their best interests has resulted in a complex body of law, fraught with inconsistencies.

193 GMC, *Confidentiality: Protecting and Providing Information* (2000), para 38. Superseded by GMC, *0–18* (2007), para 51, which states that disclosures when a child lacks capacity to consent should only be made if they are in the best interests of the child.

194 Mrs Axon sought judicial review of Department of Health Guidance, *Best Practice Guidance for Doctors and Other Health Professionals on the Provision of Advice and Treatment to Young People under Sixteen on Contraception, Sexual and Reproductive Health* (2004).

195 *R (on the application of Axon) v Secretary of State for Health* [2006] EWHC 37 (Admin). See J Loughrey, 'Can you Keep a Secret?' (2008) 20(3) *CFLQ* 312.

196 DHSC, *Reference Guide to Consent for Examination of Treatment* (2nd ed, 2009), ch 3, paras 2–11.

197 Ibid, ch 3, para 5.

17.29 Authorising a deprivation of liberty

At 7.11 above we discussed safeguards that apply to adults with mental disorder who are informally detained (without recourse to sections 2 and 3 of the Mental Health Act 2003) but lack capacity to consent to their detention and treatment. We saw that a lacuna in the law breached Article 5 of the European Convention. Adults were deprived of their liberty without lawful justification. The 'Bournewood gap' was filled by an amendment to the Mental Capacity Act 2005 in the form of Deprivation of Liberty Safeguards (DoLS), which currently apply from the age of 18 to patients under 'continuous supervision and control and not free to leave'.[198] Though the meaning of deprivation of liberty is the same regardless of whether they have a physical or mental disability, the courts have made clear that DoLS will not usually need to be made for urgent medical treatment.[199]

In non-urgent cases, the situation was unclear for those under 18, where the DoLS do not apply. In *Re D*[200] Keehan J considered whether a 15-year-old was deprived of his liberty when he was informally admitted to a psychiatric hospital for assessment and treatment. Keehan J found that, provided his parents consented, D was not deprived of his liberty. When D turned 16, however, Keehan J considered that parental consent could no longer be relied upon. Whilst parents retain parental responsibility for 16–17-year-olds, Keehan J noted the various ways in which Parliament has chosen to distinguish between those aged under 16 and those of 16–17.[201] The Court of Appeal disagreed and the matter came to the Supreme Court in 2019,[202] which held that where people aged 16 and 17 cannot consent, parental consent will be insufficient to authorise a deprivation of liberty. Article 5 safeguards were therefore required. The situation is now addressed in the Mental Capacity (Amendment) Act 2019. Subject to Regulations planned for 2023, new Liberty Protection Safeguards will apply from the age of 16. They will apply when the person lacks capacity to consent to arrangements to enable their treatment that will deprive them of their liberty.

Children with disabilities who need specialist care in children's homes or residential accommodation can be lawfully deprived of their liberty under statute.[203] Sadly, there has been a recent spate of cases where a shortage of secure accommodation for vulnerable children with complex needs who pose a risk to themselves or others has led them to be placed in unregulated and unsuitable accommodation. Sir James Munby said of one such case:

> What this case demonstrates, as if further demonstration is still required of what is a well-known scandal, is the disgraceful and utterly shaming lack of proper

198 *P v Cheshire West and Chester Council and another, P and Q v Surrey County Council* [2014] UKSC 19.

199 *R (Ferreira) v Inner South London Senior Coroner* [2017] EWCA Civ 31; *Re D* [2019] UKSC 42, [119]–[120] (Lady Arden).

200 *Re D (A Child) (Deprivation of Liberty)* [2015] EWHC 922 (Fam).

201 As, for example in the Mental Capacity Act 2005 and Family Law Reform Act 1969.

202 [2019] UKSC 42.

203 Such as the Mental Health Act 1983 (for assessment and treatment of certain mental health conditions) or the Children Act 1989, s 25 (secure accommodation order).

> provision in this country of the clinical, residential and other support services so desperately needed by the increasing numbers of children and young people … It is a disgrace to any country with pretensions to civilisation, compassion and, dare one say it, basic human decency …[204]

The Supreme Court found in *Re T (A Child)*[205] that the inherent jurisdiction of the High Court could be invoked to authorise a local authority to deprive a child under the age of 16 of his liberty in a non-approved secure establishment where no placement is available by reference to the relevant statutory scheme,[206] but recently the High Court has had occasion to refuse to do so.

Wigan MBC v W, N and Y[207] is one of the saddest cases we have read. Twelve-year-old Y, who had ADHD and autism spectrum disorder and was traumatised by past abuse, was kept inappropriately on a paediatric ward because he did not meet the criteria for detention under the Mental Health Act due to his behaviour being trauma-based rather than resulting from psychiatric illness, and there was at the time simply nowhere else for him to go. The ward had to be shut to new admissions and other children moved out. Y was distressed and suicidal and the staff available were not appropriately trained to help him. The door to the shower had been removed and he slept on a mat without a pillow or sheet because those items posed a risk of suicide. Mr Justice MacDonald recognised that the hospital staff were doing their best. He further recognised the obligation on the state to make provision for Y. Notwithstanding the lack of alterative placement, he refused to authorise the deprivation of liberty on the ground that it was not in Y's best interests to do so. The current placement was an 'inappropriate, demeaning and, quite frankly, brutal one for a 12 year old child'.[208] It breached Y's rights under Article 5 and possibly also Article 3. He concluded that the 'local authority simply *must* find him an alternative placement'.[209]

The best interest test remains the gold standard, but legal, clinical and academic analysis continues to debate its meaning and application.[210]

204 *Re X (A Child) (No 3)* [2017] EWHC 2036 (Fam), [37]. (And see 3.8 above).

205 [2021] UKSC 35.

206 The Care Planning, Placement and Case Review (England) Regulations 2010, SI 2010/959. The Regulations were later amended by SI 2021/161. In *MBC v AM and Ors (DOL orders for children under 16)* [2021] EWHC 2472 (Fam) MacDonald J held that the inherent jurisdiction continues to allow the court to authorise the deprivation of liberty of an under-16-year-old post-2021 amendment, 'subject always to the rigorous application of the President's Guidance of November 2019 entitled *Placements in unregistered children's homes in England or unregistered care home services in Wales* and the addendum thereto dated December 2020'.

207 [2021] EWHC 1982 (Fam). And see *Nottinghamshire CC v LT* [2021] EWHC 2584 (Fam); *A County Council v A Mother & Ors* [2021] EWHC 3303 (Fam).

208 Ibid, [53].

209 Ibid, [61].

210 See for example, H Taylor, 'What are "Best Interests"? A Critical Evaluation of "Best Interests" Decision-Making in Clinical Practice' (2016) 24(2) *Med Law Rev* 176; G Birchley 'The Theorisation of "Best Interests" in Bioethical Accounts of Decision-Making' (2021) 22 *BMC Medical Ethics*.

Chapter 18

HEALTHCARE RESEARCH[1]

18.1 Introduction

In the COVID-19 pandemic, vaccines were the product of remarkable collaboration, funding and effort, and of the willingness of volunteers to be involved in their research and development. But volunteering to be a research participant is not risk-free. In 2006, six healthy volunteers at Northwick Park Hospital[2] were rushed to Critical Care after suffering an adverse reaction in a phase 1 clinical trial.[3] At least four of them suffered multiple organ failure, and it was feared that they may have suffered permanent damage to their immune systems. The drug, TGN1412, was a monoclonal antibody designed to treat leukaemia and rheumatoid arthritis. Volunteers were paid £2,000 to volunteer. The Medicines and Healthcare products Regulatory Agency (MHRA) concluded that the reaction resulted from an 'unpredicted biological action' of the drug in humans. It found no deficiencies in the manufacturers' work, the formulation of the drug or its administration to the participants.[4] An independent Expert Scientific Review, chaired by Professor Duff, was less sympathetic:

> Our conclusion is that the pre-clinical development studies that were performed with TGN1412 did not predict a safe dose for use in humans, even though current regulatory requirements were met.[5]

The system was at fault. The expert group made twenty-two recommendations to improve the safety of first-in-man clinical trials.

The shocking incident at Northwick Park continued a trend of diminishing confidence in the regulation of research. In 2000, inquiries were held into allegations that research was carried out on newborn babies without parental consent in a hospital in North Staffordshire.[6] Scandals surrounding retention of

1 We are grateful for the research assistance of Dr Eliza Bechtold who contributed to updates of an earlier draft.

2 See P Ferguson, 'Clinical Trials and Healthy Volunteers' (2008) 16(1) *Med Law Rev* 23.

3 Department of Health and Social Care (hereafter DHSC), *Expert Scientific Group on Phase One Clinical Trials* Final Report (2006) HMSO.

4 MHRA, *Investigations into Adverse Incidents during Clinical Trials of TGN1412* Final Report (May 2006), para 6.

5 DHSC, *Expert Scientific Group on Phase One Clinical Trials* Final Report, p 2.

6 See 18.8 below.

body parts originated in Bristol and Liverpool with evidence of children's body parts being retained for research without their parents' consent or knowledge.[7] Medical research was acquiring a bad reputation. Yet every time any one of us receives a prescription for antibiotics or a vaccine against infectious disease we benefit from research performed on others in the past. It is becoming a human guinea pig oneself, or letting one's child be so used, that may be an unattractive prospect. However, if medicine is to progress to combat cancer and continue the battle against diseases such as diabetes and multiple sclerosis, new drugs, devices, vaccines and procedures must be subject to trials.

In this chapter we consider in particular:

(1) The authority to carry out research on the human adult derives from that person's consent. How satisfactory are the principles governing consent to participation in clinical research?
(2) The law on medical treatment demands that the physician respects the confidences of their patients. How does this translate into medical research?
(3) What provision does the law make for an individual suffering injury in the course of their participation in such clinical research?

18.2 What is clinical research?

Health research ranges from clinical trials to qualitative projects such as surveys or interviews. This chapter focuses on clinical research,[8] which may be classified in a number of ways. Non-intrusive research involves no direct interference with participants, for example research into health data and epidemiological research. Intrusive research may be non-invasive, for example psychological inquiries, or invasive, involving actual contact with the patient's body, for example taking blood, administering drugs and testing new surgical techniques. Some research is combined with medical care, sometimes referred to as 'therapeutic research'. Some utilises volunteers who agree to participate in a research project not likely to confer any personal benefit to them, as in the Northwick Park study outlined above. Generally, the more invasive the research and the smaller the potential benefit to the participant, the greater are the ethical problems.[9]

18.3 Research governance

Health research governance is the responsibility of the Health Research Authority (HRA). Originally established as a Special Health Authority in

7 See 22.2 below.

8 Wider aspects of healthcare research (including sociological research) are not covered here.

9 See Medicines and Healthcare products Regulatory Agency, *Risk-adapted Approaches to the Management of Clinical Trials of Investigational Medicinal Products* (2011) setting out a three-level risk categorisation: Type A No higher than the risk of standard medical care; Type B Somewhat higher than the risk of standard medical care; Type C Markedly higher than the risk of standard medical care.

2011,[10] the HRA is responsible for co-ordinating and standardising the regulation of research[11] and overseeing the ethical review system. To facilitate the HRA's UK-wide responsibility for research governance, it was re-established in the Care Act 2014 as a Non-Departmental Public Body.[12] From 2016, a single 'HRA Approval' of National Health Service (NHS) research proposals replaced a system of shared regulation by local NHS research and development management and NHS research ethics committees (RECs). From 2018 the approval was extended to cover all NHS project-based research in England and Wales. Applications are made through a dedicated system called the Integrated Research Application System.

The HRA provides a policy framework[13] for conducting and managing research across the UK. It is supported by operational guidance and applies to both clinical and non-clinical research undertaken by NHS and social care staff. The framework sets out 19 high-level core principles highlighting the importance of safety, scientific and ethical conduct, consent, privacy, patient and public involvement, and integrity.

The HRA interacts with regulators such as the General Medical Council (GMC) (Chapter 2 above), which sets professional standards and ensures compliance. Specialist regulators such as the Human Tissue Authority (HTA) (Chapter 20 below) and the Human Fertilisation and Embryology Authority (Chapter 15 above) regulate specialist research on human tissue, gametes and embryos. The HRA also cooperates with the MHRA (Chapter 12 above), which grants authorisation for the manufacturing of medicines and medical devices and for clinical trials. The MHRA was part of the European system of clinical trials approvals which facilitated a centralised procedure for EU-wide approval, but post-EU Exit, the MHRA became a standalone body.[14]

18.4 Clinical trials

Special rules apply to clinical trials which investigate in humans the effects of one or more drugs, or 'investigational medicinal products' as they are termed. Clinical trials of investigational medicinal products (CTIMPs) cannot commence without the authorisation of both an ethics committee (see 18.6 below)

[10] The Health Research Authority (Establishment and Constitution) Order 2011, SI 2011/2323 (since revoked).

[11] The HRA's remit goes beyond legal standards to also incorporate ethical standards and responsibilities: *R (Richmond Pharmacology Ltd) v HRA and Sense about Science* [2015] EWHC 2238 (Admin), [71] per Jay J.

[12] Care Act 2014, s 109; The Care Act 2014 (Health Education England and the Health Research Authority) (Consequential Amendments and Revocations) Order 2015, SI 2015/137 and see also SI 2014/3090.

[13] HRA, *UK Policy Framework for Health and Social Care Research* (2017).

[14] Subject to the Northern Ireland Protocol 2019, whereby the European Medicines Agency retains responsibility for the authorisation of medicines marketed in Northern Ireland where EU pharmaceutical law continues to apply, subject to periodic consent of the Northern Ireland Legislative Assembly.

and the UK licensing authority,[15] the MHRA,[16] which focuses on safety and scientific assessment. Embarking on a trial without the prior sanction of a relevant ethics committee is a criminal offence.[17] A combined review service, overseen by the HRA, applied to all new CTIMP applications from 2022, allowing a single application and leading to a single UK decision. If the clinical trial commences, then the MHRA takes on a monitoring role. As we saw in Chapter 12, the MHRA goes on to provide marketing authorisation (licences) and inspect the marketing processes and is also responsible for surveillance and enforcement.

Two European Directives, the Clinical Trials Directive 2001[18] and Good Clinical Practice (GCP) Directive 2005,[19] impacted on how trials in the EU were approved, conducted and monitored. They enabled clinical trials to take place in more than one country, with a single permission, and enhanced the safety of research participants. The Clinical Trials Directive 2001 has been labelled 'arguably the most criticised piece of legislation in the Union *acquis* on medicines'.[20] It created inconsistency and burdensome bureaucracy across Europe. A new EU Clinical Trials Regulation 536/2014 was agreed but then subject to long delays in its implementation. After a period of uncertainty,[21] implementation came too late to be captured by the UK's EU (Withdrawal) Act 2018, which copied and pasted certain EU laws into UK law. By virtue of a Protocol, EU law continues to apply in Northern Ireland, but the Regulation does not apply in Scotland, Wales or England.

What did the EU Regulation seek to change? It sought to cut bureaucracy, enhance transparency[22] and drive innovation. Regulation 536/2014 is underpinned by a new EU online portal and database which harmonises the submission, authorisation and reporting of CTIMPs. The sponsor of the research submits a single application via the EU portal. Member states in which the research will be conducted participate in the review to the extent that national or local ethical issues arise. An expedited review process applies to low-risk CTIMPs – especially where the medicine is already authorised or there is an

15 Medicines for Human Use (Clinical Trials) Regulations 2004, reg 11(3).

16 The MHRA subsumed the old Medicines Control Agency.

17 Medicines for Human Use (Clinical Trials) Regulations 2004, reg 49.

18 EC 2001/20 implemented in the Medicines for Human Use (Clinical Trials) Regulations 2004, SI 2004/1031.

19 EC 2005/28 implemented in Medicines for Human Use (Clinical Trials) Amendment Regulations, SI 2006/1928.

20 European Commission, *Roadmap: Legislative Proposal on a Regulation/Directive Amending the Clinical Trials Directive 2001/20/EC* (2010), 1.

21 See G Laurie, 'How Do We Make Sense of chaos? Navigating Health Research Regulation Through the Liminality of the Brexit Process' (2018) 18(2–3) *Medical Law International* 110; E Cave, 'EU Clinical Trials Regulation 2014: Fetter or Facilitator?' (2018) 18(2–3) *Medical Law International* 179.

22 An attempt by the HRA to impose new requirements of transparency ahead of the EU Regulation's implementation was successfully challenged in a judicial review in *R (Richmond Pharmacology Ltd) v HRA and Sense about Science* [2015] EWHC 2238 (Admin).

evidence base for off-label (unlicensed) use. Reporting is largely the responsibility of a 'reporting' member state, avoiding the duplication of near-identical reports from each country involved in the trial.

Delayed implementation of the Regulation in 2022 meant that whilst EU law changed in accordance with the EU Regulation, the outdated Directive continued to apply in Britain via the Medicines for Human Use (Clinical Trials) Regulations 2004 that transposed the Directive into law.[23] This is set to change. Sections 2 and 5 of the Medicines and Medical Devices Act 2021 provided the Secretary of State with extensive powers to amend the existing regulatory framework and constituted the next step toward a bespoke UK regulatory landscape. In 2021, a Government Taskforce ('TIGRR')[24] set out a proposal for a new regulatory architecture that would repeal the existing 2004 Regulations 'to restore global UK leadership in clinical trials'. The emphasis is on maximising potential post-'release' from the EU regulatory regime, removing barriers and stimulating growth. The number of commercial clinical trials started in the UK has declined sharply and the UK is lagging behind international competitors.[25] Two challenges are these. Global leadership requires sufficient harmonisation of international protocols and alignment of multiple regulators to reduce bureaucracy in research that takes place in multiple countries. And red tape aims to protect research participants from unethical and unsafe practices, such as those that occurred at Northwick Park (18.1 above). The aims of facilitating good research and boosting the life sciences are laudable, but a balance must be struck between social and individual needs.

18.5 COVID-19 clinical trials

The COVD-19 pandemic put the precarious balance between social and individual needs to the test. In a public health crisis, utilitarian ethics that promote the overall health of the public are more readily applicable and publicly acceptable. The lack of effective treatments and the necessity for national lockdowns with consequent economic impacts triggered a global race for effective and safe treatments and vaccines. The first COVID-19-related trial to come before the HRA became known as the RECOVERY trial. It identified dexamethasone as a beneficial treatment for people hospitalised with COVID-19. Eighteen months later, the UK was the first country in the world to approve an antiviral, Lagevrio (molnupiravir), that could be taken at home, so reducing opportunities to transmit the virus. In between, around 800 studies were reviewed by RECs,[26] including the world's first human 'infection challenge'

[23] Subject to amendments in the Medicines for Human Use (Clinical Trials) (Amendment) (EU Exit) Regulations 2019, SI 2019/744.

[24] I Duncan Smith, T Villiers and G Freeman, *Taskforce on Innovation, Growth and Regulatory Reform* (2021) May, pp 67–82. The MHRA consulted on legislative proposals in 2022.

[25] See ABPI, *Clinical Research in the UK: An Opportunity for Growth* (2021).

[26] N Yamazaki, 'Blog: One Year on Since the First COVID-19 Research Studies were Approved' *HRA* (2021) 16 March.

study: a special type of study used to test vaccines by deliberately infecting people with the virus in controlled conditions.[27]

The UK's Vaccine Taskforce, set up in 2020, sought a portfolio of vaccines that could be available quickly in the largest possible quantities. Maximum short-term impact was prioritised. The four COVID-19 vaccines initially approved for use in the UK by the MHRA were not immediately given marketing authorisation. Rather, temporary authorisation[28] of identified batches was provided through a process of expedited rolling review, responding to the data as it became available.

Several ethical dilemmas arose.[29] We allude briefly to just two. Vaccine production could not meet the immediate demand. Who should get the vaccines first? The UK Joint Committee on Vaccination and Immunisation provided advice on priority groups.[30] The global picture was concerning. Whilst many high-income countries scrambled to secure supplies of more vaccines than they would use, and later embarked on booster campaigns, many inhabitants of low- to middle-income countries lacked access to a first dose.[31] And yet, a global response is critical to the reduction and control of new variants, which could prove resistant to vaccines.

Several issues flowed from the known and unknown risks associated with novel vaccines. The vaccines had gone through the full three stages of clinical trial before receiving temporary authorisation. Nonetheless, there remained an initial post-authorisation risk of unanticipated serious adverse events, as well as longer-term risks that only become apparent in time. In the 2009 H1N1 'swine flu' pandemic, for example, a link was later drawn between vaccination with Pandemrix and increased risk of narcolepsy, diagnosis of which can take up to a decade. In the case of COVID-19 vaccines, temporary authorisation did not declare that the vaccines were risk-free but rather that the risks were commensurate with those posed by COVID-19 infection, taking into consideration both the risks to particular patient cohorts, and the broader societal risks. As we discuss at 12.15 above, manufacturers were keen to secure liability protection, and in the UK the approved COVID-19 vaccines were added to the Vaccine Damage Payment Act 1979's no-fault vaccine compensation scheme.

[27] See DP Sulmasy, 'Are SARS-CoV-2 Human Challenge Trials Ethical?' (2021) 181(8) *JAMA* 1031.

[28] Under the Human Medicine Regulations 2012, SI 2012/1916 (as amended), reg 174 on 'supply in response to spread of pathogenic agents'.

[29] See E Cave and A McMahon, 'Should States Restrict Recipient Choice Amongst Relevant and Available COVID-19 Vaccines?' (2022) *Med Law Rev* fwac942.

[30] For a consideration of the ethical issues see Nuffield Council on Bioethics, *Policy Briefing: Fair and Equitable Access to COVID-19 Treatments and Vaccines* (2020) 29 May.

[31] For contrasting perspectives on global vaccine inequity see N Hassoun, 'Against Vaccine Nationalism' (2021) 47(11) *J Med Ethics* 773; K Ferguson and A Caplan, 'Love Thy Neighbour? Allocating Vaccines in a World of Competing Obligations' (2021) 47(12) *J Med Ethics* e20.

18.6 Research ethics committees (RECs)

A number of RECs exist outside the NHS. These include RECs set up by universities and pharmaceutical companies. The Economic and Social Research Council's *Framework for Research Ethics*[32] and other subject-specific frameworks provide guidance. RECs should not be confused with *clinical* ethics committees, which often serve NHS Trusts and support clinicians making ethically challenging clinical decisions.[33]

Within the NHS, the HRA is responsible for the Research Ethics Service (RES) and has powers to establish and abolish RECs in England.[34] As we have intimated above, the dual aims of protecting research participants, by ensuring their rights, dignity and safety, and facilitating research for the good of society are not always mutually conducive. Some risk to participants may be acceptable in the pursuit of medical knowledge and the independent RECs, guided by international and national guidelines and principles, exist to make that assessment.

The RES consists of around 900 REC members in sixty committees. It considers around 5,000 applications a year and can take up to sixty days to provide an opinion, though if there are no material ethical issues a proposal may be eligible for accelerated 'proportionate review' whereby a sub-committee rather than a full committee considers the application.[35] In the COVID-19 pandemic, which required new ways of working across sectors, the HRA developed a fast-track process that could review urgent proposals in as little as twenty-four hours. A pilot has since tested the fast-track process in non-COVID research for more extensive roll-out. The HRA is committed to streamlining regulation without compromising the protection of participants: research indicates that some aspects of research approvals are historical and bureaucratic rather than necessary to protect participants.[36] The MHRA consulted in 2022 on further changes that would combine regulatory and research ethics approval.[37]

Not all NHS RECs have the authority to review CTIMPs. To do so, the Committee must be given statutory authority by the UK Ethics Committee

[32] Economic and Social Research Council, *Framework for Research Ethics* 2010 (revised 2015). And see UK Research Integrity Office, *Code of Practice for Research* (2009) and UK Research and Innovation policy and guidelines on good research conduct.

[33] On which see J Brierley, D Archard and E Cave, 'Challenging Misconceptions About Clinical Ethics Support During COVID-19 and Beyond: Role, Remit and Representation' (2021) 47(8) *J Med Ethics* 549.

[34] Care Act 2014, s 115.

[35] See HRA, *Research Ethics Service and Research Ethics Committees*, at www.hra.nhs.uk.

[36] See for example M Petrova and S Barclay, 'Research Approvals Iceberg: How a "Low-Key" Study in England Needed 89 Professionals to Approve it and How we can do Better' (2019) 29(7) *BMC Medical Ethics*, recording 491 exchanges with eighty-nine individuals in the process of ethics and governance approvals.

[37] MHRA, *Consultation on Proposals for Legislative Changes for Clinical Trials* (2022).

Authority (UKECA).[38] There are three types of REC: some can review applications for phase 1 trials in health volunteers, some can review applications for CTIMPs and some, called 'authorised RECs', cannot review CTIMPs but can review other research projects. And there are specialist committees, including the Confidentiality Advisory Group (CAG)[39] (which is an independent committee that advises on the use confidential patient information without consent) and the Gene Therapy Advisory Committee (which is the UK national REC for gene therapy research).[40]

We will say more about the constitution of ethics committees under the UK Clinical Trials Regulations shortly. First it is important to note that, outside the remit of the UK Clinical Trials Regulations and the Mental Capacity Act 2005, various sanctions and ethical guidance[41] deter research without ethical approval. An NHS employee failing to seek the requisite approval is likely to be disciplined by their employing Trust. Outside the NHS, researchers may face disciplinary action by professional regulatory authorities. Conducting research without ethical review may constitute impaired 'fitness to practise'. In 2007, the GMC instigated disciplinary action against Andrew Wakefield, the author of a 1998 *Lancet* paper linking autism and the MMR vaccine. Among ten counts of serious professional misconduct was the claim that children underwent research procedures without prior approval from an ethics committee. Dr Wakefield was struck off the medical register in 2010.[42]

Section 112(3) of the Care Act 2014 requires that the HRA publish a REC policy document (currently the *Governance Arrangements for Research Ethics Committees*[43]) specifying requirements with which RECs must comply. According to this document, RECs advise as to the ethics of any NHS healthcare research and 'protect the dignity, rights, safety and well-being of people who take part in research'.[44] They can also consider private sector research if requested to do so. RECs include up to 18 members from a diverse

38 Medicines for Human Use (Clinical Trials) Regulations 2004, reg 5. Care Act 2014, s 116.

39 See 5.9 above. CAG operates under the Care Act 2014 and the Health Service (Control of Patient Information) Regulations 2002.

40 According to The Medicines for Human Use (Clinical Trials) Regulations 2004, reg 14(5).

41 See Declaration of Helsinki (2013), Article 23; Council of Europe, *Additional Protocol to the Convention on Human Rights and Biomedicine, Concerning Biomedical Research* (2005), Article 9 (the UK is not a signatory).

42 General Medical Council, *Wakefield: Determination on Serious Professional Misconduct and Sanction*, 24 May 2010. See DJ Opel *et al*, 'Assuring Research Integrity in the Wake of Wakefield' (2011) 342 *BMJ* d2. Note that in *Walker-Smith v General Medical Council* [2012] EWHC 503 (Admin) a finding of serious professional misconduct against Professor John Walker-Smith, who had carried out tests on children later used by Dr Andrew Wakefield, was quashed.

43 DHSC, *Governance Arrangements for Research Ethics Committees* (updated version published 20 July 2021).

44 Ibid, para 3.1.1.

distribution. There should be a mixture of expert and lay members, the latter constituting at least one third of the membership.[45]

18.7 A troubled history

The Department of Health first recommended that district health authorities establish local research ethics committees (LRECs) in 1975. More detailed formal guidance was issued in 1991.[46] Each local health authority was required to set up at least one, and there were over 200 LRECs in all. Multi-centre research ethics committees (MRECs) were introduced in 1997,[47] performing a single ethical review of research taking place in more than one research site. The process remained unwieldy. The Central Office for NHS Research Ethics Committees (COREC) was established in 2000, to coordinate the system.[48] In 2001, the Department of Health issued *Governance Arrangements for RECs* (GAfREC),[49] to harmonise the committees' constitutions and remit. Researchers stepped up political pressure, aimed at reducing the level of bureaucracy and facilitating research, and as a result the National Patient Safety Agency (NPSA[50]) took over responsibility for COREC in 2005.

The transposition of the Clinical Trials Directive 2001[51] in the Medicines for Human Use (Clinical Trials) Regulations 2004 wrought further changes on the system. In each Member State, the decision of one REC became valid for the whole of that country, thereby enabling research to cross borders within Europe. The Directive also brought in new standards of good clinical practice.[52] The remit of RECs was tightened.[53] In summary, the committee could consider the relevance of the trial and its design; the balance of risks and benefits; the protocol; the suitability of the investigator and the facilities; the information sheet and procedure for obtaining informed consent; indemnity, insurance and compensation arrangements and payments to the participant; and investigator Ethics committees should not concern themselves with legal and scientific evaluations.[54] The Directive went some way toward harmonising the EU ethical review process in relation to CTIMPs, but the number, purpose and remit of ethics committees across Europe remained inconsistent.[55] Efforts

45 Ibid, para 4.2.7.

46 Department of Health (DH), *Local Research Ethics Committees*, HSG (91) 5.

47 DH, *Multi-centre Research Ethics Committees*, HSG (97) 23. Replaced by the DHSC, *Governance Arrangements for Research Ethics Committees* (2001) (updated 2021).

48 The National Research Ethics Service took over from COREC in 2007.

49 DHSC, *Governance Arrangements for Research Ethics Committees* (2001) (updated 2021).

50 The NPSA was closed in 2012 and functions transferred to the NHS Commissioning Board Authority.

51 (EC) 2001/20.

52 Medicines for Human Use (Clinical Trials) Regulations 2004, Pt 4. See also Commission Directive (EC) 2005/28.

53 Medicines for Human Use (Clinical Trials) Regulations, reg 15.

54 *Governance Arrangements for Research Ethics Committees* (2021).

55 P Veerus, J Lexchin and E Hemminki, 'Legislative Regulation and Ethical Governance of Medical Research in Different European Union Countries' (2014) 40 *J Med Ethics*

to streamline the process continued. A reformed 'National Research Ethics *Service*' (NRES), launched in 2007, took over from COREC and introduced a 'Proportionate Review Service' to fast-track research proposals that raised no material ethical issues. And much more radical simplification followed the Academy of Medical Science's 2011 recommendations for reform.[56] Subsuming the NPSA, a single regulator called the Health Research Authority (see 18.3 above) took on the governance and ethical review of all NHS research.

The potential for medical research to reinvigorate the economy has spurred the streamlining of the review process. Researchers want a proportionate review system and they do not want to duplicate their applications. But national efforts can only go so far. As we have seen, the EU Clinical Trials Regulation 536/2014 came into force in 2014 but did not apply in the EU until January 2022, and does not apply in Scotland, England and Wales. The ongoing reform of the ethical review process, both in the UK and Europe, focuses on the facilitation of good research; on efficiency, effectiveness and proportionality. Article 8 of the Declaration of Helsinki[57] (2013) states that: 'while the primary purpose of medical research is to generate new knowledge, this goal can never take precedence over the rights and interests of individual research subjects'; sentiments echoed in Article 2 of the European Convention on Human Rights and Biomedicine.[58] This begs the question: how well does the law protect research participants? We attempt to answer that question in the next sections.

18.8 Consent to participation in trials[59]

In the course of the Infected Blood Inquiry,[60] described as the worst treatment disaster in the NHS's history, allegations were made that research carried out in the 1970s and 1980s on haemophiliac children at a specialist school was conducted without the knowledge of the children or parents.[61] And in 2000, allegations were made, albeit later largely not proven,[62] that research carried out a decade before on premature babies at North Staffordshire Hospital was conducted without parents' consent.[63] Since 1964 the Declaration of Helsinki

409, reporting that the number of ethics committees in each country varied from 1 to 264.

56 AcMedSci, *A New Pathway for the Regulation and Governance of Health Research* (2011).

57 World Medical Association, *The Declaration of Helsinki: Ethical Principles for Medical Research Involving Human Subjects*, WMA General Assembly, Edinburgh, October 2000. Clarifications were added in 2002 and 2004 and the Declaration was amended in 2008 and 2013.

58 Article 2: 'The interests and welfare of the human being shall prevail over the sole interest of society or science.'

59 See GMC, *Good Practice in Research and Consent to Research* (2010) (updated 2013).

60 See 11.2 above.

61 See H Siddique, 'Infected Blood Scandal: Ex-pupil Tells Inquiry he did not Know he was in a Trial' *Guardian* (2021) 21 June.

62 See Editorial, 'Babies and Consent: Yet Another NHS Scandal' (2000) 320 *BMJ* 1285.

63 MP Samuels and DP Southall, 'Negative Extrathoracic Pressure in Treatment of Respiratory Failure in Infants and Young Children' (1989) 299 *BMJ* 1253. There

has sought to protect research participants' rights by demanding rigorous consent procedures.

Special rules apply to CTIMPs under the UK Clinical Trials Regulations 2004. Schedule 1, Part 2, paragraph 9 requires that 'subject to the other provisions of this Schedule relating to consent, freely given informed consent shall be obtained from every subject prior to clinical trial participation'. The UK Regulations go on to require that informed consent:

(a) is given freely after that person is informed of the nature, significance, implications and risks of the trial; and
(b) either:
  (i) is evidenced in writing, dated and signed, or otherwise marked, by that person so as to indicate his consent, or
  (ii) if the person is unable to sign or to mark a document so as to indicate his consent, is given orally in the presence of at least one witness and recorded in writing.[64]

Though informed consent of the participant is a prerequisite for ethical approval in most types of medical research, the UK Clinical Trials Regulations, EU Regulation 536/2014 and, outside their remit, ethical codes of conduct, accept limited circumstances where alternative safeguards are acceptable. Self-evidently someone may be unable to consent by virtue of being a child or suffering from mental incapacity. In such circumstances, we shall see that other safeguards are put in place to protect the research participant.[65] Even in relation to competent adult participants, there may be trials where low risks justify research without consent. Thus, in some cases of epidemiological research (such as the collection of statistics on measles, for example) where anonymised information is used, it may be unnecessary to obtain express consent.[66] Even in epidemiological trials, however, if data is not fully anonymised, consent should usually be obtained.[67] Article 26 of the Declaration of Helsinki outlines the importance of adequate information and Article 25 stresses the importance of voluntariness. What does this mean in practice?

In any research on human beings, each potential participant must be adequately informed of the aims, methods, sources of funding, any possible conflicts of interest, institutional affiliations of the researcher, the anticipated benefits and potential risks of the study and the discomfort it may entail. The participant should be informed of the right to abstain from the study or to withdraw consent to participate at any time without reprisal. After ensuring that the

was a subsequent NHS review: NHS Executive, *West Midlands Regional Office Report of a Review of the Research Framework in North Staffordshire Hospital NHS Trust* (2000).

64 Schedule 1, Pt 1, para 3(1) implementing Article 2(j) of Directive (EC) 2001/20. See also Sch 1, Pt 3 which sets out conditions of informed consent.

65 See below 18.10 and 18.11.

66 GMC, *Confidentiality: Good Practice in Handling Patient Information* (2017) (updated 2018), para 79.

67 But see National Health Service Act 2006, ss 251–252; formerly Health and Social Care Act 2001, s 60, discussed 5.9 above and at 18.17 below.

participant has understood the information, the researcher should then obtain the participant's freely given informed consent, preferably in writing. If the consent cannot be obtained in writing, the non-written consent must be formally documented and witnessed.

The requirement of adequate information for consent to treatment has been addressed in Chapter 6 and we have seen that the decision of the Supreme Court in *Montgomery v Lanarkshire Health Board*[68] at long last abandoned the professional standard of information disclosure in favour of the 'reasonable patient' test. In the context of research, a 'reasonable participant' test now governs what researchers must disclose to research participants.[69] The volunteer is not free to accept any risk whatsoever. RECs will carefully assess the risk involved before sanctioning a research project.

Ethics committees will consider whether the volunteers are truly volunteers. Do medical students feel under compulsion to assist in trials mounted by their teachers? Do patients feel obliged to 'help' their doctor if he asks them to participate in research that is not related to their medical care? Where resort is had to volunteers outside the medical schools and hospital patients, payments are often made in this country. Amounts paid are usually relatively modest but may still constitute an inducement to impoverished students and the unemployed.[70] The principles of law are clear. Any degree of compulsion renders any written consent given invalid.[71] Proving compulsion might be the difficulty for a medical student. And for an unemployed 'volunteer', economic compulsion arising from their circumstances rather than any misconduct by the research team is as yet unrecognised in English law. Article 27 of the Declaration of Helsinki provides that where any suspicion of duress might arise, an independent physician unconnected with the research project should seek the participant's consent. The issue of free and full consent[72] is central to the propriety and legality of clinical trials.[73] The definition of what constitutes a proper consent is, as we have seen, far from easy.

18.9 Experimental and unproven treatments

The obvious benefits of speedy access to innovative healthcare must be balanced with the risks it presents.[74] Problems arise when experimental and

[68] [2015] UKSC 11.

[69] HRA, *Applying a Proportionate Approach to the Process of Seeking Consent* (2019), v 1.02, 2.2.

[70] See EA Largent and HF Lynch, 'Paying Participants in COVID-19 Trials' (2020) *J Infect Dis*, May 29 who consider three goals of payment: reimbursement, compensation and incentivisation.

[71] *Re T (Adult: Refusal of Medical Treatment)* [1992] 4 All ER 649.

[72] V Sanchini *et al*, 'Informed Consent as an Ethical Requirement in Clinical Trials: An Old, but still Unresolved Issue' (2014) 40 *J Med Ethics* 269.

[73] See L Doyal and JS Tobias (eds), *Informed Consent in Medical Research* (2000) BMJ Publishing.

[74] See discussion of Access to Medical Treatments (Innovation) Act 2016, which gives the Secretary of State power to set up a database of innovative treatment, at 8.9 above.

unproven treatment is offered to patients who have exhausted standard treatment options and have no other hope. Such patients (and their families) may be desperate and vulnerable.[75] They may struggle to assimilate the known and unknown risks of innovative therapy when providing their informed consent. The line between experimenting on a patient and doing your utmost for them is blurred.[76] For example, if a doctor caring for patients with cancer attempts a novel treatment as a last resort, knowing that there is no conventional treatment which will prolong the patient's life, have they crossed that line and made the patient a research participant?[77] One hurdle is to secure funding for such treatment. In general, the NHS will not routinely fund treatments which are considered to be experimental, but Commissioners may make exceptions, for example when a disease is very rare and unlikely to attract clinical trials.[78]

What if an adult patient lacks mental capacity to consent? In such cases the consideration of the Court of Protection is appropriate.[79] *Simms v Simms and An NHS Trust*[80] establishes that the use of innovative therapies in the best interests of the patient lacking capacity is not necessarily unlawful. Butler-Sloss P found it lawful to administer experimental treatment that had never been tested on humans to two patients suffering from new variant Creutzfeldt-Jacob Disease. Both lacked the mental capacity to give consent themselves. Both faced a dismal prognosis given their degenerative and terminal condition. The risks of treatment were unknown but as some benefit was possible, Butler-Sloss P held that administration of the drug Pentosan Polysulphate by intracerebral infusion was in the best interests of the patients.

Jonathan Simms's father fought for the treatment which might effect an improvement in his son's terrible condition. In *B NHS Trust v J*, the patient's family opposed the administration of innovative therapy.[81] J was in a persistent

75 See S Fovargue, 'The (Ab)use of Those with No Other Hope? – Ethical and Legal Safeguards for Recipients of Experimental Procedures' (2013) 22(2) *Cambridge Quarterly of Healthcare Ethics*, 181.

76 See GT Laurie, S Harmon and E Dove, *Mason and McCall Smith's Law and Medical Ethics* (11th edn, 2019) Oxford University Press, 20.65, and see discussion of Paolo Macchiarini's alleged misconduct at 18.16 below.

77 When COVID-19 vaccines were given temporary authorisation some argued that they crossed the line and were in fact research products, the deployment of which breached the Nuremberg Code. For a refutation of this argument see P Allen-Kinross, 'Why is the Nuremberg Code being used to Oppose Covid-19 Vaccines?' *FullFact Blog* (2021) 13 May.

78 NHS England, *Commissioning Policy: Individual Funding Requests* (2017), p 15. And note that in the EU a compassionate use programme that facilitates access to unauthorised therapies undergoing clinical trials is established by Regulation (EC) No 726/2004, Article 83.

79 *Applications Relating to Medical Treatment: Guidance Authorised by the Honourable Mr Justice Hayden* [2020] EWCOP 2, [11] (pending revised MCA Code of Practice in 2022).

80 [2002] EWHC 2734 (Fam). And see *UCL Hospitals NHS Foundation Trust v KG* [2018] EWCOP 29.

81 [2006] EWHC 1318.

vegetative state (PVS) after suffering a brain haemorrhage three years earlier. Against the wishes of her family, withdrawal of artificial hydration and nutrition was postponed so that an innovative therapy could be administered. Two research papers had indicated that the insomnia drug Zolpidem sometimes enhanced neural responses in PVS patients. Experts held out little hope that it would work in J's case but saw no harm in trying. The family disagreed. J had extensive neurological damage. Heightened awareness, if it could be brought about, would bring to her only distress. Sir Mark Potter P accepted the expert opinion that the therapy was in J's best interests and ordered it to proceed.[82]

A quite different problem arises if patients or families seek innovative or experimental treatment that the doctors do not consider to be in the patient's best interests. As we discussed at 17.15 above, Charlie Gard's parents argued that he should be given access to experimental treatment abroad. UK medical professionals disagreed and the courts found that, very sadly, the proposed treatment would be futile. We agree with Sara Fovargue[83] that, in cases of dispute, the courts have a legitimate role in determining whether innovative treatment is in the patient's best interests. Parents and patients may be vulnerable to unsubstantiated promises of hope.[84]

18.10 Young people in medical research programmes[85]

When can a young person give their own consent to participation in a trial? When can they withhold that consent? If the young person is incapable of giving an effective consent, may a parent give consent on their behalf?[86] When is their assent required? Once again, the answers currently depend on whether or not the study is governed by the Medicines for Human Use (Clinical Trials) Regulations 2004.[87] For studies that fall outside the ambit of the Regulations, the House of Lords' ruling in *Gillick*[88] empowers a minor to consent to medical treatment when they have reached an age and individual maturity to judge what the treatment entails and assess its benefit and disadvantages. In the case of research combined with medical care, the test might be the same, though

[82] See DHSC, *Reference Guide to Consent for Examination of Treatment* (2nd edn, 2009), ch 1, para 41.

[83] S Fovargue, 'Preserving the Therapeutic Alliance: Court Intervention and Experimental Treatment Requests' in I Goold, J Herring and C Auckland, *Parental Rights, Best Interests and Significant Harms* (2019) Hart, ch 8.

[84] E Cave and E Nottingham, 'Who Knows Best (Interests)? The Case of Charlie Gard' (2018) 26 *Med Law Rev* 500, 503.

[85] For an examination of the ethical issues see Nuffield Council on Bioethics, *Children and Clinical Research* (2015).

[86] This will be particularly difficult if the parent is themselves a minor: S Fovargue, 'Doctrinal Incoherence or Practical Problem? Minor Parents Consenting to their Offspring's Medical Treatment and Involvement in Research in England and Wales' (2013) 25(1) *CFLQ* 1.

[87] See E Cave, 'Seen but not Heard? Children in Clinical Trials' (2010) 18 *Med Law Rev* 1.

[88] *Gillick v West Norfolk and Wisbech Area Health Authority* [1984] QB 581.

professional guidelines encourage the involvement of parents.[89] If the child is over 16, the Family Law Reform Act 1969 statutorily empowering minors aged 16 and over to consent to medical treatment will offer protection to the medical team.

What of research that confers no direct benefit on the child? There is no apparent reason why the *Gillick* ruling should not apply. The basis of the judgment is not limited to medical treatment alone but concerns the general capacity of older children to make decisions for themselves. Whenever researchers wish to include in such research a research participant under 18, only the *Gillick* test can grant the minor herself authority to consent to participate in the trial. Section 8 of the Family Law Reform Act 1969, empowering young people between 16 and 18 to consent to medical treatment, is strictly limited to therapeutic and diagnostic interventions.[90] Lord Donaldson considered it to be 'highly improbable'[91] that a *Gillick* competent minor could consent to a procedure of no benefit to himself. Nevertheless, Department of Health and Social Care (DHSC) guidance encourages parental involvement but recognises that young people and children may provide a valid consent to research which is of no direct benefit to them, provided they are *Gillick* competent.[92]

What about younger children?[93] The law is unclear as to whether parental consent to research of no benefit to the child is of any effect.[94] Paediatricians emphasise the need for carefully controlled research on children.[95] Children respond differently to drugs, they suffer from illnesses not afflicting adults and, above all, their suffering when afflicted is particularly poignant. The GMC states that children can be involved in research that has either 'potential benefits for children or young people generally, as long as the research does not go against their best interests or involves only minimal or low risk of harm … or potential therapeutic benefits for them that outweigh any foreseeable risks'.[96]

89 Medical Research Council /ESRC, *Involving Children in Research* (2021), p 2; General Medical Council *0–18* (2007), para 38: '… If they are able to consent for themselves, you should still consider involving their parents, depending on the nature of the research'.

90 *Re W (A Minor) (Medical Treatment)* [1992] 4 All ER 177, at 635 and 647, CA.

91 [1992] 4 All ER 177 at 635, CA.

92 DHSC, *Reference Guide to Consent for Examination of Treatment* (2nd edn, 2009), ch 3, paras 3–5.

93 Neonatal research poses particular problems: see A Alghrani and M Brazier, 'What is it? Whose it? Re-Positioning the Fetus in the Context of Research?' (2011) 70(1) *CLJ* 51; A Alghrani, 'Womb Transplantation and The Interplay of Islam and The West' (2013) 48(3) *Journal of Religion and Science* 618.

94 See, for example, the American case *Grimes v Kennedy Kreiger Institute*, Nos 128, 129, Sept Term, 2000, cert den 2001, in which the appeal court in Maryland ruled that parents cannot consent to their child's participation in non-therapeutic research.

95 See S Conroy et al, 'Drug Trials in Children: Problems and the Way Forward,' (2000) 49 *British Journal of Clinical Pharmacology* 93.

96 GMC, *0–18 years: guidance for all doctors* (2018), para 37. And see DH, *Reference Guide to Consent for Examination of Treatment* (2nd ed, 2009), chapter 3, para 28.

In law, research can only be carried out on children if it is in their best interests. How can research of no clinical benefit to the child ever be in their best interests? Do best interests include the interests of the community?[97] The House of Lords in *S v S*[98] were asked to authorise a blood test on a child to determine his paternity. Lord Reid described the parental power to authorise such a test in this way:

> Surely a reasonable parent would have some regard for the general public interest and would not refuse a blood test unless he thought that would clearly be *against the interests of the child* [our emphasis].

Arguably where any risk to the child is minimal, parents may authorise any procedure which is not perceived as *against* the interests of the child.

The *Gillick* ruling does not apply to CTIMPs carried out under the UK Clinical Trials Regulations 2004. They require that the written consent of the person with legal responsibility[99] for the child is obtained. In the EU, Article 32(1)(c) of EU Regulation 536/2014 provides that when a minor 'who is capable of forming an opinion' and assessing the relevant information refuses to participate or wants to withdraw from a CTIMP, that wish must be respected. The 2004 Regulations do not go this far and merely require that a refusal to participate or withdraw is 'considered'.[100]

CTIMPs pose a more awkward problem where they are not combined with medical care. The Clinical Trials Regulations 2004 state that children should only be enrolled in research where it 'can only be carried out on minors' and, more prohibitively, that 'some direct benefit for the group of patients involved in the clinical trial is to be obtained from that trial'.[101] Here, too, the EU takes a different approach. Article 32(1)(g) of Regulation 536/2014 requires that either the research will benefit the individual child or that it is of minimal risk and will benefit the population represented by the child. This is a boon for children suffering rare diseases. The requirement of direct benefit under the UK 2004 Regulations is restrictive of Phase 1 trials (which test very small doses of the treatment) designed to combat diseases which affect only children.[102] The distinction between the UK and EU position on these matters is likely to influence changes resulting from the Medicines and Medical Devices Act 2021.

There is another, perhaps bigger, problem in paediatric medicine. Too many drugs that are given marketing authorisation (a licence) for use in adults are

97 P Lewis, 'Procedures that are Against the Medical Interests of Incompetent Adults' (2002) 22(4) *OJLS* 575 asks whether we should be more honest and accept a utilitarian calculus that sometimes the incompetent person's interests are not paramount. And see *Vavřička and Others v the Czech Republic*, App No 47621/13 (ECHR, 2021), on the relevance of community interests in establishing the best interests of children in the context of a mandated vaccination policy.

98 [1972] AC 24, HL.

99 The 'person with legal responsibility' will usually be a parent, a guardian or the court.

100 See Cave, 'Seen but not Heard? Children in Clinical Trials'.

101 Medicines for Human Use (Clinical Trials) Regulations, P 4, paras 9, 10.

102 See Cave, 'Seen but not Heard? Children in Clinical Trials'.

not licensed for use in children.[103] This happens because of ethical and financial restraints on clinical trials that would identify the required dosing in different age groups. This frequently results in drugs being prescribed for children for unlicensed or 'off-label' use.[104] More good quality paediatric clinical trials are needed. To tackle this problem, the EU Regulation on Paediatric Medicines 2006[105] required that new medicines (and some existing drugs) are tested on children in accordance with an agreed Paediatric Investigation Plan (PIP) in order to produce information for the drug label.[106] In addition, new networks have been established to facilitate paediatric trials.[107] But too frequently ethics committees and insurers automatically perceive paediatric clinical trials as high risk.

18.11 Adults who lack mental capacity

As problematic as the question of research involving children is the question of research involving mentally ill, mentally disabled, or unconscious patients. The UK Clinical Trials Regulations 2004 currently deal with clinical trials and the Mental Capacity Act 2005 deals with other research.[108] Consistency between the two was inevitably too much to ask.

Special rules are put in place to govern research. Section 30 states that intrusive research[109] is lawful if an 'appropriate body'[110] (normally an REC) agrees that

103 A Svobodník *et al*, 'How to Improve Children's Research' (2010) February *Applied Clinical Trials*: 'Children and adolescents represent about 25% of the European population, however, most medicines given to children are used off-label. In hospital paediatric wards this is around 45% and in the neonatal intensive care setting this can be as high as 90%.'

104 See Royal College of Paediatrics and Child Health, *The Use of Unlicensed Medicines or Licensed Medicines for Unlicensed Applications in Paediatric Practice* (2019).

105 EU Regulation on Medicinal Products for Paediatric Use Regulation (EC) No 1901/2006. See also European Commission, *Better Medicines for Children from Concept to Reality: Progress Report on the Paediatric Regulation* 1901/2006 (2013).

106 There are exceptions, for example if the illness does not affect children or the drug may be unsafe for them.

107 See European Medicines Agency, *European Paediatric Research Network Ready to Start* (2010), EMA/273427/2010.

108 Also see Mental Capacity Act 2005 (Loss of Capacity During Research Project) (England) Regulations 2007, SI 2007/679. And see guidance in HRA web guidance and learning module at www.hra.nhs.uk.

109 In essence, intrusive research is research that would normally require consent. The Mental Capacity Act 2005, s 30(2) states; 'Research is intrusive if it is of a kind that would be unlawful if it was carried out – (a) on or in relation to a person who had capacity to consent to it, but (b) without his consent.' See R Heywood *et al*, 'Lost Voices in Research: Exposing the Gaps in the Mental Capacity Act 2005' (2019) 19 *Medical Law International* 81 for criticism of the vagueness of the definition.

110 Mental Capacity Act 2005, s 30(4). Defined in Mental Capacity Act 2005 (Appropriate Body) (England) Regulations 2006, SI 2006/2810, reg 2.

the research is safe and relates to the person's impairing condition and that it cannot be done as effectively using people who have the requisite mental capacity to consent. In addition, the research must produce a benefit to the person that outweighs any risk or burden, or it will derive new scientific knowledge[111] and it is of minimal risk to the person and can be carried out with minimal intrusion or interference with their privacy.[112] Section 32 requires researchers to identify a personal or nominated 'consultee' independent of the project who is consulted about whether the person who lacks capacity should participate in the research. These requirements operate in the place of the best interests test which usually governs decision-making for those who lack mental capacity.[113]

Let us compare this with the arrangements for clinical trials under the Clinical Trials Regulations 2004. According to these Regulations, a clinical trial can only recruit adults lacking mental capacity if it relates 'directly to a life-threatening or debilitating clinical condition from which the subject suffers'[114] and '[t]here are grounds for expecting that administering the medicinal product to be tested in the trial will produce a benefit to the subject outweighing the risks or produce no risk at all'.[115] Note that this test is stricter than the test applied under the Clinical Trials Regulations to children; there the benefit need only apply to the group as a whole, rather than to the individual participant. This is probably due to the necessity to prioritise research on children whose physiology is quite different to adults. It is also somewhat more restrictive than the equivalent section dealing with adults lacking capacity in the Mental Capacity Act 2005. Under the Act, the benefits do not necessarily have to outweigh the risks, provided the study derives new scientific knowledge and is of 'minimal risk'. Under the Clinical Trial Regulations, the research must either benefit the participant or produce 'no risk at all'.[116]

Article 31 of the EU Regulation is likely to be influential when the UK reforms the clinical trials regime. It more closely aligns the requirements vis-à-vis incapacitated and minor participants and is more consistent with the Mental Capacity Act. Article 31 only allows trials that are both 'essential with respect to incapacitated subjects'[117] and relate 'directly to a medical condition from which the subject suffers'.[118] As is the case with minors, Article 31(1)(g)

111 Mental Capacity Act 2005, s 31(5).
112 Ibid, s 31(6).
113 R Heywood *et al* are critical of the separate substantive tests and argue that a best interests assessment would have achieved a better balance between empowerment and protection.
114 Medicines for Human Use (Clinical Trials) Regulations 2004, Pt 5, para 11.
115 Ibid, Pt 5, para 9. Note that the requirements are not as stringent as those relating to a minor whereby some direct benefit for the group of patients is required (Pt 4, para 10).
116 See Medical Research Council, *Medical Research Involving Adults who Cannot Consent* (2007), which gives guidance on assessing risk and other decisions relevant to research on adults lacking capacity; Royal College of Physicians, *Guidelines on the Practice of Ethics Committees in Medical Research with Human Participants* (2007) paras 4.32–4.36; GMC, *Consent to Research* (2010, updated 2013), p 13.
117 EU Regulation No 536/2014, Art 31(1)(e).
118 Ibid, Art 31(1)(f).

requires *either* direct benefit to the participant outweighing the risk and burdens *or*, where the trial poses only minimal risks and burdens in comparison with standard treatment, that it will benefit the population represented by the incapacitated subject. However, there is an important caveat. The second option applies only if the trial relates to 'the life-threatening or debilitating medical condition from which the subject suffers'. In the majority of cases, then, there will need to be grounds to suppose that the trial will directly benefit the incapacitated participant.

18.12 Emergency research

Research in emergency settings presents challenges with regards to obtaining consent. We will turn to clinical trials in due course, but first let us consider the law that applies to other research. Section 32(9) of the Mental Capacity Act 2005 provides an exception to the requirement to consult a personal or nominated consultee where there is either 'prior agreement of a registered medical practitioner not involved in the trial or the researcher acts in accordance with a procedure approved by the appropriate body at the time the research project was approved'.[119] An ethics committee will be unlikely to sanction research without the prior agreement of a medical practitioner, save in one situation: emergency research. Emergency research involves participants with life-threatening conditions who cannot give consent. It might, for example, compare two methods of treatment of stroke on admission to hospital. Were it not for section 32(9), emergency research would be severely restricted.

No such exception was to be found in the original UK Clinical Trials Regulations 2004. The MHRA, concerned at the potential ill-effects on emergency medicine, or perhaps at missing out on lucrative research, proposed an amendment in August 2005 sanctioning *deferred* consent after the commencement of the research treatment. Beyleveld and Pattinson[120] argued that the provisions in the Directive ruled out such an approach and that the duty to put the research participant before the interests of science prevents a purposive interpretation of the Directive. Nevertheless, the UK Medicines for Human Use (Clinical Trials) Amendment (No 2) Regulations 2006[121] promulgated a 'deferred consent' model. Accordingly, an exception to the requirement that a legal representative gives consent on behalf of an adult who lacks capacity is created when:

(i) treatment is required urgently;
(ii) the nature of the trial also requires urgent action;

119 See General Medical Council, *Consent to Research* (2010, updated 2013), paras 33–35.

120 See D Beyleveld and S Pattinson, 'Medical Research into Emergency Treatment: Regulatory Tensions in England and Wales' [2006] 5 *Web Journal of Current Legal Issues*.

121 SI 2006/2984.

(iii) it is not reasonably practicable to meet the conditions in paragraphs 1 to 5 of Part 5 (obtaining consent etc); and
(iv) an ethics committee has given approval to the procedure under which the action is taken.

The Clinical Trials Directive received vehement criticism for the restrictions it placed on emergency research on participants unable to consent.[122] Article 35 of EU Regulation 536/2014 now makes express allowance for trials without prior consent subject to conditions that:

- the participant is unable to give consent;
- it is not possible within the time frame to obtain the consent of a legal representative;
- the investigator is not aware of any prior objection expressed by the participant;
- the trial relates directly to the participant's condition; and
- the trial poses minimal risk and burden in comparison to standard treatment.

Provided these conditions are satisfied, the intervention can proceed and consent should then be sought in order for the participant's involvement in the trial to continue. This approach is likely to be influential when the UK model is reformed.

18.13 Randomised controlled trials[123]

At the heart of much modern medical research lies the randomised controlled trial (RCT). Patients suffering from the same illness are divided into two groups and subjected to different treatments. Most commonly, either (a) one group will receive the conventional treatment, and another be given the experimental and hopefully more effective treatment, or (b) one group will be given a new drug, and the other a placebo.[124] For an outsider there are a number of worrying features to RCTs. First, there is again the question of consent. Second, there is concern that the control group is denied a chance of superior treatment.[125] Public anxiety was highlighted by a trial

122 The European Commission, *Assessment of the Functioning of the Clinical Trials Directive 2001/20/EC: Summary of Responses to the Public Consultation Paper* (2010), p 14 recognises that: 'Most respondents agreed that the situation as established by the CTD [in relation to emergency research] was unsatisfactory'. And see S Pattinson, 'Emergency Research and the Interests of Participants' (2012) 12(2) *Medical Law International* 121.

123 For trenchant criticism of randomised controlled trials, see J Penston, *Fiction and Fantasy in Medical Research: The Large Scale Randomised Trial* (2003) London Press.

124 On which see Declaration of Helsinki (2013), Article 33 and *Additional Protocol to the Convention on Human Rights and Biomedicine, Concerning Biomedical Research* (2005), Article 23(3).

125 The ethical acceptability of placebo-controlled research is usually based on either the concept of 'equipoise' or minimal risk. See Royal College of Physicians,

involving 3,000 women at risk of conceiving a spina bifida baby. Studies had shown that similar women appeared to suffer a reduced incidence of carrying a spina bifida baby if treated with special vitamin supplements. The trial involved randomising the women into four groups. One group received the full treatment under trial, another part only of the supplement, a third the other element of the supplement, and the fourth a placebo. Why should any women at risk be denied a treatment which *might* help her avoid a spina bifida conception? Further criticism of randomised trials includes this point, that while the control group in a test may be denied a benefit, people are also concerned at the risk to the experimental group. And finally, who controls and monitors RCTs?

There are doctors and researchers who believe that the RCT is most effective if conducted 'blind', that is the patient is told nothing at all.[126] The issue then is whether consent to treatment given generally is negated by unwitting participation in the RCT. The law will decide the issue on how closely related the RCT is to the condition under treatment and whether consent to treatment impliedly includes consent to what was done in the trial. At best, a patient asked to take part in an RCT will be told just that. The nature of the trial and the purpose of random allocation may be explained. Exactly what will be done to the patient cannot be explained, by virtue of the very nature of a RCT. Consent on the strength of a proper explanation of the trial and free acceptance by the patient of its random basis would appear both sufficient and necessary. Entering the patient in a random test with no explanation and no consent places the doctor at risk of an action for battery if the patient finds out. Fears that patients, if properly informed, will refuse to participate are natural. The erosion of personal freedom resulting from allowing 'blind' trials is not justified by those fears. A patient who will not agree to, or cannot understand the implications of, a trial should not be entered in that trial.[127]

Apart from the questions of consent, the other means by which the courts may be invoked to consider the RCT arise when something goes wrong, and a participant suffers injury. Will the law enable them to obtain compensation?

18.14 Compensation for mishap

Article 76 of the EU Regulation requires there to be a compensation system in place should a participant suffer injury resulting from the clinical trial. Under

Guidelines on the Practice of Ethics Committees in Medical Research with Human Participants (2007), at 5.17, 5.20 and ch 6.

126 And see *Mason and McCall Smith's Law and Medical Ethics*, 19.39 on the ethical implications of a blind, randomised controlled trial on the treatment of Parkinsonism.

127 See the useful discussion in SJ Edwards *et al*, 'Ethical Issues in the Design and Conduct of Randomised Controlled Trials' (1998) 2 *Health Technology Assessment* 1.

the research governance framework, the sponsor of research is responsible for ensuring that appropriate insurance and indemnity arrangements are in place. RECs do not scrutinise the arrangements but are required to ensure that they at least exist.[128]

At present, compensation for personal injury suffered as a participant in a clinical trial is available only either to a participant who can prove negligence on the part of the operator of the trial, or on an *ex gratia* basis. Indemnity for non-negligent harm (caused through no discernible fault of an individual or institution involved) cannot be purchased by NHS bodies, and universities find the costs of such arrangements increasingly prohibitive.[129] A claim in negligence may arise in two contexts in an RCT. First, a participant from the control group may complain that they were denied an improved prospect of cure. Second, participants from the experimental group may allege that unjustifiable risks were taken. Neither is likely to succeed. As long as conventional treatment of the control group remains proper medical practice, participants in that group have no claim in negligence. As long as the novel procedure was a properly conducted piece of research, carried out in conformity with a well-founded and responsible body of medical opinion, the subject of that procedure is likely to fail.

Next, what about the case where something goes disastrously and unexpectedly wrong? The participant will not know why. It may be an inherent risk in the trial; it may be that the staff conducting the trial were negligent. The patients in the Northwick Park debacle[130] quickly ran into difficulties in their legal action. Not only did the MHRA conclude that the reaction was an 'unpredicted biological action', but TeGenro, the German manufacturer, offered an interim payment but then filed for bankruptcy with only limited insurance. Whilst the NHS will meet their immediate medical needs, the injured participants went under-compensated. Guidance, issued in 2012, provides detailed recommendations on a Sponsor's responsibilities and the appropriate level of cover.[131]

In principle, carelessness by the research team, be it in selecting participants on the basis of their previous medical history, in the conduct of the trial or in monitoring the effects of the trial, creates a remedy for the patient. Moreover, they also may have, in theory, a remedy against the ethics committee which approved the trial. It has been held that ethics committees can be subject to judicial review.[132] Arguably committees recognised by the UKECA have

128 HRA, *SOPs for RECs* (2021), para 3.43. And see Annex F.

129 In the European Commission *Assessment of the Functioning of the Clinical Trials Directive 2001/20/EC: Summary of Responses to the Public Consultation Paper* (2010), at para 10.3 'an EU-wide insurance was suggested and advocated as a "silver bullet" for academic research'.

130 See 18.1 above.

131 ABPI *et al*, *Insurance and Compensation in the Event of Injury in Phase I Clinical Trials* (2012).

132 *R v Ethical Committee of St Mary's Hospital (Manchester) ex parte H* [1988] 1 FLR 512.

sufficient legal personality to be a defendant in a civil lawsuit. However, for those which lack statutory recognition, both the appointing authority and each individual member of the ethics committee have direct legal responsibilities to research participants. The *Governance Arrangements for RECs* require the appointing authorities to indemnify REC members 'to relieve them of personal liability in respect of their opinions of the ethics of research'.[133]

18.15 No-fault compensation

Is the present law adequate as a means to provide compensation for injury suffered as a participant of medical research? Forty-five years ago, the Pearson Commission[134] recommended that:

> Any volunteer for medical research or clinical trials who suffers severe damage as a result should have a cause of action, on the basis of strict liability, against the authority to whom he has consented to make himself available.[135]

To date, the DHSC and the pharmaceutical industry have operated *ex gratia* compensation schemes. The injured participant's legal rights remain, in general, dependent on the vagaries of the law of negligence. When a research participant suffers injury in a drug trial they may, of course, gain some slight advantage from the regime of strict liability imposed on drug companies by the Consumer Protection Act 1987. They still have to prove that their injury resulted from a defect in the drug, and that it was that defect which caused their injury. If the drug company chooses to dispute liability, once again the matter is clumsily resolved by adversarial proceedings.[136] An individual, volunteer or patient who agrees to subject themselves to risk in the cause of medical science and the better health of the community deserves better than this.

Extra-legally, drug companies in the United Kingdom recognise the research participants' moral right to compensation independent of proof of fault. The Association of British Pharmaceutical Companies (ABPI) operates an *ex gratia* scheme whereby any healthy volunteer in a drug trial mounted by an ABPI member will receive compensation for any injury arising from that trial. However, many drug trials relate to drugs manufactured by foreign companies. Such companies may not be ready to accept the ABPI guidelines. As we have seen, the HRA requires that ethics committees are adequately reassured that 'the sponsor and investigators will have appropriate insurance or indemnity cover for the potential legal liability arising from the research, and consider provision in proportion to the risk for compensation or treatment in the event of injury, disability or death attributable to participation.'[137] Further, the Royal College of Physicians advises RECs that 'sponsors and investigators

133 DHSC, *Governance Arrangements for RECs* (2021) Annex D(g).
134 See 11.9 above.
135 Royal Commission on Civil Liability and Compensation for Personal Injury (1978) Cmnd 7054, paras 1340–1341.
136 For the problems of establishing strict liability under the 1987 Act, see Chapter 10.
137 HRA, *SOPs for RECs* (2021), para 3.43. And see Annex F.

must have insurance or indemnity cover to meet their potential liabilities arising from research'.[138] Patients agreeing to participate in research, and volunteers involved in non-drug trials, remain outside this informal no-fault provision. And the *ex gratia* nature of the ABPI scheme means that compensation remains dependent on the drug companies' generosity and is in no sense a right enjoyed by research participants. Moreover, as Joanna Manning has argued, industry-drafted guidance 'operate primarily to protect the interests of industry' rather than injured research participants.[139]

The case for no-fault compensation of persons injured in the course of research has long received wide support among doctors.[140] The burden of compensating those injured in the course of research to benefit us all should have a wide base. A fund could be financed from all bodies promoting research – from the profession, the pharmaceutical industry and the DHSC. The prospects for introduction of a scheme to compensate medical research victims along these lines may be brighter than prospects for a general no-fault scheme for all victims of medical accidents.

A scheme limited to injury suffered as a research participant will confront one very real problem. Exactly who would be entitled to benefit under the scheme? Would eligibility be confined to healthy volunteers, such as those in the Northwick Park hospital disaster? The moral case for automatic compensation for that group is overwhelming. Volunteers put their health on the line with no hope of personal benefit. But what of patients used as participants in research into conditions unrelated to their illness? Should eligibility depend on the lack of any conferral of benefits from the research? Or should it extend to all research participants? If it did, the problem of deciding eligibility moves to determining when a patient suffers injury as a result of a research enterprise, as opposed to in the course of general healthcare, which may include resorting to some novel procedure. These potential problems are not insuperable. A second problem occurs where the threat of litigation is removed without the introduction of stringent measures to ensure accountability. Abolishing legal liability in clinical research may provoke a scandal if existing controls are not seen to operate effectively.

18.16 Research misconduct

Monitoring guards against research misconduct, which was defined in 2013 by the UK's Research Council to include fabrication, falsification, plagiarism, misrepresentation, mismanagement, or inadequate preservation of data and/or primary materials, and breach of duty of care. Career promotions are

138 Royal College of Physicians, *Guidelines on the Practice of Ethics Committees in Medical Research with Human Participants* (2007), para 4.10.

139 J Manning, 'Does the Law on Compensation for Research-Related Injury in the UK, Australia, and New Zealand Meet Ethical Requirements?' (2017) 25(3) *Med Law Rev* 397.

140 See JM Barton *et al*, 'The Compensation of Patients Injured in Clinical Trials' (1995) 21 *J Med Ethics* 166. And see Manning, ibid.

dependent on research publications and grant success and competition is fierce. As 'fake news' has proliferated, so too has fake research. There have been several high-profile scandals. We consider just two.

Elizabeth Holmes, the CEO of Theranos, a consumer healthcare technology startup company, was convicted of fraud in 2022 and sentenced to eleven years in prison.[141] She and others made false claims about the efficacy of new blood tests. The valuation of the company rose rapidly to around $9 billion before crashing when whistleblowers raised concerns. In another high-profile case, Paolo Macchiarini, a regenerative medicine researcher, transplanted synthetic tracheas seeded with stem cells in three patients in Sweden. When patients sadly died, he continued his studies in other countries. Reports of research misconduct were filed, but the Karlinska University Hospital in Sweden initially cleared him. Journalists brought the matter to the fore in a documentary, and he was found guilty of misconduct.

Scandals such as those involving Theranos and Macchiarini have heightened the need for more rigorous oversight and prompted a shift from in-house investigation to the formation of independent governmental bodies. Denmark set up a government agency for serious research misconduct in 2017 and Sweden followed suit in 2019. In its first year of operation, thirty out of forty-six cases concerned medicine, health and natural sciences.[142] The UK's Research Institute reforms were more muted. A Committee on Research Integrity champions research integrity[143] but will this suffice?

Professional groups are subject to disciplinary action by the relevant regulatory bodies, such as the GMC and the Nursing and Midwifery Council. The Medical Research Council promulgates a suite of guidance on good research practice[144] and the UK Research Institute issues guidance on research integrity.[145] In relation to clinical trials it is an offence to provide false or misleading information when requesting authorisation of an opinion from an REC.[146] We have seen that the MHRA perform routine and triggered Good Clinical Practice Inspections, during which they will be alert to potential research misconduct. In addition, an NHS Counter Fraud Authority is a special health authority set up to combat fraud and corruption in the NHS. Additionally, the Committee on Publication Ethics promulgates guidelines and a code of conduct for journals, but not all misconduct comes to the attention

141 *US v Elizabeth Holmes et al*, 18-CR-00258-EJD. And see J Carreyrou, *Bad Blood: Secrets and Lies in a Silicon Valley Startup* (2018) Knopf Publishing Group; 'Elizabeth Holmes: Theranos Founder Convicted of Fraud' *BBC News* (2022) 4 January.

142 See H Else, 'Swedish Research Misconduct Agency Swamped with Cases in First Year' *Nature* (2021) 13 September.

143 See House of Commons Science and Technology Committee, *Research Integrity* (2018) HC350.

144 Accessible from their website at www.ukri.org.

145 Ibid.

146 Medicines for Human Use (Clinical Trials) Regulations 2004, reg 50. Penalties are set out in reg 52.

of journal editors. The Retraction Watch Database records 25,000 retractions of journal articles, a significant proportion of which result from misconduct and fraud. A panel for Research Integrity in Health and Biomedical Sciences was set up in 2006,[147] but its role is promotional and advisory. Investigations of research misconduct remain in the hands of employers or sponsors. Overall, there remains a substantial imbalance between the monitoring of clinical trials and the monitoring of other research.[148]

18.17 Privacy and medical research[149]

As we collect ever-increasing amounts of health data from a widening range of sources, the opportunities for commercialisation and economic growth are matched by fears for our privacy.[150] In 2015 a Nuffield Council on Bioethics report into the ethics of data use called for greater participation, accountability and governance, including criminal penalties for the misuse of data.[151] But Government failures to engage transparently with the public over data use have led to public distrust. Two schemes to improve the ways in which general practitioner (GP) data can be used in research to provide insights into population health have had to be abandoned when low levels of trust led to such extensive opt-outs that the data would be compromised.[152] From 2018, with some exceptions, NHS Digital's national data programme allowed patients to opt out, via the NHS App or website, of their confidential patient information being used for purposes of research and planning. How does current law protect our research data?

It is incumbent on us first to note that the law is in a state of flux. In 2021 a Government Taskforce set out new proposals to replace the current framework with a 'UK Framework of Citizen Data Rights'.[153] The stated aims are to maximise the potential of the lucrative digital sector by enhancing flexibility and to 'ensure that privacy is protected' by giving people better control of their data. It is unclear how the two goals are compatible.[154] More specifically in relation to research, the proposals are to bring together the statutory provisions on

[147] See UK Research Integrity Office, *Code of Practice for Research: Promoting Good Practice and Preventing Misconduct* (2009).

[148] R Smith, 'It's Time to Criminalise Serious Scientific Misconduct' *New Scientist* (2014) 15 September. For a global perspective see R Dal-Ré *et al*, 'Should Research Misconduct be Criminalized?' (2020) 16 *Research Ethics* 1.

[149] The common law duty of confidentiality and the Data Protection Act 2018 are explored fully in Chapter 5.

[150] See, for example, A McMahon, A Buyx and B Prainsack, 'Big Data Governance Needs More Collective Responsibility: The Role of Harm Mitigation in the Governance of Data Use in Medicine and Beyond' (2020) 28(1) *Med Law Rev* 155.

[151] Nuffield Council on Bioethics, *The Collection, Linking and Use of Data in Biomedical Research and Health Care: Ethical Issues* (February 2015).

[152] Care.data was abandoned in 2014 and General Practice Data for Planning and Research programme was paused in 2021. See DHSC, *Data Saves Lives* (2022).

[153] I Duncan Smith, T Villiers and G Freeman, *Taskforce on Innovation, Growth and Regulatory Reform* (2021) May, pp 49–53. See 5.19 above.

[154] See further Department for Digital, Culture Media & Sport, *National Data Strategy* (December 2020) and *Data: A New Direction* (September 2021).

research to make them less confusing, to offer a clearer definition of 'scientific research' and to set out a new ground for the lawful processing of data for scientific research, which Edward Dove fears could lead to misalignment with the EU.[155] At the time of writing the proposals are at an early stage, and so we focus in this section on currently applicable provisions.

For now, the Data Protection Act 2018, which replaced the Data Protection Act 1998, sets out the framework for data protection law in the UK. It operates in conjunction with the EU's General Data Protection Regulation (GDPR), which came into force in 2018, and is incorporated into law under the European Union (Withdrawal) Act 2018. Operational guidance for researchers is provided by the Health Research Authority, which notes that 'in most cases the impact [of data protection laws] on individual research projects will be limited'.[156]

The GDPR aimed to standardise data protection laws across the EU and to make it easier for people to control their data. The GDPR and 2018 Act are concerned with 'personal data', which is identified as 'any information relating to an identified or identifiable living individual'.[157] The definition excludes anonymised data, but can capture certain pseudonymised (coded) data. It requires first that the use of personal data in health research must have a 'legal basis'. As we saw in Chapter 5, there are six such bases and the appropriate legal basis depends on the organisation processing the data. For NHS organisations, the HRA advises that the research should be a 'task in the public interest'. This can be demonstrated by showing that it is complies with the UK Policy Framework for Health and Social Care Research.[158] This contrasts with the position under the 1998 Act which focused on consent as the justificatory principle. The 2018 Act and the GDPR recognise that an imbalance in power between a research participant and those controlling the data can render reliance on consent as the legal basis for processing personal data inappropriate. But this does not render the role of consent otiose. In addition to showing that the processing has a 'legal basis', other relevant legal frameworks such as the common law duty of confidentiality must also be satisfied. As we saw in Chapter 5, consent is integral to the use of confidential patient information in research, subject to exceptions, such as those set out in section 251 of the Health Service (Control of Patient Information Regulations) 2002 under which the CAG can sanction research using confidential information without consent. Article 89 of the GDPR and section 19 of the 2018 Act also require that data is safeguarded to ensure that it is processed and stored accurately and securely. Identifiable information should not be used if anonymised information would suffice.

The common law duty of confidentiality, which applies independently of the 2018 Act, is open to misinterpretation in relation to medical research. To advance the development of medicine and to enable research when completed to benefit other patients, the results of research must be published. Does publication of research findings amount to a breach of confidence to the patient?

155 E Dove, 'Data: A New Direction – But Which Direction?' *Mason Institute Blog* (2021) 10 November.

156 Accessible from their website at www.hra.nhs.uk.

157 Data Protection Act 2018, s 3(2).

158 HRA, *UK Policy Framework for Health and Social Care Research* (2017).

First, the patient, if they have given full and free consent to their participation in a trial, may at the same time agree to information about them being disclosed once the trial is completed and a report is prepared. This must be the preferable course of action. Whether in law disclosure in the course of a research project of confidential information about a patient without their consent amounts to an actionable breach of confidence depends yet again on the nebulous test of whether that disclosure can be justified by the public interest in the advancement of the relevant research.

The GMC[159] requires that where practicable, researchers seek consent and anonymise data, and always keep disclosures to a minimum.[160] It provides special requirements for researchers dealing with medical records and advises on the reporting of research data. Is data that is fully anonymised subject to the duty of confidentiality?

In *R v Department of Health ex p Source Informatics Ltd*[161] the applicant was a data collection company. It persuaded GPs and pharmacists to supply it with anonymised information about prescribing habits. It then sold this information to drug companies. The Department of Health issued a document ruling that to disclose such information without patient consent constituted a breach of confidence. The company challenged the ruling. The trial judge found that anonymisation did not remove the obligation of confidence. Transfer of anonymised data might in certain cases be justifiable, for example to ensure clinical audit, but information about patients was in all cases confidential, whether the patient was identifiable or not. The Court of Appeal disagreed. Disclosure of anonymised information, the appeal court ruled, did not violate the interests which obligations of confidentiality protect. The patient's privacy was not violated. He was not vulnerable to any harm.

What is clear is that disclosure should be limited to information strictly necessary to the project and that the anonymity of the patient must be protected. The NHS Ombudsman upheld a complaint from a young man who discovered in a medical textbook a full-face frontal picture of his naked body.

18.18 Genetic privacy and biobanks[162]

Genetic and genomic research[163] generates significant public concern.[164] Some deem it 'unnatural' or unethical. Others worry about the implications for their right to privacy under Article 8 of the European Convention on Human

159 General Medical Council, *Confidentiality* (2018), para 8; GMC, *Good Practice in Research* (2010, updated 2013), para 42.

160 See discussion of care.data at 5.21 above.

161 [2000] 1 All ER 786, CA.

162 See 5.14 above. And see S McLean (ed), *Genetics and Gene Therapy* (2015) Routledge.

163 'Genetics' is the study of heredity and 'genomics' is the study of an organism's genes in their entirety.

164 H Widdows, *Connected Self: The Ethics and Governance of the Genetic Individual* (2013) Cambridge University Press.

Rights (ECHR). Public databases, or 'biobanks', containing genetic information have vastly increased in number.[165] Tighter controls on medical data ushered in by the Data Protection Act 1998, and subsequently the GDPR and Data Protection Act 2018, have made it harder for researchers to access the data they desire. They are required to protect the identity of participants and to prove that the use of confidential data is in the public interest.

Genetic profiling is playing an ever-increasing role in research and, increasingly, treatment. Genomics England is a limited company owned by the DHSC, set up to deliver the 100,000 Genomes Project. The project completed in 2018 having sequenced the genomes of 100,000 patients with rare diseases or cancer, to benefit patients and facilitate scientific development. It laid the foundations for the NHS Genomic Medicine Service, which has an expanded remit to sequence 500,000 genomes and ultimately to offer whole genome sequencing as part of routine care to aid diagnosis and personalised medicine. Another dataset, the UK Biobank project,[166] has, since 2006, collected both data and samples on the health of an additional 500,000 volunteers and made them accessible in anonymised form to approved researchers. UK Biobank has approval from an REC, as well as Research Tissue Bank approval and an HTA licence.

In Chapter 21, we examine the law relating to the human body and its parts and the effects of the Human Tissue Act 2004. The doctrine of consent is central to the legislation. An exception exists for health-related research on living people where the tissue is unidentifiable, and the project has received ethical approval[167] in accordance with the Human Tissue Act 2004 (Ethical Approval, Exceptions and Licensing and Supply of Information about Transplants) Regulations 2006. The REC must consider how tissue is to be disposed of and the means by which relatives are informed of results.[168] Another exception exists by virtue of section 7(4) of the 2004 Act, which confers on the Secretary of State a power to deem consent to be in place, though it is envisaged that this will only be used where there is an overwhelming public interest in doing so.[169]

Might the public interest threshold be set so high as to inhibit valuable research? It is unlikely. As we demonstrated in Chapter 5, the right to privacy under Article 8(1) is not absolute. It can be limited under Article 8(2):

[165] Editorial, 'Genetic Privacy' (2013) 493 *Nature* 451.

[166] See *Mason and McCall Smith's Law and Medical Ethics*, at 7.81; SMC Gibbons, 'Regulating Biobanks: A Twelve-Point Typological Tool' (2009) 17(3) *Med Law Rev* 313.

[167] By an authorised research ethics committee: see the Human Tissue Act 2004 (Ethical Approval, Exceptions from Licensing and Supply of Information about Transplants) Regulations 2006, SI 2006/1260, reg 2.

[168] See Human Tissue Authority, *Code of Practice and Standards, Code E: Research* (2021).

[169] For additional guidance on research involving human tissues, see General Medical Council, *Consent to Research* (2010, updated 2013), paras 36–39 and Royal College of Physicians, *Guidelines on the Practice of Ethics Committees in Medical Research with Human Participants* (2007), paras 4.37–4.41, and ch 7.

> ... in the interests of national security, public safety or the economic well-being of the country, for the prevention of disorder or crime, for the protection of health or morals, or for the protection of the rights and freedoms of others.

Though there has been little case-law on Article 8(2) in the context of medical confidentiality,[170] the House of Lords in *R (S & Marper) v Chief Constable of South Yorkshire Police*[171] indicated how readily the judiciary put the public interest before that of the individual. The UK National DNA Database holds DNA profiles of select individuals. Since 1998 it has been instrumental in the detection of more than 300,000 crimes.[172] It was held in *Marper* that the retention and use of DNA and fingerprints by the police, after a suspect had been cleared of the offence, did not offend Article 8. Four of the Law Lords held that Article 8(1) was not invoked. Baroness Hale held that though there was an interference with privacy within the meaning of Article 8(1), it was justified as proportionate under Article 8(2). The information would not be made public and individuals were not identifiable to the 'untutored eye'. The retention of the samples to be used as comparators was appropriate.

The European Court of Human Rights disagreed and, in *S and Marper v UK*,[173] ruled the UK's policy incompatible with the ECHR. The Protection of Freedoms Act 2012 resulted in the deletion of more than a million DNA profiles and fingerprint records and the destruction of DNA samples.[174] What are the implications for the storage and retention of genetic data for healthcare research? Laurie, Harmon and Dove argue that the decision does not necessarily prevent long-term retention of genetic data but makes it imperative that it is justified as both necessary and proportionate.[175] Strong governance is essential.

The government will not shackle researchers.[176] Research is lucrative. Let us not forget that it also advances medicine and saves lives. In England and Wales, regulation and review of research is going through a period of unprecedented change. Efforts to facilitate good research have been matched by significant improvements in the level of participant safety. Provided this equilibrium is maintained (though, as domestic reform proposals and reforms of the UK Clinical Trials Regulations unravel, this cannot yet be assumed), the changes are to be celebrated.

170 Though see Strasbourg cases *MS v Sweden* (1997) 28 EHRR 313 and *Z v Finland* (1997) 25 EHRR 371 protecting children's medical confidentiality.

171 [2004] UKHL 39.

172 Home Office, *Helping the Police Fight Crime More Effectively* (2013).

173 (2009) 48 EHRR 50.

174 Protection of Freedoms Act 2012, s 1, inserting a new s 63D into the Police and Criminal Evidence Act 1984.

175 *Mason and McCall Smith's Law and Medical Ethics*, 2.46.

176 See UK Gov, *Genome UK: The Future of Healthcare* (2020): A strategy setting out the vision to extend the UK's leadership in genomic healthcare and research.

Chapter 19

DEFINING DEATH

19.1 Introduction

The single certainty in human life is that we shall die. Death cannot be evaded, albeit it may be delayed. Medical technology has created real questions about just how we identify the threshold between dying but alive, and death itself. The development of transplantation played a major role in prompting doctors to rethink definitions of death. It would be wrong to conclude that a desire to maximise the number of viable organs suitable for transplant is the only or the most important factor in the imperative need to define the moment of death.[1] The question is far from straightforward and a legal definition of death is required for several purposes.

19.2 Defining death[2]

Defining death is difficult because, biologically, death is a process and not an event. Different organs and systems supporting the continuation of life cease to function successively, and at different times. The need to determine an exact or, at best, approximate time of death is important for many reasons. The law often requires such a finding. Establishing the date of death may be important for property purposes. Until death is established, steps cannot be taken to obtain probate or letters of administration to that person's estate. The timing of death is relevant to the calculation of inheritance tax and if the victim has a claim for damages for the injuries sustained, the amount of damages will differ substantially depending on whether the victim is comatose yet living, or dead.[3] And self-evidently, doctors cannot remove organs for transplant under the rules governing cadaver donations unless the donor is legally dead.

Determining whether a person was dead once posed little difficulty. Historically, the key factors in the process used to determine whether death had occurred were the cessation of breathing and the cessation of heartbeat.

1 See C Machado *et al*, 'The Concept of Brain Death Did Not Evolve to Benefit Organ Transplants' (2007) 33 *J Med Ethics* 197.

2 For an excellent analysis of all the medical and ethical conundrums surrounding a definition of death, see GT Laurie, SHE Harmon and ES Dove, *Mason and McCall Smith's Law and Medical Ethics* (11th edn, 2019) Oxford University Press, ch 17.

3 See *Lim Poh Choo v Camden and Islington Area Health Authority* [1980] AC 174.

Advances in medicine gradually demonstrated that this was not a valid test for all purposes: elective cardiac arrest during open-heart surgery, for example, or cases of spontaneous cardiac arrest followed by successful resuscitation. The heart stops but the patient is not dead. Machines such as mechanical ventilators or respirators have effected major improvements in techniques of resuscitation and life support for those who are desperately ill or injured. Where these efforts are successful and the patients recover, one may praise the advances in medical techniques. Sometimes such measures do not provide any satisfactory outcome, for example where the person's heart continues to beat on the machine long after breathing has stopped but his brain is irreversibly damaged. In such circumstances, keeping a body 'alive' on a machine can be as undesirable as it is pointless. It is distressing to relatives. It can have an adverse effect on nursing staff morale; the cost of maintaining the patient in such intensive care is high, and the use of machines in these cases can mean that other patients better able to benefit from them may be denied access to them. Developments in life support made rethinking death inevitable.

Nonetheless, a significant trigger to rethinking our definition of death was the development of transplantation, which highlighted the need for speed in diagnosing death and removing organs from the body. Thus, pressures developed to consider a redefinition of death based upon a new concept of 'irreversible brain damage' or 'brain death'. This concept can be illustrated dramatically by considering a guillotine victim. Nobody would consider the body, after the head has been severed, to represent an individual living being; yet the decapitated body could be resuscitated and the organs kept 'alive' for a considerable period. In most cases, brain death follows the cessation of breathing and heartbeat in the dying process, but occasionally that order of events is reversed. This occurs as a result of severe damage to the brain itself, from perhaps a head injury or a spontaneous intracranial haemorrhage. In such cases, instead of failure of such vital functions as heartbeat and respiration eventually resulting in brain death, brain death results in the cessation of spontaneous respiration; normally followed within minutes by cardiac arrest. If, however, the patient is supported by artificial ventilation, the heartbeat can continue for some days[4] and this will, for a time, enable the function in other organs, such as the liver and kidneys, to be maintained.

This condition of what was then described as a 'state beyond coma' or 'irreversible coma' or 'brain death' was first advanced as a new criterion of death in 1968.[5] In such cases (it was said) a doctor could pronounce as dead a 'comatose' individual who had no discernible central nervous system activity; and then the ventilator could be switched off. But public opinion was unwilling to surrender control of such matters lightly to the medical profession. Unease was expressed about the relationship between attempts to redefine death and the needs of transplant surgeons to ensure that organs taken from a deceased

[4] And occasionally much longer: See discussion of *Re M* [2020] EWCA Civ 164 at 19.3 below. Baby Midrar was ventilated for four months.

[5] 'A Definition of Irreversible Coma' (1968) 205 *JAMA* 337.

person should be taken as soon as possible after death. In 1975, the British Transplantation Society expressed concern at the poor quality of cadaver kidneys being transplanted, mainly because of delay between the determination of death and the removal of the kidneys from the body. It was also important, for transplantation, that a ventilator should not be switched off permanently, but rather that the donor's body be kept on the machine to preserve the quality of the organs until they were required. Two major fears were voiced. First, was the pressure to redefine death being made simply to enable transplant surgeons to obtain better results? Second, was it ethically or legally permissible to remove organs from a donor before the ventilator had been turned off? The British Transplantation Society recommended that the death of a potential organ donor should be certified by two doctors; neither of whom were a member of the transplant team and, most important, that the decision to stop a ventilator should be made quite independently of transplant considerations.

From the late 1970s the medical establishment in Britain[6] agreed that 'brain death'[7] or, preferably, 'brain stem death' (which is the 'irreversible loss of brain stem function') could be diagnosed with certainty; and in these circumstances, the patient is dead whether or not the function of some organs, such as a heartbeat, is still maintained by artificial means.

Some commentators continued to reject the notion that 'death' could be equated with 'irreversible loss of brain stem function'.[8] They argued that only the cessation of the heartbeat truly indicated the end of life. In January 2011, the Chief Rabbi, Lord Sachs, re-ignited controversy relating to brain death. He issued a rabbinical ruling that only 'cardiac death' was acceptable as the definition of death in Orthodox Jewry.[9] The consequences for organ donation are discussed in the next chapter.

Official endorsement of 'brain stem death' in the UK is now to be found in a comprehensive Code of Practice issued by the Academy of Medical Royal Colleges:[10] '[D]eath involves the irreversible loss of those essential characteristics which are necessary to the existence of living human person and thus the definition of death should be regarded as the irreversible loss of consciousness

6 See Conference of Medical Royal Colleges and their Faculties in the UK, 'Diagnosis of Brain Death' (1976) 2 *BMJ* 1187; and 'Memorandum on the Diagnosis of Death' (1979) 1 *BMJ* 332; C Pallis and DH Harley, *ABC of Brainstem Death* (2nd edn, 1996) BMJ Books.

7 For an analysis of the confusing terms in debates on 'brain death' see *Mason and McCall Smith's Law and Medical Ethics*, 16.10–16.21.

8 See M Evans, 'A Plea for the Heart' (1990) 3 *Bioethics* 227; and note that in Japan 'brain stem death' was only accepted as a lawful definition of death in the late 1990s, see J Wise, 'Japan to Allow Organ Transplants' (1997) 314 *BMJ* 1298. And see JL Verheijde, MY Rady and M Potts, 'Neuroscience and Brain Death Controversies: The Elephant in the Room' (2018) 57(5) *Journal of Religion and Health* 1745 challenging the scientific legitimacy of the definition of brain death.

9 And see A Bedir and S Aksoy, 'Brain Death Revisited: It is not "Complete Death" According to Islamic Sources' (2011) 37(5) *J Med Ethics* 290.

10 Academy of Medical Royal Colleges, *A Code of Practice for the Diagnosis and Confirmation of Death* (2008).

combined with the irreversible loss of the capacity to breathe.' Brain stem death is defined as follows:

Death following the irreversible cessation of brain stem function

> The irreversible cessation of brain stem function (brain stem death) whether induced by intra-cranial events or the result of extra-cranial phenomena, such as hypoxia, will produce this clinical state and therefore irreversible cessation of the integrative function of the brain stem equates with the death of the individual and allows the medical practitioner to diagnose death.[11]

Importantly, the Code of Practice also sets out detailed and careful instructions for rigorous criteria for tests to confirm death.[12]

19.3 The law

There is still no statutory definition of death in the United Kingdom. There is, however, sufficient judicial authority in England to support a definition of 'death by neurological criteria' based on 'brain stem death'. The question first arose where persons accused of murder claimed that it was not they who killed the victim, but the hospital team who disconnected the life-support machine. The courts did not react favourably, even though they side-stepped the issue as to what, in law, constituted death.[13] Subsequent cases concerned disputes as to when ventilation of a brain-stem-dead patient can cease. In *Re A* (1992)[14] a 2-year-old boy suffered a serious head injury and he was put on a ventilator. Tests established that he was, undoubtedly, brain-stem-dead. His parents vehemently opposed the decision to switch off the ventilator. The hospital sought a declaration that doctors in disconnecting the child from the ventilator did not act unlawfully. Endorsing the definition of death by neurological criteria then encapsulated in a Department of Health Code of Practice, the judge declared that the child was for all purposes legally dead. The House of Lords in *Airedale NHS Trust v Bland*[15] lent further authority to a legal definition of death dependent on proof of 'brain stem death'.

In 2015 the Code of Practice criteria for death[16] were once again affirmed in *Re A* (2015).[17] The case concerned a 19-month-old boy who, having tragically choked on food, was brought to hospital and ventilated. There he was declared clinically dead based on two brain stem tests. Extubation was opposed by A's parents. Forty-eight hours later, the coroner assumed jurisdiction over the body and asked that ventilation be withdrawn. Such a move is unprecedented.

11 Ibid, ch 2.1.
12 Ibid, chs 4–6.
13 *R v Malcherek*; *R v Steel* [1981] 2 All ER 422. And see *Finlayson v HM Advocate* 1978 SLT 60.
14 [1992] 3 Med LR 303; and see *Mail Newspapers plc v Express Newspapers plc* [1987] FSR 90; *Re TC (A Minor)* (1993) 2 Med LR 376.
15 [1993] 1 All ER 821, HL. See 22.15 below.
16 Academy of Medical Royal Colleges, *A Code of Practice for the Diagnosis and Confirmation of Death* (2008).
17 [2015] EWHC 443 (Fam).

Whilst the coroner has legal jurisdiction to remove a body[18] so too does the High Court, which is clearly better placed to deal with the sensitive question of withdrawal of treatment from a clinically dead child. Hayden J stated:

> I cannot conceive of any circumstances in which the Coroner should seek to intervene, where a body remains ventilated, beyond those circumstances concerning the removal of organs where the family are consenting. Any other approach I regard as likely to generate immense distress and contribute to an atmosphere where sound judgment may be jeopardised.[19]

In *Oxford University Hospital Trust v AB (a minor)*[20] Francis J applied the Code of Practice criteria, confirming the brain stem death of a 14-year-old girl who was tragically found hanging at home. Francis J concluded that it was therefore in AB's best interests for all support to be withdrawn. This aspect of the decision raised an important question: if AB was dead, were her best interests relevant? The Court of Appeal in *Re M (declaration of death of child)*[21] held that they are not. Noting the urgent and 'most fraught' circumstances of the hearing, McFarlane P held that Francis J 'inadvertently fell into error': 'Once death has been established, then the concept of "best interests" no longer has any legal relevance'.[22]

In *Re M* the 'death by neurological criteria' was confirmed again. Against the parents' objections, the Trust sought permission to remove ventilatory support from baby Midrar, who had been starved of oxygen at birth. Granting the application, the court confirmed that he was clinically dead and that it was 'not open to this court to contemplate a different test'.[23] The appropriate standard of proof was the balance of probabilities, 'but the Court should apply anxious scrutiny to the evidence.'[24]

But *Re M* raised another thorny issue: is informed consent required for the assessment to take place? If family members can prevent assessment, they might also prevent withdrawal of support. Disputes as to the best interests of adult patient or a refusal of a parent to consent to the assessment could be dealt with by the courts, which would be likely to consider assessment to be in the patient's best interests.[25] But at first instance in *Re M*[26] Lieven J opined

18 Under the Coroners Act 2009, s 15.

19 [2015] EWHC 443 (Fam), [22]. See KA Choong and MY Rady, '*Re A (A Child)* and the United Kingdom Code of Practice for the Diagnosis and Confirmation of Death: Should a Secular Construct of Death Override Religious Values in a Pluralistic Society?' (2018) 30(1) *HEC Forum* 71.

20 [2019] EWHC 3516 (Fam).

21 [2020] EWCA Civ 164.

22 Ibid, [49] per McFarlane P. And see *North West Anglia NHS FT v PN and PS* [2022] EWHC 663 (Fam).

23 Ibid, [91] per McFarlane P.

24 *Manchester University NHS FT v Namiq* [2020] EWHC 180 (Fam), [35].

25 The Trust could apply for a specific issue order under the Children Act 1989, s 8: *Barts Health NHS Trust v Dance* [2022] EWHC 1435 (Fam), [16].

26 *Manchester University NHS Foundation Trust v Midrar Namiq and Or* [2020] EWHC 180 (Fam), [45].

that consent would not necessarily have to be given for such a test.[27] In any event she did not need to decide the issue because the parents knew the test was being conducted and consent could be inferred from their conduct.[28]

As two sad cases demonstrate, the standard test for 'death by neurological criteria' set out in the Code of Practice is neither universally applicable nor immune to further scientific development. In the case of 12-year-old Archie Battersbee, discussed at 17.18 above, Archie did not react to a peripheral nerve stimulation test, which is a necessary precursor to the brain stem test. As a result the brain stem test, if performed, would not be reliable. At first instance it was found in light of evidence based on other tests and expert opinion that, on the balance of probabilities, Archie was dead.[29] But on appeal counsel for both sides agreed that where the standard brain stem test could not be relied upon, it was appropriate to make a best interests evaluation on the basis that the patient was alive, which the Court proceeded to do.[30]

The evidential uncertainty in *Re A* (2022)[31] was of a different nature. A was 3 months old when he was brought to hospital after multiple fractures and cardiac arrest. Repeated brain stem testing indicated that he was dead, but A's parents wanted him to be given more time. The Trust originally applied for an order that brain stem death had occurred, but in a development that shocked clinicians and fuelled the hope of A's parents, Baby A recommenced to breathe and settled into a regular breathing rhythm. The hospital immediately rescinded the brain stem death diagnosis and the court was asked instead to make a best interests evaluation. The Code of Practice applies to all patients, but *Re A* revealed its inadequacies in relation to infants with an open fontanelle. The Code of Practice is not static. As science advances so the test must be updated.

19.4 Should there be a statutory definition of death?

The case for a statutory definition of death is less compelling than when such arguments were first advanced,[32] as the courts have introduced a degree of certainty into the debate. Nonetheless, the cases discussed in the previous section demonstrate that the issue remains live. Had there been a statutory definition of death in 1976 (a definition based upon the longstanding medical criteria of irreversible cessation of breathing and heartbeat), then the medical redefinition of death to take into account irreversible cessation of brain function would have had no legal effect, in those cases where there was a difference in

27 And see T Pope, 'Brain Death Forsaken: Growing Conflict and New Legal Challenges' (2017) 37(3–4) *Journal of Legal Medicine* 265.

28 This argument was accepted on appeal: [2020] EWCA Civ 164, [68].

29 *Barts Health NHS Trust v Dance* [2022] EWHC 1435 (Fam).

30 *Barts Health NHS Trust v Dance* [2022] EWCA Civ 935. See also *Re X (Catastrophic Injury: Collection and Storage of Sperm)* [2022] EWCOP 48, [6] (the court proceeded on the basis that X was alive in circumstances where brain stem death was suspected but not confirmed).

31 *Re A (A Child)* [2022] EWHC 1873 (Fam); [2022] EWCA Civ 1221.

32 For example, see 14th Report of the Criminal Law Reform Committee, *Offences Against the Person* (1980) Cmnd 7844.

time between the two definitions, until the existing definition had itself been changed by statute. As long as the matter is treated as a question of medical fact, changes in medical approach can be accommodated within the law without any requirement for further legislation.

Those in favour of legislation regard the ease with which, without legislation, definitions of death can alter, and have altered, as a source of disquiet. Doctors, supported by judges, changed the goalposts. Visceral fears that doctors continue to be eager to declare A dead to give B her organs have not gone away.[33] A debate on a statutory definition of death would allow wide public involvement in that debate, and an opportunity for public education.

Formulating a statutory definition of death is not straightforward.[34] Section 26(2)(d) of the Human Tissue Act 2004 empowered the Human Tissue Authority (HTA) to prepare a Code of Practice in relation to the definition of death, but for the purposes of that Act only. No such Code has been developed by the HTA. While the HTA may be well placed to consult widely in relation to its preparation of such a Code, it is regrettable that their Code of Practice would be narrowly focused within the 2004 Act. This could reinforce fears that a different standard applies where the primary question is removal of organs and tissue from the body.[35]

Open debate about how we define death would allow two other questions to be explored, namely those relating to anencephalic infants and pregnant women. In anencephalic babies, the conventional criteria for 'brain stem death' are unworkable. An anencephalic baby is born lacking a higher brain. He is bound to die, usually in a matter of days and, were his interests alone to be considered, such an infant would not be ventilated. Other babies are born with intact brains but defective hearts or kidneys. Doctors may want to use organs from the anencephalic baby to save the life of a baby with other defective organs. In 2015, the parents of Teddy Houlston learned during the pregnancy that their son was anencephalic but elected to continue the pregnancy so that Teddy could be an organ donor. He lived for about a hundred minutes and died in his mother's arms. Once his heart stopped, surgeons removed the kidneys, which were then transplanted into an adult.[36] Teddy was thus a Donation after Circulatory Death (non-heart beating) donor. If newborn infants are to be used more often as organ donors, brain death in newborns and anencephalic infants

33 See JM Appel, 'Defining Death: When Physicians and Family Disagree' (2005) 31 *J Med Ethics* 641.

34 For an argument against a statutory definition see DN Banyubala, 'Death in Ghana: Socio-cultural Implications for Organ Transplant Legislation' (2014) 14 *Medical Law International* 52. For an attempt to resolve international disagreement about brain death criteria see DM Greer *et al*, 'Determination of Brain Death / Death by Neurological Criteria: The World Brain Death Project' (2020) 324(11) *JAMA* 1078.

35 See C Machado *et al*, 'A Definition of Human Death Should Not be Related to Organ Transplants' (2003) 29 *J Med Ethics* 201. Note discussion at 20.12 below on technological advances in Donation after Circulatory Death whereby it is sometimes possible to retrieve a heart for donation after it has stopped beathing.

36 'Newborn Baby Teddy was UK's Youngest Ever Organ Donor' *BBC News* (2015) 23 April.

needs to be clarified to allow the baby to be ventilated while arrangements for a transplant are made. That poses a problem in defining *when* he dies. Tests for 'brain stem death' are not applicable to newborn babies under two months old,[37] and there is some evidence that, if ventilated, an anencephalic infant's brain stem may remain active, 'alive', for some considerable period of time. In 2015 the Royal College of Paediatrics and Child Health[38] issued a report providing recommendations of diagnosis of brain death in infants under two months old. The guidance may enable doctors to diagnose death in newborns without waiting for the heart to stop and so increase the numbers of organs available for transplant especially into child recipients.

One objection, regardless of how we define death in such cases, is that in ventilating an anencephalic baby to retrieve her organs we use her solely as a means to an end. A similar problem surrounds ventilating brain-dead pregnant women.[39] We do no more than pose a series of questions. If a pregnant woman suffers head injuries during pregnancy and brain stem death is diagnosed, should her corpse be ventilated to allow the fetus the opportunity to be delivered alive? Who should make such decisions? In a recent report of a case from Portugal, a woman who was nineteen weeks pregnant was diagnosed as brain-stem-dead just days after suffering an asthma attack. She was maintained on a ventilator for fifty-six days to allow the fetus to survive in her womb, and the child was eventually born at thirty-two weeks.[40] Could a similar decision be taken in England and Wales? Where a woman has herself contemplated such a possibility and in an advance decision expressed her wish that her body be sustained so her child can live, the outcome might seem clearer. She has authorised the use of her body for that purpose but such a use of a dead body is not contemplated in the Human Tissue Act 2004. The temptation for doctors wishing to comply with the 'dead' woman's instructions might be to fall back on earlier definitions of death based on cessation of heartbeat and declare that this woman is not dead. What of instructions *not* to ventilate her 'corpse' from a woman in the later stages of pregnancy when a few further days in the womb might give the fetus a fighting chance of survival? Can her wishes be ignored? Absent any instruction from the woman herself, does her husband, partner or parent have a right to determine whether or not the fetus survives? Or is this a case where an independent fetal interest can be asserted? In the Portuguese case described above, it is reported that the ethics committee recommending ventilation was influenced by the family's support and the fact that the woman

[37] See Working Party of the British Paediatric Association, *Diagnosis of Brain-Stem Death in Infants and Children* (1991) endorsed in the Academy of Medical Royal Colleges, *Code of Practice for the Diagnosis and Confirmation of Death* (2008) see para 6.2 and Appendix 4.

[38] Royal College of Paediatrics and Child Health, *The Diagnosis of Death by Neurological Criteria in Infants Less than Two Months Old* (2015). A revised guideline is expected in late 2023.

[39] See R Heywood, 'Live or Let Die?: Fine Margins Between Life and Death in a Brain-Dead Pregnancy' (2017) 25(4) *Med Law Rev* 628; and see *Mason and McCall Smith's Law and Medical Ethics*, 17.28–17.31.

[40] See 'Portugal Baby Born to Woman Brain Dead for Three Months' *BBC News* (2019) 29 March.

had not opted out of the presumed consent organ donation law. The committee considered this to be indicative of a will to make a sacrifice so that another might live. As we shall see in the next chapter, England, Scotland and Wales have all moved to opt-out organ donation legislation, strictly restricted to certain activities which do not extend to posthumous fetal incubation.

The Irish case of *PP v Health Service Executive*[41] illustrates the complexity and poignancy of the dilemma of the brain-dead pregnant woman. NP was fifteen weeks pregnant when she was diagnosed as brain-stem-dead. Her father and her partner sought to have the ventilator switched off. Doctors sought to maintain NP on life support to allow the fetus to survive. Note that in Ireland, until the Eighth Amendment was repealed in 2018,[42] Article 40(3) of the Constitution expressly acknowledged the 'right to life of the unborn and, with due regard to the equal right to life of the mother, guarantees in its laws to respect, and as far as practicable, by its laws to defend and vindicate that right'. The Irish High Court heard medical evidence that indicated that the fetus was unlikely to survive. The judges therefore concluded that it was not in the best interests of the fetus for its mother to be maintained on life support. They noted, too, the terrible distress caused to her family if this largely 'futile' exercise was to continue and that NP herself would be deprived of 'dignity in death'. An apology was issued to the family in 2019. The case leaves open a number of questions. First, what would be the situation if a similar factual scenario occurred in a jurisdiction that did not provide any constitutional protection for the fetus? Indeed, given that the Eighth Amendment has now been repealed, should a similar case arise once again in Ireland, there is no guarantee that judges would reason the best interests question through the lens of the fetus in the same way. Secondly, and perhaps more importantly, what would be the outcome if the same incident happened but the gestational development of the fetus was significantly more advanced, either much closer to, or even beyond, the point of viability.[43] Whatever your conclusion as to the continued ventilation of brain-dead pregnant women, the notion of 'brain-dead incubators'[44] challenges our understanding of death, and could undermine confidence in definitions of brain stem death.

The brutal reality may be that, however death is defined and whether such a definition is enshrined in statute or not, diagnosing death will always be a matter of concern.[45] Few people wish their final moments to be cut short by others. Accepting the death of someone close to you is more than an exercise in logic.

41 [2014] IEHC 622. And see R Heywood, 'Live or Let Die?: Fine Margins Between Life and Death in a Brain-Dead Pregnancy' (2017) 25(4) *Med Law Rev* 628.

42 See 16.1 above.

43 See for example, 'Portugal Baby Born to Woman Brain Dead for Three Months' *BBC News*.

44 See NS Peart, AV Campbell and AR Manara, 'Maintaining a Pregnancy Following Loss of Capacity' (2000) 8 *Med Law Rev* 275.

45 See LF Ross, 'Respecting Choice in Definitions of Death' in Defining Death: Organ Transplantation and the Fifty-Year Legacy of the Harvard Report on Brain Death Special Report (2018) 48(6) *Hastings Center Report* S53.

Chapter 20

ORGAN AND TISSUE TRANSPLANTATION

20.1 Introduction

This chapter explores legal questions surrounding organ and tissue transplantation. Closely related questions addressing organ retention for the purposes of education and research are dealt with in Chapter 18. The Human Tissue Act 2004 was enacted to regulate most of the questions relating to removal, retention and uses of human body parts and tissue, including transplantation, in England, Wales and Northern Ireland. Scotland enacted its own statute, the Human Tissue (Scotland) Act 2006. In 2013, the Welsh Assembly passed the Human Transplantation (Wales) Act. The major change implemented by the Welsh Act was the introduction of deemed consent for cadaver transplantation. Where Wales led, England and Scotland followed suit, making provision for deemed consent in the Organ Transplantation (Deemed Consent) Act 2019 and Human Tissue (Authorisation) (Scotland) Act 2019, respectively. A consultation is under way in Northern Ireland with a view to similar changes. The chapter focuses on the application of the 2004 Act (as amended) in England. The origins of the 2004 Act owed more to the controversy surrounding revelations about the practice of organ retention than the needs of transplant medicine.[1] A fundamental principle embodied in the original Act was that all donations, including cadaver donations, had to be based on 'appropriate consent', and such consent must be explicit.[2] 'Deemed consent' for donations is a radical change in the law.

Certain sorts of tissue transplantation, such as blood donation and skin grafts, have been routine for decades. Despite the number of lives saved, solid organ donation has had a stormy history. Debates involving clinical, ethical, scientific, financial and resource considerations continue to rage.

Scientific developments in transplantation continue to be amazing.[3] The principal problem remains the gap between supply and demand. At the beginning

1 See 21.2 below.
2 For an overview of the Act, see D Price, 'The Human Tissue Act 2004' (2005) 68 *MLR* 798; M Brazier and S Fovargue, 'A Brief Guide to the Human Tissue Act 2004' (2006) 1 *Clinical Ethics* 26.
3 See, for example, 'Covid Patient Receives World's First Living Donor Lung Transplant' *BBC News* (2021) 8 April.

of 2022, nearly 6,000 people were waiting for a transplant.[4] For the last two years the number of suitable donors has dropped due in part to the average age of donors and lifestyle choices.[5] In its 2021 report on transplant activity, NHS Blood and Transplant (NHSBT) considered the year to have been 'the most challenging in our history' as a result of the COVID-19 pandemic. Due to extreme system pressures, some transplant centres temporarily closed. Additionally, the virus was thought to pose risks for donor recipients who would be immunocompromised and donor numbers sharply declined.[6] In 2020/1, 474 patients died on the active waiting list, up 26 per cent on the previous year.[7]

When considering the supply of organs, four factors must be noted.

(1) Living donors play a central role in organ donation.
(2) One single cadaveric donor is often the source of multiple transplants.
(3) Criteria for selecting cadaver donors are becoming less stringent.[8]
(4) Demand for organs steadily increases with ever higher rates of heart, renal and liver disease.

Additionally, the success of transplant medicine increases demand as people restored to health by a transplant will later in life need a second or third transplant. To meet the gap, proponents of 'deemed consent' (also referred to as presumed consent or opt-out) have long argued that doctors should be allowed to remove organs from the dead unless the deceased had registered an objection to organ donation.[9] As we have seen, England, Wales and Scotland have all now legislated to introduce deemed consent.[10]

Several other strategies to increase the supply of organs exist. Many ethicists advocate a 'market' in organs. The potential of 'regenerative medicine': medical devices, artificial organs and engineered tissue with prosthetic devices seeded with growth hormones (called 'scaffolds') offers hope.[11] We get ever closer to the possibility of 'growing' new organs from stem cells and the possibility of xenotransplantation, using genetically modified organs harvested

4 NHS Blood and Transplant (NHSBT), *Statistics About Organ Donation* (2022) January.
5 NHSBT, *Organ Donation and Transplantation 2030: Meeting the Need* (2021).
6 L Gumber and A Gumber, 'COVID-19 and "Lockdown" in Organ Transplantation in the UK' (2020) 185 *Public Health* 55. Note however, remarkable efforts to sustain the service notwithstanding the system pressures. See for example 'Five Receive Organs after Staffordshire University Student Dies' *BBC News* (2021) 29 March.
7 NHSBT, *Organ Donation and Transplantation: Activity in the UK 2020/21* (2021).
8 See A Cronin, 'Making the Margins Mainstream: Strategies to Maximise the Donor Pool' in A-M Farrell, D Price and M Quigley (eds), *Organ Shortage: Ethics, Law and Pragmatism* (2011) Oxford University Press, p 104.
9 *The Potential Impact of an Opt Out System for Organ Donation in the UK: An Independent Report from the Organ Donation Taskforce* (2008).
10 The Organ Donation (Deemed Consent) Act 2019 came into effect May 2020; The Human Tissue (Authorisation) (Scotland) Act 2019 came into effect March 2021.
11 But see discussion of research misconduct relating to experimental regenerative medicine at 18.16 above.

from non-human animals, looks more likely to materialise than some years ago.[12] But at present there remains a pressing need for organs donated by human donors. The focus is on developing better systems of identifying and recruiting potential organ donors and improving ways of maintaining the quality of organs removed from deceased donors.[13] Transplantation technology advances at a pace. Whereas prior to 2015 all heart donors came from people who were brain-stem-dead but whose hearts were beating, it is now sometimes possible to retrieve a heart after it has stopped beating. And whereas, previously, livers for transplant were placed in static cold storage, normothermic perfusion is increasingly used to reduce the risk of damage to the organ.

Before examining the law in detail, three points need to be understood. First, the organ must be suitable for transplant – that means it should be 'healthy enough' and retain a reasonable 'shelf life'.[14] Second, the organ must remain viable – in good condition. Either the transplant must take place a very short time after its removal from the donor, or means must be found to preserve it while it is transported to the potential recipient. Finally, there should be a tissue match between donor and recipient. Improvements in drugs used to prevent rejection of 'alien' organs have made it possible to use a wider range of donors with less emphasis on the perfect tissue match but a live transplant from a close relative is still an optimal choice.

20.2 The Human Tissue Act – an overview

The Human Tissue Act 2004 repealed all previous legislation including the Human Tissue Act 1961 and the Human Organ Transplants Act 1989.[15] The 2004 Act regulates all aspects of human transplantation, whether the organs (or tissue)[16] are removed from the living or the dead. There are few express

12 See EC Rabin, 'In a First, Surgeons Attached a Pig Kidney to a Human, and it Worked' *NY Times* (2021) 21 October. The recipient was brain-dead at the time of the transplant, with no hope of recovery. And then in January 2022 David Bennett was the recipient of the first transplanted heart from a genetically modified pig. He did well for several weeks but then deteriorated and sadly died: 'Man Given Genetically Modified Pig Heart Dies' *BBC News* (2022) 9 March.

13 NHSBT, *Organ Donation and Transplantation 2030: Meeting the Need* (2021).

14 See 'Patients Given Kidneys Rejected "Unfit" by Other Hospitals' *BBC News* (2014) 18 November. And see Advisory Committee on the Safety of Blood, Tissues and Organs, *Transplantation of Organs from Deceased Donors with Cancer or a History of Cancer* (2014, revised 2020) emphasising the need to balance risks and benefits and ensure informed consent of the recipient.

15 The Act also repeals the Human Tissue Act (Northern Ireland) 1962; the Corneal Tissue Act 1986 and the Anatomy Act 1984.

16 The Act adopts the term 'relevant material' and defines such material in s 53 as '… material other than gametes, which consists of or includes human cells'. Embryos outside the human body, hair and nail clippings are expressly excluded from the Act. This very broad definition covers more than organs, such as kidneys, and tissue, such as bone marrow, but does not mean that every section of the Act applies to every speck of 'human material'; see Price, 'The Human Tissue Act 2004', at 800.

references to transplantation. The Act sets out rules for twelve scheduled purposes involving the use of human organs and tissue. Transplantation is just one of the twelve.[17] For the most part, the broad rules which the Act imposes apply generally to transplantation. Only a few sections of the Act apply exclusively to transplants. The Act offered no more than a framework to regulate transplantation. The details are supplied by regulations made by the Department of Health and Social Care, and Codes of Practice promulgated by the Human Tissue Authority (HTA).[18]

The HTA is central to the Act,[19] established to regulate all matters concerning the removal, storage, use and disposal of human tissue (except for gametes and embryos).[20] The HTA must have a majority of lay members. Its remit in the context of this chapter is principally to regulate transplantation. Another authority, the NHSBT, is charged with operational matters relating to transplantation, and it is required to encourage donation and ensure the quality of the transplant service. The HTA has, however, also played a role in working to increase the number of organs made available for transplant; for example in 2006 it promulgated a policy designed to increase the numbers of living donors by allowing new kinds of altruistic donation.[21]

20.3 Live donor transplantation

For one person to subject themselves to an unnecessary procedure for the benefit of another requires courage and altruism. A distinction must be made between donation of regenerative and non-regenerative organs. The blood donor undergoes temporary discomfort. Their body replaces the blood they have lost. Blood and bone marrow are regenerative tissue. Some non-regenerative organs, such as the heart, are impossible for a living donor to donate in normal circumstances. However, domino transplants are possible, involving organ 'swaps'. A cystic fibrosis patient needs a lung transplant. The success rate is higher and the operation easier if a heart and lung transplant is performed. The recipient may receive a heart and lungs from a cadaver donor and opt to donate her own healthy heart to another patient.[22]

The most common non-regenerative organ donated by a living person remains the kidney. There were 1,836 living kidney donors in 2020/21.[23] Techniques

17 See Sch 1, Pt 1(7).
18 See 21.8 below.
19 See ss 13–15 and Sch 2. Note that although different legislation applies in Scotland and has done in Wales from December 2015, the HTA performs various roles in Scotland and Wales.
20 Already regulated by the Human Fertilisation and Embryology Authority; see 14.2 above.
21 HTA, *Press Release* (2006) April 26.
22 As a domino transplant involves treatment of both patients, such procedures are not as such regulated by the HTA: see HTA, *Code F (part one): Living Organ Donation* (2020), para 34.
23 See NHSBT, *Organ Donation and Transplantation: Activity in the UK 2020/21* (2021).

allowing transplants of lobes of the lung and segments of liver have increased the utility of live donations, but at a cost. According to NHSBT, the risk of death in a live kidney donation is about 1:3,000 but rises to 1:200 for living right lobe liver donations. In 2020/21 there were twenty-two living liver donations.[24] The donor agrees to major surgery and accepts a significant risk to their own health.

The law should be designed to ensure that living donation is informed, truly voluntary, and not the result of coercion. It has been argued that no part of a person's body should be treated as a commodity subject to the pressures of the market.[25] Section 32 of the Human Tissue Act 2004 continues the prohibition on sale of organs (or other bodily material) for transplantation, a ban initially imposed by the Human Organs Transplant Act 1989.[26] Markets remain illegal in the United Kingdom. Whether this should be so, we discuss later.

20.4 Adult donors

In the early days of transplantation, doubts were cast about whether it was lawful for a person to agree to donate a solid organ, such as a kidney, to another during his lifetime. As we have seen, inflicting actual bodily harm on another person can constitute a crime regardless of consent.[27] By 1995, the Law Commission[28] could say with confidence that 'once a valid consent has been forthcoming, English law now treats as lawful donation of regenerative tissue and also non-regenerative tissue not essential to life'.[29] The Human Tissue Act 2004 provided a statutory basis for live donation of organs and tissue for transplantation.

Sections 1 and 3 of the Act provide in effect that it is lawful to remove *relevant* material[30] including organs from a living adult for transplant with, but only with, his *appropriate* consent. The law empowers a person to choose to give a kidney, or a lobe of lung, or segment of liver, to another in need of a transplant. But what is an appropriate consent?[31] Living donors are often closely related to the potential recipient. The potential donor may be the best match as a person whose compatibility is such that a relative's life can

24 Ibid.

25 See RM Titmuss, *The Gift Relationship: From Human Blood to Social Policy* (1971) Allen & Unwin.

26 This Act was a hasty response to a scandal involving the sale of human kidneys by four impoverished Turkish citizens in circumstances where it seemed highly likely that the 'vendors' were cruelly exploited.

27 See *R v Brown* [1994] 1 AC 212, HL, discussed at 10.9 above.

28 Law Commission, *Consent in the Criminal Law* (1995) Consultation Paper No 139, para 8.32.

29 For ethical analysis see G den Hartough, 'Is Consent of the Donor Enough to Justify the Removal of Living Organs? (2013) 22(1) *Cambridge Quarterly of Healthcare Ethics* 45.

30 Defined in s 53 as '...material other than gametes, which consists of or includes human cells'.

31 See further 21.8 below.

be saved.[32] In such circumstances, the psychological pressure can be enormous. It becomes crucially important to establish that the donor did give a genuinely free and informed consent. The Act itself does not define what *appropriate* means. That task is left to the HTA, which has set out guidance on consent in two key Codes of Practice.[33] The potential donor must be given information about what will be done to them and the risks involved. They must be given reliable information about the chances of success. They must be warned about some of the risks of tissue typing. Tests might reveal that apparent siblings are not full siblings. Donors should be offered counselling, given time to make a decision and reassured that they are free to withdraw consent at any time up to the operation.

Nor is the donor's consent alone sufficient to make a live organ donation lawful. Section 33 of the 2004 Act gives the HTA powers to oversee all live donations, including those between family members. The HTA must be satisfied that no money has changed hands and that other conditions prescribed by Regulations are met.[34] All potential donations, whether by a stranger, a friend or a sister, will be scrutinised. Is this right? The need to ensure a tissue match between donors and recipients means doctors will normally prefer a living donor closely related to the potential recipient. Close genetic relationships maximise the chances of a successful transplant. It might be argued that if we (as adults) choose to give a kidney, or a segment of liver, to a dying sibling, this is nobody else's business. Within the family, emotional pressure may be as potent a threat to our free will as poverty could be were sales of organs allowed.

The regulations made under section 33 of the 2004 Act need to be read together with the HTA *Code F (part one)* for living donation of solid organs, or *Code G for donation of Allogenic Bone Marrow and Peripheral Blood Stem Cells*. We focus first on adults with capacity and consider children and incapacitated adults below. Clinicians responsible for a potential live donor of a solid organ, or part of an organ, must refer the case to the HTA. The HTA must satisfy itself that the organ or bone marrow is not being sold. All live donations must be scrutinised to ensure a genuinely free consent has been given by the donor. The HTA appoints Accredited Assessors (AAs) who interview potential donors and recipients, satisfy themselves that the conditions set out by the HTA are fully met, and report to the HTA, which makes the final decision. The AAs will be specially trained and senior health professionals. The Regulations and the Code of Practice distinguish between different kinds of live donation.[35] In the first two categories, both donor and recipient will be interviewed by the AA and then be assessed by an HTA living donation assessment team:

32 In one American case a court, not surprisingly, refused to *order* the only possible donor to submit to a bone marrow transplant; *McFall v Shimp* (1978) 10 Pa D & C 3d.

33 See HTA, *Code A: Guiding Principles and the Fundamental Principle of Consent* and *Code F part one: Living Organ Donation* (2020, updated 2021).

34 See The Human Tissue Act 2004 (Persons Who Lack Capacity to Consent and Transplants) Regulations 2006, SI 2006/1659, discussed at 20.5 and 20.6 below.

35 *Code F part one* (2020), para 28.

(1) 'Directed donation' where a donor names a specific recipient with whom they have a genetic or pre-existing emotional relationship.
(2) 'Directed altruistic donation' where the donor specifies a recipient but has no pre-existing relationship with them. For example the two may have been 'introduced' via a social network site.

The next two categories require additional safeguards.[36] In addition to AA interviews, each case must be considered by a panel of at least three members of the HTA:

(3) 'Non-directed altruistic donation' where a healthy person donates an organ to a person in every sense unknown to them, with no conditions, and no expectation of any exchange benefiting those close to them. A recipient interview with the AA cannot take place here because there is no identified recipient when the interview takes place.
(4) 'Paired/pooled organ donation' where a healthy person cannot donate to their chosen recipient because the pair are incompatible. They can be matched with another donor and recipient in the same situation and the donor organs swapped. The donation is 'paired' where two pairs are involved. Assume your partner needs a kidney transplant but you are not a suitable tissue match. If you agree to donate your kidney to B, a relative of B will provide a kidney for your partner. It is 'pooled' if there are more than two pairs. For example, donor A gives a kidney to the son of donor B. Donor B gives a kidney to the husband of donor C. Donor C's kidney is given to the wife of donor A. 'Exchange' donations increase the likelihood of live donations. Should a brother be dying of renal failure and none of his relatives are a tissue match, his family could volunteer to give an organ to someone else for whom one of them is a match. And then, in exchange, directly or indirectly, a relative of the recipient will donate an organ to the brother.

For lower-risk donation of allogenic bone marrow and peripheral blood stem cells (PBSCs), there is no need for HTA approval, provided the adult has capacity.[37] The clinician must still secure the donor's valid and informed consent.

20.5 Child donors

More difficult questions arise where organs or tissue are to be taken from children. Should children ever be used as organ donors?[38] Until the Human Tissue Act 2004, this was a 'grey' area of law but it became routine practice for

[36] SI 2006/1659, reg 12(4).
[37] Ibid, reg 10(3); HTA *Code G* (2017), para 11.
[38] See D Price and A Garwood-Gowers, 'Transplantation from Minors: Are Children Other People's Medicine?' (1995) 1 *Contemporary Issues in Law* 1. And see 19.4 above on organ donation in anencephalic infants.

parents to authorise bone marrow donations (and skin grafts) from a healthy child to a sick sibling. Solid organ donations from one living child to another appear to have been ruled out by the transplant community itself.

The Human Tissue Act 2004 clarifies the law. As is the case in relation to adults, a distinction is drawn between using a child (defined in the Act as a person under the age of 18) as a living donor of a solid organ or part organ[39] and using a child as a living donor of bone marrow or PBSCs,[40] which carries less risk. In relation to the former, the HTA states that 'Children can be considered as living organ donors only in extremely rare circumstances'.[41] Three hurdles must be overcome before donation of a solid organ or part organ can be countenanced:

(1) There must be a valid and informed consent. For younger children, donation will require appropriate consent from a person with parental responsibility for the child.[42] That means in most cases consent from the child's parents. It will not be strictly necessary for both parents to consent, even when they share parental responsibility for the child,[43] but we submit that the nature of the procedure is such that a court would be likely to wish to ensure that both parents agreed to the donation. What of older children? Prior to the 2004 Act it was doubtful whether any minor was legally competent to consent to organ donation.[44] Section 2(2) now empowers the *competent* minor to donate organs and tissue.[45]
(2) The approval of a court must be obtained.
(3) Regulations made under the Act require that any proposal to use a child[46] as a solid organ donor must be referred to the HTA for advice, and considered by a panel of three members of the Authority.[47]

For bone marrow or PBSC donation, the Human Tissue Act 2004 (Persons who Lack Capacity to Consent and Transplants) Regulations 2006 provide an exception to the requirement for HTA approval when a competent child provides a valid consent.[48] The HTA must assess all cases where the child lacks competence. It must be satisfied that appropriate (usually parental) consent is in place and no reward has been given. In such cases, court approval is not required, though the HTA advises that it be considered in cases of dispute or

39 See HTA *Code F part one*, paras 44–46.
40 See HTA, *Code G* (2017), pp 11–13.
41 HTA, *Code F part one*, para 44.
42 See Human Tissue Act 2004, s 2(3).
43 HTA *Code A* (2020), para 90.
44 See *Re W (A Minor) (Medical Treatment)* [1992] 4 All ER 627, at 635 and 647.
45 HTA, *Code A*, para 88.
46 SI 2006/1659, reg 12(2)(a).
47 See HTA, *Code F part one*, para 46.
48 SI 2006/1659, reg 10(3). Accordingly, if a competent child consents, then their bone marrow or stem cells are not classified as 'transplantable material' for the purposes of s 33. HTA *Code G*, paras 41–48 advises that in assessing the competence of children, *Gillick* competence applies to those under 16 and the Mental Capacity Act 2005 presumption of capacity applies to those aged 16–17.

doubt as to best interests.[49] Conversely, as we discuss in the next section, if an adult donor lacks mental capacity, the approval of the Court of Protection is required. When *A NHS Trust v MC*,[50] which involved a young adult, came before the Court of Protection Cohen J ended his judgment with a cautionary note relating to children. He had been informed that around sixty-five cases a year involving minors are approved by the HTA. Cohen J warned that a 'vacuum' exists in relation to the protection of bone marrow and stem cell donors under the age of 18. Not only is the principal duty of care owed by the Trust to their patient, the recipient of the donation, rather than the donor, but the HTA focuses predominantly on consent and inducements: 'Nowhere is there at the centre of what is being considered either by the treating Trust or the Human Tissue Authority, the best interests of the donor.'[51] Cohen J advised that the HTA pays close attention to the best interests of potential donors under the age of 18 when they are not competent to consent for themselves.

20.6 Mentally incapacitated 'donors'

Before the Human Tissue Act 2004 came into force, Connell J granted a declaration in *Re Y*[52] that bone marrow donation from a severely learning-disabled woman of 25 to her 36-year-old sister, who was dying of leukaemia, was lawful. Of the elder sister's relatives, only her learning-disabled sister proved to be a compatible donor. She was, it was agreed, incapable of giving consent to the procedure. The relationship between the sisters was not especially close. The older sister's illness had meant that visits had become fewer. The relationship between the younger sister and her mother was close, as was the relationship between mother and her older, sick daughter. The judge found that if the older daughter died, her death would have an adverse impact on the mother. She would be less able to visit Y and much occupied in caring for her grandchild if the child's mother died. If the transplant went ahead the 'positive relationship' between Y and her mother would be enhanced, as would the relationship between the sisters. The risk and discomfort to Y would be minimal. Accordingly it was in Y's best interests to allow the bone marrow transplant to go ahead. Connell J made it clear that he was not setting a precedent for kidney 'donation' by a learning-disabled person. Should he have sanctioned a transplant which amounts to enforced donation? The 'benefit' to Y seems somewhat remote on the facts of the case.

49 *HTA Code G*, para 48.

50 [2020] EWCOP 33.

51 Ibid, [21].

52 *Re Y (Mental Incapacity: Bone Marrow Transplant)* [1997] Fam 110. And see influential USA cases *Strunk v Strunk* (1969) 35 ALR (3d) 683 where a Kentucky court gave permission for a kidney donation from the mentally incapacitated brother of a man dying of kidney disease; *Re Peslinski* 226 NW 2d 180 (1975) at 181 (Wisconsin); *Re Richardson* (1973) 284 So 2d 185.

The 2006 regulations[53] made under section 6 of the Human Tissue Act 2004 provide that organs or tissue can be removed from a person lacking mental capacity for transplant if, but only if, such a procedure is in that patient's best interests. Any such proposal must first receive approval from the Court of Protection[54] and must then be referred to an HTA panel.

The first case to come before the Court of Protection was *A NHS Trust v MC*.[55] Cohen J held that it was 'overwhelmingly' in 18-year-old MC's best interests for her blood stem cells to be harvested to treat her mother, who had chronic leukaemia. Without the procedure the mother was unlikely to live more than a year. MC, who lived at home with her parents and siblings and lacked capacity to make the decision, was the only suitable match in the family. Cohen J recognised that there was some risk and no *direct* benefit to MC in undergoing the procedure. But he considered that the *indirect* social, emotional and psychological benefits of her mother's life being extended were considerable.[56] This included benefits she might perceive from being 'seen by others positively by acting altruistically'.[57] Would the assessment differ if the risks to the donor were greater? It is difficult to see how the discomfort and surgery needed to remove a solid organ could be justified by a supposed emotional benefit. And if the proposed donor cannot comprehend what is done to her, the balancing exercise becomes somewhat mythical.

20.7 Cadaver transplantation

The need for more cadaver donors remains acute. At common law, a person had no legal power to donate organs from his body after his death; equally nobody has any right to interfere with a corpse, and any such interference would be a criminal act.[58] It was feared that cadaver transplantation might be illegal. Legislation was needed. In 1952, the Corneal Grafting Act, later amended by the Corneal Tissue Act 1986, authorised the removal and use of eyes for therapeutic purposes in some circumstances. This statute attracted

53 See SI 2006/1659 and see HTA, *Code F part one*, paras 47–51.

54 HTA, *Code F part one*, para 55 and see the Mental Capacity Act Code of Practice (updated 2014), para 8.18 and interim practice guidance pending revision of the Code at [2020] EWCOP 2, [11].

55 [2020] EWCOP 33. We discount a previous case, *Re SW* [2017] EWCOP 7, [37] of which Sir James Munby said 'this scarcely coherent application is totally without merit, it is misconceived and it is vexatious. It would be contrary to every principle of how litigation ought to be conducted in the Court of Protection, and every principle of proper case management, to allow this hopelessly defective application to proceed'.

56 Ibid, [15]. And see B Venter, '*A NHS Foundation Trust v MC* [2020] EWCOP 33: Revisiting Best Interests and "Altruistic" Incapacitous Stem Cell Donation' (2021) 29(2) *Med Law Rev* 337.

57 Ibid, [17].

58 In *R v Lennox-Wright* [1973] Crim LR 529. An unqualified person removed eyes from a cadaver for further use in another hospital. He was successfully prosecuted for contravening Human Tissue Act 1961, s 1(4) which prohibited removal save 'by a fully registered medical practitioner'.

little publicity, nor was there much more public interest when the Human Tissue Act 1961 widened the law to cover any other parts of the body. Although the 1961 Act served as a model for similar legislation in many other countries, it was unsatisfactory in almost every respect.

20.8 Deemed consent[59]

The Human Tissue Act 2004 required appropriate *explicit* consent for cadaver donations as it did for living donations. The case for consent to be presumed if an adult died without registering an objection to the removal of their organs for transplant was largely unheard in the thick of controversy generated by revelations about non-consensual organ retention. More recently, a media campaign[60] and support for a Private Member's Bill indicated a more favourable public attitude towards a change in the law, hence the legislation introducing deemed consent in Wales (2013) England (2019) and Scotland (2019).[61]

'Deemed consent', sometimes styled 'presumed consent' or 'opt-out', means in effect that the law should allow organs to be removed for transplant unless the deceased has expressly put on record that either they object to or put conditions on such use. 'Deemed/presumed consent' is much more complex than first appears and what we say here is merely introductory. A distinction must be made between 'soft' opt-out, which allows for the consultation of relatives and if they object their objections are normally respected, and 'hard' opt-out, whereby doctors may remove organs unless the deceased's name is entered on a register of objectors. Very few countries have legislated to implement 'hard' opt-out.[62]

Wales was the first jurisdiction in the UK to introduce a system of deemed consent / presumed consent. England followed suit with the Organ Donation (Deemed Consent) Act 2019, amending the 2004 Act. The 2004 Act requires *appropriate* consent for transplantation where the person has died. As we discuss in the next section, appropriate consent can be based on the deceased's own prior decision, or, if not, the decision of a proxy nominated by them

59 See M Brazier and A Mullock, 'Body Parts and Baleful Stars?' In E Dove and N Shuibhne (eds), *Law and Legacy in Medical Jurisprudence: Essays in Honour of Graeme Laurie* (2022) Cambridge University Press, pp 209–231.

60 The Organ Donation (Deemed Consent) Act 2019 is otherwise referred to as 'Max and Keira's Law' after Keira (aged 9), who was killed in a road traffic collision in 2017 and whose organs helped four people (including 9-year-old Max), which sparked a media campaign to change the law.

61 The implementation of the Human Tissue (Authorisation) (Scotland) Act 2019 was delayed by COVID-19. For a detailed comparison of the Scottish and English models, see JA Parsons, 'Deemed Consent for Organ Donation: A Comparison of the English and Scottish Approaches' (2021) 8(1) *Journal of Law and the Biosciences*, DOI: 10.1093/jlb/lsab003. Parsons points to differences in the requirements to consult close relatives and different approaches to raising public awareness.

62 Austria and Singapore have a system of 'hard' presumed consent: See E Jackson, *Medical Law: Text, Cases and Materials* (5th edn, 2019) Oxford University Press, p 652. The positive effects on the transplant waiting lists have been dramatic.

(a 'nominated representative'), or, if not, the decision of a person in a qualifying relationship. A new section 3(6)(ba) provides that appropriate consent can also be *deemed* in certain circumstances. It will only apply if the deceased or nominated representative have not made a decision to consent or to opt out, though where a nominated representative exists and cannot be reached or cannot decide, then consent can potentially be deemed.[63]

Deemed consent is restricted to certain organs and tissue,[64] and it will not apply to 'excepted adults' who either lacked capacity to understand the notion of deemed consent for a significant time before their death, or had not been resident in England for at least a year immediately before their death.[65] The HTA interprets the deemed consent provisions as a 'soft' opt-out model[66] and as such requires that reasonable steps are taken to contact family members to give them an opportunity to provide information that would lead a reasonable person to conclude that the potential donor would not have consented.[67] It is clear that 'when there is no family found or available, donation should not proceed',[68] but an objection from a family member is not necessarily determinative unless it would 'lead a reasonable person to conclude that the person did not want to be a donor'.[69]

A year after the deemed consent model was introduced, NHSBT reported that 296 people in England had donated their organs by deemed consent. This amounted to 29 per cent of the donations taking place that year.[70] As we have seen, 474 patients died on the active waiting list in 2020/1. Deemed consent is a positive step forwards but the donor shortage remains severe. Nor must we forget that other routes to posthumous removal, storage and use of organs and tissue for transplantation set out in the 2004 Act remain valid and relevant. In 2020/21 NHSBT recorded 2 million opt-out registrants, whereas 26.7 million had opted in to the NHS Organ Donation Register.[71] We turn now to the alternative mechanisms for establishing appropriate consent.

63 HTA, *Code F part two* (2020), para 86.
64 See Human Tissue (Permitted Material: Exceptions) (England) Regulations 2020, SI 2020/521. Relevant material that is not 'permitted material' includes (*inter alia*) the brain, face, spinal cord, hand, embryo (inside the body), testicle, uterus, penis and vagina. The result is that certain organs, such as reproductive organs, cannot be transplanted without express consent. Brazier and Mullock, 'Body Parts and Baleful Stars?', p 225 question whether and how the 'eclectic' list will change as the pool of body parts utilised in transplant medicine expands.
65 See Human Tissue Act 2004, s 3(9) and HTA, *Code F part two* paras 34, 69 and 185–188.
66 On the human rights implications of a soft opt-out see E Dove *et al*, '*Elberte v Latvia*: Whose Tissue is it Anyway – Relational Autonomy or the Autonomy of Relations' (2015) 15 *Medical Law International* 77.
67 HTA, *Code F part two*, paras 87, 189–198.
68 Ibid, para 191 and see para 91.
69 HTA, *Code F part two*, para 87.
70 NHSBT, 'Family and Public Support Helping Save Lives One Year on from the Introduction of Max and Keira's Law' (2021) 20 May.
71 NHSBT, *Organ Donation and Transplantation: Activity in the UK 2020/21* (2021).

20.9 The Human Tissue Act 2004

A deceased person over the age of 18's organs and tissue can be removed for transplantation under section 3(6) if either:

(a) the deceased himself gave appropriate consent before he died, for example by registering on the organ donor register or by ticking the relevant box when applying for a driving licence; *or*

(b) if he gave no consent, but nor did he veto organ donation, consent is given by the deceased's nominated representative – that is a person expressly nominated by the deceased to make decisions about the use of his body parts before his death; *or*

(ba) if neither (a) nor (b) apply, his consent is deemed, subject to the conditions we have set out in 20.8 above; *or*

(c) if the above do not apply, consent is given by a close family member or friend – what is described as 'a person who stood in a qualifying relationship with the deceased before his death'.

Where donation is a possibility, the first job for staff at the hospital where the potential donor dies is to check the register. When evidence of the deceased's wishes is available, their wishes are not subject to deemed consent and should not be subject to any family veto.[72] The objections of a grieving widow do not in law override her husband's ante-mortem consent. Implementing such a policy in practice is harder. The HTA urges doctors to discuss this dilemma sensitively with the family. They should be encouraged to accept the deceased's wishes.[73]

The second means of authorising organ donation is by way of a nominated representative. The Act states that a nomination may be made orally or in writing.[74] It may be asked why one should delegate such a task to someone else. If a person has given the thought to donation required to make a nomination, you might expect them to express their own wishes directly. One reason for nominating a proxy may be a case where the potential donor is aware of divisions in their family about organ donation. The family might belong to a faith where more orthodox adherents rule out organ donation.

In the absence of express authorisation by the deceased, or the consent of a proxy chosen by them, then deemed consent can be considered as we explored above. If consent cannot be deemed, then the power to donate organs falls to the family. The Act sets out a hierarchy of relatives (or exceptionally, a friend).[75] Staff seeking consent should first approach the deceased's spouse or partner.[76] If he or she declines to make a decision, or the deceased had no

72 HTA, *Code F part two*, paras 82, 89.

73 HTA, *Code F part two*, para 88.

74 Section 4. An oral appointment must be made in the presence of two witnesses; a written appointment must be signed and witnessed or contained in a will. HTA, *Code F part two*, paras 125–126.

75 Section 27(4).

76 '[A] person is another's partner if the two of them (whether of different sexes or the same sex) live as partners in an enduring family relationship.' Section 54(8).

spouse or partner, those seeking consent then work their way through the following list:[77] (1) parent or child; (2) siblings; (3) grandparent or grandchild; (4) nephews or nieces; (5) stepparents; (6) half siblings; (7) friend of longstanding. In what will often be the case, where more than one individual falls into any of these categories, the consent of one person alone will suffice to make removal of organs for transplant lawful.[78] If there is no one standing in a qualifying relationship to the deceased, organs cannot be taken for donation.[79]

Section 2 of the 2004 Act addresses cadaver donations from minors. As we noted above, deemed consent is restricted to adults over the age of 18. The Act provides that where a person under 18 has given advance consent to organ donation at a point in her life when she was sufficiently mature and intelligent to make such a decision for herself, her consent authorises cadaver transplantation. The *Gillick* competent minor can determine what happens to her body after her death too. In theory, her parents have no say in the matter. Establishing *Gillick* competence retrospectively will be hard. Overriding grieving parents will be painful. Where a child has expressed no wishes of their own, the decision falls to a person with parental responsibility[80] immediately prior to their death. This will normally be their parents. Again, in theory, the consent of one parent alone will be enough.

20.10 Violating the Human Tissue Act 2004

One of the principal criticisms of the Human Tissue Act 1961 was that no provision was made for a criminal penalty or civil redress for breach of the Act.[81] The 2004 Act[82] imposes criminal sanctions for any failure to comply with the Act's rules requiring consent for removal of organs for transplant. Any removal of cadaver organs without appropriate consent is a criminal offence unless the person removing the organs reasonably believes that he acts on the basis of such an appropriate consent. Any false representation that such a consent has been obtained is equally a criminal offence. Both offences carry the possibility of a gaol sentence of up to three years. Any prosecution requires the consent of the Director of Public Prosecutions.

20.11 The coroner

The kinds of death likely to yield organs for transplant may often be the kinds of death likely to involve referral to the coroner, for example a fit, healthy

77 See s 27(8).
78 See s 27(6).
79 *CM v The Executor of the Estate of EJ (deceased)* [2013] EWHC 1680 (Fam). See 21.6 below.
80 Or if there is no such person, if, for example, parents and child died together in a road traffic collision, consent must be sought from the nearest qualifying relative, usually a grandparent.
81 See PDG Skegg, 'Liability for the Unauthorised Removal of Cadavers Transplantation Material' (1974) 14 *Medicine, Science and the Law* 153.
82 See s 5.

adult suffers massive brain injuries in a road traffic collision. Where there is reason to believe that an inquest may have to be held on a body, or a post-mortem examination may be required by the coroner, it will also be necessary to obtain the consent of the coroner to the removal of any part of the body and so risks delaying the opportunity to remove organs. The government has issued guidance to coroners, stressing that it was not part of a coroner's function to place obstacles in the way of the development of medical science or to take moral or ethical decisions in this matter, and that the coroners should assist rather than hinder the procedure for organ removal. A coroner should refuse his consent only where there might be later criminal proceedings in which the organ might be required as evidence, or if the organ itself might be the cause or partial cause of death, or where its removal might impede further inquiries.[83] The HTA advises doctors and donor co-ordinators how to proceed in case of potential organ donation that may properly involve the coroner.[84]

20.12 'Donation after Brain Death' and 'Donation after Circulatory Death'

Whatever the legal rules governing consent to donation, account must be taken of the practical need for the shortest possible period between removal of an organ and its transplantation into the intended recipient. A successful transplant requires that the organ to be transplanted remains viable – so it has not, to put it brutally, begun to decay in the time between removal from the dead donor and implantation in the recipient. A distinction must be made between 'Donations after Brain Death' (DBD), previously called 'beating heart donors', and 'Donations after Circulatory Death' (DCD), previously called 'non-beating heart donors'. When a DBD heart donor is used, the donor will usually have been placed on a ventilator in the hope that treatment could be instituted to prolong their life. Once they are diagnosed as brain-stem-dead, but with the heart still beating, arrangements may be made for organ donation. Oxygen will have continued to perfuse the organs up to the time that the organ is removed. In contrast, organs removed from a donor after circulatory death need to be rushed to the recipients as lack of oxygenation will swiftly trigger the start of decay. In 2020–21 deceased donors comprised 766 DBD and 414 DCD.[85]

A possible measure to increase the number of viable organs available for transplant, elective ventilation, was mooted in the 1990s and implemented at a hospital in Exeter.[86] Elective ventilation would involve patients dying from strokes or similar cerebral injury being transferred from a medical ward to the

[83] HC (65) 1977. And more recently, see Chief Coroner, *Organ Donation: Guidance No 26* (2017).

[84] HTA, *Code B* and *Code F part 2*, para 219.

[85] NHSBT, *Organ Donation and Transplantation: Activity in the UK 2020/21* (2021). This represented a 25 per cent fall in numbers of deceased donors on the previous year.

[86] TG Feest *et al*, 'Protocol for Increasing Organ Donation After Cerebrovascular Deaths in a District General Hospital' (1990) 335 *Lancet* 1133.

intensive care unit and then ventilated until brain stem death occurs. Organs are maintained in optimum condition for organ retrieval. Ventilation would be performed *solely* to enable the patient to become a potential organ donor and confer no benefit on them. The practice was abandoned well before the enactment of the Human Tissue Act 2004 on the grounds that the ventilation of the dying patient was unlawful, an assault on the dying person. At the time a decision is made to transfer the patient to intensive care he is unlikely to be able to consent to such a procedure himself. And so it is argued that the transfer to benefit the potential organ recipient is unlikely to be judged to be in his interests[87] and might fall foul of section 4 of the Mental Capacity Act 2005.[88]

There is nothing in the Human Tissue Act 2004 expressly authorising or prohibiting elective ventilation. Should elective ventilation be lawful?[89] The Law Commission's original report on the treatment of adults lacking mental capacity suggested that, with proper safeguards, such a procedure could be ethical and lawful. The Mental Capacity Act 2005 did not expressly implement this proposal. Could one argue nonetheless that if a person expressly requested elective ventilation to bolster their wish to be an organ donor, then that procedure does, paradoxically, become something done in his best interests?[90]

Other strategies to improve the rate of organ donation in the UK focus on DCD.[91] The donors' hearts would have stopped and death diagnosed by the traditional cardio-respiratory criteria. The statement by the Chief Rabbi for England in January 2011 that Jewish law only recognised a definition of death based on traditional cardio-respiratory criteria is reminder that brain death is still not universally accepted.[92]

The problem arsing where a donor is a DCD donor is that organs removed after circulatory death will start to decay due to a lack of oxygenation. Section 43 of the 2004 Act allows hospitals, or other relevant authorities, to take whatever steps are immediately necessary to preserve parts of the body for transplantation. What is done must be the minimal and least invasive steps possible. Machine perfusion of the organ will extend the time in which organs remain viable. Such a procedure needs to be done as soon as the heart stops beating, at a time when it cannot necessarily be ascertained if the deceased had consented to donation and relatives may not be at the scene. The HTA advises, however, that machine perfusion of the organs 'cannot be considered

87 See JV McHale, 'Elective Ventilation – Pragmatic Solution or Ethical Minefield?' (1995) 11 *Professional Negligence* 23.

88 See 7.10 above.

89 See J Coggon, 'Elective Ventilation for Organ Donation: Law, Policy and Public Ethics' (2013) 39 *J Med Ethics* 130.

90 D Price, 'End of Life Treatment of Potential Organ Donors: Paradigm Shifts in Intensive and Emergency Care (2011) 19(1) *Med Law Rev* 86.

91 For discussion of the ethical issues raised, see D Price and J Samanta, 'Supporting Controlled Non-Heart-Beating Donation – An Ethical Justification' (2013) 22(1) *Cambridge Quarterly of Healthcare Ethics* 22.

92 See 19.2 above. And see NHSBT, *Organ Donation and Religious Beliefs* (2012).

to be minimum steps' and so should only be used if there is appropriate consent to donation.[93]

Other steps (short of elective ventilation) could feasibly be taken prior to the patient's death to increase the potential that the dying patient could become an organ donor. Such steps could include delaying for a short time the withdrawal of treatment, and measures such as administering drugs close to the point of death to protect the viability of the organs destined for donation.[94] As with elective ventilation, the steps taken would be in the interests of the potential organ recipient and not in the clinical interests of the dying patient. Thus some doctors argue that doing anything to the patient before his death, however minor, is unethical and unlawful given that patients unable to consent for themselves must be treated in their best interests. But, as we have seen, best interests embrace more than narrow clinical considerations and, for the many dying patients who wish to be organ donors, interventions to assist in the realisation of that wish once there is no hope of recovery are part and parcel of their best interests.[95]

20.13 Establishing death

In Chapter 19, we noted that DBD donors were not under traditional definitions of death strictly 'dead'. The needs of transplant medicine provided part but not all of the impetus to reformulate that traditional view of death as the irreversible cessation of heartbeat and respiration. The difficulty in persuading the public that 'brain' or 'brain stem' death truly constitutes the death of a person has beset organ transplantation for decades. And, as we have seen, in 2011, both Jewish and Islamic scholars and leaders voiced the judgement that within their religious laws 'brain stem death' could not be accepted, the person was only dead when the heart stopped beating.[96]

20.14 A market in organs

The introduction of deemed consent, married to efforts to improve the systems for identifying potential cadaver donors and to use public education to encourage voluntary altruistic donations, is at the centre of national policy relating to organ donation. Whether that strategy will suffice to make up the shortfall in organs needed for transplant remains to be seen. Those who doubt its efficacy attack the tradition that bodily products should be freely given and not traded.[97] Section 32 of the Human Tissue Act 2004 bans payments for live or cadaver organs, although NHS England allows financial reimbursement of

93 HTA, *Code F part 2*, para 217–218.

94 Fully discussed in Price, 'End of Life Treatment of Potential Organ Donors'.

95 See J Coggon *et al*, 'Best Interests and Potential Organ Donors' (2008) 336 *BMJ* 1346; and see 20.6 above.

96 See 19.2 above.

97 J Radcliffe-Richards *et al*, 'The Case for Allowing Kidney Sales' (1998) 351 *Lancet* 1950.

living donors to ensure the impact on them is cost neutral.[98] The European Convention on Human Rights and Biomedicine states forcefully: 'The human body and its parts shall not, as such, give rise to financial gain.'[99]

And yet organs are frequently shipped across borders.[100] And paid donation abroad is not uncommon.[101] In support of maintaining a prohibition of a market in organs are a cluster of arguments. They centre on four questions.

(1) Would financial incentives to sell your own, or your deceased relative's, organs risk endangering the safety of organ transplants? In their anxiety to obtain payment might people conceal medical conditions which could endanger the recipient?[102]
(2) Is there a risk that financial pressure on potential vendors is such that they would give a less than voluntary and informed consent? There is evidence from the developing world that economic duress operates to pressure the poor into selling organs to the rich.
(3) Is it intrinsically wrong that, even if properly informed, poorer people should 'have' to 'earn' part of their living by selling off body parts?
(4) In sum, do markets degrade?[103]

Those proposing markets do so cautiously. They stress the vulnerability of the person needing the transplant. Their life is at risk. Harris and Erin argue that a regulated market,[104] where the National Health Service is the only permitted 'purchaser', would (1) ensure the quality of organs 'sold' and (2) rigorously monitor the consent process. Provision would be made to ensure that the vendor was adequately informed and acted freely. Fears of exploitation could be met in a regulated market. As to the distastefulness of the poor becoming

98 See HTA, *Code F part two*, para 40 and NHS England, *Clinical Commissioning Policy: Reimbursement of Expenses for Living Donors* (2018).

99 Article 21.

100 See 2012 EU Directive 2012/25/EU to facilitate EU cross-border exchange of information about organs and their donors. Post-EU Exit a licence is required to import or export tissue to or from a country outside the UK. See Human Tissue (Quality and Safety for Human Application) Regulations 2007, SI 2007/1523 as amended by SI 2019/481, SI 2020/1306.

101 On the legal and ethical issues of paid donations abroad (that would be prohibited in the UK under the Human Tissue Act 2004) see J McHale, 'Organ Transplantation, the Criminal Law, and the Health Tourist: A Case for Extraterritorial Jurisdiction?' (2013) 22(1) *Cambridge Quarterly of Healthcare Ethics* 64. For an international perspective see I Cohen, 'Transplant Tourism: The Ethics and Regulation of International Markets for Organs' 41(1) (2013) *Journal of Law, Medicine and Ethics* 269.

102 At the heart of Titmuss's argument in *The Gift Relationship; From Human Blood to Social Policy*.

103 See M Radin, 'Market – Inalienability' (1987) 100 *Harvard Law Review* 1849; N Duxbury, 'Do Markets Degrade?' [1996] 59 *MLR* 331.

104 See C Erin and J Harris, 'An Ethical Market in Human Organs' (2003) 29 *J Med Ethics* 137.

organ banks, it is contended that worldwide the rich have benefits denied the poor. Laurie, Harmon and Dove[105] question whether commercialism and altruism are irreconcilable values. They ask why one poor and needy person is allowed to risk his brain in the boxing ring, when another is barred from selling his kidney. They remind us that illegal markets across the world already exploit the poor. Janet Radcliffe-Richards,[106] leading the advocates for markets, sums up the debate:

> The weakness of the familiar arguments suggests that they are attempts to justify the deep feelings of repugnance which are the real driving force of the prohibition, and feelings of repugnance among the rich and healthy, no matter how strongly felt, cannot justify removing the only hope of the destitute and dying. This is why we conclude that the issue should be considered again, with scrupulous impartiality.

For the most part, advocates for markets focus on living vendors. But why not allow payments for cadaver organs? The risk of harming the donor's health is nil. 'Donors' might see the promise of an organ for payment as an alternative, or a supplement, to life insurance. Relatives auctioning off Grandma's kidneys might be distasteful, unless your child was dying for want of a kidney. Laurie, Harmon and Dove find 'payment for organs of the dead far less easy to justify than payment to a living donor'.[107] But they somewhat reluctantly suggest that this may come to pass. The justification for banning payments needs more careful thought. Exploitation arguments are less compelling and the 'safety' arguments advanced by Titmuss[108] have proved fallible in the context of blood donation.[109]

20.15 Other inducements[110]

In debating the ethics of payments for organs, other forms of inducement to donate need to be considered. Is there an issue about any form of inducement or incentive to donate or is it simply money that is seen as 'evil'? In permitting 'paired' and 'pooled' donations, inducements are sanctioned. The potential 'reward' of a kidney for your husband or child may be a much more powerful inducement than money. What of the promise of priority for registered donors or families who have agreed to donation should they later require an organ? Such a scheme is now embodied in Israeli law. Registered donors of at least three years' standing are granted priority should they themselves need an organ transplant. A similar priority is given to close relatives of registered and

105 GT Laurie, SHE Harmon and ES Dove, *Mason and McCall Smith's Law and Medical Ethics* (11th edn, 2019) Oxford University Press, 18.24–18.29.

106 Radcliffe-Richards *et al*, 'The Case for Allowing Kidney Sales'.

107 *Mason and McCall Smith's Law and Medical Ethics*, 18.53.

108 Titmuss, *The Gift Relationship and Social Policy*.

109 See A-M Farrell, 'Is the Gift Still Good? Examining the Politics and Regulation of Blood Safety in the European Union' (2006) 14 *Med Law Rev* 155.

110 See M Brazier and J Harris, 'Does Ethical Controversy Cost Lives?' in Farrell, Price and Quigley, *Organ Shortage: Ethics, Law and Pragmatism* (2011), pp 15–34.

deceased donors.[111] Then if non-monetary inducements are considered acceptable we return to the issues of cash payments and must consider if a moderate financial 'reward' short of a sale might be considered. In many countries the state will at least meet the funeral expenses of the deceased donor.[112]

20.16 Conditional donations

Conditional donation, whereby families seek to direct to whom a cadaver organ might go or to place some restrictions on who may benefit from a cadaver donation, was initially banned when a family sought to restrict the use of a relative's organs to white recipients only. Such an attempt to restrict donation to persons of one's own racial group, or religious persuasion, appears fairly odious at first sight, and after an investigation the Department of Health ruled out acceptance of conditional donations.[113] But should any form of conditional directed donation be banned? We allow living donors to direct to whom their gift should be donated. Consider this example. A young man dies in a road accident. His twin sister has end-stage renal failure. His parents are prepared to donate all his organs if one of his kidneys is made available to his sister. In 2008, something not dissimilar occurred. A young woman, Laura Ashworth, died suddenly after an acute asthma attack. Before her death she had discussed donating a kidney to her mother but had not taken any formal steps to become a living donor. The family asked that one of her kidneys be given to Laura's mother but that wish was overruled and both kidneys went to strangers. The Department of Health[114] subsequently diluted the ban on conditional donations to allow account to be taken of wishes to donate to a person related to the deceased 'genetically socially or by way of friendship' who is in urgent need of a transplant.

20.17 Xenotransplantation

A once much-vaunted development in the field of organ transplantation involves the use of non-human animals. Non-human animal to human transplant attempts are not new. Early efforts resulted in disastrous rejection episodes. Scientists responded by seeking to develop procedures to modify the genetic make-up of pigs to provide tailor made organs suitable to transplant into humans. The technical progress with xenotransplantation has been slow, but recent innovations have awakened interest.[115] The range of problems

111 See J Lavee, T Asheknazi and D Steinberg, 'A New Law for the Allocation of Donor Organs in Israel' (2010) 375 *Lancet* 1131–1133 and M Quigley, 'Incentivising Organ Donation' in Farrell, Price and Quigley, *Organ Shortage: Ethics, Law and Pragmatism*, pp 89–103.

112 See 'Patients May be Asked about Organ Donation on Hospital Admission' *Guardian* (2012) 12 October, recounting possible incentives such as payment of funeral expenses.

113 See DH, *An Investigation into Conditional Organ Donation* (2000).

114 DH, *Requested Allocation of a Deceased Donor Organ* (2010).

115 DK Cooper and H Hara, '"You Cannot Stay in the Laboratory Forever": Taking Pig Kidney Xenotransplantation from the Laboratory to the Clinic' (2021) 71

associated with it is vast.[116] Is it right to use non-human animals in this way?[117] What about infection risks? How would the first human volunteers be recruited?[118] The UK government initially responded cautiously, setting up an interim regulatory body, the United Kingdom Xenotransplantation Interim Regulation Authority (UKXIRA).[119] For those that are satisfied that breeding animals for transplant is ethical, the major problem becomes the risk to humans. Zoonoses are diseases that cross the species barrier, as it would appear swine flu and coronaviruses have done. Genetically engineered pigs may carry viruses harmless to pigs but lethal to humans. In the light of this risk, it is argued xenograft recipients would have to consent to lifelong monitoring, sterilisation and abstention from unprotected sexual intercourse. How would such draconian rules be policed? Should recipients be allowed to create risks for us all?[120] Yet in 2006 the government announced its decision to abolish UKXIRA, and the Medicines and Healthcare products Regulatory Agency and research ethics committees are now charged with making any necessary decisions about clinical trials of xenografts in humans.[121]

20.18 Liability for mishaps

Questions about potential liability arise if organ transplantation goes awry. In February 2011 a living donor whose life was wrecked when the operation to remove his kidney was botched was awarded £6.75 million pounds in damages. Massive blood loss destroyed his remaining kidney and the donor had himself to receive a kidney from his sister.[122] A failed transplant will not of itself give rise to any legal claim by the recipient. The renal surgeon does not guarantee success any more than any other medical practitioner. But what if, for example, donated blood or kidneys prove to be infected, perhaps with HIV? Might the donor, or the transplant team,[123] be liable in tort? It would seem unchallengeable that donors owe a duty of care to recipients which is breached by a donor knowingly donating organs or tissue when he is aware

Lancet, DOI: 10.1016/j.ebiom.2021.103562. And see 'Man Gets Genetically-Modified Pig Heart in World-First Transplant' *BBC News* (2022) 10 January.

116 See Nuffield Council on Bioethics, *Animal to Human Transplants* (1996); S Fovargue, *Xenotransplantation and Risk: Regulating a Developing Biotechnology* (2011) Cambridge University Press.

117 See W Cartwright, 'The Pig, The Transplant Surgeon and the Nuffield Council' (1996) 4 *Med Law Rev* 250.

118 See S Fovargue, 'Oh Pick Me, Pick Me – Selecting Participants for Xenotransplant Clinical Trials' (2007) 15 *Med Law Rev* 176.

119 See HSC 1998/126.

120 See S Fovargue, 'Consenting to Bio-Risk: Xenotransplantation and the Law' (2005) 25 *Legal Studies* 405.

121 See L Williamson, M Fox and S Mclean, 'The Regulation of Xenotransplantation after UKXIRA: Legal and Ethical Issues' (2007) 34 *Journal of Law and Society* 441.

122 *Times* (2011) 15 February, p 16.

123 See R Day, 'A Dad Missed Out on Potentially Life-Saving Treatment After a Doctor Filled Out a Form Incorrectly, Inquest Heard' *Manchester Evening News* (2019) 14 February: Smith died after a double kidney transplant. The kidneys were infected with Cytomegalovirus and due to a transcription error, he was not given

that he is infected by, say, hepatitis or HIV.[124] The recipient's problem may be tracing the donor. Public policy grounds for protecting the anonymity of donors may be found to outweigh the recipient's individual right of action.[125]

Most claims in respect of contaminated body products will be brought against the hospital supplying those products. The Pearson Commission recommended that strict liability should be imposed on authorities responsible for the supply of human blood and organs. It is now clear that the Consumer Protection Act 1987, imposing strict liability for defective products, includes human tissue in its definition of a product.[126] Group Litigation against the government by Jason Evans and others in 2017 was stayed in light of the Infected Blood Inquiry, which has yet to report.[127] His father died in 1993 having been infected with both HIV and Hepatitis C from contaminated Factor VIII products used to treat haemophilia. He is the lead claimant in group litigation which seeks to determine whether the national blood service and other public bodies owed a duty to take care to prevent personal injury to people receiving blood and blood products in the 1970s, 1980s and early 1990s.

20.19 Fetal tissue and neonatal transplants

The potential for the use of fetal tissue for transplantation initially aroused much ethical debate. Fetal brain cells can be taken from aborted fetuses and transplanted into the brains of patients with Parkinson's disease, and perhaps other neurodegenerative conditions in the hope of improving the recipient's condition. Many doctors see stem cell therapies as a better potential line of treatment.[128] Fetal tissue is governed by the Human Tissue Act and the HTA[129] has issued guidance that makes it clear that fetal tissue is to be treated as the mother's tissue and that, as with any other human tissue, her informed consent is needed for any use of tissue that she elects to donate and she must be told of the proposed purposes to which the tissue will be put.

necessary treatment. At the inquest, apologies were made and the Trust reported that systems and processes had been changed to prevent recurrence.

124 And might be criminally liable for causing grievous bodily harm? See *R v Dica* [2004] 3 All ER 593, CA.

125 A Scottish court so found in relation to a claim against a blood donor; see *AB v Scottish Blood Transfusion Service* [1990] SL 203.

126 See *A v The National Blood Authority* [2001] Lloyd's Med Rep 187 discussed at 12.6 above. And see also 12.9 above discussing vCJD contaminated blood products.

127 *Jason Evans & Others v Secretary of State for Health*, Claim No HQ17C03611; *Contaminated Blood Products Group Litigation* (2017) at www.gov.uk/guidance/group-litigation-orders#contaminated-blood-products-group-litigation; and see 12.8 and 20.14 above.

128 See *Mason and McCall Smith's Law and Medical Ethics*, 18.65.

129 HTA, *Code A*, para 141. Note that the guidance differentiates fetal tissue of less than twenty-four weeks' gestation and stillbirths (after twenty-four weeks) or neonatal deaths, where consent should be handled in accordance with the guidance on use of tissues of the deceased: HTA *Code A*, para 142. And see HTA, *Guidance on the Sensitive Handling of Pregnancy Remains* (2021).

A rather different question arises in relation to anencephalic neonates. Could a baby born without a brain be used as a donor of organs for a baby born with a defective heart, for as we have seen the usual criteria for brain stem death are not applicable to newborn babies?[130] Nonetheless the removal of organs for donation (with parental consent) was endorsed in a report from the medical Royal Colleges in 1998 when 'two doctors, who are not members of the transplant team, agree that spontaneous respiration has ceased'.[131]

20.20 Transplantation: the future?

Developments in transplant medicine create the potential for transplant of an ever greater range of organs and tissue. Face transplants have excited popular attention, but it is doubtful that they pose any new ethical or legal questions.[132] Womb transplants may create more dilemmas. Globally, around seventy women have received womb transplants, resulting in at least twenty-three births.[133] If it is possible to transplant a womb into a woman born without one, then it may also become possible to transplant a womb into a trans woman and unlawful under the Gender Recognition Act 2004 to refuse on grounds that relate to the person's status as a woman. Finally, if a womb can be transplanted into a trans woman, it may become possible to transplant a womb into a man. Male pregnancy, once the stuff of tawdry drama and cheap jokes, may become reality. One legal problem stands in the way of the pregnant man. He would need IVF to create embryos for implantation into his donated womb. At present the Human Fertilisation and Embryology Act only allows licensed clinics to provide treatment services 'for the purposes of assisting *women* to carry children'.[134]

Advances in transplantation, gene therapy, stem cell research and medical devices together bring new potential to replace or repair damaged organs, tissues and cells. The emerging field of 'regenerative medicine'[135] has the potential to match exactly and to create a potentially inexhaustible supply. The ethical and regulatory issues,[136] particularly those surrounding patents, have yet to be resolved, but in an increasingly ageing population regenerative medicine – focusing on repair rather than cure – is set to have an ever-increasing role.

130 See Academy of Medical Royal Colleges, *Code of Practice for the Diagnosis and Confirmation of Death*, Appendix 4.

131 *Report of the Working Party of the Conference of Medical Royal Colleges and their Faculties in the United Kingdom on Organ Transplantation in Neonates* (1988). And see 'Newmarket Baby Becomes UK's Youngest Organ Donor' *BBC News* (2015) 1 December.

132 See RS Hartman, 'Face Values: Challenges of Transplant Technology' (2005) 31 *American Journal of Law and Medicine* 7. Though see 'Face Transplant Patient Meets Donor's Sister' *BBC News* (2015) 29 May.

133 BP Jones *et al*, 'Uterine Transplantation: RCOG Scientific Impact Paper No 65' (2021) 128(10) *British Journal of Obstetrics and Gynaecology* e51.

134 See discussion of *R (McConnell and YY) v Registrar General for England and Wales* [2020] EWCA Civ 559 at 14.13 above.

135 Medical Research Council, *A Strategy for UK Regenerative Medicine* (2012).

136 See S Devaney, *Stem Cell Research and the Collaborative Regulation of Innovation* (2014) Routledge.

Chapter 21

THE HUMAN BODY AND ITS PARTS[1]

21.1 Introduction

We take our bodies for granted most of the time. The purpose of our organs and tissue is to sustain us, the people who live in those bodies. We refer without reflection to 'our' hands, 'our' hearts. Whether that language of ownership is reflected in the law may be doubted, although the decision of the Court of Appeal in *Yearworth v North Bristol NHS Trust*[2] issued in a new era in debates about owning at least some parts of 'ourselves'. What is beyond doubt is that our human body parts have value to others.[3] 'My' kidney may save 'your' life. That kidney could become 'yours' while I remain alive. 'My' heart could also save your 'life', but only when my 'life' has ended. The development of transplantation highlighted the usefulness of human body parts, taken from both the living and the dead. However, doctors and scientists have been learning from the bodies, and body parts, of the dead for centuries. Medicine has developed from the knowledge gathered from the dissection of corpses. Dissection, however good its ends, has a murky history.[4] Bodies were stolen in the seventeenth and eighteenth centuries. The Anatomy Act 1832 conscripted the bodies of the poor to help train medical students in anatomy and provide material for early medical research. In the twentieth century, the public knew little about practices whereby doctors retained organs and tissue for both research and education. Post-mortem examinations were rarely discussed. Only when the controversy surrounding organ retention erupted at the end of that century was public attention drawn to the uses of bodies and their parts. That controversy obscured the fact that donation of tissue for research and education, and donation of bodies to train doctors, has an even greater role in saving lives and preserving health than the better-known practice of organ transplantation.

1 For an analysis of different theoretical and legal approaches see I Goold *et al* (eds), *Persons, Parts and Property: How Should We Regulate Human Tissue in the 21st Century?* (2014), Hart Publishing. And see D Price, *Human Tissue in Transplantation and Research* (2009) Cambridge University Press.

2 [2009] EWCA Civ 37.

3 See M Brazier, 'Human(s) (as) Medicine(s)' in SAM McLean (ed), *Do No Harm* (2006) Ashgate, p 187.

4 See R Richardson, *Death, Dissection and the Destitute* (2nd edn, 2000) University of Chicago Press.

In this chapter, we examine how (outwith the context of transplantation) English law regulates the removal, retention and uses of human body parts and we consider briefly how far (if at all) we own our own bodies. We examine the relevant provisions of the Human Tissue Act 2004 and the role of the Human Tissue Authority (HTA). In addition, we address some aspects of the role of the coroner, a key factor in the regulation of the use of bodies and body parts post-mortem. The Coroners and Justice Act 2009 was enacted to reform both the substantive law on the investigation of deaths in England and Wales and to reform the operation of the coroners' service, a central part of the latter being the creation of the office of Chief Coroner.[5] We noted in the previous chapter that Scotland enacted its own legislation in relation to the removal and uses of human tissue from the dead in the form of the Human Tissue (Scotland) Act 2006 (as amended). It must also be noted that the system for investigation of deaths in Scotland is wholly different to the coronial system applying south of the border.[6] While Wales has enacted separate legislation (the Human Transplantation (Wales) Act 2013)[7] to introduce an opt-out system for cadaver organ transplants, the Human Tissue Act 2004 continues to regulate other matters relating to organ retention and use in Wales and the law relating to the role of the coroner is the same in both England and Wales.

21.2 Removal of body parts from the dead

It was organ retention from the bodies of the dead that resulted in the enactment of the Human Tissue Act 2004. For this reason, we reverse the natural order, and consider first the questions relating to the use of corpses before addressing retention of organs and tissue from the living. In the course of the Inquiry[8] established in 1998 to investigate the paediatric cardiac service at Bristol Royal Infirmary, evidence emerged of a widespread practice of organ and tissue retention. Over a long period of time, organs and tissue had been taken at, or after, post-mortem examinations from children's bodies and used 'for a variety of purposes, including audit, medical education and research, or had simply been stored'. The Bristol Inquiry Team, led by Professor Ian Kennedy, issued an Interim Report in 2000.[9] Subsequently, an Independent Confidential Inquiry under section 2 of the National Health Service Act 1977 was chaired by Michael Redfern QC to investigate the removal and disposal of human organs and tissue following post-mortem examinations at Alder Hey.

5 See the Coroners and Justice Act 2009, s 35 and Sch 8.

6 The provisions of the Fatal Accidents and Sudden Deaths Inquiry (Scotland) Act 1976 apply to fatal accidents occurring in Scotland.

7 See 20.8 above.

8 *Learning from Bristol: The Report of the Public Inquiry into Children's Heart Surgery at the Bristol Royal Infirmary 1984–1995* (2001) Cm 5207 (1).

9 The Inquiry into the Management of Care of Children Receiving Complex Heart Surgery at the Bristol Royal Infirmary Interim Report, *Removal and Retention of Human Material* (2000).

The 2001 Redfern Report[10] proved to be political dynamite. It revealed long-standing practices of removing and retaining children's organs without the consent or even knowledge of their grieving parents. In some cases, infants were literally stripped of all their organs and what was returned to their families was an 'empty shell'. In some instances, the whole of a fetus or still born infant was kept and stored in pots. The Report addressed not only the retention of organs without consent, but also the subsequent mishandling of organ return, and a range of other appalling practices and mismanagement. In this chapter, we focus on the legal issues arising out of organ retention.

Simultaneously with the publication of the Redfern Report, the Chief Medical Officer published a census carried out to ascertain the extent of organ retention since 1970 across the National Health Service (NHS) in England and Wales.[11] What became apparent was that practices whereby pathologists simply took and retained human material after post-mortem examination were routine. The extent to which the deceased's family was involved at all in such decisions varied radically. Adequate and free consent was rarely obtained, or even thought necessary. Nor was this a practice limited to children. Many families were to learn about organs stripped from adult relatives.[12]

The value of taking and retaining organs after post-mortem examination in certain cases should not be doubted. Ascertaining the cause of death is self-evidently important. And often, especially with infants, tests on organs and tissue may have crucial value to the child's family. Investigations which reveal genetic disease may be the key to helping that family have further healthy children. In the wider public interest, medical research is dependent on access to human organs and tissue. Medical education requires such material. But it can only be ethical to do so with the family's consent. For the devout Jew or Muslim, it is a religious imperative to bury the body intact. For other families, the pain of not laying their relative to rest complete is overwhelming. However, for many families involved in the organ retention controversy, what motivated their anger was the loss of control over their relative's burial or cremation. Many relatives said publicly that had they been consulted they would have agreed to doctors retaining the organs of the dead child or other relatives. What they abominated was the lack of respect shown to them and their relative. They felt that someone whom they loved dearly had been treated as a mere convenience, treated with contempt.[13]

10 *The Royal Liverpool Children's Inquiry Report* (2001) HC 12–II.

11 DH, *Report of a Census of Organs and Tissue Retained by Pathology Services in England* (2001).

12 The Retained Organs Commission Regulations 2001, SI 2001/741, set up the NHS Retained Organs Commission to manage the process by which NHS Trusts provided information to families about organ retention, oversee the process of organ return, act as an advocate for families and develop a new regulatory framework for organ and tissue retention. (This was abolished by SI 2005/6.)

13 For diametrically opposed views about the ethics of organ retention, see J Harris, 'Law and Regulation of Retained Organs: The Ethical Issues' (2002) 22 *LS* 527; M Brazier, 'Retained Organs: Ethics and Humanity' (2002) 22 *LS* 550.

21.3 Post-mortem examinations[14]

Death certification feeds into research and planning and provides assurances about the cause of death. It follows one of two routes. In some cases, death may be certificated by a registered medical practitioner. In 2019, influenced by the case of Harold Shipman who murdered patients and limited suspicion by certifying their deaths, a new Medical Examiner system was rolled out to scrutinise certification by medical practitioners. Section 169 of the Health and Care Act 2022 inserted a new section 18A into the Coroners and Justice Act 2009 to put the system on statutory grounds. The second route to death certification is through the coroner. Medical practitioners must report deaths to the coroner in certain circumstances,[15] as must the police, and others can do so if they have concerns. The coroner then decides whether further inquiries are needed, such as an inquiry or a post-mortem examination and subsequently whether an inquest is needed.

Post-mortem examinations in England and Wales can either be compulsory on the orders of the coroner, or voluntary, conducted with the consent of the deceased or his family. This latter form of post-mortem examination, we shall refer to as a hospital autopsy.

Post-mortem examinations must be distinguished from anatomical examinations. Anatomical examinations involve what is more commonly known as dissection. People donate their whole bodies to medical schools to assist in medical education, primarily to educate students in human anatomy and train them in dissection.

Before looking at the law relating to retention of dead bodies, organs and tissue, we need to say more about post-mortem examinations, sometimes referred to as autopsies. A post-mortem examination is conducted by a pathologist to investigate (*inter alia*) the cause of a death, and to understand more fully the nature of the patient's disease, including an evaluation of any medical or surgical treatment given to them. Such examinations are a key tool of modern scientific medicine. Forensic anthropologist Professor Dame Sue Black's best-selling books have helped to demystify death for the layperson,[16] but what is done to the body in a full post-mortem examination may still seem grisly. The body is opened and organs removed, weighed and sometimes dissected. In some cases, organs must be retained for a period of time to be treated before they can be fully examined, or organs and tissue may be sent away for tests elsewhere. Cultural issues cannot be ignored in deciding how to regulate the use of the bodies of the dead.[17] Some religious faiths, including Orthodox Judaism and Islam, mandate the swift burial of the intact body. Post-mortem examinations (save in exceptional circumstances) thus offend those faiths.

[14] For comprehensive guidance on the regulation of post-mortem examinations today see HTA *Code B: Post-mortem examination* (2020).

[15] Notification of Deaths Regulations 2019, SI 2019/1112.

[16] See S Black, *All That Remains* (2019) Black Swan; *Written in Bone* (2020) Doubleday.

[17] See DN Banyubala, 'Posthumous Organ Retention and Use in Ghana; Regulating Individual, Familial and Societal Interests' (2016) 24(4) *Health Care Analysis* 301.

21.4 The law before 2004: complex and obscure[18]

Doctors, especially pathologists, endured odium in the wake of revelations in the Bristol Interim and Redfern Reports. Some of the blame lay with the unsatisfactory state of the law prior to the Human Tissue Act 2004, when a complicated mixture of ancient common law principles and statutes governed the retention and use of body parts taken from the dead. The common law asserted that there was 'no property in a corpse'.[19] This principle remains untouched by the 2004 Act. When a family member dies his family have no claim by which they can assert 'this is now our body and we have unfettered rights to dispose of it or its parts'. However, the executors or administrators of the deceased's estate are subject, ultimately, to a common law duty to dispose of the body decently. This duty confers on them a right to possession of the body to fulfil that duty of decent disposal of the body.[20] A distinction must be made between removal of organs and tissue after a hospital autopsy, and removal of body parts subsequent to a coroner's post-mortem examination. The Human Tissue Act 1961 governed removal and retention of organs after a hospital autopsy. A person was not empowered to authorise an autopsy on themselves in advance of their death. If body parts were to be retained after completion of the autopsy, a further enquiry was supposed to establish that there was no objection to retention and use of those parts. 'Consent' to an autopsy should not have been judged to presume consent (or no objection) to organ retention.

In relation to transplants, doctors were reluctant to exercise the powers granted by the 1961 Act. They sought positive and explicit consent from families before removing organs for transplant, even if the deceased carried a donor card. In the context of organ retention, the opposite ethos seems to have prevailed. The 1961 Act was obscure. It did not require explicit consent. Rather it set up a 'no objection' rule. Put crudely, hospitals thought that they could take organs and tissue for purposes of education and research if no family member voiced dissent. The flaws in the Human Tissue Act 1961 became patent. Even if it could be shown to have been flouted, the lack of sanctions punishing violation of the Act rendered it toothless.

The position in relation to coroners' post-mortem examinations was no better. The overwhelming majority of post-mortems were and are performed on the orders of the coroner. Rules made under the Coroners Act 1988 placed a duty on the pathologist to remove and preserve 'materials' which in his opinion bore on the cause of death. If a baby died in the course of cardiac surgery, the pathologist might lawfully remove and retain his heart until it was possible to ascertain why the infant died. However, there was no power to retain organs for research or teaching purposes. Once the cause of death was established,

18 See D Price, 'From Cosmos and Damian to Van Velzen: The Human Tissue Saga Continues' (2003) 11 *Med Law Rev* 1.

19 *Doodeward v Spence* (1908) 6 CLR 906.

20 *Williams v Williams* (1882) 20 Ch D 659.

neither the coroner nor the pathologist had any further legal power to retain body parts. Such 'material' should have been disposed of, unless the relatives of the deceased authorised retention for research or teaching purposes. In practice, coroners simply allowed pathologists to do what they wished with human material no longer required for the purposes of verifying cause of death. Pathologists, in ignorance of the law in many cases, retained organs and tissue over long periods of time and for a multiplicity of purposes. By 2001, NHS hospitals were in possession of literally tens of thousands of organs and vast collections of blocks and tissue slides. Leading teaching hospitals and medical museums such as the Royal College of Surgeons had extensive archival material of body parts, some including collections long predating the NHS. Families had no say either in the decision to order a post-mortem or in the subsequent retention of parts of the body of their dead relative.

21.5 The Coroners and Justice Act 2009

Section 1 of the Coroners and Justice Act 2009 now provides that a senior coroner who is made aware that the body of a deceased person is within that coroner's area must conduct an investigation into that person's death if the coroner has reason to suspect that the deceased:

(a) died a violent or unnatural death,
(b) the cause of death is unknown, or
(c) the deceased died in custody or otherwise in state detention.[21]

The coroner is empowered to make whatever enquiries seem necessary and this includes ordering a post-mortem examination.[22] The family of the deceased have no right to object to the conduct of the post-mortem, however strong their religious beliefs relating to the burial or cremation of the intact body may be. However, the Act and regulations made under it do provide for notification to next of kin and an emphasis is placed on respect for the needs of bereaved families. Section 40 of the 2009 Act originally provided for an appeal against a coroner's decision to order a post-mortem but this provision was repealed without ever coming into force. It is the law relating to retention of organs after a coroner's post-mortem that has been radically changed by the combination of the Coroners and Justice Act and the Human Tissue Act 2004.

21.6 The Human Tissue Act 2004: the dead[23]

The Human Tissue Act 2004 governs the removal, retention and use of body parts taken from the dead, except where body parts are removed and retained solely for the purpose of investigating a death under the authority of the coroner. The Act also governs the performance of hospital autopsies. The Anatomy

[21] See also ss 2–4 and Schedule 10.
[22] See the Coroners and Justice Act 2009, s 14 and the Coroners (Investigation) Regulations, SI 2013/1269 (as amended).
[23] See D Price, 'The Human Tissue Act 2004' (2005) 68 *MLR* 798.

Act 1984 and the Human Tissue Act 1961 were wholly repealed. The Act, as we have seen in Chapter 20, makes 'appropriate' consent the fundamental principle governing retention and use of whole bodies and body parts. The Act also introduces extensive regulation of hospital autopsies[24] and retention and use of both bodies and what is styled 'relevant material'. It is tortuous to read. It does not apply in Scotland.[25] The scope of the Act will surprise many for it covers much more than organs such as hearts or kidneys and encompasses nearly all human bodily products. Defining organs and tissue and attaining a common understanding of what those words meant had been a major source of controversy in the debates surrounding organ retention. Section 53 defines 'relevant material' as 'material, other than gametes, which consists of or includes human cells', save that embryos outside the human body are excluded,[26] as are hair and nails from living subjects.[27]

Let us start with the circumstances in which it is lawful to conduct a post-mortem examination. All post-mortem examinations must now be performed in premises licensed by the HTA. The 2004 Act does not govern when a post-mortem examination can be ordered by the coroner. If a person dies in hospital and there is suspicion that their death may be as a result of some crime or medical malpractice, the coroner will be informed. If the coroner orders a post-mortem examination, as we have seen the family have no right to object. The Coroners and Justice Act is supported by guidance to assist families coping with the trauma of the investigation into a relative's death.[28]

Beyond the jurisdiction of the coroner, there are many other circumstances when doctors might want to conduct a post-mortem examination, to carry out a hospital autopsy. There may be uncertainty about the exact cause of death. There may be a wish to learn more about why treatment failed and the underlying disease or injury. Doctors (and families) may want to explore whether any genetic factors are implicated in the deceased patient's disease. Any such hospital autopsy will be lawful only if[29] the deceased themselves gave appropriate consent to the autopsy in advance of their death, or such consent is given by his nominated representative,[30] or, failing any advance consent by the deceased or authorisation by their nominated representative, appropriate consent is obtained from a person who stood in a qualifying relationship to the deceased.[31] Whatever the purpose of the hospital autopsy, be it to determine

24 See HTA, *Code B: Post-mortem Examination.*

25 See the Human Tissue (Scotland) Act 2006.

26 Regulated by the Human Fertilisation and Embryology Act 1990; see above Chapters 14 and 15.

27 See HTA, *List of Materials Considered to be 'Relevant material' under the Human Tissue Act 2004* (2021) at www.hta.gov.uk. The current list includes blood, saliva and urine and excludes sweat, serum and plasma (provided it does not contain platelets and other blood cells).

28 Ministry of Justice, *A Guide to Coroner Services for Bereaved People* (2020) issued under the Coroners and Justice Act 2009, s 42.

29 Human Tissue Act 2004, ss 1, 3, and Sch 1, paras 2 and 3.

30 Ibid, s 4.

31 For discussion of who constitutes such a person, see 20.9 above.

the cause of death, investigate the effect of treatment on them, or examine genetic factors, what is done can only be done with appropriate consent.[32]

Should doctors wish to retain body parts after the hospital autopsy, explicit consent to both the retention and the projected use of those parts must be obtained additionally, and separately, from any consent to the autopsy.[33] Imagine that, knowing she is dying from ovarian cancer, a woman consents in advance to an autopsy, especially in order to assess any genetic risk to her daughters. In the course of the autopsy, pathologists identify further tumours in her kidneys and liver. They want to retain those organs for further investigation and research. For such retention and use to be lawful, appropriate consent will have to be obtained from the woman's husband or partner, if she had one, or from one of her daughters. Retention of body parts from the dead must be authorised by appropriate consent, whether the purpose of retention be research, audit, education, performance assessment, public health monitoring or surveillance.[34]

If there is no advance consent from the deceased person or their nominated representative and no one who stands in a qualifying relationship to the deceased and so able to consent, nothing can be done to the body of the deceased that falls within the scope of the Human Tissue Act.[35] The consequences of this 'rule' are graphically illustrated in the extraordinary case *CM v The Executor of the Estate of EJ (Deceased)*.[36] CM, a senior doctor, was driving home off duty when she saw a body lying on the pavement. She stopped and went to help the woman (EJ). EJ was seriously injured and bleeding profusely. She died at the scene. When CM reached her home, she noticed abrasions on her hands, hands that had been covered with the deceased's blood. Concerned that she might have contracted a blood borne disease such as HIV or hepatitis, CM commenced a course of antiviral drugs but the drugs made her very unwell and so she wished to know if EJ had suffered from any such disease and thus have EJ's blood or tissue tested. Tests need to be done swiftly. Thus, the matter came to court. The judge ruled that the coroner, while able to order a post-mortem to investigate EJ's death, had no power to authorise tests for the benefit of a third party. Unless a person in a qualifying relationship to EJ gave consent, tests to benefit CM were unlawful. EJ proved to be a foreign national. EJ was unmarried and her parents were abroad, as yet unaware of their daughter's death and tracking them down would take time. They would of course be first in the hierarchy of qualifying relatives. EJ's mother's cousin OP was contacted. The judge referred to section 27(8) of the Human Tissue Act that provides that if it is not reasonably practicable in the time available

32 The bare rules of the Human Tissue Act 2004 are elaborated in this context by two Codes of Practice: HTA, *Code A: Guiding Principles and the Fundamental Principle of Consent* (2020) and *Code B: Post Mortem Examination* (2017).

33 See the Human Tissue Act 2004, s 1 and Sch 1.

34 See also HTA, *Code E: Research* (2021).

35 HTA, *Code A: Guiding Principles and the Fundamental Principle of Consent* (2020), para 33.

36 [2013] EWHC 1680 (Fam).

to contact the highest ranking qualifying relative, the next person in the hierarchy may give the necessary consent. He went on to find that although section 27 makes no reference to remoter relatives such as a mother's cousin, OP as 'a reasonably close relative' was enabled to give appropriate consent as a friend of longstanding. Had OP not lived in England and the judge not been so innovative in his interpretation of the Act, CM, the Good Samaritan, would have been left in limbo, ill and unable to work. A happy postscript to the case is that tests on EJ proved negative and CM was able to resume her career.

Albeit no consent is required when the coroner orders a post-mortem examination, once that examination is complete, should a pathologist wish to retain body parts removed in the course of that investigation, appropriate consent must be sought to make such retention and any projected use of those parts lawful. If our hypothetical patient who died of ovarian cancer died unexpectedly on the operating table, the coroner may well order a post-mortem. Should the examination establish that her death was in no sense caused by any error or lack of care, but pathologists still wish to retain her organs, consent must be sought for the retention and use of those organs even though it was not required for the post-mortem examination itself. The Coroners (Investigations) Regulations 2013[37] require that a coroner ordering a post-mortem examination and notified about retention of organs[38] and tissue must inform the deceased's family (*inter alia*) that organs and tissue will be retained, about the options[39] once examination of retained material is complete and (if the relatives wish the material to be returned to them) about what arrangements may need to be made.[40]

Somewhat surprisingly, the Human Tissue Act 2004 prescribes no formalities for consent to a hospital autopsy, or in general to retention and use of organs after post-mortem examination. There is no statutory rule requiring that consent must be given in writing. Greater formality is required for two particular uses of dead bodies, and their parts. A person who wishes to donate their body for anatomical examination or for public display must (normally) do so in writing and in the presence of at least one witness.[41] Moreover *only* the individual themselves can donate their body to anatomical examination[42] or public display.[43] Should the authors of this book die in advance of our spouses, having given no instruction about the use of our corpses, those spouses could authorise a hospital autopsy and donate our organs and tissue for medical research or education. Only we can donate our whole bodies to

37 SI 2013/1629, reg 14.

38 Regulation 13.

39 Disposal of the material by the pathologist, return to the 'family' or consent to retention of the materials for research, education or any scheduled purpose within the Human Tissue Act.

40 And see HTA, *Code B Post-mortem Examination*, paras 30–32.

41 See ss 3(4) and (5).

42 For further information about anatomical examination, see HTA, *Code C: Anatomical Examination* (2017).

43 HTA, *Code D: Public Display* (2021).

the local medical school or gain a strange sort of immortality in exhibitions such as *Bodyworlds*, where plastinated human bodies are on display as public 'entertainment'.

Section 2 of the 2004 Act makes express provision in relation to children and young people who die before reaching the age of majority at 18. If a young person was sufficiently mature and intelligent to make an advance direction about the conduct of an autopsy or retention of body parts, their advance direction authorises implementation of their wishes. A *Gillick* competent minor can in theory determine what happens to their body after death.[44] Establishing *Gillick* competence retrospectively after death will not be easy. In relation to younger children, normally their parents will be the designated decision-makers. Autopsy and organ retention are lawful only on the basis of appropriate consent from a person with parental responsibility[45] for the dead child. Consent from one parent alone will in theory suffice to make the relevant activity lawful. Overriding an objecting bereaved parent will pose ethical and practical difficulties. Consider this dilemma. A child dies of cancer at the age of four. His Orthodox Jewish father objects to any retention of his organs. His mother desperately wants to know if his disease has any genetic implications for her other children, and so want his organs retained and samples tested.

21.7 The Human Tissue Act 2004: the living

The Human Tissue Act 2004 was enacted in the wake of controversy about the (mis)use of the bodies of the dead. The Act, however, also regulates the retention and use of 'relevant material' from living patients. The original Human Tissue Bill imposed almost the same regime of requirements for explicit consent in relation to surgical or surplus tissue from living patients, as for body parts removed and retained from the dead. The Bill caused an outcry with senior scientists claiming that such burdensome rules would paralyse medicine.[46] Hence a modified set of rules govern retention of surgical or surplus tissue from living patients. Many doctors still regard the regulations as unreasonably onerous.

The 2004 Act does not regulate the initial removal of body parts from the living. That continues to be governed by the common law. Any surgery is normally unlawful and a criminal assault unless properly authorised by the patient's consent. A hysterectomy on a mentally competent woman self-evidently requires her consent. But what if doctors want to retain her diseased uterus, either to help train medical students or to pursue research[47] into the kind of cancer that necessitated the surgery? Must doctors seek the woman's explicit consent to retain her uterus, or even any specimens of diseased

44 See s 2(3). Only such a *Gillick* competent minor can authorise donation of her body for anatomical examination or public display. Parents cannot donate their children's bodies for such purposes.

45 See ss 1, 2 and Sch 1. Where there is no such person, the nearest person in a qualifying relationship to the dead child is the designated decision-maker.

46 See P Furness and R Sullivan, 'The Human Tissue Bill' (2004) 328 *BMJ* 533.

47 And see HTA, *Code E: Research* (2021).

tissue? It depends on their purpose.[48] If retention is intended for the purposes of audit, education or training, performance assessment, public health monitoring or quality assurance, her consent may be presumed.[49] Retention to acquire genetic or other information relevant to others will normally require an explicit consent. However, in relation to material taken from the body of living persons the HTA can exceptionally dispense with the need for consent if (*inter alia*) the donor cannot be traced or reasonable efforts to obtain consent have been unsuccessful.[50] Had EJ survived but remained unconscious, the HTA would have been able to authorise tests on her blood to establish if CM was at risk of contracting a blood borne disease.[51]

Retention for research will require specific consent if the identity of the patient will be ascertainable. The Act empowered the Secretary of State to make regulations allowing retention of material from the living for research, without an explicit and specific consent, where the research has been approved by an accredited research ethics committee and the 'source' of the material has been anonymised.[52] Research on surgical or surplus tissue taken from us must be explicitly authorised by us if researchers will be able to discover that the source is Brazier, Cave or Heywood. Very often, researchers will require this information about our identity to be able to, for example, access our medical records, which may be crucial to the research project. Only research, approved by a research ethics committee, where that link is *not* necessary, and has not been broken, will not require our explicit consent.[53]

The final version of the Act operates on the assumption that more people have little concern about what happens to 'bits of their living body' removed at surgery. They would be indifferent to whether such 'bits' were incinerated or put to some good use. Two *caveats* should be stated.

(1) Some religious faiths attach an almost equal value to parts separated from the living body as from the dead. When an Orthodox Jew has to have a limb amputated, they will make arrangements for that limb to be stored and ultimately interred with them.

(2) Surplus tissue is not necessarily mere 'waste'. It can be the source of crucial and sensitive genetic information. It can be the source of medical advances of commercial value.

48 See HTA, *Code A Guiding Principles and the Fundamental Principle of Consent*, Annex C.

49 See ss 1(d) and (f) and Sch 1.

50 See Human Tissue Act 2004, s 7.

51 *CM v The Executor of the Estate of EJ* [2013] EWHC 1680 (Fam), see 21.6 above.

52 See ss 1(7), 1(8) and 1(9); see also The Human Tissue Act 2004 (Ethical Approval, Exceptions from Licensing and Supply of Information about Transplants) Regulations 2006, SI 2006/1260.

53 Section 6 empowers the Secretary of State to make regulations relating to 'deemed consent' by persons who lack the requisite mental capacity to consent on their own behalf. See the Human Tissue Act 2004 (Persons Who Lack Capacity to Consent and Transplants) Regulations 2006, SI 2006/1659 (amended SI 2008/3067) regs 3 and 8.

21.8 'Appropriate consent'

We have so far indicated when explicit consent is required by the Act. The Act refers to 'appropriate consent'. Just what those two words may mean is crucial to how the Act will operate in practice. The HTA was expressly required by the Act to address what constitutes consent and has done so in a number of Codes of Practice and Standards, including a general Code on *Consent*,[54] and more specific Codes, some with separate Standards and Guidance, relating to post-mortem examinations,[55] anatomical examination,[56] public display,[57] research,[58] living organ donation,[59] deceased organ and tissue donation[60] and donation of allogenic bone marrow and blood stem cells for transplantation.[61] An additional Code deals with the Welsh 2013 Act.[62] All were updated in 2021.

In Code A on *Consent* the HTA stresses that health professionals seeking consent:

> ... need to tailor the information they provide to each specific situation ... [as] some people may require in-depth detail, whereas others may prefer to give consent having only had the basics of the procedure explained to them.[63]

While written consent is only mandatory for consent to anatomical examination or public display, written consent should be obtained wherever possible for any donation of tissue post-mortem.[64] A valid consent must be given voluntarily and on the basis of sufficient information. What degree of information is sufficient is difficult. Some families asked to consent to a hospital autopsy and organ retention may not want comprehensive and graphic descriptions of what will be done to their newly dead relative.[65] Some living patients will be happy simply to 'give away' excess tissue or diseased organs, uninterested in its fate. Doctors should not assume either that acute distress in the first case or indifference in the second justifies failing to *offer* information. A number of families brought claims against hospitals retaining organs without consent. In *AB v Leeds Teaching Hospital NHS Trust*,[66] the judge stressed that (even under the old Human Tissue Act 1961) families were 'entitled to have their wishes in respect of their deceased [relative's] body respected and complied with ... [and] those wishes cannot be complied with unless it is explained to the [relative] what is involved'. He rejected any blanket view that information

54 HTA, *Code A: Guiding Principles and the Fundamental Principle of Consent* (2020).
55 HTA, *Code B* (2017).
56 HTA, *Code C* (2017).
57 HTA, *Code D* (2021).
58 HTA, *Code E* (2021).
59 HTA, *Code F part 1* (2020).
60 HTA, *Code F part 2* (2020).
61 HTA, *Code G* (2017).
62 HTA, *Code of Practice on the Human Transplantation (Wales) Act 2013* (2020).
63 HTA, *Code A*, para 96.
64 HTA, *Code A*, para 103.
65 See D Knowles, 'Parental Consent to the Post Mortem Removal and Retention of Organs' (2001) 18 *Journal of Applied Philosophy* 215.
66 [2004] EWHC 644.

would have been distressing to all relatives saying: 'In so far as it involved the exercise of a therapeutic privilege it was one which does not appear to have been exercised on a case by case basis'.

Doctors should offer to disclose to the person giving consent all the information that any reasonable lay person would need to make a sensible choice about whether or not to give the requested consent.[67] Especially in the context of sudden bereavement, time and support for the decision-maker will be crucial. Information must neither be withheld nor forced on the unwilling recipient. Evidence of compliance with HTA Codes of Practice will weigh strongly with the courts.

The HTA endorses the applicability of seeking a *general* consent, for multiple purposes.[68] Donors may be asked to make an unconditional gift of their tissue (or that of their deceased relative). The key factor will be to establish what kind of consent was sought and given. Did the patient or relative consent only to the use of the relevant material for Project X alone, or Project X plus any related research or teaching activities, or did they consent to surrender all control of that material, and 'gift' the body parts in question to the hospital or university?

21.9 Regulation

We have focused in this chapter on the legal requirements for consent to removal, retention and use of body parts. The Human Tissue Act 2004 also imposes substantial regulatory requirements on such activities. We touch on these only briefly. As we saw in relation to transplantation, the HTA plays a major role in regulation. Its mandate to prepare Codes of Practice means that the HTA profoundly influences how the Act works in practice.[69] More directly, a number of activities require a licence from the HTA.[70] These include carrying out anatomical examinations and storing anatomical specimens. Medical schools have to be licensed by the HTA to carry out and train students in dissection.[71] Post-mortem examinations must be carried out in licensed premises. Storage of any body or part of a body for any of the purposes covered by the Act must be licensed, as must the use of bodies and their parts for public display. Pathology museums and archives of tissue will also need to be licensed in respect of acquisitions after the Act came into force. It remains lawful to retain existing holdings (even where there is no evidence of consent).[72] The HTA nonetheless advises that if the views of the deceased person or their relatives

67 Modelled on *Montgomery v Lanarkshire Health Board* [2015] UKSC 11 (discussed at 6.12 above).

68 See HTA, *Code A*, paras 105–107.

69 See ss 26 and 27.

70 See s 16.

71 Continuing the regulatory regime previously imposed by the Anatomy Act 1984; and see ss 16(2)(a), 17 and 21.

72 See s 9. And the licensing requirement does not apply to bodies of people who died before the Act came into force and are at least 100 years old (ie archaeologists are exempt). An example is the remains of King Richard III discovered under a car park in Leicester.

are known, those views should be respected,[73] and it gives extensive advice on the respectful disposal of existing holdings.[74]

The 2004 Act, unlike its predecessor, the Human Tissue Act 1961, has teeth. Proceeding without appropriate consent where consent is required is a criminal offence unless the person reasonably believed that he acted on the basis of an appropriate consent.[75] To ensure doctors charged with seeking consent do their part, it is also a criminal offence to represent falsely to another that appropriate consent has been obtained.[76] Carrying out unlicensed activities where such a licence is required equally engages criminal liability.[77]

21.10 Ownership of body parts[78]

The vexed question of whether we own our bodies is only fleetingly addressed in the Human Tissue Act 2004. We noted earlier the ancient common law assumption that there is no property in a corpse. That statement must be qualified. Consider the Egyptian mummies held in the British Museum. Do they belong to the British Museum?[79] Or might we lawfully help ourselves to one or two? *R v Kelly*[80] confirmed that, once a body or body parts had been changed in nature by work done on them, such parts become capable of being property. A technician was accused of stealing body parts from the Royal College of Surgeons and selling them to an artist who wished to use the parts as moulds for his sculptures. Both were charged with theft. Their defence was the College did not own the parts and so they could not steal them. Upholding the convictions, the Court of Appeal found that body parts became capable of being property for the purposes of the Theft Act 1968 because they had 'acquired different attributes by virtue of the application of skills, such as dissection or preservation technology, for exhibition or teaching purposes'. The notion of 'property' however is complex in this context. The Court of Appeal in *Kelly* did not find that the Royal College of Surgeons *owned* the stolen body parts. A right to lawful possession of property is all that is required for that property to be stolen from you.

Does it follow from *Kelly* that whenever organs or tissue have been retained and, for example, have been preserved in formalin or put in blocks, the hospital

73 HTA, *Code B*, para 7.
74 HTA, *Code B*, paras 71–75.
75 See s 5(1).
76 See s 5(2).
77 See s 25.
78 For an analysis of English law see M Quigley, 'Property in Human Biomaterials-Separating Persons and Things' (2012) 32 *OJLS* 659 and see JW Harris, 'Who Owns My Body?' (1996) 16 *OJLS* 55. Laurie, Harmon and Dove devote a whole chapter to 'The Body as Property': see *Mason and McCall Smith's Law and Medical Ethics* (11th edn, 2019) Oxford University Press, ch 15.
79 We do not consider here when museum pieces should be returned to their countries of origin. See M Wilding, 'Museums Grapple with Rise in Pleas for Return of Foreign Treasures' *Guardian* (2019) 18 February.
80 [1998] 3 All ER 741.

in possession of the specimen can assert a property right to it? *Dobson v North Tyneside Health Authority*[81] appears to undermine such an argument. The family of a woman who had died of a brain tumour brought a claim in clinical negligence against the health authority alleging failure to diagnose her condition sufficiently swiftly to offer her effective treatment. To succeed in their claim, they needed to ensure that their expert witnesses could examine samples of the brain. The brain had been removed at a coroner's post-mortem, preserved in paraffin, and later disposed of. The family sued the hospital for conversion alleging unlawful disposal of the brain. They argued that on completion of the coroner's investigation the family were entitled to the return of the brain. They enjoyed either ownership or, at least, a right of possession of the deceased's brain. The Court of Appeal dismissed their claim. Fixing the brain in paraffin was not a sufficient exercise of skill or labour to give that brain any different attributes to the organ initially removed from the body in the course of the post-mortem.

Identifying exactly what must be done to transform an organ taken from a body into property is difficult and somewhat artificial, and *Dobson* may be a decision soon to be consigned to legal history. Nonetheless the 'no property rule' received further support in *AB v Leeds Hospital NHS Trust.*[82] Parents whose deceased children had been subject to post-mortem examinations and organ retention without their consent brought claims for psychiatric injury to themselves and wrongful interference with the bodies of the children. Gage J, rejecting the latter claim, re-asserted the rule of 'no property in a corpse'. He also confirmed that nonetheless separated parts of the body subjected to the application of work and skill might become property – the property of he who expended that work and skill. So, pathologists who dissected and fixed organs from the body and transformed them into blocks and slides could acquire ownership of that 'property'. The skill and labour rule creates the odd paradox whereby our bodies and their parts are not our property (or at least do not form part of our estate) but put 'to the uses of medicine, their body parts become, as if by magic, property, but property owned by persons unknown for purposes unforeseen by the deceased'.[83]

However, in *R v Kelly*[84] Rose LJ had suggested *obiter* that the common law could develop to recognise a body part as property even without the acquisition of different attributes if it had acquired 'a use or significance beyond … mere existence'. He even indicated that in such a case outright ownership may be recognised. The Court of Appeal in *Yearworth v North Bristol NHS Trust*[85] took a small further step towards recognising property in separated body parts. Claims were brought by five men and the widow of a sixth in respect of the alleged negligence of the defendant Trust in allowing their stored sperm to

81 [1996] 4 All ER 479.

82 [2004] EWHC 644. And see the Scottish decision *Stevens v Yorkhill NHS Trust* 2007 SCLR 606.

83 See Brazier, 'Retained Organs: Ethics and Humanity', at 563.

84 [1998] 3 All ER 741, at 750.

85 [2009] EWCA Civ 37.

perish when the temperature in the storage tanks dropped and no attempt was made to ensure the sperm remained safely frozen. All the men had stored sperm for future use before undergoing chemotherapy for cancer. The men's claim that the loss of their sperm constituted personal injury failed. The appeal court allowed their claims for damage to their property, stating that 'developments in medical science now require a re-analysis of the common law's treatment of and approach to the issue of ownership of parts or products of a living body'.[86] The Court acknowledged that they could have used the 'skill and labour' notion to find that the complex process of storing sperm in liquid nitrogen was enough to transform the sperm to property.[87] Lord Judge CJ was clear that the Court of Appeal was scornful of that principle, saying that its 'ancestry did not commend it as a solid foundation'.[88] Their Lordships preferred to derive their findings from Rose LJ's dictum in *Kelly*. The men had, for the purposes of a claim in negligence, 'ownership of the sperm which they ejaculated'. They alone had generated and ejaculated the sperm and done so solely to ensure that it could later be used for their benefit. The storage of the sperm was governed by the Human Fertilisation and Embryology Act 1990. The 1990 Act restricted how the men could use the sperm, but entrenched the ability of the men to ensure that 'their' sperm was not used contrary to their direction; their 'negative control over its use remains absolute'. Furthermore, as the Authority could not continue to store the sperm without the continuing consent of the men, the Act recognised a fundamental feature of ownership in that the men and they only could require destruction of the sperm at any time. Analysis of the rights relating to the use and storage of the men's sperm led the Court to conclude that no individual or authority had any *rights* in relation to the sperm.

Yearworth could be seen as a narrow judgment[89] heavily dependent on the context of the claim relating to storage of gametes under the Human Fertilisation and Embryology Act.[90] It is hedged around by qualifications as will have been noted. The judgement of ownership was for the purposes of a claim in negligence and relates to property in products of the living body. Lord Judge is clear that the old rules must be revisited and the law must keep up with modern science. Another feature of *Yearworth* is this. The restrictions on use of the sperm imposed by the Human Fertilisation and Embryology Act did not undermine the men's ownership claims. It thus does not follow that by

86 Ibid, [45(a)].

87 Ibid, [45(c)].

88 Ibid, [45(d)]. And see discussion in Scottish case *Holdich v Lothian Health Board* [2013] CSOH 197, per Lord Stewart at [31–34].

89 But see also the latter part of the judgment relating to bailment. And note the extension of the narrow ruling in *Yearworth* in the decision of the Supreme Court of British Columbia in *JCM v ANA* 2012 BCSC 584. Also note that the Outer House of the Court of Session in Scotland allowed a claim to proceed to trial where a leak of liquid nitrogen resulted in damage to sperm in a cryogenic storage facility. Lord Stewart in *Holdich v Lothian Health Board* [2013] CSOH 197 acknowledged that it is not possible to 'put a kilt on Yearworth' [15].

90 See SHE Harmon and GT Laurie, '*Yearworth v North Bristol NHS Trust*: Property, Precedents and Paradigms' (2010) 69 *CLJ* 476.

allowing ownership you open the door to wholesale commodification. Policy-based restrictions on sale and use are not incompatible with ownership.

As we have seen, section 32 of the Human Tissue Act 2004 prohibits commercial dealings in body parts for transplant purposes, the Act exempts from this prohibition 'material which is the subject of property because of an application of human skill'.[91] The Bill had originally sought to ban commercial dealings in body parts for any purposes. Such a broad rule would have been unworkable as human tissue is fundamental material in medical research and trade among laboratories is well established. What seems to be objectionable is not for University A to sell human material excess to its requirements to Company B but for the human originator of that material to receive any recompense or property rights in his or her body.

The fundamental question of whether we should own our bodies would constitute a book of its own. We might ask – does it matter? The Human Tissue Act 2004 grants us and our families fairly extensive control of what may be done with our bodies and their component parts. A number of reasons suggest that it might matter. Common law dicta that there was no property in a corpse did not derive from any belief that such bodies were without value. Quite the contrary – the dead should not be seen 'as other inanimate objects, but were to be treated quite differently, even reverently'.[92] Our bodies were too valuable to be 'things', to be mere property. Would classifying bodies as property devalue them or endorse that value?

There is no avoiding the evidence that in the modern world bodies have certain sorts of tangible value. Sometimes this value is crudely commercial. Consider the famous case of Mr Moore.[93] Cell lines developed from his excised and diseased spleen made his doctor $15m and much greater profits for the drug company who bought the potential cell line. Yet Mr Moore was held to have no ownership rights in the body part removed. Another value secreted in our body parts is our genetic information. What may seem to be redundant surplus tissue carries within it information about the whole of our health and much about ourselves. We may prefer to retain control of that information.

Until recently, proponents of property models and bodies tended to be motivated by a belief in markets in human tissue. We should own our bodies so we can sell them. The debate is much more sophisticated now. Mason and Laurie[94] have made a powerful case for a modified property model. Finally, we have not touched on the vexed question of intellectual property and refer you again to Laurie, Harmon and Dove.[95]

91 See s 32(9)(c).

92 See P Matthews, 'The Man of Property' (1995) 3 *Med Law Rev* 237, p 254.

93 *Moore v Regents of the University of California* 793 P 2d 479 (Cal 1950).

94 JK Mason and GT Laurie, 'Consent or Property: Dealing with the Body and its Parts in the Shadow of Bristol and Alder Hey' (2001) 64 *MLR* 710. And see L Skene, 'Property Rights in Human Bodies, Body Parts and Tissue: Regulatory Contexts and Proposals for New Laws' (2002) 22 *LS* 102.

95 *Mason and McCall Smith's Law and Medical Ethics*, 15.45–15.65.

Chapter 22

THE END OF LIFE[1]

22.1 Introduction

Society has never been comfortable with issues surrounding the process of dying; and as healthcare staff are involved with the dying, they inevitably become involved in ethical as well as medical dilemmas.[2] For the last few years the heat of the debate has focused on whether the law should permit some sort of assistance for those who are terminally ill to end their lives. But this, as we shall see, is just one of a host of difficult dilemmas.

One is whether efforts should always be made to keep a dying person alive despite the additional suffering incurred by that person and the cost in terms of human dignity. The practice of, what some regard as, 'striving officiously to keep alive' has been facilitated by the increase in high-technology equipment capable of postponing inevitable death. The benefits of such equipment may often be great; yet there is a cost, in both human and economic terms. Further treatment may sometimes be said to be futile. A vast literature has developed around the concept of medical futility. The very word generates controversy. Laurie, Harmon and Dove[3] prefer to talk of non-productive treatment, treatment which cannot offer even a minimal likelihood of benefit to the patient. Part of the difficulty in this debate is the problem of separating human and economic considerations. Refusing to order doctors to continue to ventilate a severely injured infant, Balcombe LJ said openly:

> [A]n order which may have the effect at compelling a doctor or health authority to make available scarce resources and to a particular child ... might require the health authority to put J on a ventilator in an intensive care unit, and thereby possibly deny the benefit of those limited resources to a child who was much more likely than J to benefit from them.[4]

Language invoking medical futility could be seen as disguising rationing decisions, or even covert euthanasia. Whatever the economic considerations, few

1 We are grateful for the research assistance of Dr Eliza Bechtold, who contributed to updates of an earlier draft.

2 GT Laurie, S Harmon and E Dove, *Mason and McCall Smith's Law and Medical Ethics* (11th edn, 2019) Oxford University Press, ch 16.

3 Ibid, 16.06.

4 *Re J (A Minor) (Wardship: Medical Treatment)* [1992] 4 All ER 614 at 625, CA. And see GMC, *Treatment and Care Towards the End of Life: Good Practice in Decision Making* (2010), paras 38 and 39.

would deny the personal cost to the patient and to those close to the patient in terms of human dignity. Do the 'rights' of patients include the right to die with dignity? If so, does that 'right' extend to being 'helped to die'? In preserving and sustaining the life of a patient with a hopeless prognosis, is it in the interests of the patient, the family or the doctor to prolong his suffering? Unlimited access to technology may sometimes be as cruel as the illness itself. Doctors concerned with terminally ill patients must make professional and human decisions to give up treatment which may be merely sustaining the function of the organs, and turn to appropriate care at the terminal stage.

In 1993, the tragic case of Tony Bland thrust this question into the public domain.[5] Did the law demand that a young man grievously injured in the horrific disaster at Hillsborough Football Stadium should continue to be kept alive by artificial means? The Law Lords concluded that it did not. The *Bland* judgment rekindled debates on euthanasia, albeit their Lordships and many commentators[6] vehemently rejected suggestions that the decision to allow Tony Bland to die was in any sense sanctioning euthanasia.[7]

End-of-life decisions relating to adults lacking capacity now fall under the Mental Capacity Act 2005. The Act sets down principles by which the social and medical care of persons lacking the mental capacity to make their own decisions should be conducted. A Code of Practice provides guidance on the interpretation of the Act. We examined the wider effects of the Act in Chapter 7. In this chapter, we will consider the implications of the Act for adults, like Tony Bland, lacking capacity.

But what of patients who retain capacity? Since *Bland*, the courts have been deluged with cases seeking clearer definition of an individual's right to determine the manner of their death, or life. The Human Rights Act 1998 focused attention on what exactly is entailed in the right to life embodied in Article 2. Does the prohibition on inhuman and degrading treatment in Article 3 assist those dying in distress? Does a right to privacy in Article 8 encompass autonomy in decisions on the end of life? The case-law remains confused and confusing.

The Suicide Act 1961 decriminalised suicide and attempted suicide, but section 2[8] makes it an offence to encourage or assist the suicide (or attempted suicide) of another. In 2002, the President of the Family Division endorsed a tetraplegic patient's right to demand that doctors switch off the ventilator keeping her alive,[9] but when Dianne Pretty argued that she had a right to assisted suicide, the House of Lords found against her.[10] Doctors cannot be forced to administer treatment which they believe to be clinically unnecessary,

5 *Airedale NHS Trust v Bland* [1993] 1 All ER 821, HL.
6 *Mason and McCall Smith's Law and Medical Ethics*, 15.79.
7 See in particular *Airedale NHS Trust v Bland* [1993] 1 All ER 821 at 856, CA, per Hoffmann LJ.
8 As amended by the Coroners and Justice Act 2009, s 59(2).
9 *B v An NHS Trust* [2002] EWHC 425.
10 *R (Pretty) v DPP* [2002] 1 All ER 1, HL. Mrs Pretty's appeal to the European Court of Human Rights also failed: *Pretty v United Kingdom* (2002) 35 EHHR 1.

futile or inappropriate.[11] Does this include artificial nutrition and hydration? The Court of Appeal held that it does.[12] An appeal to the European Court of Human Rights (ECtHR) was ruled inadmissible.[13] In 2009 Debbie Purdy[14] enjoyed partial success when she approached her battle for a right to assisted suicide from a different angle, claiming that the Director for Public Prosecutions[15] (DPP) was required to clarify guidance on the circumstances when a prosecution would be brought under the Suicide Act 1961 in order to comply with Mrs Purdy's rights under Article 8. In February 2010 the DPP issued new guidance identifying more clearly when prosecution would be deemed in the public interest and controversially placing emphasis on the motive of the suspect.[16] But these changes did not address the potential incompatibility of section 2 of the Suicide Act 1961 with Article 8. This matter came before the Supreme Court in 2014 when Tony Nicklinson and others challenged the restrictive nature of the law on assisted suicide before nine Supreme Court justices.[17] Two of the Justices declared the law on assisted suicide to be incompatible with Article 8. Elizabeth Wicks warns that apparent progress is marred by judicial division:

> Overall *Nicklinson* reveals a Supreme Court divided on two of the most fundamental and controversial legal issues facing the UK at present: the appropriate legal response to assisting or encouraging a suicide, and the respective roles of Parliament, domestic courts and the European Court of Human Rights in protecting human rights.[18]

The division is evident in the Supreme Court's refusal to allow Noel Conway's permission to appeal a decision that the ban on assisted suicide is compatible with his rights under article 8 in 2018.[19] Though Conway's appeal did not offer sufficient prospects of success, the carefully worded refusal did not rule out future claims of incompatibility.

Nor are the courts the only forum for debates on the end of life. A series of failed attempts to enshrine a right to assisted suicide in legislation has not dampened the ardour of reformers. Opponents argue for the sanctity of life and for better palliative care.

11 *Aintree University Hospitals NHS FT v James* [2013] UKSC 67, [18].
12 *R (Burke) v GMC* [2005] EWCA Civ 1003.
13 *Burke v United Kingdom*, App No 19807/06 (ECHR, 2006). And see discussion of *Lambert and Others v France*, App No 46043/14 (ECHR, 5 June 2015) (Grand Chamber), at 22.18 below.
14 *R (Purdy) v DPP* [2009] UKHL 45.
15 Prosecution requires the consent of the DPP. Suicide Act 1961, s 2(4).
16 DPP, *Code for Crown Prosecutors and the Policy for Prosecutors in respect of Cases of Encouraging or Assisting Suicide* (2010, updated October 2014).
17 *R (Nicklinson and another) v Ministry of Justice; R (AM) v The Director of Public Prosecutions* [2014] UKSC 38.
18 E Wicks, 'The Supreme Court Judgment in Nicklinson: One Step Forward On Assisted Dying: Two Steps Back on Human Rights [2014] UKSC 38' (2015) 23(1) *Med Law Rev* 144.
19 *R (Conway) v Secretary of State for Justice: Application for Permission to Appeal*, 27 November 2018.

The *Concise Oxford Dictionary* defines euthanasia as: 'Gentle and easy death; bringing about of this, especially in case of incurable and painful disease.' It is a term much used and misused. It may be popularly invoked to include conduct characterised as 'mercy killing', when somebody, usually a relative, deliberately and specifically performs some act, such as administering a drug, to accelerate death and terminate suffering. Prosecutions for mercy killing, while rare, are sometimes reported, and the courts tend to deal with such cases with compassion. Mercy killing, where doctors are not usually directly involved, may also be termed active euthanasia. This can be contrasted with 'passive euthanasia', which might describe, for example, withholding of life-support treatment. The terminology of the debate is complex and confusing.[20] Active euthanasia involves an act done deliberately designed to shorten life, by however short a span. *Active* euthanasia may involve *voluntary* euthanasia where the act done, the killing of the patient, is done at their specific request. *Non-voluntary* euthanasia may be the term used to refer to ending the life of someone who cannot express a view on the prolongation of their life at the relevant time. A proxy speaks on their behalf and what is done is done at least purportedly for the patient's own good. *Involuntary* euthanasia involves killing a person without their own or any proxy authority. The patient's life may be ended for what others perceive as their good or could be terminated because of the burden the patient's continued life places on society. *Passive* euthanasia can itself be voluntary, non-voluntary or involuntary. As we shall see any boundary between passive and active euthanasia is less clear than it might at first be thought to be.[21] Now we must explore the legality of this range of decisions.

22.2 Mercy killing

Deliberately taking the life of another person, whether that person is dying or not, constitutes the crime of murder. Accordingly, any doctor who, no matter how compassionately, has practised voluntary euthanasia or mercy killing can be charged with murder, if the facts can be clearly established. As Lord Mustill puts it:

> '[M]ercy killing' by active means is murder ... that the doctor's motives are kindly will for some, although not for all, transform the moral quality of his act, but this makes no difference in law.[22]

A doctor convicted of murder faces a mandatory life sentence in gaol. Dr Cox was in a sense lucky.[23] He injected his patient, Mrs Lillian Boyes, with potassium chloride. Mrs Boyes suffered unbearable pain from rheumatoid arthritis and begged Dr Cox to end her suffering. Potassium chloride stops the heart. It kills and has no therapeutic or painkilling properties. Before Dr Cox's action

20 See *Mason and McCall Smith's Law and Medical Ethics*, 18.01; E Jackson, *Medical Law: Text, Cases and Materials* (5th edn, 2019) Oxford University Press, p 906.

21 See D Shaw 'The Body as Unwarranted Life Support' (2007) 33 *J Med Ethics* 519.

22 *Airedale NHS Trust v Bland* [1993] 1 All ER 821, at 850, HL.

23 *R v Cox* (1992) 12 BMLR 38. See E Jackson, 'Whose Death Is It Anyway? Euthanasia and the Medical Profession' (2004) 57 *Current Legal Problems* 415.

came to the attention of the police, Mrs Boyes was cremated. It could not therefore be proved beyond reasonable doubt that the injection administered by Dr Cox killed her. Dr Cox was convicted only of attempted murder. The judge imposed a suspended sentence, and the General Medical Council (GMC) allowed him to continue to practise subject to certain conditions. Had the link between his action and Mrs Boyes's death been clearly established, no such merciful course would have been open to the judge.[24] This applies equally to family members and loved ones.

Any judicial sympathy for a perpetrator of 'mercy killing' is currently restricted to discretion in sentencing. In 2010 Francis Inglis killed her 22-year-old son, Tom, with a lethal injection of heroin.[25] Tom was in a coma following a road collision. Inglis contended that she acted out of compassion and love but was convicted of murder and sentenced to a minimum of nine years' imprisonment. The verdict was much criticised and on appeal the sentence was reduced to five years.[26]

22.3 Double effect

Until the law is changed, or the DPP revises his guidelines to extend beyond assisted suicide,[27] active euthanasia, whatever the circumstances, equals murder in English law.[28] The only exception to that rule was spelled out by Devlin J in the case *R v Adams*[29] in 1957. Dr Adams was charged with the murder of an 81-year-old patient who had suffered a stroke; it was alleged that he had prescribed and administered such large quantities of drugs, especially heroin and morphine, that he must have known that the drugs would kill her. In his summing-up to the jury, Devlin J first stated:

> [I]t does not matter whether her death was inevitable and her days were numbered. If her life was cut short by weeks or months it was just as much murder as if it was cut short by years. There has been much discussion as to when

24 Though the judge might reduce the sentence: See for example R Ford, 'Life May Mean Just 3 years for Mercy Killing Husband' *The Times* (2007) 25 May.

25 Unreported. See S Burns, 'Showing Mercy' (2010) 154(1) *Solicitor's Journal* 6, 8, also commenting on *R v Gilderdale* (2010) unreported, 25 January (Crown Court at Lewes). Kay Gilderdale helped her 31-year-old daughter, who suffered from ME, to die. Gilderdale admitted assisting suicide (for which she received a conditional discharge) and was acquitted of attempted murder.

26 *R v Inglis* [2010] EWCA Crim 2637. See also *R v Webb* [2011] EWCA Crim 152, [19]–[20]. Note that at the time of writing the CPS is considering responses to its 'Consultation on Public Interest Guidance for Suicide Pact and "Mercy Killing" Type Cases' (2022) 14 January. The consultation proposed revised public interest factors that prosecutors should consider if the suspect acted out of compassion for the deceased.

27 DPP, *Code for Crown Prosecutors and the Policy for Prosecutors in respect of Cases of Encouraging or Assisting Suicide* (2010, updated 2014), para 33: 'It is murder or manslaughter for a person to do an act that ends the life of another, even if he or she does so on the basis that he or she is simply complying with the wishes of the other person concerned.'

28 See Jackson, *Medical Law: Text, Cases and Materials*, pp 907–908.

29 *R v Adams* [1957] Crim LR 773.

> doctors might be justified in administering drugs which would shorten life. Cases of severe pain were suggested and also cases of helpless misery. The law knows no special defence in this category …

However, he went on to say:

> … but that does not mean that a doctor who was aiding the sick and dying had to calculate in minutes, or even hours, perhaps, not in days or weeks, the effect on a patient's life of the medicines which he would administer. If the first purpose of medicine – the restoration of health – could no longer be achieved, there was still much for the doctor to do and he was entitled to do all that was proper and necessary to relieve pain and suffering even if the measures he took might incidentally shorten life by hours or perhaps even longer. The doctor who decided whether or not to administer the drug could not do his job, if he were thinking in terms of hours or months of life. Dr Adams's defence was that the treatment was designed to promote comfort, and if it was the right and proper treatment, the fact that it shortened life did not convict him of murder.

Devlin J introduced into English law a version of the 'double effect' principle, whereby if one act has two inevitable consequences, one good and one evil, the act may be morally acceptable in certain circumstances.[30] His ruling is endorsed in *Bland*.[31] It is not crystal clear in its meaning. In one passage, Devlin J referred to the incidental shortening of life by hours and, in another passage, he referred to the shortening of life by hours or months. It must be a matter of judgement in each case.[32] Clearly he was dealing with terminally ill patients where, in order to alleviate pain, it is permissible to disregard the fact that the treatment involved may accelerate the patient's death.

An Inquiry in 2018 revealed the practice of shortening the lives of patients at Gosport War Memorial Hospital by administering high doses of medication that were not clinically indicated.[33] Over 450 patients' lives were unnecessarily shortened, many unjustifiably put on a terminal care pathway. Warnings went unheeded, deference unchecked. Gosport is a stark lessen as to the limits of the doctrine of double effect.

In recent years there is evidence of increased use of continuous deep sedation (CDS) – medically induced unconsciousness at the end of life – as a form of

30 For insightful analysis see S Pattinson, *Revisiting Landmark Cases in Medical Law* (2019) Routledge, ch 2.

31 *Airedale NHS Trust v Bland* [1993] 1 All ER 821at 868, HL. But consider the impact of *R v Woollin* [1999] AC 82, HL (jury may infer intent to kill even if causing death is not the accused's primary purpose); see E Jackson *Medical Law: Text, Cases and Materials*, p 894.

32 See, for example, the investigation surrounding forty-three cases of patient deaths under GP Howard Martin. In 2005 Martin was cleared of murdering three patients by injecting them with morphine. See 'Morphine Doctor Cleared of Murder' *The Times* (2005) 14 December. Further investigation followed and Dr Martin was struck off by the GMC in 2010 on the basis that he had hastened the death of eighteen patients.

33 *Gosport War Memorial Hospital: The Report of the Gosport Independent Panel* (2018) HC 1084.

palliative care. Use of CDS is inconsistent and poorly documented but one study claims that it is used in around 18 per cent of medically attended deaths in the UK.[34] Provided death is imminent, Laurie, Harmon and Dove are of the view that 'terminal sedation' can be 'accommodated within the acceptable processes of good medical practice – as defined by double effect'.[35] Savulescu and Radcliffe-Richards argue for a right to unconsciousness to limit suffering in the dying process and that anaesthetic rather than CDS might more effectively prevent suffering.[36] Charles Douglas is less optimistic, particularly when CDS may be accompanied with removal of artificial life support, which might hasten death: '[T]he fact that sedation to unconsciousness is available at all will surely remain a source of tension in the debate about assisted death.'[37] The spectre of *early* terminal sedation is particularly worrying. Where it is used on patients whose death is not imminent we would agree with Laurie, Harmon and Dove that the practice constitutes 'euthanasia hiding under emollient terminology'.[38]

The application of laws relating to murder and suicide are central to an understanding of law controlling treatment of the dying. It will be appropriate to consider first the case of the 'competent' patient, that is a person with full legal and mental capacity who is aware of what is happening and who may wish to make decisions themselves about their quality of life: the way they will be treated and how they will continue to live or die. Second, the case of the adult 'incapacitated' patient will be considered: unconscious patients or persons who do not have the mental or physical capacity to make their own wishes known at the relevant times.[39]

22.4 Is there a 'right' to die?

Does a patient have a 'right' to die? The answer will depend on the circumstances in which they seek to exercise such a 'right'. The Court of Appeal in *Re T*[40] made it clear that an adult patient with mental capacity enjoys an absolute right to refuse further treatment even where refusing treatment means certain death. The patient who is terminally ill or who, even if not terminally ill, suffers from intractable pain or unbearable disability can refuse further

34 C Seale, 'Continuous Deep Sedation in Medical Practice: A Descriptive Study' (2010) 29(1) *Journal of Pain and Symptom Management* 44.

35 *Mason and McCall Smith's Law and Medical Ethics*, 19.45.

36 J Savulescu and J Radcliffe-Richards, 'A Right to be Unconscious' (2019) 74(4) *Anaesthesia* 557; And see calls for wider use of general anaesthesia to aid dying patients: A Takla *et al*, 'General Anaesthesia in End-Of-Life Care' (2021) 76(10) *Anaesthesia* 1308.

37 C Douglas 'Commentary: Moral Concerns with Sedation at the End of Life' (2014) 40 *J Med Ethics* 241.

38 *Mason and McCall Smith's Law and Medical Ethics*, 19.45.

39 It should be noted, of course, that it may not always be an easy issue to determine whether a person is clinically or legally competent; see above, Chapter 7. Children and infants are considered in Chapter 17.

40 *Re T (Adult: Refusal of Treatment)* [1992] 4 All ER 465, CA; discussed above at 6.3.

treatment. The only *caveat* is that the evidence that their refusal of treatment was free and informed must be unequivocal. Their reasons to refuse treatment are not material. A patient dying of cancer has the right to say 'no more', however strongly their doctor may argue that more chemotherapy would offer them some additional months of life. A person paralysed by multiple sclerosis can refuse to be ventilated. A patient whose condition is no longer bearable to them can take their own life if they have access to the means to do so, and they are still independently capable of such action. There is a right to prevent others forcing you to live.

The first major difficulty is this. A patient who wishes to die may already be receiving life-sustaining treatment. She is hooked up to a ventilator or receiving artificial nutrition via a naso-gastric tube or intravenous drip. She wants her life support withdrawn and to be permitted to die. Intrinsically her position seems indistinguishable from the patient who refuses further chemotherapy or instructs her doctors not to ventilate her. However, someone will have to intervene in this scenario to switch off the ventilator or remove the feeding tube. Will a doctor who does the relevant act risk prosecution for murder or assisting suicide?

The decision in *Bland*[41] made it clear that if a doctor disconnects a patient from life support at their specific request, that act does not constitute either murder or assisting suicide. *Bland* exposes the fragility of distinctions made between active and passive euthanasia.[42] Three principles emerge from *Bland*.

(1) Treatment involving any invasive procedure constitutes a battery, unless authorised by the patient or, if they are unable to authorise their own treatment, it is justified by other lawful authority.
(2) Continuing invasive treatment once justification for that treatment is withdrawn becomes a battery and therefore unlawful.
(3) Artificial nutrition and hydration constitute treatment as much as drug therapy or ventilation. If a patient instructs doctors to switch off a ventilator or withdraw a naso-gastric tube, failure to act on those instructions renders continuing treatment unlawful.

In *B v An NHS Trust*,[43] Ms B suffered a haemorrhage in the spinal column in her neck. Her condition deteriorated rapidly. Within two years she was paralysed from the neck down and could breathe only supported by a ventilator. Doctors told her that she was unlikely to recover. Rehabilitation programmes to allow her to live outside hospital on the ventilator were proposed to her. Ms B was adamant that she did not want to survive in such a condition. She

41 [1993] 1 All ER 821, HL; and see *Nancy B v Hôtel Dieu de Quebec* (1992) 86 DLR (4th) 385 (Canada); *Auckland Area Health Board v A-S* [1993] 1 NZLR 235 (New Zealand); *Bouvia v Superior Court* (1986) 225 Cal Reptr 297 (USA).

42 But see A McGee, 'Finding a Way Through the Ethical and Legal Maze: Withdrawal of Medical Treatment and Euthanasia' (2005) 13 *Med Law Rev* 357 and J Keown, 'A Futile Defence of Bland: A Reply to Andrew McGee' (2005) 13 *Med Law Rev* 393.

43 [2002] EWHC 429.

instructed doctors to switch off the ventilator. The doctors treating her refused, citing conscientious objections to such a course of action and challenging Ms B's mental capacity to refuse further treatment. Butler-Sloss P held that Ms B retained mental capacity.[44] That being the case, continuing to ventilate her against her will was unlawful. She was entitled to demand that the ventilator be switched off, though not to require an individual clinician to act contrary to their conscience. Yet there can be no doubt that switching off a ventilator or removing a naso-gastric tube is an act hastening death. The Law Lords in *Bland* skirt around the logical implications of their findings. Lord Browne-Wilkinson is honest in his appreciation of the dilemma. He says:

> Mr Munby QC … submits that the removal of the naso-gastric tube necessary to provide artificial feeding and the discontinuation of the existing regime of artificial feeding constitute positive acts of commission. I do not accept this. Apart from the act of removing the naso-gastric tube, the mere failure to continue to do what you have previously done is not, in any ordinary sense to do anything positive; on the contrary it is by definition an omission to do what you have previously done.
>
> The positive act of removing the naso-gastric tube presents more difficulty. It is undoubtedly a positive act, similar to switching off a ventilator in the case of a patient whose life is being sustained by artificial ventilation. But in my judgement in neither case should the act be classified as positive, since to do so would be to introduce intolerable fine distinctions. If, instead of being removed, the naso-gastric tube was left in place but no further nutrients were provided for the tube to convey to the patient's stomach, that would not be a positive act. If the switching off of a ventilator were to be classified as a positive act, exactly the same result can be achieved by installing a time-clock which requires to be reset every twelve hours; the failure to reset the machine could not be classified as a positive act. In my judgment, essentially what is being done is to omit to feed or ventilate; the removal of the naso-gastric tube or the switching off of a ventilator are merely incidents of that omission.[45]

Eliding acts and omissions enabled the Law Lords to achieve the desired result. Consider its implications. Luis is sustained by a ventilator. He asks his wife, Anna, to switch it off because his doctor refuses to do so. Luis rejects advice to seek a declaration from the courts to overturn his doctor's advice. Reluctantly, Anna pulls the switch and Luis dies. Is Anna exempt from a charge of murder, or is a *Bland* defence exclusive to doctors? In the light of *B v An NHS Trust*, could Anna argue thus? Continuing to ventilate Luis against his will constitutes the tort of battery and the crime of assault. When Anna switched off the ventilator all she did was use reasonable measures to prevent a crime. Then there is the most awkward question of all. What of the patient whose illness renders their life intolerable, but who is not reliant on treatment or life support to survive? Their condition is such that they cannot take their own life.

44 Discussed more fully at 7.4 above.
45 [1993] 1 All ER 821, at 881.

22.5 Assisted dying

Since the Suicide Act 1961, it is no longer a criminal offence to commit, or attempt to commit, suicide. However, section 2 of the Act, as amended in 2009,[46] provides that:

> A person (D) commits an offence if
> (a) D does an act capable of encouraging or assisting the suicide or attempted suicide of another person, and
> (b) D's act was intended to encourage or assist suicide or an attempt at suicide.

It is a crime that may be committed for diverse reasons, ranging from the avaricious to the compassionate. In *R v McShane*,[47] a daughter was found guilty of trying to persuade her 89-year-old mother in a nursing home to kill herself so that she could inherit her estate. A secret camera installed by the police showed the daughter handing her mother drugs concealed in a packet of sweets, and pinning a note on her dress saying 'Don't bungle it'.

Clear evidence of aiding and abetting a particular act of suicide is necessary before a prosecution can be successful. In *Attorney General v Able*,[48] the court was asked to declare that it was an offence for the Voluntary Euthanasia Society to sell a booklet to its members aged 25 and over, setting out in some detail various ways in which individuals could die by suicide. The Society neither advocated nor deplored suicide; it had a neutral stance and regarded such decisions as matters of personal belief and judgement. Evidence in the case suggested that over a period of eighteen months after the first distribution of the booklet, there were fifteen cases of suicides linked to the booklet, and nineteen suicides where documents were found which showed that the deceased was a member of, or had corresponded with, the Society. The court concluded that in most cases the supply of the booklet would not constitute an offence. Normally, a member requesting the booklet would not make clear his intentions, and the booklet would be supplied without any knowledge by the supplier of whether it was required for general information, for research, or because suicide was contemplated. To establish an offence, it would have to be proved that the Society distributed the booklet to a person who, at the time of the distribution, was known to be contemplating suicide, with the intention of assisting and encouraging that person to die by suicide by means of the booklet's contents, and, further, that that person was in fact assisted and encouraged by the booklet to die by suicide or to attempt to die by suicide. A doctor who knowingly provides someone with sufficient tablets with which to end a life, and advises how best to take them, risks prosecution.

The well informed and able may kill themselves. The patient dying of degenerative disease, or in the terminal throes of cancer, may need help to do so.

46 The Coroners and Justice Act 2009, s 59 reframes the offence, modernising the wording and combining the offence of assisting in a suicide and the offence of attempting to assist in a suicide into one single offence. The scope of the law is unchanged.

47 (1977) 66 Cr App R 97.

48 [1984] QB 795.

If Ava can breathe only with the aid of a ventilator, she can require her doctor to switch off the ventilator. If Ava is slowly choking to death with motor neurone disease, but can still swallow enough lethal sleeping tablets, Ava can end her misery. If Ava is so weakened by the disease that she cannot reach for the tablets or swallow, she must endure her suffering.

An increasing number of commentators now advance the case for legalising physician-assisted dying.[49] But what does this mean? As we discuss at 22.12 below, several countries have legislated to allow doctors to comply with a patient's request for medication to end their life. But this does not meet the truly hard cases where the patient, even if supplied with medication, cannot take the dose independently. Recent attempts to introduce legislation legalising assisted dying in England and Wales have so far proved unsuccessful. A Scottish Terminally Ill Adults (Scotland) Bill was proposed in 2022.[50]

22.6 The patient who cannot die by suicide – the *Pretty* case

Does the patient who cannot, or does not wish to, administer the means of suicide themselves have a right to assistance? Articles 2, 3, 8, 9 and 14 of the European Convention on Human Rights (ECHR) have been employed, to date unsuccessfully, in defence of such a right.

This matter first came before the UK courts in the sad case of Dianne Pretty. Mrs Pretty was dying of motor neurone disease. Gradually she had lost all ability to use her muscles. She could barely speak and could not swallow. She was fed by a tube. Mrs Pretty sought an assurance from the Director of Public Prosecutions (DPP) that no charge would be brought against her husband should he help her to die at a time of her choice. The DPP refused to give any such assurance. Mrs Pretty brought an application for judicial review. She argued that the DPP acted unlawfully. He failed to pay due regard to Mrs Pretty's fundamental human rights. Her application failed before the Divisional Court,[51] as did her subsequent appeal to the House of Lords.[52] She took her case to the ECtHR at Strasbourg, but lost again.[53] The Law Lords held that the decision not to promise immunity to Mr Pretty should he help his wife to die was not, in the circumstances, amenable to judicial review.[54]

What human rights arguments did Mrs Pretty raise? It was put to the judges that Article 2, endorsing the right to life, carried with it the corollary of a right to die at a time and in a manner of one's own choosing. The Law Lords were unimpressed. They could read nothing into Article 2 to confer a right to be

49 Notably and eloquently, DW Meyers and JK Mason, 'Physician Assisted Suicide: A Second View from Mid-Atlantic' (1999) 29 *Anglo-American Law Review* 39.

50 Liam McArthur MSP, *Consultation: Assisted Dying for Terminally Ill Adults (Scotland) Bill* (2021) September 22. Final proposal lodged September 2022. See 22.12 below.

51 [2001] All ER (D) 251.

52 [2002] 1 All ER 1, HL.

53 *Pretty v United Kingdom* (2002) 35 EHHR 1.

54 Although at least some of their Lordships left open the question of whether on different facts such an application might succeed.

helped to die. Lord Bingham regarded Article 2 as embodying the traditional doctrine of sanctity of life. He put it thus:

> Whatever the benefits which, in the view of many, attach to voluntary euthanasia, physician-assisted suicide and suicide without the intervention of a physician, these are not benefits which derive protection from an article framed to protect the sanctity of life.[55]

Nor did an argument based on Article 3 prohibiting inhuman or degrading treatment find any greater favour. Dignity in sickness and dying should be protected. Nothing in Article 3 conferred a positive obligation to help an individual end her life.[56] The Divisional Court declared:

> [F]ar from having the effect contended for by Mr Havers, Article 2 and 3 between them are aimed at the protection and preservation of life and the dignity of life, because of its fundamental value, not only to the individual but also to the community as a whole. It is to stand the whole purpose of these articles on its head to say that they are aimed at protecting a person's right to procure their own death.

In the House of Lords, Lord Bingham[57] doubted whether any positive obligation to prevent citizens being subjected to degrading treatment could translate into a duty to ensure a person could seek help to die. Lord Steyn was clear that: 'article 3 was not engaged'. It was:

> ... singularly inapt to convey the idea that the state must guarantee to individuals a right to die with the deliberate assistance of third parties. So radical a step, infringing the sanctity of life principle, would have required far more explicit wording.[58]

Lord Hope[59] was not convinced that Mrs Pretty's condition met the minimum level of severity required in Article 3. Since she could not be compelled to accept treatment and, in his view, palliative treatment was available, Lord Hope doubted that her state was degrading.[60]

Arguments centred on Article 8, the right to respect for private and family life, fared a little better. The Divisional Court conceded that Article 8 could extend to embrace a right to bodily integrity, including a right to refuse life-saving treatment. They were even prepared to assume Article 8(1) could extend to a right to be allowed to take one's own life. In some of their speeches, the Law Lords suggest Article 8 does not even go that far. Lord Steyn put it bluntly:

55 [2002] 1 All ER 1, at 7, HL. The ECtHR concurred that Article 2 'could not be interpreted as involving a negative aspect'.

56 But see the persuasive arguments of J Coggon, 'Could the Right to Die with Dignity Represent a New Right to Die in English Law?' (2006) 12 *Med Law Rev* 219.

57 [2001] EWHC Admin 788, [51].

58 [2002] 1 All ER 1, at 11–12, HL.

59 Ibid, at 37.

60 Ibid, at 37.

> [A]rticle 8 prohibits interference with the way in which an individual leads his life and it does not relate to the manner in which he wishes to die.[61]

The ECtHR, on the other hand, was

> ... not prepared to exclude that this constitutes an interference with [Dianne Pretty's] right to respect for private life as guaranteed under Article 8(1) of the Convention.[62]

However, the ECtHR and House of Lords concurred with the Divisional Court that, even if some sort of right to choose one's manner of dying can be inferred from Article 8(1), Article 8(2) (placing restrictions on privacy rights) justifies the state in criminalising assisted dying. The need to afford protection for vulnerable people, especially the elderly, justifies the provisions of the Suicide Act as they stand. Lord Bingham said:

> It is not hard to imagine that an elderly person, in the absence of any pressure, might opt for a premature end to life if that were available, not from a desire to die or a willingness to stop living, but from a desire to stop being a burden to others.[63]

Arguments grounded on Articles 9 and 14 of the Convention also failed. Two policy questions perhaps influenced the judges in the Divisional Court and the Lords. First note that Mrs Pretty did not seek physician-assisted suicide, which might have been subject to external scrutiny, but rather sought her husband's help to die.[64] Second, the Law Lords recognised the diversity of cultural and religious views across Member States party to the European Convention and the need, therefore, for flexibility in its interpretation.[65]

22.7 Death tourism

With the development of the freedom of movement in Europe some patients have travelled abroad to take advantage of laws permissive of assisted dying in a practice labelled 'death tourism'.[66] In Switzerland, assisted dying is not illegal provided it is not motivated by self-serving ends.[67] The practice of assisting dying is not limited to doctors, and the suicide organisations in Switzerland are some of the few in the world willing to accept foreign patients.[68] The

61 Ibid, at 29.

62 (2002) 35 EHRR 1.

63 [2002] 1 All ER 1, at 18. A view endorsed by the ECtHR.

64 [2001] EWHC (Admin) 788, [60]. See also [2002] 1 All ER 1, at 21, per Lord Bingham.

65 [2002] 1 All ER 1, at 27. In recognition of the lack of consensus in Europe, the ECtHR accords member states a wide margin of appreciation. See *Haas v Switzerland* [2011] 53 EHRR 33; *Koch v Germany* [2012] ECHR 1621; *Nicklinson and Lamb v UK*, App Nos 2478/15 and 1787/15 (ECHR, 16 July 2015).

66 See 'Covid-19: Assisted Dying Travel Allowed During Lockdown, Says Hancock' *BBC News* (2020) 5 November, on the difficulties in accessing help during the COVID-19 pandemic.

67 Swiss Criminal Code, Article 115.

68 Between 1998 and 2013, 244 Britons undertook assisted suicide in Switzerland: S Warnes, 'How Many People Choose Assisted Suicide Where it is Legal? *Guardian*

English courts are powerless to intervene unless someone 'does an act capable of encouraging or assisting the suicide or attempted suicide of another person'. Many applicants are too ill to make all the arrangements themselves and are helped by a doctor or loved one.

In *Re Z (An Adult: Capacity)*,[69] Mr Z informed his Local Authority that he and his wife, Mrs Z, would travel to Switzerland where arrangements had been made for her to end her life at the Zurich-based assisted-suicide clinic, Dignitas. Could the court prevent him from assisting his wife? The judge satisfied himself that Mrs Z remained competent and was not subject to any undue influence. The decision to travel to Switzerland was hers. Any question of her husband's criminal liability was a matter for the DPP, who had not authorised any prosecution: '[A]lthough an act may be criminal, it is not always in the public interest to prosecute in respect of it.'[70]

Hirst argues that no offence is committed in these circumstances on the basis that, unless statute provides otherwise, the criminal law has no application outside this country.[71] Nor, Hirst argues, would initial preparations in this country necessarily lead to a prosecution, because arguably[72] assisted suicide is criminal only when the assisted suicide or attempted assisted suicide actually occurs. Consequently, rather than relying on jurisdictional arguments, those travelling abroad to assist a loved one in his suicide should pay heed to the DPP's guidelines about prosecution.[73]

Debbie Purdy was diagnosed with multiple sclerosis in 1995, after which her condition deteriorated. Like Dianne Pretty she was concerned that she would need the support of her husband to travel abroad to an assisted-suicide clinic, in which case he might be prosecuted under section 2(1) of the Suicide Act. Her argument was that the lack of specific guidance on assisted suicide in the Code for Crown Prosecutors breached her right under Article 8 of the ECHR. That lack of clarity prevented her from identifying the facts and circumstances relevant to any future prosecution. The House of Lords, in their final decision before moving to the Supreme Court, overruled the Court of Appeal decision. The House of Lords did not rule whether or not it was lawful to assist another in their suicide by travelling abroad to a suicide clinic, but it did require the DPP to clarify his guidance.[74]

(2014) 18 July. And see S Knapton, 'Nearly a Quarter of Suicide Cases at Dignitas are Brits' *Telegraph* (2015) 20 August.

69 [2004] EWHC 2817 (Fam). See P De Cruz, 'The Terminally Ill Adult Seeking Assisted Suicide Abroad' (2005) 13 *Med Law Rev* 257.

70 *Re Z (An Adult: Capacity)* ibid, [14] per Hedley J.

71 M Hirst, 'Suicide in Switzerland – Complicity in England?' (2009) *Criminal Law Review* 335.

72 There is some doubt following *Smith (Wallace Duncan) (No 4)* [2004] EWCA Crim 631.

73 M Hirst, 'Assisted Suicide after Purdy: The Unresolved Issue' (2009) *Criminal Law Review* 872.

74 For commentary see N Cartwright, '48 Years On: Is the Suicide Act Fit for Purpose?' (2009) 17 *Med Law Rev* 467.

R (Purdy) v DPP[75] has connotations for public law[76] but is also significant in its application of Article 8. Purdy argued that the Article was engaged, as was indicated in the ECtHR decision in *Pretty*. But the lower courts were bound by the House of Lords decision, concluding: 'it is their Lordships who, if they think it appropriate, must release the knot'.[77] The House of Lords acknowledged not only that Article 8(1) was engaged but also that the level of discretion exercised by the DPP was not justified under Article 8(2).[78]

22.8 The DPP's policy for prosecutors

Following a public consultation exercise, the DPP issued a *Code for Crown Prosecutors and the Policy for Prosecutors in respect of Cases of Encouraging or Assisting Suicide*, in February 2010 (updated in 2014). The Code shifts emphasis from the characteristics of the victim, to the motives of the suspect.[79] It encompasses not only those travelling abroad for assisted dying but also those who assist or attempt to assist dying in England and Wales.[80] It imposes a two stage test. For the evidential stage to be satisfied, the prosecution must prove that the victim attempted suicide and the suspect has done an act capable of encouraging or assisting the suicide or attempted suicide of another person. At the public interest stage each case is considered on its merits. The Code lists sixteen factors in favour of prosecution (for example where the victim is under 18; the suspect was not motivated purely by compassion; or the suspect acted in his capacity as a health professional[81]) and six against. The factors tending against prosecution are:

1. the victim had reached a voluntary, clear, settled and informed decision to commit suicide;
2. the suspect was wholly motivated by compassion;
3. the actions of the suspect, although sufficient to come within the definition of the offence, were of only minor encouragement or assistance;
4. the suspect had sought to dissuade the victim from taking the course of action which resulted in his or her suicide;

75 [2009] UKHL 45.

76 R Daw and A Solomon, 'Assisted Suicide and Identifying the Public Interest in the Decision to Prosecute' (2010) *Criminal Law Review* 737.

77 *R (Purdy) v DPP* [2009] EWCA Civ 92, [54].

78 [2009] UKHL 45, [106]: 'Our decision is simply that the article 8 rights of Ms Purdy entitle her to be provided with guidance from the director as to how he proposes to exercise his discretion under section 2(4) of the 1961 Act…', per Lord Neuberger.

79 See R Heywood, 'The DPP's Prosecutorial Policy on Assisted Suicide' (2010) 21 *King's Law Journal* 425. But will it adequately safeguard the 'victim'? See A Mullock, 'Overlooking the Criminally Compassionate: What are the Implications of Prosecutorial Policy on Encouraging or Assisting Suicide?' (2010) 18(4) *Med Law Rev* 442.

80 P Lewis argues that this makes the informal changes brought in by the Code more significant than was originally thought would be the case: 'Informal Legal Change on Assisted Suicide: The Policy for Prosecutors' (2011) 31(1) *Legal Studies* 119.

81 Regarding the latter factor, see 22.10 below.

5. the actions of the suspect may be characterised as reluctant encouragement or assistance in the face of a determined wish on the part of the victim to commit suicide;
6. the suspect reported the victim's suicide to the police and fully assisted them in their enquiries into the circumstances of the suicide or the attempt and his or her part in providing encouragement or assistance.[82]

To date, the guidelines have resulted in a permissive approach. The Crown Prosecution Service (CPS) had the required evidence to prosecute Michael Bateman who helped his wife to die by suicide. She was in chronic pain and had a settled wish to die. Bateman put a plastic bag over her head and assembled helium gas apparatus, but Mrs Bateman tightened the bag and turned on the helium.[83] The CPS concluded that it was not in the public interest to prosecute. Between 2009 and 2021 there were 171 cases referred to the CPS, of which 111 were not proceeded with and 32 were withdrawn by the police. Of those remaining, one was charged and acquitted, three were prosecuted, and eleven are ongoing.[84] The first prosecution since the guidelines were issued was made in 2013. Mr Kevin Howe was found guilty of encouraging or assisting attempted suicide when he intentionally supplied his friend, Mr Walker, with the means by which to set himself on fire. Mr Walker had a mental health condition and had previously attempted suicide. Nineteen-year-old Howe purchased petrol and a lighter, which Mr Walker poured over his head and lit. Walker suffered terrible burns, but miraculously survived.[85]

The permissive nature of the DPP's policy did not receive universal acclamation. Jacqueline Laing questions the constitutionality of the DPP's Code, suggesting that the lenient approach it endorses will gradually alter criminal law without recourse to Parliament.[86] On the other hand, campaigners argue that the reformed Code is not permissive enough.

The matter came before the Supreme Court in 2013. The 'Nicklinson litigation' was in fact a series of claims by three individuals: Tony Nicklinson, Paul Lamb and an individual referred to as 'Martin'. Each wanted his life to end but lacked the ability to bring this about. The Lamb / Nicklinson claim was a bid to change the law to sanction assisted suicide. Martin's claim was an attack on the DPP's guidelines. Let us take them in order.

82 DPP, *Code for Crown Prosecutors and the Policy for Prosecutors in respect of Cases of Encouraging or Assisting Suicide* (2010, updated 2014), para 45.

83 CPS, *Assisted Suicide Charge Not in the Public Interest* (2010) 24 May.

84 CPS, *Latest Assisted Suicide Figures* (2021) 31 July.

85 CPS, *Kevin Howe Convicted of Assisted Attempted Suicide* (2013) 12 September. And see CPS, *One Woman Charged with Encouraging or Assisting Suicide* (2014) 15 September. Howe successfully argued for a reduction in sentence (from twelve years to ten) in *R v Howe* [2014] EWCA Crim 114.

86 J Laing, 'On the Wrong Track' (2010) 154(2) *Solicitor's Journal* 8. The lack of prosecutions predates the DPP's Code and indicates that this phenomenon had been going on for some time. See for example A Mullock, 'Prosecutors Making (Bad) Law? (2009) 17(2) *Med Law Rev* 290, on the DPP's decision regarding the death of Daniel James.

22.9 Challenging the prohibition on assisted suicide in court

Unlike Martin, Tony Nicklinson and Paul Lamb would be physically unable to undertake assisted suicide.[87] After his claim failed in the High Court,[88] Mr Nicklinson refused food and contracted pneumonia. He died six days after the decision. His wife Jane Nicklinson and Paul Lamb, who was paralysed in a road accident, took the case to the Court of Appeal arguing (on the grounds of necessity) that voluntary euthanasia would not be unlawful. The claim was dismissed[89] and they went on to the Supreme Court.[90]

In the Supreme Court, the Nicklinson / Lamb case centred on the alleged incompatibility of the law with Article 8. The first matter was to determine whether the courts have the authority to declare the prohibition on assisted suicide incompatible with Article 8. Lords Neuberger, Wilson, Mance, Kerr and Lady Hale (a majority of five to four) held that it does. Lord Neuberger (President) concluded that:

> [E]ven under our constitutional settlement, which acknowledges parliamentary supremacy and has no written constitution, it is, in principle, open to a domestic court to consider whether section 2 infringes article 8. The more difficult question, to which I now turn, is whether we should do so.[91]

In answer to his question, Lord Neuberger concluded that the timing was not (yet) right:

> In my opinion, before making such a declaration, we should accord Parliament the opportunity of considering whether to amend section 2 so as to enable Applicants, and, quite possibly others, to be assisted in ending their lives.[92]

Lords Clarke, Sumption, Reed and Hughes called for Parliament to address the issue. Lady Hale and Lord Kerr, however, favoured granting a declaration of incompatibility. Lady Hale (dissenting) said:

87 An alternative was postulated by the Supreme Court, but this was not the method preferred by Mr Nicklinson: '[Mr Nicklinson's] preference was for someone to kill him by injecting him with a lethal drug, such as a barbiturate, but, if that was not acceptable, he was prepared to kill himself by means of a machine invented by Philip Nitschke, an Australian doctor. This machine, after being loaded with a lethal drug, could be set up so as to be digitally activated by Mr Nicklinson, using a pass phrase, via an eye blink computer.' *R (Nicklinson and another) v Ministry of Justice (CNK Alliance Ltd and another intervening)*; (*R (AM) v Director of Public Prosecutions and another (CNK Alliance Ltd and another intervening)* [2014] UKSC 38, [4] per Lord Neuberger.

88 *R (Nicklinson) v Ministry of Justice* [2012] EWHC 2381. See J Herring, 'Escaping the Shackles of Law at the End of Life: *R (Nicklinson) v Ministry of Justice* [2012] EWHC 2381 (Admin)' (2013) 21(3) *Med Law Rev* 487; S Michalowski, 'Relying on Common Law Defences to Legalise Assisted Dying: Problems and Possibilities' (2013) 21(3) *Med Law Rev* 337.

89 [2013] EWCA Civ 961.

90 [2014] UKSC 38.

91 Ibid, [76].

92 Ibid, [113].

> Like everyone else, I consider that Parliament is much the preferable forum in which the issue should be decided. Indeed, under our constitutional arrangements, it is the only forum in which a solution can be found which will render our law compatible with the Convention rights. None of us consider that section 2 can be read and given effect, under section 3(1) of the Human Rights Act 1998, in such a way as to remove any incompatibility with the rights of those who seek the assistance of others in order to commit suicide. However, in common with Lord Kerr, I have reached the firm conclusion that our law is not compatible with the Convention rights. Having reached that conclusion, I see little to be gained, and much to be lost, by refraining from making a declaration of incompatibility. Parliament is then free to cure that incompatibility, either by a remedial order under section 10 of the Act or (more probably in a case of this importance and sensitivity) by Act of Parliament, or to do nothing. It may do nothing, either because it does not share our view that the present law is incompatible, or because, as a sovereign Parliament, it considers an incompatible law preferable to any alternative.

By a majority of seven to two the appeal was dismissed. Lord Neuberger offered Parliament the chance to change the law. Lady Hale and Lord Kerr had run out of patience. The subsequent application to the ECtHR in 2015 was ruled inadmissible for non-exhaustion of domestic remedies.[93]

As we shall see, proposals for legislative change in 2003, 2004, 2005, 2009, 2015, 2016 and 2021 led to naught. Lady Hale retired from the Supreme Court in 2019 and Lord Kerr sadly died in 2020. Three new attempts were made to persuade the courts to act. Noel Conway, a 68-year-old man with a form of motor neurone disease, argued that the blanket ban on assisted suicide breached his Article 8 rights. The High Court ruled that the interference was proportionate.[94] His appeal was dismissed[95] and his proposed alternative scheme for assisted suicide, which contained certain conditions and safeguards, including the approval of a High Court judge, was said to raise wide-ranging policy issues that would be more suitably addressed by Parliament.[96]

In a second case, Mr T had Multiple Systems Atrophy and sought assisted suicide in England. His case did not proceed to a full judicial review hearing on the incompatibility of section 2(1) of the Suicide Act with his human rights. Judicial reviews usually focus on the law rather than evidence. Relying on a Canadian case, *Carter v Canada*[97] his argument in a preliminary issue hearing was that it was necessary for the court to hear primary evidence to determine the policy issues surrounding the assessment of proportionality. For example, he wanted to include expert evidence to show that objections to legalising

[93] *Nicklinson and Lamb v UK*, App Nos 2478/15 and 1787/15 (ECHR, 16 July 2015).

[94] *R (Conway) v Secretary of State for Justice* [2017] EWHC 2447.

[95] *R (Conway) v Secretary of State for Justice* [2018] EWCA Civ 1431. Permission to appeal to the Supreme Court was denied.

[96] See C Hobson and N Papadopoulou, 'Regulating Risk and Autonomy in Assisted Suicide: *Conway v Secretary of State for Justice*' (2021) 29(1) *Med Law Rev* 128.

[97] 2015 SCC 5 in which the Supreme Court of Canada in a unanimous decision overturned an absolute ban on assisted dying and gave Parliament a year to create a 'stringently limited, carefully monitored system of exceptions'. (At [29].)

assisted suicide were unfounded and he wanted key witnesses arguing the contrary to be cross-examined. Due to significant overlap, the case was delayed until *Conway* had been heard, by which time his suffering had become too great and he had travelled to Switzerland where he died with assistance. The Court dismissed the application.[98] Whilst Parliament would consider the evidence in a review of the law, it would not be appropriate to hear oral evidence with cross-examination in a judicial review of the assisted suicide policy.[99]

A third case was brought by Phil Newby shortly after Mr T's death. Like Noel Conway, Mr Newby had motor neurone disease. Like Mr T, he requested that primary evidence be allowed. Permission was denied. The Divisional Court was clear that Parliament and not the court is the appropriate forum for debating sanctity of life. The door has been closed on an evidence-based approach to judicial review of the prohibition on assisted dying. Natalie Papadopoulou has argued that an evidence-based inquiry of all the available evidence is needed.[100]

22.10 Prosecution policy on physician-assisted suicide

Returning to the *Nicklinson* litigation, Martin (as he was known for the purpose of the proceedings) suffered a brain stem stroke and had very limited movement. He wanted to travel to Dignitas in Switzerland for assisted suicide, but to do so would require assistance from another. His wife respected his decision to end his life but did not want to play a role in bringing about his death. Like Nicklinson and Lamb, Martin also relied on Article 8, but rather than challenging the compatibility of the Suicide Act with the Convention, his claim focused on the lack of clarity in the DPP's guidelines. If someone who had no personal connection to him – a health professional or carer, for example – decided out of compassion to help him to die, would they be more likely to face prosecution? The lack of clarity, he claimed, was a disproportionate interference with his rights under Article 8(2) of the European Convention.

The DPP's Code distinguishes between loved ones and doctors assisting suicide. One factor in *favour* of prosecution is:

> The suspect was acting in his or her capacity as a medical doctor, nurse, other healthcare professional, ... *and the victim was in his or her care*. [original emphasis][101]

98 *T v Secretary of State for Justice* [2017] EWHC 3181.

99 But see N Papadopoulou and C Hobson, 'The Omid Litigation: Should Courts Hear Oral Evidence when Determining the Proportionality of Section 2(1) of The Suicide Act 1961?' (2021) 30(2) *Med Law Rev* 348.

100 N Papadopoulou, 'Dying with Assistance: The Call for an Inquiry, the Power of a Declaration, the Role of Evidence' (2021) 31(1) *Med Law Rev* 81.

101 DPP, *Code for Crown Prosecutors and the Policy for Prosecutors in respect of Cases of Encouraging or Assisting Suicide* (2010, updated 2014), para 43.14 (emphasis, underlined, in original). See 22.8 above. The BMA have issues guidance advising doctors how to handle patients who make requests relating to assisted suicide: BMA, *Responding to Patient Requests Relating to Assisted*

Whether this component of the policy was designed to target doctors who use undue influence to persuade a patient to access assisted suicide or also to incorporate doctors whose involvement in the final stages of illness is entirely motivated by compassion was initially unclear. The GMC attempted to fill the lacuna, issuing guidance in 2013 stating:

> Where patients raise the issue of assisting suicide, or ask for information that might encourage or assist them in ending their lives, doctors should be prepared to listen and to discuss the reasons for the patient's request but they must not actively encourage or assist the patient as this would be a contravention of the law. Any advice or information they give about suicide should be limited to an explanation that it is a criminal offence for them to encourage or assist a person to commit or attempt suicide.[102]

The GMC's approach is highly restrictive. Is this what the DPP intended? Martin's challenge was unsuccessful in the High Court, but in a two-to-one Court of Appeal judgment it was held:

> In our view, the Policy should give some indication of the weight that the DPP accords to the fact that the helper was acting in his or her capacity as a healthcare professional and the victim was in his or her care.[103]

Martin's success was short-lived. On appeal, the Supreme Court unanimously allowed the DPP's appeal. It was not, the Court held, for judges to dictate matters of policy.

Nonetheless, in 2014 the DPP amended the policy, emphasising that the factor for prosecution will apply only where the doctor has exerted influence on the 'victim'.[104] Those who act out of compassion are unlikely to face prosecution. In light of this policy change, Martin launched a bid to require the GMC to follow suit and amend its guidance.[105] Martin's application for judicial review sought to ensure that doctors assisting those in his position would

Suicide: Guidance for Doctors in England, Wales and Northern Ireland (February 2015) (updated 2021).

102 GMC, *Guidance for the Investigation Committee and Case Examiners when Considering Allegations about a Doctor's Involvement in Encouraging or Assisting Suicide* (2013), para 10. And see GMC, *When a Patient Seeks Advice or Information about Assistance to Die* (2013).

103 *R (AM) v Director of Public Prosecutions and another (CNK Alliance Ltd and another intervening)* [2013] EWCA Civ 961, [140] per Elias LJ.

104 DPP, *Code for Crown Prosecutors and the Policy for Prosecutors in respect of Cases of Encouraging or Assisting Suicide* (2010, updated 2014), para 43.14. The 2014 update includes a footnote that reads: 'For the avoidance of doubt the words 'and the victim was in his or her care' qualify all of the preceding parts of this paragraph. This factor does not apply merely because someone was acting in a [professional] capacity described within it: it applies only where there was, in addition, a relationship of care between the suspect and the victims such that it will be necessary to consider whether the suspect may have exerted some influence on the victim.'

105 See C Dyer, 'Man with Locked-in Syndrome Challenges GMC Ruling on Doctors' Involvement in Ending his Life' (2015) 350 *BMJ* h3524.

not face disciplinary action. In *R (AM) v The General Medical Council*[106] the court found that the GMC's guidance did not breach Articles 8 or 10 of the Convention and neither was the GMC required to ensure that its guidance is in line with the DPP's. A subsequent challenge to the lawfulness of the DPP's policy was rejected in 2015.[107]

Should patients be able to turn to their doctor for help? To have adopted a permissive approach to physician-assisted suicide might have been hailed a radical (and unconstitutional) change in law. Doctors are primarily concerned with preserving life. Though in 2005, the British Medical Association (BMA) adopted a position of neutrality, the BMA reverted to opposition from 2006, and back to neutrality in 2021.[108] The Royal College of Nurses also moved to a position of neutrality in 2009 as did the Royal College of Physicians in 2019. Neutrality does not signal support for a change in law. The matter is finely balanced and nuanced. A BMA survey in 2020[109] indicated that 50 per cent of doctors surveyed would support a change in the law on prescribing drugs for eligible patients to *self-administer* to end their own life, whilst only 30 per cent would support a change in the law on *doctors* administering drugs with the intention of ending an eligible patient's life. What are the options for legislative reform?

22.11 The assisted dying debate[110]

English law is imprecise and uncertain. Doctors cannot always be given clear advice about the legality of various procedures. Is this fair to the medical profession? Is it right that some doctors, even acting with the best of motives, may under a screen of silence do things which they believe may be unlawful? There is some evidence that doctors practise covert euthanasia.[111] If what is taking place in medical practice is acceptable to society, it is argued that the law should be changed to set out clearly the parameters within which they should be acting. If society disapproves of certain procedures, how can they be

106 [2015] EWHC 2096 (Admin).

107 See *R (Kenward) v DPP* [2015] EWHC 3508 (Admin).

108 BMA, 'The BMA's Position on Physician-Assisted Dying' (2021) September. Note the World Medical Association Declaration on Euthanasia and Physician-Assisted Suicide (2019) is 'firmly opposed to euthanasia and physician-assisted suicide'.

109 BMA, 'Physician-Assisted Dying Survey' (2020) 8 October.

110 For an excellent examination of pro-euthanasia, anti-euthanasia and compromise positions (respectively) see A Alghrani, R Bennett and S Ost (eds), *The Criminal Law and Bioethical Conflict: Walking the Tightrope Volume 1* (2012) Cambridge University Press: J Griffiths 'Euthanasia and Assisted Suicide Should, When Properly Performed by a Doctor in an Appropriate Case, Be Decriminalised', pp 15–29; J Keown, 'Five Flawed Arguments for Decriminalising Euthanasia', pp 30–48 and R Huxtable, 'Euthanasia Excused: Between Prohibition and Permission', pp 49–68. And see E Jackson and J Keown, *Debating Euthanasia* (2011) Hart: a debate in which E Jackson argues for and J Keown argues against legalising euthanasia.

111 See RS Magnusson, 'Above Ground, Below Ground' (2004) 30 *J Med Ethics* 441; S Ost, *An Analytical Study of the Legal, Moral and Ethical Aspects of the Living Phenomenon of Euthanasia* (2003) Edwin Mellor Press; J Keown, *Euthanasia, Ethics and Public Policy* (2002) Cambridge University Press.

controlled? Is it right, again, for the law to be left obscure, yet that when clear evidence of euthanasia occurs prosecutors may elect not to enforce the law? On the other hand, there are those who oppose legislation on the grounds that the current fudge allows for maximum flexibility for a caring medical profession.

Once any proposal to clarify the current fudge surfaces, opinions polarise sharply. As Kennedy and Grubb note, 'whenever the topic of voluntary euthanasia is broached, rational argument becomes an early casualty'.[112] The case for voluntary euthanasia is deceptively simple. It rests on the principle of autonomy. The individual is the 'final determinant of his or her destiny'.[113] We enjoy the right to control our death just as we enjoy the right to control our lives. Moreover, dignity and welfare, it is contended, impel us to allow the individual the right to end an intolerable life. A compassionate society should not force people dying, or living, with pain and disability, to continue to live. The patient in the terminal stages of motor neurone disease should not be compelled to suffer all the consequences of a drawn-out death. Human rights are invoked in support of the pro-euthanasia case. Article 3 prohibits inhuman and degrading treatment. Does the absence of an assisted dying option in effect impose such degrading treatment? Article 8 protects our private and family lives. Do laws preventing my doctor, or indeed my husband, from helping me to end an intolerable life violate my privacy? We have seen that the Supreme Court decision in *Nicklinson* heralded renewed interest in the relevance of Article 8.

Those opposed to legislation permitting physician-assisted suicide and voluntary euthanasia advance several objections. For many, though not all, opponents of euthanasia, central to their opposition to euthanasia is their commitment to the doctrine of sanctity of life.[114] But other concerns are voiced. Just how voluntary would such euthanasia be? Would the introduction of such laws result in a change of attitude by society towards the sanctity of life generally, towards the elderly, infirm, and the mortally sick? Would the existence of such laws impose pressures upon elderly and terminally ill patients to seek euthanasia, rather than remain a burden on relatives or on society? Would the existence of such legislation provide opportunities for fraud and abuse, and undermine the relationship of trust between doctor and patient? How easy would it be to apply such a law?

Let us examine what kind of form legislation might take. It seems increasingly likely that any reform would centre on human rights rather than the criminal law. Two rather different sorts of laws might be envisaged – both of which have models in other jurisdictions.[115] Legislation could sanction physician-assisted

112 Kennedy and Grubb, *Medical Law: Text and Materials* (2000) Butterworths, p 1997.

113 See M Otlowski, *Voluntary Euthanasia and the Common Law* (1997) Oxford University Press, p 189.

114 See L Gormally (ed), *Euthanasia, Clinical Practice and the Law* (1994) The Linacre Centre. And see 4.10–4.13 above.

115 The number of comparators has grown significantly in recent years. Direct comparisons are difficult given variation in political and cultural contexts: see S Blouin and M Pott, 'Assistance in Dying: Conditions for International Comparison' 46(7)

dying (as is the case in the States of Oregon, Vermont and Washington, USA, for example) or could allow voluntary active euthanasia (as is the case in the Netherlands and Belgium).

22.12 Legislating to allow assisted suicide

A growing number of countries allow assisted suicide, including various US states, Switzerland since 1942, Victoria Australia since 2017, Canada since 2021, Austria since 2022 and – in a first for the British Isles and Channel Islands – potentially soon to be Jersey. The Oregon Death with Dignity Act 1994 came into force in 1997 and has been an influential model. It applies only to adults who have been diagnosed as terminally ill. A prescription for oral medication is the only assistance sanctioned. Direct assistance with suicide is prohibited.[116] The Washington State Death with Dignity Act 2009 allows terminally ill adults with less than six months to live to ask their doctors for a life-ending prescription. Vermont's Patient Choice and Control at End of Life Act 2013 provides criminal, civil and professional protections for doctors who prescribe life-ending medication to capacitous, terminally ill patients.[117]

Many attempts have been made to form proposals that would find favour in England and Wales. Lord Joffe's Patient (Assisted Dying) Bill 2003 was modelled on the Oregon Act but incorporated voluntary euthanasia for those physically incapable of taking the final steps to end their life. It did not progress beyond a Second Reading. His ill-fated Assisted Dying for the Terminally Ill Bill 2004 ran out of time. The Select Committee on the Assisted Dying for the Terminally Ill Bill reported in April 2005.[118] Nine recommendations were made for any future bills, including (*inter alia*):

- a clearer delineation between euthanasia and physician-assisted suicide;
- a statement of the actions which a doctor may or may not take in providing assisted suicide or administering voluntary euthanasia;
- a clinical definition of terminal illness (if terminal illness is a qualifying condition);
- a definition of mental competence so as to differentiate between applicants lacking mental capacity and those suffering a mental disorder.[119]

(2021) *Death Studies* 1541. But see N Davis, 'Euthanasia and Assisted Dying Rates are Soaring. But where are they Legal?' *Guardian* (2019) 15 July.

116 Upheld by the US Supreme Court in *Gonzales v Oregon* (04-623) 546 US 243 (2006).

117 A 5:2 decision in *Baxter v Montana* No DA 09-0051 (Montana Supreme Court, 2009) upholds the right to die for competent, terminally ill patients in the state of Montana.

118 HL Paper 86.

119 Ibid, para 269(c).

Lord Joffe accepted four of the nine recommendations when introducing his third Bill in 2005. It was outvoted in the House of Lords by 148 to 100.[120] Lord Falconer's Assisted Dying Bill 2013[121] was shaped by the findings of the Commission on Assisted Dying.[122] It aimed to allow competent terminally ill adults with a life expectancy of up to six months to self-administer (by swallowing medication or activating a syringe driver) medication that will end their lives. The Bill included a conscientious objection clause[123] and legislation would be accompanied by a Code of Practice. It focused on terminal illness and excluded from its remit those in the position of Nicklinson and Lamb. Thus, Alexandra Mullock warned that it would not resolve the tensions between their position and Article 8 of the European Convention.[124] In any event, the Bill ran out of time in 2015. It was introduced again in 2015[125] but did not have government backing and so failed to make it to the statute book. In 2016, Lord Hayward introduced another Assisted Dying Bill, which was prorogued and did not get beyond the first reading in the House of Lords. Baroness Meacher's Assisted Dying Bill 2021–22 was the first such Bill in seven years to reach the Committee Stage in the House of Lords. It sought to allow adults who were terminally ill to request assistance to end their own life, provided they could satisfy the High Court that their decision was capacitous and consensual. It ran out of time in 2022. Change in the UK might come from Scotland where the Terminally Ill Adults (Scotland) Bill was proposed in 2022 following a consultation.[126] It would allow people who have lived in Scotland for at least a year[127] to access medication to take their own lives, subject to two doctors finding that safeguards have been met and that the person has mental capacity. This is the third attempt to change the law in Scotland,[128] and has attracted significant public commentary.

A consistent problem is the discomfort many feel with doctors taking a role in assisted suicide. Not only does it potentially raise conflicts of interest, but it can impact on conscience and public trust. Lucy Thomas has called for demedicalisation that would separate doctors from decisions relating to both

120 See J Keown, 'Physician-Assisted Suicide: Lord Joffe's Slippery Bill' (2007) 15(1) *Med Law Rev* 126.

121 See A Mullock, 'The Assisted Dying Bill and the Role of the Physician' (2015) 41 *J Med Ethics* 621.

122 Commission on Assisted Dying, *The Current Legal Status of Assisted Dying is Inadequate and Incoherent…* (2012) Demos.

123 For a discussion of conscientious objection in relation to assisted dying see R Huxtable and A Mullock, 'Voices of Discontent? Conscience, Compromise and Assisted Dying' (2015) 23(2) *Med Law Rev* 242.

124 A Mullock, 'The Supreme Court Decision in Nicklinson: Human Rights, Criminal Wrongs and the Dilemma of Death' (2015) 31(1) *Professional Negligence* 18, at 28.

125 Assisted Dying Bill (No 2) 2015–16, introduced by Rob Marris MP.

126 Liam McArthur MSP, *Consultation: Assisted Dying for Terminally Ill Adults (Scotland) Bill* (2021) 22 September.

127 So avoiding the potential for 'death tourism' explored at 22.7 above.

128 End of Life Assistance (Scotland) Bill 2010; Assisted Suicide (Scotland) Bill 2013.

patient eligibility and the administration of medication. Neither, she claims, are 'straightforward medical solutions to a medical problem'.[129] But on the other hand, the trust we place in doctors and their compassion at the end of life are what make the case for their assistance so compelling for those patients who seek a greater degree of control over their deaths.

22.13 Active euthanasia

Meyers and Mason[130] envisaged the doctor 'providing or *administering* a lethal dose of medication'. Yet, surely a lethal injection performed by the doctor must be killing and not simply assisting a suicide? Do we have to resort to complex mechanical devices whereby the doctor sets up a machine to inject the patient with a lethal dose and somehow (maybe via a computer) triggers the mechanism delivering the injection? The line between assisted dying and killing becomes as fragile as the artificiality of the current law. In *Pretty*, Lord Bingham exposed the dilemma:

> If article 2 does confer a right of self-determination in relation to life and death, and if a person were so gravely disabled as to be unable to perform any act whatsoever to cause his or her own death, it would necessarily follow in logic that such a person would have a right to be killed at the hands of a third party ...[131]

Several countries allow both assisted suicide and euthanasia, including the Netherlands, Belgium,[132] Luxembourg, Canada, Colombia and, recently, Spain. In the Netherlands, an informal agreement between the prosecution authorities and the medical profession allowed active euthanasia for several years. The *Postma*[133] case was the first in a series of rulings easing restrictions on euthanasia. Dr Postma gave his disabled mother, who had previously attempted suicide and no longer wanted to live, a fatal dose of morphine. The court imposed a suspended sentence of one week imprisonment and indicated that euthanasia might be acceptable provided that the patient was incurably ill, was suffering unbearably, had requested assisted suicide, and that the act was performed by the patient's own doctor or in consultation with her. Nine years later, the prosecution authorities agreed not to prosecute any doctor who ended his patient's life within the parameters set by agreed guidelines.[134] The patient must have freely requested 'help in dying' and the physician must assure themselves that that request is truly voluntary and well considered. The patient and their doctor must be satisfied that there are no other means of

129 HL Thomas, 'Demedicalisation: Radically Reframing the Assisted Dying Debate' (2020) 371 *BMJ* m2919.

130 (1999) 29 *Anglo-American Law Review* 39.

131 *R (Pretty) v DPP* [2002] 1 All ER 1, at 6–7, HL.

132 However, see the recent case of *Mortier v Belgium*, App No 78017/17 (ECHR, 4 Oct 2022), which concerned a partially successful challenge under Article 2 to the procedural aspects of the law in Belgium.

133 *Nederlandse Jurisprudentie* 1973 No 183 District Court of Leeuwarden, 21 February.

134 *Wertheim, Nederlandse Jurisprudentie* 1982 No 63, Rotterdam Criminal Court.

relieving the patient's suffering or other incurable condition. A second doctor must be consulted. Until 2000, euthanasia remained formally unlawful in the Netherlands. Legislation to give legal effect to the earlier informal arrangements came into force in 2002.[135]

The impact of Dutch practice and laws is much debated. Opponents argue[136] (*inter alia*) that (1) the incidence of active euthanasia is under-reported; (2) there is evidence of termination of life without an explicit request from the patient (in perhaps as many as one in five cases); (3) withdrawal of treatment with minimal safeguards is common; and (4) depressed and mentally disturbed patients are helped to die.[137] The nub of the case is that what is supposed to be a limited provision to allow free and informed choices by competent patients to end their lives has become a convenient means of disposing of the elderly and grievously sick. Supporters, equally passionately, refute these allegations. Dispassionate analysis of how voluntary euthanasia 'works' in the Netherlands is hard to find.

The first Euthanasia Bill in this country was introduced into Parliament in 1936. The Bill was quickly rejected. Another Voluntary Euthanasia Bill, introduced in 1969, was designed to allow a patient or prospective patient to sign in advance a declaration requesting the administration of euthanasia if they were believed to be suffering from a fatal illness or were incapable of rational existence. Again, the Bill failed. The *coup de grâce* was applied with the following comment:

> Such a Bill is medically unnecessary, psychologically dangerous and ethically wrong. Unnecessary, because legal rigidity should not be substituted for medical discretion. Dangerous, because this Bill would diminish the respect for life, blurring the line between crime and medicine. Ethically wrong, because it infringes on the absolute value of life.

Subsequent Bills in the mid-1970s were more modest and attempted to avoid being seen as attempts to legalise euthanasia or 'mercy killing'. In the wake of the decision in *Bland*, the House of Lords set up a Select Committee on Medical Ethics[138] to investigate legal, ethical and social issues surrounding treatment decisions at the end of life. The Committee endorsed the judges' ruling in *Bland*, commended, but refused to endorse legislation to give effect to,

135 Termination of Life on Request and Assisted Suicide (Review Procedures) Act 2000. Discussed in J de Haan, 'The New Dutch Law on Euthanasia' (2002) 10 *Med Law Rev* 57.

136 See J Keown, 'The Law and Practice of Euthanasia in the Netherlands' (1992) 108 *LQR* 51; H Jochenson and J Keown, 'Voluntary Euthanasia under Control? Further Empirical Evidence from the Netherlands' (1999) 25 *J Med Ethics* 16.

137 A Netherlands doctor was acquitted in 2019, having sedated and administered a lethal drug to an Alzheimer's patient: D Boffey, 'Dutch Doctor Acquitted in Landmark Euthanasia Case' *Guardian* (2019) 11 September; and three Belgian doctors were acquitted of murder following administration of a lethal injection: M Nanu, 'Doctors Cleared in Landmark Euthanasia Trial of Women' *Independent* (2020) 31 January.

138 *Report of the Select Committee on Medical Ethics*, 1993–4, HL 21.

advance decisions, and in total delivered a Report of almost amazing banality. Their recommendations in effect were no change and leave such difficult questions to the doctors. The Report came out firmly against legalising voluntary euthanasia. Their Lordships considered that argument based on autonomy, the right to choose to die, constituted 'insufficient reason to weaken society's prohibition on intentional killing'. It was not, in their view, possible to set secure limits in voluntary euthanasia, and vulnerable people might be pressured into requesting early death. Moreover, there was good evidence that palliative care could relieve pain and distress in the majority of cases. The debate intensifies. It does not seem to move on.[139]

22.14 The unconscious patient[140]

The patient who retains mental capacity can thus refuse further treatment to bring an end to their life but active euthanasia is contrary to the law. What of the fate of the patient whose illness or injury has rendered them unconscious and unlikely ever to regain consciousness? What test should be employed to determine the appropriate course of action? Two tests were examined in Chapter 7: the substituted judgement test[141] and the best interests test. English law has rejected a test whereby the next of kin should automatically enjoy proxy powers of consent. Instead, the Mental Capacity Act 2005 embraces a best interests test. The Act introduced important changes in practice. The Court of Protection can appoint a 'deputy' to act for the patient. Alternatively, the patient themselves can, whilst competent, appoint a donee of a Lasting Power of Attorney (LPA) to make certain decisions on their behalf if, or when, they lose capacity to decide. They may also make an advance decisions refusing treatment. Decisions of the LPA and the relevance and applicability of advance decisions are subject to stringent controls.[142] The best interest test in the Act adopted earlier case-law. As we shall see, the best interests test involves a careful balancing of the sanctity of life, the quality of life and the individual's rights and interests in dignity and autonomy.[143]

22.15 *Bland*: crossing the Rubicon?[144]

At the age of 17, Anthony Bland suffered crush injuries at Hillsborough football stadium. He suffered catastrophic and irreversible damage to his brain.

139 S Holm, 'The Debate about Physician Assistance in Dying: 40 Years of Unrivalled Progress in Medical Ethics?' (2015) 41(1) *J Med Ethics* 40.

140 See Parliamentary Office of Science and Technology, *Postnote: Vegetative and Minimally Conscious States*, No 498 (March 2015).

141 See discussion of *In re Quinlan* (1976) 355 A 2d 647 at 7.5 above.

142 See 22.18 below.

143 The law is supplemented with professional guidance. See BMA and RCP, *Clinically-Assisted Nutrition and Hydration (CANH) and Adults who Lack the Capacity to Consent* (2018); GMC, *Treatment and Care Towards the End of Life*.

144 *Airedale NHS Trust v Bland* [1993] 1 All ER 821, HL.

The condition from which he suffered was known as a persistent vegetative state (PVS).[145] He had lost all cortical (higher brain) function, but his brain stem continued to function. PVS patients continue to breathe independently and their digestion can continue to function. Tony Bland was incapable of voluntary movement and could feel no pain. He could not see, hear, taste or smell.[146] He remained alive, fed through a tube. All his excretory functions were managed mechanically. Doctors were agreed that there was no hope of recovery of any sort. In this condition, the young man existed for two years until, with the concurrence of his family, the hospital applied for a declaration that they might lawfully discontinue artificial nutrition and hydration. The House of Lords unanimously granted that declaration.

We have seen[147] how their Lordships managed to find that withdrawing the naso-gastric tube was not an act hastening death such as to expose doctors to liability for murder. Tony Bland, however, could not instruct his doctors to cease treatment. The Law Lords fell back on *F v West Berkshire Health Authority*.[148] When a patient was incapable of deciding whether to continue treatment for himself, what could lawfully be done to him depended on what constituted treatment in his best interests and in conformity to responsible medical practice. For Lords Goff, Keith and Lowry, the evidence of medical opinion and professional guidelines on diagnosis and confirmation of PVS assisted them to conclude that, as Tony Bland received no benefit from treatment, it was not in his best interests to continue naso-gastric feeding. They reasoned – the regime of artificial feeding constitutes treatment, an overwhelming body of medical opinion supported withdrawing artificial nutrition and hydration from patients confirmed in PVS.[149] Therefore withdrawing 'treatment' was lawful.

Lord Mustill acknowledged[150] the complexity of best interests in this context. Tony Bland was not suffering; he felt no pain.

> By ending his life the doctors will not relieve him of a burden become intolerable, for others carry the burden and he has none. What other considerations could make it better for him to die now rather than later? None that we can measure, for of death we know nothing. The distressing truth which must not be shirked, is that the proposed conduct is not in the best interests of Anthony Bland, for he has no best interests of any kind.

Lord Mustill turned traditional analyses of best interests on their heads. He looked at the justification for what was being done to Tony Bland's body; the tubes feeding him, the tubes excreting his waste. Absent evidence that such invasive treatments were necessary to promote his best interests, they were

145 Since *Bland* the terminology has changed, as we explore below.
146 This incontrovertible physical evidence and irreparable damage to the brain distinguishes *Bland* from some subsequent cases.
147 At 22.1 above.
148 [1989] 2 All ER 545, discussed fully at 7.6 above.
149 The Royal College of Physicians offers clinical guidance: RCP, *Supporting People who have Eating and Drinking Difficulties* (2021).
150 [1993] 1 All ER 821, at 894, HL.

themselves unlawful, a trespass on the youth's unconscious body. Thus, treatment not in his interests could and must be withdrawn. *Bland* is a difficult case. No one could fail to sympathise with a family whose child was breathing, but effectively a 'living corpse'. Yet where does *Bland* lead?[151] Can something as basic as feeding be withheld to bring about death? Would this mean staff caring for a patient in advanced stages of dementia who could swallow, but did not demand food, could stop spoon-feeding?

The Law Lords saw the dangers of their decision. They advised that before treatment was discontinued, a declaration should be sought from the courts. They warned that their ruling covered only patients in PVS. They sought to restrain any slide down slippery slopes. Withdrawal of artificial nutrition and hydration required evidence that: (1) every effort should have been made to provide rehabilitation for at least six months; (2) diagnosis of irreversible PVS should not be considered confirmed until at least twelve months after the injury; (3) diagnosis should be agreed by two independent doctors; and (4) generally the views of the patient's immediate family will be given great weight.[152]

Bland is a limited and cautious decision. Even on its own facts it provokes numerous questions. The experts who gave evidence in *Bland* expressed total confidence in medical ability to judge that a patient was irreversibly in PVS, but there are limits to diagnostic accuracy. The legerdemain by which their Lordships classified removal of a feeding tube as an omission not an act provokes charges of covert legalisation of euthanasia.[153] Lord Mustill[154] recognised that it is difficult to find any moral difference between inaction resulting in a slow death and action resulting in a swift one. Can the legal distinction be maintained?[155] If it is a matter of policy rather than legal principle, then should the mantra of sanctity of life be swapped for that of quality of life and euthanasia legalised?[156] If Tony Bland's life was sacred, for itself, not its quality, how can withholding basic food and water be acceptable?

22.16 After *Bland*: PVS to 'near PVS'

Bland has led to radical change in the law governing the ending of life. The carefully constituted limitations built into *Bland* to keep that decision within bounds were eroded step by step. In *Frenchay Healthcare NHS Trust v S*,[157] the patient was said to have been in PVS for two and a half years following a drug overdose. His feeding tube was accidentally disconnected. The

151 For critical appraisal of *Bland* see JM Finnis, 'Bland: Crossing the Rubicon?' (1993) 109 *LQR* 329; J Keown, 'Restoring Moral and Intellectual Shape to the Law after *Bland*' (1997) 113 *LQR* 481.

152 And see BMA, *Withholding and Withdrawing Life-Prolonging Medical Treatment*.

153 See the incisive arguments of Finnis, 'Bland: Crossing the Rubicon?' and Keown, 'Restoring Moral and Intellectual Shape to the Law after *Bland*'.

154 [1993] AC 789, at 885, HL.

155 See L Doyal, 'Dignity in Dying Should Include the Legalization of Non-Voluntary Euthanasia' (2006) 1(2) *Clinical Ethics* 65.

156 See P Singer, *Rethinking Life and Death* (1994) Oxford University Press, p 75.

157 [1994] 2 All ER 403.

hospital immediately sought a declaration that it could lawfully refrain from re-inserting the tube. The Court of Appeal granted the declaration in haste and without any independent medical opinion confirming that S was irreversibly in PVS. The court recognised that the evidence as to S's condition was neither as unanimous nor as emphatic as in *Bland*. The judges found that in the emergency which had arisen because of the disconnection of the tube, there was no benefit conferred on S by re-inserting the tube. Indeed, following Lord Browne-Wilkinson's reasoning in *Bland*, it might be construed as an assault on S to do so. In these circumstances, the further inquiry necessary to take an independent medical opinion could be dispensed with. A fortuitous event affected the criteria set out in *Bland* to protect patients. On the facts of S, some doubt exists whether S was truly in PVS. There was evidence of restlessness and distress for which S was receiving medication.[158] Condition 3 set by Lord Goff in *Bland*, independent evidence confirming PVS, survived barely a year.

Subsequent decisions eroded the *Bland* limitations yet further. In *Re D*,[159] the patient had suffered serious brain damage after a road accident. As in *Frenchay*, her feeding tube became disconnected. Stephen Brown P accepted evidence that D's condition did not fully conform to guidelines for diagnosis of PVS laid down by the Royal College of Physicians (RCP). He was satisfied that there was 'no evidence of any meaningful life whatsoever' and held that it was lawful to refrain from re-inserting the tube. In *Re H*[160] a 43-year-old woman had suffered brain injuries in a car crash. She retained some rudimentary awareness and, like D, did not fit squarely within the RCP definition of PVS. The President of the Family Division approved cessation of artificial feeding. He was 'satisfied that it is in the best interests of this patient that the life sustaining treatment currently being artificially administered should be brought to a conclusion'.[161]

Another lesson which may be drawn from post *Bland* cases on PVS, or near PVS, is that PVS cases are no longer 'special'. Nor is withdrawal of feeding seen as much more of a dilemma than withdrawal of any other form of treatment, such as dialysis.[162] Best interests is a phrase easy to utter and difficult to interpret. It inevitably involves judgements of quality of life. In *W Healthcare NHS Trust v H*,[163] the feeding tube of KH, a 59-year-old woman with multiple sclerosis, fell out. KH was conscious but lacked the capacity to make her own decisions. She recognised nobody, had difficulty swallowing and had required a feeding tube for the past five years. The family opposed the carers' wish to replace the tube. In the absence of a valid advance decision, the court held that it was in KH's best interests for the tube to be reinserted: Death by starvation would be even less dignified than the death she would face if the feeding tube

158 See J Stone, 'Withholding of Life-Sustaining Treatment' (1995) *NLJ* 354.
159 *Re D (Medical Treatment)* [1998] FLR 411.
160 *Re H (A Patient)* [1998] 2 FLR 36.
161 [1998] 2 FLR 36, at 41.
162 For example, *Re D (Medical Treatment: Mentally Disabled Patient)* [1998] 2 FLR 22.
163 [2004] EWCA Civ 1324.

was reinserted.[164] Whether judges like it or not, the effect of the long series of judicial decisions relating to withdrawal of treatment is that judges are making life or death decisions.[165] Furthermore, as more cases are determined in the healthcare setting,[166] this role is transferred to health professionals. The Royal College of Physicians and the BMA produced guidance on clinically assisted nutrition and hydration in 2018 to help health professionals make legally and ethically sound decisions.[167]

22.17 Changing terminology: 'Prolonged Disorders of Consciousness'

The law has struggled to keep up with advancing medical understandings of consciousness. The terminology has moved on since *Bland*. A 'minimally conscious state',[168] unlike a 'vegetative state', is characterised by evidence of awareness of self or environment. As Baker J has pointed out, 'there is a spectrum of minimal consciousness extending from patients who are only just above the vegetative state to those who are bordering on full consciousness'.[169] The term 'prolonged disorders of consciousness' is now used to capture those in a coma or in a vegetative or minimally conscious state.[170]

Though some of the cases in the preceding section may well have featured patients in a minimally conscious state, the first application to a court to withhold artificial nutrition and hydration from a patient diagnosed as being in a minimally conscious state was *W v M and others*.[171] Refusing the application, Baker J in the Court of Protection distinguished vegetative state (in which case, 'the balance falls in one direction in every case – in favour of withdrawal'[172]) from minimally conscious state. In cases falling into the latter category, best interests are assessed by the 'balance sheet' approach.[173] On the facts before them, the court ruled in favour of preserving life. Whilst the 'do not attempt CPR' notice should continue, assisted nutrition and hydration should be maintained.

164 [2004] EWCA Civ 1324 per Brooke LJ, [22] and [27].

165 A series of cases involving the withdrawal of treatment from children is examined above in Chapter 17, 17.6–17.12.

166 See discussion of *NHS Trust v Y* [2018] UKSC 46, 22.20 below.

167 RCP/BMA, *Clinically-Assisted Nutrition and Hydration (CANH) and Adults Who Lack the Capacity to Consent* (2018).

168 See R Heywood, 'Moving on from *Bland*: The Evolution of the Law and Minimally Conscious Patients' (2014) 22(4) *Med Law Rev* 548.

169 *W v M and others* [2011] EWHC 2443, [46].

170 See NHS Website at www.nhs.uk/conditions/disorders-of-consciousness/: 'A disorder of consciousness, or impaired consciousness, is a state where consciousness has been affected by damage to the brain.'

171 [2011] EWHC 2443, [56] per Baker J.

172 Ibid, [35] per Baker J.

173 See A Mullock, 'Deciding the Fate of a Minimally Conscious Patient: An Unsatisfactory Balancing Act?: *W v M and Others [2011] EWHC 2443 (Fam)*' (2012) 20(3) *Med Law Rev* 460 for discussion of the tensions that arise between the balance sheet approach and the Mental Capacity Act requirement to respect to the patient's previously expressed wishes.

Rigorous collection of evidence is necessary to establish an accurate diagnosis. In *St George's Healthcare NHS Trust v P and Q*[174] family members took video recordings to dispute the hospital's contention that the patient was in a vegetative state. Newton J, holding that withdrawal of renal replacement therapy would not be in the patient's best interests, cautioned:

> [T]hose video recordings provided a watershed insight to the proper conclusion in this case. ... [B]ut for [the family's] persistence, ... I could have so easily concluded on inadequate evidence, as it transpired, a conclusion that would have led to P's demise.[175]

The courts will not, however, require doctors to administer futile treatment. In *An NHS Foundation Trust v VT*,[176] VT, who had previously suffered a stroke, was admitted to hospital after suffering a cardiac arrest. He was without oxygen for around seventeen minutes and meaningful recovery was unlikely. The Trust sought a declaration that it would be unlawful to resuscitate VT (other than by bag and mask) or to provide intensive care. The family disagreed:

> If CPR would, they say, cause further brain damage and distress but, nonetheless, their father survives it, that, they believe, is the will of Allah. Moreover, to deprive their father of the opportunity to suffer is to deprive him of the chance to purify his soul in preparedness for death. These are the strongly held views of this family.[177]

Intensive care is intended to be restorative but the evidence was that, at best, such care would preserve VT's minimally conscious state. Hayden J concluded that 'these interventions are wholly contrary to the central medical objectives of intensive care'.[178] There was no justifiable medical reason for cardio-pulmonary resuscitation (CPR) or intensive care and the declaration was granted.

The question of how to gauge when treatment of a patient in a minimally conscious state is futile was raised in the case of *Aintree University Hospitals NHS Foundation Trust v James*.[179] In this important case, the Supreme Court considered for the first time the best interests of a patient in a minimally ('or very limited'[180]) conscious state under the Mental Capacity Act framework. Lady Hale gave the sole judgment with which the other Supreme Court Justices agreed.

David James was admitted to hospital in 2012. Recurring infections led to a gradual deterioration in his condition. He was fed and hydrated through a naso-gastric tube. The Trust applied for a declaration that three specific treatments (*not* including assisted ventilation or nutrition and hydration) should be withheld. The treatments included CPR, invasive procedures and renal replacement therapy. The clinical team felt that such treatments were not in Mr James's best interests. The family disagreed. The declarations were refused

174 [2015] EWCOP 42.
175 Ibid, [7].
176 [2013] EWHC B26 (Fam).
177 Ibid, [20] per Hayden J.
178 Ibid, [19].
179 [2013] UKSC 67.
180 Ibid, [6] per Lady Hale.

at first instance but granted by the Court of Appeal. Lady Hale in the Supreme Court disagreed with the *reasoning* of the Court of Appeal but granted the declarations on the basis of a change in facts – Mr James's condition had deteriorated. Lady Hale upheld the principles applied in the first instance decision. These include: recognition that best interests incorporate the patient's welfare in the widest sense; and the assertion that treatment is not futile if it brings benefit to the patient, even if that benefit does not extend to impacting on the underlying medical problem.[181] Pointing out the limited nature of the guidance provided by section 4 of Mental Capacity Act,[182] Lady Hale reiterated the common law presumption that it is in the person's best interests to stay alive.[183] We would agree with Shaun Pattinson's assertion that it is a weakness of section 4 that the presumption is not explicitly stated.[184] Lady Hale also pointed to the limits of the court's powers with regard to best interests decision-making. Because the court can do no more than a patient with capacity could do it 'cannot order a doctor to give a particular form of treatment'.[185] To this, Lady Hale added in *N v ACCG* that nor can the court order a Clinical Commissioning Group to fund treatment that patients or families desire: the court can only choose between 'available options'.[186]

22.18 A right to Clinically Assisted Nutrition and Hydration (CANH)?

The entry into force of the Human Rights Act raised questions about the legality of the reasoning in *Bland* and the cases which followed *Bland*. Were decisions to cease feeding, especially to withdraw CANH, lawful? Or did they contravene Article 2 of the European Convention protecting the right to life? In *NHS Trust A v M*,[187] the President of the Family Division ruled that in the circumstances of cases such as *Bland*, where a recovery allowing the patient to enjoy any sort of cognitive abilities was nigh on impossible, nothing in Article 2 required measures to ensure prolongation of survival.

The matter recently came before the ECtHR. The French Supreme Court, the Conseil d'État, had authorised the withdrawal of the artificial nutrition and hydration from Vincent Lambert, who had suffered severe brain damage and quadriplegia in a road traffic accident in 2008 when he was 32 years old. Lambert was said to be minimally conscious in 2011 and vegetative in 2014. His wife supported the removal of treatment, but his devout Catholic parents

181 Ibid, [39–40]. And see *University Hospitals Birmingham NHSFT v HB* [2018] EWCOP 39 where treatment was authorised, despite clinical objections based on futility and burden, based on evidence of the patient's wishes.

182 *Aintree*, [23].

183 Ibid, [35].

184 S Pattinson, *Medical Law and Ethics* (6th edn, 2020) Sweet and Maxwell, 14–038.

185 *Aintree*, [18].

186 *N v ACCG* [2017] UKSC 22, [35] and [44]. And see *London North West University Healthcare Trust v M, A, H & T* [2022] EWCOP 13.

187 [2001] 1 All ER 801 and see E Wicks, 'The Right to Refuse Medical Treatment Under the European Convention on Human Rights' (2001) 9 *Med Law Rev* 17.

sought continued treatment. The parents made an emergency appeal to the ECtHR in 2014. Lambert's wishes could not be ascertained. He had made no relevant advance decision. The Court relinquished jurisdiction to the Grand Chamber, which upheld the French court's decision and ruled, twelve to five, that there was no violation of the Article 2 right to life.[188] The dissenting judges feared that depriving a severely disabled person of food and water in circumstances when he could not communicate his views constituted a 'retrograde step' in the protection afforded to vulnerable people.[189] The wide margin of appreciation afforded to Member States in matters relating to the beginning and end of life recognises the lack of consensus across Europe but makes for sparse guidance from the Strasbourg court. Provided Member States fulfil their duties under Article 2, they will be left to determine whether or not to allow withdrawal of life-sustaining treatment and the balance between the rights to life and autonomy.[190] On this basis, the Grand Chamber held that there was no need to rule separately on the potential violation of Article 8. Member States must look elsewhere for guidance.

The GMC produced guidance in 2002 indicating that, where a patient's disease is severe and the prognosis poor, CANH will not always be appropriate, even if death is not imminent.[191] This prompted Leslie Burke, who suffered from a degenerative neurological condition, cerebellar ataxia, to fight for the right to artificial nutrition and hydration in the event that he was unable to voice his wishes. His condition gradually reduced his coordination while his mental faculties were unimpaired. His condition would cause the loss of abilities to walk, hear, see and swallow. He could make an advance decision, but his worry was that, after a significant deterioration, the GMC guidance would sanction the discontinuation of CANH in spite of it, and that he would be aware of great pain and suffering caused by malnutrition and dehydration. His argument was that, in his personal view, knowing as he did the likely progression of his disease, CANH would never be futile.

Mr Burke argued that the GMC guidance offended his human rights in four ways. First, the right to life in Article 2(1) contains both a negative obligation not to unlawfully take life and a positive obligation to protect it. The guidance failed to adequately protect his life. Second, by failing to protect him from death by malnutrition and dehydration, it offended Article 3, which protects

188 *Lambert and Others v France*, App No 46043/14 (ECHR, 5 June 2015) (Grand Chamber). Vincent Lambert died in 2019 aged 42, when his feeding tubes were removed by doctors following a final ruling by the French appeals court.

189 Ibid, dissenting opinion, [1].

190 Ibid, [148].

191 GMC, *Withholding and Withdrawing Life-Prolonging Treatments: Good Practice in Decision-Making* (2002). Para 16 provided: 'Doctors must take account of patients' preferences when providing treatment. However, where a patient wishes to have a treatment that – in the doctor's considered view – is not clinically indicated, there is no ethical or legal obligation on the doctor to provide it.' The 2002 guidelines were replaced by GMC, *Treatment and Care Towards the End of Life*. The GMC have endorsed RCP/BMA, *Clinically-Assisted Nutrition and Hydration (CANH) and Adults Who Lack the Capacity to Consent* (2018).

him from inhuman and degrading treatment. Third, by failing to give his advance decision legal force, the guidance offended Article 8, which protects his right to a private and family life. Finally, it discriminated against those incapable of making a competent decision and therefore offended Article 14, which protects from discrimination. At first instance, it was held that the GMC guidance was incompatible with Articles 3 and 8 of the Human Rights Act 1998.[192] Munby J's decision was controversial because it suggested a positive right to demand treatment that was not, in the clinicians' views, in his best interests.[193] Could the principle be extended beyond the provision of CANH, to other forms of treatment? The GMC feared that it might and took the case to the Court of Appeal, where Munby J's decision was overturned.[194] Mr Burke's concerns, the Court held, were already addressed by the law. Where a competent patient indicates his wish to be kept alive through CANH, a doctor who deliberately brings that life to an end by removing CANH may be guilty of murder. Mr Burke was more concerned about what should happen in the event that he loses capacity. The Court is clear. An advance request to receive CANH will carry weight, but it is not determinative of best interests. There is no discrimination, as the law applies equally to both a competent patient demanding treatment and an incompetent patient whose demands are expressed through an advance decision. Doctors are guided by the indistinct and complex concepts of futility and best interests. The Court of Appeal decision (on the facts of this case) is a setback to patient autonomy and a victory for medical paternalism. In 2006, Leslie Burke lodged an appeal with the ECtHR. His application was ruled inadmissible.[195] There was no imminent risk that CANH would be withdrawn in circumstances that would lead to death by malnutrition and dehydration. In many ways, Mr Burke made his case too early: the emphasis on 'imminent' risk and the court's view that no issue arose under Articles 2, 3 and 8 on the basis that 'the applicant cannot pre-determine the administration of specific treatment in future unknown circumstances'[196] must have come as a blow given that by the time the issues became 'imminent', Mr Burke would be unlikely to be competent to bring the proceedings himself. Nor is there any discrimination within the meaning of Article 14: neither competent nor incompetent patients can require a doctor to provide treatment that they do not believe is clinically justified.[197]

192 *R (Burke) v GMC* [2004] EWHC 1879 (Admin).

193 See R Gillon, 'Why the GMC is Right to Appeal Over Life-prolonging Treatment' (2004) 329 *BMJ* 810. In support of the High Court judgment see H Biggs, 'In Whose Best Interests: Who Knows?' (2006) 1(2) *Clinical Ethics* 90; D Gurnham, 'Losing the Wood for the Trees: *Burke* and the Court of Appeal' (2006) 14 *Med Law Rev* 253, Also see J Coggon (2006) 12 *Med Law Rev* 219, who argues that a right to die with dignity cannot exist in the absence of a right to die.

194 *R (Burke) v GMC* [2005] EWCA Civ 1003.

195 *Burke v United Kingdom*, App No 19807/06 (ECHR, 2006).

196 Ibid, per Casadevall J.

197 Though subsequent case-law has indicated that the courts will give weight to previously autonomous requests made by those lacking capacity: see S Pattinson, '*R (Burke) v GMC*; *Burke v UK*: Contemporaneous and Advance Requests: The Fight for Rights at the End of Life' in J Herring and J Wall (eds), *Landmark Cases in Medical Law* (2015) Hart, pp 255–269.

As we shall see, section 4(5) of the Mental Capacity Act 2005 offers further guidance. It provides that decisions relating to life-sustaining treatment must not be motivated by a desire to bring about the patient's death. This has not been interpreted to mean that there is a positive obligation on doctors to provide life-sustaining treatment. Those in Mr Burke's position can make an advance decision refusing treatment, or appoint a health and welfare lasting power of attorney.

22.19 The Mental Capacity Act 2005[198]

As we have noted, the Mental Capacity Act 2005 now governs decision-making on behalf of adults who temporarily or permanently lack mental capacity and thus affects decision-making concerning incapacitated patients at the end of life.

How does the Act affect end-of-life decisions? As we have seen, the test of lawfulness remains the best interests of the patient, but an element of substituted judgement is incorporated into the statutory checklist for best interests. As a result, the law has moved on since *Bland* to make the incapacitated person's views, wishes, beliefs and values integral to best interests decision-making.[199] In the Supreme Court decision of *Aintree University Hospitals NHS Foundation Trust*[200] (examined above at 22.17), the Supreme Court made an assessment of what the patient would want.[201] There is no clinical obligation to provide futile treatment, but treatment is not necessarily futile just because it will not return the patient to good health. The patient's past and present views as to what constitutes an adequate quality of life are a relevant consideration.

Particular attention must be paid to any written statement made by the patient when they had capacity.[202] An advance decision purporting to *demand* treatment may be persuasive, but it is not binding.[203] Many patients in Mr Burke's condition might prefer to ensure that life-sustaining treatment was not prolonged. The Act gives force only to advance refusals and as we saw in Chapter 7 under section 25 of the Act, advance decisions to *refuse* treatment are not valid if:[204]

- the treatment in question 'is not the treatment specified in the advance decision'; or
- 'any circumstances specified in the advance decision are absent'; or

198 See also above Chapter 7.
199 Mental Capacity Act, s 4(6)(b). And see, for example, *Royal Bournemouth and Christchurch Hospitals NHS Trust v TG & Anor* [2019] EWCOP 21, [19].
200 [2013] UKSC 67.
201 As we have seen, the deterioration of Mr James's health led Lady Hale to accept the Court of Appeal's conclusion that treatment should be withdrawn.
202 Mental Capacity Act 2005, s 4(6)(a) and see ss 24–26 on advance decisions to refuse treatment.
203 This was also the case in common law: *R (Burke) v GMC* [2005] EWCA Civ 1003 CA, [35].
204 Section 25(1).

- 'there are reasonable grounds for believing that circumstances exist which [the patient] did not anticipate at the time of his advance decision and which would have affected his decision had he anticipated them'.

In addition, where the advance decision to refuse treatment relates to life-sustaining treatment, special conditions apply. It must incorporate a statement that the decision stands, even if life is at risk. It must be in writing, signed, witnessed and verified by the author.[205] If so, it is as binding as a statement refusing life-sustaining treatment made by a competent patient such as Ms B. Yet there is no requirement that the patient discuss the content or implications of the statement with a health professional or that they be fully informed.

The legal requirement for a witness is not necessarily obvious to patients and their families. In *An NHS Trust v D*,[206] D fell into a vegetative state following surgery. He had made an advance refusal of treatment in the form of a signed letter but did not get it witnessed. As a result, it did not satisfy section 25 of the Mental Capacity Act. Though his decision was upheld on the basis that it was in his best interests to do so, the failure to comply with section 25 resulted in court proceedings and delay with consequent distress to his family.

Rather than making an advance decision, a competent patient may appoint a proxy to act for them via a lasting power of attorney (LPA) and make decisions on their behalf in the event that they lose capacity.[207] Again, special conditions apply if the LPA is to make decisions regarding life-sustaining treatment. The LPA may only make such decisions if the donor of the LPA expressly enabled them to do so.[208] Even then, the decision of an LPA is subject to the conditions of the Act. If the LPA and the doctors or carers disagree about what is in the best interests of the patient, the court will usually be called upon to make a decision or declaration.[209] The court as 'decision-maker' will be guided, but not bound, by the views of the LPA.

Whoever is making the crucial decision (doctors, or any attorney, or the Court), section 4(5) of the Mental Capacity Act contains special considerations relating to life-sustaining treatment (which is defined as 'treatment which in the view of a person providing health care for the person concerned is necessary to sustain life'):

> Where the determination relates to life-sustaining treatment [the person making the decision] must not, in considering whether the treatment is in the best interests of the person concerned, be motivated by a desire to bring about his death.[210]

This peculiar statement was framed to appease those who feared that the Mental Capacity Act would sanction covert euthanasia. It forbids the decision-maker

205 See ss 25(5)–(6).
206 [2012] EWHC 885 (COP).
207 Lasting Powers of Attorneys are governed by ss 9–14.
208 See s 11(8)(a).
209 See for example *Re AVS v An NHS Trust* [2010] EWHC 2746 (COP).
210 Section 4(10).

from being 'motivated by a desire to bring about the person's death'.[211] We are at a loss to define 'desire' in this context. The Code of Practice states:

> There will be a limited number of cases where treatment is futile, overly burdensome to the patient or where there is no prospect of recovery. In circumstances such as these, it may be that an assessment of best interests leads to the conclusion that it would be in the best interests of the patient to withdraw or withhold life-sustaining treatment, even if this may result in the person's death.[212]

The Code recognises that those making the treatment decision might wish the patient dead (either to ease his suffering or for other reasons) but insists that this is not the motivation for the discontinuation of treatment.

22.20 The role of the courts

It is good practice to seek prior judicial sanction in cases of dispute or uncertainty as to the patient's capacity or his best interests, but is there a legal requirement to do so? We saw in Chapter 7 that there is not. In *Burke*, Lord Phillips MR stated:

> Good practice may require medical practitioners to seek such a declaration where the legality of proposed treatment is in doubt. This is not, however, something that they are required to do as a matter of law.[213]

Nor does the Mental Capacity Act 2005 mandate resort to the court. The Court of Protection Rules, however, direct practitioners to bring to court certain decisions concerning serious medical treatment. This included proposals to withdraw artificial nutrition or hydration[214] and most controversial cases therefore appeared before the Court of Protection. In 2018, however, the Supreme Court clarified that court approval is not necessarily required before treatment can be withdrawn from a patient with a prolonged disorder of consciousness. In *NHS Trust v Y*,[215] a man in his fifties suffered a cardiac arrest which resulted in severe cerebral hypoxia and extensive brain damage. He was kept alive by means of CANH. The question before the Supreme Court was whether a court order must always be obtained before CANH may be withdrawn.[216] The Court held that neither the common law nor the ECHR, in combination or separately, gives rise to a mandatory requirement for court

211 Office of the Public Guardian, *Mental Capacity Act: Code of Practice* (2007) (revised July 2013, updated October 2020), para 5.29.
212 Ibid, para 5.31. And see J Coggon, 'Ignoring the Moral and Intellectual Shape of the Law after *Bland*: The Unintended Side-effect of a Sorry Compromise' (2007) 27 *Legal Studies* 110.
213 [2005] EWCA Civ 1003, [80].
214 Court of Protection Rules 2007, Pt 9, Direction E, *Applications Relating to Serious Medical Treatment*, para 5(a); Replaced by *Serious Medical Treatment, Guidance* [2020] EWCOP 2 pending a revised Mental Capacity Act 2005 Code of Practice in 2022.
215 [2018] UKSC 46.
216 Ibid, [2].

involvement to decide upon the best interests of every patient before CANH may be withdrawn.[217] Specifically, if the relevant provisions are followed and guidance observed, and there is agreement regarding the best interests of the patient, he may be treated accordingly without application to the court.[218] However, if at the conclusion of the medical process, 'it is apparent that the way forward is finely balanced, or there is a difference of medical opinion, or a lack of agreement to a proposed course of action from those with an interest in the patient's welfare, a court application can and should be made'.[219] However, as we noted in Chapter 7, where there is consensus regarding a course of action, there may be no one to enforce recourse to the court. The patient will lack an advocate.

22.21 DNACPR notices

DNACPR (do not attempt cardio-pulmonary resuscitation) notices are not expressly referred to in the Mental Capacity Act 2005. What is in issue is not withdrawing treatment, but whether or not the patient should be given CPR if they suffer a cardiac arrest.

The validity of DNACPR orders came before the English courts in *Re R (Adult: Medical Treatment)*.[220] R was 23. He was born with a severe malformation of the brain. He developed epilepsy in infancy. He suffered from multiple disabilities and had no real means of communicating with others. He had severe and debilitating intestinal troubles including ulcers 'all the way through his guts'. He appeared to experience quite acute pain. His only real response to others seems to have been to being cuddled. He was not in PVS or anything akin to 'near PVS'. Since he was 19, he had lived in a nursing home, attending a day centre and going home to his devoted family most weekends. In the year before the court proceedings, R had been hospitalised five times. His doctors, with the full agreement of R's parents, issued a DNACPR notice. Should R suffer from a life-threatening condition involving a cardiac arrest he should not be resuscitated. Staff at R's day centre were concerned about the use of DNACPR notices in R's case, and made an application for judicial review of the order. Sir Stephen Brown P upheld the DNACPR notice. He was persuaded that the evidence established that in cases such as R's, CPR was unlikely to succeed. R had never been able to articulate his wishes. Nonetheless, the judge concluded that it was permissible to consider the patient's quality of life in assessing his best interests. DNACPR notices do not involve measures to terminate life or accelerate death. Where continued existence involved a life 'so afflicted as to

217 Ibid, [46].

218 For discussion of the potential implications, see E Wicks, '*An NHS Trust v Y* [2018] UKSC 46: Reducing the Role of the Courts in Treatment Withdrawal' (2019) 27(2) *Med Law Rev* 330; R Huxtable, 'Dying Too Soon or Living Too Long? Withdrawing Treatment from Patients with Prolonged Disorders of Consciousness After *Re Y*' (2019) 20 *BMC Med Ethics* 91.

219 See interim practice guidance giving effect to this case at: *Serious Medical Treatment, Guidance* [2020] EWCOP 2 (pending revised MCA Code of Practice).

220 (1996) 31 BMLR 127.

be intolerable',[221] policies designed to limit life-saving intervention could be approved. In the absence of consent from the patient, the decision to institute a DNACPR notice should usually be made by the physicians, family and carers.

Whose decision should determine whether or not a DNACPR notice is made? In some cases, the patient can be consulted. Where they lack capacity, the Mental Capacity Act 2005 will apply. An advance refusal of treatment may be effective, or where the donor expressly authorises it, the Lasting Power of Attorney may 'authorise the giving or refusing of consent to the carrying out or continuation of life-sustaining treatment'.[222] In other cases, guidelines on DNACPR notices make it clear that decision-making is not an exclusively medical role.[223] The patient's wishes and preferences, if known, should be taken into account.

In *R (Tracey) v Cambridge University Hospitals NHS Foundation Trust & Ors*[224] the Court of Appeal held that a DNACPR notice that was applied without consultation of or notice to Mrs Tracey (who retained capacity) and her family breached Article 8 of the ECHR. The DNACPR notice was withdrawn when her family complained and a second notice imposed when Mrs Tracey lost capacity to decide for herself. Mrs Tracey died shortly afterwards. The claim focused on the first DNACPR notice. The Court of Appeal stopped short of requiring that (capacitous or otherwise) patients are consulted. There must, however, be a convincing reason for not involving a patient, such as the likelihood of causing harm (which is more than mere distress).[225] 'Particularly convincing justification' is needed to justify not telling a patient that the clinicians consider CPR to be futile in a particular case. A failure to inform the patient in these circumstances robs them of the opportunity to seek a second opinion. And even if the patient cannot demand CPR that the clinician considers futile, they are, *prima facie*, entitled to know that the decision has been taken.[226] In *Tracey*, the claim against the Trust was upheld in part. A second claim against the Secretary of State focusing on the lack of clear national guidance on DNACPR was dismissed. The government's policy is to encourage local decision-making and this policy does not breach Article 8.[227]

Guidelines developed jointly between the BMA, the Resuscitation Council (UK) and the Royal College of Nursing were revised in light of *Tracey*.[228] The guideline reiterates the presumption in favour of involvement of the patient in the decision-making process, encourages advance care planning (which gives

221 See *Re J (A Minor) (Wardship: Medical Treatment)* [1990] 3 All ER 930, CA.
222 Section 11(8)(a).
223 GMC, *Treatment and Care Towards the End of Life*, paras 129–131.
224 [2014] EWCA Civ 822. See J Samanta, '*Tracey* and Respect for Autonomy: Will the Promise be Delivered?' (2015) 23(3) *Med Law Rev* 467.
225 [2014] EWCA Civ 822, [54] per Dyson MR.
226 Ibid, [55] per Dyson MR.
227 Ibid, [84] per Dyson MR: '[T]o hold that article 8 requires the formulation of a unified policy at national level, rather than having individual policies at local level, is unwarranted and would represent an unjustified intrusion into government healthcare policy.'
228 BMA/RC(UK)/RCN, *Decisions Relating to Cardiopulmonary Resuscitation* (updated 2021).

people the opportunity to say 'no' to treatment they do not want) and reiterates the importance of making decisions on an individual basis (not simply on the basis of the person's age or condition).[229] Decisions should be made after appropriate consultation with other staff and the patient's family. Once a DNACPR notice is in place, the guidelines state: 'A DNACPR decision does not override clinical judgement in the unlikely event of a reversible cause of the person's respiratory or cardiac arrest that does not match the circumstances envisaged.'[230] Where a DNACPR notice has not been made and the wishes of the patient are unknown, CPR should generally be attempted if cardiac or pulmonary arrest occurs, though there may be cases where this is not appropriate, for example, if the patient is in the final stages of terminal illness and has not requested CPR.

Fears about DNACPR decisions focus on *who* makes the decision about life or death, whether such decisions may be made arbitrarily or in a discriminatory fashion, and whether the patient will be treated well once a DNACPR notice is in place.[231] DNACPR notices are made more often in relation to elderly patients. That of itself may not be surprising. It is the quality of decision-making which counts and how prospects of successful resuscitation and future quality of life are assessed. A greater number of very elderly patients who are also gravely ill may be more unlikely to recover than their grandchildren in their twenties and thirties. Junior doctors in particular require training to understand the needs of their elderly patients.[232] The criteria governing the assessment of the patient and the weight given to his or her family's wishes should not vary with age. Recourse to the courts is rare indeed and should be reserved for cases of serious disagreement.

Unprecedented pressures were placed on healthcare services in the COVID-19 pandemic. A Care Quality Commission review[233] conducted in 2020 found over 750 cases where DNACPR decisions were made without involving patients or their families and, in some cases, were applied to groups of patients, particularly in care homes. It found evidence of variation in training and advance care planning and set out an urgent need for improved oversight and assurance.[234]

229 Ibid, p 4.

230 Ibid, p 5.

231 See T Shakespeare and B Vernon, 'Disability Rights and Resuscitation: Do Not Attempt Reconciliation' in L Clements and J Read (eds), *Disabled People and the Right to Life: The Protection and Violation of Disabled People's Most Basic Human Right* (2007) Routledge Cavendish, ch 5.

232 GT Laurie, SHE Harmon and ES Dove, *Mason and McCall Smith's Law and Medical Ethics* (11th edn, 2019) Oxford University Press, 19.32.

233 CQC, *Protect, Respect, Connect: Decisions About Living and Dying Well During COVID-19* (2021).

234 And see empirical research reported by H Bows and J Herring, 'DNACPR Decisions During Covid-19: An Empirical and Analytical Study' (2022) 30(1) *Med Law Rev* 60 which did not find evidence of increases in DNACPRs for older adults in the pandemic: 'Overall, approximately one in five patients was not consulted about the DNACPR decision, but during the first Covid wave more patients were consulted than pre-Covid.'

The report recognises the immense value of advance care planning and the role that DNACPR decisions can play within it. Correctly implemented, DNACPR notices can enhance autonomy and control and reduce the need for invasive and ineffective procedures. Incorrectly applied without necessary consultation, they can cause distress, harm and untimely death.

22.22 Conclusion

The debate around assistance in dying arises out of tragic facts and raises ethically and socially intractable issues. The courts have begun to tackle medical advances which facilitate, with increasing accuracy, differentiation between vegetative and minimally conscious states. Judicial interference with assisted suicide is, in principle, open to domestic courts but should the Court so intervene? In *Nicklinson* Lady Hale and Lord Kerr's minority judgments proposed a declaration of incompatibility of section 2(1) of the Suicide Act 1961 with the appellants' rights under article 8 of the ECHR. Lady Hale opined:

> [W]e have no jurisdiction to impose anything: that is a matter for Parliament alone. We do have jurisdiction, and in some circumstances an obligation, to form a professional opinion, as judges, as to the content of the Convention rights and the compatibility of the present law with them.[235]

Legislative reform proposals have, so far, led to naught. Principles of justice, autonomy and non-discrimination vie with slippery slope arguments, resulting in pragmatic reform proposals to assist the terminally ill that fail to fully satisfy either camp. Support for reform is mounting.

235 [2014] UKSC 38, [325].

Index